KING HUSSEIN OF JORDAN

KING HUSSEIN
OF JORDAN

A POLITICAL LIFE

NIGEL ASHTON

YALE UNIVERSITY PRESS
NEW HAVEN AND LONDON

For information about this and other Yale University Press publications, please contact:

U.S. Office: sales.press@yale.edu   yalebooks.com
Europe Office: sales@yaleup.co.uk   www.yaleup.co.uk

Set in Minion by SX Composing, Rayleigh, Essex
Printed in the United States of America by Sheridan Books

Library of Congress Cataloging-in-Publication Data

Ashton, Nigel John.
    King Hussein of Jordan : a political life / Nigel Ashton.
        p. cm.
    Includes bibliographical references and index.
    ISBN 978-0-300-09167-0 (ci : alk. paper) 1. Hussein, King of Jordan, 1935–1999.
    2. Jordan—Kings and rulers—Biography. 3. Jordan—Politics and government—
    1952–1999. I.
Title.
    DS154.55.A84 2008
    956.9504'4092—dc22
    [B]
    2008010803

A catalogue record for this book is available from the British Library.

10 9 8 7 6 5 4 3 2 1

For Danielle, Isabelle and Sophie

CONTENTS

ACKNOWLEDGEMENTS

I began work on this biography of King Hussein of Jordan in the spring of 1999, shortly after his untimely death. From the outset, it was clear that while the King's political longevity and personal charisma made him an excellent subject for a biography, there would be many challenges to be negotiated in researching and writing such a book. Top of the list was the problem of access to sources. Until now, no biography of a contemporary Arab leader has been written with the benefit of full access to his papers. This book breaks the mould. The breakthrough was a long time in coming, but during 2007, with the gracious permission of His Majesty King Abdullah II and the Director of his Office, Dr Bassem Awadallah, I was afforded full and unfettered access to King Hussein's correspondence files. Despite this unprecedented and generous assistance, it should be stressed that I have not written an official biography of King Hussein. The opinions expressed in this book are my own. They do not in any way represent official Jordanian views, or the views of any member of the Hashemite family.

With these disclaimers out of the way, I can perhaps say a little more about the impact which the King's files had on my own research. In contrast to Western archival sources which, as a general rule, become fuller due to declassification the further back in recent history one goes, I found that Hussein's files were richest for the late 1970s, 1980s and 1990s. This much will be clear to anyone scanning the notes appended to this volume. The willingness of the Jordanian authorities to allow me access to such contemporary material is, I believe, a remarkable testimony to their openness. The papers in the Royal Archives have served considerably to complement and enhance archival material available to me elsewhere.

Access to these files gave me another, much more welcome challenge. I had to rewrite the book extensively, adding whole new chapters on the 1980s and

1990s in particular. The King's files also helped me to understand better his approach to certain issues, particularly in the final two decades of his reign. A full knowledge of his role as intermediary between the United States and Iraq during the Iran–Iraq war, for instance, is essential in order to understand his attempt to play the same role during the 1990–91 Gulf crisis. The documents also threw up some remarkable surprises. The exchanges between President Ronald Reagan and the King over the Iran-Contra scandal in November 1986, for example, reveal not only that Reagan personally authorised this shabby affair, but also that Hussein was effectively undercut by the president.

The documents in Hussein's files have also served to increase the focus of this biography on the King's conduct of regional and foreign policy. While some might see this as an unbalanced approach, my own view is that it reflects the King's own interests. He spent a lot of his time dealing with such issues, and he was personally most engaged in politics when handling regional crises. Of course, in the case of Jordan, any attempt to divorce regional policy from domestic policy would be artificial; for Hussein the two were intimately connected. The crisis of September 1970, when a clash between the Jordanian army and Palestinian guerrilla groups provoked a Syrian invasion, illustrates the point perfectly.

In the course of writing this book I have incurred a large number of debts. Numerous Jordanians have helped me along the way, often by offering their own reflections on the late King. I am grateful to Her Majesty Queen Noor, who was generous enough to grant me my first interview back in the summer of 1999, not long after her husband's death. I am also particularly indebted to Prince Raad and Princess Majda for their frequent hospitality during my many subsequent trips to Jordan, and to Awn Khasawneh for helping me to understand the intimate relationship between international law and international history. During my earlier visits to Jordan, Marwan Qasim was generous in offering me both his time and his hospitality, and Maan Abu Nowar, himself a noted scholar of Jordanian history, provided me with useful advice at an early stage of my work. In the Royal Hashemite Archives the assistance provided by Dr Baker al-Majali was generous and indispensable. I am very grateful for his assistance in finding pictures of King Hussein for the picture section and back cover, and for permission to include these in the book. Finally, my friend Zeid Raad, who understands the importance of history, has offered unstinting advice and support as this project has developed. Without fail, everyone I have encountered in my dozen or more visits to Jordan across the last eight years has been courteous, helpful and supportive of my work.

Closer to home, I am grateful to my research assistants, Aziz Abdalli and Rasha Khalil, for assistance with the translation of Arabic documents. All quotations from correspondence between Hussein and other Arab leaders cited in this book are translations from the original Arabic. Hussein's letters to Western and Israeli leaders, by contrast, were always written in English. I have used familiar Anglicised spellings of Arabic names wherever possible: thus 'Hussein', not 'Husayn'. Where there is no familiar Anglicised form, I have used the transliteration favoured by the individual concerned. Finally, in citing original documents, I have preserved the transliteration adopted at the time, even though this has occasionally resulted in inconsistencies in the book as a whole. On the same theme, I would also like to thank my own Arabic tutors, Vehbi Baysan and Luay Hassan, whose efforts have helped to give me a basic understanding of the beauty and logic of the language.

At the London School of Economics and Political Science, my academic home for the past nine years, I have benefited greatly from conversations with several colleagues in the International History Department. I am particularly indebted to the departmental convenor, Arne Westad, for his help in the later stages of my research, particularly for his support in securing the sabbatical during 2006–7 that enabled me to complete this book.

My editors at Yale University Press, Robert Baldock and Phoebe Clapham, deserve special thanks. Robert took on this project at an early stage and thereafter proved very supportive of my requests for extensions to the original deadline. Once the manuscript was finally complete, Phoebe showed a skilled eye in detecting the points in the text where I had assumed too much and explained too little. Her efficiency and engagement during the editorial process have been exemplary.

At a personal level, my wife Danielle has shared the ups and downs of my research, and has been most understanding and supportive of my frequent absences abroad. To her I owe my greatest debt of gratitude. Our daughters Isabelle and Sophie, meanwhile, who were both born and grew up during the extended process of gestation of this book, have contributed to it in their own inimitable ways. They have all helped remind me that there are ultimately more important things in life than research and writing. It is to them that I dedicate this book.

LIST OF ILLUSTRATIONS

Maps

Plate section

Jordan and its neighbours

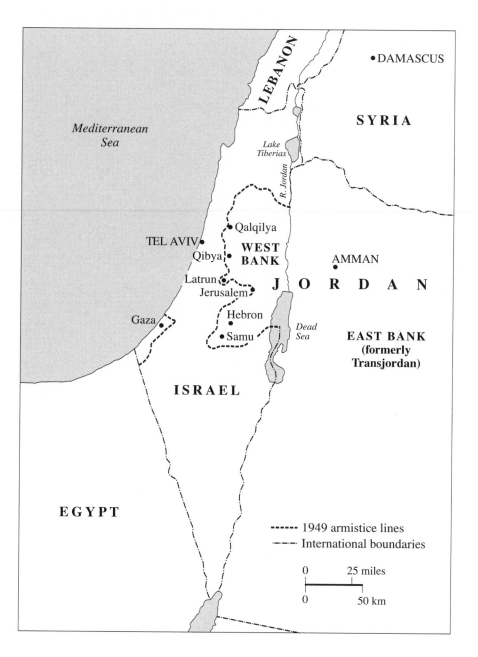

Jordan and Israel: the 1949 armistice lines

A CONTESTED DESTINY

'My only hope is that people, long after I am gone, will judge me kindly and cast their verdict for me and not against me.'[1]

It was a funeral procession like no other. First came the outpouring of grief and emotion from the ordinary Jordanians who lined the route of the King's cortège, struggling to catch a final glimpse of his coffin as it made its last journey through the streets of Amman on 8 February 1999. Then came the remarkable stream of dignitaries: not just Jordanians, or Arabs, or even Muslims, but a cosmopolitan gathering of leaders of all faiths from all around the world. Kings, queens and presidents – some fifty heads of state in all – were accompanied by princes, dignitaries and ministers too countless to name. Even more remarkable than the size of the gathering were the unlikely bed-fellows it threw together. Stealing the show with his unexpected arrival was Syrian President Hafez al-Asad. Frail, ashen and, as it transpired, close to the end of his own life, he still made the spur-of-the-moment decision to fly to Amman to see off his former friend and sometime enemy. The Syrian leader was not the only mourner whose relations with Hussein had been turbulent across the decades. While Asad prayed over Hussein's coffin as it lay briefly in state at the Raghadan Palace, Yasser Arafat, chairman of the Palestine Liberation Organisation and Hussein's long-time political rival, who in September 1970 had given Hussein twenty-four hours to leave the country or face the consequences, paid his own tribute in a way which summed up the ambivalence of his relationship with the King: first he bowed over the coffin and then he saluted it.

Arafat and Asad were not the only former enemies who came to pay their respects. As most of the mourners made their way up the hill, another group came down the hill towards the Raghadan Palace from the opposite direction, approaching as though their entry had been planned for maximum dramatic effect. A mere five years earlier the presence of this party would have been unthinkable, composed as it was of the past and present leaders of the state of Israel. Prime Minister Benjamin Netanyahu, whom Hussein had once condemned as not belonging to the 'peace camp' at all, was flanked by another figure who for most Jordanians had come to personify the enemy: General Ariel Sharon. There was a rich irony here, for the first major political crisis faced by the young King Hussein, nearly half a century earlier, had been caused by an Israeli reprisal raid against the village of Qibya led by none other than Ariel Sharon. Sharon, like Arafat, had for much of his political career seen Hussein as expendable, an obstacle in the way of a satisfactory solution to the Palestinian problem. As the King put it with some venom in a private letter written in 1981: 'General Ariel Sharon, born to Polish immigrants in Palestine, ironically once stated that he considered me an intruder on Palestine and the Palestinians.'[2] And yet, as if to prove he never held a grudge, after the conclusion of the 1994 peace treaty with Israel Hussein struck up a personal correspondence with Sharon, welcomed him to Jordan, and even came to treat him as one of the more sympathetic figures in the Israeli government. Sharon and Netanyahu had not made the journey from Jerusalem to Amman alone. Other past and future Israeli prime ministers, including Shimon Peres, Yitzhak Shamir and Ehud Barak, accompanied them to Hussein's funeral, though their movements had to be carefully choreographed to ensure that they did not happen to find themselves standing next to an Arab enemy.

From the Raghadan Palace the King's coffin, mounted on a gun carriage, made its way up the hill to the Hashemite family mosque and cemetery. Here Hussein was to be buried alongside his grandfather Abdullah and his father Talal, whose descent into mental illness had brought Hussein to the throne as a boy of seventeen back in 1953. Flanked by Bedouin troops with their rifles reversed, and followed by the King's white charger, with his riding boots reversed in the stirrups, the funeral procession was accompanied by a bagpipe lament. At the graveside, after the King's body had been lowered into the ground in a simple white shroud, the sound of the 'Last Post' completed the British-inspired martial theme. The procession was a blend of traditions, Western and Arab, reflected in the red-and white-checked keffiyeh head-dresses accompanying the dark suits worn by many of the Jordanian mourners. Informality and dignity were its hallmarks, qualities which had typified Hussein's approach to the kingship. The spontaneous and self-disciplined organisation of the illustrious mourners in the procession behind the King's coffin provided a fitting epitaph for the Jordan he had striven to build: no one was told where to go, but everyone found his place.

The stature that Hussein had attained during nearly half a century as King of Jordan, then, was amply illustrated in the international attendance at his funeral. But this stature was perhaps even more remarkable considering the challenges he had faced to his very survival across the decades. Sandwiched between Israel to the west, Syria to the north, Iraq to the east and Saudi Arabia to the south, Jordan had been dealt a poor hand by geography. As a weak buffer state at the heart of a turbulent region, the country was bound to be dragged into the Arab–Israeli conflict and inter-Arab rivalries. This was even more the case since Hussein's grandfather, King Abdullah, had joined the battle for Palestine in 1948 and had emerged holding the area of land which became known as the West Bank. In addition to gaining land during the war, Jordan also accepted hundreds of thousands of Palestinian refugees who fled from what became the state of Israel. These dispossessed and often destitute Palestinians constituted a huge political and economic challenge, and his grandfather's troubled bequest would later bring Hussein into conflict with the Palestinian national movement.

To make matters worse, Hussein's Jordan did not possess the natural resources, notably oil, which many of its Arab neighbours boasted. This, together with its relatively small settled population and the under-developed state of the economy when Hussein acceded to the throne, meant that Jordan was afflicted by a chronic budget deficit. The domestic tax base was simply not big enough to fund basic services, never mind the substantial military establishment which was essential for the defence of the country and the preservation of the regime. This meant that for the bulk of his reign one of the dominating facts of Hussein's political life was the search for foreign benefactors to support his country.

If money was one of Hussein's main concerns, security was another. Hussein was obliged to balance his more powerful enemies off against each other. This led him into a succession of close, if transient, friendships with his Arab neighbours. The shifting cast of Hussein's allies reads like a 'who's who' of the region's major leaders across the decades. During the 1960s, it was to King Feisal of Saudi Arabia that Hussein turned, hoping to form a monarchical bloc which might defend his regime against the rising forces of revolutionary Arab socialism. Then, after the 1967 Arab–Israeli war, Hussein formed an unlikely partnership with his former enemy, Egyptian President Gamal Abdel Nasser, which lasted until Nasser's death in September 1970. After the 1973 Arab–Israeli war, it was Syrian President Hafez Asad to whom Hussein turned, until their alliance broke down in mutual recriminations at the end of the decade. Finally, during the 1980s, Hussein forged a close relationship with the Iraqi President Saddam Hussein, which endured until after the Iraqi invasion of Kuwait in 1990.

Hussein did not rely only on Arab allies to buttress his regime. He also maintained close relations with the Western powers. When he came to the throne in 1953, Jordan was still effectively under British protection. Britain not only funded the Jordanian army, known as the Arab Legion, it also provided key members of its officer corps, including its overall commander General Sir John Bagot Glubb. One of the main themes of the early years of Hussein's reign was the casting off of what was increasingly seen as this yoke of British influence. But the termination in 1957 of the treaty which had committed Britain to Jordan's defence did not mean the end of Hussein's connections with the West; far from it. While continuing to maintain close diplomatic relations with Britain, he also built up a deep and enduring relationship with the United States. Washington sought anti-communist Arab allies who were open to compromise in the struggle with Israel, and in both respects Hussein seemed to fit the bill. This is not to say that he became an American client or puppet. In fact, at several junctures in his reign he fell out spectacularly with the United States. But, despite these disagreements, Hussein always returned before long to the path of cooperation with the United States, which he saw as ultimately the most reliable military and financial backer of his regime.

Hussein's relations with the West reflected his astute understanding of power. His shift to the United States for support during the late 1950s and 1960s tracked the rise of American hegemony in the Middle East. This same sense of realism influenced his approach to many of the crises which swept through the region during his long reign. It also helps explain his covert relations with the state of Israel across the decades, until the formal conclusion of a peace treaty between the two states in 1994. Israel was a fact on the map of the region as far as Hussein was concerned; he never believed the Arab propaganda about driving the Jewish state into the sea. But he was all too well aware of Israel's military strength, and he consistently sought to establish a relationship which would ward off potentially damaging Israeli reprisal raids against Jordan. Over the years, Hussein's perception of the character of the Israeli threat changed. The Likud Party's accession to power in Israel in 1977 brought with it the more pressing danger posed by their 'Jordan is Palestine' slogan. During his final two decades on the throne, what Hussein most feared was an Israeli attempt to resolve the Palestinian problem by driving the Palestinians out of the occupied West Bank and into Jordan, overthrowing his regime in the process.

Hussein also sought to use his dialogue with Israeli leaders to explore the possibilities of a broader peace in the region. For the most part, he found the Israelis cautious and evasive. Particularly after the 1967 war, when Hussein was prepared to agree to full peace in exchange for a return to the pre-war lines, his approach did not find a receptive audience amongst Israeli leaders. In fact, the covert dialogue with Hussein after 1967 seems to have been pursued from the Israeli side more as an extension of domestic political rivalries, and as a holding operation, than as a serious peace process. Despite this, Hussein showed remarkable tenacity, returning time and again to the negotiating table in the hope that the situation might change.

In order to understand his approach to these negotiations we need to grasp another important strand of Hussein's character. More than just a realist, he was also an idealist. In the final years of his life, he spoke increasingly of the need to forge peace between what he termed the 'children of Abraham', a quasi-religious formulation that also reflected his fundamental belief in the leadership role of his family, the Hashemites. This claim rested on two foundations, one political – his great-grandfather Sharif Hussein's leadership of the Arab revolt against the Ottomans during the First World War – and one spiritual – the Hashemites' descent from the Prophet Mohammad via his daughter Fatima and her husband Ali. This spiritual claim was reinforced by the Hashemites' traditional status during the Ottoman era as guardians of Mecca and Medina, the most holy Muslim sites.

These political and spiritual foundations provided the explanation for Hussein's conviction that his family was destined to provide leadership for the Arab nation. This ideology of Hashemite Arab nationalism was never precisely codified. But, beyond the obvious element of the Hashemite claim to leadership, it also comprised the search for Arab unity, solidarity and independence, for Arab solutions to Arab problems, and the rejection of external, imperialist domination. In King Hussein's hands, and under the impact of the Cold War struggle which formed a critical backdrop for most of his reign, it also took on an anti-communist flavour. In his early autobiography *Uneasy Lies the Head* Hussein described communist atheism as anathema to his brand of Hashemite Arab nationalism. Of course ideology did not always trump interest; in the wake of the 1967 war Hussein visited Moscow and in subsequent decades purchased limited quantities of arms from the Soviet Union. But despite these tactical shifts he continued to believe that communism was the wrong path towards the realisation of Arab unity and independence.

Hussein's preference for an alliance with the United States, his opposition to communism, his widely rumoured covert contacts with Israel, and his belief in his family destiny made him a controversial figure in the Arab world. He always believed that he could punch above his weight in the battle for Arab leadership, and he was never prepared to cower in the corner of the ring, hoping his more powerful opponents would leave him alone. On the contrary, throughout his five decades on the throne, Hussein was in the thick of the fight. Despite the rhetoric of Arab solidarity, the central reality of Arab politics throughout Hussein's reign was one of struggle; not the struggle with Israel as one might expect, but a struggle amongst Arab regimes for the prize of leadership, with the Arab–Israeli conflict playing the role of a stick with which to beat opponents. Hussein, the one Arab leader who maintained consistent clandestine contact with the Israelis, and who sided with the West, made a very tempting target. This was apparent in the succession of assassination plots, coup attempts and bouts of externally sponsored disorder which plagued Jordan during his reign. Perhaps Hussein should have kept his head down and his guard up more. But he believed attack was the best form of defence, and his personal sense of destiny always kept him in the ring.

These formulations of Hussein the idealist and Hussein the realist take us a long way towards understanding his statecraft. But one example goes to show that, as with any individual, his decisions cannot always be attributed to neatly devised categories. In September 1970 Hussein finally decided to move against the Palestinian guerrilla groups, which had become so powerful in Jordan that they constituted almost a state within a state. He had fixed the beginning of the operation against them for first light on 16 September when Princess Firyal, the wife of his brother Prince Mohammad, intervened, warning him that according to her fortune-teller that would be a very inauspicious day for the Hashemites. And so at the last moment the King postponed the operation to the following day, to the puzzlement of British and American representatives in Amman. The story of the fortune-teller reminds us that one should never forget the role of impulse, emotion or intuition in informing Hussein's actions.

Inevitably, experience also shaped and changed Hussein. The teenage King of the mid-1950s was not the same man as the statesman of the 1990s. Those who served him in the final years of his reign recollect that by this stage he had 'seen it all before', and rarely bothered to read position papers presented to him by advisers, trusting instead to his own accumulated political wisdom. This did not necessarily mean that his early statecraft was more prone to error while his final years were a record of unbroken success. On the contrary, his political instinct was not always a sure guide to successful action. The early 1990s found him personally and politically isolated and disillusioned as a result of his stance during the Gulf crisis. But Hussein rarely remained passive or politically paralysed for long, and in the face of this isolation he struck out actively on the one remaining course open to him, engagement in the American-instigated peace process, which culminated in the 1994 Jordanian–Israeli peace treaty.

While he was certainly persistent in the face of adversity, Hussein was not always engaged to the same degree in the day-to-day affairs of state. Economic or administrative matters did not excite his attention, and from the late 1960s he entrusted part of the task of overseeing them to his Harrow- and Oxford-educated younger brother, Crown Prince Hassan. In one way the bookish Hassan made an unlikely partner for his practical brother, and there was always an underlying tension to their relationship, which came to the fore dramatically in the succession struggle during the final year of Hussein's life.

Hassan was not the only other political actor of significance in the Kingdom. In the 1950s, Hussein was served by a small group of advisers whom he inherited from his grandfather King Abdullah, and who helped guide his initial actions. By the 1960s, he had started to promote his own contemporaries to high political office, and from the 1970s onwards Jordanian politics came to be dominated by a relatively small cast of close friends and advisers of the King. This restricted the breadth of advice Hussein received, a fact which helps explain some of the misjudgements of his later years, including the domestic economic and political crisis which overtook Jordan in 1989 and his stance during the 1990–91 Gulf crisis.

While the King was at liberty to choose his own close political advisers, formally his actions as head of state were governed by the 1952 constitution. It was his task as monarch to appoint a prime minister and government. Although the system deteriorated in his final years, with prime ministers being allowed less and less time to prove themselves in the job, Hussein normally liked to give them free rein to implement their political programmes to the point where he could judge whether they were successful or not. It was only in periods of crisis, particularly regional crisis, that the King was fully engaged in politics. By personal and political inclination, Hussein was a risk-taker, a man whose mind was fully concentrated only when faced with danger. Still, as King of Jordan, he suffered no shortage of such danger; it is hard to identify a period of longer than two years through-out his whole reign when he was not faced with a serious political crisis of one sort or another.

One of the key personal qualities that enabled Hussein to survive these many crises was empathy. He was an extremely shrewd judge of character in others, and was very good at putting himself in their place and thereby predicting their likely actions. Put rather less nobly, he always knew what others were up to. As he described it himself in a letter to President Ronald Reagan in 1986:

> Throughout my many years of public service, and whenever I was confronted with a shocking situation, I have always attempted to take my time before dealing with it. I have often tried to place myself in the position of others, with the purpose of trying to understand their deeds from their vantage point.[3]

But this quality of empathy could be as much a source of frustration as it was an asset to his statecraft. Even if he could see matters through the eyes of others, and predict how they might act or react, this did not necessarily mean that he could influence the course of events. As he said in his final television interview, 'the worst part was that there were many crises that passed through this area that I could see coming and I warned and did whatever I could to prevent them happening. But no one listened.'[4]

It is perhaps understandable in these circumstances that there was a streak of escapism in Hussein's character, a desire to break away from the grind of everyday political survival and dream other dreams. Often, these dreams had a military flavour. Hussein was never happier than when mixing with military men, discussing the attributes of the latest jet fighter or, better still, sitting behind its controls. In a report delivered in January 1973, one British air attaché noted:

> In July [1972] a Mystère 20 arrived to join the Royal Flight. Probably because of the mourning period [for King Talal], delivery was taken at Aqaba. With typical exuberance the King was quickly airborne carrying out simulated low level strikes on the local hotels and his own summer chalet. I asked him later what speed he was doing and he replied 'the maximum, 350 knots' . . .[5]

It later transpired that one other chalet had been a particular target for the King on this occasion. 'Where else', asked the British officer concerned, can you 'bowl the King out at cricket and have the Monarch take his revenge by dusting the roof of your beach chalet with his Mystère 20?'

If flying was always top of the list of the King's ways of escape, one of his other long-term hobbies gives another clue to his character. Hussein was an enthusiastic amateur radio operator. This became a way for him to speak to people all round the world, outside the normal boundaries imposed by protocol. He had a fundamental, unfeigned interest in others, and a prodigious memory when it came to recollecting their individual needs, worries and interests. He was also always happy to go out of his way to do someone else a favour. So, mixed in with all of the important political correspondence in the file of his exchanges with President George Bush senior is a letter he wrote to the president on behalf of an American amateur radio enthusiast, a Mr McMillen Sr., with whom he had been in contact over the airwaves. Evidently, Mr McMillen was prevented by a disability from taking the Morse Code Test, which barred him from gaining his General Class Amateur Radio License. 'I thought that perhaps through your good offices', Hussein wrote to the president, 'he, and others in a similar position, might be given some hope for the future . . . It would be very heartening to know that Mr McMillen might achieve his life's ambition together with many others.'[6]

This reputation for helping others left the King open to requests which were rather less noble in nature. One anecdote illustrates the point. As far as possible, Hussein strove to maintain the tradition, honoured by his grandfather and father, of hearing petitions put to him by his subjects. In this case the petition he heard was of a rather unusual nature: one of his subjects came to the King requesting that he should provide him with a red Range Rover. Not disposed to grant this material request without good reason, Hussein was also puzzled as to its specific detail and asked why the car had to be red. 'Sire, is he who owns a *red* Range Rover somehow better than I?' was the petitioner's reply. Hussein's solution to the problem was typically adroit: he gave the man a car, but not a *red* one.

Hussein's ability to judge character in others was one of the key skills which helped him to maintain his throne. Paradoxically, one way he demonstrated this was through his well-known practice of rehabilitating his political opponents. There was more to this than a simple personal preference for forgiveness; part of his reasoning was that the enemy he knew was always better than the enemy he had not yet discovered. Although calculation played its part in his approach, it still threw up some startling examples of what could only be termed recklessness. For instance, in March 1963 the King received information from CIA sources about a plot against him hatched from within the Jordanian army, led by Brigadier Mashur Haditha al-Jazy.[7] On 6 April 1963 Hussein sent a well-publicised letter to the commander in chief of the armed forces, Field Marshal Habes al-Majali, in which he referred to measures taken against 'a number of officers involved in aspersions and allegations'.[8] And yet at a time of great danger for his regime in June 1970, he appointed the very same Mashur Haditha al-Jazy to command the Jordanian army. The risks involved in such actions were obvious, but by and large Hussein seems to have been well served by those he rehabilitated.

No doubt part of the explanation for this was the King's own personal charisma. While this quality is necessarily an intangible one, Hussein's mixture of monarchical gravity and personal charm struck many of those who met him. There is an interesting contrast to be drawn with one of his political contemporaries, the Egyptian leader Gamal Abdel Nasser. Both men possessed charisma, but Nasser's was of a more physical variety. He could dominate a room or a crowd through the weight of his physical presence, and through his rough, down-to-earth, often rabble-rousing rhetoric. Hussein's charisma, by contrast, was of a much more reserved, understated, almost spiritual nature. It was distilled in his voice, which was deep, rich and distinctive, and in his manner of speech, which was slow, deliberate and thoughtful. Without pushing himself forward, he nevertheless managed to attract others to his side.

Although the stresses and demands of politics were many, in his private life Hussein was for the most part quiet, reserved and informal. Perhaps because of the family troubles which, as we will see, affected his own childhood and adolescence, he took particular care to make sure that he always had time for all of his children, and the members of his extended family. But he also had an impish sense of fun, deciding on one memorable occasion to dress up as Santa Claus and deliver presents by helicopter to the children of his closer relatives. His sense of humour was not dry or sarcastic, but slapstick. Once, descending the steps of the Basman Palace on a rare icy day in Amman, he slipped and fell flat on his back with his arms and legs waving in the air. His companions' concern was only broken when the King burst out in laughter at his undignified posture. This slapstick humour was reflected in his younger years in his fondness for practical jokes, even extending to food fights at private parties. But there were clear limits to his tolerance for fun at the expense of others; when a joke was made at the dinner table about the alleged sexual orientation of one of the Gulf sheikhs, the King was furious. The individual concerned was one of his closer friends amongst Arab leaders, and had helped Jordan out financially on many occasions. Hussein was not prepared to hear fun made at his expense.

While Hussein was undoubtedly a family man, his private life was not without its complications. His first marriage to Queen Dina in 1955 was a failure, while his second, to Princess Muna, ended in divorce in 1972. His swift re-marriage to his third wife, Queen Alia, caused tensions and disagreements within the family, while the marriage itself ended in tragedy less than five years later, when Alia was killed in a helicopter crash. In 1978, Hussein married Queen Noor, with whom he remained until the end of his life. This restless search for happiness in his private life was in part the corollary of the stresses imposed by his public duties. As Hussein put it in a private letter to one close confidant on 8 January 1973, shortly after his marriage to Alia, 'one needs a certain amount of comfort and peace of mind to be able to continue to cope with responsibilities of such magnitude'.[9]

As he grew older, Hussein had to adjust the pace of his private life to accommodate his increasingly uncertain health. The water-skiing expeditions which had been the focus of his weekend excursions to Aqaba in his youth gave way, in the final years of his life, to more sedate boating trips on the Red Sea. Here Hussein was most often to be found at the wheel of his own vessel, contemplating in silence the horizon and the rocky shoreline where Jordan, Israel, Egypt and Saudi Arabia came together in close proximity. In these final years, alongside a persistent and growing sense of disillusionment with politics, close family members also observed in him an increasing spirituality.

This found expression in his formulation of the peace process with Israel as a quasi-religious mission.

While the account which follows of Hussein's reign might seem in one sense to be simply the chronicle of one crisis after another, and little more than a struggle for political survival, it is important to bear in mind that for the King himself this was only part of the picture. Survival was a means to an end. The kingship of Jordan was a means to an end. Even the development of the state of Jordan itself was a means to an end. No doubt the goal of Arab unity under Hashemite leadership was a quixotic one in the context of Arab politics in the second half of the twentieth century. But for Hussein, much as for his grandfather Abdullah before him, Jordan always had to have 'a larger future than a few thousand square miles of sand'.[10]

CHAPTER 1

THE TRAGEDY OF KING TALAL

Tragedy ended the reigns of both Hussein's grandfather Abdullah and his father Talal, but they were tragedies of very different kinds. Abdullah's was that of the political martyr, felled at the door of the al-Aqsa Mosque in Jerusalem by an assassin's bullet. Talal's tragedy was personal. He was the reluctant king, who had to bear the burden not only of the crown, but – far worse – of his father's disapproval. The fates of Abdullah and Talal made a deep impression on Hussein, and he carried their burdens with him for the rest of his life.

How the Hashemite kings came to reign over Jordan in the first place is a fascinating story in its own right, combining historical accident with design and determination. During the last years of the Ottoman Empire, the area of land which would become Jordan was a marginal one, at the fringe of the empire, which fell notionally under the authority of the province of Syria.[1] It was the First World War that changed the face of the region. As part of their search for allies against the Ottomans during the early part of the war, the British government entered into correspondence with Arab leaders, particularly Hussein's great-grandfather, Sharif Hussein of Mecca, to see if they would foment a rebellion against Ottoman rule. The classic account of the subsequent Arab Revolt was written in the 1930s by George Antonius, a political adventurer turned historian who had privileged access to the Hashemite family's private papers and held extensive conversations with Sharif Hussein and his sons Feisal and Abdullah. Antonius was more than just an ordinary historian: he was a family insider. If we want to understand King Hussein's perception of the roots of his own ideology there is no better place to look than Antonius's book.

In essence, Antonius identified the origins of twentieth-century Arab nationalism in movements spawned during the final decades of the Ottoman era, particularly what he termed Arab nationalist secret societies. Of these, the two most important were al-Fatat ('the Young Arab Society'), founded by Muslim students in Paris in 1911, and al-Ahd ('the Covenant'), founded in 1914 by Ottoman army officers. Antonius chronicled the establishment of links between these two secret societies and Sharif Hussein of Mecca, via his third son Feisal, who would later become the first king of Iraq. The crucial contacts took place in early 1915. In January the Sharif received an emissary from al-Fatat, Fauzi al-Bakri, who brought with him a message to the effect that Arab officers in the Ottoman army would be prepared to raise the standard of revolt to attain Arab independence if the Sharif were prepared to lead them.[2]

The Sharif did not immediately accept this invitation, but, instead, sent Feisal on a mission to Damascus to sound out the plotters. Antonius chose his words carefully in describing what now transpired: 'Feisal was let into the secret of the society and sworn in as a member.'[3] Thereafter, he was also sworn in as a member of al-Ahd, the secret association of army officers. In June 1915 he returned to see his father in Mecca, bringing with him a proposal from the two secret societies to cooperate with the British in defeating the Ottomans in order to create an independent Arab state.

Sharif Hussein treated the proposal cautiously. He wanted first to sound out the British government himself, and did this through correspondence with a British representative, Sir Henry McMahon, who was the High Commissioner of Egypt. The famous (or, to Hashemite minds, the infamous) Hussein–McMahon correspondence provided, as the Sharif saw it, a British guarantee of the creation of an independent Arab state covering the whole of Arabia, including Palestine, after the defeat of the Ottomans. This was a promise which was destined to remain unfulfilled. Instead, the subsequent Anglo-French 'Sykes–Picot' agreement of January 1916 laid the foundation for the eventual imperialist carve-up of the region, with Britain securing control over Palestine and Iraq, and France securing Syria and Lebanon. The British government proved keener to placate its French ally than to honour its commitments to the Hashemites. This double-dealing was the basis for the Hashemite claim that the Sharif was betrayed at the hands of the Allies after the war. As King Hussein put it in a letter written in 1981, 'Hashemites can never shirk their sense of duty and commitment to the Arab and Muslim cause. The leader of the Great Arab Revolt, betrayed by the Allies together with the Arab Nation, chose death in exile, although his body was returned to be buried in Jerusalem.'[4]

Antonius's account of the genesis and impact of the Arab Revolt was of course somewhat romanticised and one-sided. Subsequent historians, beginning with the scholar C.E. Dawn and including such luminaries as Albert Hourani, have questioned his version of the origins of Arab nationalism, the significance of the Arab Revolt, and the role of the link between the secret societies and the Hashemites in raising it.[5] But, when reading Antonius's account after the passage of seven decades, it is important to remember that he knew more about the relationship between the Hashemites and the secret societies than he was able to divulge in the pages of his book. There is no doubt that the intense loyalty of the members of these societies to the Arab nationalist cause, inspired in part by the nature of the oath they swore when learning the societies' secret, had a galvanising effect on the movement.

In the context of the life of King Hussein, what matters more, then, is not whether subsequent historians have accepted Antonius's claims about the impact and aims of the Arab Revolt and its eventual betrayal by the Allies, but whether Hussein himself believed them. All the evidence suggests that he did, and that his attachment to the Hashemite brand of Arab nationalism was firm and sincere. Others might have disagreed with his approach and questioned his methods, but it is clear that in key crises of his reign Hussein often fell back on this personal ideological reference point in framing his actions.

Despite Hussein's belief in the Allied betrayal of his great-grandfather, the Hashemites did not emerge empty-handed from the First World War – far from it. Feisal, who had led the Arab army into Damascus at the end of the war, became the first king of the newly created state of Iraq, one of several successor states to the Ottoman Empire which were entrusted initially to the Western powers as 'mandates' of the League of Nations. Meanwhile, Hussein's grandfather, Abdullah, who was in many ways the moving spirit behind the Arab Revolt, and who had commanded the Arab armies which had engaged the Ottoman forces for much of the war, now staked his claim to what would become Jordan. In advancing his claim, Abdullah showed a shrewd grasp of political opportunity, for the British remained undecided as to what to do with this area of land lying between Syria to the north, Palestine to the west, Iraq to the east and the Arabian peninsula to the south. Initially, the territory, which was known as 'Transjordan', was administered as part of Palestine, but in November 1922 the mandate was amended to permit its separation. In confirming his position as ruler of the territory Abdullah was helped by the advocacy of two individuals: T.E. Lawrence, the 'Lawrence of Arabia' of wartime legend, and the British Colonial Secretary, Winston Churchill, with whom Abdullah shared a particular bond.

Abdullah's ambitions were always too large to be contained within the emerging state of Transjordan. He did what he could to advance his interests beyond its frontiers, particularly in Syria, where his contacts with Arab nationalists excited the wrath of the French authorities and rebukes from the

British. But an even greater threat to his rule than the displeasure of the imperial powers was posed by the raiding activities of the fanatical Ikhwan forces loyal to the Hashemites' dynastic enemy Abdul Aziz ibn Saud. In October 1924 the Saudi forces defeated the Hashemites in the Hejaz, seizing the holy cities of Mecca and Medina and forcing Sharif Hussein into permanent exile. In November 1925 Abdullah had to recognise the authority of Ibn Saud over what became the Kingdom of Saudi Arabia through the Hadda agreement, which was negotiated under British auspices. Thereafter dynastic suspicion was never far below the surface in Saudi–Hashemite relations.

The southern frontier of Transjordan was secured through the Hadda agreement, but there was much work to do to build up central authority in the embryonic state. In February 1928 an agreement was reached between Abdullah and the British authorities whereby a young British army officer, Major John Bagot Glubb, arrived to set up a Desert Mobile Force, the nucleus of what became the Arab Legion, which co-opted the Bedouin tribes into the process of providing security. Glubb, who remained in Jordan for more than a quarter of a century, would play an important role in the early years of Hussein's reign. His continuing attachment to Jordan even after he left was reflected in private letters to Hussein, in which he referred to '*our* country', and commented that he would 'always remain a Jordanian'.[6]

As in other parts of the British Empire, the Second World War brought great changes to Transjordan. Abdullah tried to persuade the British to agree to some form of union between Syria and Transjordan after Damascus fell under Vichy French rule in 1941, but, failing in this, he increasingly focused his attention on developments in neighbouring Palestine instead. Abdullah's attitude towards the Jewish community in Palestine as it increased in size during the 1920s and 1930s can perhaps best be termed 'Ottoman' in its inspiration, harking back to the semi-separate status of the Jews as a *millet* or autonomous religious community under the Ottoman Empire.[7] Although the Hashemites saw the Balfour Declaration of 1917, which had committed the British government to establishing a 'national home' for the Jewish people in Palestine, as part of the Allied betrayal of the promises of independence made to Sharif Hussein, in practice Abdullah took a pragmatic attitude towards the Jewish presence in Palestine. During the 1930s he maintained sporadic contacts with the Jewish Agency, exploring amongst other issues the possibility of some form of bi-communal state in Palestine under his leadership. After the end of the Second World War, with the situation in Palestine deteriorating and communal strife increasing, Abdullah held meetings with Jewish representatives during which it was tentatively agreed that partition might be the best solution to the problem, with Abdullah coming to rule over the land allocated to the Arab inhabitants of Palestine.[8]

These discussions coincided with changes in the status of Transjordan itself. On 22 March 1946 an Anglo-Transjordanian Treaty was concluded granting Transjordan independence, with the qualification that the country would continue to provide Britain with defence facilities in exchange for an annual subsidy which would support the Arab Legion. During an ensuing parliamentary session in May, two decisions were taken: to declare the Emir Abdullah 'King', and to rename the state over which he ruled 'the Hashemite Kingdom of Jordan'.[9] Events in neighbouring Palestine were now to change the nature of that state dramatically.

Abdullah's role in the war for Palestine during 1948–9 remains hotly contested.[10] It has a special importance in understanding both his legacy to his grandson Hussein and Hussein's own subsequent conduct of relations with the state of Israel. As his earlier consideration of the possibility of partition suggested, Abdullah was prepared to countenance the formation of a Jewish state in part of Palestine, even though his real preference was for an Arab–Jewish confederation under his leadership. But, as the commander of the only effective Arab army to engage in the conflict, and the titular overall commander of Arab forces, he also had to accommodate the broader Arab hostility to the creation of any Jewish state. Unlike many of his Arab contemporaries, though, Abdullah seems to have had a realistic respect for the strength of the Jewish forces, and a corresponding recognition of the weaknesses and division evident in the Arab camp. Under the stresses of war in 1948, his pre-war understandings with representatives of the Jewish Agency (including Golda Meir, the subsequent Israeli prime minister, whom he met in November 1947 and May 1948) broke down. After the Israeli declaration of independence in May 1948, the Arab states, including Jordan, joined the battle for Palestine. Although the Jordanian forces suffered setbacks, particularly in the final phase of the conflict, they emerged at the beginning of 1949 holding a large section of the territory earlier allocated to an Arab state under the 1947 United Nations partition plan, together with the Old City of Jerusalem.

With the war over, recriminations escalated in the Arab camp. Abdullah's pre-war contacts with Jewish leaders and his continuing willingness to contemplate a peace settlement with the new state of Israel constituted in the eyes of his enemies a betrayal of the Arab cause. But the fact remained that the only significant portion of mandate Palestine saved for the Arabs had been held by Abdullah's forces. In Hussein's subsequent negotiations with Israeli leaders there are echoes of the dilemma which Abdullah had faced. On the one hand Hussein came to see it as part of his Hashemite destiny to bring together what he would call 'the children of Abraham'. On the other hand he was well aware, both from his grandfather's and his own experience, that Israeli leaders were hostile and inflexible on the subject of the acquisition and retention of land. This was amply illustrated in the negotiations for an armistice between Jordan and Israel during 1949, which saw Jordan first coerced into relinquishing further territory in the southern Negev as a result of an Israeli violation of the ceasefire, and then forced to give up land in the Wadi Araba.[11] Mindful of his grandfather's experiences, in his own subsequent negotiations with the Israelis Hussein held firmly to the position that he could not be responsible for the relinquishment of one inch of Arab land.

Abdullah's success in holding on to part of Palestine went some way towards fulfilling his sense of Hashemite destiny. His kingdom had been expanded through the addition of a populous and well-developed area of land on the West Bank of the River Jordan, which was officially incorporated into Jordan through the Union of the Two Banks, passed by the Jordanian parliament in April 1950. But this achievement also made the Palestinian question an irrevocable part of Jordan's domestic politics, as well as its foreign policy. Abdullah was not destined to live long enough to grapple with the issue, but integrating and governing the two Banks became Hussein's greatest political problem between 1953 and 1967, and the clash between Hashemite and Palestinian nationalism was one of the enduring challenges of Hussein's reign. In essence Hussein held the same paternalistic view of the Palestinian question as his grandfather. On the one hand, he supported Palestinian rights both to land and to political self-determination. On the other hand, he believed that the Hashemite Kingdom, incorporating the West Bank, was the best home for the Palestinians, and he saw no essential conflict between the two. On the contrary, he felt that he was better placed to secure Palestinian rights than the leaders of the Palestinian nationalist movement, which coalesced as the Palestine Liberation Organisation during the 1960s. The gap between his perception and that of many Palestinians caused him a great deal of frustration and disappointment across the decades.

While in this and other respects Hussein enthusiastically embraced his grandfather's legacy, and shared his sense of the destiny of the Hashemites, the same could not be said of his own father. The turbulent personal relationship between Abdullah and his elder son, Talal, who had been born in 1909, deeply affected the young Prince Hussein during his childhood. Whether it was in the form of disagreements over Hussein's education, resulting in his frequent changes of school, or of his grandfather's refusal to entrust Talal with any significant political role, or of Abdullah's evident lack of faith in Talal's suitability to accede to the throne, the tension between the two men frequently impinged on Hussein's life. Talal, who was thoughtful and introverted by nature, seems never to have recommended himself to the exuberant extrovert Abdullah. Handsome, and blessed with considerable natural dignity and charm of manner, Talal preferred to mix with small groups of friends at lunch parties and seldom went out. In conversation, he showed an excellent grasp of politics, and was a shrewd and humorous judge of character. According to one observer, he had 'no illusions about the Arabs' and was 'unlikely to follow his father's habit of surrounding himself with favourites'. Also unlike his father, he had no personal or dynastic ambitions. Abdullah's dreams of Hashemite destiny, and of the creation of a 'Greater Syria' under his leadership, were likely to die a death if Talal became King. Talal was progressive too in his social attitudes. He disliked the veiling of women and took a more liberal outlook on religious issues than his father. He was a firm believer that the Crown's role should be strictly limited. All in all, according to one British observer, Talal had the makings of 'a good constitutional monarch'.[12]

Talal's personal qualities and his liberal views did little to recommend him to Abdullah. Probably the most important, unspoken source of tension between father and son was jealousy; Abdullah may have felt that his son's intelligence rivalled and perhaps exceeded his own.[13] Divided by temperament and belief, father and son moved still further apart during the late 1920s and 1930s as Talal disappointed Abdullah's expectations. Unlike Abdullah, who had revelled in his role as military commander during the revolt against the Ottomans, Talal seems to have had an instinctive aversion to the military profession. During his time at the British Army Training Academy of Sandhurst in 1928 he rebelled against the military regimen, and found himself unceremoniously dunked by his fellow cadets in the pond in the college grounds for his trouble.[14] In contrast to his son, Hussein, who was to develop a certain respect for British military methods and discipline as a result of his own time at Sandhurst, for Talal the experience of England was not a positive one. Whilst it would be too simplistic to suggest that his difficulties at Sandhurst lay behind his widely rumoured German sympathies during the Second World War,[15] Talal found himself much less attracted to, and impressed by, the British than either Abdullah or Hussein.

During the 1930s, the relationship between Abdullah and Talal deteriorated still further, with the Emir giving his son little or nothing to do while he languished in his modest rented home in Amman.[16] Talal's many suggestions that he should be given some administrative or ministerial appointment were rebuffed by Abdullah, who effectively forced on him a life of complete idleness which would have been trying for anyone.[17] Talal's position was also affected adversely by an element of sibling rivalry with his younger half-brother Nayif, whom his father evidently favoured. Not blessed with any particular intellectual ability or good judgement, Nayif did at least share his father's extroverted temperament, which made relations between him and Abdullah somewhat easier. No doubt Abdullah was aware of Nayif's shortcomings in respect of intellect and industry, but by the time the Second World War broke out he had come to the conclusion that Nayif would be the better prospect as his successor. With the assistance of the British Resident in Amman, Alec Kirkbride, who described Talal at this point as 'at heart deeply anti-British', King Abdullah signed a secret decree excluding his elder son from the succession.[18]

Beyond Talal's widely rumoured German sympathies, other factors seem to have lain behind Abdullah's decision. Frustrated and with nothing to do, Talal had taken to drinking during the pre-war years. By his own subsequent admission, he had reached 'the bottle a day mark in whisky drinking' during this period.[19] This, together with the intermittent flashes of what Alec Kirkbride initially termed 'mild eccentricity', and later 'peculiar behaviour' bordering on 'mental abnormality',[20] undermined what little remaining confidence Abdullah had in his elder son as successor to the throne. But, to his credit, Talal managed to turn himself round during the course of the war. He stopped drinking completely during 1942–3 and made great efforts to reconcile himself to Abdullah and the British. While Talal was striving to prove himself trustworthy, Nayif's innate shortcomings became all the more apparent. The result was that after the war, in 1946, Abdullah cancelled his secret change to the succession and, in a public decree issued in March 1947, formally bestowed on Talal the title of heir to the throne.[21]

The key stabilising influence in Talal's life during these years was undoubtedly provided by his wife, Sharifa Zein. Married in 1934, the couple ultimately had four children, of whom Hussein, born on 14 November 1935, was the eldest. Zein was a fascinating and complex woman. Born in Egypt on 2 August 1916, she was subsequently educated in a convent. After her marriage to Talal, she conformed in public to the contemporary Muslim social conventions, which largely excluded her from any formal political role. In private, though, and in the company of Westerners, she showed herself to have an informed and astute grasp of politics. Indeed, in later years, the British Foreign Secretary Selwyn Lloyd was to dub her 'the Metternich of the Arab world', such was the sophistication of her political manoeuvring.[22] But there was much more to Zein than intelligence and political skill. The contemporary testimonies to her strength of character, her fortitude in the face of adversity and her personal courage are numerous. Steadfast in her affections, she did her best to guide and protect her husband, even as severe mental illness overtook him in later years. She also played her part in attempting to salvage his relations with Abdullah. If Zein had a weakness it lay in the fact that her strength of character led her to try to dominate both her husband and children, a tendency much in evidence in her handling of Hussein's education and in her role during his early years on the throne. During the late 1930s and 1940s, Zein proved a rock of stability in her husband's personal life. With his family, Talal proved himself to be 'a model of the domestic virtues'. He was devoted to his wife and young children, and one of his friends commented, 'I fully believe him when he tells me that he is never really happy out of their company.'[23]

With Abdullah apparently reconciled to Talal's succession, one might have expected that relations between father and son, and Talal's mental state, would have been placed under much less strain. Unfortunately, the respite was short-lived. The tensions between the two men soon erupted once again, with Abdullah refusing to give Talal any significant role during the 1948–9 war in Palestine. Meanwhile, Talal began to show increasing signs of instability. In a character sketch written in July 1949, the British diplomat Martin Pirie-Gordon noted that Talal's two greatest failings were his temper, 'which is unpredictable and violent', and 'a certain timidity as regards social obligations and public life which takes the form of sudden last minute panic and cancellation of arrangements'.[24] His instability also manifested itself in his financial affairs, which were described as 'mysterious'. Before independence from Britain in 1946, Talal had been kept on a very tight allowance of about £1,500 per year. The result was that he got into debt. After Jordan's independence, the government progressively raised his allowance to £5,000 per year by 1949, but still Talal accumulated debts, even though by this stage he had no obvious vices or expensive hobbies. There was speculation that he had used the money to buy jewellery, which he was hoarding against the day when he might cease to be heir to the throne.[25]

But the crux of Talal's problems remained his bad relationship with his father, which 'had a profoundly depressing effect on him'. Pirie-Gordon wrote:

> I believe the fault to be mainly the King's, but Talal, who really admires the old man, although he laughs at him, has believed the continual squabbling to be due to some weakness of his own and has thereby grown something of an 'inferiority complex' to which I think many of his present faults can be attributed.[26]

Talal's spirits actually revived slightly when 'on reading the history of the House of Hanover he found that strained relations between the sovereign and the heir were by no means confined to the Hashemites!'

By the end of 1950 relations between Abdullah and Talal had reached another low point, with the King discussing once again the question of excluding him from the succession.[27] Although he took no action at this point, matters came to a head in early 1951. By this stage, Talal had accumulated debts totalling £11,000, even though his allowance had been raised again to £6,000 per annum. The King, who paid off Talal's debts, was furious when he broke his subsequent promise to live within his means, and threatened not to appoint Talal as regent during his absence on a planned trip to Turkey in May.

Although he grudgingly relented on this issue, Abdullah left the country promising to reconsider the question of Talal's succession when he returned.[28] This altercation was sufficient to tip Talal over the brink. A few hours after Abdullah's departure, he called up the British Minister, Alec Kirkbride, and 'put a series of questions which showed that something serious had happened to his mind'. Next he sent for the prime minister, Samir Rifai, telling him that he knew there was a plot unfolding: first the King had been sent into exile, next he himself was to be assassinated and finally Nayif would be made king. He accused both Rifai and Kirkbride of having been party to the conspiracy. According to Kirkbride's account, written immediately after the events:

> This was bad enough but worse was to come. Talal's wife was in the Italian hospital where she had given birth to a daughter [Princess Basma] a few days before. At 3am the next morning Talal forced his way into the hospital, and . . . attacked his wife with a dagger. He was disarmed before he hurt her . . .[29]

Talal was taken to his home and a guard placed outside the door. In the final scene of the drama, the Minister of Health, who had been Talal's family doctor for some years, went to visit him at home, only to find him 'trying to extort information from [Prince Mohammad] his second son (ten years old) with violence. He had to knock Talal down to get the child away from him.'[30]

It was immediately decided that Talal would have to leave the country for medical treatment in Beirut in the care of a mental health specialist, Dr Ford Robertson. According to Kirkbride, Talal left the country 'most willingly as he was still convinced that he was about to be assassinated'.[31] Once Talal had reached Beirut, Dr Robertson quickly reached the conclusion that the root of his problem was his relationship with his father. He felt that Talal's condition was not beyond treatment; with a long period of convalescence outside Jordan, the chances were about even that he would recover sufficiently to live a relatively normal life. Dr Robertson did not believe, though, that Talal would ever be fit enough to take up the kingship, arguing that the strains of high office would be too much for him to bear. This was an opinion shared by the other doctors who had seen him before he left Jordan.[32]

By now the question of the succession was drawing in outside powers which had an interest in the future of Jordan and the Hashemite dynasty. In this sense, there was a parallel between the events at the beginning and the end of Hussein's reign. During 1951–2 it was the Iraqi and Saudi royal families who battled for influence over the Jordanian succession. Their basic interests in what happened in Jordan were not hard to identify. The Iraqis hoped for some form of Iraqi–Jordanian union, in which Iraq would play the leading role, or the straightforward succession of a member of the Iraqi branch of the family to the Jordanian throne. The key figure on the Iraqi side was the Regent, later Crown Prince, Abdul Ilah, whose approach was complicated by his very poor relations with Talal and by an intense sense of personal and familial dignity which bordered on the neurotic. The Saudis, led by King Ibn Saud, sought to block the extension of Iraqi influence in Jordan at all costs, for fear of a united Hashemite bloc which might exercise regional leadership or, worse still, attempt to recover the lost Hashemite lands in the Hejaz.

Talal's departure to Beirut in May prompted an immediate upsurge in Iraqi interest. When Abdullah went to visit the now somewhat recovered Talal in Lebanon on 1 June, he was accompanied by Abdul Ilah, together with the veteran Iraqi Prime Minister Nuri as-Said.[33] Whatever the pressures exerted by the Iraqis, King Abdullah decided to wait on events before taking a final decision on the succession. On 27 June, though, Talal returned unexpectedly to Jordan, leaving the care of another mental health specialist to whom he had been referred earlier in the month in London.[34] In a heart-to-heart discussion with Abdullah about the succession, Talal reportedly told his father that he did not feel he could assume the responsibilities of kingship, and was prepared to write a letter renouncing his rights to the throne. As a result of the conversation, Abdullah gave serious consideration to making Nayif heir apparent once again. The main obstacle in his path was the prime minister, Samir Rifai, who argued that installing Nayif as Crown Prince would require an amendment to the constitution, something which his government was very reluctant to seek.[35]

Within three days of his return to Amman, however, Talal suffered a relapse in his condition, launching a further serious assault on his wife and younger children. Dr Robertson arrived in Amman and recommended that Talal should be committed to a clinic in Geneva for at least a month, where he should undergo electro-convulsive therapy. This further violent episode evidently made up Abdullah's mind. In the absence of his trusted confidant, Alec Kirkbride, who had returned to England for what would turn out to be a particularly ill-timed spell of leave, Abdullah called in Malcolm Walker of the British legation on 10 July. In the presence of Nayif, he announced, according to Walker, that:

> The Arab tradition in this matter was that the bravest, wisest, strongest and, generally, the most suitable member of the reigning family should succeed. Since Talal was incapable and Talal's eldest son [Hussein] was an untried boy, the only man who fulfilled all the requirements was the Amir Naif. Whether Naif should be King or only Regent for Talal's son did not matter so much, but there was no alternative to him as head of the State.[36]

Abdullah concluded by noting, with what proved to be ominous prescience, that although he did not propose to take any action until after Kirkbride's return to Amman, 'he wanted His Majesty's Government to know that if in the meanwhile anything should happen to him, those were his wishes'. In a handwritten annotation to his report, Walker commented, 'I now learn that the King was speaking not so much to me in the Amir Naif's presence as to the Amir Naif in my presence! It was a manoeuvre to overcome Naif's reluctance to having the succession thrust on him as much as a means of preventing me from making any criticism!'

At the same time as Abdullah was giving his final blessing to Nayif as his successor, Talal left by plane for Geneva, where he began his treatment. The next act in the tragedy was played out in Jerusalem. There, on Friday 20 July, with the young Prince Hussein at his side, Abdullah was shot through the head at point-blank range at the door of the al-Aqsa Mosque by a Palestinian tailor's apprentice, Mustafa Ashu. The murder of his grandfather had a profound effect on Hussein. It was the event with which he chose to begin his early autobiography, *Uneasy Lies the Head*, where he also wrote of Abdullah's premonition of his fate, this time in another conversation three days before he left for Jerusalem.[37]

During the weeks following Abdullah's assassination, the succession to the throne and, indeed, the very survival of Jordan as an independent Hashemite kingdom, hung in the balance. Although an initial effort was made to keep the news of Abdullah's assassination from Talal in Geneva,[38] probably for fear of worsening his condition, he quickly found out what had happened, impatiently cabling his brother Nayif: 'have heard the sad news of assassination of my beloved father. No news from you. Please write full details and situation of my family.'[39] Talal's telegram was accompanied by a cable from Dr Ford Robertson about his condition, intended for the Jordanian prime minister: 'treatment proceeding but not yet well enough to meet crisis at Amman. Hope you will not insist on return. May need full time before a decision is possible.'[40] On 23 July Nayif cabled his brother, telling him what was known about their father's assassination.[41]

Prime Minister Rifai now held urgent discussions with the British Minister Kirkbride, who had returned to Amman immediately after the assassination. The best solution, Rifai argued, would be for Talal to remove himself willingly from the line of succession, with Nayif made regent for Hussein. If Talal would not agree to this, then he would have to be removed from the succession by a decision of the Council of Ministers.[42] However, Rifai could not take matters further, since it was the convention that a new prime minister should be chosen after the death of the sovereign, and hence Rifai was succeeded by the veteran statesman Tawfiq Abu'l Huda. An able administrator with the reputation for being incorruptible, Abu'l Huda was by nature a circumspect political operator. He held his cards very close, making it difficult for friend and foe alike to determine where his sympathies lay, or what his next political move might be. He, like Rifai, was aware of Abdullah's final wishes concerning the succession, but, in keeping with his usual approach, he proceeded cautiously, preferring to avoid taking any immediate decision on the issue.

The events of the next five weeks remain somewhat murky, although the basic outline of what transpired can be deciphered. For various reasons, including an improvement in his health, the vigorous sponsorship of his wife Zein, the backing of the Saudis and the political ineptitude of Nayif, Talal emerged as Abu'l Huda's favoured candidate for the throne. How far Abu'l Huda had already made up his mind as to which successor he would support when he took up the premiership is unclear. Similarly, how far the Saudis were able to influence his judgement in favour of Talal is difficult to divine, although it seems that Abu'l Huda did receive some personal financial support from King Ibn Saud's coffers.[43]

Of all the factors which finally tipped the balance of succession in favour of Talal, though, his status as the constitutional incumbent and his swift apparent recovery from illness probably loomed the largest. After visiting Talal in the middle of August, Deputy Prime Minister Said al-Mufti returned pronouncing him to be 'normal and apparently happy'.[44] During Mufti's visit, Talal also approved an idea first broached by Zein that Hussein should be sent to school in England, to Harrow.[45] The main reason behind this was concern about the prince's security should he return to Victoria College in Alexandria, where he had hitherto been educated. In view of a suspected Egyptian connection to Abdullah's assassination, England was considered a safer place for the prince.

The trial of those accused of Abdullah's assassination ended on 28 August, with guilty verdicts handed down on four of the defendants. The conspiracy was believed to have been orchestrated from Egypt by a Jordanian exile, Abdullah al-Tall, a former confidant of the King, although Tall himself continued to protest his innocence, and was indeed welcomed back to Jordan and pardoned by Hussein at the beginning of the 1970s.[46] This remarkable political rehabilitation casts doubt on whether Hussein believed in his guilt, and the real origins of the plot to murder Abdullah remain unresolved. Nevertheless, with the trial concluded, Abu'l Huda felt able to move on the other key outstanding issue: the question of the succession. In the final weeks before Talal's return to Jordan on 6 September, Nayif proceeded to over-play his hand, first threatening to refuse to sign the death warrants for his father's killers unless his own position as successor to the throne was confirmed, and then conspiring with members of the Hashemite Regiment to stage some form of military coup against Abu'l Huda's government. Nayif has traditionally been portrayed as the 'villain' of the succession saga as a result, but his behaviour is easier to understand in the knowledge that Abdullah had told him ten days before his death that he should succeed to the throne.[47] Nevertheless, the result of his inept manoeuvres was that by the time Talal flew back into Amman, the Jordanian political establishment had turned decisively against Nayif, and he meekly accepted his brother's coronation as King. From his position as Abdullah's chosen heir before his assassination, Nayif had been turned in the space of less than two months into a political pariah in Jordan. To be sure, he made mistakes during this time, but there is little doubt he was also out-manoeuvred in the succession struggle by the Prime Minister Abu'l Huda and Sharifa Zein.[48]

Apart from Nayif, the biggest losers in the saga were probably the Iraqis, who had opposed the succession of Talal.[49] Commenting bitterly on the outcome of the succession struggle, Abdul Ilah expressed particular suspicions of Zein's role, believing that she was manoeuvring to secure Hussein's succession once he came of age, as this would leave her a freer hand to dominate the throne from behind the scenes.[50] Hussein himself, though, was not about to let his mother take all the decisions about his future without having his own say. During his childhood he had become accustomed to his mother's domineering tendencies. It was only when he left Amman in his early teens to attend Victoria College in Alexandria that he could begin to assert his independence, and, perhaps as a result, he recalled in his autobiography that his two years at Victoria 'were among the happiest in my life'. It is plain that Hussein was opposed to his parents' decision to move him from Victoria College to Harrow School in England in the summer of 1951, acquiescing only reluctantly in view of the strained relations between Egypt and Jordan following his grandfather's assassination.[51]

During his time at Harrow School from September 1951 until July 1952, and then at the Sandhurst Military Academy from September 1952 until February 1953, Hussein became more confident and assertive. This was no doubt the result both of being thrown in at the deep end in the English public school system, and of acting as the male pillar of the family during his father's illness. Hussein's experience at Harrow was a difficult one. First, there was the language barrier. Although he had had lessons in English at Victoria College, he found that his accent was heavier and his level of comprehension lower than he had realised. Then, there was the cultural transition. Although Victoria College had been established along English public school lines, the majority of its pupils had, like him, an Arab background. Now he found himself to be the only Arab in his peer group, with the exception of his cousin Prince Feisal. The linguistic and cultural barriers made it very difficult for him to establish contact with the other boys, meaning that he was initially very lonely. Partly as a result of his language difficulties, Hussein also struggled academically. Probably his only outlet was 'games' – he threw himself into rugby, although even here his slight build and short stature were disadvantages against which he had to labour.

Two other distractions made it difficult for Hussein to settle at Harrow. The first was the constant attention of the Jordanian ambassador in London, Fawzi al-Mulqi. Mulqi was a thirty-nine-year-old diplomat, who held degrees from both the American University of Beirut and the University of Edinburgh. As ambassador in London, it was of course his duty to make sure that the Crown Prince was properly looked after during his time in England. But Mulqi's attentions went far beyond those required by simple diplomatic propriety. From an early stage, Mulqi believed that by ingratiating himself with Hussein, he might open the way to his eventual appointment as Jordan's prime minister. Consequently, he kept up a constant stream of invitations for Hussein to attend parties and other functions in London, and his frequent weekend absences from Harrow made it even more difficult for him to settle in.

The other distraction for Hussein was the continuing uncertainty surrounding his father's state of health. Talal's 'recovery', if such it ever was, proved sadly short-lived. The first obvious signs of his relapse came during a family vacation in January 1952. There were evidently several other minor incidents during the early part of the year which Queen Zein managed to contain, but she was fighting a losing battle. The stresses of the kingship had led Talal to take up drinking once again. As the new British Minister Geoffrey Furlonge reported at the end of March, 'it now transpires that for some time past he has gradually been becoming re-addicted to whiskey, off which Dr Ford Robertson specifically warned him . . .'[52] Zein's attempts to manage her husband's condition were made all the more difficult by the fact that from the end of 1951 she was herself seriously ill, suffering from a blood circulation disorder accompanied by repeated heart attacks.[53] By 19 March she had no alternative but to travel to Switzerland for an operation. The consequences of Zein's departure for Talal's own mental state were serious. On 27 March he had a further breakdown. Summoning the former prime minister, Samir Rifai, he demanded 'to be told the truth about the plot to murder him'.[54] Although Prime Minister Abu'l Huda managed to calm him down, his condition was once again a major political concern. Talal's physician, Ford Robertson, was consulted and his advice was sobering: 'the King is not dangerous to a grown man, nor probably to a woman, but is liable at any time, now that he has again taken to whiskey, to do serious harm to his young children, who must therefore be got out of his way'.[55] Abu'l Huda, who had up to this point been confident in his ability to manage the situation himself, now turned to the British Minister Furlonge to seek his advice. At this stage, though, he was saved from taking any difficult decisions by the fact that the

King seemed to recover quickly from his attack, and showed considerable remorse. According to Abu'l Huda, the King now spoke constantly of abdicating when his son Hussein came of age on 2 May 1953, which at least suggested that the problem might be one of limited duration.[56]

How much of this reached Hussein at Harrow is unclear, but the Crown Prince had his own problems to deal with at this stage. In mid-March 1952 he raised concerns that he was being watched 'by unknown persons (apparently Arabs) whenever he left the precincts of the school'.[57] Although both the British Foreign Office and the Special Branch police were inclined to make light of the incidents, the investigation into them revealed that apparently no measures at all were being taken to protect Hussein.[58] In view of the fact that his grandfather had been assassinated the previous year this seems extraordinary. In any event, Hussein's concerns were taken more as a symptom of his unhappiness at Harrow than as any serious threat to his security. In a bid to broaden his contacts with English families and improve his impression of England, efforts were now set in train, with the agreement of his housemaster at Harrow, Mr W.H. Stevenson, to secure him weekend invitations to tea with neighbouring families. In a letter addressing the Foreign Office's concern that the prince should take away a positive impression of England, Stevenson wrote:

> He is a likeable boy and gets on quite well here but it is not easy for anyone, and particularly someone from the East, to join a community like a House at the age of 16 when his background is so different from that of those he is with. In Italy last holiday he was made much of and he therefore thinks highly of that country and associates England largely with work and discipline. I would welcome anything which gave him the best possible impression of this country.[59]

On 27 March Hussein left Harrow for Switzerland to support his mother during her operation and subsequent convalescence. As Zein recuperated during April, there was also some improvement in Talal's condition back in Amman. He cut down on his drinking and behaved normally for the most part, the only disturbing development being his tendency to take unescorted rides around town, during which he entered shops and made purchases incognito. 'It would look as though he has been reading stories of Harun el Rashid,' commented the British Minister Furlonge wryly. Furlonge also noted that the Prime Minister Abu'l Huda was keeping his fingers crossed, and looking forward to the Queen's expected return at the beginning of May, which he hoped might stabilise Talal's condition.[60]

In the event, these hopes were dashed. Talal was evidently already troubled about the activities of his half-brother Nayif, who had fled to Beirut. However unlikely it was, Talal believed that Nayif was still manoeuvring to seize the throne, and wanted him to be expelled from Lebanon.[61] Zein's return to Jordan on 7 May brought about a further serious deterioration in Talal's condition. For the first three days after her return to Jordan, the Queen did not sleep at all for fear of Talal's constant physical threats. This left Abu'l Huda with no choice but to take action. Unable to find a local Jordanian doctor with sufficient courage to pronounce Talal unfit to rule, an assistant of Dr Robertson had to be summoned from abroad, arriving in Amman on 11 May. In the meantime, the Queen had taken what measures she could to protect herself, including persuading Talal to hand over his revolver, which she hid. Still weak from her operation and without any sleep for the best part of a week, Zein had understandably reached breaking point. By 17 May, when the crisis peaked, Abu'l Huda, whom Talal still continued to treat as his one trusted confidant, was also very near to physical breakdown. The key to resolving the problem seemed to lie in persuading Talal to leave the country, but this he persistently refused to do, claiming that it was part of the plot against him orchestrated by the British. It was only early on the morning of 18 May, in a brief moment of lucidity, that Talal was finally persuaded to board a British-chartered aircraft and leave Amman for Paris. In his absence, a Throne Council headed by Abu'l Huda was appointed to exercise the functions of regency.[62]

The final unfortunate scenes of the tragedy of King Talal were now played out in Europe. Although Talal had been persuaded to leave Jordan, he had not yet accepted that he should be hospitalised. Consequently, a ministerial delegation comprising Interior Minister Said Mufti and Defence Minister Suleiman Tuqan was sent after him to Paris in a bid to persuade him to accept treatment. The mission was a failure, and Talal's attacks continued, forcing Zein to seek refuge with her three younger children in the British embassy in Paris on 29 May.[63] There, the following evening, Hussein arrived from England to join her. According to the British ambassador, he 'made an excellent impression' on arrival, before moving on to join his father who was staying at Versailles. The two cabinet ministers who had been sent out from Jordan, by contrast, proved to be 'quite useless'.[64] Even Ambassador Mulqi, who had travelled with Hussein, soon turned out 'to be a broken reed and too frightened to be trusted'. It was up to Hussein, at the age of sixteen, to manage the crisis and support his mother. His goal was to do what he could to calm his father and persuade him to accept treatment. Unfortunately, Talal's condition was too far advanced to be susceptible to reason. On 31 May he attacked Hussein with a knife and he was forced to take refuge at another hotel.[65] Hussein was evidently on his own by this stage, since Mulqi had now attached himself to the King. In a final bid to force access to his wife and children, Talal turned up at the British embassy accompanied by Mulqi, 'beating on the door and making a scene in the courtyard' before eventually driving off.

The following evening Zein, with Hussein's support, decided that it would be best for her to leave Paris and travel to Lausanne, where she hoped to escape her husband's attention. She asked that the British minister in Amman should impress on Prime Minister Abu'l Huda the urgency of a decision about the King's treatment since his health was deteriorating and 'at any moment a tragedy may occur if he is not confined'.[66] On the evening of 2 June, Zein, accompanied by Hussein and his brother and sister, Mohammad and Basma, flew to Geneva en route for Lausanne. (Oddly, Zein elected to leave her five-year-old son Hassan behind in the care of his father together with his nurse, a woman whom Talal apparently trusted.) Hussein himself had taken the place of Zein's lady-in-waiting, Sharifa Fatma, on the flight to Geneva 'principally in order to ensure that malicious tongues should not accuse the Queen of leaving unescorted with the Chamberlain'.[67] The fact that such precautions had to be taken showed the depths to which some people were prepared to descend in seeking gossip about Zein.

Zein's escape was short-lived. Talal quickly discovered her destination and followed her to Lausanne, although once there he could not find out where she was staying. By this stage it was impossible to keep the drama quiet, and the international press ran a number of stories between 9 and 11 June about the King's attempts to catch up with the Queen.[68] With his mother in a position of relative safety, Hussein himself returned to England, where he remained in telephone contact with both of his parents at their separate locations in Lausanne.

The unhappy saga of King Talal was now drawing to its close. On 3 July, the King returned to Jordan, where he was subsequently examined by two Egyptian physicians who confirmed the gravity of his condition. Zein meanwhile remained in Switzerland. Prime Minister Abu'l Huda's intention at this stage was to send Talal away for an extended period of treatment in Egypt, but this plan was dropped when a military coup resulted in the fall of the Egyptian monarchy on 23 July. At this point, Abu'l Huda used his Saudi connections to approach King Ibn Saud to see if he would accept responsibility for Talal. Although Ibn Saud's response was positive, Talal's behaviour was now so erratic, including contacts with disaffected elements in the army who feared a British-inspired conspiracy against the throne, that Abu'l Huda decided there was no alternative to deposing him. On 7 August he wrote to Zein informing her that the King had made 'a dangerous attempt to upset the welfare and security of the country'. In these circumstances, it was 'possible that Parliament will make a decision to terminate his rule and to declare Prince Hussein his successor'.[69] On 11 August a special session of parliament was convened at which a committee was appointed to review the medical evidence on Talal's condition. At the committee's recommendation, parliament then voted to depose Talal and appoint Hussein in his place.[70] Talal accepted his fate with dignity and on 16 September departed the country for Egypt, where all of the expenses for his medical treatment were met by King Ibn Saud.[71] Thereafter, following a serious car accident in July 1953, Talal was relocated to a private home in the Ortakoy district of Istanbul where he lived until his death on 8 July 1972. With his father deposed, the responsibilities of the kingship, which had ultimately proved too great a burden for Talal to bear, would now fall on Hussein.

As the final dramatic events of Talal's reign were unfolding, Hussein found himself at first back at school in England, where he still had to finish his final term at Harrow. There, to distract him from the travails of his father's illness, and to further the British Foreign Office's plan of giving him a positive impression of England, he was invited at the end of June to visit the home of a senior official who lived near Harrow. His report of Hussein's visit provides a further snapshot of the young prince's interests and character at the time. Although Hussein was still shy in company, he was gifted with 'a very ready and engaging smile'. In terms of his pastimes, while he showed some interest in horses, and discussed his grandfather's stud, it was clear that his pride and joy was his car, a pale blue Rover, which he drove himself. Overall, Hussein's hosts were particularly struck by his good manners, which would serve him well in the years to come.[72]

Hussein's schoolboy days were now nearly over. Not long after this visit, near the end of July, he left England to join his mother in Switzerland. If his father's illness had cast a shadow over his year at Harrow, and forced him to grow up quickly, Talal's deposition from the throne now thrust on him the role of monarch before his seventeenth birthday. Until Hussein formally came of age according to the Islamic calendar on 2 May 1953, the royal prerogatives would be exercised by a regency council acting in his stead. On 25 August Hussein, now King, returned to Jordan accompanied by his mother in order to meet the prime minister and other dignitaries. Hussein also had a brief encounter with his father, who was staying near Irbid before his departure from the country. The young King was shocked at both the mental and physical condition of his father, who had lost a considerable amount of weight since he had last seen him in June. As could only be expected, the atmosphere during their meeting was fraught with emotion.[73]

Hussein's first visit back to Jordan as King was a brief one. He soon returned to England, where he began a compressed officer's training course at Sandhurst in early September. As with his schooling at Harrow, some advance consideration was given by the British Foreign Office to the impact that his course at Sandhurst might have on the young King's impressions of England. Concern was expressed that the rigorous discipline, spartan conditions and attention of warrant officers 'who are scant respecters of persons (not excluding Royalty)' might 'prejudice him against this country for the rest of his days'. On the other hand, it was recognised that singling Hussein out for special, privileged treatment might only make him a lonely figure and would deprive him of the 'undoubted benefits which a somewhat Spartan regime can bestow'.[74] The agreed compromise was not to make special provision for Hussein, but to ensure that the commandant of the college, Major General Dawnay, kept a close eye on his progress. In the event, some minor extra privileges were afforded 'Officer Cadet King Hussein', as he was known, including a room to himself complete with modern conveniences, and a servant specially selected to help him clean his military equipment. It was also agreed that he should spend eight weeks instead of the regular six months in each of the Junior, Intermediate and Senior terms, allowing him to pass out in the Sovereign's Parade after only five months.[75]

As his course at Sandhurst progressed, Hussein showed further signs of increasing self-assertiveness, particularly when it came to opposing his mother's plans for organising his time between passing out at Sandhurst in February and his coronation in Amman in May. Zein was evidently worried that if Hussein returned to Amman too soon he might become caught up in palace intrigues. She therefore wanted to keep him out of the country for as long as possible and privately sought the cooperation of the British authorities in achieving her goal. The Queen's idea was that Hussein should be attached to a 'royal regiment' of the British army for a limited period after Sandhurst which would prevent him returning to Amman. Unfortunately, through some injudicious remarks made by his company commander at Sandhurst, Hussein got wind of the scheme. He promptly marched down to the local post office with a telegram addressed to his mother in which he angrily opposed the plan, insisting that he wanted to return to Jordan to be with his people after the conclusion of his term at Sandhurst. The telegram, which was to be sent unencrypted, was intercepted by the Post Office and passed on to Ambassador Mulqi, who knew nothing of the plan.[76] In the event, Hussein's impulsive intervention stopped the scheme in its tracks. Instead of an attachment to a British regiment, plans were developed to provide the young King with a brief 'royal tour' of Britain in which he would have the opportunity to visit various important cultural, political and industrial sites.

Hussein's progress at Sandhurst, as reflected in his half-term reports delivered at the end of November 1952, was very good. Commandant Dawnay wrote that he had been impressed by 'his ability, commonsense and eagerness to learn. He has charm, poise and excellent manners. But best of all is the impression that he has made on Instructors and Cadets of straight-forwardness, integrity and a strong sense of duty.'[77] The instructors' reports themselves add some further detail to the picture of the King at Sandhurst. According to one, Hussein possessed 'decided opinions which command respect, but not always assent'. Another noted that 'he has a pleasing personality, quite unassuming, although one feels at times that he is aware of the heavy responsibilities which lie on his shoulders'. Another spoke of his 'alert mind', but commented that at times 'the edge has been taken off his concentration'. This last observation pointed to what was the only minor blot on Hussein's copybook, noted also by Commandant Dawnay in a confidential cover note sent to the British Foreign Office: 'I have omitted references to his duties at the Jordan Embassy interfering with his work and causing him at times to be very sleepy. This difficulty is now lessened and the situation is under control.'[78] The 'duties' concerned evidently included the continuing programme of parties and nightclub visits organised for him by Ambassador Mulqi.

If Queen Zein's attempts to attach Hussein to a British regiment had been thwarted, she was still busy with other important plans for the young King's future. On 5 December, in conversation with the British Ambassador Furlonge, the Queen revealed in the strictest confidence that 'she was anxious to get Hussein married off as soon as possible and had been giving considerable thought to the choice of a suitable bride'. While she recognised that there were limits to her influence, she had come to the conclusion that by far the most suitable choice would be the only daughter of Sharif Abdul Hamid ibn Aun, a Hashemite who had resettled in Egypt after the fall of the Kingdom of the Hejaz in 1925. Sharifa Dina was, as far as Zein was concerned, 'in all ways desirable, as she is sensible, intelligent, and well educated'. To further the match, Zein confided that she had invited Dina to spend part of the Christmas holidays with her and Hussein in Switzerland.[79] For her part Dina was evidently uncertain how to respond to the Queen's approach. She wrote in private to her cousin, Abdul Ilah, the Regent of Iraq, asking for his advice as to how she should proceed. Abdul Ilah meanwhile described Dina as a suitable wife for Hussein, although he did note that she was some seven years older than the young King.[80]

Zein's plan worked. According to her account Dina spent three weeks with her in Switzerland, during part of which time Hussein was present too. Relations between the two of them 'evolved very satisfactorily' from Zein's perspective, culminating in what she termed 'a private betrothal', which she expected would be officially announced immediately after Hussein's coronation.[81] After Hussein's return from Switzerland Ambassador Mulqi also confided to A.D.M. Ross of the British Foreign Office that 'King Hussein was "sort of engaged" to his cousin, the Sharifa Dina – the fact to be kept secret until after the King's return to Jordan when, having assumed his royal powers, he would announce his intention also to take a wife.' In what would prove to be a significant comment, Mulqi implied that 'it was not a love match', but rather a choice which could not be criticised on the grounds of the suitability of the bride.[82] The news soon leaked, with the London *Evening Standard* running a story on 19 January 1953 headed 'A King's Romance' which claimed that the King would announce his engagement to Princess Dina Abdul Hamid before long, and was expected to marry her in Amman during the summer.[83] Dina's presence, at Zein's suggestion, at Hussein's Sandhurst passing-out parade on 5 February lent further substance to the story.

Some indication of how Hussein was passing his private time after his graduation from Sandhurst was provided by one story which also made its way into the otherwise rather restrained British tabloid press of the day. Under the heading 'Royal Tunes', the *Sunday Express* carried the following piece in its regular gossip column:

> 'Your Majesty', called bandleader Paul Adam across the nightclub floor, 'you're on'. Jordan's young King Hussein, who has become one of the brightest lights in London's flickering bright lights business, left his table. 'No smoking on the stand', said the bandleader. The King stubbed out his cigarette. Then he sang 'Luna Rossa', [and] followed it with a smart rendering on the maracas of 'Don't Let the Stars Get in Your Eyes'.[84]

By the standards of early twenty-first-century international royal exploits, this story would hardly merit a single column inch. But in the staid atmosphere of early 1950s London, an Arab king singing and smoking in a nightclub was newsworthy. The Jordanian embassy and British Foreign Office also showed some concern about the story, although no significant attempt was made to block it.

The 'royal tour' planned at the request of Queen Zein for Hussein's final two months in Britain during February and March 1953 had in the end to be considerably curtailed. First, on 18 February Hussein entered a nursing home for follow-up treatment resulting from an earlier sinus operation which he had undergone in London. This sinus problem would subsequently prove to be one of his most chronic ailments, requiring repeated treatment through-out his life. Then, a week after beginning his tour on 1 March, Hussein caught the flu in a wintry Keswick in the English Lake District and was confined to his bed for several days. The final stage of his tour, when he had planned to visit Queen Elizabeth II at Windsor, also had to be cancelled due to court mourning for the death of Queen Mary. Nevertheless, the message of goodwill which Hussein sent after his return to Jordan on 5 April suggested that the King had taken away positive impressions with him.[85] In future years he was a frequent visitor to Britain, where he subsequently owned three properties. His time at Sandhurst in particular seems to have made a mark on his character, helping him to develop his sense of discipline and duty.

Once back in Jordan Hussein had just over three weeks to prepare for his coronation on 2 May. The date of his accession provoked a further controversy in relations with the Iraqi branch of the Hashemite family. It transpired that the Regent Abdul Ilah had approached Hussein personally in 'unjustifiably pressing' terms, to try to persuade him to change the date of the ceremony so that it would not clash directly with the coronation of his cousin Feisal II in Baghdad. Whatever Hussein's own view, the Jordanian Prime Minister Abu'l Huda refused the request because he wanted to avoid the presence of a senior Iraqi delegation including Abdul Ilah at Hussein's coronation.[86] The clash suited his purposes, though it once again stoked up Hashemite family rivalries.

Hussein passed the weeks leading up to his coronation by making a series of tours around the country to show himself to the people and meet local dignitaries. He specifically chose frontier villages on the West Bank which had been the site of recent Israeli raids for his first visit. Meanwhile, speculation surrounded his first choice of prime minister. In private conversation, Mulqi indicated to Furlonge that Hussein had promised him the post while he had been recuperating from influenza in Keswick.[87]

Hussein's coronation on 2 May passed off peacefully and successfully. The King made his constitutional oath in a firm and clear voice, and was greeted by loud and prolonged applause from the assembled dignitaries. After prayers, he visited the tomb of his grandfather and thereafter received a stream of dignitaries. The following day he attended a ceremonial parade of the Arab Legion in which General Glubb, its British commander, made sure that the British officers were not conspicuous. Summing up the ceremonies, Ambassador Furlonge commented:

> throughout what must have been an exhausting ordeal King Hussein bore himself with confidence, dignity, and composure which was remarkable in a young man of 17½ and which was favourably commented on in all quarters. What degree of authority and influence he will be able to exert in the future remains to be seen; but first impressions certainly suggest that he may have just those qualities of leadership and firm decision which the country will chiefly require.[88]

With Hussein's coronation a further formal line was drawn under the reign of King Talal. Subsequently, the King spoke little about his father's mental breakdown although he regularly visited him in Istanbul during the remainder of his life. But his father's fate must have affected him deeply, as must the political manoeuvres surrounding Talal's succession and subsequent deposition. In his autobiography he wrote bitterly of 'rapacious politicians' who 'fought for the crumbs of office like the money-hungry relatives that gather for the reading of a will'.[89] If nothing else, the memory of this episode must have affected his own thinking during the final months of his life, when he too faced a difficult decision over the succession. He wanted there to be no doubt that he was in full command of his faculties when he decided to disinherit his brother, Prince Hassan.[90]

But by far the most striking thing about Hussein's role during the turbulent political transition which led to his accession to the throne is his remarkable maturity. Some commentators have been inclined to pour cold water on the 'lonely at the top' image Hussein sought to fashion in his autobiography.[91] But we must not lose sight of the fact that as these events unfolded Hussein was a teenager. In rapid succession, between his fifteenth and seventeenth birthdays, he saw his grandfather assassinated at his side, his father suffer successive mental breakdowns, and his seriously ill mother suffer a number of assaults at the hands of his father, which he himself also endured. At the same time, he was moved from school in Egypt into an alien cultural environment in England, and designated Crown Prince and then King within the space of a year. The phrase 'a life packed with incident' would hardly do justice to this bewildering series of personal wrenches. Throughout it all, there was no one else Hussein could fully rely on. True, his mother was a pillar of strength, but often it was Hussein who had to support her, rather then the other way around. If the measure of a man lies not just in his handling of the challenges he faces, but also in the scale of those challenges, Hussein passed this extraordinary test with flying colours.

CHAPTER 2

BREAKING THE BRITISH CONNECTION, 1953–6

Hussein's first few months on the throne of Jordan during the summer of 1953 were deceptively calm. The young King faced no immediate challenge to his authority either from any Arab opponent or from Israel. But this period of calm could not last. The Arab–Israeli conflict was only in temporary abeyance while the new state of Israel consolidated itself domestically and the Arab states recovered from the shock of defeat in the 1948–9 war. Similarly, the struggle for leadership in the Arab world, in which Hussein's grandfather had played such a central role, was bound to resume, albeit with a changed cast of characters. In both respects Hussein would face stern tests before he had had the chance to learn much about statecraft, or to judge the loyalty of key individuals in Jordan.

While the conflict with Israel and rivalries in Arab ranks were one part of Hussein's troubled inheritance, Jordan's relationship with Britain was another. Although the Hashemite Kingdom had gained its independence in 1946, the continuing British role in officering and funding the Arab Legion meant that Britain was still seen as the power behind the Hashemite throne. Moreover, British priorities in the region were different from those of Hussein. The British wanted to entrench their influence in the Middle East by promoting links between the Arab states and London. They also wanted to block the expansion of Soviet influence into the region, a threat which seemed much greater under Stalin's successor in the Kremlin, Nikita Khrushchev, who pursued an active role in the 'Third World'. The Americans also sought to limit Soviet influence, although the United States at this stage still played second fiddle to Britain in the region.

Hussein's own initial priorities were much closer to home. In addition to defending Jordan he needed to bolster and entrench the authority of the Hashemite regime over its subjects. He was also well aware that the main enemy as far as Jordanian public opinion was concerned was Israel; the global Cold War seemed remote and irrelevant to the man in the street in Amman or East Jerusalem. Moreover, Britain was tarnished in the eyes of most Jordanians through its perceived collusion in the creation of Israel. The continuing British role in Jordan was thus the object of deep popular suspicion, but Hussein could not abandon it without some viable alternative method of funding the army on which the survival of the country and his regime depended.

As if these difficulties were not enough, Hussein also faced other considerable domestic challenges. The kingdom he inherited was made up of two parts: the East Bank, formerly Transjordan, and the West Bank, formerly part of the Palestine mandate. In April 1950 a new forty-member chamber of deputies composed of equal numbers of representatives from each Bank had confirmed their unification, but there remained much work to be done to turn this union into a social, economic and political reality. While the East Bank comprised 94 per cent of Jordan's territory, it contained only around one-third of the total population, which numbered about one and a half million. In social and economic terms, there was also a mismatch between the two Banks: the East Bank was under-developed with no manufacturing industry, low levels of literacy and only rudimentary educational provision. The West Bank, by contrast, boasted significantly higher levels of economic activity and schooling. The presence of 458,000 Palestinian refugees, constituting roughly one-third of the population, presented a further huge economic and political challenge for the Jordanian state. Settled mainly in camps, the refugees were dispossessed, impoverished and embittered. Despite the international relief effort, institutionalised in the form of the United Nations Relief and Works Agency (UNRWA), their presence created large new administrative burdens for the Jordanian state. Amman became the hub for the organisations involved in addressing these challenges, and as a consequence witnessed a remarkable building boom in the years leading up to Hussein's coronation. Indeed, there was no doubt that the centre of gravity of the Jordanian state during this period tilted in most respects towards the East Bank.[1]

In terms of the political system Hussein inherited, Jordan was a constitutional monarchy. The King's actions as head of state and his relations with the chamber of deputies and senate were governed by the 1952 constitution. This contained guarantees of personal freedoms and provided for the separation of powers, which limited to some degree the monarch's freedom of manoeuvre. However, the King was still endowed with significant powers, including the right to dissolve the chamber of deputies and senate, call elections, and appoint a prime minister and ministers. He was also supreme commander of the Jordanian armed forces, with the right to declare war and conclude treaties. Crucially, he was empowered to declare martial law by royal decree when faced with a state of national emergency.[2] In practice, then, Hussein was by far the most important political actor in the kingdom. In fact in his early years, he was probably constrained more by cultural than by constitutional factors: as a young man in a society which valued age and experience, he found that it was initially difficult to make his mark with tribal elders and the circle of veteran politicians he inherited from his grandfather.

In terms of potential external threats to Jordan, Hussein later admitted that when he came to the throne he knew very little about Israel and its leaders, and – most crucially – what they wanted to achieve in the region.[3] Of all the frontline Arab states, Jordan had by far the longest border with Israel. Policing it or indeed defending it effectively was all but impossible, and infiltration and reprisal were the realities of the West Bank frontier during the early years of Hussein's reign. Palestinians, who in many cases could still see their former lands, crossed into what was now Israel for a variety of reasons: sometimes to gather crops, sometimes to retrieve possessions, and sometimes to seek revenge. The Israelis, meanwhile, responded with reprisal raids designed both to punish Jordan and to impress on the Jordanian authorities the need to restrain the trespassers. The Jordanian army, the Arab Legion, stood in the front line. The fact that the higher levels of its officer corps were dominated by the British promoted a whispering campaign on the West Bank suggesting that they were somehow colluding in Israeli actions, and doing too little to protect the Palestinians. In truth, the army was doing all it could in the face of an insurmountable challenge, but perception perhaps mattered more than reality.

Israel was only part of the regional picture for Hussein. In many respects the bigger threat to his survival came from his Arab rivals. Chief among these was the new revolutionary regime in Cairo established by the Egyptian 'Free Officers' who overthrew King Farouk in July 1952. Initially the figurehead of the new regime was General Neguib but, by the beginning of 1954, Colonel Gamal Abdel Nasser had emerged from the shadows as its real leader. Hussein initially expressed his enthusiasm for the Free Officers' coup, and was not at first inclined to see the new Egyptian regime as a threat. His mother, who took an altogether more disapproving view of the overthrow of the Egyptian monarchy, was far less sanguine.

Zein's opinions mattered. In part because of his youth and in part because of his uncertainty as to whom he could trust, during the early years of his reign, Hussein continued to pay considerable deference to her views.[4] Zein had to exercise her influence cautiously from behind the scenes since court etiquette still barred her from overt political interventions, such as meeting a Western male ambassador. During one clandestine meeting with the British Ambassador Furlonge in January 1954, Zein confided her concern that Hussein was 'still too inexperienced to realise the depth of Egyptian intrigues'.[5] Zein feared the new post-revolutionary regime in Cairo was attempting to entangle Jordan in an anti-British policy, something she was determined to block. To this end, she worked behind the scenes to persuade Hussein to postpone a planned visit to Cairo in February 1954, which he duly did.[6] Zein confided to Furlonge that:

> She was now happier about Hussein than she had been when he first returned here. He had settled down, had acquired certain interests (of which flying was of course the chief), and suffered less from boredom than at first. She had persuaded him to take a course of study in international law, and he was now buckling down to this.[7]

As had been foreshadowed before his coronation, Hussein's first choice of prime minister to replace Abu'l Huda was Fawzi Mulqi, with whom he had developed a close personal and political relationship. Having spent most of his career in posts outside Jordan, Mulqi had little by way of domestic political experience to fall back on, in sharp contrast to his predecessor Abu'l Huda.[8] No doubt this also helped recommend him to Queen Zein, who hoped to play a dominant role behind the scenes without the inconvenience of an assertive prime minister.

As ambassador in London, Mulqi had not only proved to be a ready source of social introductions and entertainment for the then Prince Hussein. He had also been the host of a reception during the spring of 1953 where Hussein had met one of the leaders of the embryonic Jordanian 'Free Officers' movement, a man named Abu Shahut, who was then in England on an artillery training course. This secret group within the British-led Arab Legion would come to play an important political role during the pivotal years of 1956–7. Their central goal was to 'Arabise' the Jordanian army, securing the dismissal of the British and the promotion of a new generation of Arab officers. This apparently limited military aim also had broader political overtones in the shape of the officers' attachment to Baathism, an ideology which was revolutionary socialist as well as Arab nationalist in inspiration. These ideological roots meant that any alliance with Hussein, a hereditary monarch, was bound to be an uneasy one in the long run.

During this first meeting in 1953, Abu Shahut was introduced to Hussein by his friend Ali Abu Nowar, who was later to become the figurehead of the movement.[9] How much Mulqi knew of the nature and inspiration of the Free

Officers movement when he facilitated the meeting is unclear. But the suggestion that Hussein voiced sympathy for their aims would fit in with other accounts of his youthful enthusiasm for Arab nationalist causes, including that of the Free Officers in Egypt.[10]

Mulqi was to prove to be a poor choice as prime minister of Jordan. Indecisive and vain by nature, his premiership was characterised by a lack of strategic vision and clear direction. He seemed to regard the holding of office as an end in itself, rather than as the means to achieve political goals, and was consequently prey to the competing interests of the coalition of ministers he assembled.[11] Anxious to cultivate the image of a moderate after the authoritarian rule of Abu'l Huda, Mulqi allowed the press much greater freedom to express criticism, particularly of the British role in Jordan. As US Ambassador Lester Mallory put it, 'Mulqi, either because of conviction or through want of a strong character, embarked on a laissez-faire regime during which the press ran rampant and extremist groups including the communists increased in influence.'[12]

Although the new government won initial popularity for its domestic liberalisation measures, developments on the frontier with Israel soon threatened to undermine it. Following an upsurge of border incidents, on 14 October 1953 a detachment of Israeli troops under the command of a young officer named Ariel Sharon levelled the village of Qibya, deliberately killing around fifty men, women and children in the process.[13] The raid was out of all proportion to previous incidents on the frontier. Even some Israeli officials were shocked in private by its brutality, with Ambassador to the United Nations Abba Eban calling it 'a cruel reprisal', and an act that Israel 'cannot be proud of and that cannot be excused even by the Arab crimes that preceded it'.[14]

The raid provoked street demonstrations on both the East and West Banks, together with calls from the opposition for the expulsion of the British officers from the Arab Legion, who, it was claimed, had not done enough to protect Qibya. Mulqi's handling of the crisis was incompetent, and as a result Hussein began, during the early months of 1954, to take a more active political role.[15] In particular, Mulqi was undecided as to whether to accept the United Nations Security Council's call for an Israeli–Jordanian meeting under the terms of the General Armistice Agreement, and vacillated in the face of public opposition. By May, Hussein had had enough of Mulqi's dithering and the prime minister was forced to resign. The aftermath of the Qibya raid showed that the Arab–Israeli conflict played an inescapable role in Jordan's domestic politics. It was an early lesson in one of the dominating facts of Hussein's political career.

In the wake of Mulqi's dismissal, Hussein opted for experience and brought back Abu'l Huda as prime minister. In the view of US Ambassador

Mallory this move was satisfactory; the ambassador felt that 'Jordan was getting out of hand politically' and 'the return to power of the hated but respected Tawfiq Abu'l Huda will reverse this trend'.[16] Abu'l Huda's task was to oversee the run-up to elections planned for 16 October 1954, which he did, although not without accusations that the whole process had been rigged. In an attempt to bolster his position in the aftermath of the elections, Abu'l Huda took up the populist banner of reform of the treaty arrangements that governed Jordan's relations with Britain. This was to prove to be his undoing. During a visit to London in December, the prime minister found the British government in no mood to compromise over the existing terms of its financial subsidy to Jordan, and he returned to Amman empty-handed.

The following year, 1955, was to prove to be a year of decision in Arab politics, in which the domestic and regional tensions threatening Hussein's regime would be dangerously exposed. It was also a year in which Hussein made what quickly proved to be an unfortunate choice in his private life. The King's marriage to Sharifa Dina Abdul Hamid took place on 19 April 1955. As we have seen, Queen Zein had begun preparing the ground for the match in late 1952, with the original expectation that the engagement would be announced, and the wedding would follow, shortly after Hussein's coronation in May 1953. In the event, there was a further delay of nearly two years before the engagement was eventually made public in February 1955. The available sources provide no clear explanation for this; it may be that either Hussein or Dina had misgivings about the marriage, which, as Ambassador Mulqi had earlier observed, was not a love match. Nevertheless, the wedding ceremony on 19 April passed off smoothly. The groom's party included Hussein's cousin, King Feisal of Iraq, his brother Prince Mohammad, King Saud's son Mohammad, Crown Prince Abdul Ilah of Iraq, and the bride's father. The presence of the Iraqi King and Crown Prince in Hussein's party reflected Dina's good relations with the Iraqi branch of the Hashemite family, who were reported to be delighted at her marriage to Hussein.[17] The assessment of the new British ambassador, Charles Duke, was also very positive:

> The marriage seems highly popular. The general sentiment in informed circles seems to be that the new Queen, with her greater maturity and wider education, cannot fail to influence the King for good, and it is hoped that this will offset the somewhat narrow and unedifying influences to which he has hitherto been exposed.[18]

Just what Duke meant by these 'unedifying influences' soon became clear. The chief individual concerned was Hussein's uncle Sharif Nasser, his mother's younger brother, who had become his ADC. The British records from this period are full of unflattering references to Sharif Nasser, who was described as Hussein's 'wicked uncle' in despatches sent back from Amman.[19] A character sketch written some years later by the US State Department described him as 'one of the most hated and feared men in Jordan', notorious for his 'illegal traffic of arms and drugs'.[20] According to General Glubb, Dina quickly developed a dislike for her new uncle,[21] and their rift soon came into the open when the Egyptian press published stories about a court case involving a substantial hashish-smuggling operation in which Sharif Nasser was rumoured to be involved – and for which Queen Dina had allegedly provided information for the prosecution.[22] Clearly, part of the intention behind these rumours was to blacken the reputation of the Jordanian royal family. But the credence given to them in Amman was largely due to the fact that the rift between Queen Dina and Sharif Nasser was becoming obvious.

This might not have mattered so much if relations between the royal couple had developed smoothly. Unfortunately the marriage experienced strains from the very outset. Preparations for a visit by the couple to England in June 1955 provided a glimpse of some of their difficulties. Writing to London about arrangements for the visit, Ambassador Duke noted that the King himself had few interests beyond 'aircraft, racing cars and on occasion, without too much publicity, lively parties which he greatly enjoys (though he hardly drinks at all)'. Dina by contrast was 'much more widely educated' and interested in intellectual pursuits.[23] The preparations for the visit threw up another fact that caused some raised eyebrows in London. Fawzi Mulqi, who by this stage was court minister, approached Ambassador Duke to inquire about the royal couple's accommodation at the Dorchester Hotel. When told that a suitable suite of rooms would be provided, 'Fawzi, with slight sign of embarrassment, said that he was sure the accommodation would be comfortable and appropriate, but if possible they would like it to consist of two bedrooms, each with its own bathroom, separated by the sitting room'. At the bottom of the telegram reporting this request, Duke noted, 'I refrain from comment!'[24]

In fact, Duke's exclamation mark proved misplaced for, a little less than nine months later, on 13 February 1956, Dina gave birth to a daughter, Alia. It seemed briefly that this might help to bridge the growing divide between the couple. Hussein was reported to be very pleased with his daughter, and managed to conceal any disappointment he may have felt at not having a son as his first child.[25] But the improvement in their relations was short-lived. Not only was Dina at loggerheads with Sharif Nasser, she seems also to have progressively alienated Queen Zein, her original sponsor, which in view of Zein's continuing influence over Hussein was a more significant impediment to the success of their marriage. During a trip to Istanbul to visit her husband Talal in August 1956, Zein 'made plain her dislike of the young Queen', telling the British ambassador that Dina was 'very leftish in her sympathies (as a result, she said, of her earlier associations at Cairo University)'.[26] The Suez crisis, which was already under way by this stage, seems to have brought the rift between Zein and Dina to the fore. Zein remained a supporter of the British connection in Jordan, using her influence with the King, according to Ambassador Duke, 'to keep him on our side and to resist Egyptian blandishments (backed by secret offers of Iron Curtain armaments)'.[27] Later Zein told British Chargé Heath Mason laughingly that 'she was known as the English woman in the household as it so frequently turned out that she said the same as we did'.[28] When Dina went to visit relatives in Egypt in September 1956, a surprising destination given the precarious situation there, Zein made it clear that 'she thought it was not a bad thing anyway as Queen Dina was a very great admirer of Colonel Nasser and took very much the Egyptian line with the King'. Zein went on to recount a conversation with Hussein in which he had told her that Dina had teased him about 'supporting the "Colonizers"', to which he had replied that she should not use that term of the British since as far as Jordan was concerned they had done a great deal of good for the country and proved real friends.[29]

Hussein himself provided no direct explanation in his autobiography for the decision he now took to divorce Dina, noting that it was 'a sad and difficult period', but that 'it was far better, and only fair to both of us, to end it'.[30] Part of the explanation may well have been Dina's active interest in politics, which seems to have displeased Hussein almost as much as his mother. Dina's frequent political activities also meant that Hussein did not find the companionship and support in his home life which he may have been seeking to compensate for the instability of his adolescence. With a dominating mother continuing to exercise a strong hand in his affairs, Hussein may well have felt that the last thing he needed was an independently minded and politically active wife. The breakdown of his marriage may also have been influenced by his relationship with Flavia Tesio, the daughter of a well-respected Italian doctor and a friend of Hussein's since childhood, who was widely rumoured to have begun an affair with the King at this time. They shared an interest in fast cars, competing in the same speed trials and hill climbs, with the King driving a silver Mercedes and Flavia a scarlet MG.[31] Interestingly, Flavia also left Jordan unexpectedly in mid-October 1956, and subsequently applied to the British Foreign Office for a visa to take up a two-year business contract in Kenya. However, not everyone was convinced by the rumours concerning her relationship with the King; commenting on her visa application, the new British ambassador in Amman, Charles Johnston, noted: 'there is no reason whatever as far as I know to believe that she is anything more than a childhood friend of the King who happens to share his enthusiasm for motor racing and dancing the samba'.[32]

In any event, after Dina's departure for Cairo in mid-September, the King wrote to her, giving his opinion that their marriage was failing and it would be better if they stayed apart. When Dina wrote back requesting that their daughter, Alia, should be sent to her in Cairo, Hussein refused, largely because of Zein's now implacable hostility towards Dina, although there were also sound political arguments against sending his daughter to Egypt in the circumstances prevailing at the end of 1956. In addition, Hussein may well have been angered by the press leaks in Cairo about the break-up of his marriage. During the next six years, Dina was only allowed to see her daughter once, despite sending numerous letters to Hussein requesting regular access, to which she did not receive any reply. Finally, at the beginning of 1962, she decided to try to break the deadlock by publishing her ghost-written memoirs. The timing could not have been worse, since the initial instalment appeared just before the birth of Hussein's first son Prince Abdullah by his new bride Muna, and the ghost-writer immediately betrayed Dina's trust, publishing a claim which Dina subsequently denied that Hussein had originally threatened to abdicate if he did not marry her.[33] It was left to another British journalist who apparently had Dina's confidence, John Osman of the *Daily Telegraph*, to act as a go-between with Hussein. Osman passed on in person another letter from Dina to the King during three meetings he held with him in Amman in February 1962. According to Osman's account at the close of their final interview, the King told him to 'take a message to Dina saying that the door was not yet entirely closed'. Osman's impression was that the King's words were sincere, and that he still retained some affection for Dina.[34] Overriding the opposition of his mother, Hussein was as good as his word and allowed Dina access to her daughter Alia on a more regular basis. This helped to repair what by this stage had become an increasing personal embarrassment, and a public blemish on Hussein's reputation for generosity and forgiveness.

Back in 1955, Hussein had also begun another relationship which was to prove rocky and controversial, although this time its nature was political rather than personal. During the same February 1955 visit to Cairo when he had announced his engagement to Dina, Hussein had also held his first meeting with the Egyptian President Gamal Abdel Nasser. Hussein's relations with Nasser were to loom very large for the following decade and a half of his reign. In later life the King came to describe Nasser, alongside Iraqi President Saddam Hussein, as the two 'demi-gods' who had done untold harm to the Arab cause.[35] Coming from a poor background, Nasser had risen through the ranks of the Egyptian army, and had been a central figure in organising the July 1952 coup that had overthrown the Egyptian monarchy. Intelligent, quick-witted and secretive by nature, Nasser was also a natural demagogue, and exuded a brash and physical charisma. Partly because of his own experiences as a revolutionary leader, Nasser had an instinctive distrust of hereditary monarchs, though, according to his confidant Mohammad Heikal, Nasser came to regard Hussein with a mixture of admiration and astonishment.[36] Heikal insists that Nasser made no subsequent attempts to plot Hussein's death, although some of the propaganda pumped out by Radio Cairo incited others to do so. Ultimately, it was politics rather than any insuperable personal enmity that divided the two men. Hussein was unwilling to cut his ties to the Western powers, or to acknowledge Nasser's leadership of the Arab world. He thus acted as an obstacle to the fulfilment of Nasser's political goals. With the exception of the 1956 Suez crisis and 1967 Arab–Israeli war and its aftermath, the two leaders found themselves on opposite sides of the political divide in the Arab world.

Although it was not clear at the time, Hussein's six-day visit to Cairo, between 21 and 26 February 1955, marked the beginning of the parting of their ways. It coincided with the signature on 24 February of a defence pact between Iraq and Turkey and just preceded a major Israeli raid on the Egyptian-held Gaza Strip on 28 February, both events that Nasser saw as threats to Egypt's position, and which were to play a significant role in shaping his subsequent strategy. While Nasser saw the pact between Iraq and Turkey as throwing down the gauntlet in the struggle for regional leadership, its origins in fact lay in an American initiative to encourage what was termed the 'Northern Tier' defence of the Middle East against the Soviet Union. US Secretary of State John Foster Dulles envisaged Pakistan, Iran, Turkey and Iraq banding together in a new defence organisation directed against Moscow. The British were initially wary of this American initiative, seeing it as an encroachment in their traditional sphere of influence and a threat to their existing defence treaty with Iraq, which was due to expire in 1957. However, once Iraq and Turkey had taken the plunge and signed their defence pact, the British quickly stepped in, negotiating a renewal of their own defence relationship with Iraq under the auspices of an Anglo-Iraqi special agreement which was appended to the renamed Baghdad Pact when Britain joined it in April. Now it was Washington's turn to play the diffident party, with Secretary of State Dulles backing away from his 'foster' child for fear that it had become both the vehicle for the renewal of British imperial influence and a source of regional instability.

King Hussein's initial reaction to the Turco-Iraqi Pact also seems to have been negative. He took on board Nasser's fears that it would undercut the existing collective security arrangements provided by the Arab League.[37] The official position of the Jordanian government towards the pact was one of neutrality, but in early March Nasser upped the stakes by negotiating a rival pact with Syria and Saudi Arabia, leaving Jordan uncomfortably isolated. By the middle of March, Hussein had abandoned his initial sympathy for the

Egyptian stance, and he told US Ambassador Mallory that he was prepared to consider a request to join the Baghdad Pact, depending on the military benefits available to Jordan.[38]

The British government was enthusiastic about the idea of Jordanian membership of the Baghdad Pact, seeing it as a way to bolster the position of the Anglophile Iraqi regime, but the unexpected strength of Nasser's opposition, and the pact's apparent potential to divide the Arab states and thus stoke up the Arab–Israeli conflict, made US Secretary of State Dulles wary of its extension.[39] While means were sought to resolve the Arab–Israeli conflict via the secret Anglo-American 'Alpha' peace plan, Dulles asked the British government to accept a temporary freeze on further Arab membership of the pact.[40]

Paradoxically, it was a series of Egyptian political successes that subsequently opened the way for London to make its attempt to secure Jordanian entry to the pact. First, in September, came the news of the so-called 'Czech' arms deal, under which Nasser secured extensive quantities of Soviet weaponry to modernise Egypt's armed forces. The arms deal was firm evidence that the Cold War had arrived in the Middle East, as the Soviets under Khrushchev sought to build close relations with Arab nationalist regimes in order to compete with the West for influence in the region. From Nasser's perspective the arms deal underlined Egypt's independence and dignity. If the Western powers would not sell him the arms he needed then the 'Czech' arms deal proved that he had an alternative. Hard on the heels of the arms deal, Nasser engineered a further coup in the shape of the mutual defence pacts signed with Syria on 20 October and Saudi Arabia on 27 October 1955, which provided the bilateral underpinning for the Egyptian–Syrian–Saudi alliance announced in March. Although he was not yet firmly set on the path of confrontation with the West, Nasser's diplomacy showed that he was determined to assert Egypt's leadership role in the Arab world. This was a particularly worrying development for the British government, which had invested its prestige in the Iraqi-led Baghdad Pact. These Egyptian successes also left both the Turkish and Iraqi governments fearing for the future of the Baghdad Pact: would Nasser succeed in persuading further Arab states to join his grouping, leaving the existing Baghdad Pact members isolated? With these fears in mind, the renewed impetus towards Jordanian membership of the pact came from the Turkish government,[41] although the British Foreign Secretary, Harold Macmillan, took little persuading as to the justice of the cause.[42]

In the midst of these developments, Hussein visited London at the end of October 1955, though there appears, perhaps surprisingly, to have been little said directly about the Baghdad Pact; there were other pressing issues that needed to be resolved first. Hussein's greatest concern was with the question of the development of the Jordanian Air Force. Specifically, he was very unhappy at the prospect of the British government recalling the RAF officer Colonel Jock Dalgleish.[43] Dalgleish had taught Hussein to fly, thus fuelling a lifelong passion on the part of the King, and in the process had become very close to him personally: too close as far as London was concerned. Not only did Dalgleish tend to fuel what the British government saw as unrealistic expectations on Hussein's part as to the likely level of British support for his proposed air force, his personality clash with General Glubb was a matter of concern in London. In a private conversation with Hussein, the Foreign Office official Evelyn Shuckburgh directly tackled rumours that the King himself was not pleased with Glubb. While describing Glubb as 'one of us', Hussein commented, in a portent of troubles to come, that 'Glubb had formed the Arab Legion a long time ago and there were those who thought his methods were becoming a little out of date. He the King was bound to watch this with concern since neighbouring states were only too quick to say that the British connection was holding Jordan back.'[44]

Pressure for Jordan to join the Baghdad Pact began in earnest with the visit of Turkish President Jelal Bayar to Amman at the beginning of November 1955.[45] The British government decided to capitalise on the Turkish initiative, sending Chief of the Imperial General Staff Sir Gerald Templer to Amman on 6 December to present a formal proposal for Jordanian accession, baited with what London hoped would be appealing offers of extra aid for the Arab Legion. Templer was somewhat ill suited to the role of diplomat in such delicate circumstances. An arrogant and sometimes abrasive man, one of his less endearing traits was the habit of stubbing out his cigarettes in the sherry glasses of subordinates.[46] Impatient by nature, Templer could not readily sit still, which in view of the leisurely fashion in which most business was typically conducted in Amman was an unfortunate weakness. Templer had little sympathy for the difficulty of the Jordanian government's position, fulminating in his despatches back to London about the opposition of the West Bank ministers who 'are completely blind to any aspect of the problem except the Israel issue about which they bleat continuously'.[47] Nor was Templer impressed with the approach of Prime Minister Said Mufti, who had replaced Abu'l Huda at the end of May, and whom Templer described as 'a jelly who is frightened of his own shadow'.[48] Although Hussein took a more positive stance, he emphasised that Jordanian public opinion, fanned by Saudi-backed propaganda, was deeply hostile to the prospect of joining the pact.[49]

To Templer's frustration, the King procrastinated, and several days passed after his initial audience before he managed to see him again. In the interim, he learned that Hussein had been whiling away the time, and perhaps relieving the stress caused by the crisis, by 'driving his fast cars on a sand track'.[50] On 13 December matters came to a head, with Templer pressing the King and prime minister to initial a letter of intent to join the pact. Although the King indicated a willingness to sign, Prime Minister Mufti refused to do so. Without the backing of Jordan's government, Templer told the King that he did not think it would be wise for him to sign. This marked the effective collapse of the negotiations, with Templer cabling London: 'I am afraid I have shot my bolt.'[51] Templer's explanation for his failure was straightforward: 'the trouble is none of them has got any bottom'.[52]

Amplifying his thoughts in a report written after his return to London, Templer dwelt on the 'spineless pusillanimity' of Prime Minister Mufti and the preoccupation of all Jordanian politicians with the Palestine problem. On Hussein's own role in the saga, Templer was much more positive. He believed that the King had been impressed and pleased with the amount of the initial British military offer as a sweetener for pact membership and that he 'seems to have made up his mind at once in favour of accession'. Thereafter 'he was an active ally in pressing for an immediate decision from his government'.[53]

Templer's view that the King favoured accession to the pact seemed to be borne out by subsequent events. Mufti's resignation just before Templer left Amman opened the way for Hussein's appointment of a new cabinet under the pro-pact leadership of Hazza al-Majali. But Majali had no time to act on the King's wishes. On 17 December the worst rioting Jordan had ever witnessed broke out throughout the country. Foreign missions and institutions were the principal target of the rioters, and the Arab Legion and police force proved powerless to restore order. In the face of such unrest, Majali was forced to resign as prime minister on 20 December. Hussein's choice for his replacement was Ibrahim Hashim, one of the old guard of politicians who had served his grandfather Abdullah. When the British Ambassador Charles Duke saw the King on the afternoon of 21 December, he found him still considerably shaken by the disturbances, although more confident that order could now be restored.[54] In the event, Hussein's assessment proved too optimistic, with another round of rioting breaking out in early January. This precipitated Ibrahim Hashim's replacement as prime minister by Samir Rifai on 8 January 1956. Rifai moved to secure his position by declaring that Jordan would not accede to 'a new pact'.[55]

The principal cause of the rioting seems to have been genuine public hostility to the Baghdad Pact, fuelled by Egyptian subversive activities financed by Saudi money.[56] Defending his role in the crisis, King Saud wrote to Hussein in its immediate aftermath, admitting that he opposed the Baghdad Pact but denying any hostile intentions, and specifically refuting the British claim that Saudi troops were massing on the Jordanian border, which he argued was part of an 'outside plot' to divide the Arabs.[57] Saud's emotional protestations of friendship belied his regime's undoubted attempts to block what was seen as the advance of Iraqi and British influence. Dynastic rivalry accounted for the anti-Iraqi element of Saud's policy, while the forcible British reoccupation on 26 October of the disputed Buraimi Oasis, on the border between Saudi Arabia and the British-protected Gulf sheikhdoms of Abu Dhabi and Muscat, accounted for the anti-British element. But, in truth, the Egyptians and Saudis were pushing at an open door in terms of Jordanian public opinion. There was a fundamental discrepancy between the focus of Jordan, its people and politicians, on the threat posed by Israel, and the focus of the pact, designed as it was to counter the Soviet Union. Put simply, the pact looked like a device to divert attention from what most Jordanians saw as the real enemy. The fact that the Israeli government itself was hostile to the pact, manoeuvring behind the scenes with the help of its friends in Congress to block any prospect of US membership, seems to have made no difference to Arab opinion. In a rather cold reply to Saud's emotional letter, Hussein pressed precisely this point: that what had happened in Jordan was only 'in the interests of the enemy' and that the Arabs must work together and unite.[58]

In any event, the question of Jordan's accession to the pact was now effectively buried. Hussein's own role in managing the situation had been somewhat uncertain and inconsistent. This perhaps mirrored the fact that on the one hand he was attracted by the military benefits promised in return for pact membership, while on the other he was conscious of the overwhelming hostility of public opinion. By focusing attention once more on the unpopularity of the British connection in Jordan, the Baghdad Pact riots must surely have played their part in preparing the ground for the King's next crucial political initiative: the dismissal of the commander of the Arab Legion, General Sir John Bagot Glubb, on 1 March 1956.

Hussein's personal relationship with Glubb was a troubled one. Glubb himself cites an incident during the then Prince Hussein's schooling at Harrow, when he took him out in London for the day: 'We went to the Battersea Festival Gardens, but he was not amused. He did not want to go on the merry-go-rounds or the scenic railway. I must have misunderstood his age-group, or his early introduction to public affairs in such tragic circumstances had sobered him prematurely.'[59] There was of course a huge gap in age and experience between the two men, which Hussein evidently felt keenly once he became King. He was aware that he had much to gain from Glubb's experience, but the general's reputation as the uncrowned King of Jordan, the man who made the important decisions about defence and security behind the scenes, was a source of increasing frustration for Hussein. When Glubb took the King along to a meeting with tribal leaders early in his reign, it was the general who played the leading role, greeting all the elders by name, and Hussein who stayed quietly in the background.[60] Mahmud al-

Mu'ayta, one of the Free Officers, recalls a joint visit by the King and Glubb to their barracks in Zerqa early in February 1956. During the visit, Glubb stood up and made a speech about the costs involved in quelling the Baghdad Pact riots, claiming that the sum of money involved would have been enough to equip an extra brigade for the Arab Legion. Glubb then made the King stand up and repeat word for word what he had just said. This was a humiliation for Hussein in front of his men, and Mu'ayta believed it contributed to the King's subsequent decision to approach the Free Officers to coordinate action against Glubb.[61]

In the wake of this incident, a crucial meeting took place in late February between the King and the Free Officers' leadership. Accounts vary as to its location, with Mu'ayta suggesting that it took place at the house of Adib Abu Nowar, a relative of Ali Abu Nowar's, in Zerqa, and Marwan al-Qasim suggesting that it was at the house of Zeid bin Shaker, then one of the King's ADCs, in Amman.[62] Nevertheless, there is substantial agreement between their accounts as to what transpired. The King was accompanied to the meeting by his principal ADC Ali Abu Nowar and by Munthir Innab, one of his assistant ADCs, who had played an important role in re-establishing contact between the Free Officers and the King from mid-1955 onwards when he and Mazen al-Ajlouni had become assistant ADCs to Hussein at the King's request.[63] During this meeting, the King asked the Free Officers a crucial question: could they succeed in removing the British officers and accomplishing 'Arabisation' in one smooth operation? The officers assured him that it could be done quickly and effectively. With the overall principle agreed, the meeting moved on to consider the question of timing. Mu'ayta himself suggested that they should begin the move against the British officers at 2 p.m. on Thursday 29 February 1956, since there was an inspection due to finish at that time and so all of the officers would be gathered together. The plan was that Mu'ayta and the Second Regiment would surround Amman airport, isolating the RAF contingent stationed there. Telephone lines would be cut to prevent the British officers communicating with one another. The roads into Amman were to be closed, while the First Regiment was deputed to prevent any of the British officers based at Zerqa from leaving.[64] The plan had to be executed swiftly before Glubb had time to react, rallying Bedouin elements in the Arab Legion who were personally loyal to him and blocking the intrigues of the Free Officers.

In the event, the 29 February operation could not have run more smoothly. By the end of the day, everything was secure. At 9 that evening Ali Abu Nowar telephoned Glubb to make sure that he still had no inkling of what was afoot. The following morning the King called a meeting of the cabinet and delivered his handwritten order for the dismissal of Glubb to Prime Minister Samir Rifai, telling him, 'These are my orders. I want them executed at once.' It fell to the stunned Rifai to carry out the thankless task of breaking the news to Glubb.

As if the blow of dismissal was not enough for Glubb, Rifai made plain that the King wanted him out of the country at once. 'Can you leave in two hours?' he asked the stunned general. 'No sir! I cannot! I have lived here for twenty-six years. Almost all my worldly possessions are here, to say nothing of my wife and children,' Glubb exclaimed. 'You could go and leave your family behind,' countered Rifai. 'I'm afraid I can't do that either,' Glubb replied.[65] In the end, a compromise was fashioned by which Glubb was asked to leave by plane at 7 a.m. the next day. As his plane took off the following morning Glubb looked back on Jordan for the last time. Despite repeated entreaties from Hussein, he would never return. Glubb's dismissal was not only a personal tragedy for a man who had devoted his life to Jordan, it was also a considerable blow to British prestige throughout the region.

How did Hussein himself explain his actions? In his first meeting with Duke after Glubb's dismissal, he told the ambassador that he had discovered grave deficiencies in the equipment and stores of the Arab Legion, particularly in respect of ammunition. He was also aware of serious discontent among the Arab officers over the question of promotion. He mentioned Egyptian propaganda attacks on Glubb's role, and said that he had also been 'upset by constant articles in the press, even in England, representing Glubb as everything that mattered in Jordan'. He concluded by claiming that 'he had felt bound to do what he considered essential for the preservation and honour of the Kingdom . . .'[66] In a further interview with Duke five days later, during which the ambassador noted that Hussein spoke with 'more appearance of frankness and sincerity than I have ever seen him show and frequently with tears in his eyes', the King insisted that the 'whole affair had been directed against Glubb personally and solely'.[67] He went on to catalogue what he saw as a series of shortcomings on Glubb's part, together with what he believed were a series of personal insults. He had often warned Glubb of the need for reform in the army, he claimed, but nothing had been done. Moreover, Glubb had reinstated an officer dismissed by the King in the aftermath of the Qibya incident without any consultation. On the day before Glubb's dismissal, he had not only received figures as to the parlous state of the reserves of ammunition, he had also received a proposal from Glubb for the dismissal of fifteen officers merely on the grounds that 'they were hot-headed and undisciplined'. Finally, in a rather extraordinary outburst, the King claimed that Glubb had tried to bribe him to accept this measure with £50,000 per year from the Arab Legion subsidy.

Behind the King's accusations about Glubb's personal shortcomings, Duke identified two main factors that had shaped the King's decision. The first was the role of the Free Officers, who 'brought the King's resolution to the point by continually working him up against Glubb and who executed the King's plan for his dismissal'.[68] It was they who supplied the King with the information about the shortage of ammunition. The second factor was Hussein's need to deflect criticism from the Egyptians and other extreme nationalists and communists, who had focused their attacks on Glubb. 'He may have believed', Duke wrote, that 'the only way to ensure his own survival was to remove Glubb, the focus of hostility from inside as well as outside the country.'[69]

Sir Alec Kirkbride, the former British minister in Amman, was asked by the British government to conduct inquiries into the causes of the King's decision, investigating amongst other things whether Hussein's actions had been determined by his mother, and whether she in turn was being bribed by the Saudis to secure Glubb's dismissal.[70] Zein hotly denied any foreknowledge of her son's plans, telling Kirkbride that 'the plot against Glubb was the first important matter which Hussein had hidden from her'.[71] This was a significant development in terms of Hussein's increasing maturity and self-confidence.

But overriding all of the explanations for Hussein's actions detailed above, there is one element in the King's handling of Glubb and his contacts with the Free Officers that deserves further attention. Hussein's sympathy for the Free Officers dated back at least as far as early 1953, when he had expressed enthusiasm for the Egyptian revolution, and Glubb's dismissal can be seen as an expression of Hussein's personal attachment to Arab nationalism, the same nationalism that had drawn him to the Free Officers' cause in the first place. Hussein's attachment to his personal brand of Hashemite Arab nationalism was to be a persistent feature of his reign, conditioning among other key decisions Jordan's entry into the 1967 Arab–Israeli war, his refusal to join the Camp David peace process, and his neutrality during the 1990–91 Gulf war.

Glubb's dismissal, then, was a clear expression of Hussein's desire to assert his personal authority in Jordan. Its immediate result, though, was a period of uncertainty, in which various nationalist forces struggled to assert themselves, and Hussein cast around for a clear strategy which would preserve his throne in the face of rising tensions both between the Arab states and with Israel. The events of March 1956 marked the beginning of Hussein's political coming of age. It was not until he had successfully weathered the storm, first of the Suez crisis, and then of the nationalist coup attempt of early 1957, that he would finally emerge as the dominant political actor in Jordan.

CHAPTER 3

To Hold a Throne, 1956–7

In the aftermath of Glubb's dismissal, internal politics in Jordan entered a period of confusion. On the one hand, the King did what he could to repair relations with Britain and to maintain the British subsidy for the Arab Legion. On 17 March 1956, Hussein wrote to King Saud of Saudi Arabia, President al-Quwatly of Syria and Egyptian President Nasser stressing that while he welcomed their 'brotherly' offer of aid to replace the British subsidy for the Arab Legion, this was only one aspect of the defence treaty between the two countries. While that treaty remained in force, Hussein argued, Jordan still had the right to claim financial support from Britain.[1] Hussein's letter made it clear that he did not want to abandon the British connection completely just yet. On the other hand, he pressed ahead with the promised promotion of Arab army officers. Far from restoring the morale of the officer corps, however, Arabisation opened a Pandora's Box of factional, tribal and personal divisions within the army. In particular, the Free Officers movement, largely composed of younger officers, was opposed by the older guard who had risen through the ranks,[2] and who resented the leadership role accorded to new-comers like Ali Abu Nowar, whom they saw as an unprincipled opportunist.[3] These divisions within the ranks of the Arab Legion constituted a serious threat to Hussein's position. Although he had allied himself with the Free Officers in the coup against Glubb, Hussein needed a united and loyal army to maintain his throne. With Glubb gone, the danger for Hussein was that he might become the next target for revolutionary Arab nationalists. His position was more precarious and uncertain than at any time since he had acceded to the throne, with Jordan at the heart of the battle for hegemony in the region that now directly pitted Britain on one side against Egypt on the other.

In view of this broader Anglo-Egyptian struggle it is not surprising that the British did not abandon their position in Jordan in the wake of Glubb's dismissal. On the contrary, they began to build up a 'separate secret service', intended to improve contacts and intelligence gathering within the army in particular.[4] This was part of a broader plan, including information and propaganda activities, which was designed to reassert British influence in Jordan and reduce that of Egypt. One of the more interesting revelations to emerge from recently declassified British official papers is that Ali Abu Nowar now indirectly approached the British government, offering to work for it in return for personal financial reward. Abu Nowar's motives probably did not extend further than a desire to seize any opportunity he could to line his own pockets. More surprising was the British decision, authorised at the highest level, to pay the bribe. Prime Minister Anthony Eden was initially sceptical about the advice he received from Foreign Secretary Selwyn Lloyd on the matter, writing that he had understood that Abu Nowar was 'the most unreliable of the lot'. He continued:

> The only possible course in these Arab countries, I believe, is to try to fix relations of confidence with somebody. This may not always be possible but Kirkbride did get the King to promise that he would talk frankly to Duke. Surely that should be the basis of our policy rather than trying to bribe the least reputable military character with £2000, though I would not be against this if it fitted in with a general plan.[5]

Nevertheless, armed with Kirkbride's support and a telegram from Duke in which he argued that 'Abu Nowar gives the impression of being a Jordanian nationalist' rather than a disciple of Nasser, Lloyd evidently persuaded Eden to change his mind.[6] His hope was that Abu Nowar might be prepared to betray his former friends in the Free Officers movement, helping the more pro-British 'old guard' faction in the army to win the struggle for power. A telegram was despatched to Amman authorising Duke 'to offer him some personal financial assistance', subject to Duke's judgement as to whether discreet support for Abu Nowar would strengthen or weaken the 'stable elements in the Legion'. The ambassador was also told to make it clear to Abu Nowar that he was being paid off because 'we believe his policy is the same as ours, i.e. to support the independence of Jordan and the Hashemite dynasty and to maintain the efficiency of the Arab Legion'. The British evidently suspected that Hussein was beginning to have doubts about the loyalty of some of the Free Officers who had helped him stage the coup against Glubb. In the same telegram, Foreign Secretary Lloyd noted:

> It seems possible that Nowar's approach to us was made with the

knowledge of the King and may be the first step towards the establishment of a military government in Jordan. If that is what the King and Nowar are aiming at we must expect that they will eventually fall out when it comes to deciding which of them is to rule.[7]

This observation at least was to prove prophetic. But in hindsight it seems to have been a misjudgement on the part of the British government to extend 'personal financial assistance' to Ali Abu Nowar, who proved an unreliable guarantor of anyone's interests, except his own.

As the British sought to retrieve their position in Jordan, the Egyptians also attempted to advance their influence. In the aftermath of Glubb's dismissal the Egyptian military attaché in Amman, Salah Mustafa, contacted the Free Officers. According to Mahmud Mu'ayta, in early summer, shortly before his assassination by Israeli intelligence, Mustafa brought Abu Shahut, the real leader of the movement, 'a suitcase full of money', saying it was available for his use should he need it. The Egyptians wanted to buy the allegiance of the Free Officers, but Abu Shahut apparently refused the bribe.[8] The point which Mu'ayta wanted to make in relating this tale is clear: the Free Officers were patriots and idealists, not the Egyptian puppets the British suspected. Standing back from all of these machinations, then, one is left to contemplate a puzzling situation in which the public face of the Free Officers movement, Ali Abu Nowar, was in the pay of the British, while the officers themselves had been offered and refused money from the Egyptians: all this against the background of the fact that their one concrete achievement was the dismissal of the British commander of the Arab Legion, General Glubb.

What of the suggestion in Lloyd's telegram to Duke that the King might have been behind Abu Nowar's approach? The possibility that Hussein might have contemplated a military government at this stage is given some credence by the extent of his dissatisfaction with his Prime Minister Samir Rifai, who (British sources suggest) he believed was in the pay of the Saudis.[9] Hussein's lack of trust in Rifai at this stage is demonstrated in his decision to keep the planning for Glubb's dismissal secret from the prime minister.[10] Abu Nowar probably also played a part in undermining Rifai's position. Whether by coincidence or not, in May 1956 Hussein requested Rifai's resignation and promoted Abu Nowar to the post of Chief of Staff of the Arab Legion.

With Rifai gone, and Abu Nowar trying his best to seem at one and the same time the friend of the British, the Egyptians and the King, the political landscape was uncertain, and became even more so when the King dissolved parliament and called new elections to be held on 21 October. Then, on 26 July 1956, came Nasser's announcement that he had nationalised the Suez Canal Company, a move which brought him into direct conflict with Britain and France, the main shareholders. The British government, which had turned decisively against Nasser in the wake of Glubb's dismissal, with Eden believing that the Egyptian leader was behind King Hussein's decision, now had to face the reality that a man whom some likened to Hitler or Mussolini was in direct control of Britain's most important economic artery. The French government, meanwhile, believed that Nasser was aiding the independence movement in Algeria, a French colony. Arab public opinion, of course, stood firmly behind Nasser in his struggle with the imperialist powers.

Paradoxically in view of his reputation as a pro-Western figure, Hussein was the first Arab leader to respond to Nasser's coup with a public letter of congratulation, in which he declared: 'The shadow of exploitation is fading from the Arab world. The wrong is eliminated and substituted by the right.'[11] Hussein's reaction was no doubt partly defensive: with elections looming he wanted to protect himself against Arab nationalist criticism. But inevitably his response worsened his already strained relations with the British government,[12] which seriously considered withholding the next instalment of the British subsidy to the Arab Legion.[13]

In the event the money was paid over.[14] But these further strains in relations with Britain, which under the terms of the Anglo-Jordanian Treaty acted as the ultimate guarantor of Jordanian security, could not have come at a worse time. Tensions on the West Bank had been rising for some time, with the cycle of infiltration and reprisal intensifying markedly during the summer of 1956. Although Israel's main strategic preoccupation at this stage was with dealing with the threat posed by Egypt, which was rearming with Soviet weaponry, the Israelis remained determined to respond forcefully to any infiltration from the West Bank. The looming threat from Israel was one of the reasons Hussein cited in a discussion with Ambassador Duke for his congratulatory message to Nasser,[15] which had also spoken of standing together 'in the face of the common enemy'.[16] There is little doubt that the Israeli threat was Hussein's main preoccupation as the Suez crisis developed.[17] Britain was still committed to helping defend Jordan against any full-scale attack by Israel, although how the British would respond to a large-scale raid was left purposefully vague. The problem this presented for Hussein was two-fold. Firstly, could he trust the British to honour their defence commitment, especially if, as he increasingly came to suspect, they might collude with France and possibly Israel in an attack on Egypt? Secondly, even if he could trust the British, what would be the domestic impact of calling for British aid to defend Jordan against Israel? No doubt there would be a clamour from all quarters to call in Arab, especially Egyptian, assistance, but, with Nasser preparing for a possible Anglo-French assault, this was unlikely to provide an effective defence for Jordan.

In this precarious position, it is surprising that Hussein adopted such a critical tone in his dealings with the British. He may well have thought that an attack from Israel was coming whatever he did, but, if he still wanted British military aid, which most of the evidence suggests that he did, he might have been advised to tone down his criticisms of the British handling of the Suez crisis. For instance, in a meeting with Ambassador Duke on 4 September, in which he spoke with 'considerable vehemence and bitterness', Hussein warned that the British government:

> should not be misled into thinking that if we use force against Egypt it would be only Egypt that we had to deal with. Force against Egypt would be regarded as a blow against all the Arab States. It would leave them, and in particular Jordan, at the mercy of Israel since the Egyptian forces, which were the strongest in the Arab world, would be mobilized. Our action would be added to the list of Arab grievances against the West . . .[18]

In a bid to enhance Jordan's security in the face of his uncertain relations with Britain, Hussein explored the avenues open to him for securing Arab military backing. On 3 October he received a letter from Syrian President Shukri Quwatly expressing sympathy and support for his position, and promising military aid. In passing, Quwatly also expressed his sorrow that Hussein's negotiations to secure an Iraqi troop commitment to Jordan had so far not succeeded.[19] In fact the main focus of Hussein's efforts to secure other Arab forces to help defend Jordan against Israel was on Baghdad, where Prime Minister Nuri Said, overcoming his initial reluctance, eventually indicated a willingness to move Iraqi forces into Jordan. The plan ran up against the suspicions of the Israeli government, though, which feared that if anything more than a token Iraqi force moved into Jordan it could threaten their flank during any conflict with Egypt.[20] Ultimately, Iraqi forces did move up to the Jordanian border in mid-October, but not into Jordan itself, at Hussein's request. Meanwhile, Hussein's scepticism about the defence commitment from Britain had not been allayed by a further discussion at the beginning of October. Foreign Secretary Selwyn Lloyd had instructed Ambassador Duke to tell Hussein that 'the Anglo-Jordan Alliance is in bad shape'. He went on to note:

> In the last year we have put up with a succession of public rebuffs from Jordan. It is hardly surprising that the Jordanians themselves cannot but wonder whether we will really come to the assistance of a country which has treated us, their ally, in such a manner. But this is not our way. Although Jordan's recent actions and pronouncements have been unfriendly we have a solemn Treaty with that country . . . There can therefore be no question of our not carrying out our obligations.[21]

When Duke came to convey the foreign secretary's views to Hussein on 4 October, he found that 'the King clearly rather resented the message'.[22] He interrupted to ask what were the 'rebuffs and unfriendly pronouncements' from Jordan to which Lloyd referred, before going on to warn again that he faced the constant threat of Israeli attack and that 'he was fighting for the existence of Jordan'. He did not want to imply that he doubted the British commitment to defend Jordan, but he had faced many 'dangers and unpleasant surprises from people from whom he would not have expected them and whom he had regarded as friends'. The King concluded by saying that 'at least as a result of these exchanges Jordan now knew where she stood, but whatever happened, if Israel attacked, Jordan would fight with whatever she had to defend herself'.

Hussein did not have to wait long for a major challenge from Israel. The culmination of an escalating series of border incidents came on the night of 10–11 October, when a brigade-sized Israeli raid, mounted by paratroops supported by armour and artillery, resulted in the destruction of the Jordanian police fort at Qalqilya.[23] During the course of the engagement, Hussein called on the local British RAF commander to provide air cover over Qalqilya, but the Israeli raid was over before London had time to make a decision. In its aftermath, though, the Foreign Office did warn Israel that a full-scale attack on Jordan would result in the activation of the Anglo-Jordanian Treaty. This was not enough for Hussein, who was disappointed by the lack of air cover for his forces. The response from London was to note pointedly that the King had reduced the effectiveness of the Arab Legion himself by dismissing Glubb and the British officers.

These Anglo-Jordanian exchanges in the aftermath of Qalqilya need to be set alongside the subsequent Anglo–French exchanges with Israel over a possible attack on Egypt. In secret meetings at a villa in the Parisian suburb of Sèvres on 22 and 24 October, it was agreed that Israel would attack Egypt on 29 October, with Britain and France landing forces posing as peacekeepers on the Suez Canal. It was further agreed that there would be no Israeli attack on Jordan, nor any British assistance to Jordan should it launch hostilities against Israel. The deal thus eliminated the theoretical possibility of Britain being dragged into war with Israel to protect Jordan, at the same time as it committed all of the parties to engage in hostilities against Egypt. Since Britain, France and Israel had all along been mostly preoccupied with Nasser, it served their interests to remove Jordan from the military equation.

Hussein was of course not privy to the secret Anglo-French–Israeli exchanges, but his reaction to the Israeli attack on Egypt, and the duplicitous Anglo-French attempt to pose as peacekeepers, suggests that he may have expected all along that Britain would turn to Israel for help. Once the operation began, Hussein wrote to King Saud of Saudi Arabia describing it as the 'treacherous British-French-Israeli attack', and asking him to do all he could to evict Israel from the two Saudi islands which dominate the mouth of the Straits of Tiran.[24] When the British Ambassador Duke came to discuss the situation with the King, the new Prime Minister Suleiman al-Nabulsi and Chief of Staff Ali Abu Nowar, late on the evening of 31 October, he noted:

> Surprisingly . . . their attitude towards the military action we had taken against Egypt was almost more one of sorrow than anger. They were all convinced that the Israel aggression in Sinai had been started with our encouragement. They placed no reliance whatever on Israel assurance to us that they would not attack Jordan . . . On the contrary, they thought the West Bank of Jordan was probably the price that we had undertaken to let Israel have for her assistance to us against Egypt.[25]

Duke recorded that when he repeated the assurances the British government had received from the Israelis, 'the King and Ali Abu Nowar both smiled incredulously and remarked that the Israelis appeared, for practical purposes, to be our new allies'.

From the King's point of view it was fortunate that the Anglo-French–Israeli action had been launched at the end of October and not a week earlier. Had it coincided with the Jordanian election on 21 October, the result might have been even worse from his point of view. As it was, the elections produced a parliament which, although it represented many different groups and shades of opinion, was dominated by Arab nationalists of various hues. The unfortunately named National Socialist Party of Suleiman Nabulsi represented the largest single political voice and as a result of this the King called on Nabulsi, who had failed to win a seat in parliament himself, to form a government on 27 October. Nabulsi's background was in finance, although he had been politically active in support of what may broadly be termed Arab nationalist causes since his twenties. Perhaps the best word for his approach to politics is 'populist'; he tended to follow the mood of the street, rather than to lead it. Nevertheless, there was nothing in his earlier career to suggest that he might be disloyal to the Hashemite throne. Once in office, Nabulsi's response to the Suez crisis was similar to the King's, though more measured; when Hussein called for an attack on Israel, Nabulsi exercised a restraining influence.[26]

The ill-fated Anglo-French intervention in Egypt came to a close at the end of the first week of November, when American diplomatic and financial pressure forced the British government to break ranks with its allies and accept a ceasefire. Once the hostilities in Egypt had been concluded, the paths of the Nabulsi government and the King started to diverge. Jordan's relationship with Britain had effectively collapsed, and Hussein turned to

Washington for aid; he had written to President Eisenhower during the hostilities to prepare the ground, praising US support for the principles of right and justice which had 'won her the appreciation of all peace loving nations'.[27] The Nabulsi government, by contrast, preferred Arab aid, although Nabulsi proved once again to be one of its more cautious members in pursuing this course.

Interestingly, in view of his earlier role in seeking 'personal financial assistance' from the British, it was Ali Abu Nowar who was the initial standard-bearer for the King's approach to the Americans. On 9 November he told the US military attaché in Amman, James Sweeney, that he could guarantee a crackdown on communists and the imposition of martial law in Jordan in exchange for American financial aid. If this did not come, Jordan would be forced to accept aid from the Soviet Union. Abu Nowar's appeal was followed a week later by an appeal from the King himself in the same terms.[28] Neither was received enthusiastically by Washington, which was not willing to take over the British financial commitment to Jordan at this stage.

Nabulsi, who was unaware of Abu Nowar's and the King's approach to Washington, found himself in a difficult position. He favoured the end of the British connection, but wanted first to secure firm promises of Arab aid to replace it. Nabulsi's caution was reflected in the government's decision to seek a negotiated termination of the Anglo-Jordanian Treaty, rather than its unilateral abrogation, conditional on the prior guarantee of Arab aid to replace the British subsidy. Here the Jordanians were pushing at an open door. The dismissal of Glubb and the British officers, the deterioration in the Legion's efficiency and finally the Suez defeat had all contributed to a change in London's position. The Jordanian connection was no longer viewed as value for money and the goal was now to shed it as quickly as possible. The only proviso was that the British exit should look like a graceful retreat rather than a forced withdrawal.[29]

As part of this strategy, the British government sought a commitment from Washington to take over the role of Jordan's Western financial backer.[30] This coincided with a review of American strategy in the region which took place in the wake of the Suez crisis and resulted in the promulgation of the Eisenhower Doctrine, which was enunciated by the president to a Joint Session of Congress on 5 January 1957. This committed the US administration to provide American military and economic aid to friendly Middle Eastern countries and also extended the offer of direct military protection to any 'nation or group of nations requesting assistance against armed aggression from any country controlled by international communism'.

The Eisenhower Doctrine helped open the way for overt and covert American support for Hussein. At the time, of course, this was not clear to the King, whose initial efforts to secure financial support from Washington had been rebuffed. Jordan's economic situation was critical; adequate funding for his armed forces was vital for both the survival of the Hashemite regime and the defence of Jordan, but he had no domestic means of raising the large sums of money required. In the absence of any alternative, he had no choice but to go along with the Nabulsi government's attempts to secure Arab aid, and as a result on 19 January 1957 he reluctantly signed the Arab Solidarity Agreement with Nasser, King Saud and Syrian Prime Minister Sabri al-Asali in Cairo. According to the terms of the agreement, the three Arab states agreed to provide Jordan with 12.5 million Egyptian pounds per annum for ten years to replace the British subsidy.[31] Subsequently, Syrian President Shukri Quwatly wrote a series of letters to Hussein suggesting that Syria, Egypt, Jordan and Saudi Arabia should also coordinate their defence policies in the face of Israel's evident reluctance to withdraw fully from the territory it had seized during the Suez war. Quwatly was particularly concerned that Israel intended to hold on to Sharm al-Sheikh with a view to dominating the Gulf of Aqaba. Much like the promised Arab subsidy, though, these grandiose plans for defence cooperation remained no more than paper proposals.[32]

On 4 February negotiations for the termination of the Anglo-Jordanian Treaty were set in train between a British delegation led by Ambassador Charles Johnston and a Jordanian one led by Nabulsi, who wanted to conclude the negotiations swiftly to bolster his domestic popularity and secure his position against the King's displeasure. The final settlement provided for the termination of the treaty with effect from 14 March 1957. The remaining British troops were to be withdrawn within six months, and in exchange the Jordanian government would pay compensation of £4.25 million over six years.

As foreshadowed by the King's repeated public warnings about the dangers posed by communism to the kingdom, the question of whether or not Jordan should now accept aid under the terms of the Eisenhower Doctrine proved to be the main battleground between Hussein and the Nabulsi government. On 18 February the King instructed the cabinet that the press should not attack the Eisenhower Doctrine, that the diplomatic service should not be reorganised, and that no action should be taken to establish relations with communist states.[33] In the meantime, the King had evidently begun his covert contacts with the CIA. The first link was established by a young CIA officer who became part of the King's close social circle, and whose initials were 'JD'.[34] Both the nature and the purpose of these contacts have tended to be somewhat sensationalised. The early financial assistance provided by the CIA was certainly not of the order of the 'millions of dollars' later suggested. In fact, throughout the 1960s and into the early 1970s, the monthly sum passed by the CIA station chief directly to the King was only 5,000 Jordanian dinars (about $14,000), a subsidy aimed at helping him maintain the loyalty of key individuals within the army, a task which he had to carry out personally since at this stage he had no domestic intelligence service. If one accepts this explanation as to the destination of the money and the amount involved, then claims that the CIA somehow bought the King's loyalty through its payments from 1957 onwards seem far-fetched and exaggerated. Indeed, far from the 'suitcases of cash' postulated by some, the money handed over fitted neatly into a regular brown manila envelope, which the King never opened or drew attention to in the presence of the CIA station chief.[35]

Against the backdrop of the King's developing American connections, his confrontation with the Nabulsi government soon became open. On 2 April, Nabulsi informed the King of the government's intention to establish diplomatic relations with the Soviet Union. He followed this up on 7 April by giving the King a list of twenty-seven officials whom he proposed to retire, including Hussein's director of security, Bahjat Tabara. Although the King acquiesced to these measures, a further list sent by Nabulsi on 10 April, which included the name of the Chief of the Royal Diwan, Bahjat Talhuni, proved to be the final straw. Hussein sent Talhuni to see Nabulsi instead with a letter demanding the government's resignation. His tough action may well have been prompted by the events of 8 April, when the First Armoured Car Regiment under the command of Captain Nadhir Rashid, one of the Free Officers' leaders, had surrounded Amman in what Rashid later argued was only a traffic census.[36] Hussein was far from convinced, later claiming that the move could have meant only one thing: 'imminent danger to Jordan, a possible attack on the Palace'.[37] If Hussein was right, the plotters lost their nerve, for no move against him was made at this point.

Nabulsi accepted the King's call for his resignation, apparently confident that Hussein would not be able to form an alternative government and that he would soon be called back to office. For a couple of days this seemed possible, but then, on the evening of 13 April, a dramatic event intervened.[38] During the day reports had reached Hussein that a coup might be in the making, and that Rashid's armoured car regiment had been ordered to move out once more, this time with the goal of surrounding the palace and kidnapping the King.[39] How immediate the threat really was is difficult to ascertain. In view of the factional struggle within the army between the 'old guard' and the Free Officers it is at least possible that the threat was concocted with the goal of persuading Hussein to move against the Free Officers.[40] If this was its purpose, then it succeeded spectacularly.

Impulsively, Hussein decided to drive out to the Zerqa camp himself to find out what was going on. His arrival was preceded by that of his cousin, Zeid bin Shaker, who was one of the Free Officers. Bin Shaker found a mêlée of confusion, rumours and sporadic gunfire, and was himself taken into custody by suspicious troops.[41] As Hussein's own car arrived a further round of firing broke out. Without a moment's hesitation, he jumped out of the vehicle and waded into the crowds to rally the troops in person. It was a huge gamble. In the midst of an agitated throng of troops in the darkness, anything could have happened. Shaking hands, embracing and being embraced, Hussein rallied his men. His personal bravery had saved the day. But there remained the question of how to deal with the suspected coup plotters. Aware that they had been out-manoeuvred, most of the Free Officers' leaders immediately fled from Jordan to Syria. Ali Abu Nowar, who, in fear of his own life, had begged the king to let him return to Amman rather than face the troops at Zerqa, was allowed to leave the country the next day. There are indications that US intelligence officials played their part in subsequent efforts to blacken his name. In a phone conversation with his brother, Secretary of State Foster Dulles, CIA Director Allen Dulles commented that 'someone in prison is bitter re Nuwar. They think they can pin a shortage of Army accounts on him. The Sec. said we should get it out even if it is gossip.'[42] Evidently the Dulles brothers were prepared to use evidence from any source about Abu Nowar's personal corruption in order to help discredit him.

Although Hussein had now passed the point of greatest personal danger, he still had to form a new government to replace that of Nabulsi. Here Hussein once again demonstrated that he had come of age politically. His first moves were cautious, involving the creation of what was to prove to be a caretaker cabinet under Fakhri al-Khalidi, which included Nabulsi as foreign minister. At the same time, Ali al-Hiyari, a suspected Free Officers sympathiser, was appointed as the new chief of the general staff to replace Ali Abu Nowar. (The appointment of Hiyari may well have been intended to test his loyalty, something he dispelled any doubts about by defecting during a trip to Syria on 20 April.) At the same time, though, the King managed to neutralise the external threat to his regime from Syria and Egypt, by astutely ensuring the support of Saudi Arabia, Iraq and the United States for his actions. King Saud had already placed Saudi troops which had been stationed in the Jordan Valley since the Suez crisis at Hussein's disposal should he need them. In the face of suspicious Syrian troop movements in the vicinity of Irbid on 14 April, the day after the Zerqa affair, Hussein readied himself to move north at the head of a combined Jordanian and Saudi force. In the event, military action proved unnecessary. Divisions of opinion in Damascus together with Hussein's resolute stance led President Quwatly to send a message confirming that the Syrian troops, which had also been stationed in Jordan since Suez, had no hostile intentions and were 'unreservedly under King Hussein's command'.[43] All the same, Hussein made sure he covered his position further by contacting the Iraqis and requesting that they should put forces on standby just over the Jordanian border.[44]

Hussein's resolute action at Zerqa did much to raise his stock in Washington. American support constituted the third string to Hussein's bow and, although the intervention of US troops was neither requested nor offered, the Eisenhower administration lent the King both overt and covert backing as the political crisis unfolded. The stop-gap Khalidi government was quickly undermined both by the opposition of the Arab nationalist parties and by Nabulsi's decision to resign from the cabinet on 24 April. It was at this point that the King moved to assure himself of American support, with a message communicated through intelligence channels on 24 April indicating his intention to impose martial law.[45] He asked the US administration to use its connections with the Israeli government to make sure that they did not intervene militarily in Jordan. In addition to warning off the Israelis, and issuing a public statement in Hussein's support, Eisenhower also ordered the US Sixth Fleet to move into a forward position in the Eastern Mediterranean, a gesture intended to help face down any Soviet-backed move against the King. Discussing the crisis with Foster Dulles, the president commented that 'the young King was certainly showing some spunk and he admired him for it'.[46]

With his external position covered, Hussein moved decisively against the domestic opposition. Calling together a small circle of loyal supporters, including Ibrahim Hashim and Samir Rifai, on the evening of 24 April, the King persuaded them to join a new government. The nerve of those prospective ministers who wavered was strengthened by the formidable presence of Queen Zein, who warned that none of them would be allowed to leave the palace until he had agreed to serve. The King followed up the next day by dismissing the Khalidi government, and announcing its replacement by the new cabinet led by Ibrahim Hashim. Martial law was declared and all political parties were banned.[47] Assessing the new cabinet over in Washington, Foster Dulles told his brother Allen, 'things are going along fairly well. The only change is R is FM rather than PM. H is PM and is all right and respectable. R did not want it yet.'[48] Evidently the Americans had been told in advance to expect the appointment of Samir Rifai ('R') as prime minister, but were prepared to see Ibrahim Hashim ('H') take his place as a short-term measure.

The day after the formation of the new cabinet, on 26 April, Hussein, accompanied by his new Foreign Minister Samir Rifai and his Chief of Diwan Bahjat Talhouni, held a meeting in Riyadh with King Saud, whose support had been a valuable asset during the crisis. For Saud's benefit Hussein offered his own summary of what had taken place in Jordan. According to the King, there were 'groups' linked to a 'big foreign country' who had been working to undermine and take control of Jordan. They had 'tried to infiltrate into the army and some of their actions were directed at his person from inside and outside the army'. To mollify Saud, who remained an opponent of the British- and Iraqi-led Baghdad Pact, Hussein indicated that he did not intend to change his foreign policy, or 'throw his country into foreign alliances and invite the occupation back'. However, the King made it clear that Egypt and Syria should 'take their hands off our internal affairs'. If they did so, he would be prepared to attend a summit in Riyadh to 'clear things between us'. For his part, Saud expressed his sympathy with Hussein's position and agreed that no Arab country should interfere with the internal affairs of another.[49] Over the ensuing months Hussein's relations with the Saudi monarch became closer still. Hussein commended Saud's stand against Syrian propaganda attacks, and worked to forge closer relations between Saudi Arabia and Iraq in an effort to build a monarchical alliance to counter-balance Egypt and Syria.[50]

Meanwhile, the King's decision to opt for a scarcely disguised form of palace rule was welcomed by both Britain and the United States. As British Ambassador Charles Johnston saw matters, 'our interest is better suited by an authoritarian regime which maintains stability and the Western connection than by an untrammelled democracy which rushes downhill towards Communism and chaos'.[51] The fate of Suleiman Nabulsi, the central figure in Jordan's brief experiment with 'untrammelled democracy', was, in the short term at least, an unhappy one. The King had him put under house arrest which, as Queen Zein observed to Ambassador Johnston, involved shutting him up alone with his 'rich and ugly wife whom he detests'. Johnston could not resist a smirk at Nabulsi's expense, noting that he would no doubt have preferred to be locked up in prison instead, where 'he would be the centre of an admiring circle to whom he could make speeches all day long. Nabulsi is of course as queer as a coot and the punishment devised for him is in accordance with the best modern thinking about Hell as propounded by M. Sartre.'[52]

The April 1957 crisis represented Hussein's full political coming of age. In dismissing the Nabulsi government, putting down the Zerqa 'mutiny' and facing down his domestic and regional opponents, the King had shown considerable personal and political courage. Nevertheless, Hussein did not act in isolation. While British protection of Jordan was now a thing of the past, the King received valuable support from Iraq, Saudi Arabia and particularly the United States, with which the April crisis was to cement a new, closer relationship. The King could also thank the domestic political legacy of his grandfather, Abdullah, for the successful reassertion of Hashemite rule in April 1957. Just as Abu'l Huda, one of Abdullah's men, had successfully overseen the awkward political transition which had brought Hussein to the throne in 1953, so Ibrahim Hashim and Samir Rifai, two more of Abdullah's political protégés, headed the government which reasserted Hashemite authority at the end of April 1957. As an exhausted Hussein prepared to go to bed at 5 a.m. on 25 April after taking the decisive steps required to form a new government, his Head of Diwan, Bahjat Talhuni, intervened to stop him. There was one more thing for His Majesty to do before he retired, Talhuni suggested. He should kneel down and recite a verse of the Koran, giving thanks to Allah for his grandfather, since without Abdullah's training there would have been no ministers to whom he could turn in this time of crisis. The King promptly knelt and prayed.[53]

CHAPTER 4

A DYNASTY UNDER THREAT, 1957–61

H ussein may have come of age politically during the April crisis, but
many still believed that his days as king were numbered. Determined to
prove them wrong, Hussein undertook a series of measures intended to
strengthen his position. The April coup plotters were put on trial before a
special military court. But, although the prosecutor asked for the death
sentence for twenty-one out of the twenty-two accused, when the court
delivered its verdict on 25 September 1957 five men were acquitted, while the
remaining seventeen received prison sentences ranging from ten to fifteen
years. There can be little doubt that the King's inclination to show clemency
to political opponents conditioned their relatively light sentencing. As such,
it was another measure of his increasing self-confidence. Despite the light
touch he employed in dealing with the plotters, Hussein recognised the
importance of developing security services to support his regime, and to
ensure his personal safety, he created a special Bedouin Royal Guards
regiment formed from hand-picked men under the command of his uncle
Sharif Nasser. When the National Assembly reconvened on 1 October 1957,
Hussein's speech from the throne made it clear that he would brook no
further challenges to his authority from within or without Jordan's borders.
'We shall fight to keep our independence', he declared.[1]

Hussein's determination also paid dividends in his relations with
Washington, where the State Department described the question of the future
stability of Jordan as a 'matter of deep concern to [the] US'.[2] In addition to
the grant of $10 million which had been announced on 29 April, the
Eisenhower administration followed up with another $10 million at the end
of May and $30 million during the summer. In order to make Hussein's

position easier, all of the US financial aid was offered under the terms of the 1954 Mutual Security Act, rather than the more controversial Eisenhower Doctrine.[3] This financial aid was accompanied by an emergency airlift of military hardware on 9 September, precipitated in part by the crisis which had broken out in Syria during August. A covert American attempt to overthrow the government of Prime Minister Sabri al-Asali, which included Baathists and other leftists, had been unmasked by the Syrian intelligence service run by Colonel Abd al-Hamid Sarraj. Three American embassy officials were expelled from the country. With the influence of leftist groups including the Syrian Communist Party advancing, fears about a possible communist coup in Damascus were rife in Washington, and military aid to Hussein looked like a reliable means of bolstering pro-Western forces in the region.

Hussein took an active interest in the political crisis in Syria, telling King Saud in a letter on 18 August that the Syrian Communist Party had signed an agreement with Moscow which, he warned, meant that Syria would come under the 'complete influence' of the Soviet Union. He also noted in passing that one of the conspiracy theories manufactured by the Syrian communists was the so-called 'Jordanian warning': the claim that Jordan was preparing to declare war on Syria. Hussein dismissed this at the time as a complete lie.[4]

In fact, there was more to this claim than Hussein admitted. During the second half of August and early September 1957 the US and UK developed a secret 'Preferred Plan' which would involve coordinated action by Syria's neighbours, especially Jordan and Iraq, to overthrow the regime in Damascus.[5] The final report of the Anglo-American 'Working Group', produced on 18 September, suggested deliberately provoking border incidents between Syria and Iraq and Jordan, especially on the Syria–Jordan border, as a pretext for military action. The plan envisaged enlisting King Hussein's cooperation to induce one or two of the Bedouin tribes in southern Syria to stage a rising of sufficient scale to provoke a Syrian counter-attack. Tribal forces would then withdraw across the border, pulling Syrian units after them in hot pursuit into Jordan, where the Jordanian army would be waiting to engage them. In addition, the CIA and MI6 planned to gather Syrian opposition groups together in Jordan under the auspices of a 'Free Syria Committee'.

Whether or not the Preferred Plan in its final form was agreed with King Hussein is unclear, but during a meeting in late August in Istanbul, Eisenhower's special representative, Loy Henderson, who had been deputed by the president to tour the region to muster support for operations against Syria, suggested to Hussein that retaliation against Damascus need not wait for aggression in the usual sense. Rather, 'Syrian provocations', which might include staged border incidents, would be sufficient grounds for attack.[6] Whatever the enthusiasm for action against Syria in Washington and

London, Hussein evidently did not think the matter pressing enough for him to cancel a planned European vacation, which kept him out of Jordan from late August until 12 September 1957, just before the Preferred Plan was finalised.[7]

In the event, the plan was undercut by further developments in the region. The Iraqis, under Prime Minister Ali Jawdat al-Ayubi, were unenthusiastic about involving themselves in covert action in Syria. Their position was not helped by the escalation of tensions on the Syrian–Turkish border, which allowed the regime in Damascus to portray the crisis as a struggle against external interference in Arab politics. This, together with King Saud's decision to pose as a neutral mediator rather than a pro-Western protagonist in the crisis, meant that Hussein would have been isolated in the Arab world had he chosen to participate in the plan. The King fell somewhat grudgingly into line with the moderate Iraqi and Saudi approach, accepting a Saudi-brokered truce in his propaganda war with the regime in Damascus. In mid-October the Jordanian government issued a statement pledging support for Syria if it was subject to external aggression.[8] In the event, it was Nasser's intervention, involving the landing of a small contingent of Egyptian troops at the Syrian port of Latakia on 13 October, that decided the outcome of the crisis.[9] Nasser's action enabled him to pose, somewhat improbably, as the defender of Syrian independence and the guardian of Arab unity, while also advancing Egyptian influence in Syria.

Nasser's aggrandisement was a worrying development for Hussein. With the exception of a brief détente during the Suez crisis, his relations with the Egyptian leader had been difficult ever since the Baghdad Pact riots of the winter of 1955.[10] The prospect of Nasser gaining control over Syria presented Hussein with a potential threat to his position from across Jordan's northern border. In fact, Nasser's aim in Syria was to secure influence without the responsibility of power, and developments there during the winter of 1957–8 may have forced his hand. The two main rival political forces in Syria by this stage were the Baath Party and the Communist Party. Briefly put, their struggle for political leadership resulted in the Baathists turning to Nasser to strengthen their position. When a delegation of Baathist Syrian army officers arrived in Egypt on 11 January 1958, Nasser was initially diffident about their call for complete union. During a second round of talks on 17–20 January, however, he changed tack.[11] He now agreed to the officers' proposal for an immediate union between Egypt and Syria, but only on terms which would give him control over its political direction, including the dissolution of political parties in Syria and the withdrawal of the Syrian military from politics. Provisional agreement on Nasser's terms was reached on 20 January, with the creation of the United Arab Republic of Egypt and Syria being formally announced on 1 February 1958. The new union gave a major boost to Nasser's prestige in the struggle for leadership in the Arab world, and constituted a significant blow to the Hashemite monarchies of Iraq and Jordan. The 'struggle for Syria' which had been waged intermittently throughout the 1940s and 1950s, and which ultimately dated back to Feisal's proclamation of a short-lived, independent Arab kingdom in Damascus at the end of the First World War, seemed now to have been decided in Egypt's favour.

In response, Hussein set in train negotiations for an Iraqi–Jordanian union. On 7 February he wrote to King Saud informing him of his progress and asking for his support in refusing to recognise the new United Arab Republic.[12] In view of past Saudi sensitivities about the creation of any Hashemite union, Hussein no doubt thought it prudent to keep the Saudi monarch up to date with the negotiations. A federation agreement between Iraq and Jordan was now hastily concluded and signed in Amman on 14 February 1958. However, this Hashemite attempt to create a counterpoise to the UAR was beset by problems. Firstly, the relationship between the Iraqi and the Jordanian branches of the House of Hashem was poor. Although personal relations between Hussein and his cousin Feisal were good, the Iraqi Crown Prince, Abdul Ilah, remained a controversial figure in Amman, and Hussein thought he exercised an unwarranted degree of influence over the young King Feisal.[13] Abdul Ilah, for his part, had argued since the days of King Talal that the Jordanian branch of the Hashemite family was not fit to rule, and that the kingdom should have reverted to the Iraqi branch. The bad blood between the two branches of the family undoubtedly affected the negotiations for union. How far the potential marriage of King Hussein to his Iraqi cousin, Princess Husaima, the elder daughter of Princess Rajiha and a granddaughter of King Feisal I, might have gone towards healing this breach is a moot point. Certainly, there was gossip about the proposal in Amman during June 1958, and Queen Zein seems to have retained her enthusiasm for the idea even after the Iraqi revolution.[14] Hussein's own views remain unknown, although the fact that the match never took place leads one to suspect that he was at best unenthusiastic.

On top of the difficult family politics of the Hashemite union, from the outset it suffered from a lack of popular appeal. On the street in Amman and Baghdad, just as elsewhere in the Arab world, it was Nasser's Egyptian–Syrian union which excited the imagination.[15] During the civil crisis which broke out in neighbouring Lebanon during May and June 1958, it was evident that the United Arab Republic exercised a significant attraction for Arab nationalists in the country. With a justified sense of foreboding, Hussein wrote to King Saud on 6 June, warning that events in Lebanon would have 'dangerous consequences' for the neighbouring countries, including Iraq, Jordan and Saudi Arabia.[16] Meanwhile, the practical implementation of the Iraqi–

Jordanian union proved problematical. The Iraqis had been unenthusiastic about Hussein's initiative from the outset and seem to have been persuaded to press ahead only by the King's willingness to cede the title of head of the union to his cousin Feisal. Even so, the Jordanian and Iraqi officials charged with working within the confines of the new union found the task largely uncongenial.[17] In view of the compromises necessary on both sides, but particularly for the Jordanians, who had ceded leadership, this is not surprising. Moreover, despite British support, the Americans were unenthusiastic about the idea. The Iraqi perception was that the Americans were 'trying to make a deal with Nasser' instead of backing the Hashemites. Crown Prince Abdul Ilah went so far as to send a message to Secretary of State Dulles in early June 'requesting advance notice so that the pro-Western leaders would have time to clear out to save their lives'.[18] This was to prove an eerily prescient warning.

The troubled Hashemite union never had the chance to establish itself. Events, in the shape of a military coup d'état in Baghdad on the morning of 14 July, overtook it. To this day, controversy still surrounds the question of whether the Iraqi coup might have been thwarted had more heed been paid to information gathered beforehand by the Jordanians. As the Iraqi plotters awaited their opportunity to act, a conspiracy was uncovered within the Jordanian army, led by one Colonel Mahmud Rusan, the former military attaché in Washington. Since Jordan had no intelligence service of its own at this stage, a CIA officer was specially despatched to Amman, together with a skilled foreign interrogator, to help the Jordanians investigate the plot.[19] In pursuing this investigation, this CIA officer worked closely with Mohammad Rasool Kilani, a public prosecutor whom the King had deputed to oversee matters. Kilani and the CIA officer subsequently formed a lifelong friendship.

Nearly half a century later, though, they recollected the fruits of their investigation differently. According to Kilani, Rusan had not only admitted to a conspiracy against the Jordanian monarchy, he had also revealed under questioning that there was a broader plot in the offing, which was intended to take place between mid-June and mid-July, and which was aimed not just at the Jordanian but also at the Iraqi branch of the Hashemite family.[20] The recollection of the CIA officer concerned is different: according to him, the Jordanians' concern about a possible threat to the Iraqi monarchy was the result not of Rusan's interrogation, but of suspicions about the eventual leaders of the coup in Baghdad, Brigadier Abd al-Karim Qasim and Colonel Abd al-Salam Arif, which had originally been formed when they had been stationed together in Jordan in 1956–7.[21]

However, both Kilani and the former CIA officer were clear about one thing. When the Jordanian concerns were raised with the Iraqi Commander-in-Chief of the Arab Union armed forces, General Rafiq A'rif, during a hastily arranged visit to Amman on 10 July, he dismissed them, refusing to believe that a plot could be brewing within what he regarded as the disciplined officer corps of the Iraqi army.[22] Events were to prove his confidence misplaced.

For some time discontent had been brewing within the Iraqi officer corps, coalescing during 1957 in the form of a Free Officers' movement loosely modelled on that which had seized power in Egypt. The Iraqi Free Officers condemned the Hashemite regime's close ties with Britain and sought the establishment of a republic which would pursue an Arab nationalist foreign policy. The overall leader of the movement was Brigadier Qasim, who enjoyed a privileged position as a favourite of Prime Minister Nuri Said. He was assisted by Colonel Arif, who was to prove the principal man of action on 14 July.

With an irony that later came to trouble King Hussein, it was the aftermath of the Rusan plot in Jordan that gave the Iraqi army conspirators their opportunity to act. In order to bolster Hussein's position, the Iraqi regime gave the order for the Twentieth Brigade Group, which included forces under the command of Colonel Arif, to move towards the Jordanian frontier from its base east of Baghdad on 13 July. On its way through the capital, the brigade mutinied.[23] Furtively, under cover of darkness, Colonel Arif led his troops into Baghdad, where they seized the radio station and proclaimed the establishment of the republic of Iraq. Meanwhile, Arif sent troop detachments to Prime Minister Nuri Said's house and to the Rihab Palace, the residence of King Feisal and Crown Prince Abdul Ilah. Shots were fired as the Royal Guard resisted. A parley ensued. At 8 a.m. Feisal, Abdul Ilah and the royal princesses made their way out into the palace courtyard. Whatever their message, they had no chance to deliver it. A young army captain opened fire, spraying the courtyard with bullets. In seconds the Hashemite dynasty of Iraq was no more.

Nuri Said, who had been tipped off, fled his house and remained in hiding for the rest of the day. But the following day, escaping in disguise, he was spotted on the street and shot. His body was then dragged through the streets and mutilated as a vehicle was reversed repeatedly over it. Meanwhile, in the ultimate indignity, Crown Prince Abdul Ilah's body was disinterred from its grave by the mob, dragged naked through the streets and strung up outside the Ministry of Defence. With the old order destroyed, the Free Officers were able to assert control. Brigadier Qasim, who had arrived in the capital later on 14 July, now became the first leader of the Republic of Iraq.

The initial reports King Hussein received from Baghdad were sketchy. But, as the day progressed, it became clear to him that military conspirators had successfully overthrown the monarchy, murdering King Feisal and Crown Prince Abdul Ilah in the process. It was a terrible personal blow. Feisal, his friend and cousin, was dead. His family had been butchered. Now he alone bore the burden of Hashemite expectations. Hussein lost no time in staking his claim to the Iraqi throne. He assumed the leadership of the Arab Union, and despatched Jordanian forces under the command of his uncle, Sharif Nasser, over the Iraqi frontier. In order to secure his own position and release further forces for possible operations in Iraq, Hussein appealed to the British and American governments for support. His message found a receptive audience in London, but a much more reluctant one in Washington. The King himself was probably not initially aware of the differences between Britain and the US over how best to respond. In fact, a key theme of post-Suez British policy in the Middle East had been a continuing enthusiasm for blocking the advance of Nasser's influence. This was balanced by a rather more complex and cautious American approach, which was ultimately dominated by broader Cold War strategy.

Now, faced with the disaster of the overthrow of the Iraqi regime, London reacted by pressing for a wide-ranging operation to extirpate Nasser's influence from the region. From the perspective of the British prime minister, Harold Macmillan, this should involve not only the landing of Anglo-American forces in Lebanon, but also intervention in Jordan, with a view to providing a possible platform for further action in Iraq. Macmillan told President Eisenhower in a crucial phone conversation on the evening of 14 July: 'If you do this thing in the Lebanon, it is really only part of a much larger operation, because we shall be driven to take things as a whole. I want to feel that we both regard it as a whole. It looks like a showdown.' Eisenhower's response was much more cautious: 'So far as we are concerned we cannot undertake anything beyond Lebanon. The situation elsewhere is going to be much more complicated.'[24]

Despite the president's evident reluctance, Macmillan raised the question of King Hussein's request for an assurance of Anglo-American military support should he require it. The open phone line on which he was speaking to the president led the prime minister to resort to a bizarre form of code in conveying Hussein's message, the key to the understanding of which is provided by the short physical stature of Hussein and his cousin Feisal: 'we have had a request from one of the two little chaps – one is gone and the other is there – we do not really know the final reports, but the second one is going on alone. We have this request. His being deputy gives him a legal right over the whole. What are we going to do?' Evidently the only person fooled by Macmillan's description of Hussein and Feisal as 'two little chaps' was Eisenhower himself, who later recorded in his memoirs, 'I had to smile at Harold's efforts at code over the telephone – "We have had a request from the two little chaps", meaning Hussein and Chamoun [the president of Lebanon].'[25] Whatever his amusement or bemusement at Macmillan's code, the president reserved his position on King Hussein's request, telling the prime minister that he needed authority to act.

During the ensuing forty-eight hours, the British government kept up its pressure, both on the US administration to commit itself to joint military action in Jordan, and on King Hussein to persuade him to make his request for Anglo-American intervention before it was too late. The events of 16 July, when Hussein finally called for British and American military intervention, remain somewhat murky. The King's decision was apparently prompted by fresh intelligence about an imminent coup planned for 17 July. According to Secretary of State John Foster Dulles, 'this intelligence came from the British who gave a digest of it to Hussein'.[26] The British chargé d'affaires in Amman told his American opposite number he

> had given [the] King information from what HMG considered [a] 'most reliable source' indicating UAR agents had penetrated not only [the West] bank refugee camps but also [a] considerable portion [of] East Jordan, that they had responsive groups within [the] security forces including [the] Army who in all probability would not 'fire on their brothers' once mob action began.[27]

Although Israeli sources confirmed the British information, one CIA officer who was present on the ground in Amman during the summer of 1958 is sceptical as to its veracity. As far as he is concerned, the only definite plot uncovered against Hussein that summer was Rusan's, which had already been unmasked and investigated by the time the British issued their warning to Hussein on 16 July.[28]

Indicative of the haste with which the British operation to aid King Hussein was now launched was the failure to gain firm agreement from the Israeli government for the over-flights which brought in the first British paratroops from Cyprus to Amman.[29] The Israeli government demonstrated its displeasure by intercepting some of the British planes near the end of the first wave.[30] In more general terms, the Israeli position during the July 1958 crisis was ambivalent. On the one hand, Prime Minister David Ben Gurion saw the crisis as an opportunity to be exploited in order to promote closer relations with the Western powers, in particular the United States. On the other hand, Israel could ignore neither the opportunities nor the threats which might be created should Hussein be overthrown. If Hussein were to be succeeded by a pro-Nasser regime then the arguments in favour of a pre-emptive move into the West Bank might prove irresistible. Ben Gurion himself, in common with other key figures such as Foreign Minister Golda Meir, was somewhat equivocal on this question. Although he could see the potential security benefits of occupying the West Bank and the ideological appeal of uniting

Jerusalem under Israeli control, he recognised the potential dangers to Israel of ruling over the Palestinian Arab population of the West Bank as an occupying power. Ben Gurion's view at this stage of his political career was that the most pressing problem facing Israel was not a shortage of space, but a shortage of Jews. In any case, the situation in Jordan stabilised without Israel needing to consider whether to launch any formal military action.[31]

While the Eisenhower administration had agreed at the outset to give diplomatic and logistical support to the British operation in Jordan, both Secretary of State Dulles and President Eisenhower continued to resist the idea of any American ground force commitment. As Eisenhower put it, the US should avoid getting into the position of 'supporting Kings against their people'.[32] They did, though, decide to provide Hussein himself with an escape route from Amman should the crisis deepen. At the request of CIA Director Allen Dulles, planes stationed with the US Sixth Fleet were put on standby to evacuate the King from Amman should this prove necessary.[33] The King himself, and his Prime Minister Samir Rifai, pressed the administration hard over the decision not to send in American troops. During a meeting with US Chargé Thomas Wright, Rifai launched into a 'tirade accusing United States Government [of] having failed [to] fulfil its commitments', and contrasted the American attitude with that of the British who had 'rushed to our side in [a] moment of peril'. Although Wright argued that a token US force would make little difference to the defence of Jordan from external attack, Rifai in a fit of anger shouted: 'the King and I are not concerned with outside aggression, it is the psychological effect of having only British troops in Jordan that we wish to offset'. Evidently, the British were still associated with the 'mandate days' in the minds of many Jordanians, who feared that once their troops returned they would never leave. In any event, Rifai made clear that the King's overall goal remained that of using foreign troops to stabilise the situation in Amman, while reorganising the Jordanian army into an attacking force at the head of which he could march into Iraq and restore the rightful government.[34] Indeed, the following day, the King made an official request to the two Western powers for help in restoring the Arab Union through the movement of Jordanian forces into Iraq. Neither power proved willing to back up Hussein's plan.[35]

In the face of evident American and British reluctance to support any move into Iraq, Hussein and Prime Minister Rifai changed tack. In a meeting with US Chargé Thomas Wright on 21 July, Rifai maintained his pressure for the despatch of US troops, but, on behalf of the King, now disavowed any intention to move Jordanian forces into Iraq. Wright was at a loss to explain this 'incredible' change of approach. After a follow-up meeting with the King, Rifai and British Ambassador Charles Johnston that same evening, Wright voiced his suspicions that the King was involved in hatching a new plan for intervention in Iraq 'involving [a] joint attack by Turkey, Iran, [and] Pakistan with some assistance [from] Jordan'. This would, in Wright's view, explain the King's supposed need for 7,000 foreign troops to maintain internal security.[36] If such a plan was considered by the Baghdad Pact powers and Jordan, nothing further came of it. The belief that the Eisenhower administration had been less than forthcoming in his hour of need lingered with the King and may have contributed to the sense of personal crisis and paralysis which overtook him at around this time.[37] It also did not help matters that his prime minister, Samir Rifai, had a mild heart attack towards the end of month and had to reduce his workload.[38] The main explanation for the King's depression, though, was undoubtedly the gruesome fate of his Iraqi cousins and his own inability to do anything about it after the event.[39]

By the end of July, the King had begun to emerge from his shell, and he undertook a round of successful visits to army units which did much to rebuild his personal prestige. Demonstrating his courage once again, Hussein insisted on dismissing his guards before going amongst the troops. Indirectly, the King also showed his appreciation of the Israeli role in the crisis, telling Queen Zein afterwards that 'for the first time on such an occasion he had omitted any attack on Israel from his speeches'.[40] Meanwhile, domestic security continued to improve. Despite Nasser's hostile rhetoric no serious external threat to the King's position emerged. Nasser himself, in conversation with the US envoy, Robert Murphy, claimed, 'he felt sorry for Hussein who was a nice young man in an impossible situation'. According to the Egyptian leader, their mutual hostility stemmed from the influence of Hussein's mother Queen Zein, who blamed him for the overthrow of the monarchy in Egypt. He himself disavowed any intention to overthrow Hussein.[41]

The private talk in Washington and London nevertheless continued to be of the longer-term inevitability of Hussein's fall. It was believed that he could not indefinitely withstand the challenges posed by revolutionary Arab nationalism. In the short term, though, both of the Western powers contributed to the shoring up of his rule, the British through their troop commitment, and the Americans through petroleum, oil and lubricants (POL) supplies and short-term budgetary support. The Americans remained cautious, as Eisenhower's remark about the dangers of supporting kings against their people illustrated, and insisted on supplying aid no more than one month in advance. This conveyed the impression that the administration thought the life of King Hussein's regime could be measured in weeks. Discussing Jordan in a phone conversation on 23 August, Secretary Dulles commented that 'he did not know how long we could keep this show going'.[42] After a strenuous lobbying campaign by the British government, prompted by Ambassador Charles Johnston in Amman, the Americans did agree by the end of August to supply budgetary aid on a quarterly basis, which at least suggested that they thought Hussein might have months rather than weeks left on the throne. The fatalistic attitude of US Chargé Thomas Wright and of key officials back in Washington, such as Assistant Secretary of State William Rountree, caused much anger on the British side. Ambassador Johnston was particularly scathing in his assessment, noting, 'Mr Rountree perhaps imagines that the alternative to King Hussein could be a nice cosy pro-American and anti-British republic. If he does, he could not be more mistaken.'[43] Throughout the late summer and autumn of 1958, Johnston continued to rail against what he saw as the defeatism of his American colleagues in Amman.

One concrete indication of the Jordanian regime's renewed confidence in the wake of the crisis came in the form of King Hussein's ceremonial opening in October of the new road from Amman to the Dead Sea and also the new Dead Sea Hotel. Given the opportunity to report home for once about developments beyond the King's simple struggle for political survival, Ambassador Charles Johnston wrote of an event which was typical of contemporary Jordan in 'its mixture of heavy security precautions and jocular informality'. The Dead Sea Hotel, Johnston wrote, is:

> a typically grandiose Jordanian achievement. Built regardless of cost, with a night-club over the water designed to put the Beirut industry out of business, with three taps in each bathroom (hot, cold, and Dead Sea), with an imported staff of Swiss managers and Sudanese waiters in brand-new gallabiehs and turbans, it will need to be permanently full of guests at about £10 a night in order to pay. Jordan will have to become as stable as Stratford-on-Avon before it can attract tourists on that sort of scale.[44]

The opening of the Dead Sea Hotel confirmed that, whether or not Washington and London had faith in his future, Hussein was determined to continue Jordan's development.

His political position was now eased further by action at the United Nations. Initially both Hussein and Prime Minister Rifai were sceptical about the likely usefulness of any UN guarantee of Jordan's security and independence.[45] However, the emergence of a split between Nasser and the new Iraqi regime of Brigadier Abd al-Karim Qasim opened the way for unexpected cooperation on the part of the UAR in the framing of a resolution designed, in effect, to make Jordan a temporary 'ward of the United Nations'. Nasser evidently did not want to find himself embroiled in a struggle with the Western powers over the future of Jordan, while a new rival for Arab leadership emerged in Baghdad. The result of this new climate of cooperation was the passing by the UN General Assembly of the so-called 'Arab resolution' on 21 August 1958. This gave UN Secretary-General Dag Hammarskjold new responsibilities in Jordan, which he discharged by developing a UN 'representative office' in Amman aimed at promoting good relations between Jordan and the neighbouring Arab states and facilitating the departure of British troops. The UAR Foreign Minister, Mahmoud Fawzi, played a central role in the drafting of the resolution, which suggests that Nasser had opted for a peaceful resolution rather than a confrontation over Jordan. The passing of the Arab resolution, together with the improvement in internal security, paved the way for the withdrawal of British forces from the country by 2 November 1958.[46]

Just over a week after the departure of British forces, a puzzling incident took place that casts some doubt on Nasser's intentions towards Hussein.[47] With the domestic crisis apparently over, Hussein decided to take a vacation in Europe. At 8.20 a.m. on the morning of 10 November 1958 his plane, an aged propeller-driven Dove of the Royal Jordanian Air Force, took off, headed for the Syrian border. Although the aircraft was initially cleared to enter Syrian airspace, a few minutes later air-traffic control contacted the King and his pilot, Jock Dalgleish, to tell them that they were not cleared to over-fly Damascus, and must land there. The King sensed trouble. He ordered Dalgleish to take over the controls, turn the plane around and return to Amman. Diving to near ground level to avoid Syrian radar, they were almost immediately intercepted by two Syrian MiGs. Although the Syrian jets did not fire on the King's plane, they made repeated attacking passes, trying to force it down. Partly through Dalgleish's skill, and partly through the incompetence of the Syrians, the King's plane made it back into Jordanian airspace unscathed. Whether the Syrian pilots were under orders to bring the plane down at all costs, or whether they had simply been told to buzz it in the hope of frightening the King into landing, is unclear. Had the King landed, in the opinion of British Ambassador Charles Johnston, he would have been forced to abdicate the throne.[48]

Hussein's safe return to Amman was greeted with frantic scenes of celebration by loyal Bedouin army units. According to Ambassador Johnston, the episode had 'strengthened the already potent "Hussein Legend"'. The King himself was 'completely unmoved by his experience and inclined to treat it as a joke'.[49] As to culpability for the incident, although Johnston acknowledged in hindsight that there had been a failure to obtain the necessary clearance for the flight on the part of the RJAF, he still considered the Syrians' behaviour inexcusable. It was no secret that the King intended to leave via Syrian airspace, and the two MiGs which intercepted his plane had evidently been lying in wait. It is unlikely that such a trap could have been prepared without Nasser's knowledge as president of the UAR. We are left to conclude that Nasser's cooperation in the framing of the Arab resolution at the UN during August had been no more than a tactical move, and that it did not represent any strategic shift in his relations with Hussein.

In most accounts of Hussein's reign, the question of his dynastic ambition in relation to Iraq lapses around this point, within a matter of weeks of the 14 July revolution.[50] In fact, the King never gave up hope of the lost Hashemite kingdom returning to the fold. Across the ensuing four decades, openings periodically presented themselves for the King to pursue this goal, most obviously his participation in the failed CIA effort to overthrow Saddam Hussein in 1995–6. However, during the period 1958–63 attempts to exploit the weakness of the Qasim regime in Baghdad with a view to advancing his own claim to the Iraqi throne were a persistent theme of Hussein's regional strategy. During a conversation between British Foreign Secretary Selwyn Lloyd and US Secretary of State Christian Herter in Geneva in May 1959, Herter asked whether Lloyd had 'heard anything of King Hussein's megalomaniac ideas? He had apparently gone to Turkey and said that the right policy for the West was that he should become the Hashemite King of both Iraq and Jordan. That was the answer to all the problems.' Although Lloyd stressed that the King had 'never mentioned the idea of uniting Iraq and Jordan into a joint kingdom' during his recent visit to London, he had spoken of a time coming when Syria and Jordan might grow closer together, apparently reviving his grandfather's idea of a Greater Syria under Hashemite control. According to Lloyd, Herter concluded the conversation with 'some rather disparaging remarks about Queen Zein', whose influence he perhaps saw as helping to prompt the King's Iraqi designs.[51]

Despite this State Department impatience over his Iraqi ambitions, Hussein's visit to the United States in March–April 1959 proved a personal success. A State Department assessment of the visit concluded that Hussein had initially found it difficult to adjust to the fast pace of life in the US.[52] However, as the trip advanced he fulfilled his engagements with increasing confidence. His improving popular touch led Governor Williams of Michigan to comment, 'I would hate to run against him in an election.' Unfortunately, the governor balanced his praise with an obvious gaffe when greeting the King at Detroit airport with the words 'the last time I saw Your Majesty was on the happy occasion of your marriage to Dina'. The King was not best pleased to be reminded of his dissolved marriage. When pressed in more general terms in private about his future personal plans, the King was non-committal, saying that he had other things to think about than a second marriage. On the same theme, the report noted somewhat coquettishly that 'the King showed himself discreet in his contacts with American ladies, but it is clear that his preference is for brunettes who are smaller than he is'. One lady who fitted the description was the actress Susan Cabot, whom the King met while in southern California. Rumours about a possible romance made their way into the newspapers during Hussein's stay in the United States.[53]

For the benefit of his American audience, Hussein laid particular stress during his visit on his ideological opposition to communism, describing himself as destined, as a descendant of the Prophet, 'to save Islam in general and the Near East in particular from communism'. In terms of his broader dynastic ambitions, the report noted that 'over the long run, Hussein thinks that he will take over the leadership of Syria and Iraq, probably along with the Hejaz, and thus fulfil his grandfather's Fertile Crescent ambitions'. On Iraq specifically, 'hardly a day passed on the trip but that he asked about developments in Baghdad . . .' Hussein argued that he had foreseen the danger of a communist takeover in Iraq as far back as the 14 July coup. This anti-communist packaging of Hussein's dynastic ambitions was a shrewd piece of presentation for an American audience, but there is no doubt that the King still saw communism as inimical to Hashemite Arab nationalism.

During the business sessions of the visit, a gap was evident between King Hussein's position, which remained trenchantly anti-Nasser, and that of the Eisenhower administration, which was increasingly prepared to contemplate working with Nasser over Iraq. In the eyes of most US officials, the danger that a communist takeover might result from the Iraqi leader Qasim's increasing reliance on the local communist party trumped fears about Nasser's regional ambitions, and policy-makers again started to envisage Nasser as an 'independent ally' working against the advance of Soviet influence in the region, a view which had motivated the CIA's original sponsorship of the Egyptian Free Officers' movement. Hence, Hussein's emphasis on the dangers posed by a Nasserite coup in Baghdad did not find a receptive audience in Washington, probably partly because of US suspicions about his own ambitions in relation to Iraq.[54] In any event, the King's meeting with President Eisenhower on 25 March was more successful than those with State Department officials, with the president praising Hussein's courage and leadership and stressing their similarity of outlook on many questions. The only hint dropped by Hussein as to his wider ambitions was his comment to the president that he did 'not want to live only for Jordan', but rather 'to help all Arabs'.[55] In a telephone conversation after the meeting, the president described Hussein as 'a nice boy', while Secretary Herter commented that he showed 'a maturity beyond his years and was very courageous'.[56]

During the rest of 1959 and into 1960, Hussein's rivalry with Nasser, and his continuing concern that the Eisenhower administration was much too willing to work with the Egyptian leader over Iraq, remained at the forefront of his mind. During a visit to Iran in early June, Hussein 'made remarks about his destiny to liberate Syria and Iraq'.[57] The King also professed still to believe that Nasser had been largely responsible for bringing about the 14 July coup in Baghdad, even though all independent commentators now acknowledged that its planning had been an indigenous Iraqi affair.[58] During a December 1959 visit to London, the King emphasised his concern at developments in Iraq, and spoke of the possibility of Iraqi émigrés organising themselves into 'a group which could express responsible opinions'. Although Hussein claimed that neither he, nor the émigrés reaching Amman, planned to initiate action against the Iraqi regime, he also noted that it was always possible circumstances might change:

> Supposing Qasim disappeared from the scene, the Communists in Iraq attempted a coup, or civil war broke out, the Jordanians would feel obliged not only to organise themselves against any emergency but also to develop their links with the Iraqi émigrés in order to save them from joining up with Nasser or even with groups on the Left.[59]

When he visited Morocco in April 1960, Hussein was still preoccupied with the same themes. In conversation with Charles Duke, the former British ambassador to Amman who had now moved to Rabat, 'it seemed . . . that his dream of reviving the old united Arab kingdom of Sharif Hussein' was 'as vivid in his mind as ever'. Duke's own view was that 'looking at the present rulers of the Middle East and the mess there, who can say that he is not right and that he would not make the best man to rule the lot of them'. Evidently some of King Hassan of Morocco's own advisers shared Duke's view. 'C'est le seul élément valable dans tout le Moyen Orient' ('He's the only worthwhile figure in all of the Middle East'), they commented in private.[60] Back in London, the Foreign Office was much more sceptical:

> We find it rather discomfiting to see how far wishful thinking still colours King Hussein's views . . . Although we and the Americans are content to subsidise the regime for the time being . . . we are apt to be sceptical of the King's tendency to see the Middle East revolving around Jordan, rather than vice versa, and certainly lose no opportunity of discouraging him in any dreams of a Hashemite restoration in Iraq which he may cherish.[61]

The culmination of the tensions between Jordan and Nasser's UAR came on 29 August 1960, when the Jordanian Prime Minister Hazza Majali was killed by a bomb planted in his desk drawer by Syrian agents. Majali had been appointed to his post the previous May, and had initially seemed to exert a positive influence on Jordan's relations with the UAR. In August 1959 formal diplomatic relations between the two states had been resumed, but this breakthrough proved more apparent than real.[62] The King seems to have been reluctant to make a real effort to improve relations with Nasser at this stage, and Majali's earlier political career, most notably as the prime minister called briefly to office in December 1955 to push through Jordanian membership of the Baghdad Pact, and as a former friend and confidant of Nuri Said of Iraq, also made him ill-suited to the role of bridge-builder to Nasser. From the spring of 1960 onwards, a renewed propaganda battle raged between the UAR and Jordan, sparked by differences over the Palestinian question, which were aired at the Arab League Council meeting in Cairo in February 1960.[63] This time round, words were not the only weapons employed by both sides. The King himself was the target of several assassination plots in 1960, two of which Hussein offered lurid accounts of in his memoirs. The first involved an attempt to substitute acid for his nasal spray, a plot uncovered by chance by Hussein himself on the evening after Hazza Majali's murder. The second involved an attempt to poison him by one of the cooks in the palace kitchens, who had been recruited by the UAR intelligence service. This latter plot was uncovered after the putative poisoner, somewhat foolishly, first elected to test his wares out on a number of feral cats living in the palace grounds.[64] The result was a number of dead cats but no harm to the King.

It may be that the bomb plot which cost Hazza Majali his life was also aimed at the King himself. The first bomb, which killed the prime minister, was followed by a second explosion at the scene less than forty minutes later. Had the King followed through on his initial intention to visit the bomb site, he might well have been caught in the second blast.[65] The King's reaction to Majali's assassination is also interesting from the point of view of his regional ambitions. During the fortnight following the assassination, Jordanian forces massed on the Syrian frontier. This military build-up seems to have been in part a result of the King's own determination to stand up to Nasser and in part a result of pressure from the Majali family, who wanted revenge for Hazza's death.[66] According to one source, the King also despatched a representative to meet with Chaim Herzog, the head of Israeli military intelligence, to ask Israel not to take advantage of the reduction of Jordanian forces on the Israeli front. In response, Israeli Prime Minister Ben Gurion forwarded a message to the King in which he pledged not to attack Jordan.[67] Hussein's approach to the Israeli government at this stage fitted in with the pragmatic stance he took in private on the Arab–Israeli conflict. He had already told US Ambassador Mills at the beginning of the year that 'the Arab legend' that Israel should be pushed into the sea should be abandoned, and that 'it was time to put aside emotionalism and take steps toward a final settlement between Israel and the Arabs'.[68]

The possibility of an attack by Jordan on Syria at this point was taken very seriously in the Western capitals, with both the British and American governments exerting significant, sustained pressure on Hussein to restrain him from any rash move against Damascus,[69] which they feared would fail, leading to Hussein's overthrow.[70] There was a certain irony here. Three years earlier, when it had suited their purposes, both London and Washington had subscribed to the secret Preferred Plan for the toppling of the Syrian regime, which would have been based around the manufacturing of incidents on the Jordan–Syria frontier and the use of Jordanian tribal connections in southern Syria. Now, when tribal forces of a different kind, together with Hussein's own feud with Nasser, threatened a similar outcome, both the British and American governments demurred. By the summer of 1960 it did not suit either government to see Hussein spoiling for a fight as they were both engaged in trying to improve their relations with Nasser's UAR.

In terms of Hussein's own state of mind at this juncture, the British Ambassador Charles Johnston, who conveyed his government's warnings to the King, made a number of interesting observations. Hussein, as Johnston saw matters, seemed to have been overtaken by a sort of fatalism, typified by his frequent references to 'preferring death in battle to assassination'.[71] The ambassador attributed this to a potentially dangerous loss of morale on the King's part, and a belief that his friends in the West were deserting him in his hour of need. Johnston did what he could to persuade Hussein that seeking death in battle rather than continuing the political struggle would be to take the easy way out. Reflecting on the 'September crisis' in his memoirs, written a decade later, Johnston also noted with some amusement that at the time he had not realised the efficacy of one particular warning which he had been authorised by London to deliver to the King. This was that if hostilities against the UAR seemed to be in the offing, the British army training mission then based in Jordan would be withdrawn. One officer attached to the mission was Lieutenant-Colonel Gardiner, whose daughter Antoinette had already attracted the King's attention.[72] She was later to become Hussein's second wife, Princess Muna.

In the event, war was averted in September 1960, and the romance between Hussein and Antoinette Gardiner was able to grow further. 'Toni', as she was known when Hussein met her, was a vivacious, outgoing, attractive teenager without any affectations. Her family background was modest but respectable. Born on 25 April 1941 at Chelmondiston, near Ipswich in England, she was the only daughter of Lieutenant-Colonel Walker P. Gardiner of the British army's Royal Engineers. Part of her childhood had been spent abroad, in Kuala Lumpur, during her father's posting to Malaya. Thereafter, she had come with her family to Jordan. How she and Hussein first came to meet in 1960 is the subject of rather different tales. Hussein himself recollected that she had approached him at a fancy-dress party which he had arranged in his house at Shuneh on the shores of the Dead Sea. According to one account of this meeting Toni accosted him with the words 'You look pretty scruffy, Your

Majesty'.[73] In fact, this tale probably makes her seem more precocious than she really was. The normal convention at such parties was that ladies would have to approach the King to ask him to dance, rather than vice versa. And the nineteen-year-old Toni was apparently racked by nerves before plucking up the courage to speak to him.[74]

From then on, throughout the autumn and winter of 1960–61, their relationship blossomed and flourished. Sharing his time with Toni, whether dancing, go-carting or horse-riding, Hussein could forget his cares. It helped a lot that Toni, unlike his first wife Dina, had little or no interest in politics. Hussein could compartmentalise his life, socialising with her without ruminating over his political troubles. Their relationship culminated on 1 May 1961 with the announcement by the royal palace of their engagement. Although concerns were voiced that marriage to an Englishwoman might present an easy target to Hussein's enemies, in the event little capital was made of it, even in Cairo and Damascus. For Hussein himself, the cross-cultural nature of the match was without doubt one of its attractions. Throughout his life, Hussein moved between the Arab world and the West, feeling as much at home with European and American friends as he did with his long-time Jordanian associates. His own education in Britain and his experience of social life in London in 1951–3 left him with a lingering attraction to Western culture and company of which Toni no doubt reminded him. The marriage, then, was without doubt a love match. It afforded Hussein some welcome domestic stability in the midst of the turbulence of regional politics.

Perhaps partly to forestall criticism of his potentially controversial marriage, early in 1961 Hussein made an attempt to improve relations with both the Iraqi regime and Nasser's UAR.[75] Between 23 February and 7 May 1961, Hussein and Nasser swapped four letters, two each way. The exchange was initiated by Hussein but all it served to reveal was that the two leaders had very different notions both of the right path towards Arab unity and of the main threats to be confronted along the way. For Nasser 'imperialism' remained the true enemy, while for Hussein it was communism. Already by the summer of 1961 this half-hearted bridge-building attempt was petering out, giving way to a new period of what may best be termed 'armed truce' in Jordanian–UAR relations.[76]

Relations with the Qasim regime in Baghdad, by contrast, improved during this period. In one sense, this is surprising, given that Qasim and his comrades had murdered Hussein's cousin Feisal. However, for all his dynastic ambitions, by the summer of 1960 Hussein had come round to accepting that a refusal to deal with the Iraqi regime achieved little beyond increasing Jordan's own regional isolation. Abandoning the attempt to retrieve Iraq for the Hashemite cause by confrontation, the King now sought to bolster his position and perhaps build a constituency in the country through indirect means. During his visit to New York for the UN General Assembly meeting in the autumn of 1960, Hussein held talks with the Iraqi Foreign Minister, Hashim Jawad, which presaged Jordan's official recognition of the Iraqi regime on 1 October 1960. This was followed by the appointment of Wasfi al-Tall, soon to become a key figure in Jordanian domestic politics, to the post of ambassador in Baghdad. Of course, shared hostility to the UAR was a crucial lubricant in Iraqi–Jordanian relations during this period, and Tall, who had previously shaped anti-UAR propaganda at the Jordanian Information Ministry, was well placed to exploit this.[77]

The improvement in Iraqi–Jordanian relations survived a further regional crisis which broke out at the end of June 1961, precipitated by the granting of independence to Kuwait by Britain. Qasim reacted with fury to the announcement, warning in a press conference on 25 June that Kuwait was part of Iraq, and that the Baghdad regime would accept no 'false agreements'. In London, Harold Macmillan's government elected to take no chances with the substantial British economic interests in Kuwait, despatching a deterrent force to the emirate at the beginning of July. The Iraqi threat to Kuwait, probably little more than bluster on Qasim's part, quickly melted away, leaving the British government to resolve the thorny question of when and how to withdraw its forces from Kuwait without further incident. Here Hussein played an important role. The Arab League's decision to admit Kuwait to membership on 20 July, contingent on the withdrawal of British forces and their replacement by Arab troops, provided an opportunity for Jordan to prove itself a friend of both the oil-rich Gulf emirate and the Western powers. The British government was particularly concerned that the UAR should not make a substantial troop commitment to the so-called Arab Deterrent Force established by the Arab League. Fears of Nasser-inspired subversion in Kuwait were strong, and there was considerable relief in London when King Hussein offered to make the largest single troop contribution.[78] Perhaps surprisingly, Hussein managed to take on this leading role in the ADF without causing substantial damage to relations with Baghdad. Qasim seems to have recognised that one motive for Hussein's participation was to prevent Nasser from controlling the force.[79]

That rivalry with Nasser continued to dominate Hussein's thinking was confirmed by his reaction to the next regional drama. The army coup in Damascus which led to the break-up of the union of Egypt and Syria caught Hussein, as much as Nasser himself, by surprise. As the news broke on the morning of 28 September 1961, Radio Amman enthusiastically relayed the proclamations of the Damascus rebels. Hussein reacted immediately, putting the Jordanian army on alert. It seemed possible that he intended a rash military intervention to block any Egyptian attempt to restore the union.

Fearing the worst, both London and Washington warned Hussein in strong terms against intervening in Syria.[80] Nasser, meanwhile, was devastated by the break-up of the union. It was a turning point in his political career, dashing his hopes of Arab unity under Egyptian leadership. When, the following day, Hussein decided to recognise the new regime in Damascus, Nasser reacted strongly, breaking off diplomatic relations with Jordan.[81]

Less immediately apparent was the link between the King's reaction to the break-up of the UAR, the Kuwaiti crisis and his dynastic ambitions in Iraq. The view in the British Foreign Office was that 'the Syrian <u>coup</u> will . . . add substance to Hashemite dreams and to [the] hope that Qasim may soon go the way of Nasser'. In respect of Hussein's involvement in the Kuwaiti ADF, the fear in London was that Hussein might now choose to withdraw his troops so as 'not to appear as the opponent of what he believes to be an Iraqi national aspiration'.[82] In the event, the crisis caused by the collapse of the UAR simmered down, and Hussein did not withdraw his forces from the ADF. By the end of the year, though, his relations with Iraq had seriously deteriorated. Although some sources attribute this deterioration to the King's decision to receive an ambassador from Kuwait in January 1962,[83] his reaction to the rumours of a renewed Iraqi threat to Kuwait, which circulated during the second half of December 1961, may also have played a role. While protesting that Jordan had no intention of intervening in Iraq directly, Hussein told British Prime Minister Harold Macmillan in a meeting on 18 December that 'Qasim would not last another six months'.[84] When Foreign Secretary Lord Home asked the King 'whether the Hashemite supporters were numerous in Iraq and whether in the event of a revolution there would be an attempt to restore the monarchy', Hussein replied that 'more and more Iraqis were establishing contact with Jordan and that a restoration of the monarchy was a possibility'. The King also noted in passing that his ambassador in Baghdad, Wasfi Tall, might well be sent out of the country within a matter of days for being, as he put it, 'too active'. Overall, Hussein was upbeat about his position, noting that 'in the past he had always been on the defensive', and that in the future he hoped to play a more pro-active regional role.

Not for the first time, Hussein's Iraqi ambitions caused concern in London. In a conversation after the King's return to Amman, the British ambassador once again warned the King on behalf of his government not to embark on any Iraqi adventure.[85] On 17 January 1962, Wasfi Tall was recalled to Amman for consultations. He did not return to Baghdad. Instead he was promoted to the post of prime minister at the end of the month. Little further came of Hussein's Iraqi ambitions at this stage, although Tall's promotion suggests that whatever activities he had been engaged in in Baghdad had met with the King's approval. Hussein's promise of a more pro-active foreign policy, in effect of attack being the best form of defence, was soon to be borne out by his reaction to the coup in Yemen at the end of September 1962, which involved the despatch of Jordanian forces to Saudi Arabia. As we will see, the fruits of this activism were to prove decidedly mixed.

Looking back, it is clear that in the wake of the coup in Baghdad Hussein felt an extra burden of responsibility as the sole surviving standard-bearer of the Hashemite cause. It is also evident from his conduct of policy in the years which followed the coup that he clung to the hope that circumstances might change, and that a local or regional crisis might open the way to the restoration of Hashemite rule in Baghdad. At the same time, Hussein could not resist engaging in a broader propaganda battle with Nasser, whose concept of Arab nationalism was fundamentally at odds with his own. For all the prompting of the British and American governments, which urged him to concentrate on Jordan's domestic development, Hussein could not help being distracted by larger ambitions. Alongside the 1967 war and the 1990–91 Gulf crisis, the 1958 Iraqi revolution was to prove to be one of the key watersheds in Hussein's reign.

CHAPTER 5

ARAB COLD WAR AND DÉTENTE, 1962–6

For Hussein, 1962 began on a joyous note. On 30 January, his first son, Abdullah, was born to his wife, Muna. The popular reaction to the birth was enthusiastic; according to one Western observer, downtown Amman was seized by a 'holiday spirit'.[1] The King moved quickly to name his newborn son Crown Prince, and to confer on his wife Muna the title of Princess. The birth of a direct heir to the throne after a decade of uncertainty was a clear cause of celebration for both Hussein and the kingdom.

The stability promised by the birth of a male heir was matched by apparently positive developments elsewhere. For many, the appointment as prime minister of Wasfi Tall on 27 January seemed to mark the beginning of a new era in Jordanian politics. Aged only forty-two when he took office, Tall bore a mane of thick black hair that lent him the appearance of an even younger man. Serious, ascetic and tough in character, Tall was intensely loyal to his friends and often disdainful of his enemies. His self-confidence, which sometimes manifested itself as arrogance, made him an indefatigable believer in his ability to change Jordan and to get things done. Tall was also a loyal adherent of the Hashemite brand of Arab nationalism, and a stern critic of Nasser's attempts to spread his influence through the Arab world during the 1950s. His political sympathy and skills were recognised by King Hussein from an early stage, and he began a rapid rise after his appointment as director of the Department of Publications during the Baghdad Pact riots of December 1955. Thereafter, he held a succession of posts in the Foreign Ministry, before becoming director of the Ministry of Information in Hazza Majali's government in 1959.[2]

Tall's final key appointment before becoming prime minister was as ambassador to Baghdad from December 1960 to January 1962. Tall had always stressed the need for close relations between Jordan and Iraq, favouring a federation between the two countries, and the overthrow of the Iraqi monarchy had been a particular blow for him. Indeed, it has been suggested that part of the reason for Tall's advancement under King Hussein was that he played on the King's continuing desire to pursue influence, and possibly even Hashemite dynastic ambitions, in Iraq. While he was in Baghdad, Tall made covert contact with surviving sympathisers of the former regime, something that did little to endear him to the post-revolutionary leader Abd al-Karim Qasim.[3]

But, beyond his activities in Iraq, Tall owed his appointment as prime minister to the conviction he shared with the King that it was time for Jordan to move forward through economic development and administrative efficiency. Nepotism and graft should be squeezed out of the system, in the hope that economic wellbeing would foster political stability.[4] This manifesto meant that Tall's appointment was met with initial optimism by informed observers of Jordan's affairs. After meeting him on 1 February, US Ambassador William Macomber commented that he found the atmosphere reminiscent of the 'excitement and optimism which surrounded [the] "New Lookers" in 1953 and [the] "New Frontiersmen" of 1961'.[5]

As befitted Macomber's characterisation of him as a sort of Jordanian 'New Frontiersman', back in Washington the Kennedy administration welcomed Tall's appointment as prime minister.[6] Had the new government been able to maintain the domestic focus of its programme, it is possible that it might have become one of the longer-lived and more successful in Jordan's history. Unfortunately for Tall, regional politics in the shape of the outbreak of civil war in Yemen in September 1962 intervened to thwart this goal.

From its outset, the Yemeni civil war promised to be more than a local struggle. There are strong suspicions that Nasser was aware of, and may have supported, the plans of the group of army officers, led by Colonel Abdullah Sallal, to overthrow the regime of the new Imam of Yemen, Mohammad al-Badr, on 27 September 1962.[7] After the coup, the Imam fled to the north of the country to rally tribal backing with the assistance of Saudi Arabia. The Sallal regime meanwhile turned to Nasser for support. The reasons why Crown Prince Feisal of Saudi Arabia[8] and Egyptian President Nasser became involved in the conflict can be readily discerned. Feisal sought to prevent any threat to Saudi stability from across the Yemeni border, while Nasser wanted to retrieve prestige lost through the collapse of the United Arab Republic a year earlier. However, King Hussein's interest in the conflict is at first sight less clear. In fact, he seems to have seen opportunities for Jordan both to improve ties with Saudi Arabia and to thwart Nasser's drive for regional hegemony. This fitted with his new strategy of moving from the defensive to the offensive, which he had outlined in his meeting with British Prime Minister Harold Macmillan in London the previous December. Friendship with Saudi Arabia might provide Jordan with a longer-term and domestically more acceptable alternative to economic support from the United States and Britain, while a defeat for Egypt might diminish the external threat to Jordan's stability. To these considerations may be added a personal factor. Hussein was in the process of developing a close bond with Feisal, who was probably the Arab leader for whom he developed the most respect during his reign. While he always rejected the notion of reactionary and revolutionary camps in the Arab world, preferring instead to use the label 'evolutionary' for the brand of Arab nationalism he espoused,[9] it is clear that despite the troubled history of Hashemite–Saudi relations Hussein felt more affinity with the conservative, monarchical regime in Saudi Arabia than with any of his republican neighbours.[10] By the beginning of the 1960s, although dynastic tensions still lurked beneath the surface, Saudi–Jordanian relations were entering a new, more positive phase, founded on common interests and a shared ideological hostility to communism and Nasserism.

Jordan's active engagement in the Yemeni civil war threw up a number of problems for Wasfi Tall's government. In the first instance, it was domestically unpopular: few Jordanians, whether East or West Bankers, could see good reasons for backing the Yemeni royalists, a policy many saw as yet another instance of Jordan isolating itself from mainstream Arab opinion. Secondly, Jordan's intervention in Yemen caused a good deal of tension in relations with the United States. The Kennedy administration had been pursuing a policy of 'constructive engagement' with Nasser, and was anxious not to sacrifice this for the conflict in Yemen.[11] Despite the threat to relations with Saudi Arabia, the US believed that the conflict could best be damped down by recognising the new republican regime, in exchange for guarantees from Nasser and Sallal that they would not seek to subvert either Saudi Arabia or the neighbouring British-backed South Arabian Federation.

Even before the outbreak of the polarising war in Yemen, Hussein had expressed his unhappiness about the Americans' attempt to work with Nasser and their stance in relation to the Arab–Israeli conflict. In discussion with Ambassador Macomber in August 1962, Hussein had commented, 'I continue to be saddened by Western policies towards the Arab states and increasingly troubled as to whether I am doing the right thing in following a policy of unilateral alignment with the West.'[12] Although a conciliatory personal exchange of letters between President Kennedy and Hussein the following month may have done something to smooth matters over, in his reply the King still communicated his lingering sense of frustration: 'At least to me and for the benefit of my Jordanian Family, I feel that a continued exchange of views would help clear much of what remains to us both puzzling and even disheartening. I refer to the policies of our friends in some fields and areas connected with the Near East.'[13]

Against the background of the conflict in Yemen, the King's disenchantment with US policy towards Nasser increased once again. In a meeting with Macomber on 15 October, Hussein declared, 'as a friend, I must warn you that your current UAR policy will have disastrous consequences for you and your friends in the Eastern Arab states.'[14] Hussein was right that the American attempt to woo Nasser would backfire. Nevertheless, his decision to lend substance to his support for the Yemeni royalists and Saudis by despatching a Jordanian air squadron to Taif in Saudi Arabia brought 'disastrous consequences' for Jordan. US reaction to the deployment was forthright: the administration was 'utterly opposed to [the] useless frittering of Jordanian resources'.[15] Tall and Hussein's position was further damaged when, in the middle of November 1962, the commander of the Jordanian air force detachment defected to Egypt, followed by two further pilots from the squadron. As prime minister, Tall had to take responsibility for the propaganda disaster, but a slip of the tongue when discussing the matter with Ambassador Macomber, in which he referred to 'his' rather than 'my' policy, made it clear that the King was the driving force behind the Yemeni engagement.[16] Despite his vigorous public advocacy, in private Tall was distressed and unhappy with the part that Jordan played in the civil war,[17] and he admitted that 'his enemies might be able to force [the] fall of his government in the near future'.[18] Although the King ordered the recall of the remaining elements of the air squadron soon after the defections, implicitly recognising his inability to influence the outcome of the conflict militarily, he continued to adhere to his pro-Feisal, anti-Nasser line, accompanied by repeated expressions of exasperation with US policy.[19]

The damage to Jordan's domestic and regional position was now reinforced by what looked like another major propaganda coup for Nasser: the overthrow of the governments in Iraq and Syria during February and March 1963 and their replacement by Baathist regimes which opened negotiations for a new union with Egypt. At a stroke, the possibility of a new, Nasser-led union with broad popular appeal in the Arab world opened up once again. For Hussein, who had founded his Arab policy on opposition to Nasser, the position was an extremely uncomfortable one. Although he could count on reasonably solid support amongst the East Bank elite, the tripartite unity negotiations served to highlight the enthusiasm of many of his subjects, especially the West Bankers, for Nasser's brand of Arab nationalism. The belief was widespread that Arab unity under Nasser's leadership still provided the most promising path to the defeat of Israel. Worse still, in the region as a whole, with the exception of Saudi Arabia, Hussein seemed almost friendless.

As a result, April 1963 was a month of crisis for him. The domestic political and security situation began to deteriorate during the second half of March. On 20 March Hussein indicated to a CIA representative in Amman that he intended to dismiss Wasfi Tall's government within a few days; Tall's hardline anti-Nasser stance was no longer appropriate now that Hussein was trying to accommodate the renewed upsurge in Nasser's pan-Arab popularity. The King also commented to his CIA interlocutor that he realised that 'an assassination attempt could be made against him at any time by an individual or a relatively small group of people. In this eventuality, it would be essential that a strong and experienced Cabinet be in office to provide continuity.'[20]

The King's precarious domestic position was highlighted by a further CIA report on 22 March, which detailed a plot against Hussein from within the army. This was to be led by Brigadier Mashur Haditha, commander of an armoured brigade stationed at Zerqa, and involved a number of middle- and high-ranking officers. Their plan was to move on 22 March or, if their plot was postponed, within two months at the latest. They intended to assassinate the King's uncle, Sharif Nasser, and then to attempt to persuade the King to leave Jordan. 'If the King refuses, he will be killed,' the CIA report noted. The plotters would attack the royal palace, seize the radio station, call on other units of the army to join them, and proclaim the establishment of 'the Arab Republic of Jordan'.[21] It is not clear from where the CIA officers on the ground obtained their information, but the level of detail suggests a source close to the conspirators themselves.

Whether because of the leak of information to the CIA, or the King's absence from Amman on 22 March, the plot was evidently postponed. On 6 April Hussein sent a well-publicised letter to the commander in chief of the armed forces, Habes al-Majali, in which he referred to measures taken against 'a number of officers involved in aspersions and allegations . . .'[22] These measures dated back to 21 March so it is evident that Hussein was made aware of the CIA information about the plot, and took seriously the threat against him. Meanwhile, on 27 March, Wasfi Tall tendered the resignation of his government. To replace him, the King chose Samir Rifai, the veteran politician who had served his grandfather as prime minister in the 1940s and enjoyed spells in office under Hussein during the 1950s. While Rifai's reputation for toughness in a crisis seemed to make him the right man for the job, his position was undermined by the announcement, on 17 April 1963, of the creation of the tripartite Arab Federation of Egypt, Iraq and Syria. The popular response in Jordan, particularly on the West Bank, was over-whelming. Demonstrations in favour of Jordanian accession to the union quickly turned into riots and, on 20 April, four people were killed and thirty injured in Jerusalem. Under the impact of the demonstrations, the government failed to win a majority for a planned vote of confidence in the chamber of deputies for the first time in Jordan's history, forcing Rifai's resignation.[23]

Whatever the errors that had contributed to the 20 April débâcle, Hussein proved to be at his pugnacious best when confronting the political crisis. Falling back on a 'Palace Cabinet' of regime stalwarts, he appointed his great-uncle Sharif Hussein bin Nasser as prime minister and dissolved the chamber of deputies. Meanwhile the army imposed a curfew and restored order on the West Bank. As far as US Ambassador Macomber was concerned, the King had adopted an 'in extremis defensive stance entailing [a] form of scarcely disguised direct rule supported by key East Bank henchmen. He will clearly be [his] own Prime Minister', Macomber argued, 'as Sharif Hussein is [an] elderly, amiable cipher lacking physical and mental energy.'[24]

Despite Hussein's tough action, his position was far from secure. As the plot of 22 March had shown, the key to his survival would lie in the loyalty of the army. On 26 April, information reached US intelligence sources that another army coup was in the offing, planned 'with the complete knowledge of the UAR'.[25] The immediate concern in Washington was that a pro-Nasser coup in Jordan might lead to an Israeli move into the West Bank and a new Arab–Israeli war; Israel saw the Nasser regime as the main strategic threat in the region, and a pro-Nasser government in Jordan was unlikely to strive to keep the frontier quiet. Although it was Saturday morning when the news reached Washington, a crisis meeting involving President Kennedy and his key advisers was immediately convened, showing how seriously the administration took the threat; there had been no such reaction to the intelligence about the planned 22 March coup. During the crisis meeting, Under Secretary of State George Ball outlined the situation in Jordan, noting 'the reported coup group seemed Baathist but friendly to Nasser'.[26] The conclusions of the meeting were that the administration should put pressure on Nasser to try to block the coup, while pressing the Israelis not to take precipitous action in the event that the coup went ahead. Meanwhile, carriers of the US Sixth Fleet would be moved into forward positions in the Eastern Mediterranean, and preparations would be made with the UK for possible military intervention.

As in March, King Hussein was told of the planned coup.[27] Since it did not take place, White House Middle East expert Bob Komer concluded that 'our warning to Hussein was probably smart preventive action'. George Ball had rather less success in his efforts to restrain the Israelis. The Israeli Ambassador, Avraham Harman, whom Special Assistant for National Security Affairs McGeorge Bundy called 'a hard bitten cookie',[28] reserved his government's right to respond to events in Jordan as it saw fit, though he claimed that US and Israeli objectives in the crisis were similar, with both countries 'determined to help Hussein hang on'.[29]

The real nature of Israeli attitudes to Hussein's regime is the most intriguing issue thrown up by the April 1963 crisis. Some commentators have argued that the crisis highlighted a shared strategic interest between Israel and Hashemite Jordan, suggesting that the possibility of Israeli intervention in the West Bank may have exerted a restraining influence on Nasser, who was their common enemy. Both feared his influence on the West Bank and the radicalisation of its Palestinian population.[30] Nevertheless, it seems more likely that the Israeli government was motivated less by solicitude for Hussein's regime and more by its territorial aspirations in relation to the West Bank. Even during the crisis itself, US officials speculated that there might be a Machiavellian purpose behind the Israelis' support for Hussein. According to Komer, 'Israel's patent attempt to embrace Hussein . . . is so much a kiss of death to the brave young king as to raise suspicions [the] Israelis want him to fall so they could take [the] West Bank.'[31]

Indirect support is lent to this line of argument by Israeli Prime Minister David Ben Gurion's description of a meeting which took place between him and two of his closest ministerial associates, Moshe Dayan and Shimon Peres, on 3 May. Ben Gurion noted in his diary entry: 'Moshe Dayan thinks that if the King is overthrown, or if a change occurs in the Jordanian regime, we have to take over Mount Scopus [a key strategic hill overlooking Jerusalem].' If the Jordanians responded to this militarily it would be 'good' as it would be a justification for an Israeli move deeper into the West Bank. Shimon Peres's view was that if a change of regime occurred in Jordan, Israel would have to take further territory on the West Bank and 'nominate an Israeli of Arab origin as a King of Jordan, and then negotiate with him peace'.[32] The Israeli government's attitude towards Hussein's survival during the April–May 1963 crisis can perhaps best be characterised as ambivalent. The formal position remained that Israel favoured the status quo on the West Bank – and there is no evidence of a direct Israeli attempt to undermine Hussein – but, in private, Israeli leaders do seem to have entertained hopes that the crisis might bring about a favourable alteration in Israel's territorial position.[33]

In the event, a combination of King Hussein's firmness in responding to the challenge to his rule and inter-Arab politics brought about a rapid diminution in the political temperature in Jordan during the latter part of May and June 1963. Parliamentary elections scheduled for 6 July passed off smoothly. The rivalry between Nasser and the Baath Party, which re-emerged soon after the tripartite April declaration, lessened calls for Arab unity in Jordan and worked to the King's advantage.[34] The general public, according to the US embassy in Amman, was 'disgusted, disappointed and confused by [the] struggle between Nasser and [the] Baath'.[35] After the experiment of the Tall government, the King decided to play matters safe politically, keeping

Sharif Hussein on as prime minister, supported by a cabinet that was of a decidedly 'old guard' tinge.[36]

Despite the rapid American response to his predicament in April, the King remained bitter about US policy in the region, believing that the Kennedy administration's attempt to cultivate good relations with Nasser had aided and abetted the latter's aggressive Arab policy. This much was clear from Hussein's private conversation with the Deputy Director General of the Israeli Foreign Ministry Yaacov Herzog on 24 September 1963. Most historians believe that this was the first encounter between Hussein and a representative of the Israeli government, though one very well-informed source close to the King believes that Hussein may already have begun cultivating a personal relationship with Moshe Dayan, who had been the Chief of Staff of the Israeli Defense Forces in the 1950s.[37] Dayan's personal link to Hussein was as much temperamental as political. Both men were military adventurers by nature, political 'loners' who found the excitement of highly secret, independent initiatives appealing. Although it is not clear precisely when their personal contacts began, the possibility that Hussein may have already met Dayan before he met Herzog has to be taken seriously.

The meeting between Hussein and Herzog, which, by contrast, was authorised by the Israeli Foreign Ministry, had been arranged through the good offices of the King's Jewish physician, Dr Emmanuel Herbert, and it was at his surgery in north London that it took place. Dr Herbert had earlier passed messages from the Israeli government to Hussein via his mother, Queen Zein, who was also his patient. The Israeli government had cultivated this channel of communication since 1960, seeking opportunities to arrange a meeting with the King. The 24 September meeting came about after Dr Herbert asked Queen Zein to pass on a message to Hussein about a border incident at the end of August. To Herbert's astonishment the Queen had replied, 'Why meet with me? His Majesty is in London and is willing to meet an authorised representative of Israel's Prime Minister.'

Herzog, who was chosen as this representative, found the King understandably nervous when they met, aware of the risk he was taking in speaking to an Israeli official. In the course of their conversation, the King's main preoccupations became clear. His troubles, Hussein explained, were more to do with his friends than his enemies. Specifically, the King complained that the Americans were supporting Nasser unconditionally at the highest level while, he felt, they were taking Jordan for granted. Herzog expressed sympathy with the King's position, and proposed that they explore the possibilities of covert cooperation in the fields of intelligence, international relations and Jordan's economic development. In particular, Herzog suggested they might consider forging closer connections between a group comprising Jordan, Turkey, Iran and, covertly, Israel. The meeting concluded amicably, with an agreement between the two men that their contact should be maintained in future.[38]

In the wake of the meeting, during 1964, Hussein's position in inter-Arab politics was eased by the emergence of a temporary détente in the Arab Cold War. Faced with deadlock in the Yemeni conflict, and worried by the threat of war with Israel over the latter's planned diversion of the River Jordan, Nasser turned instead to summitry as a means to try to resolve his differences with his Arab opponents. In a speech to a mass rally at Port Said on 23 December 1963 he called for a meeting of all Arab heads of state, ostensibly to address the political implications of the Israeli plans for the River Jordan. In reality, his appeal was also a shrewd device aimed at reducing the pressure exerted on him by both his conservative and his radical Arab critics. By convening an anti-Israeli talking shop, Nasser hoped to avoid the far more unpalatable contingency of being dragged into an Arab–Israeli war. Nasser's tactics also unintentionally brought about a temporary improvement in King Hussein's position. On 15 January 1964, while the first Arab summit conference was in session in Cairo, diplomatic relations between Jordan and Egypt, which had been broken off after the collapse of the UAR in September 1961, were restored. Hussein also pardoned or released a number of his political opponents and on 22 July transferred Jordan's formal recognition from the royalist to the republican side in the Yemeni conflict.[39] These moves were accompanied by a show of personal cooperation between Hussein and Nasser.[40] Evidently the rivalry of earlier days had still not vanished from the King's thinking, though. In a meeting with a British official on 30 April, Hussein argued that he could play the role of mediator in the Arab world, putting a brake on Nasser's more provocative behaviour. He also talked of 'bringing together a wider group of countries – including Iran, Turkey and Pakistan – in which Nasser would be one voice in a collective leadership instead of being able to be the boss as he tends to be among the Arabs'. The King, reported his British interlocutor, 'naturally sees himself in the role of the architect of all this'.[41]

Interestingly, the King's ideas echoed the proposals made by Yaacov Herzog during their meeting in September 1963. Indeed, Hussein's meetings with British officials were immediately followed by a further covert meeting with Herzog on 2 May 1964. Herzog found the King more confident and assertive than during their first encounter. Hussein returned to the idea of a wider grouping of states in the Middle East, including Iran, which would help rein in the Arab radicals and strengthen the moderates. During their conversation, Herzog noted that Hussein was inclined to defend Nasser's actions, arguing that the Egyptian leader did not want war, and that he now recognised that he had made mistakes in his conduct of relations with the other Arab states in the past.[42]

Despite his defence of Nasser in conversation with Herzog, persisting tensions between the Egyptian president and Hussein were evident over the development of the United Arab Command (UAC) established as a result of the Cairo summit. The force goals agreed for the UAC required Hussein to expand and modernise the Jordanian armed forces. Nasser, through the UAC, pressed Jordan to purchase Soviet weaponry. The ostensible reason for this was the goal of standardising the equipment used by the Arab forces, but the political overtones of the move were clear. Since Jordan was the only frontline state which relied on Western suppliers for its armed forces, the pressure was intended to highlight Hussein's links with Washington, and, better still, force him to break them. The corollary of this would be that if Hussein were forced to turn to Moscow for the re-equipment of·his armed forces, he would sacrifice a great deal of his political independence vis-à-vis the Soviet Union and the UAR.[43] In a conversation with US Ambassador Barnes, Brigadier Amer Khammash, the King's closest military adviser, claimed that ever since the first day of the Cairo summit there had been constant pressure on Jordan to accept Soviet military equipment. Although the King was determined to resist this pressure, Khammash argued that he could only succeed if Washington came up with a substantial arms package.[44] Of course, this argument was not without a degree of self-interest. The US administration was well aware that the King had long cherished the goal of expanding the Jordanian armed forces, and that the pressure from the UAC gave him the opportunity to pursue his case in Washington with the added advantage afforded by a Cold War bargaining chip.[45]

From the perspective of officials of President Johnson's new administration, selling arms to Hussein presented a complex problem. Since the 1950 Tripartite Declaration, the basic American strategy had been to limit arms supplies in the region as far as possible. Now, if Hussein were to secure the modern tanks and supersonic aircraft he had requested, the Americans would immediately face demands from Israel for compensatory supplies. Any substantial arms deal with Israel would, in turn, result in further damage to Washington's already strained relations with the Arab world. It would also set a very awkward precedent, making it even more difficult to refuse subsequent Israeli requests for additional arms supplies. As befitted a president with sensitive domestic political antennae, Lyndon Johnson was particularly alert to the dangers of any charge that he was arming Jordan, a member of the UAC, without addressing the resulting increased threat to Israeli security.[46]

Initially, the administration's strategy was to stall for time in the hope that the 'Arab unity scheme will fold up and we'll never have to deliver'.[47] However, by February 1965 it was apparent that Hussein could not be strung along any further, and veteran diplomat Averell Harriman and National Security Council staff member Bob Komer were despatched to secure Israeli acquiescence at the minimum price in terms of compensatory sales. By early March a deal had been struck by which Israel would not oppose Jordan's receiving 100 basic M48 tanks and other ancillary equipment, subject to the proviso that they should not be moved on to the West Bank in normal peacetime circumstances. Meanwhile, the US offered if necessary to make good the balance of a stalled West German tank sale to Israel, involving 150 modern M48 A-3 tanks which had both a longer range and a more powerful armament than those sold to Jordan. The Johnson administration promised in addition to 'ensure the sale directly to Israel at her request of at least the same number and quality of tanks that it sells to Jordan'. To sweeten the pill even further for the Israelis, the memorandum of understanding committed the United States to ensuring 'an opportunity for Israel to purchase a certain number of combat aircraft, if not from Western sources, then from the United States'. In return, the only commitment that the Johnson administration managed to secure to preserve the strategic balance in the region was the Israeli government's reiteration of its commitment not to be 'the first to introduce nuclear weapons into the Arab–Israel area'.[48]

The Jordanian and Israeli arms deals of March 1965 established a pattern: whatever the Americans sold to Jordan, they would sell larger quantities of more modern comparable weaponry to Israel. So, the following spring, Hussein had to be content with up to thirty-six secondhand F-104A/B 'Starfighter' interceptors, whilst Israel secured forty-eight modern Skyhawk A4-E ground-attack jets.[49] Although Hussein indicated his gratitude for the sale of the Starfighters in a personal letter to Johnson,[50] he saw the wrangling which had preceded these deals and the administration's evident reluctance to move unless it could secure Israeli agreement as an affront. At the very least, the protracted arms sales battles seemed to show that the US's commitment to Jordan's security came a distant second to their commitment to Israel.

There was one further major development during this period of Arab summitry which would in the longer run prove very dangerous to Hussein's position. This was Nasser's sponsorship of the formal creation of the Palestine Liberation Organisation (PLO) in 1964. During the early 1960s, the King had paid a good deal of attention to the question of how best to encourage loyalty to the Hashemite throne among his Palestinian subjects, particularly those living on the West Bank. In December 1962, a White Paper presented to parliament by Wasfi Tall, and drafted in the main by Hazem Nusseibeh, a Palestinian from Jerusalem, had proposed the establishment of a 'United Kingdom of Palestine and Jordan'. Nasser saw this proposal as an attempt on Hussein's part to outbid him in the struggle for leadership of the Palestinian cause, and accordingly subjected it to fierce propaganda attacks.[51] Behind the scenes, though, Nusseibeh continued to work on the King's behalf, seeking to build a bridge to the Palestinian national movement that was emerging under the leadership of Ahmad al-Shuqayri. Nusseibeh invited Shuqayri to Amman to see if they could work out together a formula that would allow for cooperation between Palestinians and Jordanians within the same state. But the sticking point, according to Nusseibeh, was always the demarcation line between Palestinian and Jordanian political authority within the Hashemite kingdom.[52] Hussein could not permit the establishment of any power within Jordan that acted as a rival for the loyalty of his Palestinian subjects.[53]

Initially, the improved climate in inter-Arab politics and Shuqayri's careful politicking prevented any full-blown conflict between the PLO and the Jordanian state. Hussein signed up to the resolution of the first Arab summit at Cairo calling for the creation of the PLO, and also to the resolution of the second summit at Alexandria endorsing Shuqayri's work in establishing the organisation. In the interim, the founding congress of the PLO had been held in Jerusalem, with Hussein's permission, at the end of May 1964. In his opening remarks to the congress, Hussein was downbeat, terming it merely 'a new stage of planned effort', and stressing that it was an extension of the recent Cairo summit. This seems to have been an attempt on his part to emphasise the continuing leading role of the Arab heads of state. Shuqayri, for his part, went out of his way to reassure the King: 'The emanation of the Palestinian entity in Jerusalem does not aim at carving the West Bank from the Hashemite Kingdom of Jordan . . . We are in no way touching on the Jordan entity.'[54] Even the Palestinian National Covenant adopted at the congress explicitly repudiated the creation of Palestine at the territorial expense of Jordan, although this commitment was later dropped in 1968. Moreover, of the 388 delegates to the congress, 242 lived in Jordan, and were individuals who the King expected would be 'prudent and moderate'. But despite these genuflexions on the part of Shuqayri, the threat to Hussein's authority posed by the nascent PLO remained. US intelligence reports indicated that in private Hussein was disturbed by the security implications of Shuqayri's activities on the West Bank,[55] and this was apparent from the subsequent negotiations between Shuqayri and the Jordanian government over the question of the PLO's status and role within Jordan.

Two issues dominated this increasingly troubled relationship during 1965 and 1966, both of which stemmed from decisions taken by the Arab summits in 1964 and both of which were fundamental problems that impinged directly on the sovereignty of the Hashemite kingdom. The first concerned the right of the PLO to raise levies within Jordan, as endorsed by the Alexandria summit in 1964, and the second its right to receive taxes. Setting the stage for conflict over these issues, in January 1965 the first guerrilla raid on Israel across the Jordanian armistice lines was mounted by Fatah, a Palestinian faction which was at this stage outside the control of Shuqayri's PLO. Founded in Kuwait in 1957 by Yasser Arafat and a small circle of dedicated associates, Fatah rose quickly in prominence after the formal establishment of the PLO, and its emphasis on the role of guerrilla action against Israel won it many adherents.

In February 1965 Hussein brought back Wasfi Tall as prime minister. It is reasonable to assume that he wanted a tough figure at the head of the Jordanian team charged with negotiating with the PLO and blocking Palestinian guerrilla action from Jordanian territory. Still, in an effort to avoid precipitating a crisis, Hussein stressed in his letter of commission to Tall the need to cooperate with the PLO in the domestic and inter-Arab arenas.[56]

The first move of the Tall government in respect of the question of levies for the Palestine Liberation Army (PLA) was the abolition of the Jordanian National Guard at the beginning of March. The King and his new government clearly feared that this 40,000-strong militia, based principally in frontier villages, might become the nucleus for Shuqayri's force. Members of the Guard were, where possible, transferred to the regular army, where they could be watched over more carefully. But the government's actions did not bring a halt to Fatah raids across the frontier, which on 27 May brought about Israel's first major retaliatory action against Jordan since the Suez crisis. The lack of progress on the question of the raising of PLA forces on Jordanian soil came into the open at the third Arab summit conference at Casablanca in September 1965, at which Shuqayri pointedly omitted Jordan from the list of countries cooperating in this process. Shuqayri's criticism brought forth a response from Hussein himself on 4 October, when he stressed that no organisation, meaning the PLO, could work outside the bounds of the United Arab Command established at the Cairo summit.[57] Just as at the Jerusalem congress the previous year, Hussein had once again emphasised the leading role of the Arab states vis-à-vis what was a non-state actor, the PLO.

At the same time as it blocked the PLO's attempts to raise levies, the government procrastinated over the question of the PLO's right to tax revenues. Although in talks between Tall and Shuqayri in June, the prime minister agreed in principle to the collection of a so-called 'liberation tax' from all civil servants, whether Palestinian or Jordanian, in practice nothing was done to implement this decision.[58] A visit by Shuqayri to Amman during November 1965 at the behest of Nasser did nothing to advance matters. Tall, whom Shuqayri pompously referred to as a former 'clerk of mine in the Arab Office in Jerusalem in 1946', was steadfast in his insistence that defence had to be dealt with by the Jordanian army.[59]

Hussein was not the only one who was concerned about the implications of allowing the PLO to fund and raise levies in Jordan. During his third meeting with Yaacov Herzog in London, on 19 December 1964, the Israeli representative also raised this issue, expressing concern that the creation of a PLO army might threaten the Hashemite throne and the integrity of the state of Jordan. Hussein made it plain that he was aware of the danger, and that he had no intention of allowing any units which Shuqayri might raise to be based in Jordan. Moreover, the King stressed that whatever Jordan's obligations under the UAC, he had no intention of allowing other Arab states to base their forces in Jordan. The King's comments were of course specifically tailored to his audience. As if to emphasise the point, when Herzog raised the issue of the movement of three brigades of the Jordanian army on to the West Bank, the King asked, 'What are you afraid of? You know how strong you are!' Well aware of the potential danger of Israeli retaliatory raids, Hussein dwelt on his determination to retain full military control within his kingdom.[60]

During a subsequent meeting in Paris in autumn 1965 with Israeli Foreign Minister Golda Meir, which Herzog was unable to attend due to illness, the King's pledge not to deploy Jordan's American-supplied tanks on the West Bank and the question of Palestinian guerrilla activities were both considered. Meir also shared with Hussein her memories of his grandfather, Abdullah, whom she had met secretly before the 1948 war. But the meeting was more about atmospherics than substance: both Meir and Hussein spoke warmly about their hopes for a future era of peace.[61]

As relations with the PLO subsequently deteriorated during 1965, Hussein made two further crucial moves to buttress his position. On the inter-Arab level, Hussein moved to shore up his relations with King Feisal of Saudi Arabia, reaching agreement in August 1965 on a treaty newly delimiting the Saudi–Jordanian frontier. This involved the first formal recognition on the part of Saudi Arabia to the right of the Hashemite kingdom to a foothold on the Red Sea shoreline. Hussein also dropped broad hints that he would be interested in an Islamic congress, an idea which Feisal was later to carry forward in competition with Nasser's promotion of secular Arab unity.

Possibly of even greater significance in the longer term, though, was Hussein's decision to change the line of succession on 1 April 1965. In place of his three-year-old son, Abdullah, Hussein appointed his eighteen-year-old younger brother, Hassan, as Crown Prince. This was not a move to be made lightly, involving as it did an amendment to the constitution. The installation of Hassan as Crown Prince was the foundation for a political partnership that was to prove crucial to the survival of the Hashemite kingdom across a period of more than three decades. At the time, in view of the increasing dangers facing the state, the move was justified in straightforward, pragmatic terms. As Hussein himself put it, he had changed the order 'to choose the most suitable for the task, and to prepare the one who can continue carrying the responsibility'.[62] Should anything happen to the King, then Hassan, unlike Abdullah, was old enough to step straight into the breach. However, this alone does not explain the choice of Hassan since the King had also passed over Hassan's elder brother Prince Mohammad in making his decision. A large part of his motivation seems to have been based on his judgement of Hassan's personal qualities and the way in which they might complement his own leadership skills, a judgement that was to be thoroughly vindicated across the coming years.

Hussein was well aware of his own weaknesses as well as his strengths. Although he was at his best in a crisis, he was less well suited to framing a longer-term strategy. His attention span was short and he often lost interest in affairs of state once the point of a crisis had been passed. There were also crucial areas of state activity, particularly in terms of economic development and administrative efficiency, in which he could muster little consistent personal interest, even though he recognised their importance. Finally, the King was overwhelmingly a practical man, with little time for intellectual theorising. Nevertheless, he recognised the role of ideas in galvanising the populace and providing an overall sense of purpose and direction. In all of these respects, Hassan's personal strengths seemed well suited to make up for the King's own deficiencies. Although he was only just finishing his schooling at Harrow, Hassan's successful application to Oxford, where he was later to perform creditably as an undergraduate, marked him out as the family intellectual. In future years he took on an extensive portfolio of political and economic interests. Moreover, during the King's frequent absences from the country, he was to prove a tough and able regent.

But a simple detailing of their respective strengths does little to explain the frisson of the Hussein–Hassan relationship. On one level, it was that of brother to brother, fraught with the potential for competition and tension, but also more intimate than any other blood relationship apart from parent and child. The same aspects of Hassan's character that commended him to Hussein for the role of Crown Prince could also be the source of tension in their relations. On the one hand, Hassan's reputation as an intellectual was a useful asset to the King in communicating Jordan's case to an educated Western audience. On the other, because intellectual theorising ran counter to his own instincts, Hussein was often impatient with Hassan's mode of expression. Political intimates of the two men recall many occasions on which Hussein would shrug his shoulders as Hassan embarked on an extended verbal excursion around a particular problem. In later years, Hussein would also come to entertain suspicions about Hassan's own political ambitions, particularly in respect of the future line of succession. However, back in the mid-1960s this problem, and the further tensions engendered between them by that most pernicious of poisons in fraternal relations, warring wives, were very much in the future. For the present, Hussein had exercised a shrewd piece of political judgement in bolstering his domestic position.

Up to the beginning of 1966, then, Hussein had not had to pay a particularly high price for the active Arab policy he had followed against the backdrop of the Yemeni conflict during 1962–4. Nor had he been confronted with the implications of his decision to attach himself to the 'conservative' Saudi-led Arab camp. The main reason for this was that Nasser's pursuit of détente during 1964–5 had temporarily diminished the polarisation of the Arab world. But, even during this era of apparent harmony, the creation of the PLO, together with the development of the UAC, had put Jordan in an increasingly awkward position. As détente broke down in 1966, the full implications of the King's earlier approach became apparent. Jordan was to find itself caught between Israel on the one hand and the emerging Egyptian–Syrian alliance on the other, unable to influence developments as the region slid towards war.

CHAPTER 6

THE PATH TO DISASTER, 1966–7

Hussein may have negotiated one crisis after another during his first years on the throne, but all of these events paled in significance next to the existential clash he was to face in 1967. During the early months of 1966, pressure began to build throughout the region. With the progressive breakdown of the brief phase of détente in the Arab world, Hussein's concerns about relations between Jordan and the PLO grew rapidly. Both the PLO leader Shuqayri and the King were trying to avoid a complete break in their relations at the same time as presenting their respective positions in the best possible light for a broader Arab audience. The result of this manoeuvring was an agreement between the PLO and the Jordanian government, signed in March 1966, which once again tried to lay down mutually acceptable terms for the PLO's activities within Jordan. According to Shuqayri's account, this agreement would not have been reached without a last-minute intervention on the part of the King himself.

It was all to no avail. Inter-Arab relations continued to deteriorate and the 'radical/conservative' divide in the region reopened, with King Feisal calling for an 'Islamic Summit' during a visit to Tehran in December 1965 and another coup in Damascus on 23 February 1966 which brought to power a more radical faction of the Baath Party. Since Shuqayri was under Nasser's protection, and Hussein had attached himself to Feisal, the renewed trend towards polarisation during 1966 cut the ground from under both parties' attempts to finesse their fundamental differences. In a speech on 14 June 1966, Hussein finally declared: 'all hopes have vanished for the possibility of cooperation with this organisation [i.e. the PLO] in its recent form'.[1] The King's speech heralded the near elimination of the PLO from public life in

Jordan.[2] Shuqayri for his part now denied that Jordan had any right to exist, while Nasser announced his disillusionment with summitry. The end of the détente era was formally confirmed on 22 July 1966, when the acting secretary-general of the Arab League announced the indefinite postponement of the fourth Arab summit, scheduled to meet in Algiers on 5 September.

As yet oblivious to the storm which would break over Jordan during the autumn, Hussein was abroad once more in the summer of 1966, this time on an official state visit to the United Kingdom. His comments during talks with Prime Minister Harold Wilson give an insight into his reading of inter-Arab politics at this juncture. In a meeting on 22 July, Hussein told Wilson that 'there was a good deal of talk about the reappearance of a division between the Arab states into a group of "revolutionary" states ranged against what were sometimes called "reactionary" states, but which he would like to call "evolutionaries", those who believed in the evolutionary process and in stability as the best foundation for future development'.[3] Hussein evidently still hoped that a way could be found to bridge this 'revolutionary/evolutionary' divide.

The visit to Britain also provided a snapshot of Hussein the man at the age of thirty. The list prepared by the British Foreign Office of 'topics of conversation' for social occasions with the King included 'water-skiing, motor-boats and skin diving; motorcars; aircraft; youth work; Crown Prince Hassan at Christchurch, Oxford (reading Oriental Languages); the armed forces . . .', before going on to list a collection of economic and social issues. According to a later Foreign Office report of the trip, the British press had seized on the story of King Hussein's visit to the Royal Armoured Corps Centre at Bovington on 25 July. Here, encouraged by a British colonel to 'give it a little more gas', the 'sudden pressure of the Royal foot upon the accelerator of an armoured fighting vehicle caused that same colonel to break a front tooth'. *The Times* reported the incident under the heading 'Colonel's Stiff Upper Lip'. The King's trip to a Royal Air Force base at Little Rissington, where he performed a series of aerobatic rolls in a jet trainer, also attracted much attention.[4] There was evidently still life after thirty for Hussein the action man.

Once back home, the King's challenges proved to be of a much less welcome nature. During the summer of 1966, Fatah had stepped up its guerrilla raids against Israel, launched from Jordan with the active encouragement of the Syrian regime. Between October and mid-November 1966, Syrian-backed Palestinian guerrillas carried out eleven raids into Israel, six of which were launched from Jordanian soil.[5] The Syrians saw this as one means of destabilising the Hashemite kingdom, alongside a propaganda campaign calling for the overthrow of Hussein as the essential first step along the road to the liberation of Palestine. These attacks on Hussein were all part of a battle for leadership of the 'revolutionary' camp in the Arab world, which at this stage pitted Damascus against Cairo. Not to be outdone, Nasser gave Shuqayri free rein to attack Hussein via the 'Voice of Palestine' radio station broadcast from Cairo, although he himself carefully avoided criticising Hussein by name. Shuqayri for his part began to lend his support to Fatah operations about which he had previously expressed reservations.[6] Jordan thus found itself once more at the fulcrum of inter-Arab tensions.

Much worse was to come. On the night of 11–12 November an Israeli army half-track was blown up by a mine laid by Fatah inside Israeli territory south of Hebron. Three soldiers were killed and six wounded. The guerrillas' tracks led across the border into Jordan, and the Israeli government resolved to retaliate. Early on the morning of 13 November an Israeli infantry brigade supported by tanks, artillery and Mirage jet fighters crossed the border. Their target was the Palestinian village of Samu, and the raid was carried out with ruthless efficiency. Sweeping into the village, the Israeli force destroyed everything in its path: the police station, a girls' school and ninety-three houses were demolished. Worse still for Hussein, an outgunned Jordanian army column now stumbled unprepared into the area, only to be decimated by the Israelis. Fifteen Jordanian soldiers, including two officers, were killed.[7] Hussein desperately committed his tiny air force to the battle, only to see the Israelis shoot down one of the planes. For the King, who knew all of his small band of pilots personally and felt himself to be one of their number, this was a particularly grievous loss.

The Samu raid was a key landmark on the road to war the following June. It was also a deep personal loss and humiliation for Hussein. Indeed, the incident presents a significant problem of interpretation for those historians who believe that from 1963 onwards a strategic partnership had emerged between Israel and the Hashemite regime.[8] The problem is simple: if the Israelis wanted to see Hussein survive, why did they launch a major, brigade-strength raid into the West Bank which served to highlight the King's inability to protect its Palestinian population, and made him the central target of the Arab radicals? The conventional explanation is that Samu was a miscalculation on the part of an Israeli government which was itself divided as to the best course of action to take to protect the security of its citizens.[9] Most sources argue that Yitzhak Rabin, the architect of the operation, planned it in the expectation that there would be no significant resistance and no direct engagement with the Jordanian army.[10] But it is difficult to believe that the Israeli cabinet which authorised the operation could have been convinced by the argument that Hussein's forces would stand idly by in the face of such a large-scale incursion.[11]

Aside from the reaction in the Arab world, the Israeli operation provoked consternation in Washington, where officials were sceptical of Israeli

explanations for the attack. In a 15 November memorandum to President
Johnson, his Special Assistant Walt Rostow provided a prescient summary of
the likely effects of Israel's action. Not only had the Israelis undercut the tacit
system of cooperation which had developed over the West Bank frontier, they
had undercut Hussein's personal position. He was now likely to be subjected
to pressure to take a strong anti-Israeli stance, not only from Syria and his
own Palestinian subjects, but also from within the Jordanian army.[12] The US
administration did not pull its punches in expressing its disapproval of the
Israeli action. The State Department refused to pass on a conciliatory message
from Prime Minister Eshkol to Hussein and American officials privately
threatened that if Israel repeated its action the US 'military pipeline would
begin to dry up'.[13] As Rostow saw things, Israel

> for some machiavellian reason, wanted a leftist regime on the Left [sic]
> bank so that it could then have a polarized situation in which the
> Russians would be backing the Arabs and the U.S. would be backing
> Israel, and that Israel would not be in an embarrassing position where
> one of its friends among the Great Powers would also be a friend of an
> Arab country.[14]

Rostow's view was shared by Hussein himself, who argued that the Israeli
strategy involved the 'toppling of [the] Hashemite throne'. The succession of
a left-wing regime would polarise the region, leaving Washington 'little
alternative but to support Israel'.[15] Hussein believed that the Israelis intended
to escalate the conflict to the point where they would be able to seize the West
Bank.[16] As he told one American official, he considered the unwritten agreement which had neutralised the Jordanian–Israeli border to have 'now been
permanently shattered'.[17] As far as the King was concerned, the attack had
'completely changed his outlook on trying to live with Israel . . . I no longer
have a shred of faith in Israeli intentions', he commented bitterly.[18]

Hussein's bitterness was heightened still further by what he regarded as the
particular duplicity of Israeli actions leading up to the raid. In what Rostow
characterised to President Johnson as an 'extraordinary revelation', Hussein,
in conversation with US Ambassador Findley Burns and CIA station chief
Jack O'Connell, set the raid in the context of his hitherto undisclosed clandestine dealings with Israeli representatives over the course of the preceding
years.[19] These contacts included the meetings with Herzog and Meir and the
messages passed by Dr Herbert. Hussein had also met privately with Israeli
Foreign Minister Abba Eban while the two were holidaying on the French
Riviera.[20] But even beyond this web of contacts, Hussein also evidently had
still further undisclosed channels to Israeli leaders. In an emotional exchange
which is worth quoting at length, he confided to Burns and O'Connell that

there was one element affecting the whole picture which no one in his country, except himself, knew about:

He did not believe in war as a solution to the Palestine problem . . . He had consistently followed a course of moderation on the whole question of Palestine in the hope that reasonable men could one day negotiate a just settlement. He had done his utmost to eliminate terrorism against Israel from across Jordan's border. The US knew all these things and so did the Israelis. The Israelis knew it, he said, because 'I told them so personally'.

'For the past three years,' the King said, 'I have been meeting secretly with Golda Meir, Eban and others. We have discussed these problems at length and agreed on all aspects of them. I told them, among other things, that I could not absorb or tolerate a serious retaliatory raid. They accepted the logic of this and promised that there would never be one. Moreover, in addition to these secret personal meetings, I have maintained a personal and confidential correspondence with the Israeli leaders. These exchanges have served to "underscore and reinforce our understandings".

'The last message I received from the Israelis was further to reassure me that they had no intention of attacking Jordan. I received the message on Nov. 13, the very day the Israeli troops attacked Samu.' The King added that the message was unsolicited, and had been despatched presumably between 24 to 48 hours before he received it.

'As far as I am concerned this attack was a complete betrayal by them of everything I had tried to do for the past three years in the interests of peace, stability and moderation at high personal political risk. Strangely, despite our secret discussions and correspondence, despite secret agreements, understandings and assurances, I never fully trusted their intentions toward me or toward Jordan. In assessing Israeli intentions I ask you to put my experiences with them into your equation.

'You will excuse me,' he added 'if I find it ironic that the same Eban who expressed to me such understanding of the problems here and gave such firm assurances is now on his way to Washington to tell you, I am sure, that Jordan's needs should not be met.'

The King closed the discussion by saying bitterly: 'This is what one gets for trying to be a moderate, or perhaps for being stupid.'[21]

Back in Washington, Rostow's estimate of the King's startling revelation was that 'it could be that the contacts existed in a very narrow circle and were not known to the whole government or to the Israeli military. In that case, as they faced heavy pressure to retaliate, those who had the contacts would

have been in a most difficult bind.'[22] Hussein's own reading of the Samu raid
was evidently much simpler and more direct: it was an act of deliberate
treachery.

Whatever the degree of displeasure displayed by US officials to the Israeli
government over the raid, it did little to alleviate the position in which
Hussein now found himself. Discontent within Jordan manifested itself not
only in the form of extensive street protests in the wake of the raid, but also
through more plots against the regime from within the armed forces.
According to one CIA report, the plotting was not confined to Palestinian
officers, but also extended to East Bankers.[23] Paradoxically, though, divisions
between these groups worked in Hussein's favour, since the 'basic distrust
and suspicion within the JAA [Jordan Arab Army] between Palestinian and
East Bank officers . . . prevents close cooperation and trust between the two
factions'. The East Bankers were convinced that should the Palestinians
mount a successful coup, they would 'relegate all East Bank officers and
citizens to second class status'. One anti-regime faction thus served to balance
the other, although from Hussein's point of view this was a precarious
equilibrium.

On the inter-Arab level, the King's inability to defend the villagers of Samu
undermined his refusal to allow the Palestine Liberation Army to recruit on
the West Bank or to allow other Arab forces to move in under the United
Command. The King's own view was that 'it is [in] our interest to keep all
foreign troops out of Jordan. They will merely create [a] new avenue of
trouble.'[24] Hussein's refusal was reinforced by intelligence reports, considered
by a meeting of his top advisers on 22 December, which indicated that Iraq,
Syria, the UAR and the PLO were colluding with a view to using the entry of
UAC troops into Jordan as a means of undermining internal security. These
reports suggested that there was an agreement to include PLA troops wearing
Iraqi insignia among any Iraqi contingent moved into Jordan. In the light of
this intelligence, it was agreed that the Jordanian representative, Amer
Khammash, should seek to prevent the entry of Iraqi troops at the UAC
meeting on 24 December by the Machiavellian tactic of calling instead for the
despatch of forces from all thirteen members of the UAC to defend the West
Bank. Hussein's calculation was that assuming Nasser wanted to avoid war he
would have to refuse such a request, and that this refusal would provide
useful anti-UAR propaganda material.[25]

These Jordanian suspicions and manoeuvres underlined the fact that the
UAC was now effectively a dead letter. Indeed, the conclusion of the
Egyptian–Syrian Defence Treaty on 4 November just before the Samu raid
had confirmed as much. Both Nasser and the regime in Damascus evidently
now thought the only way forward was to plan for military action on a
bilateral basis. More importantly, from Hussein's point of view, the bilateral

pact also evidenced Nasser's move firmly back into the Arab 'radical' camp. By tying his fortunes to those of the Syrian regime, which was engaged in an escalating confrontation with Israel, he had greatly increased the chance of general war.[26]

The ensuing deterioration in Hussein's relations with Nasser was rapid. On the evening of 2 December 1966 the King made a speech to 'the nation and all Arabs', in which references to the Yemen and the United Nations Emergency Force (UNEF) stationed in Sinai as a buffer force between Egypt and Israel since the 1956 war left no doubt that his target was Nasser. The presence of UNEF on Egyptian soil was used by Nasser's critics to suggest that he was cowering behind the UN because of his fear of Israel. The King argued that 'some Arab factions are trying to destroy Jordan, and this is exactly what the enemy wants',[27] and that 'these regimes' had boasted in public that they had sufficient aircraft to 'eclipse the sun from the enemy's skies', but that in private they admitted that they could not even defend their own airspace, never mind send planes to help Jordan. Although Hussein avoided mentioning Nasser by name in his speech, Nasser himself entertained no such personal inhibitions. In a speech on 22 February 1967, he labelled Hussein the 'whore of Jordan', a personal attack which contributed to Hussein's decision to recall his ambassador from Cairo.[28] For his part, Hussein played further on the fact that Egypt was unwilling to take any initiative on its own frontier to face down the Israelis, instead continuing to hide behind UNEF. Hussein had developed this theme in a speech on 25 January, when he declared, 'if UNEF remains there can only be one explanation for its presence – that there is an agreement that this force stays until the Palestine question is settled or until reconciliation is achieved'.[29] The presence of UNEF was to prove an important point of pressure on Nasser. His request for its removal in May would be one of the catalysts for war.

If UNEF acted as a buffer to action on the Egyptian front, there was no such hindrance on the Syrian front. After the Samu raid, the Israeli government turned its attention to the threat it saw posed by the Soviet-backed regime in Damascus. Syrian propaganda and actions only served to confirm Israeli perceptions. Radio Damascus proudly proclaimed on 16 January 1967: 'Syria has changed its strategy, moving from defence to attack . . . We will carry on operations until Israel has been eliminated.'[30] An escalating series of clashes on the Syrian front beginning during that month culminated in a major land and air engagement on 7 April. In a dogfight near Damascus witnessed by the population of the city the Syrian air force was soundly defeated, with Israeli jets performing a victory loop to proclaim their supremacy. The absence of any Egyptian help underlined the hollowness of the November defence treaty. It also further increased the pressure on Nasser to put military substance behind his rhetoric.

Hussein tried to exploit the clash to relieve the pressure on Jordan, with Radio Amman hammering home the point that Nasser had not come to Syria's aid in its hour of need. Unfortunately for the King, Jordan was by this stage so isolated that the effort rebounded, and the Egyptians accused Jordan of colluding in the attack on Syria. In fact, despite the feisty anti-Egyptian propaganda coming out of Amman, Hussein seems to have recognised by this stage that Jordan would have to trim its sails to the warlike winds blowing through the region. Just how far he would have to tack was not yet clear. His attempts to build up relations with the conservative states in the Arab world, principally Saudi Arabia, had done nothing to afford Jordan a defence against the Syrian, Egyptian and PLO propaganda attacks, or to ward off the potential threat of Israeli action. Jordan's isolation was such that Hussein was contemplating withdrawing from the Arab League, where Shuqayri was seeking to indict him on thirty-three counts of treachery.[31] Within the Jordanian political establishment, there was also opposition to the strident anti-Egyptian line pursued by the Wasfi Tall government. Bahjat Talhuni, a long-standing rival of Tall's, opposed the policy and he and his supporters tried to persuade the King to have Tall removed.[32] At first the King stuck by Tall. However, in a move probably intended to increase his domestic and regional room for manoeuvre, Hussein accepted Tall's resignation as prime minister on 4 March, moving him on to the post of chief of the Royal Court.[33]

Tall was replaced as prime minister by Saad Juma'a who, although he had previously espoused an anti-Nasser line, had changed course during the early part of 1967. One of Juma'a's first acts after forming a new cabinet on 23 April was to call for a resumption of the Arab summits. This was a clear signal of the new government's attempt to resurrect the middle ground in Arab politics.[34] The response of Syria and Egypt was dismissive, and they continued their propaganda attacks against the Hashemite regime. On 21 May Syria went even further. A truck loaded with explosives was detonated at the Jordanian border post of Ramtha, claiming the lives of twenty-one Jordanian bystanders. The government was left with little choice but to break off diplomatic ties with Syria.[35]

The Ramtha incident took place against the background of a gathering regional crisis. During the second week of May, Israeli leaders had made a series of public statements warning that unless Syria ceased its sponsorship of aggressive acts against Israel, the government would regard itself as justified in taking action in self-defence.[36] In an awkward balancing act, at the same time the Israeli government tried to dispel rumours circulated by the Soviet Union that Israel was concentrating troops on northern border for a pre-emptive strike against Syria. The reasons for Moscow's propagation of the so-called 'false intelligence report' remain the subject of debate, although the controversy is somewhat outside the scope of this book.[37] Whatever the details, Nasser seems to have taken the rumour-mongering as a signal of Soviet backing for a more pro-active Egyptian stance against Israel. He was certainly well aware that if a full-scale attack on Syria took place he could not afford to ignore the provisions of the Egyptian–Syrian defence treaty, as he had during the 7 April incident.

Nasser now initiated a series of escalatory steps which helped create the circumstances for the outbreak of war. These began with his 14 May decision to move additional Egyptian troops ostentatiously across the Suez Canal into the Sinai desert. On 16 May, Nasser escalated the crisis further. Finally responding to the criticism of the presence of UNEF in the Sinai, levelled by Hussein among others, he called on UN Secretary-General U Thant to remove the force. Thant's decision to comply with Nasser's request, a move for which he has been roundly criticised,[38] opened the way to further escalation. Nasser's forces moved to occupy Sharm al-Sheikh at the tip of the Sinai Peninsula and the Egyptian leader followed up the move with a public declaration on 22 May that the Straits of Tiran, now overlooked by his forces, were closed to Israeli shipping.

In all of these events, Hussein was a bystander. He may well have been shocked that Nasser had finally taken the initiative and acted on the charges which Hussein himself had levelled against him. Discussing Nasser's move with the British ambassador in Amman on 23 May, the King said that 'he found Nasser's threat to close the Straits of Tiran incomprehensible and extremely dangerous'.[39] He had, he candidly admitted, 'no appreciation of the military situation' since Nasser's statement, despite the fact that he had sent General Khammash, his chief of staff, to Cairo on 21 May with instructions to find out Nasser's military intentions and to see whether any form of coordination was possible. Nasser's refusal to meet Khammash personally, or to take up the offer he conveyed from the King for the stationing of other Arab troops on Jordanian soil, showed that their mutual enmity remained undiminished.[40] Hussein commented that for his own part he was 'determined to keep calm and to avoid incidents'. Overall, the King considered Nasser to be 'behaving like a madman'.[41]

Despite the steely demeanour Hussein presented to the emissaries of Western powers, Nasser's move in respect of the Straits of Tiran, although primarily directed against Israel, also increased pressure on Jordan, which depended economically on the free passage of goods to and from its port of Aqaba. Or, as British Ambassador Adams put it, Egyptian control of the Straits 'posed a potential mortal threat for Jordan . . . In any future dispute with Nasser Jordan would find his thumb on her windpipe.'[42] The King's immediate response to the deepening crisis was to order general mobilisation of Jordanian forces on 24 May. He also offered Iraq facilities for stationing its forces in Jordan, an offer which was disdainfully rejected by the Baghdad regime.

These events further marked Jordan's isolation in the face of a clear trend towards war. In essence, the King was faced with two unpalatable choices. He could throw in his lot with Nasser, which would mean accepting whatever terms the Egyptian leader offered for Jordan's participation in the joint struggle, and running the risk of a military confrontation with Israel which might well entail the loss of the West Bank. This course also carried domestic risks in the shape of a likely increase in Egyptian influence and the probable return of the PLO as an open political force in Jordan. Alternatively, the King could endeavour to stand aside from the coming conflict and hope that the Israelis would respect his neutrality. The risks involved here were perhaps even greater. If the King's estimate of Israeli intentions was right, they might still manufacture some pretext to launch an attack on the West Bank. Jordan, Hussein told the *New York Times* on 29 May, would inevitably be attacked 'because Israel views the Arab world as one'.[43] Even without an Israeli attack, the King would probably be faced with domestic disturbances on a scale that would dwarf even those which had followed the Samu raid. How far he would be able to hold the country together and rely on the support of the army in these circumstances was a moot point. There were many imponderables in both courses of action and, either way, the King's domestic political authority seemed likely to be challenged. However, when Hussein distilled the problem to its essence, it boiled down to a choice between accepting the embrace of Arabism and accepting the embrace of Israel. Viewed in these terms, the decision must have seemed rather more straightforward.[44] As he put it himself in a later interview:

The atmosphere that I found in Jordan, particularly in the West Bank, was one where, frankly, we had the following choice: either to act at the right time with no illusion of what the results might be but with a chance to do better than we would otherwise, or not to act and to have an eruption occur . . . which would cause us to collapse and which would obviously immediately result in an Israeli occupation of probably the West Bank or even more than the West Bank . . . That was really the reason why I went to Egypt to meet Nasser to his surprise.[45]

On 24 May Radio Jordan officially proclaimed the nation's support for Nasser. At a meeting at Prime Minister Juma'a's home on 28 May, in an attempt to sound out Nasser, King Hussein told the Egyptian ambassador that he would like to fly to Cairo as soon as possible to consult over the coordination of battle plans. The following day, Nasser's reply came: 'come as soon as you can'.[46] The King's dramatic flight to Cairo on the morning of 30 May at the controls of his own plane took Western and Israeli commentators by surprise. Even the CIA station chief in Amman, Jack O'Connell, who had developed a close personal as well as professional relationship with Hussein, received no advance warning of the King's move.[47] When he heard the news, he hurried to the airport to try to prevent the King from being taken in by what he regarded as an 'Egyptian trick', only to find that he had arrived too late to stop Hussein's departure.

Nasser now proceeded to 'double-cross' Hussein on his arrival in Cairo. Beforehand, the two men had agreed that the meeting would be kept secret unless they failed to reach agreement. In fact, when Hussein arrived at Cairo airport he was met by Nasser amid full publicity, with the first Egyptian press release on their meeting issued a mere hour and forty minutes after Hussein's plane touched down.[48] The encounter between Hussein and Nasser was not an easy one. Hussein strode down the aircraft steps in full military uniform with a pistol at his hip, while Nasser stood waiting in his civilian suit. Their first exchanges increased the tension still further. In an ill-timed piece of irony, Nasser asked the King, 'What would happen if we chose to arrest you on the spot?' Hussein replied testily, 'The possibility never entered my mind.'[49]

Once they reached the presidential palace the atmosphere improved. Hussein made it clear that he had come prepared to do whatever was necessary to secure a military pact. This even extended to an offer to accede to a carbon copy of the Egyptian–Syrian Defence Treaty, which committed each party to come to the defence of the other in the event of an attack. The combined forces of the Eastern Front, including those of Syria and Jordan, were now to be placed under the overall command of the Egyptian Chief of Staff, General Mohammad Fawzi. In order to strengthen the Jordanian front Hussein also agreed to the entry of troops from Egypt, Iraq, Syria and Saudi Arabia into the country. In what the King regarded as a particular personal humiliation, Nasser also pressed him into taking Ahmad Shuqayri on his plane with him back to Amman. Shuqayri appeared alongside Nasser and Hussein at a press conference where news of the agreement was announced. These moves, much like the rest of the publicity given to Hussein's visit, were, according to a CIA estimate, 'designed to emphasize that Hussein is going to Canossa'.[50] In return for these significant concessions on his part, Hussein received the promise of air support from Egypt and Iraq, together with the symbolic end to his isolation in the Arab world.[51] The CIA station chief Jack O'Connell, who had arrived at the airport too late to stop Hussein's departure, was there to witness his return. As he saw the King step off the plane followed by Egyptian army officers, O'Connell's heart fell. He knew the die had been cast.

Although the public face was one of Arab unity, Hussein's supporters privately continued to tell Westerners that he did not trust Nasser. In a conversation with a US official on 3 June, Chief of Staff Amer Khammash stressed that Hussein and his government did not want war. He had hoped through the signing of the defence agreement to shift his burden in respect of the Palestinian problem onto Nasser's shoulders, allowing the latter to take the blame for any 'sense of let-down in the Arab man-in-the-street' should the war not go ahead.[52] How far these reassurances genuinely represented Hussein's views and how far they were intended to mollify the King's Western backers in an attempt to avoid a complete break in relations is unclear. In public, Hussein ostentatiously distanced himself from the American and British governments.[53]

No doubt part of the explanation for the King's stance was the attempt to court domestic and broader Arab opinion, but disillusionment with the Anglo-American approach to the crisis does seem to have been a central factor. This approach had initially involved efforts, led by the British with Washington's encouragement, to put together a multinational naval force to convoy ships through the Straits of Tiran, thus breaking Nasser's blockade. By the beginning of June, however, the plan had run into trouble, with divisions in the British cabinet and doubts about its feasibility persuading the British government to step back.

On the other side of the Atlantic, the Johnson administration took an even more equivocal position, reflected by the fact that officials had encouraged the British to take the lead in trying to break the blockade rather than doing it themselves.[54] Once it became clear that the British were not prepared to carry the plan forward, the Americans resigned themselves to Israeli action to open the Straits. This, it was assumed, would mean an Arab–Israeli war in which Israel would emerge victorious. This forecast was based largely on CIA information, with the State Department taking a consistently more sceptical view of the likelihood and speed of any Israeli victory. CIA Director Richard Helms, however, stuck by his analysts' estimate of overall Israeli air and ground superiority, and according to some sources told Johnson in advance that the war would last no more than seven days.[55] The CIA certainly seems to have had very detailed information about Israeli battle plans as a result of its contacts within the Israeli intelligence services, where the operation against Egypt was being planned. There is reason to believe that this allowed Helms to warn Johnson in advance as to the planned date of the Israeli attack, which was moved up from approximately 15 to 5 June at short notice, because the Israelis, who continued to see Egypt as the main strategic threat in the region, wanted to make sure that Nasser did not have time to find a way out of the exposed position in which he had put himself. The advance warning Johnson received from Helms would explain his subsequent rather smug comment to Congress that he had been expecting the Israeli move, and Helms's observation that it was 'a fairly tidy package'. It would also explain why Helms was ushered into the president's 'magic inner circle' after the war, a dramatic improvement in his status.[56]

The CIA director was not the only person who received advance intelligence about the planned date of the Israeli attack. This information, it now transpires, also reached Hussein himself. Extraordinarily, Hussein apparently passed the warning he had received on to Nasser in two telephone calls which he made during the final three days before war broke out.[57] The Israelis must have monitored these warnings, which might help to explain the panic which gripped certain members of the civilian and military leadership, including Prime Minister Eshkol and Chief of Staff Rabin, in the final hours before the attack. They need not have worried. Nasser did not react. Why not is unclear, although two possible explanations suggest themselves. Firstly, Nasser may have suspected that Hussein was simply trying to trick him into backing down, and losing face in the crisis. He was no doubt aware that Hussein might be manoeuvring to put him in a position whereby he made the decision to retreat from military action and (as Amer Khammash had suggested earlier) incurred the subsequent wrath of Arab public opinion. Secondly, one should not underestimate the dysfunctional state of the Egyptian leadership in the period leading up to the outbreak of war. The Nasser regime resembled nothing more than a paralysed rabbit trapped in the headlights of an approaching juggernaut.

While the final timing of the operation against Egypt was being decided in Israeli intelligence circles, a national unity government was formed in Tel Aviv on 1 June, with the controversial but charismatic Moshe Dayan entering the Israeli cabinet as minister of defence. On the same day, the Egyptian general Abdul Munim Riad arrived in Jordan to take up command of all forces, including those of Jordan, on the eastern front. There was very little time for preparation and there is no doubt in hindsight that Riad would have been better advised to rely on the existing Jordanian battle plans. After all, the Jordanian high command was far better acquainted with the capabilities of its own forces, and the nature of the ground. But Riad's mission was overwhelmingly political. If Cairo was in charge of the Arab forces then Cairo would impose its own battle plans on them.

Hussein may not have expected victory but he was certainly not prepared for the speed and scale of the defeat that was inflicted on the combined Arab armies.[58] The lightning attack launched by the Israeli air force on Egyptian airfields early on the morning of 5 June to all intents and purposes decided the outcome of the battle before it had even been joined on the ground. The IAF followed up its devastatingly successful attacks on Egypt with a series of raids that afternoon which also eliminated the Syrian, Iraqi and Jordanian air forces. Without air cover, the Arab armies could not hope to withstand the Israeli assault. It was clear from the reports provided by the Jordanian radar station at Ajloun that a major air operation was taking place. But the information relayed by Cairo to Amman at 9 that morning was the opposite of actual events. The Egyptians proclaimed a great success, declaring that three-quarters of the attacking Israeli force had been knocked out, and that Egyptian air and ground forces were now assuming the offensive. General Riad was ordered in turn to attack on the Jordanian front.[59]

The reports from Cairo were followed up by a phone call to Hussein from Nasser, who repeated the false claims about Egyptian successes and asked that Hussein try to take possession of as much land as possible before the UN intervened to impose a ceasefire. Riad's instructions from Cairo required him to move Jordanian forces forward in a broad offensive along the eastern front, a move vigorously but fruitlessly opposed by the Jordanian high command. Hussein himself, faced with what he knew to be a dangerous and ill-thought-out manoeuvre, did not intervene to stop it. As far as he was concerned, the die had been cast a week earlier during his visit to Cairo. He could not agree to place Jordanian forces under Egyptian command only to withdraw that authorisation if Cairo sent orders with which his own commanders disagreed. The same calculation seems to have applied to one of the more puzzling incidents of the first morning of the war, a message from the Israeli government to Hussein relayed by General Odd Bull, the chief of staff of the UN Truce Supervision Organisation in Jerusalem. In it, the Israelis warned Hussein to stay out of the fighting; in exchange, they would not attack Jordan.[60] Hussein's reason for ignoring the message was the same as that which he gave for accepting Cairo's battle plans. He later stated: 'I did receive the message but it was too late in any event. I had already handed over command of the army to the unified Arab command.'[61] What calculations led the Israeli government to send the message remain unclear. It may have been intended to give Hussein an honourable way out of the crisis,[62] or to cover the Israeli international position should a particularly destructive battle in and around Jerusalem ensue, or it may simply have been intended to delay the outbreak of fighting on the eastern front while the Israelis dealt with the Egyptians to the south.

In any event, it is clear that, in what Hussein saw as a response to the Israeli attack on the Egyptians, Jordanian forces took the initiative in escalating the engagement in Jerusalem. The use of Jordanian artillery against what Hussein subsequently insisted were military targets in West Jerusalem,[63] which began late in the morning, was the cue for the Israeli forces to go on the offensive. In a series of actions during the afternoon, they steadily cleared Jordanian forces from their positions in and around the city. Dayan also authorised further limited offensive operations in the West Bank aimed at preventing the encirclement of the Israeli forces fighting in Jerusalem.[64] By the end of the first day's fighting the Israelis had captured southern Jerusalem and were in a commanding position to roll up the remaining Jordanian positions the following day.

Further insight into Hussein's state of mind at this point is provided by a telephone exchange that took place with Nasser during the early hours of 6 June. Rumours had begun to circulate the previous day, partly fuelled by Nasser himself, that Egypt had been the victim of a Suez-style surprise attack from the British and Americans. Hussein lent further sustenance to the claim by alleging that Jordanian radar had picked up the arrival of sixteen planes at the Israeli airfield of Ramat David from two carriers stationed offshore.[65] Although there was no conclusive evidence to back this up, it was a comforting device to help rationalise the scale of the emerging defeat. Hussein's disillusionment with the Anglo-American response to the May crisis has already been noted. When he failed to get a positive response from Washington to his requests for help in arranging a de facto ceasefire during the night of 5–6 June,[66] he went further, and, in a conversation with Nasser which was monitored by Israeli intelligence, lent his own name to what would become known in London and Washington as the 'Big Lie'. 'Will we say that the U.S. and Britain [are attacking] or just the United States?' Nasser asked. 'United States and England,' Hussein replied, and the two men agreed to issue coordinated statements to this effect.[67]

During daylight hours on 6 June, the Jordanian forces on the West Bank were subjected to relentless air attack. Although a Jordanian contingent held on within the walls of the Old City of Jerusalem, it was clear to Hussein that a ceasefire was essential to preserve what was left of his armed forces. Not wanting to break ranks with the United Arab Command, however, the King refused to move openly without Nasser's agreement. It was not until 11.15 that night that a message finally arrived from Nasser acknowledging the destruction of his own forces and the need to 'evacuate the West Bank of the Jordan tonight, and hope that the Security Council will order a ceasefire'.[68] The final act in the military débâcle was played out the following morning. Resisting calls from Britain and the United States for an immediate ceasefire,[69] Israeli forces moved in to occupy the Old City of Jerusalem.

With defeat on the West Bank complete, Hussein, who by this stage was close to physical and nervous exhaustion, tried to rally his remaining forces for the defence of the East Bank, while repeating his call for a ceasefire. Although the King seems to have feared that the Israelis might cross on to the East Bank,[70] the Israelis stopped their advance once they had completed their roll-up of the remaining Jordanian forces, and took up defensive formations at the River Jordan. By midday on 8 June the struggle on the Jordanian front had come to an end.[71] Its price was the total loss of the West Bank. Reflecting on the outcome of the war, Hussein was bitter about the effects of Arab coordination on Jordan's war effort:

If our men had known from the beginning that they could not expect support from either Egypt, Syria or Iraq our strategy would have been different and Jerusalem would have been ours today. For during those first few days of this rapid war we placed Arab interest above our own. This is how I understood solidarity. Unfortunately no one else adhered to the same principle.[72]

There is no doubt that Jordan had suffered the hardest blow of any Arab country as a result of the war. Its air force had been annihilated and 80 per cent of its armoured forces destroyed. Seven hundred soldiers had been killed, together with six thousand wounded or missing. The loss of the West Bank, which had accounted for 35 to 40 per cent of Jordan's Gross National Product, also had a devastating impact on the Jordanian economy. A quarter of Jordan's cultivatable land was now gone, together with nearly half of its industry. Finally, the influx of 300,000 refugees into the East Bank added significantly to Jordan's social and political problems. Despite the help of UNRWA, feeding, housing and employing these new refugees would be a burden on Jordan for the foreseeable future.[73]

Hussein's decision to join Nasser in waging war against Israel in 1967 was the greatest calamity of his reign. Although by the time of his 30 May trip to Cairo, the King had little alternative other than to seek Arab allies, the dynamics of the Arab Cold War and Hussein's inability to find a way to resolve the Palestinian question within his kingdom provide the main explanations for his isolation during the May crisis. Perhaps, if Hussein and the Tall government had taken a less pro-active stance in inter-Arab politics earlier in the decade, he might have had more room for manoeuvre in 1967. The price of Nasser's acceptance might have been much lower had the level of animosity between the two men not been so high. If he had not had to accept Egyptian command, Hussein would have retained much more of the freedom of manoeuvre that he so evidently craved after the event. But to reflect on these errors after the war was fruitless. With the end of fighting on the ground, Hussein was left to try to rebuild the East Bank, and to seek the return of the West Bank occupied by Israel through post-war peace negotiations.

CHAPTER 7

LOST IN A SANDSTORM

HUSSEIN AND THE PEACE PROCESS, 1967–8

For King Hussein, the disaster of the June war was complete. Haunted by his decision to commit Jordan to battle, the King's physical and emotional condition in the wake of the conflict was fragile.[1] The loss of Jerusalem, the decimation of the Jordanian armed forces, the plight of the refugees and the general economic dislocation within the East Bank all affected him badly. Not only that, but he felt betrayed by all sides. It was not just that his Arab allies had let him down; a degree of unreliability from that quarter was only to be expected in the light of his pre-war relations with Cairo and Damascus. More significantly, Hussein felt that his friends in the West had failed him too: he believed that London and Washington could have done much more to defuse the May crisis and that they had connived in the Israeli attack. One expression of this sentiment was the King's initial willingness to believe the canard spread by Nasser that the Egyptian air force had been the victim of an Anglo-American surprise attack. In the immediate aftermath of the war, Hussein called in the CIA station chief Jack O'Connell to show him unsophisticated but troubling radar images of aircraft apparently attacking from the sea. It was only after American specialists arrived to decipher the signature of the aircraft concerned, and to explain the Israeli mode of attack, that the King's concerns were quelled.[2] By the end of June, he admitted on American television that there was 'no evidence whatsoever' that the British and Americans had been involved in the attack, blaming the misunderstanding on 'some radar sightings of aircraft that were appearing from the sea'.[3]

Hussein's renunciation of the 'Big Lie' was an essential first step in salvaging his relationship with Washington. For all his sustained criticism of the Johnson administration's handling of the Middle East crisis, the King believed that the US was the only power that could persuade Israel to make territorial concessions. Hussein saw himself as personally responsible for the loss of the West Bank, and in exchange for recovering it in full he was prepared to pay the price of full and open peace with Israel. His initial bargaining position was thus simple: there should be a return to the 4 June 1967 lines in exchange for peace. He was prepared to be flexible in countenancing reciprocal territorial rectifications with Israel at points where the 1949 armistice agreements had left behind anomalies, but he would not agree to any settlement which left Israel in possession of substantial tracts of Arab land conquered in the June war, especially in and around Jerusalem.[4]

Even if he managed to secure these favourable terms, Hussein's pursuit of peace with Israel was still a huge personal gamble. With Arab public opinion bitter and hostile, the only way in which Hussein could have survived if it became public would be with Nasser's backing and the cover provided by a United Nations Security Council resolution. Gaining both, and exploring possible Israeli peace terms, were Hussein's main diplomatic preoccupations in the aftermath of the war. If the risks were so great, though, why did Hussein pursue the covert peace process? No doubt part of his motivation was defensive: he was well aware that Jordan would remain on the front line as long as the Arab–Israeli conflict rumbled on. But the June war had also reinforced his conviction that a comprehensive political solution to the conflict was essential: war would solve nothing.

Trying to reconstruct Hussein's contacts with Israeli leaders during this period is like piecing together an incomplete jigsaw puzzle. As we have seen, before the 1967 war Hussein had already formed a web of contacts which included the official Israeli Foreign Ministry channel via Dr Herbert, through which he had met Yaacov Herzog and Golda Meir, and exchanged letters on matters of mutual concern. But there were also apparently unofficial channels. How his pre-war meeting with Abba Eban on the Riviera was arranged is unclear. Similarly it is not known who passed on the letter which he received on the morning of the raid on Samu, 13 November 1966. To make the puzzle even more complex, as we will see, after the 1967 war, further channels surfaced. It is reasonable to assume that at least one of them, via the CIA's James Jesus Angleton, may already have existed before the June war. According to Efraim Halevy, who later became Hussein's Mossad contact, Angleton had first met Hussein in the early 1950s, when he had arranged a course in physical protection for the then young and vulnerable King. Angleton was well placed thereafter to facilitate an introduction for Hussein to Moshe Dayan, a man he knew well and for whom he had the highest personal regard. Above all, though, Angleton was a man who could be trusted to keep a secret.[5] In more general terms the CIA, with its well-established channels to Hussein personally, was uniquely placed to facilitate clandestine contacts.

Piecing together this puzzle, then, requires us to use a combination of a fragmentary and often cryptic documentary record,[6] together with oral testimony from surviving participants who in some cases must remain anonymous. Of all the participants, there is only one man who could have known the full picture: Hussein himself. Despite his willingness to discuss the covert peace process in later life, there were inevitably parts of it about which he still kept silent. One final point should also be made here: this is a historical detective story with a purpose. With the Palestinian–Israeli conflict still unresolved four decades later, and the fate of the West Bank and Jerusalem lying at its heart, the question of whether opportunities were missed to negotiate a solution to their status in the aftermath of the 1967 war is of much more than academic interest.

In what would prove to be an ironic choice, the codename the Johnson administration now chose for Hussein's covert search for peace was 'Sandstorm'.[7] The name proved appropriate, for over the course of the next eighteen months there unfolded a secret diplomatic process in which the participants found themselves groping forward blindly, without ever arriving at a solution.

Hussein's initial contact with an Israeli representative after the war took place by his own account during the first week of July 1967, when he was on his way back to Jordan after a visit to the emergency UN General Assembly meeting in New York. He later told Jack O'Connell that this contact had taken place through a 'channel' in Europe, warning him that 'very few people in the Israeli Govt knew of this channel and therefore we should hold this information very tightly'. Via this channel, the Israelis urged him to open up a 'direct secret dialogue'. Hussein had replied that he would be prepared to do so 'if and when such action appeared [that] it might lead to an acceptable agreement'.[8]

Hussein was probably referring here to the meeting he had in London on 2 July with Yaacov Herzog, who was by now director-general of Prime Minister Levi Eshkol's office. As before, the meeting was brokered via Dr Herbert and took place at his surgery. According to Herzog's account, during it he emphasised that the King must tell him formally that he was willing to open peace negotiations before they could discuss any details of a possible settlement. Herzog recorded that the King did not press him to outline the Israeli position on the future of the West Bank at this point, instead asking for a little more time to develop his views on the subject.[9] Assuming Hussein was referring to the same meeting in his conversation with Jack O'Connell, there are significant differences between the two parties' accounts; Hussein himself claimed that he expressed willingness to enter into formal peace negotiations provided he knew in advance that all of the substantive issues, including the status of the occupied territories, would be open for serious discussion.

The King was well aware of the dangers he faced in pursuing this approach. Even British Prime Minister Harold Wilson, a strong supporter of Israel, and Foreign Secretary George Brown, who met the King the day after his encounter with Herzog, expressed anxiety at the possible effect on his position of negotiating a separate peace at this stage. Brown was even more explicit in his warnings, arguing that 'the King had shown himself by his recent behaviour to be one of the bravest men alive; but he believed that the King could not afford, without serious risk to himself, to take any position in regard to Israel which put him too far ahead of his Arab colleagues in other countries'.[10] For his part, though, Hussein ruled nothing out:

> As regards a separate peace, his first objective was an Arab Summit Conference, to try to concert an agreed Arab strategy and a common line on what their objectives should be – including acceptance of a peace settlement. If this failed, then he might indeed have to 'go it alone' – including some kind of separate settlement with Israel.[11]

A subsequent exchange of letters with George Brown which can be found in Hussein's private files suggests that Brown himself was one of the channels via which Hussein communicated with the Israelis.[12] In a letter he sent to Hussein after visiting Israel in January 1970, Brown wrote cryptically, 'I think I should let you know that I am *still* being used as a post-box',[13] and went on to suggest a private meeting with Hussein to discuss a covert message he had received from an Israeli leader. It is unclear when Brown began to play this role, which on the surface seems an unlikely one. His public image was pro-Arab, with Israeli Prime Minister Levi Eshkol later calling him an 'enemy of Israel', while Golda Meir labelled him a 'Judas' after he publicly advocated Israeli withdrawal from the occupied territories following the 1967 war.[14] On the other hand, 'Judas' was an interesting choice of label. Behind the scenes, Brown adopted a more pro-Israeli stance and, like other leading members of the British Labour Party, had friends within the Israeli Labour movement.[15] During the 1950s he had been introduced, by the pro-Zionist Labour leader Hugh Gaitskell, to key Israelis including Yigal Allon and Moshe Dayan. Gaitskell evidently saw these introductions as an antidote to Brown's extensive network of friends in the Arab world, to whom he had been introduced in the 1950s by the Lebanese businessman Emile Bustani.[16] Brown's relationship with Hussein himself, whom he had met through Bustani, had been reinforced when, in the wake of the 14 July 1958 revolution in Iraq, he broke with his shadow cabinet colleagues and refused to vote against the Conservative government's decision to send troops to Jordan to support the King. Brown subsequently explained that his action 'had been influenced by . . . personal knowledge of many of the personalities who had been killed in recent happenings in Iraq'.[17]

If Brown was one intermediary, according to a later cryptic memo written by CIA Director Richard Helms, yet another covert channel was also opened at this point. Through it a secret meeting between Hussein and an Israeli leader was planned to take place in Switzerland during July. However, the meeting 'was cancelled at a late moment . . . when the U.S. terminated an emergency communications channel between the two parties that had been established during hostilities and used by both parties after the war in making arrangements for a clandestine Switzerland meeting'.[18] Helms's memo was deliberately obtuse.[19] The impersonal sounding 'emergency communications channel' he referred to was provided by the CIA's James Angleton and its termination was due in part to bureaucratic in-fighting in Washington. What had transpired via this channel before it was terminated was remarkable to say the least. Israeli Defence Minister Moshe Dayan, who in public was to take the toughest of stances regarding the need to hold on to Israel's wartime gains, had privately contacted Angleton, who oversaw all dealings with Israel within the Agency, telling him that he was greatly concerned that General Ariel Sharon, among others, wanted formally to annex the West Bank; if this was not prevented, any future resolution of the Arab–Israeli conflict would be impossible. Hence, Dayan proposed that a meeting with Hussein should be arranged as soon as possible to initiate a covert peace process which might provide a way out of the situation. Angleton was a more than willing intermediary in arranging the meeting which was scheduled to take place in Geneva. According to a recently declassified CIA history, he was also deeply concerned about the prospect of an endless cycle of conflict in the Middle East, and advocated a 'dramatic move to break through this destructive pattern'.[20] Dayan's initiative in his opinion was just such a move. It also reflected the Israeli Defence Minister's character; like Hussein he was a political loner by nature, attracted by the excitement of independent initiatives and unwilling to subordinate himself to a broader government line.

Unfortunately, through a remarkable example of bureaucratic myopia, this opportunity for peace was allowed to slip away. Helms's memo deliberately obfuscated the main reason for the last-minute cancellation of the meeting, which was that the State Department at the highest level had got wind of what was afoot and vetoed it, claiming that Hussein was in too weak a position to enter such a dialogue at this stage. Although Israeli Prime Minister Levi Eshkol was plainly unenthusiastic about this CIA channel,[21] it is likely that inter-agency rivalry over what the State Department saw as a CIA initiative in its own territory was a deciding factor in the veto. According to the authors of the CIA history: 'in the embittered views of both Angleton and [CIA

Middle East chief] James Critchfield, an opportunity of possibly historic proportions had been allowed to slip away'.[22]

Angleton and Critchfield were not the only ones embittered by the collapse of this initiative. Dayan himself withdrew into what might be termed a temporary sulk, rejecting repeated requests to participate in the broader Israeli delegations which met with Hussein during 1968. And Prime Minister Eshkol, who had got wind of his independent approach after the June war, refused to allow him to meet Hussein alone.[23]

While these immediate post-war initiatives were unfolding, Hussein's next port of call in July after his return from Europe was Cairo. Hussein's relationship with the Egyptian president now came to form one of the essential props for his post-war diplomacy. Nasser too had learnt lessons from the conflict, not the least of which was that division had been one of the main causes of the Arab defeat. Despite his rapid rearmament, Nasser was realistic about the prospects of regaining lost Arab territory by force. Although he remained reluctant to enter into any negotiating process with Israel, Nasser agreed, during a summit in Cairo during the second week of July, to give his backing to Hussein's covert diplomacy, with two provisos: there should be no direct negotiations with Israel and no peace treaty; the King should instead work through the US to see what terms could be secured from Israel.[24] Nasser's support for Hussein's negotiating position, and their much-improved personal relationship, may well have been the result of the unheeded warnings which the King had delivered to him before the Israeli attack on 5 June. Nasser recognised that Hussein had behaved honourably before and during the war and that he was now in his debt. But Nasser also recognised the weakness of his own position as the man who bore the main responsibility for the Arab defeat: it was less risky for him to back Hussein's covert search for peace than to engage directly in the process himself.

After his return to Amman, Hussein put out his first formal peace feeler via the Americans on 13 July 1967,[25] stating in a conversation with US Ambassador Burns that he was now prepared to make a unilateral settlement with Israel.[26] The King, whom Burns described as being on a 'razor's edge' due to loss of sleep and exhaustion, said 'he had been responsible for bringing Jordan to its present state and he had a solemn obligation to Jordan to do his utmost to repair the damage that had been done'. Somewhat dramatically, Hussein professed himself to be willing to go anywhere in the world to conclude a settlement, a statement which Burns took as a hint that Hussein would be prepared to meet face to face with Israeli leaders. If a diplomatic settlement could not be achieved, the King warned, Jordan would have to join the other Arab states in preparing for another war, in which case he would feel bound to abdicate since it went against his beliefs. Recognising the danger posed to the King's domestic position should knowledge of his approach leak

out, Burns noted in his report to Washington that he had asked Jack
O'Connell to get in touch with him after their meeting to 'persuade him to
pursue a course of the utmost discretion and caution at this time'. Burns also
noted that the King had made the same approach to the British ambassador,
asking the British government to ascertain what terms the Israelis might be
willing to offer. Burns had agreed with his British counterpart that their
respective approaches would have to be carefully coordinated due to the
sensitivity of the operation.

Hussein's approach was immediately relayed on by Secretary of State Dean
Rusk to Israeli Foreign Minister Abba Eban.[27] Rusk argued that it
represented:

> a major act of courage on the part of King Hussein and offers the first
> important breakthrough toward peace in the current period following
> active hostilities. It is an opportunity in our judgment that must not be
> lost, offering as it does a chance to embark on a course in the Arab
> world which could lead to an acceptance of Israel by its neighbors and
> to steps which could well change the whole course of history in the
> Middle East.

Unfortunately from Hussein's point of view, the time was not ripe for such
revolutionary change. The Israeli reception for his initiative was cautious and
defensive. Apart from anything else, following the war they had little trust in
Hussein. Abba Eban subsequently told George Brown that:

> the Israelis' current disillusionment with Hussein derived partly from
> the too high hopes they had had of him before the summer. No one in
> Israel had wanted a war with Jordan but when Hussein threw in his lot
> with Nasser on 30 May the Israelis had been shocked. It was also an
> important psychological factor that the Israelis had suffered more
> casualties on the Jordan front than elsewhere.[28]

Even more importantly, there was no agreement within Israel as to whether
the country should be prepared to return West Bank territory to Jordan in
exchange for a peace agreement.[29] As the victorious power Israel was in no
hurry to sacrifice its territorial gains, and it is not surprising that the Israeli
preference at this juncture was to prevaricate and to limit any discussion to
generalities.

In conversation with US Ambassador Walworth Barbour the day after
receipt of Hussein's message, Prime Minister Levi Eshkol expressed
'considerable agitation' over what he perceived to be US backing for
Hussein's suggested peace terms. Eshkol was particularly disturbed by Rusk's

suggestion that Israel should respond with concessions over Jerusalem. The Israeli position was that the city must remain undivided and under Israeli sovereignty, as reflected in the cabinet's 18 June decision to annex East Jerusalem. Eshkol argued that he had 'stretched his cabinet like a rubber band on a number of problems which had been considered in [the] last few weeks but that rubber band would break immediately if he authorized Eban to make any statements that measures to reunify [the] city [were] only "interim" and subject [to] further debate'.[30] Although Foreign Minister Eban was somewhat more positive in discussion with Rusk the following day, he too dwelt on the Jerusalem issue, on the danger that 'Nasser may only want to get Hussein into trouble by not interposing [any] objection', and on the vagueness of Hussein's proposals.[31] In further discussion with National Security Advisor Walt Rostow, Eban also acknowledged the difficulties posed by Israeli domestic politics, conceding that, 'The people of Israel and its leaders were split in this matter.' US officials privately shared the Israeli concern that Nasser might 'booby trap' the US if it became involved too directly as an intermediary. In other words, he might publicly expose Hussein's contacts, presenting them as some kind of American plot to divide the Arabs. Moreover, partly for domestic political reasons, the Johnson administration was reluctant to put Israel under any significant pressure to compromise. This, together with concern that the gap between the Israeli and Jordanian positions over Jerusalem might be too wide to bridge at this juncture, dictated a cautious approach in Washington.[32]

The administration's formal response to Hussein's initiative reflected this caution. While telling the King that the Israelis wanted direct negotiations, Ambassador Burns was instructed to warn Hussein that the administration did not know whether there was any flexibility in the Israeli position on Jerusalem or whether an overall settlement was feasible at this point. 'Hussein should keep very much in mind', Burns was instructed to warn, 'that we do not trust Nasser, Boumediene [the Algerian president] and Atassi [the Syrian leader], who are aware of the King's intentions. We doubt if the King should trust them either.'[33] In the event, Hussein informed Burns on 28 July that 'taking all considerations into account, he had concluded his own position was too weak to try to undertake bilateral negotiations with the Israelis at this moment'.[34] He agreed that Nasser might still decide to pull the rug out from under him, and that the Jerusalem problem looked insoluble at this point; he would need to know that the Israelis were prepared to be flexible over Jerusalem before entering into negotiations. He also pointed to the weakness of his internal security situation. The King was evidently disappointed with the level of US support for his position over the return of the West Bank to Jordan, which he claimed had been on a 'descending curve' ever since his visit to Washington a month earlier.

With bilateral negotiations ruled out for the time being, the focus of diplomatic activity during the ensuing months shifted back to the possibility of multilateral action through the UN. At the end of August, the Arab leaders held a summit in Khartoum, following which they issued the famous 'three noes of Khartoum': no to recognition of Israel, no to negotiations with Israel and no to peace with Israel. In private, however, the discussions between the Arab leaders were very different. Richard Helms forwarded an upbeat report of the conference to President Johnson, based on a discussion between Jack O'Connell and Hussein.[35] In it, Hussein claimed that 'the conference was a complete victory for the moderates, exceeding all expectations . . . The road for peace definitely was open.' Moreover, Nasser was 'a changed man, even within the past six weeks'. Hussein's improved personal relationship with Nasser had really proved its worth, with the Egyptian leader playing the key role in supporting him. As for the radicals, Syria was 'isolated and blamed as most responsible for provoking hostilities . . . "Fatah" activity [was] unanimously condemned, past and future.' As for the PLO leader Shuqayri, he was 'unanimously repudiated and all his statements expunged from the record'. Hussein concluded that 'if Israel gives evidence she really wants peace, the mood of the Arabs is to meet her half way, but there is much skepticism (based on recent Israeli behaviour) whether she would not prefer [the] occupied territories to peace'. Essentially, Hussein saw the Khartoum communiqué, designed for the consumption of Arab public opinion, as no real reflection of the underlying position of his fellow heads of state.

Despite what he regarded as the success of Khartoum, Hussein's frustration rose during October and November 1967. The diplomatic dance at the UN in New York seemed to move in circles rather than towards the kind of 'land for peace' resolution which Hussein believed he needed to provide cover for subsequent negotiations with Israel. In a personal letter to President Johnson on 7 October, the King expressed his deep sense of grievance at what he considered to be the US's increasingly pro-Israeli stance. 'Double standards seem to exist in the treatment of people in our area,' he observed bitterly.[36] 'The United States would appear at present to have chosen to forsake her friendships and friends amongst us Arabs and to mainly concern herself with attempting to enforce on them what Israel might or might not wish.' To the extent that the US emphasised the need to secure a resolution to which all parties, including Israel, could subscribe, the King was right. The principle of securing territorial integrity for all now took second place to the pragmatic desire to secure Israeli acquiescence. This meant that it was essential from Washington's point of view to fudge as far as possible the question of Israeli withdrawal, ensuring that any draft resolution did not lay down a timetable which required withdrawal before a peace agreement could be concluded. Thus, by October, the US supported the use of the ambiguous phrase 'withdrawal of armed forces from occupied territories', rather than the direct call on Israel to 'withdraw all its forces from all territories occupied by it as a result of the recent conflict', which had been incorporated in a Latin American draft resolution supported by the US in July.

In his 7 October letter to Johnson, Hussein noted in passing that one of the factors limiting his engagement in the peace-making process was his state of health. The stresses of the June war, followed by a period of several months in which Hussein, by his own admission, slept no more than a couple of hours each night, exacerbated his already existing health problems, which included asthma and a chronic jaw condition. His general state of health can hardly have been helped by an incident which took place during August 1967, and which must rank as one of the most bizarre of the many 'assassination' attempts mounted against him. Over the weekend of 4–5 August, the King was accompanied to his holiday home in Aqaba by a party of guests which included Linda Christian, a lady described by US Ambassador Burns as 'a faded minor movie actress with [a] Mexican passport and [an] unsavoury reputation in Hollywood circles, who was at one time married to the late Tyrone Power'. That night the King was taken violently ill and 'came near to expiring'. The cause was 'a heavy dose of LSD' with which Linda Christian had laced his drink. Apparently the actress had also put LSD in his food, but, luckily for Hussein, he did not eat it. Linda Christian, who admitted to her actions, was subsequently held by the Jordanian police on suspicion that 'she was trying either to poison the King or at the very least, to loosen his tongue'.[37] Neither explanation seems particularly likely, both because LSD would hardly be any poisoner's first choice of drug, and because the actress evidently laced the food and drink of other guests at the party, as well as the King's. Her real motive thus remains unclear. In any event, one should not under-estimate the seriousness of the incident. One American official who was summoned to help Hussein in its aftermath was shocked to find him apparently locked in a catatonic state; only when two American doctors who specialised in treating drug overdoses were summoned from Athens to treat him did the threat to his life recede.

Arriving in New York for a further round of negotiations at the UN during early November, Hussein's health was once more put under severe strain. As a briefing paper prepared for his visit by the State Department acknowledged, 'Hussein comes here worried, and with a sense of grievance.'[38] He was convinced that the US was 'upping the ante in New York and backing off, as the Israeli position has become harder'. Despite this, the State Department assessment was that Hussein remained 'valuable' and 'possibly indispensable' to the US because of the role he could play in starting and sustaining negotiations for a general political settlement between Israel and its neighbours. The paper acknowledged candidly:

the Israeli evaluation of Hussein does not jibe with ours. Israeli representatives have gone out of their way to give us the impression Israel is writing Hussein down, and maybe off. Their motive may be to make sure Hussein comes to the bargaining table alone; or their view may reflect a diminished interest in negotiations. Manifestly they do not want continued close US/Jordan relations. We shall have to have this out with the Israelis.

The tortuous progress of negotiations during November once more proved to be a major trial for the King. The British ambassador to the UN, Lord Caradon, commented after a meeting with Hussein on 11 November that he had 'found [the] King greatly disturbed', and Caradon feared that for the first time the entire situation might be too much for him.[39] In the event, the logjam in New York was broken by a compromise resolution advanced by the British delegation, led by Caradon, during the second week of November. Caradon was backed by Foreign Secretary George Brown who, through his network of personal contacts on both sides, worked in the background to achieve agreement on a resolution which was acceptable to Israel, Egypt and Jordan. The British were ultimately much better placed to broker a compromise than the American delegation, which was handicapped by the leadership of Ambassador Arthur Goldberg, who was viewed with deep suspicion by the Arab parties. Even the temporary drafting of Jack O'Connell to act as middleman to the Arab delegations could not fully overcome their suspicions.[40]

The final, British-sponsored United Nations Security Council Resolution 242, adopted unanimously on 22 November, coupled the principles of withdrawal from occupied territories with the negotiation of peace in a fashion which was sufficiently ambiguous, or at least open to interpretation, to satisfy most of the parties. The resolution, which was supposed to provide the compass with which all of the belligerents could navigate their way through the sandstorm of conflict to reach peace, proved to be an uncertain guide; in effect, the direction to be followed depended on who was holding the compass. For Hussein, its interpretation was straightforward: full Israeli withdrawal in exchange for full peace. Hence its references to the 'inadmissibility of the acquisition of territory by war' and its call for the 'withdrawal of Israeli armed forces from territories occupied in the recent conflict'.[41] For Israeli leaders, meanwhile, the text left the extent and timing of Israeli withdrawal open for future discussion within the context of full peace in the region: hence the omission in the resolution of the definite article before the word 'territories', and the coupling of withdrawal with the requirement for the 'termination of all claims or states of belligerency'. This carefully constructed ambiguity, a masterpiece of British obfuscation, was to be the source of the durability of the resolution but also of its incorrigibility.

In the wake of his visit to New York, Hussein pursued the prospect of peace through two channels. The public channel was led by a special representative chosen by the secretary-general of the UN to carry forward the peace-making process under the terms of the resolution. Gunnar Jarring, a Swedish diplomat with limited experience of the Middle East, was appointed to this demanding role, and his mission proceeded tortuously, with little sign of progress, through the early months of 1968. The private channel consisted of the King's continuing direct meetings with Israeli officials, and of messages conveyed between the two sides, often by means of intermediaries, such as the West Bank notable Hikmat al-Masri.[42] Face-to-face contact between the King and Israeli representatives, which had apparently been in abeyance since his meeting with Yaacov Herzog on 2 July, was resumed when the two men met in London on 19 and 20 November 1967. In the interim, the former British Minister of Aviation Julian Amery, among others, had made attempts to facilitate contact between the two sides, only to see them deflected or rebuffed by the Israeli government. As Michael Bar-Zohar has astutely observed, the reasons for this included 'personal interests, rivalry among Israeli leaders, the selfish impulses of government ministers, as well as bureaucratic pettiness and continual external pressure'.[43] For all of these reasons, prevarication remained the favoured Israeli strategy. If Hussein could at least be kept in play in the peace process, the Americans would be discouraged from launching any peace initiative of their own, which might require much greater concessions from the Israeli government. Yaacov Herzog himself now adopted an inflexible position, believing that the Israeli gains in the 1967 war were providential, and that they should not be sacrificed through negotiations with Hussein. Rather, such negotiations should be pursued merely to gain time and to reassure the United States that Israel was actively seeking peace. Thus, when he finally met once again with Hussein on 19 November, this time in the company of Julian Amery, Herzog's brief reflected his own personal inclinations. He was authorised to listen, but not to offer any formal peace proposals. So, when the King asked directly whether Israel would consider the return of the West Bank through peace negotiations, Herzog replied that he was not authorised to say anything about this topic. When the King went further and mentioned the issue of Jerusalem, Herzog did not even respond at all. Instead, he seized on Hussein's request for clarification of the Israeli position regarding the West Bank, to propose further secret meetings which would explore the possibilities for direct bilateral negotiations: effectively talks about talks.[44]

Hussein was accompanied to most of these subsequent meetings by his close friend and trusted confidant Zeid Rifai, who took the notes of the discussions for the Jordanian side.[45] What transpired proved a disappointment to both men. 'At no point during the 1967–8 meetings were the Israelis prepared to countenance complete withdrawal,' Rifai recollects.[46] Moreover, all of the ideas put forward during the course of the meetings, including the famous Allon Plan,[47] which envisaged a partial Israeli withdrawal from the West Bank and the return of the major population centres to Jordanian administration, were, as Rifai puts it, no more than 'trial balloons . . . ideas aired by individuals on an informal basis' which had no official standing and which had not been cleared with the Israeli cabinet. Had the King shown an interest in any of these schemes they would have had to be referred back to the full Israeli cabinet for further discussion.[48] Rifai's characterisation of the Israeli approach to negotiations matches that of other sources. In private, Eban described the meetings as the 'Jordanian flirtation'.[49] Eban himself met Hussein in London in May 1968,[50] but he had not been authorised by the cabinet to put forward formal peace proposals, only to sound out the King as to what his reaction would be to 'a peace treaty in which the indivisibility of Jerusalem as Israel's capital would be preserved' and 'some territorial changes' in Israel's favour would be made along the River Jordan. Eban, unlike Rifai, judged the King's initial response to these ideas to be one of interest.[51]

Hussein was understandably impatient at the Israeli failure to present a formal peace plan. It was partly to assuage this impatience that, during a further meeting on 27 September 1968, attended by Yigal Allon, Abba Eban and Yaacov Herzog on the Israeli side and the King and Zeid Rifai on the Jordanian side, the Israelis presented the Allon Plan as the basis for a political settlement.[52] Although Eban later claimed that Hussein's response was 'when do we negotiate', implying that he was interested enough not to reject the Allon Plan out of hand, most other sources, including Zeid Rifai, argue that the King showed no enthusiasm for the plan.[53] He 'took it as a bargaining position and reacted stiffly'.[54] This is supported by the King's formal written response to the proposal (presented by Rifai to Herzog in a subsequent meeting), which declared that the principle underlying the Allon Plan was unacceptable; the only way forward was to exchange territory on the basis of reciprocity.[55]

Despite the apparently 'official' nature of the September 1968 presentation, Rifai judged rightly that it was no more than an initiative from a group of individuals within the Israeli leadership.[56] Although the Allon Plan became the informal basis for the Israeli negotiating position in relation to the West Bank, the Israeli cabinet itself had not formally adopted the Plan when it had been discussed on 30 July 1967. The difficulty lay in the opposition of four members of the cabinet, including the mercurial Moshe Dayan, to the territorial compromise on the West Bank which it envisaged.[57] There thus remained an ambiguity in the presentation of the plan to Hussein, and its unofficial status made the episode look even more like a potential diplomatic ambush. Zeid Rifai later likened the Israeli negotiating style at the time to Israel's military tactics: probe for an area of weakness by infiltrating in small groups, and then strike quickly to take advantage of the opening discovered.[58] The King was determined not to be duped in this way.

Moreover, it is important not to read the warmth of the Hussein–Rabin relationship of the 1990s back into these exchanges between Hussein and Israeli leaders in 1968. Negotiating with Hussein over the West Bank was not the Israeli leadership's first choice. Allon himself had originally formulated his plan based on the idea of working with a local Palestinian leadership on the West Bank, and it was only when no such leadership emerged willing to cooperate with Israel that Allon turned to the Jordanian option. In private, Israeli leaders spoke of Hussein dismissively, with Allon arguing, 'Today, Hussein is King of Jordan, and I don't know who will be in his place tomorrow . . . I would be happier if it was Shuqayri sitting in Amman today and not Hussein.'[59]

These private sentiments fit in with the observations of informed Western commentators, who believed that the Israelis saw Hussein's role in the 1967 war as an 'act of treachery . . . for which they will never forgive him'.[60] In its aftermath, and with the upsurge of Palestinian guerrilla activity in 1968, Hussein came (in the opinion of the British Foreign Office) to be regarded by the Israeli government as 'expendable'.[61] Not only that, but should peace efforts fail:

Many Israelis, perhaps the majority, will tend to come round to the view now held by a minority of 'hawks', that it would be likely to make life easier, not more difficult for Israel if Hussein were replaced by an extremist Arab nationalist regime . . . The Western nations would be 'off Israel's back', and she would need to take less account of world reactions in determining the type and scale of future anti-terrorist operations conducted inside Jordan.[62]

Thus, while on a personal basis both Rifai and the King formed positive impressions of the individuals with whom they dealt on the Israeli side during the post-1967 meetings, Rifai's overall conclusion that 'their hands were tied' seems an astute judgement of the situation.[63] Since the King's Israeli interlocutors were not mandated to discuss full withdrawal, and since the King would not compromise on this principle, the talks made no progress.[64]

In December 1968, Hussein told US Ambassador Harrison Symmes that in spite of all the contacts, there had been no discernible change in the Israeli position, recording, 'In effect, the Israelis keep giving us their general position and we keep giving them ours.'[65] Symmes's own judgement was that 'the

Israeli "clarification process" with Jordan . . . has been singularly unrealistic, unspecific, and unproductive'.[66] This view was shared by CIA Director Richard Helms, who added his own weight to the decision to end the negotiating process for the time being. From early 1969 onwards, instead of continuing the futile dialogue over a possible peace settlement, Israeli and Jordanian representatives focused on 'functional' cooperation over matters of mutual concern, especially the tracking of Palestinian guerrilla activities. The Jordanians pursued this dialogue in the hope that if contacts could at least be maintained, they might serve to ward off any Israeli threat to Jordan and mitigate the scale of Israeli reprisal raids.

The failure to reach agreement during 1967–8, and particularly what Hussein later came to regard as the fiasco of UN Resolution 242, left a lasting mark on the King. Although the resolution remained the foundation for peace-making efforts in the region across the ensuing decades, Hussein felt bitterly that a deception had been practised on him in securing his agreement to it. The purpose of Resolution 242, as he had understood it, was to provide a 'land for peace' formula which was sufficiently general to allow all parties, including Israel, to subscribe to it. Thereafter, the resolution would provide the umbrella under which more detailed negotiations about the mechanics of Israeli withdrawal in exchange for peace would take place. But this was not what happened. Instead, the general terms of the resolution were taken by the Israelis as allowing negotiations over the extent of any withdrawal which they might make, and its timing, which could be only after there had been a broader normalisation of relations with the Arab states.

For Hussein, then, Resolution 242 became a reference point of another kind: he would never again allow himself to be drawn into negotiations on the basis of general and ambiguous statements of principle. In 1978, during the bilateral Egyptian–Israeli negotiations which led to the Camp David accords, he said in private that he was 'deeply afraid of a re-run of the resolution 242 saga'.[67] In other words, another ambiguous declaration of peace principles might give the Israeli government endless scope for prevarication rather than actual withdrawal. In an interview at the same time, he made it clear that his experiences during 1967–8 had left a lasting mark on him: 'I think they [the Israelis] are really impossible in terms of their attitude,' he lamented. 'I believe the choice was always there and I said that at the United Nations in '67: territory or peace. Unfortunately, it appears territory much more than peace at this stage.'[68]

CHAPTER 8

'SEVEN QUESTIONS OF ISRAEL'

THE SEPTEMBER 1970 CRISIS

In parallel with the faltering peace process during 1967–8, Hussein struggled to rebuild his kingdom and his shattered armed forces. He also seriously considered a major reorientation of his international position. In view of the pro-Israeli bias demonstrated by the United States during and after the 1967 conflict, should he turn instead to Moscow for the military equipment his armed forces needed? Of course, the ramifications of such a decision would be wide-ranging. Hussein would in effect be changing camps in the Arab world and jettisoning one of the main ideological pillars of his rule: the notion that Hashemite Arab nationalism was incompatible with communism.

Despite the fact that the King had committed himself in his autobiography, *Uneasy Lies the Head*, written at the beginning of the 1960s, to alignment with the West against what he portrayed as the atheistic and un-Islamic threat of communism,[1] his decision not to turn to the Soviet Union early in 1968 was a close-run thing. In one particularly tense meeting on 8 January 1968, the US Ambassador Harrison Symmes and the CIA station chief Jack O'Connell only just managed to deflect the King from his decision to accept a high-level Soviet military delegation. According to Symmes, the King had evidently come to the conclusion that the US had no intention of supplying more than token arms to Jordan and 'we were only stringing him along'. Symmes reported that Hussein had developed a deep sense of guilt about the June war and now felt cornered; only if Washington offered him a way out in the form of an acceptable arms package would he feel able to hold to his pro-Western course.[2] CIA Director Richard Helms underlined the danger that Hussein would turn East in a memo to President Johnson, noting that the Soviets had handled the King, and played on his fears, with 'considerable skill'.[3] British observers too described Hussein as tired and despairing of his past and future efforts in relying on Western backers. With regard to the armed forces, the King lamented, 'I have run out of promises. I have made so many which I have not kept and I can make no more.' For Hussein, a vital turning point had been reached: 'if the Americans did not now supply the arms he required he would be forced unwillingly to turn to the Russians'.[4]

In the event, in February 1968 US Defense Secretary Robert McNamara offered Jordanian Chief of Staff Amer Khammash an arms package just sufficient to prevent the King turning to the Soviets. Still, the King's relations with the Johnson administration remained strained. Johnson himself attempted to pour oil on troubled waters via a personal message to Hussein confirming the US arms offer on 11 February, which he termed 'a strong reaffirmation of our support'. The undercurrent of tension in the King's relations with the US remained evident in his 2 March reply to the president. Hussein repeated that he had become 'extremely disheartened by what appears to be [the] lack of genuine interest in a just and durable peace by the Israelis'. In particular, he highlighted Israel's reprisal attacks against the East Bank, noting that 'her ridiculous and totally incomprehensible excuse for doing all this is that I am not fulfilling my so-called duty of ensuring the safety and security of her forces which occupy a good portion of my country'.[5]

Hussein's letter was an attempt to highlight to the president the intractability of the position in which he found himself. In the wake of the 1967 war the Palestinian guerrilla groups, known as the *fedayeen*, had escalated their campaign of attacks against Israel. Their underlying position was clear: the war had shown that the Arab states were powerless against Israel, so the Palestinian struggle could only be advanced through Palestinian self-reliance and guerrilla warfare. With its large Palestinian population and long border with Israel, it was no surprise that Jordan became the front line in this struggle. The problem this presented for Hussein was straightforward: he was caught in the middle. The more Israel punished Jordan for incursions on the part of Palestinian guerrilla groups the weaker the foundations of his rule became. And the weaker those foundations became, the weaker was his ability to rein in the fedayeen and so forestall the next round of Israeli reprisals. This anarchic spiral resulted in an inexorable decline in Hussein's authority between June 1967 and September 1970. As Hussein put it in private conversation with former US Treasury Secretary Robert Anderson: 'how can I devote my army to the service of the Israelis in protecting them from hostile Arab attacks by a passionate and displaced people when the inevitable consequence of a failure on my part would be retaliation by the Israelis which would contribute even further to my own downfall?'[6]

In terms of Israel's reprisal policy, as Abba Eban has eloquently argued, the years between 1967 and 1973 were the era of Moshe Dayan. Publicly Dayan expounded a thesis of unrelenting struggle between the Arabs and Israel, requiring that Arab incursions should be ruthlessly punished. As he put it in an interview with *Haaretz* on 19 January 1968, 'if we are stubborn on all fronts, both against Hussein and Nasser, pressure will not decrease – I said that there is no way to avert a struggle – but it will be easier for us to hold our present positions, at least from the viewpoint of Arab psychology'.[7] As far as Dayan himself was concerned this policy was logical. 'If Israel had not reacted so sharply to sabotage operations undertaken from Jordanian territory, the government of Jordan would have reached a *modus vivendi* with the terrorists,' he later wrote.[8] But Dayan's public stance stood in remarkable contrast to his private willingness after the June war to pursue dialogue with Hussein as a means to resolve the conflict. In essence the conundrum of Dayan's role during this period can be resolved in the following way: while there was war he was the harshest of Israel's leaders; if peace could be negotiated, he might be prepared to be the most generous. This was certainly how Hussein saw matters. Given that Dayan dominated Israel's defence strategy in this period, and that the conflict persisted, it is little wonder that, despite Hussein's best efforts, there was no diminution in the pressure exerted on the Israeli jaw of the military nutcracker in which he now found himself.

On the other side of the Palestinian–Israeli divide, the increasing assertiveness of the fedayeen groups based in Jordan meant that Hussein could also entertain little hope that the pressure on the other jaw of the nutcracker would be eased. A large part of Hussein's problem in negotiating with the fedayeen was the fractured and turbulent relations between the different Palestinian guerrilla groups themselves. While Fatah, led by Yasser Arafat, was prepared to countenance some degree of accommodation with the Hashemite regime, other groups, including the Popular Front for the Liberation of Palestine (PFLP), led by George Habash, and the Popular Democratic Front for the Liberation of Palestine (PDFLP), a PFLP splinter organisation formed in 1969 and led by Nayif Hawatmeh, were not. As Marxist-inspired groups, the PFLP and PDFLP were ideologically committed to the overthrow of the Hashemite monarchy as the first step on the road to the liberation of Palestine.

Less than three weeks after Hussein's 2 March letter to Johnson came the battle of Karameh, a key turning point for both the fedayeen and the Hashemite regime. The outline of what took place is relatively clear. In retaliation for Fatah's bombing of a bus carrying schoolchildren through the Negev Desert, Israel resolved to carry out a major raid on a refugee camp which also acted as Arafat's headquarters, at the village of Karameh in the Jordan Valley. The King attempted to forestall Israeli retaliation, through a top-secret message passed by the US State Department to the Israeli government, in which he expressed deep regret at the bombing and asked for any information which the Israelis might have which would help in tracking down the perpetrators. But to no avail.[9] The Israeli forces attacked on 21 March, meeting stiff resistance from the Jordanian army and Arafat's fedayeen. Jordanian artillery succeeded in knocking out a number of Israeli tanks and other vehicles while the fedayeen themselves, although largely ineffective against the Israeli armour, stood their ground and fought bravely. When the Israelis eventually withdrew at the end of the day after partially demolishing the village, they left behind a number of wrecked tanks which were later dragged back to Amman and paraded as symbols of victory.[10]

More important than the details of the battle was the propaganda victory it handed to Arafat and his fedayeen. Karameh became a symbol of Palestinian national pride and spurred the development of the Palestinian national movement.[11] Most observers argued that the attack had seriously backfired from the Israeli perspective. Not only had the image of Israeli military invincibility fostered by the 1967 war been dented, but the operation had succeeded in making the fedayeen into popular heroes in Jordan.[12] Gideon Rafael, then the Israeli permanent representative at the United Nations, later acknowledged that 'the operation gave an enormous uplift to Yasser Arafat's Fatah organisation and irrevocably implanted the Palestine problem on to the international agenda'.[13] At the fourth Palestine National Council (PNC), convened in Cairo four months later, seats were allocated for the first time to the fedayeen groups, while at the fifth PNC in February 1969 Yasser Arafat was elected chairman of the executive committee of the PLO. As Adnan Abu Odeh writes, 'to Fatah, al-Karama was a vindication of its strategy, a source of Palestinian pride, and a solid credential for soliciting Palestinian and Arab support'.[14]

For the Jordanian army, though, Karameh was their victory. The army deeply resented what they regarded as the fedayeen's appropriation of their own glory. If the battle of Karameh changed the international dimensions of the Palestinian question, it also marked the beginning of the parting of the ways between the army and the guerrillas. Hazem Nusseibeh, who was then minister of reconstruction and economic development, and who had been closely involved in the King's attempts to woo West Bank Palestinian opinion in the years leading up to the 1967 war, later argued that he felt this had been the PLO's biggest mistake in Jordan. Had it been prepared to acknowledge the role of the army at Karameh, the clash of September 1970 might never have taken place. Karameh, he argued, 'could have been the foundation of closer relations rather than of division'.[15]

In the event, the PLO's strategy left the King with an awkward dilemma. On the one hand, he could not ignore the huge groundswell of popular opinion which gathered behind the fedayeen cause. On the other, he could not afford to alienate the army, whose loyalty was the one sure guarantor of his own position. The King's solution to the problem was to try to straddle the emerging divide between the fedayeen and the army and, if possible, close it. So he strove to promote coordination with the fedayeen on the domestic and inter-Arab levels, while at the same time stressing the unity of Palestinians and Jordanians in the struggle with Israel. Only through the steadfastness of all, he argued, could victory be achieved.[16] This was the sentiment underlying Hussein's oft-quoted comment made two days after the battle of Karameh: 'I think we have come to the point now where we are all fedayeen.'[17] In private, the King even established personal contact with both the Fatah and PFLP leadership in an effort to 'influence them to cooperate with him in seeking [a] political settlement by suspending their present guerrilla activities'. According to Hussein, 'no one else even in his own government knew of these private contacts', which produced some limited dividends in terms of local ceasefire arrangements.[18] Unfortunately, though, Hussein noted that a potentially serious complicating factor in his efforts to control the fedayeen was the presence in the Jordan Valley of 'Israeli agents posing as terrorists'. He did not rule out the possibility that these Israeli agents might be involved in creating incidents.

During the rest of 1968 and 1969, the King continued to pursue the dwindling chance of unity and coordination with the fedayeen. Both conciliation and repression held out serious risks for Hussein, with Chief of Staff Amer Khammash privately likening him to 'the man who swallowed a razor blade – upward and downward movements are equally dangerous'.[19] By the spring of 1969 Hussein was, by his own admission, approaching a state of 'hopelessness' about his position, as the failure of his strategy became evident.[20] Under the weight of Israeli attacks the fedayeen were driven back from their forward bases in the Jordan Valley to the main East Bank towns and cities, particularly Amman. Here they increasingly acted as a state within a state, ignoring the authority of the local police and frequently antagonising the army. By the beginning of 1970 it was clear that the King's pleas for steadfastness and unity had been useless. On 10 February 1970 the government instead attempted to enforce law and order, issuing a list of twelve rules by which the fedayeen had to abide.[21] The results were huge demonstrations in the streets of Amman, and a hasty move by the King to instruct the government to suspend its decision.

In the wake of the crisis, the King received a private letter from his old friend, the former British Foreign Secretary George Brown, who had recently returned from a January 1970 visit to Israel. The public face of the visit had been controversial, with Brown having a flaming row with the former director of military intelligence, Chaim Herzog, at a dinner party held at Abba Eban's house on the last day of his trip. In heated exchanges, Brown had gone so far as to accuse the Israelis of having murdered King Abdullah. Earlier in his visit, though, Brown had also had a private meeting with Deputy Prime Minister Yigal Allon, who invited him to dine alone at his kibbutz. According to Brown's coded account, Allon told him that Prime Minister Golda Meir had specifically asked him, as the leader of the moderates within the Israeli government, to pass on a message that she desperately wanted a peace settlement.[22] The plot now thickened further. After Brown's return to England, Allon paid a visit to London at the end of February during which he made a completely unpublicised late-night visit to Brown's flat. Here, he repeated a proposition that he had made during the earlier dinner conversation at his kibbutz: Brown was 'authorized, if I could find some way of getting negotiations started through my personal associations with President Nasser and King Hussein, to go ahead and do so'.[23] This was the background to the letter Brown wrote to Hussein on 5 March, part of which has been quoted already:

> I watched, as you might imagine, with the deepest of interest your confrontation a week or so ago. I think I should let you know that I am still being used as a post-box. Letters these days are bad. Too many people read them. I wonder whether I could meet you, or anybody you would nominate, in any place to have a talk about the situation as I now think it to be.[24]

'I would certainly like to meet with you to discuss in detail the situation as it stands now,' Hussein wrote in reply.[25] In the event, though, Brown's initiative came to nothing: a second letter which he despatched to Nasser met with a much more cautious response. Nevertheless, it is worth noting the words with which Brown concluded his discussion of the episode in his memoirs, words which have a broader applicability to the covert role he had played between at least 1967 and 1970. 'I recall very clearly what Golda Meir said to me: "we need an intermediary. It can be anybody. It could be you . . ."'[26]

Brown's letter to Hussein gives the impression that the latter was still in a state of gloom. 'I do not think, if I may suggest it, that there is any point in spreading pessimism around,' Brown wrote. 'Anyway, I am for helping. I reckon there is still a chance and you and I together can handle the rest of the world!'[27] A further insight into Hussein's state of mind and the pressures he was under at this stage is provided by two other pieces of evidence. The first is an impassioned, handwritten letter he penned to US President Richard Nixon at the end of December 1969. Hussein had initially entertained high hopes that Nixon might be more helpful than his predecessor, Johnson, in whom Hussein had effectively lost faith by the time he left office. This much is clear from the exuberant personal letter of congratulations the King wrote to the new president after his election victory.[28] By the end of 1969, though,

Hussein was thoroughly disillusioned by Nixon's stance. In a desperate attempt to reach the president personally, and make him understand the nature of his predicament, Hussein told Nixon that Israel was waging a 'one sided war' on Jordan.[29] Examining the pretexts for the Israeli reprisals against Jordan, the King argued, 'I have honestly found them devoid of reason. It is perfectly clear that Jordan cannot accept to be held responsible for the security of Israel in the Arab areas it occupies . . . I must admit Sir to an inability to find a shred of evidence of Israel's genuine interest in an honourable final peace in our area'. Finally, in apocalyptic terms, Hussein warned, 'if my people are destined to die then we will do it well having had the satisfaction of doing all in our power to achieve peace which appears to be denied us and possibly even the world as a result'.

The second piece of evidence about Hussein's state of mind at this juncture comes from a private meeting which took place between him and the former covert US Middle East emissary Robert Anderson on 8 April 1970. Although Anderson found Hussein calm in his demeanour, he noted that the King was obviously under great emotional strain. Hussein explained that, earlier the same morning, Jordanian forces had been required to use their artillery to drive out Israeli troops who had occupied Jordanian territory near the Dead Sea.

The King was concerned not only about Israeli intentions. He also stated emphatically that he did not trust the Iraqi troops who had been stationed in Jordan, notionally for the Kingdom's defence, since the 1967 war. They were poorly trained, unstable, and ruled through fear. In an impassioned plea the King told Anderson:

> I am completely at bay, surrounded by enemies. On the West Bank I have the Israelis; to the north I have the Syrians whose Baathist leadership is opposed to my regime; and in my own country I have Iraqi troops who are not loyal to me and large elements of the resistance movement who do not wish to be subject to any authority.[30]

Hussein confided to Anderson that 'he was growing more desperate each day and saw no hope for the future, although he was a traditional optimist'.

As if to underline these points, a planned visit to Amman by US Assistant Secretary of State Joe Sisco in April 1970 was cancelled at short notice in the face of street demonstrations mounted by the fedayeen and their supporters. The King took the State Department's decision as a personal insult which implied that even his closest friends in the West did not believe that his writ ran in Amman. Hussein's ire fell in particular on the US Ambassador Harrison Symmes, whom he blamed for taking an insufficiently robust line on the Sisco visit.[31] This was only the last of a succession of incidents which had witnessed the gradual erosion of the King's confidence in Symmes.[32] The King now officially requested the ambassador's removal, an act that said much for the strained nature of his relations with the United States. As Symmes himself had earlier reported, Hussein was becoming more than ever resentful of the US's close relationship with Israel, believing that US arms supplies and support indirectly encouraged Israeli aggression against Jordan.[33]

In addition to the strain it caused to US–Jordanian relations, the Sisco affair led the regimes in Damascus and Baghdad to reconsider the durability of Hussein's rule. A senior Iraqi delegation went so far as to contact Arafat during a visit to Amman in May 1970, promising support should he mount a coup to overthrow the Hashemite regime.[34] The intentions of Iraqi forces in Jordan remained an awkward imponderable for the King and his advisers. In the wake of a PFLP assassination attempt against Hussein on 1 September 1970, the Iraqis issued an ultimatum to the effect that his forces should stop firing on the fedayeen or the Iraqi Eastern Command would take action. Hussein took this very seriously, going so far as to call for a joint four-power statement from the American, British, French and Soviet governments condemning the Iraqi threat of intervention.[35]

The potential Iraqi and Syrian threats showed that Hussein could not neglect the broader Arab context in the search for a way out of his dilemma. President Nasser showed some understanding of the King's domestic predicament, recognising that it was impossible to run a state in which lawless armed factions would not submit to his authority.[36] Unfortunately for Hussein, Nasser's sympathy for his position did not translate into support for harsh measures against the fedayeen. The main reason for this was the Egyptian leader's desire to retain influence over the PLO, a strategy which he tried to further after the 1967 war by bolstering Arafat's Fatah movement within the organisation. Thus, although the King's improved relations with Nasser gave him some diplomatic room for manoeuvre, they did not help him resolve his domestic political problem.

But probably the most important question in Hussein's mind by the summer of 1970 concerned the intentions of the fedayeen themselves. To be sure, his calls for unity and coordination had fallen on barren ground, but was this because the fedayeen were committed to the destruction of his regime, or simply because they had a different view of the right strategy to be adopted in the struggle with Israel? There were obviously differences within the Palestinian movement, with the Fatah faction taking a more moderate line than the PFLP and PDFLP. Nevertheless, Hussein's disillusionment with Arafat as a negotiating partner forms a crucial part of the explanation of his decision to opt for the use of military force in September 1970.

Indeed, one of the puzzles of the events of 1970 is why the final showdown between Hussein and the fedayeen took so long to come, particularly since there was to all intents and purposes a dry run for the crisis earlier in the summer. On 9 June, an attempt was made on Hussein's life when his motorcade was ambushed by the PFLP. Although the King escaped unscathed the incident caused an explosion in tensions between the army and the fedayeen. In an effort to avoid a major confrontation, Hussein decided to accept the resignations of two tough anti-fedayeen figures, the Commander in Chief of the Army, Sharif Nasser, and Third Division Commander Sharif Zeid bin Shaker. Taking over supreme command of the country's armed forces himself, he appointed a man more sympathetic to the fedayeen, Major-General Mashur Haditha al-Jazy, to command the army. The appointment of Mashur Haditha was a risky move since, according to CIA sources, he had been the ringleader of a putative army plot to overthrow Hussein seven years earlier in March 1963, a plot about which the King had been informed at the time.[37]

Although the King's move brought about a short-term reduction in tensions, with the PFLP releasing a group of fifty-eight foreign nationals whom they had briefly held hostage in the al-Urdun and Philadelphia hotels, Hussein's handling of the crisis further weakened his position. In the final resort, the army was the only true guarantor of his regime and his removal of Sharif Nasser and Zeid bin Shaker had significantly undermined his hold over it. Hussein later acknowledged, 'I almost lost control. The people in the armed forces began to lose confidence in me . . . At that point, some captain in the army might actually have been able to rally the rest behind him.'[38]

In the event it was a series of spectacular terrorist acts on the part of the PFLP that finally forced the King's hand. By the end of August the fedayeen movement in Jordan had reached a crossroads. The success of the US in brokering a ceasefire in the Egyptian–Israeli war of attrition at the end of July 1970 seemed to bring Nasser and Hussein closer together in their common pursuit of a political settlement with Israel.[39] In an emergency session of the Palestine National Council in Amman at the end of the month, there were calls from the more radical groups for the overthrow of the Hashemite monarchy. Although these were not endorsed by Fatah, the position of the moderates was undercut by dramatic action on the part of the PFLP. On 1 September they sprung a carefully planned ambush on Hussein, who was making his way to the airport to meet his daughter Princess Alia. Trapped in a hail of bullets, the King barely escaped with his life. Without the special training in close escort techniques which his bodyguard had received from the British SAS he might not have survived at all.

Then, on 6 September, the PFLP took their campaign a dramatic step further. They hijacked three airliners, two of which were flown to Dawson's Field, a remote desert airstrip near Zerqa, which the PFLP had hastily staked out with flares, fires and car headlamps. The third plane, a Pan-American jumbo jet, was flown to Cairo. There, the following day, under the noses of the Egyptian army, it was blown up. The passengers and crew barely escaped with their lives. The PFLP's point was clear: Nasser and Hussein were both impotent traitors. On 9 September, as if to rub it in, a further plane was hijacked and flown to join the others at Dawson's Field. The PFLP were jubilant. They now held nearly 500 hostages, including a large number of American and British nationals. There could be no clearer demonstration of the impotence of the King's position than the way in which the Jordanian security forces had to stand idly by while the PFLP practised air piracy and hostage-taking in Jordanian jurisdiction.

The hostage saga provided one of the subplots of the September showdown. Although the PFLP released all of the women and children on 12 September before staging the spectacular destruction of the hijacked aircraft, they held on to fifty-six of the male hostages, including the British and the American-Israeli dual nationals. In exchange for the latter, they demanded the release of an unspecified number of Palestinians held in Israeli jails. This caused friction between London and Washington, with the British more prepared to be flexible in trying to satisfy PFLP demands, while the US administration took a hard line.[40] Despite these tensions, the exchange of information between London and Washington during the crisis was frequent and extensive. Due to the isolation of the US embassy and communications difficulties, the new US ambassador in Amman, Dean Brown, requested that the British ambassador be designated the joint collector of information on the ground in Amman, a request which was approved by the State Department.[41]

In respect of communications, the British role during the crisis was an important one. The only secure communication link to the outside world to which King Hussein had access at his Hummar Palace had earlier been installed by the MI6 man in Amman, Bill Speares.[42] The link took the form of a radio which connected Hussein at Hummar to Speares, whose codename was 'Mary', at the British embassy in Amman. Speares, who had gained the confidence of King Hussein, and who also had a good working relationship with his CIA counterpart Jack O'Connell, played an important, if hitherto unsung, role during the crisis.

The hijackings had helped Hussein make up his mind, and he now contemplated taking decisive action against the fedayeen. As mentioned in the Introduction, he initially chose 16 September for the move,[43] then postponed it until the following day after a warning delivered by his sister-in-law Princess Firyal from her fortune-teller in London.[44] Apart from the supernatural, the King was also concerned about Syrian and Israeli plans, not to mention the movements of the Iraqi troops in Jordan. A contingency paper prepared for President Nixon by National Security Advisor Henry Kissinger omitted any reference to a Syrian threat, raising only the possibilities of a struggle between the Jordanian army and the fedayeen alone, or between the army and the fedayeen backed by Iraqi forces.[45] Although Kissinger mentions consideration of the Syrian threat in his memoirs,[46] at the time American and British officials, partly acting on Israeli intelligence estimates, gave little credence to Hussein's warnings about the possibility of Syrian intervention.[47] In response to Hussein's question about US intentions in the event of a Syrian attack, Ambassador Dean Brown cabled Washington: 'I am not sure how serious the King's request is. I can't see any real threat from Syria . . . I think the King wants his hand held.'[48]

Even more controversial is the question of the King's view of Israeli intentions in the crisis. Existing accounts, especially Kissinger's memoirs, imply that the King saw Israel as a possible counterweight to deter intervention on the part of other Arab states, particularly Iraq. Kissinger argues that the King had directly requested US views of likely Israeli intentions in the face of Iraqi intervention in early August and again in early September.[49] In a contemporary contingency paper, Kissinger had speculated that the King might already have 'clandestinely reached a tacit understanding with the Israelis that if the Iraqis intervene Israel will attack'.[50]

Nevertheless, there is evidence to support another interpretation: that the King saw Israel as a threat. His concern was that Israel might seize the opportunity presented by an internal struggle between the army and the fedayeen, or by external Arab intervention, to complete some unfinished business from the 1967 war. This might involve the seizure of the so-called 'Jordanian Golan' (the area in the north-west of the country around Umm Qais), and the foothills of the Jordan Valley overlooking Israeli settlements in the Beit Shean area.[51] Certainly, any visitor to the area cannot fail to be struck by the commanding position occupied by the 'Jordanian Golan', which constitutes a strategic location second only in importance to the Syrian Golan Heights themselves.

In the same paper in which he had speculated about clandestine dealings between the King and the Israelis, Kissinger also noted that if the King was compelled to back down in the crisis and accept a weak civilian government which would do the PLO's bidding, the 'chances that Israel would at some point feel compelled to seize more territory in Jordan would increase sharply'. Moreover, if the King appeared about to fall, the Israelis might well 'intervene on their own or at least seize the heights from which the fedayeen have been shelling Israeli settlements'.[52] In the days running up to 17 September the King's concerns focused on Israeli reconnaissance activity in the Jordan Valley. Zeid Rifai, then chief of the Royal Court, warned US Ambassador Dean Brown on 15 September that Israeli scouting expeditions were escalating, 'using maps which implied to [the] Jordanians that [the] exercise was a possible prelude to military invasion of this area'. Rifai urged the US government to take whatever measures were necessary to ensure that the Israelis took no military action.[53]

The final prelude to the launching of military action came on 15 September with King Hussein's decision to form a new military cabinet under the leadership of Brigadier Muhammad Daud. Although Daud himself was a moderate West Banker, and although known hardliners such as Wasfi Tall were not included in the cabinet, the King's move clearly signalled his intention to opt for a military solution to the crisis. According to Adnan Abu Odeh, who was appointed minister of information in the new cabinet, Tall still played an important coordinating role behind the scenes.[54] The response from the fedayeen was unequivocal. Chairman Arafat refused to conduct any negotiations with the new military cabinet. The most he could offer Hussein at this stage, he claimed, was twenty-four hours to leave the country.[55] He was candid in admitting to a parliamentary delegation that he could not fully control the actions of the guerrilla groups. This was the final straw from Hussein's point of view.

17 September dawned to the sound of tank and artillery fire. The Jordanian army had finally begun its assault on fedayeen positions. At least one American official in Amman had no doubt who would win. Shortly before the barrage began he recollected a visit to his house by one of the hard men of Hussein's army, Sharif Nasser. 'You see those three black dogs in your front yard,' Sharif Nasser told him. 'If you painted gold stripes on them, some people might say they were tigers. But underneath, you and I would still know they were dogs.' The message was clear: the fedayeen's bark was worse than their bite.[56]

As the assault began, a host of concerns were pressing on Hussein, who was trying to keep abreast of the situation from his base at Hummar. If he pushed forward with the operation would the army split, dividing into Jordanian and Palestinian factions? If he called off the offensive could he retain the loyalty of the predominantly East Bank officer corps? Would the storm of criticism which his action had evoked in the Arab world translate itself into military intervention on the part of either Iraqi or Syrian forces? What would the Israelis do in this eventuality? And finally, could he rely on the Western powers, principally the United States, for support should the situation deteriorate dramatically? Zeid Rifai, who was with the King at Hummar, conjures up a vivid picture of the uncertainties and chaos of their position, with the King isolated and unable to get accurate information, other than via Bill Speares, as to what was happening on the ground.

By the end of the second day of the operation, Kissinger's assessment of the army's progress, based on reports from the US embassy in Amman and delivered to President Nixon, was couched in gloomy terms. Although the army was proceeding methodically to root out the fedayeen and had the upper hand in the battle in and around Amman, it was meeting stiff resistance. Moreover, elsewhere in the country, particularly in the north, the fedayeen had established a strong position. Indeed, the PLO had gone so far as to announce the creation of a 'liberated area' in and around Jordan's second city of Irbid. At the same time, pressure on Hussein from other Arab states to end the fighting was increasing. In the face of these difficulties, it remained possible that rather than hunkering down for what promised to be a protracted struggle, the King might yet accept some form of compromise with the fedayeen.[57]

If the picture had been gloomy on the afternoon of 18 September, just after midnight that night the situation took a turn for the worse. Units of the Palestine Liberation Army, the Syrian-backed guerrilla group, moved across the northern border into Jordan. The PLA was acting at the behest of the Syrian regime, and their incursion into Jordan may well have been part of the internal struggle for power in Damascus which pitted the more pragmatic Hafez Asad, the air force commander, against the more radical Salah al-Jadid, deputy secretary of the Baath Party. The PLA was followed on the morning of 20 September by a Syrian armoured brigade whose tanks were hastily repainted with PLA markings. This was precisely the development which the King had feared, and about which he had warned both the British and American governments. Although the Syrian forces were engaged by the small Jordanian army contingent in the area, the outnumbered Jordanians were soon compelled to fall back. During the early evening of 20 September the King summoned a meeting of his military cabinet, whose members were driven to Hummar in armoured cars. According to Adnan Abu Odeh, who attended the meeting, the King explained that the situation in the north was grave, and that 'Jordan might need the help of foreign friends' in order to repel the Syrian invasion. The cabinet granted the King the authorisation he asked for with 'some reluctance'.[58]

Unknown to the cabinet, that morning the King had already been in touch, via the secure radio link, with Bill Speares at the British embassy, calling for 'Israeli or other air intervention or [the] threat thereof'. The King repeated his request at 6.30 p.m.[59] In London, Foreign Secretary Alec Douglas-Home was puzzled by the King's approach, wondering why he had not chosen to make this request directly to the Israelis.[60] The answer is probably because Hussein could easily and securely contact Speares with the special radio set in the attic of his Hummar Palace, and because he wanted Western intermediaries who would act as witnesses to any exchanges with the Israelis. A special cabinet committee meeting was now hastily convened in London, following which Douglas-Home contacted Ambassador Phillips in Amman.[61] After receiving confirmation from Phillips of the King's request for the British government to act as an intermediary, a further meeting was convened in London the same night, at which it was agreed that the King's approach put the British government in a position of 'some difficulty' since London wanted to avoid being dragged further into the crisis. It was decided that because of the US–Israeli special relationship, Washington would have to be consulted over the matter. As to Israeli intentions:

> Doubt was expressed whether the Israelis would go to extreme lengths to ensure the survival of the Hashemite regime; they might consider that Hussein's fall and his replacement by a blatantly pro-Fedayeen successor Government would at least end what they regard as the West's 'schizophrenia' in its present tolerant attitude towards Jordan.[62]

Sir Denis Greenhill, permanent under-secretary at the Foreign Office, reported the King's message to Washington, suggesting, as agreed by the cabinet committee, that the US administration was in a better position to contact the Israelis, particularly since Golda Meir was in Washington at that point.[63]

Just before midnight, Zeid Rifai offered Dean Brown in Amman a clarification of the King's request to the British.[64] When Brown asked Rifai specifically whether the government of Jordan was requesting an air strike of the British, Rifai replied 'not in those exact words'. 'What he thought [the] King had meant when he discussed [the] matter with [the] British Ambassador', Brown added, 'was that [the] Government of Jordan wanted to explore this possibility with [the] UK.' Rifai himself did not request an air strike at this point, although Brown's assessment was that this was what the Jordanians were hoping for if the situation got out of hand. Rifai told him that the King was convinced the Syrians were heading for Amman.

Within a matter of hours, Rifai's relatively soothing words were overtaken by a desperate personal request for aid from the King. At 3 a.m. on 21 September Hussein phoned Brown and asked him to pass the following message to President Nixon:

> Situation deteriorating dangerously following Syrian massive invasion. Northern forces disjointed. Irbid occupied. This having disastrous effect on tired troops in the capital and surroundings . . . I request immediate physical intervention both air and land as per the authorization of government to safeguard sovereignty, territorial integrity and independence of Jordan. Immediate rpt immediate air strikes on invading forces from any quarter plus air cover are imperative. Wish earliest word on length of time it may require your forces to land when requested which might be very soon.[65]

Despite the King's conviction that the Syrians were planning a full-scale invasion, Syrian intentions at this point are in fact difficult to read. As mentioned earlier, the internal political situation in Damascus was fluid, with Hafez Asad and Salah Jadid vying for power. The most commonly accepted interpretation of the Syrian actions in September 1970 is that Jadid, the more radical of the two men, ordered the remaining army division under the control of the Baath Party leadership into Jordan, while Asad, the more pragmatic, withheld the air force from the struggle. The resulting defeat for the Baath Party-controlled army division is said to have cleared the way for Asad's seizure of power in Damascus in mid-November.[66]

However, Washington perceived Syria's intervention quite differently, as a Soviet-backed attempt to unseat the pro-Western regime in Amman.[67] If the US failed to react, Kissinger argued, 'the Middle East crisis would deepen as radicals and their Soviet sponsors seized the initiative'.[68] When the King's request for an air strike was relayed by the British, Kissinger records that it 'reinforced the predisposition in favour of standing aside for an Israeli move'.[69] The US itself did not possess the intelligence or target information to respond rapidly.

After gaining the president's approval, Kissinger called the Israeli Ambassador Yitzhak Rabin at about 10 that evening to pass on the King's plea for help, and to ask that Israel should carry out reconnaissance over northern Jordan. Rabin, who was attending a dinner in honour of Golda Meir in New York, responded that he was 'surprised to hear the United States passing on messages of this kind like some sort of mailman'.[70] He told Kissinger that he would not relay the request to Meir until he knew whether the US administration was recommending that Israel should take action, though in fact as soon as he put down the receiver Rabin called Meir away from the party and told her the news. Meir phoned Israel immediately, speaking with both Acting Prime Minister Yigal Allon – who favoured a strike – and Defence Minister Moshe Dayan, who was more cautious. At 10.35 p.m. Kissinger called Rabin again with the president in the room. Nixon authorised him to say that if the Israeli reconnaissance confirmed a major Syrian invasion the US would 'look favourably upon an Israeli attack'.[71] As Rabin relates the conversation, Kissinger advised Israel to take action 'subject to your own considerations'.[72]

The following morning, 21 September, after carrying out air reconnaissance which confirmed that the Syrians were massing further forces near the Jordanian border, the Israeli government submitted seven 'considerations' – or questions – to the US administration.[73] Most were straightforward, concerning the degree of public support the US would lend to any Israeli action, but there was one crucial question the administration could not answer: 'will the King agree to request our assistance and to undertake to institute methods of communication and coordination between us?'[74] Since the Israelis believed air strikes alone would probably be insufficient to drive the Syrians out,[75] this question was really asking whether the King would be prepared to countenance Israeli ground forces moving on to Jordanian territory. Kissinger argues that this question was put indirectly to the Americans rather than directly to Hussein because the Israelis, like Hussein himself, were suspicious and wanted American witnesses to any deal.[76] In a bid to clarify the position Secretary of State Rogers cabled Dean Brown in Amman.[77] Brown's response was blunt: 'the answer is negative', he cabled. The 'request for air is "from any quarter" but land action [is] requested of [the] US and UK. I have had no intimation in any of my talks with [the] King or Rifai of any thought of Israeli ground action . . . Ground and air activity are two very different things in [the] King's mind.' Brown asked Rogers to caution the Israelis to avoid any 'premature, unilateral movement on [the] ground or in [the] air'.[78]

Within an hour of Brown's cable, the situation had changed again. Zeid Rifai phoned the ambassador to let him know that the Syrians were on the move; they had occupied Irbid and were advancing into the surrounding villages. Rifai told Brown that the King wanted an immediate air strike, adding when Brown pressed him that the King would 'much prefer a coordinated response' (rather than one from Israel alone) and that his first preference was for a US strike. But since the situation was coming to a critical juncture, 'the most important thing is to hit the Syrians now'.[79]

In the meantime the State Department had received a message from Acting Israeli Prime Minister Yigal Allon intended for King Hussein, which was forwarded to Brown in Amman. Rogers's instructions for Brown stressed that he should encourage the King to set up a meeting with the Israelis immediately since this was the best way they could concert together as to how each side could be helpful to the other in present circumstances.[80] Later in the afternoon, Israeli Defence Minister Moshe Dayan sought out the US chargé in Tel Aviv as the two men awaited the arrival of the plane bringing Golda Meir back from New York. Dayan complained that he had warned the US back in April that in the event of a breakdown in Jordan the only power which would be able to bring force to bear would be Israel. The US had failed to respond to his suggestion for joint contingency planning and had 'right down to the last few days . . . constantly urged Israel to refrain from any kind of intervention in Jordan.' 'Now', said Dayan, 'when it is too late, you come to us with [a] proposal for action.'[81]

As the situation on the ground deteriorated during the afternoon of 21 September, the King also issued a formal appeal to the permanent members of the UN Security Council to do all they could to halt Syria's invasion.[82] But there was little chance that the Security Council would be able to take effective action over the matter, hidebound as it was by Cold War rivalries. The same day, Assistant Secretary of State Joe Sisco met Yitzhak Rabin in Washington, so that Sisco could pass on the US government's official view of Israeli intervention against the Syrians, essentially the same response which had been given informally over the phone by Kissinger the previous evening. On the question of King Hussein's assent, Sisco told Rabin: 'if [the] King disagrees, we must take this into account'.[83] In other words, if the US administration felt the situation was serious enough, the King would not be allowed a veto over an Israeli incursion into Jordan.[84] This exchange highlights once again that considerations of prestige and credibility lay at the heart of US policy-making during the crisis: the Soviets' Syrian clients could not be allowed to overthrow the US-backed Jordanian regime, and in the last resort King Hussein's wishes were secondary to what the US decided was in his regime's best interests. In fact, the Soviet Union seems to have had no interest in a superpower clash over Jordan; although Soviet advisers rode with the Syrian tank forces down to the Jordanian border, it is clear that the political direction for the attack came from Damascus and not from Moscow.

With time pressing and communications with Amman and between Ambassador Brown and the King uncertain, at 10.30 the same evening the US administration gave its formal responses to Israel's seven questions to the Israeli Minister in Washington, Shlomo Argov. With no new information on the King's attitude to Israeli intervention, Rogers detailed what was known so far:

> Israel is aware of the informal exchange of messages between Deputy Prime Minister Allon and the King which we conveyed. With respect to ground operations, the only indication we have of the Jordan attitude on this question was a statement of Zeid Rifai to our Ambassador that Israeli QUOTE ground operations are fine in the area so long as they are not here in Jordan. UNQUOTE We are seeking clarification on this question from the King. Israeli air strikes have been requested or approved on several occasions by the King.[85]

In response to Rogers' message to the Israelis, Ambassador Dean Brown cabled his own views, arguing that the situation on the ground in northern Jordan had now started to improve and so the need for an Israeli attack was less imperative. If there were to be a ground offensive, Brown felt uncertain as to how units of the Jordanian army in the area would react – some might decide that the Israelis and not the Syrians constituted the greater threat. Moreover, Brown continued, the consequences of an Israeli invasion would be dangerous and unpredictable; even if the Israeli operation were limited in scope, 'its aftermath would strain [the] King's personal standing with [his] subjects and fellow Arabs. Israel's action would confirm in Arab eyes [the] libel spread by radicals for twenty years that [the] Jordanian Monarchy [is] crypto-Zionist at heart.'[86] Brown stressed that the best possible outcome from the US point of view would be if Hussein could, 'basically on his own . . . make his way to shore'.

Brown was also sceptical about the Israelis' motivations for preferring a strike into Jordan rather than Syria. The Israelis 'may have their own reasons for preferring a Jordan target to a Syrian one', he wrote. The King's desire was to see the Syrians 'so hurt that they will withdraw'. The Israeli desire, on the other hand, 'may be broader: to so smash the Syrians that they won't rise again for a long time. If this is indeed [the] Israeli aim I can see why they are massing for [a] grand attack at Irbid where [the] Syrians are stupidly open to real defeat. If [the] aim, on the other hand, is to give help to Hussein, then either [a] feint or short attack into [the] much easier country north of Tiberias would have [the] same effect without side dangers here.'

Despite his scepticism, Brown followed up on the question of Israeli intervention with Zeid Rifai later in the afternoon, with the aim of pinning down more precisely what the King wanted, a goal in which he was not assisted by the limitations of an open phone line; as Brown put it, the two men had to use 'double talk all the way' to communicate. According to Brown's account, Rifai agreed that the question of Israeli intervention would have to be discussed in a face-to-face meeting with the Israelis, and repeated that if Israeli ground action were to take place this should be 'elsewhere than Jordan'.[87] He reiterated this position several hours later after discussing it with the King.[88]

Meanwhile, the Israeli cabinet was meeting in a five-hour session to consider the same question. The positions of the main players seem to have remained unchanged. A British report of the discussion based on sources close to Prime Minister Meir noted that 'no decision was taken other than to keep options open'. Moshe Dayan among others remained 'reluctant to intervene in present circumstances on the ground that Israel's security was not threatened and that there was no reason why she should risk incurring international odium by intervening on King Hussein's behalf'. The British report also cautioned that 'this may of course be a smokescreen to cover some more positive planning'.[89] The suspicion remained that one of the reasons for the redeployment of Israeli forces to the north was 'to ensure that if Jordan is carved up, Israel gets a slice'.[90]

Other Israeli sources agree that Dayan was reluctant to intervene purely to save Hussein.[91] Indeed, he stated publicly on Israeli television on 23 September: 'We will not mourn if Hussein is replaced by someone willing to make peace with us.'[92] As the British had suspected, Dayan believed that if action were to be taken its goal should be to take and hold a large slice of

Jordanian territory. 'If we go into Irbid,' Dayan argued in the Israeli security forum debate on 21 September, 'it will be difficult for us just to return it.'[93] The divisions within the Israeli leadership were summarised by General Mordechai Gur, the commander responsible for the Syrian–Lebanese front during the crisis:

- One opinion backed the strengthening of Hussein's position and the continuation of his rule. They felt that Israel's bond with the Hashemite Kingdom was better than that with any other Arab country and that the Six Day War was a tactical error on the part of Hussein. It was impermissible to damage the positive relationship between the two countries, and in the future Hussein would be Israel's best peace partner.
- The opposing opinion supported the transformation of Jordan into a Palestinian state. The extremists in this perspective recommended that Israel offer practical assistance, in different ways, to realize the ambitions of the Palestinians in Jordan. Yasser Arafat's declaration of independence in Irbid strengthened the hands of those who held this opinion. They suggested allowing the guerrillas to achieve their aims and to take control over all of Jordan. In this they saw the ideal solution to the issue of the Palestinians.[94]

How the Israelis would have reacted if the Syrians had broken through towards Amman remains unknown, because, during the course of 22 and 23 September, Jordanian air and ground forces succeeded in driving back the Syrian armoured incursion.[95] The only significant role Israel played in this process was an indirect one, in the form of the supply of IDF intelligence information to Hussein about the retreat of Syrian forces via the Bill Speares communication link.[96] At the same time as the Jordanian forces were gaining the upper hand against the Syrians, concerns about the movement of Iraqi forces in Jordan surfaced once again. Communicating via the British and Americans, the King asked that the information he had about Iraqi movements be passed on to the Israelis, perhaps with a view to gathering their own intelligence estimate.[97] To judge by British reports, though, the Israelis seem to have been as puzzled as all of the other players about Iraqi intentions during the crisis.[98] Hussein later speculated that Iraqi intervention had not come about because the regime in Baghdad viewed its own army units with suspicion, fearing that if they acted successfully in support of the fedayeen in Jordan, they might be encouraged to take similar direct action against their own government on their return home.[99]

Although it was not clear to Hussein at the time, with the retreat of Syrian forces on 23 September the crisis had passed its point of maximum danger.

For all the manoeuvring of the Americans and Israelis in the background, the fact remains that the victory on the battlefield was won by Hussein's own troops. Indeed, as if to underline the point, IDF sources were 'very impressed with [the] fighting quality and achievements of [the] Jordan Army', and expressed 'unqualified praise for their conduct of operations against [the] Syrians'.[100] On the morning of 23 September, Hussein also received a personal message from President Nixon, who expressed his admiration for 'what you are doing to preserve Jordan's integrity in the face of both internal and external threats . . . Your courageous stand has impressed the entire free world.'[101] Just as Nixon and Kissinger had misread Syrian reasons for invading, they also misread Syrian reasons for withdrawal, crediting Israel for helping the US to achieve a Cold War victory in what was in fact a local inter-Arab struggle.[102]

Nevertheless, if the tactics used to turn back the Syrians had been successful, those used to clear the fedayeen from Amman were far less effective, and brought down on Hussein's head a great deal of opprobrium in the Arab world. As the fighting in and around Amman continued, Libya cut off financial support and diplomatic relations. Meanwhile, President Numeiry of Sudan strove to broker a ceasefire, meeting the beleaguered Arafat in Amman on 24 September. The following day Arafat broadcast his acceptance of Numeiry's ceasefire terms, and thereafter flew to Cairo where he met with Nasser in preparation for a summit of Arab heads of state, which the Egyptian president called for 27 September.

Hussein's decision to fly to Cairo for the meeting was undoubtedly courageous in view of the extent of his isolation in the Arab world. Whether it was sound politics is another matter. With no allies around the conference table in the Hilton Hotel in Cairo, he was forced to accept an agreement brokered by Nasser whose terms appeared much more favourable to Arafat and the fedayeen. Restrictions were placed on the movements of both the fedayeen and the army in Amman, while the agreement also called for the stabilisation of the military situation along the lines prevailing when the cease-fire had been called. A Truce Supervisory Commission under the leadership of the Tunisian Prime Minister Bahi Ladgham was established to ensure the compliance of both parties with the terms of the agreement. CIA analysts described the Cairo agreement as no more than a stopgap measure.[103]

To some extent this description was accurate, although not in the sense originally envisaged. The day after brokering the deal, Nasser died of a heart attack. Although in his final years the Egyptian president had been more cooperative with Hussein's regime, his role as sponsor of Arafat's Fatah movement within the PLO had given him a strong vested interest during the September crisis, and there is little doubt that his death weakened Arafat's position. At the very least it left a vacuum in leadership in the Arab world, meaning that Hussein was unlikely to have to contend once again with the sort of united opposition he had faced at the Cairo summit.[104]

Concern about the likely course of events in the wake of Nasser's death was clearly signalled in two letters Hussein received at this stage from members of the Soviet collective leadership: one from President Podgorny, and the other from Prime Minister Kosygin. While Kosygin praised Nasser's role in brokering the Cairo agreement, and dwelt on the threat now posed by imperialist, especially US, intervention in Arab affairs, Podgorny adopted a more hectoring tone, warning that the struggle between the Palestine liberation movement and the Jordanian regime must stop since it only served the interests of the imperialists and Israel.[105]

These Soviet rebukes had little effect. The King signalled his determination to restore his authority a month after the Cairo agreement with his decision to reappoint Wasfi Tall as prime minister on 28 October. As a firm believer in law and order, there is little doubt that Tall intended from the outset to crack down on fedayeen activity within the kingdom. However, he approached his task with some skill, protesting publicly that he sought partnership with the mainstream Fatah faction, while warning that there were certain elements within the PLO which did not intend to honour their agreement with the government.[106] Tall moved to exploit the differences within the PLO and by stages over the coming months pressed them out of the town centres and away from major lines of communication. By May 1971, the fedayeen had been driven back to the remote, wooded areas in the north-west of the country around Ajloun and Jerash. On 2 June, Hussein sent a message to Tall praising him for the measures he had taken to 'safeguard the homeland' and warning that 'if there is in our soil today a handful of people who make plotting their profession and treachery their vocation . . . then we wish our opposition to them to be firm, decisive and valiant, allowing no room for hesitation, tolerance or compromise'. In his reply, Tall promised that 'we shall . . . purge the ranks – all the ranks – of those professional criminals who pose as fedayeen'.[107]

On the morning of 13 July 1971 the final onslaught against the fedayeen was launched. Most of the fedayeen in the Jerash–Ajloun area were either captured or killed by the army, while the rest fled to Syria or Israel. Taking full responsibility for the action in a news conference on 19 July, Tall explained that the presence of the fedayeen around Jerash and Ajloun meant that this had become 'an occupied area subject to the harshest conditions of evil and terror', a situation which the government could no longer tolerate.[108] There is some doubt as to whether Tall ordered the final assault himself, or whether the initiative came from within the army high command, but whatever its provenance, there is little doubt that the move won the approval of the King himself and the vast majority of the East Bank political establishment.[109]

Tall was to pay the highest personal price for his actions. During a visit to Cairo to attend a meeting of the Arab Defence Council at the end of November 1971 he was gunned down by members of the 'Black September' organisation, a group established to avenge the crackdown on the fedayeen. Tall's death was a huge personal and political blow to Hussein.[110] Nevertheless, by the autumn of 1971 the King had completely re-established his authority within Jordan, although he remained isolated in the Arab world. How did the King himself view the confrontation with the fedayeen? He frequently described the showdown as a tragedy, an unwanted confrontation between brothers who should have been allied in the struggle against Israel. But perhaps his most telling description of the September crisis came in a conversation with the British ambassador in Amman immediately afterwards. It was, he insisted, 'a cancer operation that had to be performed to save Jordan's life'.[111]

CHAPTER 9

THE OCTOBER WAR

With the final expulsion of the fedayeen from Jordan in the summer of 1971, King Hussein had restored his personal authority, but at the price of badly damaging his relations with the rest of the Arab world. In a half-facetious remark, Crown Prince Hassan described Jordan's foreign policy during this period as one of 'deliberate isolation'; the Jordanian regime had no intention of pleading for its readmission to the Arab fold uninvited or on unacceptable terms.[1] Now that Jordan had emerged from the turmoil which had characterised its internal affairs since the 1967 war, it seems appropriate to step back and examine the King's personal position within the kingdom. This will help to answer the question as to how he had survived the fedayeen challenge. Central to the functioning of the Hashemite regime was Hussein's partnership with his brother Hassan, who, by the early 1970s, had taken on extensive responsibility in the field of economic development and internal affairs. Despite, or perhaps because of, their differences in character and temperament, the two men formed an increasingly effective working partnership. Hussein concentrated on high politics and foreign policy, whilst Hassan, in addition to his economic brief, focused on internal administrative development. Both men kept up a tough working schedule. While this undoubtedly took its toll, especially on Hussein's health, the King still managed in mid-life to maintain what one admiring observer called the 'physique of an Olympic featherweight', largely due to his frequent water-skiing excursions at his holiday home in Aqaba.

Beyond his partnership with Hassan, Hussein was for the most part loyally backed up by other members of the Hashemite family, including his other brother Prince Mohammad. His family thus formed one of the pillars of his rule, the second of which was his close circle of political advisers, which by this stage included his friend Zeid Rifai and his cousin, Sharif Zeid bin Shaker. The loss of Wasfi Tall from this close political circle, although undoubtedly a major personal blow to the King, did little to affect the process of decision-making. While other political advisers came and went over the course of the coming two decades, Zeid Rifai and Zeid bin Shaker remained at the heart of power throughout the period. The only other figure to emerge during the second half of the King's reign who came close to rivalling their personal position and authority was Mudar Badran, a politically supple former intelligence officer who rose to occupy the position of prime minister. In practice during the second half of his reign, the King made most of his important decisions closeted in a lunch room at the Royal Diwan with a small cabal of advisers, which almost always included Zeid Rifai, Zeid bin Shaker, the current prime minister and the head of the Mukhabarat. The cabinet and the ministries of government lay outside this close circle of power, and essentially acted as little more than ciphers – implementers of policies already agreed by the King and his close circle.

If the King stood at the centre of the constellation of power in Jordan, the political gravity of Zeid Rifai and Zeid bin Shaker attracted a host of lesser figures into their respective orbits. Whilst it would be too simple to characterise their personal relationship as one of straightforward political rivalry, there was certainly an element of tension in it. Both men were contemporaries of the King, although they had made their way to the top by rather different routes. Zeid Rifai was the son of the former prime minister and stalwart of the Hashemite regime, Samir Rifai. His education included spells at the American University of Beirut, Columbia and Harvard, where he had been taught by the ambitious young Henry Kissinger. Rifai had occupied a range of posts within the diplomatic service and the Royal Court during the 1950s and 1960s. Often to be found puffing on a Havana cigar, he possessed a sharp wit, the product of his incisive intellect. A consummate political operator, Rifai's grasp of international politics and Jordan's role in them was driven by a hard-headed realism. As his former mentor Henry Kissinger observed, 'of all our Arab interlocutors, Rifai was the least prone to the romanticism that occasionally caused even Sadat to bend reality to the rhythm of some epic poem'.[2]

Zeid bin Shaker, by contrast, had risen through the officer corps of the army. The son of Emir Shaker, who had accompanied Hussein's grandfather Abdullah on his original journey from the Hejaz to Transjordan in the wake of the First World War, bin Shaker was educated at Victoria College, Cairo, and subsequently at Sandhurst. By the mid-1950s, he had become one of the leaders of the Free Officers movement which helped persuade the King to dismiss General Glubb in 1956. Despite his role in securing the general's dismissal, in later life Zeid bin Shaker continued to express abundant personal admiration for Glubb's qualities of leadership.[3] After Glubb's dismissal, his early career was interrupted when he fell under suspicion for his role in the putative plot against the King in April 1957. Soon politically rehabilitated, he rose first to command the 60th Armoured Brigade and subsequently the Third Division of the Jordanian Army during the second half of the 1960s. During the 1970 crisis, he made a name for himself as a tough anti-fedayeen figure, and thereafter he became Chief of Staff of the Jordanian armed forces. Zeid bin Shaker's height and athleticism made him stand out physically from the crowd in Jordan, while socially his charm and intelligence made him an attractive personality. Within the military, his efficiency, authority and ambition quickly attracted followers to his side. Indeed, he possessed something of Hussein's own gift for putting interlocutors at their ease. Most at home in military circles, bin Shaker found himself more and more drawn into civilian politics as the King's reign progressed, but unlike Rifai his power base remained in the army, where he continued to command a large personal following. Both he and Rifai in their own ways exuded abundant personal charm, and were as much at home conversing in English as in Arabic; this made them ideal interlocutors when the King needed to conduct business with the Western powers, particularly the United States. Indeed, they were often to be found together in Jordanian delegations to Washington when, as was more often than not the case, the King needed to discuss military and financial support for Jordan.

If Hussein's close circle of advisers formed the second pillar of his rule, the third and arguably the most important pillar was provided by the army. Although minor stirrings of unrest or plots were periodically detected, including one sponsored by Colonel Gadhafi of Libya in November 1972,[4] the army's loyalty, discipline and morale were the crucial guarantors of Hussein's rule, and arguably the main factor in his survival in September 1970, when its failure to mutiny had surprised at least some of the fedayeen groups. In fact, the overall desertion rate from the army during the September crisis did not exceed one per cent, despite the fact that it was a broad church, encompassing all elements of Jordanian society including the Palestinians.[5] One Western observer who struck up a conversation with the members of a typical tank crew in July of that year noted that it included two Bedouin from the south, a Shishani (an immigrant group originating in the Caucasus) from Azraq, a villager from Irbid and an NCO tank commander from Nablus. The army held a central position in Jordanian society as a whole. In a country where unemployment remained stubbornly high, it was estimated that in the early 1970s one Jordanian soldier provided for an average of eight dependants. Not only that, but the armed forces were treated as an elite within the country, enjoying prestige, pay and the right to bear arms.[6]

Beyond the domestic structures of political power, Hussein was sustained internationally by his alliance with the United States. Although it is easy to characterise this relationship as one of client and patron or, more crudely still, puppet and puppeteer, neither depiction does full justice to its subtleties. The 1970 crisis and Hussein's successful stand against the fedayeen and the Syrian invasion had retrieved the alliance from its post-1967 nadir, but there remained significant tensions with Washington, not least those engendered by the US's special relationship with Israel. In 1969 Hussein had entertained hopes that the Nixon administration might prove more even-handed in its approach to the Arab–Israeli conflict than its predecessor, but by 1972 those hopes had been largely dashed. With US Middle East diplomacy essentially on hold while Nixon conducted his re-election campaign, Hussein became increasingly frustrated at what he saw as a dangerous period of drift in the region.

In an effort to break the deadlock in the regional peace process, and to retrieve domestic political ground lost as a result of his expulsion of the fedayeen, in March 1972 Hussein unveiled his plan for a 'United Arab Kingdom'. The essence of the scheme was straightforward. Hussein proposed that the Israeli-occupied territory on the West Bank should be joined to the East Bank in a quasi-federal structure. There would thus be two regions of the kingdom, Palestine and Jordan, each with its own elected governor and parliament and each with extensive responsibility for the management of its own local affairs. Meanwhile a national parliament, presided over by the King as head of state, would take on overall responsibility for the handling of the economy, defence and foreign affairs. The King would remain commander in chief of the armed forces. Amman would be the capital both of the Jordanian region and of the United Arab Kingdom as a whole, while Arab East Jerusalem would be the capital of the Palestinian region.[7] Hussein also expressed the hope that other territories such as the Gaza Strip would eventually be brought into the Palestinian entity. In private he was even more expansive, musing that 'in the distant future the whole "United Kingdom" might be widened to include other Arabs', an observation described by the British ambassador in Amman as 'shades of the Fertile Crescent and Hashemite rule in Damascus and Baghdad'.[8]

There were two obvious practical problems with the King's plan: how to persuade the Israelis to relinquish control over the occupied territory which would form the Palestinian region, and how to persuade the Palestinians that the United Arab Kingdom could provide a home for their national aspirations. It is possible that the King raised his plan in advance as part of his covert dialogue with certain Israeli leaders, but Prime Minister Golda Meir was evidently not consulted.[9] In a speech to the Knesset on 16 March, Meir described the plan as 'a surprise invention of its authors', and rejected it on the grounds that it unilaterally disposed of issues affecting Israel's borders and security while making no mention of a willingness to make peace, which, Meir argued, made it both pretentious and sterile.[10] The Israeli government particularly objected to the provision for Arab East Jerusalem to act as the capital of the Palestinian region of the United Arab Kingdom. While describing the plan as a whole as 'fanciful', Israeli Foreign Minister Abba Eban reserved special criticism for the Jerusalem clause, which he called 'provocative'.[11]

As if to reinforce their intention to scupper the plan, the Israeli government also connived in the leaking to *Time* magazine of information about covert contacts between Israel and Jordan in the same week as the plan was announced.[12] The leak, which suggested that the two countries had agreed to a long-term deal for a demilitarised West Bank and an Israeli-controlled Jerusalem, was a clear fabrication, but it was well framed to fuel charges that Hussein was colluding with Israel to sell out the Palestinian cause. In fact, the King's aims were different. He wanted to bolster support for his regime amongst East Bankers and, if possible, woo West Bank Palestinian opinion away from the PLO by showing that federation with Jordan offered the best route to end the occupation. The United Arab Kingdom plan thus formed another move in his rivalry with the PLO, and its promulgation at this point was a measure of Hussein's increased confidence after his defeat of the fedayeen challenge. From Hussein's point of view the plan showed that Jordan had emerged from its internal troubles and could now return to its broader mission in the Arab world. The assumption underlying the plan, and probably the key reason for its rejection by Israel, was the restoration of Jordanian sovereignty over all of the Palestinian territory occupied in June 1967, including East Jerusalem.

Hussein did meet Golda Meir secretly later in March to discuss the scheme's implications, but neither this meeting nor a subsequent covert encounter on 29 June 1972, to which Meir also invited Defence Minister Moshe Dayan, brought about any breakthrough in the deadlocked peace process. Hussein stuck to his position that he could not be responsible for the surrender of Arab land, and rejected a suggestion from Dayan that, even in the absence of a peace treaty, Israel and Jordan might still arrive at a secret mutual security agreement.[13]

PLO opposition to Hussein's plan, meanwhile, was also only to be expected. Indeed, comments which Yasser Arafat made subsequently to his biographer suggest that, for the PLO, the Israeli rejection of the scheme came as a welcome relief. In Arafat's view, had the King been able to secure a deal with Israel for the return of the West Bank on terms such as these 'the PLO would have been finished'.[14] The PLO's criticism of the plan was complemented by an almost wholly negative reception from the other Arab states.

Here Hussein may have underestimated the depth of his isolation in the wake of the September crisis. He tried to prepare the ground by writing personally to several Arab leaders. The letter which he sent to Syrian President Hafez Asad, leader of a country with which Jordan had no formal diplomatic relations at this point, is typical of the arguments he advanced in favour of his plan. Hussein claimed that his scheme was the result of consultations with representatives and opinion leaders of the Palestinian people in the occupied territories. Any isolated Palestinian state created there, he argued, would be 'emaciated', with the Israelis able to destroy it at any moment: hence the need for a federation with Jordan. After liberation, he promised, the people would be able to decide their own destiny.[15]

Hussein's pleas fell on deaf ears. While opposition from countries such as Syria was only to be expected, the Egyptian reaction was particularly severe, with Nasser's successor, President Sadat, going so far as to break off diplomatic relations with Jordan as a consequence. Sadat's initiative seems to have reflected more an attempt to strengthen his position in inter-Arab politics, and his strained personal relations with Hussein, than it did any genuine concern for the Palestinians living under Israeli occupation. Nevertheless, it reinforced Jordan's isolation in the Arab world. Adnan Abu Odeh, one of the framers of the plan and a former adviser to the King, has argued that the consequences of the plan within Jordan itself were also negative, since it implied that Palestinians living on the East Bank were little more than temporary residents waiting for the creation of a Palestinian entity on the West Bank.[16] However, the King stressed that under the terms of the plan no Palestinian would be forced to move from the Jordanian to the Palestinian region of the United Arab Kingdom, declaring that 'all Jordanians on both the East and West Banks would be given the option of choosing whether to belong to the Jordanian or Palestinian part of the Union'.[17]

Although the debate raised by Abu Odeh remains a contemporary issue in Jordan, the finer points of the United Arab Kingdom plan itself are academic; the simple fact was that the scheme was stillborn. Still, if it achieved nothing else, Hussein's initiative had at least accrued further political credit for him in Washington. In a briefing paper prepared for President Nixon in advance of a planned visit by Hussein, Secretary of State William Rogers recommended that the president welcome Hussein's 'statesmanlike proposal'. 'Jordan today', Rogers argued, 'symbolizes the success of our efforts to support moderate, self-reliant governments in the Middle East'.[18] Rogers acknowledged that Hussein would welcome US assistance in securing some movement in the peace process, but warned that the president's task in handling the King would be a delicate one, 'since Israel adamantly opposes our encouraging Hussein to expect the kind of settlement terms he seeks and which we have generally endorsed, and told Hussein we would support, in the past'. Hence, Rogers continued, the return of the whole of the West Bank to Jordan with only minor territorial rectifications was no longer practical politics: 'We now know more clearly than before that a settlement along these lines is unacceptable to Israel; their position over the last two years on territorial questions has hardened. I believe the best thing is to be frank with Hussein about the realities of the situation.'

Fortunately for Hussein, his visit to the US at the end of March 1972 was not all business. President Nixon, not often at home with the social side of his duties, invited the King to a successful dinner on the evening of 28 March. Introducing the King to his guests, the president paused in the line when he came to Richard Helms, the director of the CIA. 'Your Highness, this man you already know,' commented the president, 'but you're not supposed to. Just pretend you don't.' During his after-dinner toast Nixon mentioned that the King had piloted his own Boeing 707 into Andrews Air Force base the day before, quipping, 'he flew the plane himself, probably to avoid hijackers'. The King's response is not recorded but one observer described him in general as 'appreciative and quite relaxed'.[19]

After the Washington leg of his trip, Hussein went on to vacation in Florida. Here he showed the light-hearted, affable side of his character which helped build his profile in the United States. Under the headline 'Hiya King', the *Washington Post* reported that despite the high security surrounding the trip, the King himself proved to be 'good at small talk – especially with children – and very patient with the crowds that gather round him . . . He gets a kick out of the shouts of "Hiya King" – which happens only in America – and is quick to shake hands with everyone who comes near.' But there was also a more serious side to the public interest. 'It was almost ghoulish,' the *Post* reporter noted, 'the way people kept wishing him "good luck". Nobody seems to doubt that he needs it.' Hussein's own mood was similarly reflective and fatalistic. 'Yes, I feel I'll go out with a bang', he commented.

> I pass through different stages in life. Youth, the problems I faced as a child, gave me the feeling I had to prove something to myself . . . followed by responsibility, the feeling that everything is black and white that nothing is impossible. . . . Then disappointment and even despair. Then one finds one's equilibrium, and then the feeling that there is so much to learn and do. Then a sense of inner satisfaction . . . I think I am at that stage now. In terms of danger . . . when I'm really in it, it doesn't bother me. Then I'm at my best. It's before perhaps, and after that you feel it.[20]

If Hussein had by now reached some sort of equilibrium in his public life, the same seems not to have been true of his private life. During 1972, two controversies rocked the apparent stability of his family life. The first was his abrupt decision to move his two sons Abdullah and Feisal from school in the United Kingdom to school in the United States. The boys were two of the four children he had had with Princess Muna, the others being his twin daughters Zein and Aisha. The main reason for his decision to change Abdullah and Feisal's schools seems to have been concerns about his children's security. In the wake of the assassination of Wasfi Tall in Cairo, Zeid Rifai, who had been posted as ambassador to the United Kingdom, had also been the subject of an assassination attempt, probably on the part of Black September, in London on 15 December 1971. When his car was ambushed in Kensington, only good luck and a loss of nerve on the part of his attacker seem to have saved Rifai's life. Even so, the ambassador's car was riddled with bullets and he himself sustained a wound to the hand. Rifai blamed inadequate British security for the attack, and seems to have led attempts to persuade the King that the British authorities' attitude to his children's security was similarly lax. There seems to have been some basis for Rifai's complaints. Although the British police investigation quickly tracked down Rifai's would-be assassin, an Algerian who had fled to France, the Foreign Office privately welcomed the subsequent French refusal to extradite the suspect, fearing that any resulting trial might cast Britain as an enemy of the Palestinian cause and damage British relations with the oil-producing Arab states.[21]

The assassination attempt against Rifai brought to a head a crisis in relations between the King and the British government which had been simmering for some time. Hussein now sat down to write an anguished personal letter to the British Foreign Secretary, Sir Alec Douglas-Home, a six-page handwritten draft of which survives in his files.[22] Beginning by expressing his regret at the 'sad state of our relations', the King went on to request the recall of the British ambassador to Amman, Sir John Phillips. 'Frankly', the King wrote, 'in nearly twenty years of my political life, I have never encountered a less satisfactory link with HMG as that currently provided by the British ambassador to our court.' Hussein went on to explain that he had himself originally selected Rifai, 'one of my closest friends and associates', as ambassador to the United Kingdom 'in the spirit of friendship and concern that our relations be preserved and strengthened, and also to fill a dangerous, regrettable void. I can do no more', he concluded.

Then the King took up the subject of the security of his two sons, Abdullah and Feisal, and his daughter, Alia, whom he had also sent to boarding school in the United Kingdom, referring to what he saw as 'a sad lack of coordination between various security agencies in the United Kingdom', and 'a growing apparent lack of interest in Jordan'. He wrote that he had already taken the decision to remove his children from school in Britain, but had subsequently heard from the UK authorities that they might, after all, be able to offer satisfactory security. Uncertain what the true position now was, the King appealed to Douglas-Home: 'sir, as a friend and a father I would like and appreciate a clear position which I would be happy to accept one way or the other over this matter as soon as possible'.

With regard to the recall of the British ambassador, the King received satisfaction: Sir John Phillips was replaced by Glen Balfour Paul in the late spring of 1972. In respect of the royal children, though, the answer from the King's point of view was far less satisfactory. The US embassy in Amman subsequently reported that the new British ambassador had advised the King that the British government still could not accept responsibility for the security of the two boys should they return to school in Britain. The King had apparently been told that the British government recommended they should not return unless he himself would accept responsibility for their security. Hussein was quite naturally furious.[23] The British version of events as reported by Ambassador Balfour Paul was rather different. According to him, the decision stemmed from Zeid Rifai's 'alienation from things British' (perhaps an unsurprising sentiment in the circumstances). Other members of the royal family, Balfour Paul argued, including Queen Zein and Prince Hassan, 'none of whom were consulted before the King accepted Zaid's promptings, are all much enraged'.[24] Whatever the truth of the matter, Hussein had now made up his mind. In a further personal message to Alec Douglas-Home, the tone of which made clear his continuing sense of bitterness, he wrote:

> I would not wish to have the penalty which I am to bear for the policies I adopt out of conviction in the interest of my people and our common objective of a just and durable peace, and which it would appear has to be borne by my children, family and collaborators as well . . . to threaten in any way other boys, the staff in their school or the British Security men detailed for their protection.[25]

Hussein concluded with a comment on the state of the region: 'I sincerely hope, indeed I am rather positive, that the present wave of violence, which does not threaten us alone, will pass like a summer cloud, without leaving a mark on any of us.' The King's mind was made up, and the boys were moved to the United States from October 1972 onwards.[26]

The second, greater controversy in the King's private life in 1972 concerned his decision to divorce Princess Muna and immediately marry the daughter of a Jordanian diplomat, Alia Toukan, who now became Queen Alia. Young, beautiful and vivacious, Alia, who was to die tragically young in a helicopter crash in 1977, radiated charm, a quality still discernible from fading photographs of her at Hussein's side on state occasions in the mid-1970s.

How far Hussein's infatuation with her contributed to the breakdown of his marriage is a moot point, but the process of estrangement between Muna and Hussein had clearly been under way for some time. Under intense personal pressure during the years 1967–70, Hussein seems to have found it increasingly difficult to unburden himself of his problems, even to his wife. He managed only one or two brief phone calls to her during the June 1967 crisis, while in September 1970 he sent her to London for her own safety. Moreover, the interests which had brought them together at the beginning of the 1960s – sports, dancing and parties – no longer seemed to be a sufficient glue for their relationship. Perhaps it was in part that as politics consumed Hussein more and more in the shape of the existential struggles of 1967 and 1970, he could no longer compartmentalise his personal and political life. The King's lightning courtship of Alia during the latter part of 1972, then, seems only to have set the seal on the final breakdown of his marriage to Muna. Although the new Queen Alia was of Palestinian origin, the marriage seems initially to have pleased neither Bank of the Jordan and resulted in some short-term damage to the King's prestige.[27] It was certainly not a politically motivated move, as some of the British press speculated. On the contrary, the King's marriage to Alia, like his earlier marriage to Muna and his subsequent marriage to Noor, generated political controversy within the kingdom, particularly within the family and his inner circle. On this occasion, opponents of the King's divorce and remarriage did not finally give up the struggle until the beginning of December 1972, with the King's marriage to Alia taking place on the 24th of the month.[28] All of the King's closest relatives, including his mother Queen Zein, were against his decision to divorce Muna and marry Alia. Zein supported Muna and, thereafter, she and other members of the family were impressed with the good grace with which Muna accepted her position. Muna stuck steadfastly over the years to her agreement with Hussein never to discuss the breakdown of their marriage in public. Hussein for his part made sure that she was well provided for.

Private correspondence between the King and his friend Bill Speares, the British MI6 man in Amman, also gives some clue as to the personal anguish which he had endured. Bill Speares, it will be recollected, had played an important role during the 1970 crisis in Jordan, establishing a secure radio link between the British embassy and the King's Hummar Palace to enable him to maintain contact with the outside world when the need arose. During the nearly four years he had been posted to Amman, beginning in January 1969, Speares and his wife, Peggy, had established a close personal relationship with Hussein. Although the movements of MI6 officers are difficult to track, it appears that Speares and his wife left Jordan in the summer of 1972, before returning for a brief visit as Hussein's guests during the autumn. Shortly after Hussein's marriage to Alia on 24 December, Bill

Speares wrote to the King expressing his understanding of the difficulties he had faced:

> I have . . . come to know something of the unceasing burden Your Majesty has so cheerfully shouldered for Jordan and learned to gauge, in a small way, the loneliness which at times seems quite inseparable from supreme responsibility. These burdens of life, Sir, can as we all know become very great, never more so than when nobly and honourably discharged. But they are surely only tolerable if one can attain happiness and hence the will to great new strivings for all that one holds dear.[29]

A week later Hussein replied to Speares's letter:

> I have sensed between your lines how closely you have followed, and at the same time appraised, the heavy task I have shouldered during the past few years and the extreme devotion I have given my people while striving to serve their just cause, as well as their problems in other walks of life. I have associated myself with many of their diversified worries, but, nonetheless, one needs a certain amount of comfort and peace of mind to be able to continue to cope with responsibilities of such magnitude.
>
> I do hope there are many gentlemen in the world who are as deep-rooted in their affection, as well as in their understanding of human nature as you are.[30]

Hussein's less formal exchanges with Bill Speares's wife, Peggy, also provide a glimpse of his state of mind. On 15 December Peggy Speares wrote to the King:

> Dearest Majesty, This is about my third go at a letter to you. It was marvellous to be back in Jordan, and we greatly appreciated your hospitality. I was somewhat mystified and, being the same old Peggy, a bit hurt at your withdrawn manner. Now I begin to understand why. I had assumed you had problems, but had no idea of what kind of problems. All I can say is – you never have done things the easy way, and I would be very much surprised if you should ever change. I understand too the personal nature of such concerns and their solution and so am no longer mystified or hurt . . . We haven't always given our fullest support and who knows what our first reaction would have been this time. But it doesn't really matter because our love and respect for you are the true things – and they never change.[31]

Hussein drafted a reply to Peggy Speares' letter on the same day in early January that he wrote back to her husband:

> It was wonderful to receive your letter, and more wonderful to have seen you and Bill in Amman. I did not realize you found it so difficult to write me. But now that the air has cleared, I hope to hear from you more often.
>
> I am sorry if I had seemed withdrawn while you were here, but surely you know that this in no way reflected my feelings towards you and Bill. . . .
>
> As you would have heard by now, a lot has happened on the personal level since you were here. I am as happy as could be now, and Alia is really a wonderful person whom I am sure you will like very much. I told her a lot about you – all nice things – and she is anxious to meet.[32]

The negotiations surrounding the social arrangements for Hussein's visit to the United States in February 1973 showed that some of the tensions engendered by his swift divorce and remarriage remained below the surface. As Henry Kissinger noted in a memorandum sent to President Nixon ahead of Hussein's arrival, 'the King has been through some difficult disagreements in his inner circle over his remarriage, and this seems to have left some sensitive nerves on unrelated issues'. Specifically, since the King had been invited to dinner with President Nixon during previous visits to Washington such as that of March 1972, he now wanted the same honour to be accorded once again. 'Since he will be bringing his new bride', Kissinger noted, 'the Jordanians have said that the absence of similar social attention will be a cause of concern to him. . . .'[33] From Amman, Ambassador Dean Brown concurred. 'The King's feelings these days are very tender,' he noted. 'He has gone through [a] rather traumatic situation with his hasty marriage. We do not want him to get [the] notion [that the] US is letting him down. He is an impulsive man who has let his emotions get [the] better of his judgment in [the] past.'[34] In the event, any ruffled feathers were smoothed by the president's decision to host the King and Queen to a private dinner during their Washington visit.

As if these difficulties were not enough, the King also had to endure the death of his father, the former King Talal. Talal had lived for the final twenty years of his life in Istanbul and it was there that he died on 7 July 1972 at the age of sixty-three, by coincidence exactly the same age to which Hussein himself would live. His body was flown back to Jordan, where he was given a full royal funeral, which, with its mix of arms drill, ceremonial and music, culminating in the Last Post, was, according to one observer, 'all very British'. It was a dignified and touching close to a sad life, and one which left Hussein deeply moved.[35]

The demands of international politics did not give the King the luxury of a lengthy recovery time. The regional peace process remained stalled and Hussein was becoming more and more concerned that this paralysis might prompt renewed conflict. A briefing paper prepared by Henry Kissinger for President Nixon showed that even with the US election campaign now out of the way, movement in the peace process was unlikely. Reviewing the state of play in the King's covert discussions with the Israelis, about which he had been kept well informed both by the King personally and through outgoing CIA Director Dick Helms,[36] Kissinger noted that 'through numerous direct contacts with the Israelis . . . the King has been unable to change their position, even though a measure of trust and mutual respect has been created'.[37] Two crucial stumbling blocks remained: borders on the West Bank, where the King was only prepared to agree to minor rectifications in contrast to Israel's insistence on major changes, and Jerusalem, where the King's bottom line according to Kissinger was 'the return of part of the old city – the Muslim and Christian quarters and the Muslim Holy Places – to Jordanian authority', in contrast to the Israeli insistence on retaining exclusive sovereignty over the whole city. Hussein was convinced from his own efforts at direct negotiations that no further progress would be possible unless the US took an active role in persuading Israel to agree to compromise terms. Unfortunately for Hussein, even after his re-election Nixon was not prepared to put significant pressure on Israel to change its negotiating stance. The result was a continued impasse in the diplomatic process, not just on the Jordanian but on the Egyptian and Syrian fronts as well.

In the absence of any diplomatic progress during 1972–3, it is not surprising that the frontline Arab states turned to considering the option of renewed warfare as a means of recovering the territory they had lost in 1967. But Jordan was not one of them. Apart from anything else, in 1967 the kingdom had suffered worse economic, territorial and political losses than any of the other countries involved, and was clearly militarily unprepared for another round of fighting in 1973. Moreover, the Hashemite kingdom was still isolated in the wake of the expulsion of the fedayeen. Both Syria and Egypt required the King to agree to the return of the fedayeen groups to Jordan as a precondition for the resumption of normal relations. This was a price Hussein was unwilling to pay.

The driving force behind the renewal of the Egyptian–Syrian alliance was Sadat, and it had been clear almost since he had assumed the Egyptian presidency that there was no love lost between him and the King of Jordan. According to Kissinger, 'Sadat simply did not like Hussein, or royalty for that matter.'[38] Moreover, good relations with Hussein did not fit into Sadat's Arab strategy, the essence of which during 1972–3 was to build ties with Syria. Backing for the fedayeen at Hussein's expense also seemed a good way for

Sadat to burnish his Arab nationalist credentials, and protect himself against the charge that he was pursuing selfish Egyptian national interests. Sadat's rupture of diplomatic relations with Jordan in the wake of the King's United Arab Kingdom announcement was one obvious expression of this strategy.

Unlike Sadat, Hussein simply did not favour the renewal of conflict. He took every opportunity in his talks with a succession of Western leaders during 1973 to warn about both the dangers posed by war and its imminence in the absence of diplomatic progress. 'In such circumstances', he told British Prime Minister Edward Heath during a meeting on 12 July 1973, 'there was a strange logic which led President Sadat to believe that a disastrous war would be preferable to a continuing stalemate.' Hussein went on to warn that 'he had heard dates mentioned (sometimes for this month, and also for a more distant date) at which hostilities could commence . . . Action might occur quite soon, and would be very dangerous.'[39] 'Something spectacular was being planned,' the King predicted ominously.[40]

With their war plans advancing towards fruition, both Sadat and Asad evidently saw some merit in pursuing a limited thaw in relations with Hussein during the summer months of 1973. This process culminated in a summit meeting between the three leaders held in Cairo between 10 and 12 September. How much Hussein learnt during this meeting of Egyptian and Syrian plans is uncertain; he later claimed to have been totally excluded from any knowledge of what the plan was.[41] The summit communiqué not surprisingly gave little away, stating blandly that 'all undecided issues among the three countries and all issues and estimates connected with the battle of destiny were discussed'. Hussein made no significant concessions himself, either on the issue of the return of the fedayeen to Jordan, or that of putting Jordanian forces under joint command.[42] According to his own account, though, he did guarantee that he would fight any flanking movement Israel might make against Syria through Jordanian territory. 'We were told that they were afraid of an Israeli attack through Jordan and I said that if that ever happened we will fight it. We are not going to leave our territory open for anyone.'[43]

Probably the most fraught issue surrounding Hussein's role in the final run-up to the outbreak of war on 6 October 1973 concerns how much he learnt from his own intelligence sources about Egyptian and Syrian intentions, and how far he went in warning the Israeli government about their plans. The King was particularly sensitive to the charge that he divulged the Egyptian–Syrian plan of attack to the Israelis, a sensitivity which subsequently led him to make a not altogether candid denial that he had any knowledge of what was afoot: 'I can only say that, as far as I was concerned, I was caught completely off guard. I was riding a motorbike with my late wife behind me in the suburbs of Amman when a security car behind started flashing us to stop and then I was told that a war had started. I had no idea that anything of that nature would happen and certainly not at that time.'[44]

In fact, it seems that Hussein's own intelligence sources in Syria were good enough to give him a clear idea in advance of what was being planned.[45] The crucial link on the Jordanian side was provided by Abboud Salem, an air force pilot turned intelligence officer who had defected to Jordan from Iraq in the early 1960s. Abboud Salem was related through his wife to a divisional commander in the Syrian army, whom he had recruited as an agent well in advance of the October war. This high-ranking Syrian army officer was able to supply Abboud Salem with detailed advance information about the Syrian battle plans, even including the planned date of the attack. In fact, there was a late change in the Syrian plans. Originally, the attack was planned for the afternoon of Friday 5 October, but there was a last-minute postponement to the afternoon of Saturday 6 October which Abboud Salem also learned about from his Syrian contact. Apparently, the Syrians and Egyptians had been undecided as to whether they should make their attack on the eve of the Jewish holiday of Yom Kippur, as Israelis travelled home en masse before the Sabbath, or on the day of Yom Kippur itself, 6 October. The survival of the original attack schedule explains the otherwise puzzling decision to begin the attack at 2 p.m. rather than at dawn. Arguably, the original plan might have been more effective: on the day of the holiday, with Israeli reservists all at home and the roads empty, it was easier for Israel to muster its forces.

Even more startling than the fact that Hussein had access to such detailed information about Syrian intentions is the fact that the King also sent a warning to Washington through the CIA station chief in Amman. There, Secretary of State Henry Kissinger was briefed by CIA Director William Colby. Neither man acted on Hussein's warning, though Kissinger was evidently concerned by it. One member of his staff recalls him becoming increasingly agitated on the Wednesday and Thursday of the week before the attack.[46] The secretary of state repeatedly asked his staff what news was coming out of the Middle East, and whether there was any firm indication of a build-up for war. It is possible that Kissinger was not completely certain as to the veracity of Hussein's information, despite its level of detail. Nevertheless, even if this was so, he was apparently prepared to run the risk that a further round of conflict might break out in the region, perhaps in the hope that if this resulted in another Arab defeat it might further the US Cold War goal of diminishing Soviet influence in the Middle East.

The King also warned Israeli Prime Minister Golda Meir about the likely outbreak of war during a covert meeting between the two held at a Mossad guest house near Tel Aviv on 25 September. Israeli sources have provided their own version as to what information the King passed to Meir. Hussein, who was accompanied to the meeting by Zeid Rifai, appeared according to these Israeli accounts to be nervous and anxious. Initially, he took a similar approach to that which he had earlier followed with Western leaders. Stressing the need to resume the diplomatic process, the King told Meir that based on his conversations with Sadat and Asad at their 10–12 September summit, he did not expect them to tolerate the status quo for much longer, and that something had to be done to prevent the outbreak of war. To emphasise the urgency of resuming the diplomatic process, Hussein then went further, and gave Meir a flavour of the information he had received from his Syrian intelligence source: Syrian forces had moved to pre-jump positions and Hussein suspected that this was part of a plan of attack coordinated with Egypt, though he did not know for sure.[47] The King did not divulge the name of his Syrian source.

In fact, Hussein's approach seems to have made no difference to the Israelis' position. Because they calculated that the Arab states would not resort to waging a war they could not hope to win, they saw Hussein's intervention as self-serving at best and disinformation at worst. From the King's point of view, the issue was not so much whether his warning changed the course of history as whether it might be construed as an act of treachery to the Arab cause. Here, perhaps what matters most is the King's purpose. On one level, his visit to Tel Aviv might be described as a 'fishing expedition'.[48] He wanted to find out what information the Israelis had about Egyptian preparations from their intelligence sources, to see if this complemented his own knowledge about Syrian plans. Hussein also sought to avoid the outbreak of war by restarting the diplomatic process and persuading the Israelis to make genuine concessions for the sake of peace. His goal was most certainly not to enable them better to prepare for war and preserve the status quo. As Hussein himself put it, 'I had embarked on a course of trying to achieve peace and I could not be double faced about it'.[49] The difficulty of explaining this approach no doubt accounted for much of the King's sensitivity when questioned about this subject. In one sense, though, he need not have been so defensive. In view of what he actually knew about Syrian plans what is more remarkable is how little, not how much, he told the Israelis.

With Hussein's warnings ignored in Tel Aviv and Washington, the Egyptian and Syrian forces achieved almost complete surprise when they launched their combined assault on Israeli positions on Saturday 6 October 1973. The Israeli government's failure to anticipate this attack is a striking illustration of how faulty political understanding can cause erroneous interpretation of intelligence. Hussein's approach, together with the evidence of Egyptian and Syrian military preparations, and the evacuation of Soviet civilian personnel immediately before the outbreak of hostilities, were all dismissed as disinformation or misinterpreted as bluff. The Agranat Commission, established to investigate Israel's intelligence failure in the wake of the war, concluded that Israel's faulty conclusion rested on two assumptions: firstly, that Egypt would not go to war unless it was able to stage deep air strikes into Israel in order to neutralise its air force, a capability Egypt was far from possessing in October 1973, and, secondly, that Syria would not launch a full-scale war against Israel without Egypt.[50] While the second assumption may have been accurate, the first was most certainly not. Israeli politicians and intelligence chiefs alike underestimated Sadat's willingness to take military risks to break the political deadlock.

During the first four days of the war, Hussein was little more than a concerned spectator. With the initial plan of attack successfully executed on both the Golan and Canal fronts, neither Asad nor Sadat needed his partici- pation. At the beginning of the second day's fighting the US embassy in Amman estimated that although the King would strive to stay on the sidelines, if the conflict dragged on then pressures on him to intervene would mount. Should the Arabs sustain their initial advance, Hussein would come under domestic pressure to join the war in order to retrieve some of the territory on the West Bank lost in 1967. Should the tide turn against the Arabs, then Hussein would come under pressure to intervene to relieve the Egyptians and Syrians, especially if the Israelis pressed on past the former ceasefire lines. Although the King would probably stall for as long as possible in these circumstances, there were 'emotional limits' imposed by considera- tions of Arab honour which he would eventually reach.[51]

By 9 October, Hussein's position had started to become more uncom- fortable. After their initial successes, the Syrians had been turned back at considerable cost by the Israelis on the Golan front. Hussein was now faced with a request from King Feisal of Saudi Arabia to allow the movement of Saudi reinforcements through Jordan to Syria, which he initially rejected. At the same time, the Israelis delivered a harsh message to the King, warning him not to open a third front along the Jordan River.[52] In a bid to bolster Hussein's resolve to stay out of the conflict, Henry Kissinger wrote to him personally commending his 'responsible statesmanship' and promising that, through diplomatic action, 'it ought to be possible for the fighting to end soon'. According to the secretary of state, 'our recognition of the problem that the hostilities are causing for Your Majesty was a major factor in our decision to take the initiative in convening the Security Council, with a view to seeking an early end of the fighting.'[53]

However, as the deliberations at the UN unfolded, the King came under increasing pressure to act. Late on 10 October he received a request from President Sadat for Jordanian military intervention with 'strong forces'.[54] The Syrians followed up with their own request for the despatch of a full

Jordanian division to the Golan. While Hussein did his best to stall, he began discussing with the Syrians the possible movement of the 40th Jordanian Armoured Brigade across the Jordanian–Syrian border, to cover the Syrians' left or southern flank on the Golan. The Jordanians' initial goal was to identify a position for the brigade where the terrain would make it most unlikely that it would come into immediate contact with Israeli forces and from which it would have a clear line of withdrawal back to Jordanian territory. While negotiations with the Syrians got under way, Hussein sent General Amer Khammash to Cairo early on 11 October with a message for Sadat in which he warned him that it would be unwise for Jordan to intervene in the war without adequate air support.[55]

The King remained determined to limit Jordanian involvement in the battle, and made this clear in his communications with the Israeli government and the Western powers. On the afternoon of 11 October, the King called the British Ambassador Glen Balfour Paul to his armed forces HQ. Also present were Crown Prince Hassan, General Amer Khammash and the senior Jordanian liaison officer with the Syrians. This officer, according to Balfour Paul, 'brought news of the crumbling of the Syrian front' and an urgent appeal from Asad for the despatch of the Jordanian armoured brigade. Khammash meanwhile gave an account of his talks with Sadat, the upshot of which was that the King should either send the armoured brigade immediately, or allow the fedayeen back into Jordan to launch an assault across the Jordan River. The King told Balfour Paul that he 'had reluctantly decided that, if he was to retain any Arab credibility at all, he must make the gesture . . . i.e. despatch (in as slow time as possible) an armoured brigade to relieve the Syrian left wing'. When the ambassador asked him whether the Israelis would regard this as a *casus belli*, Hussein replied that 'he could not tell and wondered whether it would be possible for us to find out before it was too late'. At this point Crown Prince Hassan interjected, 'could not . . . the Israelis see that the future stability of the whole area depended on the survival of the Hashemites?'[56]

In London, Prime Minister Edward Heath followed the matter up with a late-night phone call to Henry Kissinger, who confirmed that he had also received the King's request via Ambassador Brown and that he would be passing it on to the Israelis.[57] True to his word, the secretary of state immediately called Israeli Ambassador Dinitz, who promised to forward the request to his government. When Kissinger also offered to pass on the planned location of the Jordanian brigade, Dinitz observed wryly that this constituted fighting 'war with all of the conveniences'.[58] In order to speed matters up, Kissinger warned Dinitz that the British had been promised an answer 'tonight' and that British goodwill was important because 'they have to promote the ceasefire and they are getting extremely restive'. Neither comment was quite accurate, but the secretary no doubt thought that anything which added urgency to the handling of the King's request in Jerusalem would do no harm.

By the afternoon of 13 October, the King had his answer.[59] The Israelis gave Kissinger an assurance that if Hussein did not move Jordanian forces into Syria itself, Israel would take no military action against Jordan.[60] Unfortunately from the King's perspective this assurance helped him more with yesterday's than today's problem. In other words, whilst the 40th Armoured Brigade had initially moved only up to a position covering the Syrian flank from the Jordanian side of their joint border, he was already coming under pressure to commit his forces to the battle within Syria itself. The King evidently feared that if Syria's forces cracked, the regime in Damascus might be overthrown by Iraqi-backed communists, although it is difficult to gauge how far these fears were genuine, and how far they were played up for the consumption of a Western and Israeli audience. Certainly, they were presented to the Israelis as one of the main reasons why Jordanian forces had to move up to the Syrian flank.[61]

By 15 October, matters had reached a critical point. Early that morning, the US State Department received a message from the Israeli embassy in Washington warning that the Jordanian brigade on the Syrian flank was now less than ten miles from Israeli forces. The embassy asked that a message be passed to the Jordanian government from the Israeli government giving the precise coordinates of a line which the Jordanian brigade should not cross if it wanted to avoid being engaged by the Israeli army.[62] The message was passed on to Prince Hassan at 5 a.m. Amman time. Hassan, who had just returned from inspecting the Jordanian brigade, had found 'total confusion with [the] Syrians pressing hard on [the] brigade commander to throw his troops into battle but with no precise plans for deployment'. According to Hassan, the 'brigade commander [was] still acting under instructions to stall, to maintain [the] cohesiveness of his unit, and not to take direct orders from [the] Syrians'.[63]

As the day progressed, it became clear to the King that the Jordanian brigade could no longer remain non-combatant. In view of the pressing nature of the situation, the King personally contacted Israeli Prime Minister Golda Meir, using a direct line to the Israeli prime minister which had been installed by an ex-CIA officer after the September 1970 crisis.[64] The upshot of the conversation, as reported by Israeli Ambassador Dinitz to Kissinger, was that 'King Hussein has informed PM Meir that after examining [the] location of various forces, Israel should consider the Jordanian expeditionary force of the 40th armored brigade as hostile as of yesterday morning.'[65] The King had explained to Meir that he had been 'under pressure directly from Assad to either withdraw the brigade or have it carry out its military duties at what was then the 8th day of the war . . . the brigade will inevitably be in action'. Ambassador Dinitz informed Kissinger that 'the least harm would be done if in addition to this force, no additional force was sent into action in this region or any other region of the front with Jordan, and that the existing Jordanian force there would receive instructions not to engage heavily in battle'. This was said in the 'hope that the engagement should it occur will be limited'.

Back in Amman, Ambassador Dean Brown sought out Crown Prince Hassan at 1 a.m. on 16 October to deliver Dinitz's message. Hassan and the King's uncle Sharif Nasser, in whose headquarters Brown found Hassan, both agreed that 'it would be madness for Jordan to commit more forces to Syria'.[66] The Crown Prince promised to wake the King and reiterate Dinitz's message to him. In passing, Hassan also noted that Jordanian forces had now taken their first casualties: one killed and two wounded by a stray artillery shell. Of course, these Jordanian casualties were small in the context of the war as a whole, which had now turned decisively against the Arabs. An Egyptian armoured thrust towards the Giddi and Mitla passes in the Sinai on 14 October designed to relieve the pressure on Syria had been turned back by Israel at a cost to Egypt of 200 tanks lost. On 16 October the Israelis executed a successful crossing of the Suez Canal, putting the Egyptian forces on the East Bank of the Canal in imminent danger of being completely encircled. Recognising that this could only increase the pressure on Hussein to agree to full-scale Jordanian intervention, Kissinger wrote to him on 19 October promising that a ceasefire was within reach and that, after its conclusion, the US would work towards a 'fundamental settlement' of the conflict. 'In such a settlement, Your Majesty,' the secretary of state promised, 'it is inconceivable that the interests of Jordan, which you so eloquently explained to me, would not be fully protected. I give you a formal assurance to this effect.'[67]

Even as the ceasefire finally approached on 22 October, pressure on the King to throw Jordanian forces into a further desperate Syrian-Iraqi assault on the Golan remained intense. According to British sources, 'whether [the] Jordanians would take part in such an offensive is uncertain. But evidently the King remains determined that, if the Syrian forces crack up and/or there are signs of an Iraqi political take-over, he will be in a position to pursue his counterpoise ploy as best he can.' Whatever the outcome, Hussein was undoubtedly 'reluctant to destroy his new-found standing in Syria and elsewhere by withdrawing from the battle without Assad's agreement'.[68] It was not until 26 October that the King, with the assistance of Prime Minister Zeid Rifai, found a way to effect a graceful withdrawal from Syria. According to Dean Brown:

Professor Kissinger's prize pupil at Harvard has exceeded himself in Machiavellianism. Zeid Rifai sent Amer Khammash to Damascus this morning. Amer is to tell Assad that Jordan knows that Israel violated [the] ceasefire in Syria and Egypt. Jordan has intelligence that it may do so as well on [the] East Bank. Jordan, therefore, must withdraw its troops to protect its own territory.[69]

As before, information about the planned movement of Jordanian forces was passed via the Americans to the Israelis, who, according to Kissinger, accepted the King's word as to their intentions 'in good faith'.[70]

Jordan's position at the end of the October 1973 war stood in stark contrast to that of June 1967. The country had emerged militarily unscathed. Furthermore, the King's assistance to the Syrians had enhanced his position in inter-Arab politics at a relatively low cost. As Dean Brown put it, 'he has played the game beautifully'. Putting himself in the King's position, Brown hypothesised:

you entered Syria in order to preserve some sort of meaningful relationship with [the] Arab states, especially Saudi Arabia, a spiritual and financial mentor. After the event you rationalized your action by saying you were preventing an Iraqi takeover of Syria . . . Underneath it all you have a hate/love relationship with Israel. Your people, your Palestinians want revenge but you know that your only long-term insurance policy is – if not a durable peace – a modus vivendi with Israel. And now, after three weeks of war, you realize that Israel agrees with you, at least the modus vivendi.[71]

CHAPTER 10

DISENGAGEMENT AND DISILLUSIONMENT, 1973–7

Despite Dean Brown's empathy, and Henry Kissinger's 'formal assurance' that he would defend Jordan's interests in the peace process, Hussein's hopes for a settlement after the October 1973 war were soon dashed. The step-by-step diplomacy promoted by Kissinger as the best method to edge the belligerents away from their intransigent post-war positions amounted, from the Jordanian perspective, to side-step diplomacy. Aware of the obstacles to any settlement over the West Bank, the US secretary of state focused instead on securing disengagement agreements first on the Egyptian and then on the Syrian front. Although Kissinger remains sensitive to the charge that he deceived the Jordanians, he showed little appetite from the outset for the challenges of securing 'disengagement' on the West Bank. Subsequently, he has argued that what he envisaged at the time was a 'staged disengagement, with the Jordanian disengagement being the last of the three'.[1] Part of the problem, of course, was that since there had been no direct military engagement on the Jordanian front in 1973 it could legitimately be argued that securing the 'separation of forces' there was much less pressing than on the Golan or along the Suez Canal. On the other hand, Kissinger had assured the King in his 19 October message that the reward for his patience and circumspection during the 1973 war would be the US administration's serious engagement in the peace process on Jordan's behalf in its aftermath. This did not happen.

Kissinger took only one covert initiative early in 1974 designed to probe the possibility of progress on the Jordanian front. In the wake of the elaborate charade that was the Geneva Peace Conference of December 1973, Kissinger brought with him to Amman a purely personal proposal from Deputy Prime

Minister Yigal Allon, which did not have the endorsement of the full Israeli cabinet. This amounted to a restatement of his eponymous plan for the West Bank, which would involve the return of 90 per cent of its territory and 95 per cent of its population to Jordanian jurisdiction. The proposal was offered to the King and Prime Minister Zeid Rifai as a plan for 'vertical', not 'horizontal', withdrawal, a form of words designed to stress that Israel would not execute a straight line pull back from the Jordan River.[2] Instead, the Israelis would hold on to a buffer zone along the river, and the King was offered control of areas behind that zone. The King rejected the Allon Plan as a final peace settlement as he had before, although he did indicate willingness to consider it as an interim agreement. In fact, both Hussein and Rifai must have been somewhat weary by this stage of hearing the Allon Plan presented as a private initiative, as it had been in 1968, rather than as a firm, cabinet-backed peace proposal. The King and Rifai offered Kissinger a counter-proposal during their 19 January 1974 meeting in Aqaba, which envisaged Israel and Jordan pulling back eight kilometres from the Jordan River and the re-establishment of Jordanian civil administration in the area vacated by Israel, including the town of Jericho. But this was rejected by the Israeli government, despite Hussein's efforts in arranging another face-to-face meeting with members of the Meir government on 7 March 1974 in the hope of persuading them of the merits of his plan.[3] Kissinger himself expressed exasperation over the Israeli position at this stage, noting that he had found them 'maddening to deal with. They had no coherent strategic plan (or coordinating machinery) and got the short and long term all muddled up.' Over the West Bank, 'they seemed unable to take decisions and would not commit themselves, for example, not to have troops in the Jordan Valley although they did not have any there at the moment'. With no small irony Kissinger recalled, 'at one meeting they had spoken of not being able to depart from the Allon Plan, so he had told Allon who was present that he had better change his Plan'.[4]

In the event there was no progress at all on the Jordanian–Israeli front during the spring and summer of 1974. Two more covert meetings took place, this time between Hussein and members of the new Rabin government, the first on 28 August and the second on 19 October 1974. Although Israeli accounts suggest that Hussein showed some interest in a proposal presented by Allon for the limited extension of Jordanian jurisdiction to Jericho, Zeid Rifai, who attended the meetings, denies this. According to Rifai, the Jordanians held fast to two proposals: either a full peace agreement involving the return of all the territory conquered in 1967 or an interim agreement involving a straight-line withdrawal of eight kilometres on both sides of the River Jordan. Neither proposal was acceptable to the Israelis.[5] Indeed, Rabin proved even more difficult to pin down in negotiations than Meir. The ambiguity of his position towards Hussein and Jordan was summed up in comments he made to British Prime Minister Harold Wilson during a private meeting on 28 June 1974. On the one hand, Rabin argued that

> He favoured the existence of two states, one Jewish, one a Palestinian–Jordanian community, within the boundaries of pre-1918 Palestine. This would involve the 'Palestinianisation' of Jordan, but he suggested that this was happening anyway, as could be seen from the membership of King Hussein's Cabinet and the Jordanian army. The Palestinian entity which he foresaw would consist of the East Bank and certain populated areas on the West Bank where refugees could settle.

On the other hand, in the same meeting he asserted that 'it was in the interest of Israel to keep King Hussein in Jordan. He had after all eliminated the terrorist bases in his Kingdom'.[6] Rabin apparently did not recognise the threat which 'Palestinianisation' was likely to present to the survival of the Hashemite regime in Jordan. Wilson's view was that Rabin 'was apt to become a slave to his own phrases'. Kissinger was even more cutting: 'if Mr Rabin said to him just once more that he would exchange "a piece of land for a piece of peace", he would physically attack Mr Rabin. He much regretted the loss of Mrs Golda Meir . . . Nothing could have been less well conceived than what he was reported to have said about Jordan'.[7] In these circumstances it is little surprise that during the spring and summer of 1974 Hussein remained an impatient and frustrated spectator to the peace process.

Meanwhile, in the occupied territories themselves, the effects of the Israeli occupation regime were becoming increasingly apparent. In the immediate wake of the 1967 war, Moshe Dayan, who was responsible as minister of defence for the administration of the territories, had instituted what became known as the 'open bridges' policy. The idea behind this was that if the Palestinians living under occupation could maintain contact with Jordan and thereby the rest of the Arab world, then economic and social dislocation might be avoided, and the occupation itself would be easier to maintain. In pursuit of this policy, economic links with Israel were also encouraged, with Palestinians allowed the right to travel and to take jobs there, provided they returned to their homes at the end of each working day. This resulted in a major shift in the Palestinian economy. Within four years of the 1967 war nearly half the workers in the occupied territories regularly commuted to jobs in Israel.[8]

If this was the relatively benign face of occupation, there was another more sinister one. Israel's economic integration of the territories, coupled with its higher level of development, meant that a dependent, colonial-style economy was created. Worse still was Israel's settlement policy. This was driven initially by security – the desire to protect the frontiers of the territories – and subsequently by ideology, the belief that they formed part of the biblical 'Land of Israel'. Israeli expropriation of land, often for the spurious purposes of public need or 'nature reserves', resulted in an accelerating programme of Jewish settlement building, especially once the Likud Party came to power in 1977. Some of these settlers bore an aggressive ideological commitment to what amounted to the colonisation of a Greater Israel, and unsurprisingly their presence evoked hostility from the indigenous Palestinian population. While this did not manifest itself in the form of widespread popular resistance until the Intifada of the late 1980s, by the mid-1970s it was already becoming apparent that the burden of the occupation on the Palestinians was increasing.

With no progress towards ending the Israeli occupation of the West Bank, the issue of Palestinian representation became all the more pressing. The competition between the PLO and the Hashemite regime for the loyalty of West Bankers, which had been a central fact of Hussein's political life for the past decade, once more came to the forefront of the broader Arab political agenda. Continuing tensions between the PLO and the regime were mirrored in Crown Prince Hassan's private description of the PLO in early 1974 as 'unrepresentative' and 'dissected . . . Its constituent parts could not agree with each other . . . The Fatah were a bunch of gungho characters. Higher up in the PLO there were two or three individuals who were looking only for personal glory.'[9] Hussein echoed these views, describing the PLO as 'representative of a small divided group, not the larger number of Palestinians who lived in Gaza and elsewhere, as well as on the West Bank'.[10] Nevertheless, at the Algiers summit of November 1973, all of the Arab states except Jordan had given their backing to the PLO's claim to be the sole representative of the Palestinians. This put the Hashemite Kingdom in the untenable position of having to negotiate for the return of the West Bank with a view to handing it over to the PLO should the negotiations prove successful.[11]

The contradiction was resolved at the Rabat summit of October 1974. By the time he arrived in Morocco, the King was already aware that he would face an uphill struggle. During the opening session, a tense, if somewhat ironic, encounter took place between PLO Chairman Arafat and King Hussein, who was accompanied by Prime Minister Zeid Rifai. The two sides had not met since the 1970 confrontation. According to Rifai, after bowing to the King whom he addressed deferentially as 'sayyidna' ('our lord'), Arafat hastened to embrace the prime minister as well, kissed him on the cheeks, and began to shake his hand vigorously. Rifai, who had been wounded in the hand during the Black September assassination attempt against him in December 1971, interrupted him with the words 'be careful of my hand, Abu Ammar. It still hurts.'[12] If this exchange amounted to a small moral victory, the Jordanian delegation was left with little choice during the business sessions but to acquiesce in the face of overwhelming pressure for a further resolution confirming 'the right of the Palestinian people to establish an independent national authority under the command of the PLO, the sole legitimate representative of Palestinian people in any Palestinian territory that is liberated'.[13] According to Rifai, he had already warned Kissinger early in the year that if Jordan was not on the other side of the River Jordan by the time of the Arab summit, it would not block the designation of the PLO as the Palestinians' sole legitimate representative.[14] An interim peace deal over the West Bank was thus the minimum requirement for Jordan to remain engaged in the peace process. Rifai also believes that Jordan was double-crossed by the supposedly pro-Western Arab states of Egypt, Saudi Arabia and Morocco at Rabat. In advance of the summit, Kissinger had assured him, according to Rifai's account, that there would be no new attempt to push the PLO's credentials to represent the West Bank Palestinians because these three states would block it. At the summit itself, however, it was precisely these three states, with Morocco in the forefront, which led the pressure for such a resolution.

Rifai concluded that there was a conspiracy at work. While Jordan was responsible for the West Bank, it would keep pushing for an interim agreement, which Israel did not want. Now the PLO had assumed responsibility as a result of Rabat, and Kissinger subsequently stipulated conditions for the PLO to enter the peace process, conditions to which it could not possibly agree at that point. As a result, the prospect of any interim agreement on the West Bank disappeared; there was no one to negotiate with. This cleared the way for the focus on the Egyptian–Israeli track and took the pressure off the Israelis as regards the West Bank. In Rifai's view this outcome suited the Americans, the Israelis and the Egyptians.[15]

Kissinger's recollections of the circumstances surrounding Rabat and its implications for the peace process are different. He claimed that the Rabat resolution had come as just as big a disappointment to him as to everyone else, and there was no question from his point of view of a conspiracy to undermine Jordan's role, although he knew that the Jordanians blamed him for what had transpired.[16] On the contrary, according to Kissinger, he had warned Israeli leaders repeatedly during 1974 that the opportunity to strike a deal with Hussein over the West Bank was fleeting and that they should seize it while they could. The interposition of the PLO as the negotiating partner approved by the Arab states condemned the West Bank to a stalemate which would last for two decades and, in Kissinger's view, constituted a 'major lost opportunity' in the peace process.[17] The resolution was also, of course, a major personal setback for the King, given that the Union of the Two Banks and the Hashemites' role as guardians of the Muslim shrines in Jerusalem were central to his conception of Hashemite destiny.

In the wake of Rabat, Hussein stopped short of cutting all ties with the West Bank, which would have required the Jordanian constitution to be amended, despite a good deal of pressure from within the royal family and the East Bank political elite for such a move.[18] In any event the new cabinet formed by Zeid Rifai on 23 November 1974 contained fewer Palestinians. Rifai argued that this was logical: after the Rabat resolution the West Bank could no longer be regarded as part of the Hashemite kingdom, so Palestinian representation had to drop. Adnan Abu Odeh by contrast sees this reduction as part of the beginning of a process of discrimination against Palestinians living on the East Bank, a process inadvertently furthered by the King himself.[19]

If diplomacy had brought Hussein only disillusionment during 1974, at the end of the year he made a decision in his private life which would bring him significant solace in future. This was the purchase of a private residence near Windsor in England, known as Castlewood. The circumstances in which the purchase came about were somewhat ironic. During his frequent visits to Britain until 1972, the King had been in the habit of staying in a house which he had bought in central London, at 7 Palace Green, near Kensington Palace. As part of his divorce arrangements with Princess Muna in 1972, however, he had given the house to her, and now had no permanent residence in or near London.[20] During 1973–4, this had been the source of some difficulties for the British government. Since Special Branch, which was responsible for ensuring the King's safety while he was in London, believed that this security could not be guaranteed in a hotel, the foreign secretary had been obliged to give up his own residence at Dorneywood on several occasions to accommodate the King and his party. By the autumn of 1974, this arrangement was causing strains, with the foreign secretary displaying evident pique and, according to FCO officials, 'mumbling and grumbling' at having to change his own arrangements to accommodate the King.[21] In the event, the King's private secretary in England, Miss Mae Cook, discovered Castlewood and persuaded the King to buy it for what would turn out to be the bargain price of £150,000.[22] Apart from providing a home from home for the King in future years, Hussein's purchase of Castlewood came as something of a blessed relief to British Foreign and Commonwealth Office officials, who no longer had to worry about where to house the King on future visits to England. 'Allah be Praised' was the FCO's response to the confirmation of the house purchase.[23]

In terms of Hussein's role in regional politics, the mid-1970s were a period of flux. With the Arab–Israeli peace process at a stalemate from Jordan's point of view, the King and Prime Minister Rifai devoted much of their energy to shoring up Jordan's position in inter-Arab politics, and in particular to building a new relationship with Syria. The logic behind this move was straightforward. Relations with Sadat's Egypt were strained, with the Jordanians believing correctly that the Egyptian president intended to strike out on his own to secure a peace deal with Israel to protect Egyptian interests when the opportunity presented itself. This created a natural community of interest between Jordan and the Syrian regime of President Hafez Asad, which was also deeply suspicious of Egyptian intentions. Indeed, in private talks with Rifai in March 1975, a furious Asad complained of having been 'exploited' by Sadat during the war and its aftermath. 'He was very worried about Sadat taking another step and then leaving him with no leverage,' Rifai noted.[24] Hussein had also built up a certain amount of credit with the Syrians as a result of his military assistance during the 1973 war, credit on which Rifai could draw through his diplomatic efforts in Damascus. Moreover, there was an intangible element which underpinned the attempt to build a rapprochement with Damascus. Many Jordanians tended to regard the Syrians as 'proper Arabs', culturally much more closely connected to them than the Egyptians, whom they often looked on with a degree of condescension. In terms of Hussein's own vision, closer relations with Syria, even with a view to some form of future political union, resonated with the traditional Hashemite idea of both states as part of a 'Fertile Crescent'. Whilst this remained a largely unspoken assumption in his Syrian policy Hussein did let his guard slip on one occasion, when he told former US Ambassador Dean Brown that Jordan had to have 'a larger future than a few thousand square miles of sand'.[25] Although such sentiments were not on their own sufficient to create an alliance, as had been amply witnessed by the tensions between the two countries during 1970, they helped facilitate dialogue in periods when political interests and strategies overlapped.

Against this promising backdrop, Hussein's personal relations with Asad blossomed. Reporting on a successful visit by Asad to Amman in June 1975, US Ambassador Thomas Pickering noted that Hussein seemed to have developed a serious liking and affection for the Syrian leader. According to the King himself, Asad was completely frank with him, even saying in the presence of his advisers, 'You can trust me, but don't trust this regime. I will stand by what I say, but beware of the people around me.'[26] This openness only served to deepen Hussein's respect for Asad. One anecdote in particular summed up the difference between Hussein's relations with Asad and those with Sadat. During their respective visits to Amman, both leaders had been entertained at the house of Hussein's cousin Zeid bin Shaker, which overlooked the Jordan valley. When the Egyptian leader and his party had been shown the lights of Jerusalem in the distance from the terrace, they had merely commented on the 'lovely view'. Asad, by contrast, had stood in silence for four or five minutes, before remarking, 'Bullshit, they'll never give that back in negotiations!'[27]

In 1976, the King defended the Syrian role in the civil war which had broken out in neighbouring Lebanon during 1975.[28] Indeed, Hussein admitted in an ABC television interview on 4 April 1976, 'we are helping Syria as much as we can'. As regards Asad personally, Hussein was effusive: 'I am impressed by his honesty, his ability, his courage, his wisdom but, above all, by the fact that he is a patriot.'[29] Hussein's public support was mirrored in private action. Later that same month, the King interceded on Asad's behalf with the Israeli ambassador in London, Gideon Rafael, asking him, in a secret meeting arranged at a mutual friend's house, to reassure Prime Minister Rabin that Asad's intentions in sending troops into Lebanon were purely defensive.[30] Rafael in turn conveyed an accommodating reply from Rabin to the King, who forwarded it on to Damascus.

Hussein also acted as an intermediary for the Syrians with the US. In particular, Asad seems to have used Hussein to lend extra legitimacy to the argument that his relations with the Soviet Union were seriously strained in the wake of his intervention against the PLO-leftist front in Lebanon. On 20 July 1976 the French newspaper *Le Monde* published a letter from Chairman of the Politburo Leonid Brezhnev to Asad in which he exhorted the Syrian leader to stop operations 'against the resistance and the Lebanese national movement'. Hussein had already been in secret contact with Washington on Asad's behalf, informing Kissinger that the Soviets had privately threatened to cancel deliveries of spare parts for the Syrian armed forces.[31] Kissinger's response was positive and appreciative. He wrote to Hussein promising that 'we will be giving this situation particular attention as a result of His Majesty's approach to us. It would be a matter of great concern to us if the Soviets were to exercise this kind of pressure on Syria. In such circumstances, we would take every step possible to enable Syria to preserve an independent national policy, and we would encourage our friends to do likewise.'[32] Asad's purpose in asking for Hussein's intercession with the Americans was no doubt to help retain his freedom of manoeuvre vis-à-vis his superpower patron, a goal he emphasised in a long public speech he made on 20 July in which he vowed that Syria would never bow to any ultimatum. Hussein interceded once more on Asad's behalf in October, requesting American backing for the latter's Lebanese policy. This was forthcoming, although Kissinger was careful to avoid any suggestion that the US might consider arms sales to Syria as a concrete gesture of support. Given the strength of the pro-Israel lobby in Congress, and the post-Watergate weakness of the executive branch, any such move would simply not have been practical politics for the Ford administration.[33]

Domestic politics also influenced the US's supply of arms to Jordan at this time. The biggest controversy concerned the sale of Hawk surface-to-air missile batteries to Jordan, which became a touchstone of the increasingly strained relationship between Jordan and the US. The Jordanian armed forces' need for an adequate surface-to-air missile-defence system had been highlighted by the 1967 and 1973 wars. In 1967, the unprotected Jordanian armoured forces had been destroyed from the air by Israel, while in 1973 Egyptian tanks had suffered the same fate once they ventured beyond the security provided by the Soviet-supplied SAM batteries deployed in the Suez Canal zone. Israeli air power had also been decisive in turning back the Syrians on the Golan. For Hussein, acquiring an air defence system for his armed forces was essential for morale.[34] It was common knowledge within the army that without one Jordan's ground forces would have little chance in a future confrontation with any of its neighbours.

In an attempt to get round the problem of Israeli opposition to such a sale, Hussein argued that Jordan needed the means to protect its territory against an incursion similar to that which Syria had mounted back in 1970. It quickly became apparent, though, through the actions of Israel's supporters in Congress, that the Israeli government preferred to see Jordan's airspace left open for the potential use of the Israeli Air Force, whether in the event of an incursion by a hostile Arab state into Jordan or of a future Arab–Israeli conflict. The Ford administration too saw advantages in this state of affairs since, as Kissinger acknowledged in a memo to the president, 'these unusual military relationships between Jordan and Israel have also generally strengthened our influence on Jordan'.[35] This position was not only incompatible with Jordanian sovereignty; it was also personally insulting to the King, whose actions during the 1973 war had made it clear that he was determined to avoid any further direct confrontation with Israel. Coming on top of what Hussein saw as the bypassing of Jordan in the peace process, the politicking and prevarication over the Hawk issue in Congress led him once more to question the basis for his relationship with the United States.

The compromise eventually hit on by the Ford administration to win over Congress involved the supply of Hawks to Jordan, but only in very limited numbers and in restricted operational condition.[36] Hussein was forced to swallow the humiliating provision that the Hawk batteries sold to Jordan would be deprived of their mobility and set in concrete into defensive positions. This would prevent their tactical deployment in support of Jordanian ground forces in the event of hostilities and would also make them easy targets for Israeli air strikes. As Hussein himself put it in a personal letter to Kissinger, 'how can the US Government maintain its credibility and continue to be able to play an effective role in the Arab world if its pledges, promises and commitments, all made seriously and in good faith are not lived up to because of Israel's friends in the Congress who seem to run the show there?'[37] In order to salvage what he could from the situation in respect of the King's personal 'position and dignity', Prime Minister Rifai issued a public statement to the effect that Jordan did not accept the special provisions for the deployment of the Hawks which the administration had negotiated with Congress, even while confirming in private to US officials that Jordan would abide by them.[38] This was no more than a figleaf to cover the King's embarrassment.

It was left to President Ford himself to attempt to pour oil on troubled waters through a personal message to the King on 20 September 1975, in which he described the problems over the Hawk sale as 'acutely painful to me', and praised Hussein's 'statesmanship and ability to take a far-sighted view of the interests of your country'. Flying in the face of the uncomfortable congressional realities laid bare by the Hawk saga, Ford proclaimed, 'you yourself have been a symbol to Americans of strength, wisdom and modera-tion, and both you and Jordan enjoy widespread respect and sympathy among the American people, in Congress and throughout our government'.[39] Whatever the President's sympathy for Hussein personally, though, the Hawk saga had confirmed that it evidently did not trump Congress's sympathy for Israel.

Hussein's diplomatic frustrations during the mid-1970s were partly redressed by the happiness of his private life with the new Queen Alia, and by the domestic economic boom which Jordan experienced on the back of the post-1973 oil price hike. In economic terms, Jordan has rightly been called an oil state without the oil. When oil prices have risen, it has tended to benefit significantly both from the remittances sent home by Jordanians working in the Gulf and from the increasing largesse of the Gulf States themselves. The 1970s boom was a classic illustration of both the benefits and the pitfalls of this spill-over of oil wealth for Jordan. Despite the ambitious plans of the Wasfi Tall government in the early 1960s, the domestic turmoil of the years 1967–71 had severely set back the development of the Jordanian economy. Between 1973 and 1975, the Kingdom launched a three-year development plan aimed at reviving the economy. At the same time, neighbouring states, especially Saudi Arabia, witnessed a huge expansion in their oil income. The redistribution of a small part of this income in the form of grants to Jordan helped to underpin the domestic economic recovery programme. Foreign grants, which had amounted to only 45.6 million Jordanian dinars in 1973, had risen to JD100.6 million by 1975, and would reach JD210.3 million by 1979. At the same time, many Palestinians holding Jordanian passports moved to take advantage of the opportunities provided by the demand for skilled labour in the Gulf. By the end of the decade, about one-third of the Jordanian labour force was working outside the kingdom.[40] Their remittances served to boost the domestic economy still further, enhancing what seemed to be a virtuous circle of rising incomes and economic growth. Economic confidence was also boosted by the relative peace and regional stability (with the exception of Lebanon) of the years between 1973 and 1979. All of this was reflected in the overall Jordanian economic growth rate, which ranged between 7 and 11 per cent during these years. Nevertheless, even while the country experienced a short-term economic boom, problems were stored up for the future in other fields. Inflation increased significantly, which in the longer run would erode the value of incomes and savings. A large trade gap opened up as the new-found domestic wealth sucked in imports of luxury goods. Furthermore, population growth surged at the same time as the process of urbanisation took off. Greater Amman expanded at a breathtaking pace, swallowing up what had previously been distinct, adjacent settlements. Before the 1973 war, one wealthy Amman resident recollected knowing to whom every car in his neighbourhood belonged. By the end of the decade, Amman had lost all such vestiges of its small-town past.

On the back of buoyant internal and external revenues, the state moved to expand its role in all walks of Jordanian life.[41] On the simplest level, as the state took on more functions it became a larger employer, with the number of civil servants rising by 200 per cent between 1970 and 1985. The state also took on a more interventionist role in the economy, witnessed by the establishment of the Ministry of Supply in 1974, which was intended to regulate the prices of staple goods such as bread and rice. Major development projects such as the expansion of the port of Aqaba and the building of Queen Alia International Airport were also undertaken. While the avowed aim of improving the national infrastructure was a worthy one, the Jordanian exchequer over-extended itself in such enterprises and fostered a culture of relative fiscal profligacy which could not be sustained when economic growth dipped.

If Jordan's 1970s economic miracle was doomed to breakdown, Hussein's own private happiness during these years was also to prove tragically short-lived. His marriage to Alia quickly blossomed from a love affair to a deep personal partnership. Together they had two children, Princess Haya, born in 1974, and Prince Ali, born in 1975. With her effervescent personality, Alia had the gift of helping the King to see the lighter side of life, and to put his personal and political troubles in perspective. Quick witted, outgoing and fluent in English, Alia also proved to be an asset for the King on his many overseas state visits and official occasions. Her nationality meant that she had fewer obstacles to overcome in securing the affection of the Jordanian people than those which had confronted the British-born Muna, or which were to face the King's American-born fourth wife, Queen Noor, in later years. A native Arabic speaker, she was also much better placed to navigate her way through the intricacies of court protocol and to hold her own in palace intrigues. Short-lived though her reign was, Alia had already shown an appetite to develop the more political side of her duties, a fact which contributed to the circumstances surrounding her death on 9 February 1977.

Responding to a letter of complaint, Alia, accompanied by the minister of health, had paid a surprise visit to a hospital in the town of Tafila in southern Jordan. On the return flight, her helicopter, piloted by the King's friend and ADC Captain Badr Zaza, ran into bad weather near Amman and crashed, killing all the occupants. Hussein was devastated. For the first and only time in his reign, he withdrew almost completely into his personal shell. While he continued to carry out his official duties, he showed little of his customary zest for life. It was to take the burgeoning of another love affair, this time with Lisa Halaby, the future Queen Noor, during the course of 1978 to draw him out of his deep melancholy. In a letter expressing his deep sympathy for Hussein's loss, the new US President Jimmy Carter wrote, 'my own family is so precious to me that I can understand your obvious sorrow'.[42]

Coinciding with the personal tragedy of Alia's death, Hussein also faced the political storm caused by a *Washington Post* story which ran on 18 February 1977, purporting to reveal the amount and purpose of the CIA payments which he had received across the course of two decades. The article, by Bob Woodward, was sensationalised and inaccurate, characterising the payments to Hussein as a kind of bribe to allow the CIA to 'operate freely in his strategically placed Middle Eastern country', and noting that 'Hussein's decisions have often been highly compatible with US and Israeli interests'.[43] As to the sums of money involved, according to Woodward, the CIA had for twenty years made 'secret annual payments totalling millions of dollars to King Hussein', although these had been 'sharply curtailed' to $750,000 by 1976.

In fact, the regular payment destined for individuals within his army and intelligence service passed by the CIA station chief to the King in cash every month from the late 1950s onwards had remained unaltered at its lowly original level of 5,000 Jordanian dinars.[44] From 1973–4 onwards, a new supplementary payment had begun which, by 1977, when the Woodward story broke, did indeed amount to the approximately $750,000 which Woodward mentioned. But its purpose was not the lurid personal pay-off implied in the article. In fact, it paid almost exclusively for a private security firm, run by the son of ex-President Gerald Ford, to provide twenty-four-hour-a-day protection for the King's children at school in the United States.

One former CIA station chief, mentioned by Woodward in a follow-up article the next day, was livid at both the inaccuracy and shallowness of the story.[45] Indeed, his secretary, who coincidentally found herself sharing a taxi with Woodward shortly after he wrote the story, took the opportunity to upbraid him for not checking the details out with her boss before running it.[46] Woodward was, according to this source, repentant in private, but whatever the weaknesses of the article, it caused Hussein significant and enduring political damage. The claim that he was a paid-up CIA stooge, doing the bidding of the US intelligence services, became a stock accusation of his Arab critics.[47] When coupled with the frequent, normally Israeli-inspired leaks about his covert search for peace, Hussein could be caricatured by his Arab enemies as a crypto-Zionist CIA lackey. The Jordanian authorities did little to alleviate the situation through their blank denials of all such dealings, and subsequent refusal to enter into any debate as to what the purpose of the King's covert relationship with the CIA or secret dialogue with Israel might have been. Hussein himself told *Newsweek* that 'the [CIA] assistance was designed only to enhance our intelligence and security capabilities. Period.'[48] Hussein's refusal to comment further in public was due to the fact that he wanted as far as possible to keep his family out of the media spotlight. Even in private, though, he was not much more expansive in his explanations. He told British Prime Minister James Callaghan on 24 February that 'he had never denied having received assistance from the United States, but this did not mean that the assistance was in the form of personal payments to the Head of State. He had in any case always assumed that the CIA was synonymous with the United States Government.'[49]

Beyond speculating inaccurately about the broader purposes of the payments, Woodward's article also asserted that President Carter had ordered them to be stopped at once when he was alerted to their existence by the *Washington Post* investigation. This lent further substance to the claim that Hussein's actions were somehow improper. While Carter did indeed order both subsidies stopped, the net result of halting the payment for his children's protection was only to provoke the King to move them away from school in the US. As for the 5,000-dinar payment, this had by now outlived its usefulness, since the CIA had established direct contact with the Jordanian Mukhabarat, and paid for its training and development through bilateral intelligence channels rather than through the King personally from now on. Attempting to draw a line under the unfortunate incident, Carter wrote in a private letter to the King:

> I want you to know how much I have regretted the embarrassment that recent press reports may have caused you and the people of Jordan. You understand, I am sure, that I have no authority to control the news media of this country and cannot prevent the publication of such misleading stories. I have, however, publicly stated that there was nothing illegal or improper in your relationship with us. I am particularly sorry that you have been exposed to unfair allegations, since I consider you one of our very close friends, whose wisdom and guidance will be of utmost importance as we work toward our common goal of peace in the Middle East.[50]

The story was without doubt 'misleading' and 'unfair', but this did not stop Hussein's critics using its claims as ammunition in their attacks on him for years to come; the damage it inflicted was lasting. The Woodward story brought to a close a painful chapter in Hussein's life. Sidelined in the peace process, slighted by his allies in Washington, and cruelly deprived of happiness in his personal life, the mid-1970s proved to be something of a mid-life crisis for the King.

1 King Abdullah, Hussein's grandfather, with soldiers of the Arab Legion in Jerusalem.

2 Hussein's father King Talal (right) and uncle Nayif, rivals for the succession to the Jordanian throne in 1951.

3 Hussein's mother, Queen Zein, who was a dominant influence during his childhood and adolescence.

4 The young Prince Hussein during his year at Harrow School in England, 1951–2.

5 Hussein indulging his lifelong passion for flying.

6 Hussein with General Glubb, the British commander of the Arab Legion, whom he dismissed on 1 March 1956.

14 The two Husseins: Iraqi President Saddam Hussein was a close political ally of King Hussein during the 1980s.

15 President Ronald Reagan (centre) and Secretary of State George Shultz entertain the King at the White House.

12 Hussein with his third wife, Queen Alia, whom he married in 1972, and who died in a helicopter crash in 1977.

13 Hussein and his fourth wife, Queen Noor, on their wedding day in 1978.

9 Hussein and Egyptian President Nasser, political rivals during the early years of Hussein's reign.

10 Hussein with King Feisal of Saudi Arabia, who was his friend and ally in the 1960s.

11 Hussein announcing Jordan's defeat at a press conference after the June 1967 war.

7 Hussein and his first wife Queen Dina, whom he married in 1955 and divorced in 1957.

8 Hussein and his second wife Princess Muna with their son Abdullah, who was born on 30 January 1962.

16 Hussein and PLO leader Yasser Arafat exchange greetings while Mahmoud Abbas, Arafat's deputy, looks on.

17 Hussein and his partner in peace-making Israeli Prime Minister Yitzhak Rabin shake hands, as President Clinton looks on.

18 Deciding the succession: Hussein nominates his son Abdullah (right) Crown Prince in place of his brother Hassan on 25 January 1999.

19 Jordanians mourn their King at his funeral in Amman on 8 February 1999.

CHAPTER 11

THE CAMP DAVID DISASTER,
1977–9

The year 1977 was not only one of private tragedy and public controversy for Hussein; it was also one of political upheaval in the region. In May, the opposition Likud Party won an Israeli election for the first time, and the following month the right-wing revisionist Menachem Begin formed a government. Begin saw the occupied West Bank as part of the biblical land of Israel, and he was ideologically opposed to giving up sovereignty over any part of it, least of all occupied East Jerusalem. His own earlier background as a terrorist in the days of the British mandate in Palestine suggested that he would go to whatever lengths were necessary in pursuit of his own ideals. With Israel's founding father, David Ben Gurion, likening Begin to Hitler, as the leader of a quasi-fascist movement, the prospects for progress in the Middle East peace process appeared bleak indeed.[1] On a visit to Washington in June 1977, Crown Prince Hassan, whose brief it was to discuss regional economic cooperation, warned National Security Advisor Zbigniew Brzezinski that:

> he feared that the Likud victory would make such cooperation difficult in the future. He also worried that Israel might try to divert attention by creating trouble in Lebanon or by playing on the weaknesses of the Syrian regime. This would buy Begin time. Jordan would try to stay out of a future war, but its ability to do so would depend on the type of war and its duration.[2]

Hussein, who had already expressed doubts at the beginning of the year about the possibility of a diplomatic breakthrough under the previous Israeli government, now had his sense of pessimism reinforced.[3] The worsening prospects for peace, together with the effects of his bereavement, the *Washington Post*'s story about the CIA payments and his punishing work schedule all seem once more to have depressed the King's health. In advance of a private visit to London in August, which the Jordanian royal court billed as being for the purposes of rest and relaxation, two interesting pieces of information reached the British government. The first concerned Hussein's health, with the embassy in Amman warning that 'the King's heart problem may be causing some concern' and that he might need to receive medical treatment in London. Just as after the 1967 war, the strains of high office seem to have taken their toll on the King. The second piece of information concerned the other, covert purpose of Hussein's visit. On a copy of the telegram from Amman confirming Hussein's intention to come to London, British Prime Minister James Callaghan added the note: 'If he asks I will see him. But I would like to know why Moshe Dayan is in London. Can someone find out?'[4] Callaghan's suspicions were confirmed, but the meeting which took place between Hussein and Dayan can have done little to improve either the King's state of mind or health. As he later noted, 'I saw my friend Moshe Dayan who had become the Foreign Minister of the Likud here in London. His attitude was even harder than it had been earlier and that was the end of that. We never had any contacts for a long period.'[5]

Against this unpromising backdrop, for much of the year the diplomatic focus was on the revival of the Geneva Peace Conference under the leadership of the new US administration of President Jimmy Carter. The December 1973 Geneva Conference had provided a multilateral framework for the resolution of the Arab–Israeli conflict, although the original meeting had broken up after little more than a formal opening session. Hussein favoured the Geneva framework since it provided a means of bringing all of the frontline Arab states into the peace process, and also provided for the US and USSR to act as co-chairmen, thus providing a counterpoise to the US's role as sole mediator. He hoped this approach might open the way to negotiations about the implementation of UN Security Council Resolution 242 within a multilateral framework. His ultimate goal remained a comprehensive peace in the region which would involve the return of all occupied Arab land and the recognition of Palestinian rights. The Israelis, meanwhile, were suspicious of the Geneva approach, believing that it would simply provide a platform for concerted Arab opposition, and further legitimacy to the Palestinian national cause.

The new president of the United States, Jimmy Carter, brought with him a close personal interest in the Arab–Israeli conflict born of religious conviction. A devout Southern Baptist, Carter felt a deep sympathy for Zionism. Nevertheless, this sympathy was balanced by his recognition of the plight of the Palestinians under occupation, whose position he saw as similar to that of the blacks in the United States. In view of Carter's fascination with the 'Holy Land', it is no surprise that he gave a high priority to the search for a breakthrough in the Middle East peace process during his first year in office.

By the autumn of 1978, it was clear that considerable progress had been made towards overcoming at least the procedural impediments to reconvening the Geneva Conference. In a letter to Hussein on 30 July, Carter wrote, 'I believe there is a common desire to resume the negotiations of the Middle East peace conference as soon as possible and to open negotiations without pre-conditions. This leads me to hope that negotiations will indeed be possible this fall.'[6] Following a visit by Secretary of State Cyrus Vance to the region in August, Carter struck an even more positive note, telling Hussein: 'I believe we have entered a new and more intensive phase of diplomacy which holds promise for genuine progress.'[7] Hussein too did his best to sound encouraging. 'I believe that American policy regarding the conflict in the Middle East is moving in the right direction and based on the right assumptions,' he wrote. 'It is in the interest of all the parties in the area as well as the United States that a comprehensive and just settlement of the Arab–Israeli conflict be achieved.'[8]

Despite Hussein's unsatisfactory encounter with Moshe Dayan in London during the second half of August, in a meeting with President Carter and his advisers on 19 September, the Israeli foreign minister indicated that he would be prepared to accept Palestinian representatives as part of a unified Arab delegation to the conference, and that he was even prepared to tolerate the presence of junior PLO members within such a delegation 'if everything else goes right'. 'Don't forget,' he commented, 'we deal at the moment with the mayors of the West Bank who are PLO sympathizers.'[9] By the beginning of October, National Security Council Middle East specialist William Quandt was able to write optimistically, 'if the Israeli Cabinet approves his recommendation, this will constitute a significant step in the direction of reconvening the Geneva Peace Conference. Only Syrian acceptance will remain difficult to obtain.'[10] Of course, getting the parties to Geneva was one thing; persuading them to enter into serious negotiations to resolve the conflict once they were there was quite another.

By November 1977, a reconvening of the Geneva Conference with all of the main parties was clearly a realistic prospect. A series of letters between the King and President Carter during the final two weeks of October reflect the sense of building momentum. On 16 October Carter wrote to Hussein, 'we have reached the point where the reconvening of the Geneva Peace Conference is a distinct possibility . . . I personally believe that little further progress can be made without meeting at Geneva.'[11] In an attempt to resolve the outstanding issue of how Palestinian representation should be achieved within a Unified Arab Delegation, Carter attached a working paper to his letter incorporating a suggested American framework which would bring this about.

Despite his continuing scepticism about the Israeli willingness to enter into negotiations in good faith, Hussein was encouraged by the evident progress towards a new peace conference, and paid Carter tribute in glowing terms for his personal efforts in bringing this change about. 'I am deeply impressed with your commitment to a just settlement for the conflict in the Middle East and your personal involvement in the construction of the structure of such a settlement,' he wrote to the president. 'Your insight into the realities of the Middle East situation is matched only by your inspiring dedication to the cause of justice and durable peace.'[12] The King promised to devote all of his energy to persuading fellow Arab leaders to remove the remaining obstacles in the way of the Geneva Conference, and to focus on substance rather than the form or procedure of the negotiations.

A turning point had now been reached. On 30 October Carter wrote back to the King, praising his constructive approach. 'I strongly believe that the time has come for us to move boldly to reconvene the Conference,' he argued, and proposed a specific set of steps which would lead to this goal, modelled on the procedure followed in 1973, but stating that in this case 'the Arab parties would agree to form a single delegation including Palestinian representatives'. Warning that his approach should be held in absolute confidence, Carter asked the King to signal his private agreement to this procedure, and concluded, 'I am convinced we are now at a critical moment in the efforts my Administration has been making since taking office nine months ago to chart a course that will lead to a just and lasting peace in the Middle East.'[13]

It was not to be. Instead, on 19 November 1977 President Sadat of Egypt crossed the Rubicon of Arab rejection of Israel in the most dramatic fashion when he arrived in person in Jerusalem to address the Knesset. Sadat's impetuous move was very much in character when one looks at his earlier career. Having grown up in Egypt under British occupation, he had been an early convert to the nationalist movement within the Egyptian army which seized power through the Free Officers coup of July 1952. Thereafter he had proved himself almost slavishly loyal to the coup's leader, Gamal Abdel Nasser, eventually succeeding to the Egyptian presidency himself after Nasser's death in September 1970. Of all the leading Free Officers Sadat probably had the most contempt for monarchy as an institution and the least respect for hereditary status of any kind. These views were apparent from a very early stage in his relationship with Hussein. But Sadat was above all a political gambler, a loner who played his own hand impetuously for the highest stakes. This much had been apparent in his earlier decisions both to abrogate the Egyptian–Soviet Treaty in 1972 and to launch the October war in 1973. Sadat's flight to Jerusalem, then, was another attempt to raise the stakes in the political poker game. His ultimate goal was clear: to win back Egypt's lost territory whatever the price in terms of relations with his fellow Arabs.

Sadat's visit stopped the multilateral negotiating process in its tracks. Its timing was no coincidence. Sadat knew, as did Hussein, that a return to Geneva was close, and he did not want to run the risk that his own interests might be lost in a resumed regional gathering. There was also an element of pride at stake. Sadat, who saw himself as the inheritor of Nasser's mantle of leader of the Arabs, did not want to submit to the authority of a unified Arab delegation. For all of these reasons, Hussein was particularly bitter about what had transpired. 'The real peace was derailed by Sadat. We were close to Geneva. We were all getting ready to go,' he later commented. It was not just that Sadat had bypassed the multilateral peace process on which Hussein had pinned his hopes; the symbolic significance of Sadat's act deeply affected the King personally:

> The visit to Jerusalem under occupation had great religious significance. My grandfather is buried there. He was involved in the Arab revolt against colonial rule and he died because he would not compromise. We lost Jerusalem in 1967 under Egyptian command. We knew we would lose, but we went into that war anyway. Under Egyptian command and responsibility the West Bank was lost. The Sadat visit was a very, very big shock.[14]

Although at the time Hussein welcomed Sadat's move in public, describing it as very brave and courageous,[15] in private his view was very different. According to his own account he subsequently asked Sadat, ' "why did you not tell me. Why not ask what you could get for 242?" I never got a positive answer.' 'Egypt has given much to unity,' he continued, 'but it cannot be a unity of one.'[16] US officials also described his views as 'very negative', noting that in practice there was not much difference between Hussein's position and that of President Asad of Syria.[17] The King was evidently worried that any isolated attempt by Sadat to secure a broader declaration of peace principles might go the way of his own efforts after the 1967 war, enabling the Israelis to prevaricate interminably.[18] In a January 1978 interview, he struck a pessi-mistic, almost despairing, note about the prospects for peace:

> I've done so much, I've hoped so much, my whole inclination, my whole feeling has been for peace, for a better future for the generations to come. All my efforts, my dreams – they are shattered. Maybe this is a reality that one has to begin to live with somehow. Maybe it's better than just living in dreams.[19]

Despite his scepticism about Sadat's chances of success, Hussein's initial refusal publicly to condemn the Egyptian president's move caused tensions in his relations with the Syrian regime. President Asad remained convinced that Sadat would sell out his former Arab allies at the first opportunity in exchange for Israel's return of the Egyptian Sinai peninsula. During a visit to Damascus in December 1977, the King found Asad 'adamant in his refusal to cooperate with Sadat' and determined to 'work for the creation of an Arab block opposed to Sadat's approach and actions'.[20] The King also remained a target for other Arab radicals; in February 1978 a further assassination plot against him was uncovered, this time involving the smuggling of a SAM 7 surface-to-air missile into Jordan, presumably for the purpose of shooting down his plane.[21]

The Sadat visit was not only the end of the multilateral peace process; it also marked a turning point in Hussein's relations with President Carter. Initially, as was shown by their early exchanges, the King had formed a positive impression of the new president, noting that Carter had given him more time to express his views during his May 1977 visit to the US than had any of his predecessors.[22] But Sadat's initiative, presenting as it did the opportunity for Carter to pursue a bilateral Israeli–Egyptian peace process with a greater chance of short-term success than the complex Geneva approach, proved too much of a temptation for the president.[23] Although Hussein travelled to Tehran in December 1977 to meet Carter again, this time in the presence of the Shah, their talks did not produce a meeting of minds. Carter wrote that he now had a much better appreciation of the King's 'concerns and requirements in the current negotiations', but this did not affect his own subsequent course of action.[24] For his part, Hussein continued to stress in a succession of letters sent to the president between March and August 1978 the need for a multilateral approach to peace-making within the framework established by UN Resolution 242, writing, 'for the present peace negotiations to progress and expand there must be some concrete indication shown by Israel that the negotiations would ultimately result in Israeli withdrawal and a just settlement of the Palestinian question based on the right of self-determination'.[25] As ever, Hussein was deeply sceptical about the Israeli approach to the negotiations. 'There are many signs', he wrote, 'that the Israeli leadership will not show the necessary historic vision to respond positively to President Sadat's initiative. If this situation continues and the initiative collapses in such circumstances, then the Arab world is likely to switch towards an extreme radicalism.'

The passages which Hussein chose to underline in the text of Carter's 18 March reply to his letter are particularly instructive as to his concerns about the Egyptian–Israeli peace process. Some of these passages, with Hussein's added emphasis, are reproduced below. Carter wrote:

It is my hope that the process which we have begun will lead <u>to broader negotiations</u> which Jordan will be able to join . . . Knowing the strength of the bonds between the Hashemite Kingdom of Jordan and the West Bank, it has <u>always been our view that final arrangements should provide for the restoration of ties between the two, and for the inclusion of Gaza in this framework as well</u> . . . The United States has, likewise, taken <u>the position that the Palestinian people must participate in determination of their own future</u> . . . I well understand the problems for Jordan in joining the negotiations. I want you to know that the United States will do its utmost to assure [sic] that they lead to a just and reasonable settlement, <u>and that Jordan's interests are fully taken into account.</u>[26]

One key element of the negotiating process was out of the president's hands. Carter repeatedly expressed the hope that, as he put it in a further letter of 13 May, 'you and President Sadat will coordinate your positions to the maximum degree'.[27] In fact, the letters which Hussein exchanged with Sadat between December 1977 and September 1978 chart the progressive deterioration in their relationship. Sadat's report to Hussein on his 25 December 1977 meeting with Begin at Ismailiya already foreshadowed the insurmountable problems in the way of making a satisfactory deal with the Israelis. Sadat told Hussein that he had made it clear to Begin that 'Palestinian sovereignty lies at the heart of the problem'.[28] Begin for his part, according to Sadat, had argued that since both the Arabs and Israel claimed sovereignty over the West Bank and Gaza, it was best to lay this issue to one side. Israel would instead grant the inhabitants of the territories self-rule, while retaining control over security and the right to seize land and build settlements. By contrast, Begin indicated willingness to negotiate a staged withdrawal from Egypt's own territory in exchange for a peace treaty. Sadat told Hussein that he found Begin's offer unacceptable since it amounted to the continued occupation of the West Bank and Gaza. He claimed to have told Begin that 'there is no running away from the sovereignty problem of the Palestinians', but that Begin was uncompromising on this issue. Sadat concluded by saying that he had 'hoped for more courage on the part of Begin', but that he realised that the Israeli prime minister was 'under great pressure from the more radical elements in his Cabinet'. In what proved to be a fateful promise at the end of his letter, Sadat assured the King that he would 'not move from his strong position in the cause of the Arab nation and the Palestinians'.

Hussein took some comfort from Sadat's letter. His reply, the warmest of the letters which passed between them during this period, updated Sadat on his meeting with Carter in Iran, noting that the president did not support Begin's position over the Palestinian territories. Carter had promised him that he would play 'a strong role in the coming negotiations'. Hussein stressed that the Palestinians would have to be drawn into the peace process. Jordan would be willing to discuss security concerns because these issues were important to everybody, not just Israel. Peace would only be possible, though, 'if Israel withdraws and the Palestinians get their right to sovereignty'.[29]

Hussein must already have suspected that any coordination between Sadat and the PLO was extremely unlikely, given the parlous state of Egyptian–PLO relations. On 28 February 1978, Arafat wrote to Hussein complaining about what he saw as a series of Egyptian attacks on the Palestinians, whom they were treating 'unjustly and viciously'. Arafat pointed in particular to the Egyptian decision to cancel legal and economic rights for the Palestinians in Egypt, which he argued would have devastating consequences for the Palestinian inhabitants of Gaza. Egypt's behaviour, according to Arafat, was only 'serving the Zionist and imperialist cause'.[30] In his reply to the PLO chairman on 22 March, the King could do no more than lament the sad state of Egyptian–Palestinian relations, and emphasise that the only real solution to the Palestinian problem was for the Arabs to start working together and show solidarity.[31] It was an appeal which fell on deaf ears.

Sadat's strategy in the negotiations, as he outlined it to Hussein in a further letter sent in the wake of discussions with the US Ambassador Alfred Atherton in April, was to try to divide the US and Israel, and persuade Carter to put significant pressure on Begin to reach a satisfactory agreement. Sadat reported that Carter wanted to 'enlarge the circle of negotiations' so as to include other Arab parties, starting with Jordan, and suggested that one useful tactic might be to produce a detailed Arab view of the transitional self-rule period in the Palestinian territories, which would emphasise the importance of self-determination. He added that he did not see any difficulty with the concept of a transitional period in itself, but that it must lead to full withdrawal. Once again, he stressed that he would refuse any compromise in relation to the sovereignty issue over the West Bank and Gaza.[32]

With the Egyptian–Israeli negotiating process approaching deadlock, Carter decided that the only way to make progress was to convene a trilateral US–Egyptian–Israeli summit at the presidential retreat of Camp David, beginning on 6 September 1978. On 15 August Carter wrote to the King explaining the reason why he had elected to call the summit. Once again, Hussein's highlighting of the text reveals the issues which concerned him most. Carter wrote:

> I am convinced that we cannot afford an impasse, since the positions would then harden and the atmosphere deteriorate to the point where the present opportunity for peace could well become another of the lost opportunities that have marked the history of this tragic conflict . . . Insofar as our efforts at Camp David are concerned, we will be guided by

our views on a just and lasting peace which we have consistently
conveyed to you over the months past.[33]

On 27 August, Hussein replied to Carter, beginning by focusing on the
concerns he had highlighted in the text of Carter's own letter. 'I am
particularly grateful and satisfied', he wrote, 'at your assurance that your
efforts at Camp David will be guided by your views on a just and lasting peace
which have been the subject of our talks and contacts since the beginning.'
But, he continued, he could not be anything other than pessimistic about the
likely outcome of the summit:

> Permit me . . . to point out that it is feared here in Jordan that the
> inability to achieve such genuine progress in the talks, as a result of
> Israel's proven intransigence, might prompt the participants to issue
> a vague and uncommiting document of principles aimed at de-
> emphasizing the differences and inviting other participants.[34]

Hussein's prediction was uncannily accurate.

Hussein's own role at the Camp David talks was somewhat paradoxical. On
the one hand, he was treated as an essential player in any settlement of the
West Bank-Palestinian question. On the other, he was not actually invited to
the summit. He was thus to be asked to take on responsibilities under the
Camp David framework without having any say in their negotiation. Even
given the greatest of goodwill, this would have been a difficult formula to
implement. Unfortunately, by this stage there was no basis for trust between
Hussein and Sadat. Furthermore, the King's relations with Carter had become
tense and distant. Hussein had also effectively broken off contact with the
Begin government, his last meeting having been that with Foreign Minister
Moshe Dayan in London in August 1977 before the breakdown of the Geneva
process.[35] Thus, although Carter scribbled 'communications with Hussein' as
one of the points for attention on his copy of the State Department summit
briefing book, his annotation on another paper – 'Jordan's timidity could
block progress' – said much about the strained nature of his relations with the
King.[36]

Before the Camp David summit convened, Sadat had written to Hussein
repeating his determination to demand Israeli withdrawal from the West
Bank and Gaza. He also told him that he had given Ambassador Atherton a
message for Carter, warning that he would quit the negotiations if Israel
remained intransigent, since in these circumstances it would be impossible to
secure Jordanian participation. Finally, Sadat promised to pursue the strategy
he had previously outlined of putting pressure on Israel by isolating it from
the United States, especially over the issue of withdrawal from the West Bank

and Gaza.[37] Hussein stressed in his reply that Jordan still wanted a joint peacemaking effort involving the Palestinians. Just as in his letter to Carter before the opening of the summit, Hussein warned Sadat of the danger of a 'possible declaration of principles which would cover Israel's negative position in vague terms', arguing that Sadat should be prepared to take the issue to the Security Council to try to secure a further resolution which would force Israel to implement UN Resolution 242. In a phrase well chosen to haunt the Egyptian leader at Camp David, Hussein concluded his letter by expressing confidence in Sadat's 'deep Arab nationalism'.[38]

In a phone conversation during the Camp David summit itself, Hussein reminded Sadat of these exchanges, and once again advised going to the UN Security Council if Israel proved intransigent. In fact, contrary to his promises in his letters to Hussein, Sadat showed little interest in pressing the West Bank and Gaza withdrawal question at Camp David. According to William Quandt, once agreement had been reached on the largely meaningless gesture of appending the text of Resolution 242 to the framework agreement, 'he showed little concern with details of how the West Bank and Gaza should be dealt with'.[39] This left the American side to try to whittle away at Begin's entrenched position over what he called 'Judea and Samaria' with little result. The final framework agreement for peace in the Middle East reflected the very modest concessions the US team had been able to wring from Begin. It was undermined still further by Begin's subsequent attempts to back away from even the very limited and ambiguous form of interim autonomy for the Palestinians provided for under the framework.

Hussein, who had embarked on a trip to Morocco, learnt of the final Camp David agreements during a stopover he made in Spain. According to the then prime minister, Mudar Badran, the King had initially wanted to meet Sadat on his way back from the US for a secret session in Morocco to try to persuade him to change his mind. Badran warned against this since if reports leaked out it might create the impression that Hussein and Sadat had coordinated the Egyptian president's actions at Camp David in advance. Instead, the King insisted that Badran arrange a meeting of the full Jordanian cabinet at the airport immediately on his return to Amman to discuss the implications of the Camp David agreement for Jordan.[40]

In fact, the 'Framework for Peace in the Middle East' invited the government of Jordan to join negotiations on the details of transitional arrangements for the West Bank and Gaza.[41] It also stipulated that 'a strong local police force will be established, which may include Jordanian citizens', and that 'Israeli and Jordanian forces will participate in joint patrols and in the manning of control posts to assure the security of the borders.' By the third year of the planned five-year transitional period, negotiations were to start both to determine the final status of the West Bank and Gaza, and to conclude a peace treaty between Israel and Jordan. The document is remarkable for the extent of the obligations it proposed to devolve on to a party which had not participated in the negotiations. Indeed, it would not be unreasonable to describe its prescription that Jordan must negotiate on the basis of this framework and conclude a peace treaty with Israel by the end of the transitional period as an affront to Jordanian sovereignty.

Despite the high-handed nature of the document, Hussein's initial public, if not private, response was measured. As he described matters:

> Then came the agreement, a very limited agreement. We were told that the vagueness was intentional. The role provided for Jordan under the Camp David agreements was that of a policeman, to ensure the security: of whom – the occupied? We tried to keep as quiet as possible. But that is not a role that we could play. What we wanted to know was what was the final object. Perhaps if we knew that, we could work it out.[42]

In a belated effort to gain Hussein's support after the conclusion of the summit, Carter sent him two letters: a formal, printed explanation of the agreements; and a handwritten, personal plea for him to join the process. In the formal letter, Carter acknowledged that the agreements reached at Camp David 'do not meet either your full expectations or those of President Sadat'. The president urged him to 'examine most carefully the documents concluded today at Camp David . . . Whether these opportunities can be translated into reality depends in large measure on Your Majesty. The framework document provides a significant role for Jordan – a role we will support and urge others to support.'[43]

The second, handwritten letter was sent the following day. In a tone which was half-pleading and half-threatening, Carter wrote:

> Egypt and Israel have proven that they want peace. A failure of our effort because of lack of support from other responsible and moderate leaders of the Arab nations would certainly lead to the strengthening of irresponsible and radical elements and a further opportunity for intrusion of Soviet and other Communist influence throughout the Middle East.[44]

To underline the point, Carter wrote on a separate line at the bottom of the page: 'I need your strong personal support.'

Sadat also wrote to Hussein after Camp David, providing his own detailed exegesis of what the terms of the 'Framework for Peace in the Middle East' actually meant. Acknowledging that the document was not a definitive solution, Sadat argued that it could still have positive consequences for the Palestinians 'if we use it rightly'. For Sadat, it exceeded the terms of

Resolution 242 by forcing the Israelis to acknowledge the political nature of the Palestinian question, rather than just treating it as a refugee problem. According to Sadat, he had 'tried his best' to get the words 'self-determination' inserted into the text, but Carter had explained that this was not possible since American public opinion would not support forcing Israel to accept this formulation. But, he asserted, the text made the eventual reaching of self-determination 'inevitable and undisputable'. Somewhat improbably, Sadat also claimed that the agreement would mean that 'the cancer-like spread of Israeli settlements will finally stop'.[45]

In order both to avoid an immediate breach in relations with the US and Egypt, and to investigate further as to the precise meaning of the ambiguous accord reached at Camp David, the King submitted a list of fourteen questions to US Secretary of State Cyrus Vance, who had flown to the region immediately after the conclusion of the summit bearing the handwritten letter from Carter. Vance agreed to provide Hussein with written answers.[46] As Hussein put it:

> we are trying to feel our way . . . through this maze of statements and what is available to us. And we feel obviously that the best possible course open to us is to ask some very definite questions. Hopefully we will get clear answers which will enable us to formulate our position . . . Certainly, there is a lot of vagueness that needs to be cleared up.[47]

The answers to Hussein's questions, under President Carter's signature, were duly delivered to him on 16 October by Assistant Secretary of State Hal Saunders. In the interim, in a speech delivered to the Jordanian people and the Arab nation on 10 October, Hussein had made clear the depth of his doubt about the Camp David formula. 'The Camp David decisions contain two main loopholes,' he argued.

> First, they do not imperatively link the Egyptian–Israeli agreement and the solution of the other aspects of the Arab–Israeli problem on the other fronts. Second, they do not clearly show the end of the road with regard to the West Bank, Jerusalem, Gaza and the right of self-determination for the Palestinians.[48]

Hussein also made his concerns very plain in a letter he sent to Sadat on 14 October 1978 in response to Sadat's earlier analysis of the Camp David agreements. The tone of the letter was cold, warning of the dangers of concluding a bilateral peace with Israel and deserting the common Arab cause. Criticising both agreements which came out of Camp David, Hussein pointed out that Israel had always tried to split the Arab world, and that

Egypt's role in keeping the Arab cause alive was crucial. For Hussein, the framework agreement on peace in the Middle East was vague, not linked to the separate Egyptian–Israeli agreement, and failed to mention key issues such as Arab sovereignty in the occupied territories and the status of Jerusalem. In his view any transitional agreement was 'useless', since Israel would continue its 'real politik' by changing facts on the ground. The only way forward, the King concluded, was to stay united, act as one bloc, and exercise maximum pressure on Israel.[49]

Despite the uncompromising nature of his letter to Sadat, in his response to the Americans the King continued to stall, telling Assistant Secretary Saunders that he would not be ready to make a decision on whether to enter into the negotiating process until after the Arab summit due to be held in Baghdad in early November.[50] In fact, the King's personal papers reveal that in a letter sent to Carter on 31 October, written just before his departure for Baghdad, Hussein finally made his views not only about the Camp David agreements, but also about the whole Egyptian–Israeli peace process, crystal clear. Of all the letters in Hussein's files, this one bears the most significant evidence of painstaking, even anguished, drafting and redrafting. Working off a partially typed-up text, dated 30 October, Hussein proceeded to strengthen the tone of his rejection of the agreements with a series of handwritten annotations. So the sentence 'there are some fundamental questions in our minds regarding the results of the Camp David agreements' in the 30 October draft became '*from the very beginning* there *were* some fundamental questions in our minds regarding the results of the Camp David agreements' in the final version. Similarly, the sentence in the draft 'allow me now to summarize to you our views here regarding the Camp David agreements and their chances of development into an acceptable and viable basis for future peace efforts' became 'allow me to summarize to you our views here regarding the Camp David agreements and *what we regard as a viable basis for future peace efforts*' in his final version. The thrust of Hussein's alterations was clear. He had been opposed to Sadat's initiative all along, and he did not believe that the Camp David agreements provided a viable basis for future peace efforts.[51]

Hussein proceeded to make quite clear what was wrong with the agreements from his perspective:

There was a major difference between the two documents which emerged from Camp David regarding the question of the future status of the occupied areas. While the Egyptian–Israeli accord was explicit on the question of Egyptian sovereignty over Sinai, the future of the West Bank and Gaza have been left open to negotiations. I believe that there was no balance in this, particularly as the document dealing with the West Bank and Gaza was very explicit in its provisions regarding the transitional agreements and the Jordanian role and responsibilities in them.[52]

As far as the answers supplied by the Americans to his questions were concerned, Hussein wrote, 'I am afraid . . . that they did not alter the situation in a major way. We still feel . . . that we are asked to participate in arrangements with the Israelis in the occupied areas prior to a definite knowledge of the outcome of such arrangements.' The agreements provided 'no definite answers to our fundamental concerns, namely the ultimate total Israeli withdrawal, self-determination for the Palestinians and the return of Arab Jerusalem to Arab sovereignty'.

The ensuing Baghdad summit merely confirmed that there was no possibility of Hussein joining the Camp David process. The concerted criticism of the Camp David Accords, and the public threat of the removal of the headquarters of the Arab League from Cairo if Egypt signed a separate peace treaty with Israel, led to Sadat's refusal to meet the delegation despatched by the Arab leaders. Sadat's pointed reference to the summit participants as 'cowards and dwarfs' must have had a familiar ring to Hussein, who had endured similar attacks from Nasser in the run-up to the 1967 war. 'I know that our US friends were upset by the Baghdad Conference,' the King told National Security Advisor Brzezinski during his brief stopover in Amman on 18 March 1979, but 'from my perspective and responsibility, this was the best that could be done'.[53] Writing to explain the outcome of the summit to President Carter on 29 December, Hussein argued that 'most Arab parties, including Jordan, see the resolutions drawn up by the United States, Egypt and Israel as successfully achieving the well-known Israeli objective of isolating Egypt from the Arab camp, and thus weakening it further, which is one of the reasons for our finding them unacceptable'. Moreover, the agreements neglected, in Hussein's view, the rights of the Palestinians, while allowing Israel to continue to 'create new facts, altering the character of the entire area'. He added, 'I believe the heart of the problem to be sadly clear . . . the United States, where the Zionist lobby is so strong, cannot be the champion of Israel . . . and concurrently the sole impartial and objective mediator with Israel's opponents.'[54]

Hussein's refusal to join the Camp David process led to a serious rupture in his relations with the Carter administration. In his memoirs, Carter noted that 'all of us were angered when Hussein subsequently became a spokesman for the most radical Arabs'.[55] Carter argued that the subsequent signature of the Israeli–Egyptian Peace Treaty in March was 'the indispensable first step toward peace for all who have suffered in this conflict'.[56] In its aftermath, the president sent a high-level delegation, including his National Security Advisor, Zbigniew Brzezinski, to Amman to press the case for supporting the treaty.[57] The meeting was a dialogue of the deaf. As a punishment for its stance, Jordan was subjected subsequently to indirect US financial pressure.[58] This did not prevent Hussein from speaking out against the conclusion of the Egyptian–Israeli Peace Treaty. 'As-Sadat [sic] has provided an opportunity which the Israelis always hoped for to divide and subjugate the Arabs', he told *Newsweek* magazine.[59] As for the Americans, Hussein was uncompromising: 'if they consider us to be a problem in pursuing their policy, then I imagine we shall continue to be one,' he countered.[60] Still, not everyone within the Carter administration blamed the King for his stance. NSC staffer William Quandt subsequently wrote that Carter too readily swallowed Sadat's view that Hussein and the other Arabs did not matter much and would simply have to accept the new facts of life. According to Quandt, 'this was a serious misjudgement. Little could have been done, in my view, to win the overt support of King Hussein for Camp David and the Peace Treaty, but we might have been able to gain his tacit endorsement for our endeavours. But we never made the necessary effort, nor did Sadat.'[61] For Hussein the problem was even simpler: 'The Egyptians regard other Arabs as a herd of sheep for whom Egypt chooses the course they are expected to follow unquestioningly,' he observed bitterly.[62]

In the event, US–Jordanian relations were partially salvaged by events further afield. The toppling of the Shah of Iran in January 1979 and the ensuing US embassy hostage crisis, followed by the Soviet invasion of Afghanistan in December, convinced administration officials, including Vance and Brzezinski, that relations with Jordan should be repaired. The King played his own part in this limited rapprochement both by expressing his personal sympathy for President Carter's plight during the hostage crisis – 'I have felt very close to you during this dangerous period',[63] he wrote – and by emphasising his strong opposition to the Soviet invasion of Afghanistan.[64] In late December, both Vance and Brzezinski recommended to the president that he should make a determination that Jordan was acting in good faith in the peace process. Without this formal presidential confirmation, under the terms of the International Security Assistance Act of 1979, virtually all US military assistance to Jordan would have to stop immediately. 'Despite our differences over Camp David and the King's ill-advised intemperance earlier this year,' Brzezinski argued, 'the fundamental relationship is very important to US interests.'[65] He cited Jordanian cooperation over the situation in Iran and Yemen, together with the possibility of joint contingency planning for operations in Saudi Arabia as examples of the relationship's value to the US. Carter himself evidently had more difficulty in putting the events of the past year behind him. On Brzezinski's memo he annotated the words: 'it is a very close call, & difficult for me – but OK this time'.

Personal relations between Carter and Hussein only made a belated and very limited recovery during the King's visit to Washington in June 1980. The unusually long interval since the King's previous visit in May 1977 said much about the strained nature of relations in the meanwhile. Much of the media attention during the trip focused on the King's dazzling fourth wife, the American-born Lisa Halaby, who was making her first official trip back to the capital as Queen Noor. The twenty-eight-year-old queen outshone all of the guests at the White House, exuding what one correspondent called a kind of Grace Kelly regality, dressed in Paris couture and diamonds. Indeed President Carter began his toast at the state dinner by noting that 'a lot of people have accused me of inviting Their Majesties to Washington just so we could have Queen Noor visit the White House . . . It's a delightful experience for us', he went on, 'and her presence vividly demonstrates the close relation-ship and the unbreakable ties between our two countries.'[66] Queen Noor later commented that while she was flattered by the implied comparison with Jackie Kennedy, with all the talk about her appearance she could not help but feel like a useless accessory.[67]

For all that she sometimes despaired of the media focus on her looks, the young Queen Noor certainly helped the King with the public diplomacy of his visit. The daughter of Najeeb Halaby, who had been President Kennedy's aviation adviser, and Doris Carlquist, the then Lisa Halaby had graduated from Princeton in 1974, majoring in architecture and urban planning. After spending some time in Iran, she came to Jordan to work for her father's aviation company in Jordan early in 1977. After a whirlwind courtship during the spring and summer of 1978, she married Hussein on 15 June 1978. As an American woman who now underwent a personal crash course in the realities of Middle East politics, Noor came to be imbued with a strong sense of the rights and wrongs of the Arab–Israeli conflict. She was also a very effective communicator. Moreover, her baptism of fire at the Hashemite court where, as a young American woman who initially spoke no Arabic, she had had to find her feet quickly amongst palace intrigues, had also helped her to develop a tough outer shell. This was a useful quality when parrying questions from typically pro-Israeli audiences in the United States. From this point onwards Noor was to prove not only a loyal wife but also a diplomatic asset for the King in helping to communicate his case in the West.

Whatever her own feelings about the matter, there is no doubt that all of the enthusiastic media attention for Queen Noor also helped Hussein and Carter to put a positive gloss on the business sessions of the June 1980 visit. Carter noted that they had been 'much better than would have been expected, because of his frankness and because of his generosity, his eagerness to understand different points of view without yielding at all on the deep principles which have guided his life and which he holds so dear'. In return,

Hussein acknowledged differences in approach, but stressed that both he and Carter shared a dedication to peace. Carter's son Chip Carter commented, 'I like him and Dad likes him too. They're very candid with each other.'[68] For all their candour, though, there was to be no meeting of minds between Hussein and Carter over the way forward in the peace process. In private, Carter remained much less effusive about the King, noting that his promise to 'try to be constructive' and 'act in parallel' with the US was 'an adequate position but only as long as the United States holds firm on Camp David'.[69]

How might one summarise the 1970s for Hussein, then? 'Three wives, one war and no peace' might be an apt epigram. But the King's attempts to build a rapprochement with Syria after the 1973 war, and his reluctance to sever all ties with the West Bank in the wake of the Rabat resolution of 1974, showed that his broader dynastic ambitions also persisted through the decade. While for the most part these remained unspoken, the King's passing comment that Jordan must have 'a larger future than a few thousand square miles of sand' provided a hint as to his broader aspirations. Domestically, these were years of rapid transformation, with the regime consolidating its position in the wake of the expulsion of the PLO. Although Hussein had spoken in 1972 of finding his equilibrium and developing 'a sense of inner satisfaction', his turbulent progress through the decade suggested otherwise. Moreover, with the conclusion of the Egyptian–Israeli peace treaty, and the weakening of his ties to the US, by 1979 the King was on the verge of striking out on a new path in regional politics. Carter's embrace of Sadat's unilateral peace initiative had left him with no choice but to seek new friends in unlikely quarters. This was one of the unfortunate consequences of Camp David. The burgeoning of the King's personal relations with the Iraqi leader Saddam Hussein against the backdrop of the 1978 and 1979 Baghdad summits and the outbreak of the Iran–Iraq war in 1980 pointed towards a new era. The 1980s were to be the decade of the two Husseins.

CHAPTER 12

THE IRAN–IRAQ WAR, 1980–88

'I am proud of the brotherhood that exists between us,' proclaimed King Hussein, speaking of his closest Arab ally, Iraqi President Saddam Hussein, in March 1981. 'He is a noble and gallant Arab, a wise leader and a man who works for the future. That's what is common between us. We live to do what we can for the good and welfare of the future Arab generations.'[1]

From the perspective of the early twenty-first century, with Saddam having been executed for crimes against humanity, and Iraq enduring virtual civil war while still under foreign military occupation, King Hussein's description of the Iraqi leader seems startling. In fact, it would not be difficult, scanning the King's speeches and statements from the 1980s, to find many more such flattering descriptions of the Iraqi president. The King's faith in Saddam was probably the biggest character misjudgement of his reign, and one for which he was to pay a high political price. Perhaps surprisingly, however, it has received comparatively little attention from his biographers.[2] One reason may be that the seemingly unlikely alliance between the Baathist dictator and the Hashemite patrician is an uneasy fit with the conventional image of Hussein in the West as an Arab moderate. Nevertheless, support for Iraq during its bitter eight-year struggle with Iran was arguably the central plank of Hussein's statecraft during the 1980s. His partnership with Saddam during these years, it seems, was born of a combination of factors, including national interest, ideology, domestic politics, budget security, dynastic ambition and personal affinity. Not all of these factors had equal weight in Hussein's own thinking, but they all played a role in cementing and perpetuating the Iraqi–Jordanian alliance.

The personal affinity between the two leaders offers some fascinating insights into Hussein's character. In their private correspondence, each often addressed the other in familiar terms, with Saddam using the family name 'Abu Abdullah' in his letters to the King, and Hussein reciprocating in letters addressed to 'Abu Uday'.[3] One Hashemite family member close to Hussein in the final years of his life suggests that the King saw Saddam as a sort of 'noble savage', a 'Bedouin' who was strict and brutal but fair. Moreover, he argues, Saddam subtly played on the King's own sensibilities, honouring the memory of the Hashemites in Iraq. During a July 1988 visit to Baghdad, for instance, the King was taken to the Hashemite royal cemetery where prayers were read for the souls of King Feisal I and King Ghazi. Soon afterwards money was granted for the renovation of the site, and the Iraqi press announced that a bronze equestrian statue of King Feisal, torn down in July 1958, would be re-erected at its original site, ironically a square which had in the meantime been renamed after the former Egyptian President Gamal Abdel Nasser.[4]

If these gestures towards the Hashemite heritage in Iraq played on the King's personal sensibilities, another theme of his eulogies for Saddam during the 1980s was the Iraqi leader's dedication to 'Arabism'. On one level, this is no surprise, since Iraq under Saddam was engaged in a bloody struggle with Iran, a traditional enemy of the Arabs. But, in the wake of what the King saw as Sadat's defection from the Arab camp through his signature of a peace treaty with Israel, he evidently felt that the Arabs sorely needed a new champion, a charismatic leader under whose banner they could all unite. Once again, Saddam subtly played on these sentiments, arguing that Iraq's struggle for its legitimate rights against Iran and the broader Arab struggle for dignity and independence were one and the same. As Saddam put it in a long handwritten letter to the King, sent on 31 May 1986:

> I agree with you that we were always in agreement regarding our analyses of the current Arab situation, and regarding many problems that our nation is suffering from . . . And this agreement and harmony between us – which is built on the foundations of commitment and mutual trust, and cooperation and keenness on the higher interests of the nation – has been a positive factor in the Arab position during the last years . . . It has likewise contributed to giving the right example of how the Arab countries should organise their relationships.[5]

In the same letter, Saddam spoke of Iraq's relationship with Jordan as being one which could never be emulated by that with any other Arab country, saying that his unparalleled relations with Jordan under King Hussein were 'the result of many years of mutual understanding and trust and solidarity and cooperation'.

Beyond their shared commitment to 'Arabism', it has been suggested rather less high-mindedly that the financial support Saddam gave to the King from 1976 onwards, even before he became Iraqi president, provided another foundation for their close relationship.[6] The extent and impact of this aid are both unclear, but it is no doubt true that the King felt more comfortable accepting funds from Saddam than from the Kuwaitis, Saudis or other Gulf sheikhdoms. Assistance from the Iraqi leader did not compromise the dignity of Hussein's throne in the same way as canvassing for money from former dynastic enemies or *nouveaux riches* Gulf sheikhs might appear to do. Not only that, but the Iraqi leader was prepared to be generous with his money, asking for little in return other than that Hussein should continue to advocate his cause.

If these were the personal factors which influenced the King's close relationship with Saddam, there were also other inducements in terms of broader Jordanian national interests. In the wake of the Camp David deal, Hussein was faced with awkward choices. US policy required Jordan to take sides and, since the King refused to enter the Sadat-led peace process, his only other alternative was to join the Arab rejectionist camp. Unfortunately even this formulation over-simplified the choice open to him, for the Arab rejectionist camp itself was split between rival poles of Baathist attraction. Hussein had built up close relations with the Syrian regime of President Hafez Asad in the wake of the 1973 war, but Sadat's visit to Jerusalem, and Hussein's initial qualified public welcome for the Egyptian president's initiative, had already put his relations with Syria under strain. Asad, astutely as it turned out, had expected all along that Sadat's démarche would result in a bilateral Egyptian–Israeli peace deal. Hussein was prepared to give Sadat the benefit of the doubt, at least in public, until the Camp David deal was done. Even then, once it was clear that Egypt had departed the Arab fold, Hussein would have preferred not to have had to make a further choice between Iraq or Syria. However, the renewed hostility between the two Baathist regimes in the wake of Saddam's assumption of the Iraqi presidency in July 1979 meant that he could not keep a foot in both camps. In the end, Iraq's oil wealth, and its ability to offer Jordan both budget and military security in the face of the crisis in relations with the US, proved to be decisive factors in determining the direction of Jordan's realignment.[7]

The tilt towards Iraq came at the cost of a serious breakdown in relations with Syria during 1980, when a Syrian military build-up on the Jordanian border in December brought the two sides to the brink of confrontation before Damascus backed off. The war of words continued into 1981, with Jordanian television publicising details of an apparent Syrian plot to kill Prime Minister Mudar Badran in February.[8] Even the King himself indulged in some unusually harsh and direct criticism of the Syrian regime, observing

in a speech in March 1981 that 'the leadership is harming the Syrian people
. . . In order to cover its failure in destroying Syria's spirit, the Syrian
leadership is finding cause for battles with us and others in the Arab world.
Syria wants to kill the Arab human being and Arab free opinion.' On Syria's
support for Iran, Hussein was equally scathing: 'Arabistan, which has always,
until the beginning of this century, been Arab, has become Iranian in the logic
of the Syrian leadership . . . Syria wants Iraq, our support, to be defeated so
that the Gulf will be undefended and the Arab holy land exposed to danger.'[9]
Tension rumbled on through the year, with Syrian accusations that Jordan
was sponsoring domestic Islamist opposition forces and Jordanian allegations
that Syria was behind terrorist activities in the kingdom, including a bomb
explosion in a grocery store in Amman. During the early 1980s at least,
Jordan's alliance with Iraq came at the cost of seriously strained relations with
its northern neighbour.

In financial terms, the emerging alliance between Jordan and Iraq during
this period was underpinned by the 1978 Baghdad summit pledges of aid to
Jordan totalling $1.25 billion per annum, which Saddam had played a major
role in negotiating behind the scenes. Subsequently, Iraqi grant aid to Jordan
for projects such as the development of the Aqaba port and the associated
road infrastructure expanded substantially during 1979–80. Aqaba played a
major role during the war with Iran, to the extent that even Hussein admitted
in private that it functioned as 'an Iraqi port', a fact that proved one of the
most visible and, from the Western perspective, controversial aspects of the
King's support for Saddam during the 1980s.[10]

Jordanian domestic reaction to the new-found closeness between Iraq and
Jordan was much more favourable. Saddam's direct financial largesse, and the
profits to be made in various aspects of the trade with Iraq, both overt and
covert, soon secured the support of a large part of the Jordanian political elite.
Allegations of corruption were widespread although they have proved difficult to substantiate against specific individuals. But Saddam's high-profile
arrival in Amman in November 1987 for the Arab summit meeting with a
fleet of new Mercedes cars, which he proceeded to distribute to chosen
members of the Jordanian elite, provided something of a leitmotif for the era.

The alliance with Iraq also became popular among broader Jordanian
public opinion. Although it was Saddam who took the initiative in invading
Iran in September 1980, most Jordanians accepted that the revolutionary
Islamist regime in Tehran posed a threat to Iraq and the broader Arab
world. Iraqi claims about Iranian provocations were lent extra weight by the
anti-Baathist propaganda campaign which the Iranian regime had mounted
before war broke out. The secular, nationalist ideology professed by
Saddam's regime was anathema to the Islamist ideologues who now ruled
in Tehran.

King Hussein, meanwhile, chose to play up a pan-Arab ideological justification for backing Baghdad. A persistent theme of his speeches during the early 1980s was that Iraq was both the shield and the heart of the Arab nation, providing its 'strategic depth'. Hussein often linked this argument to the familiar Hashemite theme of the Great Arab Revolt, suggesting that Saddam's Iraq had picked up the same banner and was advancing in the vanguard of the Arab nation. So, shortly after a visit to Baghdad in the wake of the outbreak of the war with Iran, Hussein reminded the Jordanian people that 'we Jordanians have always been heirs to the principles of the great Arab revolution'.[11] He went on to ask rhetorically:

> Where does Jordan stand? I have no doubt that the unhesitant answer of each of you is: we stand alongside Iraq. This is a decision we have taken knowing what we are doing, in championing our brothers, not out of fanaticism, ignorance or whimsical sentimentalism. Our support for Iraq is an inevitable extension of our principled stands because Iraq is right and demands nothing but justice.

The King proceeded to wax lyrical about his own experiences in Iraq:

> there, in the fraternal country, I saw and experienced the vigilance of beloved people, the steadfastness of kinfolk, the struggle of a noble Arab army and the march of one community. All these things have revived all the hopes that were nurtured in me since my birth, in a nation that rejects humiliation and disgrace and rises up to defend right and dignity.

The rhetoric was extravagant, but there is little doubt that Hussein's message struck a responsive chord with many Jordanians.

The ideological link Hussein drew between the Hashemite-led Arab Revolt and the Iraqi war with Iran also raises the vexed question of how the King's own lingering dynastic ambitions fitted in with his support for Saddam. The most straightforward answer might be to infer that they lay dormant during this period, since there was no obvious outlet for them in the region. However, Hussein's support for Iraq in its war with Iran was also likely to raise his profile in terms of Iraqi public opinion and perhaps earn him a measure of gratitude. Of course, there was nothing so crude at work here as an attempt to undermine or circumvent the existing Iraqi regime. Had the King even hinted at such a manoeuvre then his relations with Saddam would have broken down. But, as we will see, in the wake of Saddam's disastrous invasion of Kuwait and the deterioration in his personal relationship with the Iraqi leader, the King returned to the theme of Iraq's Hashemite heritage, noting that 'there were many people who were attached to us, and their loyalty continued beyond [the 1958 Revolution]'.[12]

One close adviser to the King during the 1990s believes that his backing for Iraq against Iran was one of five attempts he made to move closer to Iraq during his reign with a view to advancing his dynastic ambitions, the others being the pursuit of his claim to the Iraqi throne after the 1958 revolution, the despatch of Wasfi Tall as ambassador to Baghdad at the beginning of the 1960s, his decision to join the Arab Cooperation Council with Iraq in 1989 and his backing for the CIA-sponsored attempt to overthrow Saddam during 1995–6.[13] While this hypothesis is intriguing, it remains impossible to substantiate. If the King was manoeuvring to maintain or build up a Hashemite constituency in Iraq across the years, he was for the most part cautious, discreet and circumspect in his methods.

In terms of his international advocacy of Iraq's cause in the war with Iran, Hussein stressed, 'it is a question of conviction and commitment, conviction that Iraq is right and trying to regain its territory and rights in Shatt al-Arab together with seeking to recover the three islands at the mouth of the gulf to Arab control'.[14] This implied criticism of the 1975 Algiers agreement, which had temporarily settled the Iran–Iraq boundary dispute along the Shatt al-Arab waterway, glossed over the fact that when the agreement had originally been made, in the days of the Shah, the King had raised no objection to it. Times had clearly changed with the advent of the revolutionary regime in Tehran. In fact, Hussein, who had been very close to the Shah of Iran, took his overthrow as a personal blow. He was also extremely critical of the nature of the revolution which overtook Iran in 1979, believing that a wider movement of idealists who had the best interests of their country at heart had been subverted by a clique of clerical demagogues. Worse still, Hussein feared that the goal of the revolutionary regime in Tehran was to subvert the established social and political order throughout the Arab world, using religion not as a unifying but as a divisive force. This was a theme to which the King returned time and time again in his private correspondence.

In essence, Hussein offered three broad justifications for his opposition to the regime in Tehran. Firstly, he argued that Iran was seeking to propagate its revolution by fostering a Sunni–Shiite split in the Arab world. In a 30 January 1982 letter to President Reagan, the King warned, 'we are . . . trying to prevent the sinister Iranian objective of creating and exploiting a devastating wedge between Muslim Sunnis and Shiites'.[15] In another letter written two weeks later, he claimed that the Iranian regime's 'sinister designs aimed at exploding a Shiite–Sunni conflict in the entire area (so far stemmed by Iraq holding as one nation) holds incalculable dangers of instability, strife, bloodshed and disintegration'.[16] In yet another letter written three months afterwards, the King warned again that 'under no condition must we permit weakness to lead

to a Sunni–Shiite sectarian conflict within the area'.[17] This remained a
recurrent theme of Hussein's analysis of the Iran–Iraq conflict, cropping up
again in an important overview of the strategic position in the region which
he sent to President Reagan on 6 December 1986.[18]

Hussein's warnings about the dangers posed by an Iranian-sponsored
Sunni–Shiite split with Iraq as its first target appear remarkably prescient
from the perspective of the early twenty-first century. Moreover, the King
coupled these warnings with a critique of the fundamental nature of the
revolutionary Islamist regime in Tehran. For him, it was 'an inhuman regime
. . . probably one of the most inhuman that the world has produced'.[19] It
represented, he argued, 'an anachronism and an insult to human rights,
dignity, and the true teachings of Islam. Iran is riding on a tidal wave of
ignorance, bitterness, hatred and greed.' This remained a persistent theme. In
his 6 December 1986 strategic overview, Hussein claimed:

> What is tragically true . . . is the fact that Iran, under its present
> leadership, turned Islam, against the teachings and beliefs of Moslems,
> into a dangerous, ruthless, reactionary movement, which became a
> vehicle for questionable power hungry elements to achieve their
> objectives, rather then the stable, progressive one which is Islam.[20]

Hussein's final criticism of the Iranian regime concerned its relationship to
international communism, and hence its role in the Cold War. According
to Hussein's analysis, the Soviets had backed the revolutionary regime from
the outset and were 'its most logical inheritors'. The primary beneficiary
of the instability in the Arab world which the Iranians were attempting to
foster 'would only be Communism and the Soviet Union'.[21] As if to prove his
point about Soviet goals in the conflict, Hussein claimed that during his visit
to Moscow in June 1982, the Soviets had suggested that they might consider
pulling their remaining military units away from their border with Iran,
which would mean that extra Iranian divisions would soon be menacing the
Gulf States, Saudi Arabia and Iraq.[22] No doubt it was in the King's interests to
portray the Iran–Iraq conflict in Cold War terms for the purposes of trying to
persuade the Reagan administration to show more sympathy for the Iraqi
position. But he does seem to have been genuinely convinced that
revolutionary Iran was serving Soviet purposes in the region.

Hussein's impassioned defence of Iraq also manifested itself in his reaction
to the June 1981 Israeli air raid on the Iraqi Osirak nuclear reactor. In view of
the information which came to light through United Nations inspections in
the 1990s concerning Saddam's breaches of the nuclear non-proliferation
treaty, Hussein's defence of the nature of the Iraqi nuclear programme in
1981 was mistaken. In a public letter to President Reagan protesting against

the Israeli action, the King pointed out that Iraq, unlike Israel, was a signatory of the non-proliferation treaty.[23] Developing the point in an interview with America's NBC network, Hussein argued:

> this event has brought us to the limit of our endurance. It was an aggression against an Arab territory and an Arab state which is not even on the confrontation line with Israel. This state signed the Treaty for the Nonproliferation of Nuclear Weapons . . . Furthermore, Iraq was subjected to supervision in order to guarantee the use of the nuclear energy for peaceful purposes, whereas Israel is under no supervision.[24]

Pulling no punches, he told his American audience that 'an end must be put to the gangster methods of Israel. I frankly say that I fear the presence of an Israeli prime minister who imitates Hitler's acts and arrogance'.

In a speech delivered in Jordan at the Yarmuk University commencement ceremony, Hussein described the attack as 'a blatant expression of the Israeli mentality, which is hostile to Arab progress and development'.[25] Reinforcing his point that the attack constituted part of an Israeli attempt to block the Arab march towards modernity, in a further interview he argued that the Osirak nuclear reactor should be considered 'a cultural centre to be used by the Arab man to join the march of progress in this world, to forge ahead, to catch up with his age, to advance and to elevate his standard in every facet of life'.[26]

The ebb and flow of Iraqi fortunes on the battlefield also significantly influenced how the King saw the Iran–Iraq war. After the initial successes of the Iraqi assault in September 1980, the tide of war began to turn against Baghdad during 1981. By early 1982, with the Iranian assault on Khorramshahr, Iraq was close to being driven out of all of the remaining Iranian territory which it had occupied. Hussein now amplified his initial defence of Iraqi strategy. Speaking in February 1982, he argued:

> I know that Iraq never had any ambition to annex new Iranian territory. Its stand has always been defensive, and self-defence is legitimate. Iraq wanted only to regain its territory, waters and rights, and to stop at certain borders hoping that good will efforts and self-interest would lead to an end to the fighting and to negotiations to end the causes that led to the fighting. Iraq responded to Iranian aggression.[27]

In fact, the revolutionary Islamist regime in Tehran may well have presented a threat to the secular Baathist regime in Baghdad, but it is clear that in September 1980 it was Saddam who had taken the initiative in instigating hostilities by invading Iran.

With the war turning decisively against Iraq, Hussein now provided concrete Jordanian backing for Saddam through the despatch of a volunteer Jordanian force, the 'Yarmouk Brigade', to help bolster the Iraqi front. The King lent his direct personal support to the brigade, wearing its insignia on his shoulder and even symbolically firing an artillery shell from an advanced position on the front with Iran. As he put it when answering a question about the incident, 'I have the honour to be a soldier who performs his duty. In fact, I did fire that artillery shell on the battlefield. I am not announcing a secret when I say that that shell was made in Iraq . . . I shall go to the battlefield at every opportunity, God willing.'[28]

The despatch of the Yarmouk brigade presented the King with a problem in terms of his relations with the United States. Since Jordanian forces were largely equipped with American weaponry, Hussein had to ask formally for permission from President Reagan for the Jordanian expeditionary force to use their US weapons to defend Iraq. On 30 January 1982, the King wrote to Reagan justifying his decision:

> Such support, as you know, is in the face of Iranian aggression and intransigence, and I am privileged to have committed myself personally to this cause . . . I am naturally anxious that Jordanians there will carry the best arms available to them. Iran is using Israeli supplied weapons and munitions, possibly of American origin, as well as Eastern weapons.[29]

This was the first hint in Hussein's correspondence of an issue which would loom large – the question of American weapons supplied to Iran, whether by the United States itself or by Israel. How he had come to be aware of the covert Israeli arms channel to Iran is unclear, but it is likely that the information came from Saddam Hussein. For their part, the Israeli intermediaries who arranged the arms sales to Iran no doubt saw it as being in Israeli interests to prolong the conflict and tie down Iraq, which was seen as a future potential military threat.

Reagan's response to Hussein's request was not unexpected. In view of the formal US position of remaining neutral in the Iran–Iraq war, the president wrote, 'it would be inconsistent with this policy to permit the transfer of U.S. equipment, or articles or services subject to U.S. control, for use in the war. I appreciate the fact . . . that you have anticipated our position on this issue and will respect it.'[30] Hussein, at any rate, had played it by the book, even though the result of this had been a negative answer. As the Iran–Iraq conflict unfolded, it would become clear to the King that the Reagan administration itself was playing the game by other rules, and that official policy on arms supplies did not match up with the covert actions of US officials.

Hussein's appeal to Reagan was not entirely fruitless. As it became increasingly clear that Iraq would lose the crucial battle for the Iranian city of Khorramshahr in mid-May 1982, the King wrote to the president again, underlining the perilous nature of the position and warning that 'an always dreaded state of military conflict may shortly embroil Jordan'. Here, he apparently had in mind either a possible Iraqi collapse which might necessitate the full-scale engagement of Jordanian forces against Iran, or a possible Syrian attack on Jordan and Iraq to back up Iran, its ally.[31] Emphasising once again the Iraqi case that 'Iraq was internally subverted and militarily provoked into war for her legitimate self-defense', the King conjured up an apocalyptic vision of what might happen if Iraq was defeated: 'Sir, I believe that if things go badly the United States would inevitably lose all in this area. Peace in the world would be in serious jeopardy . . . I hope that your understanding of all the threats, and active cooperation, will help us avert disaster'.[32] The King's warning paid off. On 22 May he wrote to Reagan again, confirming that, as agreed with Washington, he had been in touch with the Iraqi president:

I have apprised Saddam Hussein of the United States Government's desire to send an Assistant Secretary of State to Baghdad at the earliest opportunity to establish direct American–Iraqi contact in the light of current developments in our area. I have now received a letter from the Iraqi President extending Iraq's welcome to the United States envoy to visit Baghdad at any time, as of the beginning of next week. I am, Mr President, most pleased with this entire development which I hope will produce constructive results.[33]

This was the foundation for a role which the King would play for the rest of the conflict: that of intermediary between the United States and Iraq. It served the interests of both sides to have the King playing this part, since it meant they could deny their contacts should anything go wrong. The King, for his part, was all too well aware of the nature of his position, and that bad faith on the part of one side or the other might leave him exposed to attack. But he regarded the situation as so perilous that he was prepared to run the risk.

Although Iraqi forces managed to stem the subsequent Iranian assault on the southern city of Basra during the latter part of 1982 and 1983, Iraq remained on the defensive as the war dragged on. The Iraqi diplomatic position was now that they were prepared to conclude a ceasefire based on a return to the pre-war border. Iran, meanwhile, sought the overthrow of Saddam Hussein's regime as an explicit war aim, meaning that from the Iraqi leader's point of view there was no scope for peace negotiations. In a further signal of an apparent tilt towards the Iraqi side in the conflict, though, in

November 1984 the United States restored formal diplomatic relations with Iraq, an outcome which owed much to King Hussein's persistent advocacy over the preceding years.

During 1985, the King did what he could to try to contain the escalation of the conflict. When Iraq resorted to the bombing of Iranian cities, including Tehran, Isfahan and Shiraz in March 1985, the King interceded with Saddam, arguing that both sides in the conflict should stop targeting civilians. In a letter sent on 21 March 1985, the King argued subtly that this would be in Iraq's own interests, since continued targeting of civilians might serve only to make the Iranian people back their government more firmly. At the same time he urged Saddam to release two British prisoners and one West German held in Iraq, a move which he claimed would benefit the Iraqi leader by securing European backing for his position. The King acknowledged that these were sensitive issues for Saddam, but, he argued, he was putting them before him because he wanted to support Saddam's policy and end the war.[34] These were clever and subtle tactics, showing that the King knew how to manipulate his close relationship with the Iraqi leader when he judged it necessary.

Saddam's attacks on Iranian cities in March 1985 were in part a response to a huge Iranian ground offensive, in which over 50,000 troops crossed the Tigris in boats, with the aim of driving into Iraq and cutting the crucial Baghdad to Basra highway. The Iraqis only just managed to stem the attack. In its aftermath, King Hussein's role as intermediary between Washington and Baghdad took on a further aspect: in a pattern which would be repeated during the following year of the war, the King passed detailed American intelligence information to Saddam in a bid to avert a further Iraqi battlefield defeat.

Hussein's files show that on 11 April 1985 he wrote urgently to the Iraqi president enclosing a 'critical' intelligence report from American sources which detailed Iranian preparations for a 'massive attack' on Iraq west of Hur al-Hawizeh, involving 700 armoured vehicles, three-quarters of the total possessed by Iran, an estimated 150,000 troops and several thousand boats intended to ferry the troops across the water. According to the report, the whole area between the Iranian town of Ahwaz and Hur was full of infantry units, and Iran was apparently building underground command posts to direct the operation. Thus far, most of the information offered might reasonably have come from satellite reconnaissance sources. But then came several items which could only have been gathered either through signals intelligence, that is, through the breaking of Iranian codes, or through human intelligence, that is from highly placed agents within Iranian ranks. Iran, the report claimed, had for the first time sent high-ranking commanders to the area including General Shirazi, the renowned commander of all Iranian ground troops. The attack, it was warned, might come at any point, but 'the main operation' was expected to take place later in April. The report also included a critical analysis of Iraqi dispositions in the face of this threat. Iraq lacked an overall strategy, it was argued, and it had thus far failed to increase its troops and defences in the area. It was crucially important to prevent the Iranians carrying out a successful river crossing, as they had done in their previous operation in March, otherwise Iraq would risk a 'great defeat'. With the warning duly delivered, King Hussein added his own concluding note to the report, wishing Iraq a great victory under Saddam's leadership.[35]

In fact, what became of the expected Iranian April offensive at Hur al-Hawizeh is not clear.[36] Iran did launch a further attack in the area in July, but this was not the decisive operation forecast in the intelligence report. It may be that the Iraqis swiftly bolstered their defences, deterring the Iranians from launching their planned offensive. At any rate, the report makes clear that the Americans must have had a range of intelligence sources open to them to predict Iranian battlefield moves.

Early in 1986, the situation on the ground once again became critical from the Iraqi point of view. On the night of 9 February, the Iranians launched a major three-pronged offensive, directed against areas respectively twenty-five miles north and south of Basra, and against the Faw peninsula in the far south. American intelligence information was once again passed via Hussein to the Iraqis, this time to the effect that the attack at Faw was a limited diversionary assault, and that the main Iranian offensive would come later in the central sector of the front. As a result the Iraqis did not react promptly to the Faw offensive, believing that it was a feint for the real attack elsewhere. Sure enough, on the night of 11 February the Iranians launched a further assault in the Hur al-Hawizeh marshes which seemed to bear out the American information. The Iraqis now moved to meet what they believed to be the main attack, allowing the Iranians to dig in and consolidate their position at Faw. By the time the Iraqis realised their error and launched a counter-offensive at Faw on 14 February, it was too late to dislodge the entrenched Iranians and recover the lost Iraqi territory. The result was a significant reverse which once again seemed to leave Iraq facing defeat in the conflict. Hussein's position in the wake of this incident was a difficult one. Convinced that the American information was genuine, and that there had been no attempt at deliberate deception of Iraq, he did his best to soothe Saddam's suspicions, arguing that the Iranians had fooled the American intelligence services. But his role as covert intermediary between Washington and Baghdad had been significantly compromised, and there remained lingering doubts about American good faith.[37]

Worse was to come. In early November 1986, news broke of what at first sight was one of the most unlikely political scandals of the decade. The

Iran-Contra affair almost completely undermined the credibility of US policy in the region. Contrary to its public stance against dealing with 'terrorists', it transpired that members of the Reagan administration had been covertly supplying arms to Iran with Israeli assistance in exchange for the release of American hostages held captive by the pro-Iranian Hezbollah group in Lebanon. To round the scheme off, proceeds from these illegal sales had been used to supply aid, prohibited by Congress, to the Nicaraguan Contra rebels. Although Hussein was not one to be surprised by conspiratorial dealings in the region, even he appears to have been astonished by American actions. As he put it in a subsequent interview, 'we were profoundly shocked, profoundly disturbed by this affair'.[38]

In private, the King felt justifiably that he had been double-crossed. In a series of remarkable private exchanges, President Reagan tried to defend the actions of his administration, while Hussein pointed out the damage which had been done to US credibility in the region, and to his own personal position. Reagan began on 15 November, with a letter in which he argued that 'there has been no change in our longstanding policy of seeking a peaceful solution of the war between Iraq and Iran. Our policy of not negotiating with terrorists and hostage takers also remains unchanged.' In view of the facts which had already come to light about the dealings between the US administration and Iranian officials, these denials seemed divorced from reality. Reagan then elaborated further on his reasons for authorising the arms sales:

> As you know, we have long been concerned over the war between Iraq and Iran and we continue to seek ways to help bring about an end to the fighting and a rapid negotiated settlement. Toward this goal, and in an effort to prevent Soviet gains in Iran and to contain Iranian radicalism, we have sought through private parties to develop a dialogue with selected members of the Iranian government . . . This initiative involved a large element of risk. Unfortunately, premature disclosure, orchestrated by those with much to lose if the contacts bore fruit, has compromised at least some of the promise inherent in this opening to Tehran.[39]

As to the charge that rather than pursuing such lofty strategic objectives, the administration had sought simply to buy the release of American hostages through the provision of arms to a hostile state, Reagan claimed:

> I can assure you that the U.S. government has not deviated, nor will it deviate, from its policy of refusing to give in to demands of terrorists and hostage takers. The objective of opening this dialogue was not to buy the

release of U.S. citizens held hostage in Lebanon, although in the end the assistance of our interlocutors did facilitate the efforts of Terry Waite and others in winning the release of several of the foreign hostages held there.[40]

So the story according to Reagan was that his administration had not simply been trying to exchange arms for hostages, and then use the funds for the illegal purpose of sustaining the Contra rebels in Nicaragua. It had been pursuing the higher strategic goals of bringing about an end to the Iran–Iraq war and seeking the means to influence the domestic political process in Iran.

Hussein wasted no time in demolishing the president's flimsy arguments. His critique was made all the more devastating by the measured tone in which it was delivered:

> Throughout my many years of public service, and whenever I was confronted with a shocking situation, I have always attempted to take my time before dealing with it. I have often tried to place myself in the position of others, with the purpose of trying to understand their deeds from their vantage point. In all honesty, sincerity and friendship, I must admit that all my efforts to comprehend the rationale for the actions of the United States over the last eighteen months were in vain.[41]

The King went on to recount the circumstances in which he had heard of the US's dealings with Iran. A few days before the scandal broke he had received in his office an American general from the Central Command, who had come to argue the case for Jordanian support for 'Operation Staunch' – ironically, a programme designed to stem the flow of arms to Iran.[42]

> The General heading this team and its members spent two and a half hours briefing me on your Government's investigations in its attempts to identify the quarters and sources responsible for supplying Iran with arms from different parts of the world, as well as its actions to put an end to this dangerous flow of arms to Iran. Our joint assessment was that Iran poses a grave danger to the entire area.

At the same time as he had been asked to give his blessing to Operation Staunch, Hussein noted, he had also attended a joint US/Jordanian military exercise centred around a scenario involving a Kuwaiti request for Jordanian assistance to repel an Iranian invasion. Meanwhile, Jordanian Special Forces were also training with their American counterparts on the most effective ways to combat terrorists. 'They, like most in our area,' Hussein argued, 'will simply not understand why the United States was conducting joint exercises

with them on how to combat the terrorists whose country, Iran, the United
States was arming.'

But probably the most devastating passage in Hussein's letter concerned
the way in which he had been used and deceived by the Reagan administration in its dealings with Iraq:

> I had, out of conviction, done much to remove Iraqi suspicions that the
> United States Government deliberately misled the Iraqi military when
> the Iranians attacked El Faw. The Iraqi army did not react to the
> invasion in time on the basis of American information that this was a
> limited diversionary attack and that the main offensive was coming a few
> days later in the central sector of the front. Will not the Iraqis now feel
> that they were misled, not only by the United States but also by anyone
> who tries to explain, justify or defend American actions? How can they
> now accept American refusal to supply them with a defensive enemy
> artillery radar locator system to locate Iranian artillery shelling their
> cities, especially when the offer to furnish them with this system came
> originally from one of your Agencies and was transmitted to them
> through me? How can I explain to them, let alone my people and Armed
> Forces, the refusal of the United States to sell arms to Jordan, its
> traditional, moderate and 'staunch' friend and ally for three decades,
> when American arms are widely and freely distributed to terrorists (or
> are they freedom fighters?) in Latin America, Africa and Asia?

Hussein's arguments were devastating, even down to the well-placed pun
on the title of Operation Staunch. He left Reagan no option but to reply,
going much further than he might have wanted to on paper in explaining
his own role in the covert arms sales to Iran. 'Your Majesty,' the president
wrote, 'I have received Your letter of November 18 and have been troubled
by it. There is no leader anywhere whose judgement and candour I value
more than Yours. Our relationship has always been one of deep trust, and
nothing must change that.'[43] The president went on to repeat that US
objectives remained to bring about an end to the Iran–Iraq war, to explore
the possibility of a more constructive relationship with an Iran prepared to
live at peace with its neighbours, to block Soviet designs in the region, and
to help gain the release of American hostages. Then came the president's
direct admission of clear personal responsibility for the decision to sell arms
to Iran:

> My representatives, in pursuit of those objectives, found that if the
> dialogue were to develop further our Iranian contacts needed to know
> that their U.S. interlocutors genuinely represented me. An authorization

to sell a limited quantity of defensive arms was seen as the one clear signal of my involvement. On that basis, and only after very careful consideration of the risks, I authorized the sale of a small amount of military equipment to our Iranian contacts. It wasn't easy for me to do so, but I felt we should pursue this channel and see if we could position ourselves to affect the struggle for power in Iran.

In belated recognition of the damage done to Hussein's own position, and relations with the Iraqi regime, Reagan continued:

> I greatly value the relationship which we have developed with Iraq, in large measure with Your assistance, and I profoundly hope that we can weather this period of difficulty by means of a full and frank discussion of our differences. I believe that the Iraqis know well that our relationship has been beneficial to them and that will help keep our differences within certain manageable bounds.

The president also promised to make it clear to Israeli leaders that their own shipments of arms to Iran must stop. In an attempt to show due contrition and humility, he concluded by asking the King whether he would like to send him his own recommendations as to the way forward in the search for peace in the region.

Hussein seized his chance and sent a long and detailed analysis of the strategic position. The result was a fascinating overview of the development of US policy in the region over the course of the previous decade as it appeared from Amman:

> I would assume from all available indications and my own observations that the United States had defined as its strategic interest – even before the Soviet invasion of Afghanistan – the encouragement of an Islamic revival which would form a solid block in the path of creeping communist expansion towards the warm waters of the Gulf . . . However, in the face of the invasion of Afghanistan, and during the final period of Iran's rule by His Imperial Majesty the late Shahanshah of Iran, a fresh revival of the idea of playing the Moslem game manifested itself in supporting a fundamentalist Iranian revolution which, it must have been assumed, would conceivably bolster, beyond Iran, Islamic feelings in Afghanistan and ignite them even inside the Iron Curtain.
>
> What went terribly wrong with this approach was that the Islamic Iranian revolution rapidly consumed the bright young idealists who might have turned the hypothesis into a reality.[44]

On the US role in the Iran-Contra scandal itself, the King offered one further pertinent observation:

> Supplying Iran with 2008 anti-tank missiles, in addition to Hawk anti-aircraft missiles and spares by the United States, which is what we know now, is thus, Sir, not only a negation of the United States declared policy of neutrality in the Iran/Iraq war, and its declared objectives of curbing military supplies to Iran under operation 'Staunch', but it is also an action which dangerously favours Iran by providing it with the means to threaten the main elements of Iraq's ability to defend its territory and our world, namely its Armour and Air Force.[45]

The point was well made. Reagan had claimed that the quantities of arms supplied to Iran were small and so would not affect the overall strategic balance. Hussein countered by arguing on the contrary, that the weapons were such that they would erode Iraq's advantage in the field of mechanised warfare, which was essential to countering the Iranian numerical advantage in battlefield infantry.

Although, in the wake of the Iran-Contra affair, Reagan now set out on a new effort to push for progress in reaching a negotiated settlement of the Arab–Israeli conflict, he did not directly engage with Hussein's plea in his letter for more direct backing for Iraq in its war with Iran.[46] For his part, Hussein remained profoundly disillusioned with the US role in the Middle East: 'US credibility is almost zero in the region and this is indeed so as far as I am concerned,' he observed in a radio interview in mid-January 1987.[47]

Despite his disillusionment, the King continued to work to garner support for Iraq and to secure an immediate ceasefire in the Iran–Iraq war. An important plank of his strategy was his attempt to negotiate a resumption of relations between Syria and Iraq. This would remove the potential threat to the Iraqi flank, and incidentally also to Jordan, which the Syrian–Iranian alliance had presented throughout the war. In fact, the split between Syrian President Hafez Asad and Saddam Hussein had deeper roots, with each representing rival wings of the Baathist movement. Nevertheless, during 1986–7, King Hussein worked hard to overcome Iraqi–Syrian differences. On 31 May 1986, Saddam Hussein wrote to him thanking him for his 'brotherly efforts', and acknowledging the need to establish 'healthy and honourable' relationships between the Arab countries. But the depths of his suspicions of Syria were clear. He referred to the harm the Syrians had caused Iraq, which he argued 'reached the level of treachery to the Arab nation . . . by forming an alliance with a transgressing and greedy enemy'. He also challenged the Syrian conception of what the future relationship with Iraq should become. In Saddam's view, Syria's desire, as reported by King Hussein, to 'establish the relationship between the two countries so that it becomes a special strategic relationship' was unacceptable. 'Iraq', he wrote, 'has Arab neighbours – and Jordan is on top of the list – with exceptional relationships the level of which can never be reached by a relationship with the Syrian regime . . . unless God changes the souls and the circumstances.'[48]

Despite Saddam's reservations, King Hussein persevered with his efforts. On 5 August 1986 he wrote to Saddam again, reporting on a meeting he had had with Asad in which the Syrian president had agreed that Iraq should not be left on its own to defend the eastern border of the Arab world. Asad was now prepared to work for 'a restoration of the Arab house', he claimed. The King apologised for persisting in seeking every opening which might lead to an improvement in Syrian–Iraqi relations, and concluded with another emotional expression of his backing for Saddam in the war with Iran.[49]

By the end of March 1987, the King's efforts seemed close to success. In his contacts with Damascus, he was aided by the excellent Syrian connections of his chief negotiator, Prime Minister Zeid Rifai, who was known by his family name of 'Abu Samir' in the letters the King exchanged with Asad. Writing to Asad on 26 March, the King detailed what he termed the latest progress towards meeting their 'noble nationalistic goal', whose success was essential to 'rebuild the ground under our feet, and to defeat the plans of our enemies, before we are too late'. Both Iraqi Foreign Minister Tariq Aziz and Syrian Foreign Minister Faruq al-Shara had reported to Hussein on the results of their meeting in Moscow, telling him that their respective presidents were ready to hold a meeting as soon as possible. A four-point agenda for the meeting had been agreed between Aziz and Shara, with two items suggested by the Iraqis and two by the Syrians. The King concluded by noting that he was sending Abu Samir to discuss with Asad various aspects of the meeting.[50]

In the end, though, the King's efforts were to no avail. Although he did succeed in bringing Saddam and Asad together at al-Jafr in the Jordanian southern desert in April 1987, he could not bring them to agree on a restoration of normal relations. Worse still from Hussein's point of view, he could not even persuade the two men to shake hands at the end of two days of intensive talks.[51] The attempt to bridge the Iraqi–Syrian divide failed in 1987, although Hussein resumed the effort in earnest after the end of the Iran–Iraq war the following year, coming much closer to success early in 1989.

Against the backdrop of these negotiations, during 1987 the Iran–Iraq conflict escalated still further, with Iraqi attacks on Iranian oil facilities, and Iranian attacks on Kuwaiti shipping in the Gulf. The result of this threat to shipping in the Gulf was a US decision to offer to re-flag Kuwaiti tankers, and to convoy them to port. This escalating danger to the Gulf oil trade finally brought about action in the UN Security Council, with Resolution 598, calling for an immediate ceasefire in the Iran–Iraq war, being passed on

20 July 1987. Hussein too had played his part in bringing about the passing of the resolution, repeatedly arguing the case with his Western friends in favour of a mandatory ceasefire.[52] The ceasefire resolution had no immediate effect on the conflict, however, since Iran, which still felt it had the upper hand in the fighting, rejected it.

It was not until the summer of 1988, when Iran suffered a number of serious reverses on the battlefield, that the possibility of an end to the eight-year war finally opened up. During this closing phase of the war, King Hussein once again played his part in helping to persuade the Western powers of the justice of Iraq's case in the negotiations at the United Nations which ultimately led to a ceasefire. On 4 August 1988, as these negotiations entered a critical phase, the King wrote to President Reagan and British Prime Minister Margaret Thatcher, both of whom, as the leaders of countries which were Permanent Members of the UN Security Council, could play a crucial role in backing Iraq's position. In identical letters sent to the two leaders, Hussein, who had just received a special envoy from Saddam Hussein, argued the case for supporting the Iraqi position regarding the implementation of Resolution 598. 'Iraq believes', Hussein argued, 'that Iran's acceptance is a tactical move aimed at halting the deterioration which is engulfing Iran internally and on the battlefront, and which is starting to threaten the survival of the regime itself.'[53] The King went on to detail the Iraqi suspicion that Iran only wanted a ceasefire so that it could recoup its losses and prepare to resume the fighting from a stronger position, and pressed the case for a termination of hostilities followed by negotiations for a permanent and just settlement of the conflict. He also backed Saddam's call for direct negotiations with Iran. He concluded with a call for Western support for Iraq's position:

> May I urge you, as a friend for whom I have the greatest respect and admiration, to appreciate Iraq's position. Your positive contribution in ensuring that the Security Council does not only call for an immediate cease-fire might convince Iran of the necessity for direct negotiations to settle the problem peacefully.[54]

In the event, the Iraqis got part of what they wanted in the form of a ceasefire on 20 August, followed by the opening of peace negotiations with Iran in Geneva on 25 August. These talks did not yield a permanent resolution of the conflict, and in an attempt to push the process forward, the King once again interceded on Saddam's behalf, with two further identical letters despatched to Reagan and Thatcher on 3 October. Here, he reported on a meeting with Saddam Hussein the previous day in which he had found him to be 'fully committed to the cause of peace. He is genuinely interested in arriving at a peace treaty with Iran expeditiously.'[55] Again, the King urged the Western powers to back Iraq's case regarding access to the Gulf and the use of its ports on the Shatt al-Arab waterway, which had proved to be a major stumbling block in the negotiations.

Hussein's approach elicited a sympathetic response from Prime Minister Thatcher, which makes for rather ironic reading in the light of her subsequent strident anti-Iraqi rhetoric in 1990. 'I share your concern that early progress should be made and welcome your assurances that President Saddam Hussein genuinely wants a peace treaty. I can understand Iraq's caution,' she wrote. The letter went on to outline the British position regarding the implementation of Resolution 598. Its relatively emollient tone was all the more surprising given that, in the concluding paragraph, Thatcher informed the King that the British government had been obliged to request the withdrawal of a number of members of the Iraqi embassy staff in London for unacceptable activities, adding, 'We have not sought this difficulty and would very much like to have a more normal relationship; but it is vital that the Iraqis should ensure that their diplomats in London do not misbehave.'[56]

In fact, it was to be another crisis in the region which ultimately produced a resolution of the Iran–Iraq dispute. In September 1990, trying to secure his flank after his invasion of Kuwait, Saddam Hussein unilaterally conceded Iranian objectives in the peace negotiations, agreeing to abide by all previous treaties with Iran, including the 1975 Algiers agreement which had fixed the boundary along the Shatt al-Arab waterway. Iraq had paid a remarkably high price in the eight-year war for what was to prove to be no gain at all. For King Hussein, though, the end of the Iran–Iraq conflict did not disrupt his alliance with Saddam's Iraq. On the contrary, the relationship continued to deepen during the immediate post-war phase, with enhanced military and intelligence cooperation. The immediate threat which King Hussein feared from revolutionary Iran might have been staunched, but he continued to believe that a close relationship with Iraq was essential to Jordan's future security. This was a belief which he would soon have ample reason to regret.

CHAPTER 13

FISHING IN THE DEAD SEA

KING HUSSEIN AND THE PEACE PROCESS, 1980–89

In terms of the Middle East peace process, the 1980s for Hussein would be a period of frustrated hopes and failed diplomacy. At the beginning of the decade, the King entertained some expectations of progress with the aid of a new US administration. He was certainly pleased to see the back of President Carter, whose Camp David initiative had to Hussein's mind simply served the Israeli purpose of dividing Arab ranks. His description in a letter to Vice President-elect George Bush of the moment he heard of the outcome of the 1980 presidential election on Voice of America illustrates his reaction perfectly: 'I recognized the voice of President Carter and within seconds realised that he was conceding defeat. It was a beautiful dawn to a new morning – a beautiful dawn to a fresh beginning and a new era, as I wrote to congratulate President-elect Ronald Reagan.'[1] To begin with Hussein saw Reagan as potentially a new Eisenhower: a Republican president with the courage to stand above the political fray in the search for a just settlement in the region.[2] Following his visit to Washington in early November 1981, Hussein declared in a press conference:

I found a lot of warmth, readiness and acceptance – readiness to listen, accept logic and show concern for the region. I can say that the picture is different now from what it was in the recent past. I can say that there is now a strong leadership in the United States, a leadership that is capable of and perhaps desirous of understanding truths and, consequently, adopting stands which I hope will be positive in the future.[3]

Unfortunately for Hussein, his hopes were quickly dashed. One story, later related by the King to Israeli Foreign Minister Shimon Peres during a clandestine meeting in London in April 1987, sums up what the King came to see as Reagan's fundamental lack of understanding of the region, never mind the intricacies of its politics.[4] Exchanging pleasantries with the president during his November 1981 visit to the United States, the King was momentarily taken aback when Reagan, endeavouring to make small talk, asked him about the quality of the fishing in the Dead Sea. As anyone with a passing knowledge of the region would be aware, the Dead Sea is the lowest place on Earth, and has a saline content so high that almost nothing can live in it. (A sixth-century mosaic map in a church in the Jordanian town of Madaba makes the point neatly, depicting a fish with a happy face swimming away from the Dead Sea up the River Jordan, and one with a sad face swimming towards it.) Still, confronted by the president's gaffe, Hussein's quick wits did not desert him, and he did not intervene as Reagan mused aloud about the possibility of introducing specially adapted fish from California into the Dead Sea.[5] Indeed, the president took the matter still further in a subsequent letter. It was left to Hussein to draw a line under this unlikely fishery. 'Mr President,' he wrote in reply, 'a while ago I received your message pertaining to the subject of the possibility of introducing fish into the Dead Sea. I was most touched by your thoughtfulness in this regard which prompted your investigating the possibility. We had, in any event, reconciled ourselves to the fact that the Dead Sea is dead . . .'[6]

Hussein was not the only one who questioned the president's detailed grasp of Middle East issues. During a stopover in London on the way back from the United States, the King found British Prime Minister Margaret Thatcher similarly sceptical. Thatcher, an ideological soulmate of the president, was close enough to him to be aware of his intellectual limitations. Her first comment to Hussein when they met in London on 17 November was that 'the media had suggested that King Hussein's visit had been extremely successful and that a close rapport had been established between the King and President Reagan. Had President Reagan in fact understood the message the King was giving him?'[7] Hussein's answer was that he had spoken bluntly to the president, telling him that 'until a solution to the Palestinian problem was found, Israel was enemy No. 1 of the Arab people, the United States enemy No. 2'. Reagan had described his presentation as an 'eye-opener', and had confessed to not having as much background on the region as he should have had. According to Prince Abdullah, who accompanied his father to the meeting, the King had spent thirty minutes alone with the president, who had come out agreeing with much of what he had said. Reagan's staff had had to back-pedal hastily and thereafter he was never allowed to spend any time alone with Hussein.[8]

Hussein should not perhaps have been surprised at Reagan's ignorance of Arab perspectives on the region's problems. Evidence of Reagan's blinkered understanding of the region had already been provided by his public statements during his election campaign about the occupied territories, especially Jerusalem. Hussein was concerned that these inadvertently implied recognition of the Israeli annexation of Arab East Jerusalem, a position which was at odds with the stated US policy since the June 1967 war. Even before his November visit to the United States, on 7 August 1981, Hussein had felt compelled to send the president a letter on the subject which was so long that it amounted almost to a historical treatise. In the letter the King dissected a number of the president's campaign statements on the occupied territories and the peace process, correcting what he saw as errors of interpretation, both of the history of Palestine and Jordan and of the relevant UN resolutions, especially Security Council Resolution 242. Some of the president's statements were simply wrong, including his claim that Resolution 242 'made it plain' that both Jews and Palestinian Arabs had the right to settle in the West Bank until its final status was determined, a topic which is not mentioned at all in the resolution.[9] Hussein also wanted to get across a broader point about the significance of Jerusalem to all Arabs and Muslims, and especially to him personally as a Hashemite:

> Hashemites can never shirk their sense of duty and commitment to the Arab and Muslim cause. The leader of the Great Arab Revolt, betrayed by the Allies together with the Arab Nation, chose death in exile, although his body was returned to be buried in Jerusalem. The Holy City is equally important to all followers of the three great monotheistic religions; no earthly power can ever reduce it to become solely the political capital of Israel.[10]

The King could not resist a dig at members of the Likud government:

> It may interest you to know Sir, that the now occupied city of Gaza is known as the Gaza of Hashem, the head of the House of Hashem and the Hashemites to which the Prophet belonged. Hashem was buried in Gaza in the fifth century A.D. General Ariel Sharon, born to Polish immigrants in Palestine, ironically once stated that he considered me an intruder on Palestine and the Palestinians. The Polish-born Prime Minister Menachem Begin has recently referred to Jordan as Eastern Israel, and General Ariel Sharon is his Defence Minister today.[11]

For a man not normally given to bitterness, Hussein's words on this subject dripped with contempt. But Reagan evidently absorbed little of this treatise.

Just after Hussein's visit to Washington in November 1981, in a private meeting with a group of Jewish leaders, the president apparently said that he preferred an undivided Jerusalem under Israeli control.[12] Although officials hastily issued a 'clarification' confirming that there was no change in the US policy that Jerusalem's status should be settled through negotiations,[13] Hussein was incensed not just by the statement, but also by its timing – just after his visit to Washington and just before the Fez Arab summit. 'The battle against polarisation of the entire area and its future may now be affected by the rug being swept from under my feet, so to speak, through the unfortunate statements on Jerusalem,' he wrote to the president.

> It is obvious that your great responsibilities cannot permit a personal examination of every issue placed before you. But, equally, I hate to be placed in the position of having to disturb you, by being compelled to do so time and again, because of obvious flagrant misrepresentations of facts with their consequent sad results. I am, Sir, deeply unhappy to find myself in such a situation.[14]

Not for the first time Reagan was forced to send a letter trying to retrieve the damage his ill-considered statement had caused. 'The United States continues to believe that unilateral actions concerning Jerusalem taken since the 1967 war should not forejudge the ultimate status of the city, which can only be resolved in a negotiating framework,' he wrote, penitently.[15]

For Hussein, however, the damage had been done. His sense that the new administration was too timid to challenge unilateral Israeli actions was reinforced by Washington's response to the Israeli decision to annex the occupied Golan Heights in January 1982. Although the US supported a UN Security Council resolution declaring Israel's actions to be without international legal effect, it subsequently blocked moves to impose sanctions on Israel. Reagan tried to sweeten the pill in a letter to Hussein by promising a new effort to advance the peace process, which had been stalled since the Egyptian–Israeli peace treaty had been signed in March 1979.[16]

Rather than a renewed peace process, however, the summer of 1982 brought a further Israeli effort to change the face of the region, with the invasion of Lebanon which began on 6 June 1982. In contrast to Israel's earlier limited incursion in 1978, it had grand goals, which included the elimination of the PLO as a regional player. Its ostensible purpose was to end the attacks mounted by Palestinian guerrillas on northern Israel. In reality, Defence Minister Sharon and Prime Minister Begin sought to overturn the political order in Lebanon, eliminating Syrian influence, destroying the PLO and signing an unequal peace with a puppet government. The effects for Lebanon's civilian population were catastrophic. From 13 June to 12 August

1982, Israeli forces laid siege to Beirut in an attempt to force the PLO and the remaining Syrian forces out of the Lebanese capital. The result of the siege was an estimated 18,000 dead and 30,000 wounded – most of them civilians. Aside from this carnage, from Hussein's perspective the Israeli invasion had other ominous implications. The aggressive anti-PLO strategy pursued by the Likud government was coupled with a revival of the 'Jordan is Palestine' slogan, which was favoured by major figures within the government including Sharon and Foreign Minister Yitzhak Shamir. As Hussein put it in a letter to President Reagan:

> Sharon's desire, I know, is to drive them [the Palestinians] eventually into Jordan that they may be joined by others driven out of the West Bank and Gaza so that in time and with more Israeli settlers in the occupied Palestinian territories when the issue of self-determination is addressed the results would be guaranteed in Israel's favour.
>
> At some point in the future and with the inevitable clashes with Jordan following this scenario written by Israel and Sharon and imposed upon us here, an Israeli occupation of Jordan which is unable to arm itself will probably give way to an Israeli withdrawal once a docile Palestinian state is created on Jordanian soil.
>
> End of problem?? No Sir, the issue has always been and will always be that of Palestinian rights on Palestinian soil.[17]

Hussein was further appalled both by the scale of human suffering caused by the Israeli invasion, and by the supine reaction of the Reagan administration.[18] Beyond the destruction in Lebanon and the threat of broader destabilisation in the region, the Israeli invasion also expelled Arafat's forces from Lebanon, weakening the PLO leadership and meaning that Hussein felt he had to become involved again in the search for a political solution to the Palestinian problem.

Meanwhile Reagan, conscious of the damage which his administration's response to the Israeli invasion had inflicted on the US's position in the Arab world, launched a new peace initiative of his own, focusing particularly on the search for a solution to the problem of the occupied territories. On 18 August he wrote to Hussein outlining his evolving ideas, which would become known as the Reagan Plan. The despatch of this letter was followed by detailed discussions in Amman between King Hussein and two American representatives, Nick Veliotes and Ambassador Dick Viets. The Reagan Plan envisaged Israeli withdrawal from the West Bank, but not the establishment of a Palestinian state. Instead, there would be a system of self-government in the territories in association with Jordan.[19] Jordan therefore played a central role in the suggested solution, but this did not mean that King Hussein agreed with all of its elements. On the contrary, he made it clear that 'no one individual or state can substitute for the Palestinians' active participation in resolving the Palestinian problem'. He added that he believed there was an opportunity to build a bridge to the PLO for the purposes of reaching a political settlement. 'I believe that the PLO will seek to become more of a political movement in the times ahead,' he wrote to Reagan. 'I shall encourage these trends for the PLO under the right conditions to remove the obstacles that bar the United States Government from recognizing and dealing with them openly as the primary and full partner in a coming peace process.'[20]

For Reagan, any potential involvement of the PLO would be an unwelcome impediment to progress. The conditions laid down by Secretary of State Kissinger for any American acceptance of PLO involvement in the peace process remained in force: recognition of Israel; renunciation of violence; and the acceptance of UN Resolutions 242 and 338. Writing back to the King, he warned:

frankly, your letter introduces elements of ambiguity which, if left unclarified, could lead us into the mistakes, disappointments and mistrust of the past . . . [the PLO] cannot replace Jordan as a credible and effective partner in the peace process. We also must work simultaneously to obtain support from the traditional, legitimate leaders in the occupied territories, whose participation is also called for in our process.[21]

Hussein saw matters very differently. 'I regret that you may have felt that my letter to you introduced "elements of ambiguity which . . . could lead us into the mistakes, disappointments and mistrust of the past",' he wrote in reply. 'For the record, Sir, I have always been completely satisfied that I was in no way responsible for that unfortunate and regrettable phase in relations between our two countries.'[22] As for the issue of his commitment to carry the peace process forward, 'I can assure you that once Jordan is given the absolutely necessary mandate of approval and support by the Palestinians and Arab colleagues, we would not hesitate . . .' Suggesting that he might be able to bring the PLO on board, the King argued: 'the Palestinians now feel they should define, with Jordan, a joint view of future Palestinian–Jordan relations, which is both a natural and welcomed development, given the special relationship which binds our peoples together'. Whatever Reagan's reservations, Hussein made it clear from the outset that he would not take up the role allotted to him under the Reagan Plan unless the PLO were allowed to be involved. However, although vital questions such as the status of Jerusalem were fudged, Hussein saw possibilities for progress in the plan. He welcomed it both in public and in private, later calling it 'the first bold and sincere attempt by the United States at influencing the course of tragic events in this area since 1956'.[23]

The broader Arab reaction was considerably more sceptical. The subsequent Fez Plan, endorsed by the Arab summit meeting between 8 and 10 September 1982, reiterated the centrality of the PLO's role, calling for the creation of an independent Palestinian state. This left King Hussein trying to reconcile the two initiatives by working to broker a deal with PLO Chairman Yasser Arafat. This was a difficult task since, as he had earlier admitted to Margaret Thatcher, 'Arafat was an unfortunate choice to portray the Palestinian cause.'[24] While Thatcher cited the PLO leader's association with terrorism, for Hussein the problem with Arafat was both political and personal. Politically, the two men were rivals for the allegiance of Palestinians on both the East and West Banks. This would have made their relationship a tense one even without the historical baggage of the 1970 confrontation. Moreover, on a personal level Hussein felt that Arafat lacked both the courage and integrity to advance the Palestinian cause. Ultimately, he believed that Arafat could not be trusted, and that he cared more about his survival as leader of the PLO than about the Palestinian cause.

To bolster Hussein's position, Reagan did what he could to marshal Arab, particularly Saudi Arabian, support for Jordan should it choose to participate in his peace plan.[25] The King, meanwhile, argued that events on the ground in Lebanon made his attempt to coordinate with the PLO much more difficult. Here he had in mind especially the massacres of Palestinian civilians perpetrated by Israeli-backed Phalangist militiamen at the Sabra and Shatila refugee camps on 16–17 September. The background to these massacres was the election of the Israeli client Bashir Gemayel, leader of the Phalange militia, as Lebanese president on 23 August. His subsequent assassination on 14 September was the signal for the Phalangists to run amok in the Palestinian camps, killing between 1000 and 2000 Palestinians with the connivance of Israeli forces. The PLO partly blamed the US, which had earlier guaranteed safe passage for the PLO fighters out of Beirut, for enabling the massacres to take place. 'They are justifiably concerned, after the Lebanon, that the words and guarantees of the United States carry little weight,' Hussein wrote.[26]

Hussein's position was now made even more difficult by a warning not to participate in the Reagan Plan which he received from the Soviet leader Leonid Brezhnev, who described the original Israeli invasion as being 'the direct result of the filthy politics of Reagan' and of the 'strategic cooperation between the US and Israel'. Brezhnev argued that the invasion had simply served to isolate the US and Israel and bolster the Palestinian cause, and that the US should not be allowed to escape from this isolated position via the Reagan Plan, which he saw as designed purely to further US and Israeli interests rather than Palestinian aspirations. The Soviet Union, by contrast, Brezhnev declared, fully supported the principles of the Arab Fez Plan, which mirrored the Soviet approach to the peace process.[27]

This Soviet warning might not have mattered so much to Hussein in previous years. But, after the breach in his relations with the US caused by the Camp David agreement, the King had turned in 1981 to the Soviet Union as an alternative arms supplier, a move which Saddam Hussein had encouraged.[28] Soviet displeasure thus mattered rather more to Hussein than it had in earlier decades when his alliance with the US had been firmer, and he had to weigh it alongside broader Arab scepticism in deciding how far he should be prepared to go in seeking to bridge the gap between the Reagan and Fez plans.

During the winter of 1982–3, Hussein did his best to reconcile the differences between the two plans through intensive discussions with both the Reagan administration and the PLO. A further visit on his part to Washington in December 1982 resulted in some concessions over the terms under which Jordan might take part in the peace initiative. These were detailed in a letter Reagan sent to him on 23 December. 'You will not be pressed to join negotiations on transitional arrangements until there is a freeze on new Israeli settlement activity,' Reagan promised, undertaking 'to do everything necessary to insure that negotiations on the final status of the occupied territories commence as soon as possible after the transitional period begins'. These points were both intended to address Hussein's misgivings resulting from the earlier Camp David process, which he believed had given Israel the scope to change facts on the ground during the transitional self-rule period and to prevaricate endlessly on the question of the final status of the territories. The president's promises did not go as far as Hussein wanted, but they were nevertheless an improvement on the vague Camp David framework. Reagan also offered important guarantees of Jordan's security in the face of the bellicose activities of the Likud-led government in Israel. 'The United States remains dedicated to the security and territorial integrity of Jordan,' the president wrote. 'I reaffirm our willingness immediately to enter discussions leading to the preparation of contingency plans in support of this relationship.' But the president's letter included one crucial condition: all of these understandings would come into effect only 'after you have publicly joined us in the peace process'.[29]

It was not to be. The continuing destabilising effect of the conflict in Lebanon, and the Israeli government's refusal to stop building settlements in the occupied territories, together with the opposition of the bulk of the PLO to any compromise with the terms of the Reagan Plan, left both the King and Arafat with little room for manoeuvre. During a week of talks held in Amman at the beginning of April 1983 Hussein failed to reach an agreement which

Arafat could sell to the rest of the PLO, and as a result he decided for the present to abandon his involvement in the peace initiative.[30] On 10 April 1983, Hussein wrote to Reagan informing him with deep regret, 'I sadly feel compelled to advise you that as matters stand I have reached a dead-end.' While praising the president's peace initiative, the King went on to outline the factors which had undercut his efforts. Firstly, there was the exclusion of the PLO from the negotiating process unless it explicitly accepted the American terms for participation, including the acceptance of UN Resolutions 242 and 338 and the recognition of Israel's right to exist. Then there was the Israeli government's outright refusal to accept the Reagan Plan, and its accelerated settlement-building activity in the occupied territories. Washington's description of such activity as merely 'obstructive rather than illegal was indeed unfortunate', the King commented. But Hussein was also critical of the broader Arab response to the president's initiative, referring to 'the complete inadequacy of constructive assistance and real support for our position throughout by some of our Arab brethren and mutual friends'. The result of all of these impediments was that it had not been possible to formulate the joint Palestinian/Jordanian position which Hussein had sought. 'I, myself, am unable to identify a single ray of hope that I have not pursued over the past several months,' he wrote sorrowfully. 'Unfortunately, Mr President, within our limited resources we have done our best but for the time being it seems to have been to no avail.'[31]

While no success was achieved in reconciling the Jordanian and PLO approaches in 1983, the episode did lay down the terms for their subsequent engagement in the peace process. This much was implied in Hussein's one qualification near the end of his letter: that the failure was only 'for the time being'. In essence, what Hussein subsequently sought in order to revive the peace process were firm PLO commitments to accept UN Resolution 242, recognise Israel, and participate in a multilateral peace process under a Jordanian 'umbrella', rather than as an independent political actor. In return, he was willing to offer the PLO a limited base for political operations in Amman. Arafat's negative response was influenced both by the dynamics of Arab politics and by the need to secure some form of consensus among the disparate elements of the PLO. In practice, these two constraints overlapped, since the key Arab states, especially Syria, sponsored different factions within the PLO, and were able to use the influence of their supporters to block any PLO move in a direction which they did not favour. So, during the winter of 1982–3, Syria had worked to mobilise the PLO against any acceptance of Hussein's terms.[32] This was part of an attempt to recoup prestige lost as a result of the reverses suffered by Syrian forces in the Lebanese war, and also a result of Syrian opposition to what it saw as the increasing influence of the Iraqi–Jordanian axis in the region.

In one sense, the failure to arrive at a definitive PLO–Jordanian agreement at this stage was academic, since the Begin government had stuck fast to its rejection of the Reagan Plan and its insistence that any further developments in the peace process must take place within the Camp David framework.[33] Although Israeli opinion was divided, with the Labour opposition supporting the Reagan Plan in principle, the Reagan administration made no serious attempt to press the Likud government to change its position. Even if Hussein could secure Arafat's agreement to the concessions he sought, there would still be no peace process in which to engage. The King therefore suffered once again the frustration of seeing an opportunity to advance, but lacking the power to influence regional politics accordingly.

As they had before, Hussein's political frustrations affected his health, which remained precarious. During this period of stalemate he had increasing difficulties in sleeping, and he also smoked even more heavily than normal. In January 1984 Queen Noor, who was waiting for him to fly down to Aqaba from Amman to receive official guests, instead received a call that Hussein had been taken critically ill. Returning to Amman at once, Noor found that Hussein had suffered a nosebleed which, due to the effects of the anti-coagulants he had been taking since the mid-1970s to alleviate his heart arrhythmia, had turned into a full-blown haemorrhage that nearly cost him his life. Indeed, at one stage the King's heart had apparently stopped, and he later recollected a near-death experience in which he had felt himself to be floating above his body towards a bright light, before dragging himself back. The tensions he had endured across the decades had taken a high toll on him physically and, after a check-up during a visit to the US in February, Hussein was told that, in view of the condition of his internal organs, he should assume that he was ten years older than he really was. As Queen Noor recollects, from that point onwards Hussein had an even keener sense of his own mortality.[34]

The King's visit to the US in February 1984 also provided the opportunity for a public rapprochement with the Egyptian leader Hosni Mubarak, whom Reagan had invited to the US capital at the same time. Between 1980 and 1983, Egypt, the most powerful player in the Arab world during the 1960s and 1970s, had effectively been consigned to the sidelines by Sadat's decision to make peace with Israel. In October 1981, Sadat himself had paid the ultimate price for his peace-making efforts when he was assassinated by soldiers linked to an Islamist group which hoped to stage a coup, establish an Islamic republic and abrogate the peace treaty with Israel. Although they had succeeded in killing Sadat, his chosen successor Hosni Mubarak, who had commanded the Egyptian Air Force and been made vice-president in 1975, took up and held the reins of power. Mubarak trod a delicate path as president, honouring Sadat's formal commitments under the 1979 peace treaty with Israel, but being careful not to establish the kind of close working relationship with Tel Aviv which might have barred Egypt's ultimate re-entry to the broader Arab fold.

Nevertheless, Egypt's isolation had continued. By the beginning of 1984, Hussein, who was ever alert to the shifting power dynamics of the Arab world, sensed an opportunity to rebuild Jordan's relationship with the new Egyptian leader. If nothing else, he hoped that the re-emergence of Egypt as a friendly regional player might strengthen his hand in future dealings with the PLO and weaken the position of Syria. Following their meeting in Washington in February 1984, Jordan became the first Arab state to restore formal diplomatic relations with Egypt in September of that year. During the same period, Arafat, who had been driven out of Lebanon for a second time at the end of 1983 as a result of a Syrian-backed challenge to his leadership of the PLO, also courted the Egyptian leader. Not surprisingly, these manoeuvres angered the Syrian President Hafez Asad, and Jordan's relations with Syria, which had been tense throughout the 1980–83 period, took a further turn for the worse, with the Syrian leader unleashing Abu Nidal's Palestinian terrorist faction in a campaign of assassination and intimidation directed against Jordanian targets between October 1983 and August 1984.[35]

Despite the Syrian pressure, Hussein continued to look for opportunities during 1984 to restart negotiations with Arafat. After preliminary meetings with the PLO leader during February 1984, the King wrote to President Reagan in a relatively optimistic vein concerning the chances for progress in the peace process: 'It is very clear to me, Sir, that he is determined to safeguard the freedom of the P.L.O., from now on, of all external and radical pressures which rendered it comatose over a long period of time. Arafat is plainly striving to have the P.L.O. reflect, in the truest sense, the feelings, hopes and aspirations of the Palestinian people.'[36] Throughout 1984, Jordan's relations with the PLO improved, culminating in the convening of the seventeenth Palestine National Council in Amman in November. In a speech at the opening session on 22 November, the King stressed the need for coordinated action to liberate the West Bank, arguing that Resolution 242 should provide the basis for negotiations conducted within the framework of an international peace conference.

A change in the political landscape in Israel as a result of the July 1984 elections also seemed to open the way for a new initiative on Hussein's part. Although the Labour Party, led by Shimon Peres, had not secured the clear victory for which Hussein had evidently hoped, it had gained enough ground to join a 'national unity' government alongside the Likud. Under the terms of the coalition agreement, Peres would assume the premiership for the first two years of the life of the new government, and would be succeeded by the new Likud leader Yitzhak Shamir for the same period thereafter. Each would act as the other's foreign minister when not prime minister. This complex political balancing act was to play a significant role in determining the outcome of Hussein's diplomacy in 1987.

In Washington, meanwhile, there was some frustration with Hussein's stance over the peace process. In a letter which he sent to Reagan on 9 December 1983 Hussein had made clear his insistence on an international conference as the essential opening forum for any renewed peace effort, arguing that it would draw Israel, all of the key Arab states and the two superpowers into the negotiations.[37] To the King's way of thinking this would avoid the pitfalls of the Camp David approach, in which the US had acted as the sole mediator and Egypt had negotiated in isolation from the other Arabs. To Secretary of State George Shultz, by contrast, this would be an obstacle to the bilateral Israeli–Jordanian negotiations which he believed were much more likely to succeed.[38] According to Ambassador Richard Murphy, Shultz also suspected that the international conference idea was some sort of 'slippery Hashemite ruse' to avoid entering into face-to-face negotiations with the Israelis.[39]

For his part, Hussein was frustrated with the American approach. In a letter to Saddam Hussein sent on 31 March 1984, the King argued that there had been a steady 'decline' in the positions taken by the US on the Arab–Israeli conflict ever since the 1967 war.[40] Citing specific examples, he argued that Israeli settlements in the occupied territories, which the US had originally termed 'illegal', were now only described as 'obstacles to peace', and he complained that, with a presidential election looming at the end of the year, the US had now 'completely surrendered' to the Israeli government. The King, though, criticised the Arabs for their lack of unity, arguing that part of the explanation for the 'decline' in the US approach was the Arabs' failure to maintain a unified position. In effect, the King's letter was an appeal to Saddam to lend substance to Arab unity by backing his efforts, both to bring Egypt back into the Arab fold, and to work with Arafat to see if they could develop a united position on the peace process.

By 11 February 1985, Hussein and Arafat had reached sufficient agreement to sign the so-called Amman Accord, which called for a 'land for peace' settlement as stipulated by UN resolutions, a solution to the refugee problem, Palestinian self-determination within a proposed confederation with Jordan, and an international conference to be attended by all parties to the conflict, including the PLO, together with the permanent members of the UN Security Council. On the face of things, the agreement offered something to both parties, giving Hussein a role in negotiating the future of the territories and Arafat a possible way into those negotiations under Jordanian cover. As far as Hussein was concerned, the ambiguity of the agreement was deliberate, 'designed to avoid creating obstacles in the path of the long sought negotiated peace settlement'.[41] Thus both parties could choose to interpret the agreement to suit their respective constituencies. Indeed, in a covering note sent to Washington, the King added two important riders. The Jordanian interpretation of the agreement stressed that self-determination for the Palestinians would be within a 'state confederally united with the Hashemite Kingdom of Jordan', and that Palestinian attendance at the international conference would be in a 'joint Jordanian Palestinian delegation equally constituted of representatives of the Hashemite Kingdom of Jordan and the Palestine Liberation Organization'.[42] Arafat, for his part, in a letter to the King on 14 February, emphasised that the joint delegation mentioned in Article 5 of the agreement should be one that was composed 'in harmony with the spirit of the negotiations'.[43] The King's earlier approach to Saddam Hussein requesting support for his peacemaking efforts had also evidently paid dividends; Saddam had played an important role behind the scenes in enabling the agreement to come about, although he did not want his role publicised in case his actions might be seen as compromising 'Baathist principles'.[44]

As soon as the agreement had been reached, it drew fire from almost all sides. The Israeli government, even under the relatively dovish Peres, opposed any formal role for the PLO in peace negotiations and was very wary of the international conference framework. Meanwhile, hardline elements in the PLO, backed as before by Syria, attacked the agreement as a sell-out of the PLO's right to act as the 'sole legitimate representative' of the Palestinian people, and of the Palestinian claim to an independent state.[45] Syria took the lead in organising these opposition elements and, by the end of March, a Palestinian National Salvation Front emerged whose avowed aim was to take over the PLO and topple Arafat. Under intense personal pressure, Arafat tried to attach conditions to any PLO acceptance of Resolution 242. Although the initial response to the agreement from President Reagan was positive,[46] Secretary Shultz was much more sceptical about the deal, arguing, 'the Hussein–Arafat agreement seemed like a big step forward but could easily become a big step backward'. The King, he believed, felt he could not move forward without Arafat, so he had taken him on board as a passenger, adding, 'But Arafat was a backseat driver who intended soon to take the wheel.'[47]

In an attempt to work around Shultz's scepticism, Hussein tried to influence the president through other channels. One such was British Prime Minister Margaret Thatcher, who was convinced of the need to bring authoritative Palestinian representatives into the peace process.[48] She wrote to King Hussein on 27 February informing him that she had used the opportunity provided by her recent summit meeting with President Reagan to draw his attention to the Jordanian–PLO agreement as 'an extremely important and positive step', adding that she saw the King's efforts as vitally important in making progress towards peace.[49] Hussein, who was always an astute reader of where power lay, endeavoured whenever possible to use Thatcher's ready and trusted access to the president to promote his own peace-making efforts.[50] This was especially important in view of the widespread hostility within the Reagan administration to dealing with the PLO.

Hussein himself remained adamant that it was not possible to move forward without the PLO. He stressed in a letter to Reagan that the organisation had made a bold decision 'to free itself of the constraints imposed upon it by the radical Palestinian minority and external formidable pressures'. As for the oft-repeated Israeli refusal to negotiate with 'terrorists', Hussein was scathing:

> Where would we be, Sir, if the Palestine Liberation Organization and the Arab nation responded to the Israeli attitude of the recent past and refused, on principle, ever to do business with known terrorists who themselves form a sizable portion of Israel's own government and political hierarchy. Terrorists and Terrorism indeed, Sir. Or has it not been in all honesty and reality, a simple and convenient way of procrastinating to avoid facing the demands of peace by a party to the conflict?[51]

During the rest of 1985, Hussein tried to advance the Amman Accord through discussions with the US administration and secret meetings with the Israeli Prime Minister Shimon Peres. His initial goal was to set up a meeting between the US Assistant Secretary of State Richard Murphy and a joint Jordanian–Palestinian delegation, which would include Palestinian representatives who were members of the PNC but not officially members of the PLO. This might then open the way to a US dialogue with the PLO, provided that Arafat found a form of words which satisfied the American conditions that the organisation should accept Resolution 242, recognise Israel and renounce violence. Thereafter an international conference involving a Palestinian–Jordanian delegation might be convened. From the US side, Secretary Shultz pressed the King hard for a commitment to enter into direct negotiations with Israel by the end of the year, irrespective of what came of the initiative with the PLO. This approach reflected Shultz's view that if the King had to wait for the PLO to move forward, he would probably not move forward at all.

Whether Hussein actually made this commitment to Shultz in private is disputed. In his memoirs, Shultz claims that during a meeting at Aqaba in mid-May, Hussein had promised to enter into direct negotiations with Israel by the end of 1985. A letter sent by President Reagan to the King following his meeting with Shultz reflects this interpretation, with Reagan claiming that

'1985 can truly be a year of destiny'.[52] By the time Hussein arrived in Washington for a summit meeting with the president at the end of the month, though, Shultz argues, he had backtracked under the influence of his advisers to a position where the PLO once again called the shots.[53] Zeid Rifai, who had returned to office as prime minister on 4 April 1985, disagrees, claiming that the King had merely listened to Shultz outlining his own preferred approach, without directly contradicting him out of politeness to his guest, and that Shultz had then presented his own proposal as though this was an agreement he had reached jointly with the King.[54] Ultimately, whatever the King may have said in private is academic. As Richard Murphy has observed, the job of the King's closest advisers like Rifai was to protect him, and to stop him entering into firm commitments which might cause him political diffi-culties.[55] Entering into direct negotiations with Israel in 1985, without the cover provided by a PLO role and an international conference, would have been just such a dangerous commitment.[56]

As part of his search for diplomatic progress, the King also met Israeli Prime Minister Peres twice in London during 1985, the first time on 19 July, and the second on 5 October. So far as Rifai is concerned, no specific plan as to how to move the peace process forward emerged from these meetings; they were just brain-storming sessions on the theme of how to get to an international conference.[57] Israeli sources offer a different picture, suggesting that in the first meeting the two men agreed on a staged approach to the peace process, involving the Murphy meeting, PLO acceptance of the American terms for a dialogue, and finally peace negotiations, while in the second they apparently discussed the international conference idea and the problems presented by PLO involvement.[58]

As matters transpired, the meetings made little difference, as a series of linked events now undercut the Amman Accord. First, in mid-August, came the failure to arrive at an agreed list of Palestinian representatives within a joint delegation which was acceptable either to the Americans or Israelis. This was followed by an attack by Force 17, a Palestinian group close to Arafat, which cost the lives of three Israelis, possibly Mossad agents, aboard a yacht in the harbour of Larnaca, Cyprus. An ensuing Israeli reprisal raid against Arafat's own headquarters in Tunis on 1 October in turn killed fifty-six Palestinians and fifteen Tunisians. This was followed on 7 October by the hijacking of the Italian cruise liner *Achille Lauro* by the Palestine Liberation Front, a minor faction of the PLO. In these circumstances, the attempt to construct a moderate PLO-Jordanian front for the purpose of entering peace negotiations appeared doomed.

This no doubt served the purpose of President Asad of Syria, who had done his best to undermine the Amman Accord from its inception. Indeed, Hussein had forecast the likely course of events as early as 30 June when, in a draft letter to President Reagan, he had warned, 'as this summer turns to fall, I fear that the PLO leadership will have been further fractured by the forces in Damascus, thus inhibiting the chances for a joint Jordanian-moderate Palestinian delegation capable of negotiating on the basis of Resolutions 242 and 338'.[59] In fact, with his appointment of Zeid Rifai as prime minister in April, the King had already given himself a fall-back option should his attempt to cooperate with Arafat fail. Rifai, who had been the architect of the Jordanian–Syrian rapprochement after the 1973 war, was well respected in Damascus. As the King's faith in a positive outcome from his agreement with Arafat ebbed away, he asked Rifai to pursue the task of rebuilding relations with Asad. At a meeting between Rifai and his Syrian counterpart, Dr Kasm, in Jeddah in mid-September, an agreement to end the proxy struggle between the two countries was reached. The price for Hussein's dignity was high. On 10 November, in an open letter to his prime minister, the King acknowledged that certain Jordanian officials had been involved in the Islamist insurrection against Asad earlier in the decade, a 'mea culpa' which, according to his biographer, Asad accepted with satisfaction.[60] Thereafter Rifai visited Asad and a joint communiqué was issued rejecting direct negotiations with Israel as well as any partial or separate solutions to the Arab–Israeli conflict. This gave Asad much of what he wanted, apparently removing the danger that Jordan and the PLO would make a separate peace as Egypt had done, leaving Syria isolated. The rapprochement been the two countries was crowned by a visit to Damascus by the King in December 1985, his first since 1979.

The Amman Accord was now effectively doomed. From Arafat's perspective, there was no point in sticking his neck out too far to meet Hussein's terms when the King himself had already trodden the road to Damascus. For Hussein, who was fed up with Arafat's refusal to commit himself, his inability to bridge the gap between the PLO and US positions, which had been a major source of frustration throughout the year, now provided him with a way out of the process. So, when Arafat insisted on US recognition of the Palestinian right to self-determination before the PLO would accept Resolution 242, the ensuing US rejection was not unwelcome from Hussein's perspective. The King handed the text of what Washington saw as an acceptable declaration in relation to Resolution 242 to Arafat with the words 'Abu Ammar, this will show you how far off you are.'[61]

On 19 February 1986 the King announced the failure of the Amman Accord, proclaiming, 'I and the government of the Hashemite Kingdom of Jordan hereby announce that we are unable to continue to coordinate politically with the PLO leadership until such time as their word becomes their bond, characterized by commitment, credibility and consistency.'[62] The speech marked the end of Hussein's cooperation with the PLO for the time being, but not the end of his interest in the search for a solution for the West

Bank. On the contrary, he instigated a series of moves designed to demonstrate and consolidate Jordanian influence on the West Bank, in rivalry to that of the PLO.

Here the fascinating question of Hussein's own 'contested destiny' re-emerges into the political spotlight. Thus far, his attempts to work with the PLO could be portrayed as little more than a pan-Arab duty aimed at the liberation of the occupied territories. The pursuit of a purely Hashemite role in the territories, in covert cooperation with Israel, looked much more like revived dynastic ambition. To his credit, the King played his hand subtly for the most part, with his actions equally explicable by an attempt to improve the position of the Palestinians living under Israeli occupation and the defence of Jordanian national interests. So, Hussein's July 1986 closure of all PLO offices in Jordan could be portrayed as a logical result of the breakdown in political cooperation, even while it also helped to weaken the PLO's links with the Palestinians living in the occupied territories.[63] In the same vein, the announcement of a projected five-year development plan for the West Bank and Gaza during the latter part of 1986 could be presented both as a social welfare measure and as an attempt to block Israeli efforts to drive the Palestinians out of the territories through economic pressure. This latter theme played well with East Bankers, who were perennially afraid of being swamped by an Israeli-inspired Palestinian exodus from the territories. If the development plan succeeded, though, it might also create a local Palestinian leadership tied economically to Jordan and free of PLO influence.[64]

Predictably, the PLO opposed these moves, which also aroused domestic opposition from regime loyalists who felt that the new approach risked Jordanian national interests and played into the hands of the Israeli government. In a letter to Egyptian President Mubarak, which was leaked to the press in October 1986, a group of Jordanian notables, including former prime minister Ahmad Obeidat and former cabinet ministers Sulaiman Arar and Hani Khasawneh, criticised the policy towards the occupied territories, warning of a 'grand plot to normalise Arab–Israeli relations in the West Bank and Gaza according to Zionist aims'.[65] The King succeeded in calming these fears to some extent by stressing that his plans were designed to forestall Israel's 'creeping annexation' of the territories. If the PLO was incapable of helping those living under Israeli occupation, he argued, it was Jordan's duty to do so. Otherwise, Jordan would suffer the consequences of any mass Palestinian exodus. 'If we do not plan for ourselves,' he added, 'we will be planned for.'[66]

Since PLO involvement had been one of the principal impediments to progress in the peace process from the Israeli perspective, the King's change of approach to the problem of the territories created more of a potential community of interest with the Israeli government, or at least with its Labour

Party element. Labour leader Shimon Peres favoured a deal with Hussein over the West Bank, the 'Jordanian option', as it was known at the time, which would have cut the PLO out of the peace process. The problem from the Israeli side, though, was that Peres was no longer in the driving seat by 1987, having honoured the prime-ministerial rotation agreement with Likud's Yitzhak Shamir in October 1986. This change of leader in Israel is an essential part of the backdrop to the April 1987 meeting in London between Hussein and Peres, which has often been seen as a great missed opportunity to advance the peace process.

At Peres's initiative, the secret meeting between the two men was set up via the good offices of a common friend, Victor Mishcon, and scheduled to take place on Saturday 11 April 1987 at Mishcon's home in central London.[67] Accompanied by his aide, Yossi Beilin, Peres flew to London via private jet and wearing a disguise, a stylish brown wig. His purpose was clear: to reach an agreement over the future of the occupied territories through face-to-face diplomacy. According to Peres's account, Prime Minister Shamir consented in advance to his attendance at the meeting. The informal setting of a private home, and the excellent lunch cooked by Mishcon's wife Joan, all contributed to an atmosphere which was relaxed and jovial. After Peres and Hussein had finished the washing-up together, both sides adjourned for a political discussion which began with the swapping of light-hearted anecdotes. These included the King's story about Reagan and the improbable Dead Sea fishery, and a tale from Zeid Rifai, whom the King had brought with him to the meeting. According to Peres's version, Rifai recounted how, when barred from his guest house late at night during a visit to Cairo, he had hit on the idea of claiming to be 'Shimon Peres' to get past the guards blocking his way. In Rifai's own recollection of the tale, though, there was a subtle difference: he had in fact declared himself to be the 'prime minister of Israel'.[68] These different accounts tell us something about Peres's mindset at the time. In concluding an agreement with Hussein, he behaved as though he was still prime minister of Israel, not its foreign minister.

The political discussion lasted for the best part of seven hours. By the end, the two sides had reached agreement on the framework for an international conference. This required that participants should accept Resolutions 242 and 338 and renounce violence and terrorism, provisions that would effectively exclude the PLO. Instead, there would be a joint Jordanian-Palestinian delegation, whose members would presumably be selected by the King. It was agreed that to avoid either party having to admit to discussing a covert agreement, the plan would be forwarded to Shultz, who would then propose it as though it were his own idea. According to Rifai, this approach was also intended to get the Americans involved in the process, as well as providing cover for Hussein and Peres.[69] This may well have reflected lingering doubts about the American commitment to the peace process in the wake of the Iran-Contra scandal.

Peres deputed Yossi Beilin to present the plan to Shultz. According to Shultz's account, Beilin presented the agreement as a historic step for Israel, opening the way to a possible comprehensive peace. After outlining the shape and scope of the international conference agreed upon by the parties, he asked that the proposal be 'taken over as the initiative of the United States', pleading, 'Don't let it evaporate. It's in your hands now.'[70]

The metaphor was appropriate, although not in the way Beilin had intended it. As far as Shultz was concerned, the Peres-Hussein proposal was too hot to handle. As Shultz saw it, Peres was asking him to sell an agreement he had made as Israeli foreign minister with a foreign head of state to Peres's own sceptical prime minister, who was the head of a rival political party. Moreover, the plan was being presented to him as US secretary of state before it was presented to Shamir. 'Peres was informing me, and wanting me to collaborate with him, before going to his prime minister,' Shultz recalled. 'The situation was explosive.'[71] Peres defended his approach by arguing that he had made Shamir aware of his intentions before leaving for London, and gave Shamir a 'full account' of the talks as soon as he returned to Israel, reading out to him the draft texts of the documents agreed with Hussein.[72]

But Shamir was scathing about Peres's approach, noting that he evidently hoped that 'if no one else, at least George Shultz would be able to persuade me to accept this so-called London Agreement'.[73] For his part, Shultz had to consider if, and how, he was prepared to involve himself in Peres's plan. Rather than presenting the Peres-Hussein text as an American proposal, Shultz telephoned Shamir to tell him that he had been informed of the agreement, and was prepared to come to Israel to discuss it with him. Although Shamir did not immediately reject Shultz's offer, he made it clear that he was firmly opposed to the international conference which lay at the heart of the plan, and insisted that he would need to meet King Hussein face to face before the peace process could move forward.[74]

These diplomatic manoeuvrings occupied a fortnight. Meanwhile Hussein was becoming increasingly frustrated at the failure to move forward.[75] By the beginning of May, he had effectively lost confidence in the agreement. Although he ultimately blamed Peres for the failure, he was also frustrated by what he saw as Shamir's intransigence and Shultz's timidity. 'Shamir took a negative stand against the London Agreement and the whole thing fell apart,' Hussein recalled later. 'But as far as I was concerned, Peres was the Israeli interlocutor. I talked with him. I agreed with him on something and he couldn't deliver.'[76] Responding in public to Israeli leaks about the agreement, the King also commented, 'Israel is not a cohesive country. There is a very dangerous, short-sighted element and there is a very reasonable element. It's a choice for Washington, and they may be encouraging the wrong side.'[77] Meanwhile, Peres blamed Shultz for not pushing Shamir to move forward.

No doubt the potential prize had the London agreement succeeded was a great one. But Peres's method of trying to work his way around domestic political opposition was an extraordinary one. Hussein, meanwhile, felt that the whole saga had been futile and frustrating, a belief reinforced by the private meeting he held with Shamir at his Castlewood home outside London on 18 July. Hussein later told his wife Queen Noor that the atmosphere at the meeting had been tense, with Shamir's staff so suspicious that they wanted to search his secretary's bags and examine the food.[78] Although Shamir himself gave an upbeat account of the talks, in which he tried to prompt the king to move forward with direct, bilateral negotiations, Hussein's own view was pessimistic. In effect, he dismissed further talks as hopeless, telling Shultz that he could not work with Shamir.[79]

In a final roll of the dice, the King now asked Prime Minister Thatcher to appeal to President Reagan directly when she met him on 17 July. Describing her efforts to Hussein, Thatcher wrote:

> In particular, I urged a strong US lead to carry forward the important understandings you have reached with Mr Peres. I used the arguments that we discussed during our meeting, in particular that it was not acceptable to give Mr Shamir an effective right of veto over a conference, and that inactivity by the United States would only leave the field free for the Soviet Union to promote its own interests.[80]

Thatcher did not have it all her own way in the discussions. She reported that she found Secretary Shultz particularly adamant that Shamir needed to be brought on board to broaden support for an international conference in Israel. Thatcher stuck to her guns: 'I made the point that as long as Shamir thought he could block a conference, he would do so. The most effective way to restrict his scope for this would be a clear statement of US support for an international conference.' Thatcher's conclusion was that she had made some impression on Reagan, but that difficult problems remained in the way of the convening of an international conference. 'We shall continue to do anything we can to help,' she added.[81]

In the event, there proved to be no way round Shamir's objections. Just as Israeli–Jordanian relations at the summit foundered during 1987, cooperation at the functional level over the occupied territories also ran into difficulties. The attempt to promote an alternative pro-Hashemite, as opposed to pro-PLO, leadership on the West Bank was undercut by the assassination of Zafir al-Masri, mayor of Nablus, by the PFLP in early March 1987. Nor did the ambitious five-year Jordanian economic development plan make much headway during the course of the year. By October 1987, Jordan had spent only $11.7 million on projects in the occupied territories. Set against the projected total of $1.292 billion over five years this was a miserly sum, reflecting in part the difficulties Jordan had experienced in persuading donors, especially the oil-rich Gulf States, to contribute to the plan.[82] The strategy of building up the Jordanian role in the occupied territories was already in difficulty before the outbreak of the Palestinian Intifada in December 1987.

The Intifada, a spontaneous local uprising against Israeli rule, took the PLO almost as much by surprise as it did the Jordanian regime. Following a road-traffic accident in which an Israeli truck driver killed four residents of the Jabaliya refugee camp in Gaza, rumours that the crash had been a deliberate act of revenge set off disturbances throughout the occupied territories. Within days tens of thousands of Palestinians had taken to the streets in full-scale revolt against the continuing Israeli occupation. On the back of this remarkable wave of mass protest, a local Palestinian leadership emerged which was initially largely independent of outside players, whether the PLO leadership or Jordan. Scrambling to catch up with events, the PLO in exile quickly established links with the new United National Command of the Uprising. Hussein, by contrast, found himself in a much more difficult position, since the local leadership were strongly critical of Jordan's role. On 11 March 1988, the United National Command called on the Palestinians to 'intensify the mass pressure against the occupation army and the settlers and against collaborators and personnel of the Jordanian regime'.[83]

Adnan Abu Odeh, who was a speechwriter and a close personal adviser to the King at the time, recollects the deep impact this announcement made on him. After Abu Odeh had read it to him, Hussein sat in silence for some time with his head resting in his hands.[84] The King was disconsolate at what he saw as a 'horrible sign of ingratitude' for all the efforts he had made on behalf of the Palestinians living under occupation over the years.[85] It was at this time that Hussein began to ponder an idea which would come to fruition in a speech announcing Jordan's 'disengagement' from the West Bank on 31 July 1988. There is some controversy as to who was the progenitor of this plan. Abu Odeh recollects discussing the idea with the King immediately after reading him the United Command's communiqué.[86] According to his account, he had first broached the idea by asking the King whether he could agree to a peace with the Israelis in which less than the whole of the West Bank including East Jerusalem was returned. The King said 'no'. Abu Odeh then asked whether the King thought the Israelis would agree to the return of the whole of the West Bank including East Jerusalem. Again, the King said 'no'. Finally, Abu Odeh asked if the King believed he could make peace with the Israelis and again the answer was 'no'. Abu Odeh went on to argue that both the Israelis and the Americans were operating on the assumption that he could make peace with Israel and that he was the one with whom they should deal over the Palestinian problem. So, Abu Odeh suggested, the King should take some action which would make it clear that he could not solve this problem for them. This was when, according to Abu Odeh, he floated the idea of 'disengagement' from the West Bank, in the form of an announcement by the King that Jordan would play no further administrative or legal role in the West Bank.

The King did not comment on the idea at first, but a fortnight later, during a meeting with his inner circle of advisers, he turned to Abu Odeh and said, 'Adnan, tell us about that idea you mentioned two weeks ago.' After Abu Odeh had outlined his idea, the King turned to Zeid Rifai and Zeid bin Shaker to ask what they thought of it. Both agreed that it was a good way out of the situation. Thereafter, Abu Odeh drafted a speech for the King which was given at the Arab emergency summit in Algiers in June in which he first floated the concept of disengagement. This was a trailer for the main announcement which the King made on 31 July, following the cancellation of the five-year development plan on 28 July and the dissolution of parliament on 30 July. In the speech, written by Abu Odeh, Hussein proclaimed:

> Of late, it has become clear that there is a general Palestinian and Arab orientation toward highlighting the Palestinian identity in full in all efforts and activities that are related to the Palestine question and its developments. It has also become obvious that there is a general conviction that maintaining the legal and administrative relationship with the West Bank . . . goes against this orientation . . . it is our duty to be part of this orientation and to meet its requirements.[87]

The one reservation the King made concerned Jerusalem; he emphasised that Jordan would continue to administer the Muslim holy shrines and al-awqaf (the Islamic endowments). As Abu Odeh comments, Hussein's attachment to Jerusalem as a Hashemite was something to which he clung irrespective of Jordan's administrative relationship with the West Bank.[88]

While Abu Odeh presents the disengagement plan as being originally his own idea, and while it is clear that, as Hussein's main speechwriter at the time, he was responsible for the text of the 31 July announcement, other members of the King's inner circle have disputed elements of his account. Zeid Rifai argues that the disengagement idea was not Abu Odeh's alone, but something which a number of the King's advisers had been pondering for some time.[89] It may well be that Abu Odeh simply articulated a position towards which others had already been moving given the impact of the Intifada and the failure of the 1986–7 attempt to build up the Jordanian position in the occupied territories.

In a letter to Arafat explaining his decision, Hussein referred to suspicions of Jordan's intentions which had grown amongst PLO supporters since the 1982 Fez Arab summit. He argued that the PLO had come to see Jordan as a competitor whose aim was to control the Palestinian people. As a consequence, the PLO had striven to end the presence of Jordanian institutions in the West Bank, despite repeated statements from Jordan that it had no interest in Palestinian land. Hussein claimed that the cancellation of the Jordanian development plan for the territories was intended to remove these PLO suspicions and help the Palestinian cause. Throughout, the King was careful to stress that this sense of competition were merely a PLO perception; he did not acknowledge the competitive nature of the relationship himself.[90]

Although it had been some months in the making, this shift in the King's strategy was a blow to the Americans, who had continued to work on the assumption that Hussein would maintain his role in the territories.[91] For the Israelis, meanwhile, Hussein's disengagement significantly narrowed the range of options available to them. A few weeks after his announcement, Hussein asked the US State Department to pass on a message to Shimon Peres saying that he had removed Jordan from the peace process in the hope that the PLO would 'see the light and come to terms with reality'.[92] This indeed was the way in which the King had presented his disengagement plan in identical letters sent to President Reagan and Prime Minister Thatcher on 28 July, shortly before the announcement was made on 31 July. 'The purpose of these measures', he wrote, 'is to enhance the Palestinian national cause and to help the Palestinian people, through their legitimate representative, to formulate a responsible, coherent and constructive position, committed to a just and comprehensive peace in the Middle East.'[93] Others have argued more sceptically that Hussein was really handing the PLO a poisoned chalice, in the expectation that the organisation would be unable to shoulder the burden in the occupied territories. Whether his disengagement announcement was strategic or tactical thus remains a matter of some controversy.[94] One commentator has described Jordanian interests in the West Bank as no more dead than a tree which sheds its leaves in winter.[95]

Rather than turning to the PLO as a potential negotiating partner at this point, which would have been too bitter a pill to swallow, the Israeli government continued to try to crush the Intifada by force. It also continued its efforts to promote Hamas, an Islamist movement whose popularity had risen on the back of the Intifada, as a rival to the PLO in the territories.[96] Both the use of force and the attempt to divide and rule the Palestinians failed, and Israel's promotion of Hamas proved to be a disastrous error in the long run, since a movement which had begun life as a peaceful Islamist alternative to the secular nationalism of the PLO subsequently turned to armed resistance.[97]

For the Israeli right, the King's disengagement was a political opportunity, giving further sustenance to the 'Jordan is Palestine' argument. With the 'Jordanian option' favoured by the Labour Party now dead and buried, it argued that a large-scale 'transfer' of Palestinians from the West to the East Bank of the Jordan was a more attractive approach. To guard against just such a possibility, Hussein announced that West Bank Palestinians would no longer be considered Jordanian citizens. Additional measures taken by the Jordanian authorities to try to discourage the movement of West Bankers into Jordan included changing the five-year Jordanian passports held by West Bank Palestinians into two-year travel documents.[98]

The PLO finally accepted Resolutions 242 and 338 at the PNC meeting in Algiers in November 1988, but there was no immediate breakthrough in the peace process. Continuing Israeli opposition to dealing with the PLO was coupled with considerable scepticism in Washington, which wanted to see the PLO officially recognise Israel and formally renounce violence. Once again, Prime Minister Thatcher used her influence to try to push the outgoing President Reagan, and the President-elect George Bush, towards a renewed effort in the peace process. She warned Hussein, 'the American reaction has been sceptical . . . and it is clear that the Palestinians have not yet convinced American and Israeli opinion that they genuinely want peace'. Nevertheless, Thatcher was appreciative of Hussein's own role, arguing, 'I believe that Your Majesty's decision last July on the relationship between Jordan and the West Bank has succeeded in inducing the PLO to adopt more realistic attitudes.'[99]

If this was the positive effect of Jordan's disengagement from the West Bank, Hussein's decision may also have had the negative effect of worsening the economic problems which confronted his country by the latter part of 1988. While these difficulties were largely the result of fundamental structural problems in the Jordanian economy, the fact that the Jordanian dinar was still common currency on the West Bank meant that the economic link with the occupied territories could not readily be severed. Economic confidence, already fragile as a result of the Intifada, now slipped still further, with a run on Jordanian banks and a rapid devaluation of the dinar as inhabitants of the West Bank, fearing that the currency might not remain legal tender for much longer, sold it in favour of US dollars or Israeli shekels.[100] Between April and October 1988, the Jordanian dinar depreciated by 23 per cent against the US dollar.[101]

The origins of the ensuing economic crisis in Jordan lay in the profligacy of successive governments throughout the 1980s. Jordan was and is particularly vulnerable to downturns in the regional economy because of its reliance on remittances from abroad, whether in the form of money sent home by expatriate Jordanian workers or direct grants from other Arab states. By 1983, only 45 per cent, or some $550 million, of the Arab aid pledged at the 1978 Baghdad summit was being received. But the Jordanian government continued its push for growth, increasing spending every year between 1983 and 1988. The underlying philosophy, in so far as there was one, seems to have been that something would turn up sooner or later to relieve the kingdom of its debts. When nothing materialised, the government resorted to running down its foreign currency reserves and to further borrowing. By 1989, when the government was forced to default on its debt, loan repayments were scheduled to consume 20 per cent of total spending. The budget deficit for 1988 was a staggering 26.8 per cent of GDP.[102]

At the end of 1988 Jordan was forced to turn to the IMF for assistance, initially in secret.[103] The deal concluded with the Fund required the government to cut the budget deficit in return for a stand-by credit and a loan to enable the Kingdom to reschedule its debt. In order to make the cuts in spending necessary to reduce the budget deficit, the government had to cut subsidies and implement a series of steep price rises. On 18 April, riots broke out in the southern town of Maan. Beginning as a protest by taxi drivers who had been led to believe that they would not be allowed to increase tariffs despite the steep rise in the price of petrol, the unrest quickly spread to other towns in the south including Kerak, Shubak and Tafila. Although Amman itself remained largely quiet, Hussein was greatly disturbed by the widespread unrest in the south. The King, who had been largely disengaged from the running of the economy, a topic which never excited his interest, now had to take action to shore up the foundations of the Hashemite regime.

The riots were a serious blow and a grave personal embarrassment to Hussein, worsened by the fact that he was abroad holding talks with the new US President George Bush when they broke out. Cutting short his visit to Washington, the King returned to Jordan where he quickly accepted the resignation of Prime Minister Zeid Rifai, whose government had become the focal point of popular resentment. In his place, Hussein appointed another member of his inner circle, former Chief of Staff Zeid bin Shaker, as interim prime minister. In an indirect admission that he had become too detached from domestic politics, and therefore bore a measure of responsibility for the crisis, the King now moved energetically to address the concerns of ordinary Jordanians. In June he embarked on a series of visits across Jordan. Travelling in an open-top car, the King passed through a host of towns and villages to show himself to the people and hear their concerns.[104] More importantly, he provided a formal political channel for popular discontent, deciding to hold the first general election in Jordan for more than twenty-two years on 8 November 1989. Discussing the reasons for his decision in private, he described the election as essential to 'let off steam', and reduce the political pressures which had built up in Jordan.[105]

The strategy was largely successful. The 8 November elections passed off peacefully, with the electoral success of Islamist opposition candidates providing proof that they had been open and fair. Of the eighty seats in the new East Bank-only parliament, thirty-two were held by Islamists of various descriptions. The main opposition bloc, the Muslim Brotherhood, succeeded in securing the election of twenty candidates from its twenty-six-man list.[106] In addition, a further thirteen MPs were elected who might be described as representing the nationalist or leftist opposition. In view of this potential majority for the opposition in parliament, the new Prime Minister, Mudar Badran, had to tread carefully in forming his government. In particular, he faced vociferous criticism from the new deputies over Jordan's economic problems, and the question of corruption in high places. As a former prime minister who had held office in the early 1980s, Badran had to face charges that he was partly responsible for the economic collapse which had overtaken the country. He was also challenged to take firm action to root out those guilty of corruption. The debate of confidence in Badran's new government lasted a full three days, and, as part of his efforts to win the vote, Badran had to offer further concessions to the opposition, including a promise to lift martial law within six months and to revoke a number of unpopular laws, including the ban on political parties. On the issue of corruption, he promised that 'those proved to have accepted bribes, exploited their post or abused it will be tried'.[107] In the end, Badran won the confidence vote comfortably, but to do so he had to promise a wide range of liberal changes to Jordan's political system.

The popular belief remained widespread that Jordan's economic crisis had resulted not just from adverse regional conditions and structural problems in the domestic economy, but from the siphoning-off of state funds by corrupt senior officials. While there was no doubt some substance to these claims, Jordan was arguably little different from other developing countries in this respect. Although the public prosecutor was instructed to investigate nine cases of alleged corruption involving senior officials, ranging from the clandestine sale of the country's gold reserves to the awarding of contracts for major public works programmes, no successful prosecutions resulted. The cases were either dropped due to insufficient evidence or thrown out by the courts, leaving the question of the role of corruption in Jordan's economic collapse unresolved.

Hussein followed up on the broader liberalising trend with a number of personal initiatives, including the granting of pardons to a group of twenty-nine long-term political prisoners in February 1990. These pardons came on top of a spate of earlier releases authorised by the previous Zeid bin Shaker government and a general amnesty for those involved in the rioting of April 1989. The King had also earlier set in train a major exercise in public consultation aimed at arriving at a new National Charter which would provide a political framework for liberalisation within the kingdom.[108] Although the exercise dragged on into 1991, the approval of the Charter by a special national assembly convened in June 1991 did pave the way for the legalisation of political parties, a measure which finally became law in September 1992. On 7 July 1991, Hussein also issued a royal decree formally ending martial law, which had been in force since 1967.

How far did this flurry of democratisation reflect the King's own personal political instincts? There is no doubt that the measures could not have been enacted without his approval, but the process of liberalisation during this period probably went further than Hussein himself wished. His own political instincts were paternalistic. Put simply, he believed that with all of his accrued political wisdom he knew what was best for Jordan and its people. Devolving power to others and opening up the political system to opposition was a process which he believed had to stay within clear limits or 'red lines'.[109] Any opposition must ultimately remain loyal both to the Hashemite throne and to the Jordanian state, and political debate was only acceptable if it avoided direct criticism of the throne. In the last resort, the King always felt that he knew what was best for his kingdom, which made it difficult for him to tolerate those who persisted in challenging his policy. While these limits were somewhat blurred during the 1989–91 period, they emerged clearly as the peace process moved forward during 1992–4. One of the ironies of this process was the fact that to pursue the domestically unpopular course of making peace with Israel, the King had to limit democratisation and openness in Jordan.

In terms of Hussein's private life, the 1980s were a period of much greater stability than the 1970s, which had witnessed both his divorce from Princess Muna and the death of Queen Alia. Throughout the 1980s, he was supported steadfastly by his fourth wife, Queen Noor, with whom he had four children, Princes Hamzeh and Hashem and the Princesses Iman and Raiyeh. While the Queen's role in Jordan was traditionally apolitical, Noor pushed at this boundary, speaking out publicly on themes such as the role of women in society, and sometimes acting in private as a sounding board for Hussein when he wanted to vent his political frustrations.[110]

Beyond this, Noor also contributed a new dimension to the international image of the Jordanian monarchy. Although she complained of being treated by the media as a political accessory or a fashion icon, Noor's beauty, and the uncanny knack she shared with Hussein of making most interlocutors feel valued and important, made her a favourite with the international news media. She could also turn this quality of empathy to the rougher business of ensuring her survival within the royal household. In her autobiography, she is candid about some of the difficulties she encountered as an outsider, a non-

Arabic speaker, and a woman of American background. Any one of these problems would have been difficult to negotiate in isolation, but put together, they made for a formidable challenge.[111] Nevertheless, by the end of the 1980s Noor's persistence had allowed her to weather the worst of these difficulties.

Although the 1989 riots had been a profound shock to the King, by the summer of 1990 the regime seemed to be emerging from the worst of the domestic political storm. The economy was still in trouble, but the King's gamble in opening up the political system seemed to be paying dividends, and the foundations of the regime seemed secure once again. But, like a boxer who staggers back to his feet after a knock down, Hussein was now struck by another unexpected blow. The Iraqi invasion of Kuwait on 2 August 1990 presented Hussein with a grievous dilemma, and his handling of the crisis was to result in regional and international isolation for Jordan. Much of his statecraft for the remaining years of his life would be devoted to finding a way out of the corner into which he had backed himself during the Gulf crisis. During 1990–91, then, he was to find himself truly trapped between Iraq and a hard place.

CHAPTER 14

BETWEEN IRAQ AND
A HARD PLACE

KING HUSSEIN AND THE GULF CRISIS, 1990–91

Great international crises are about much more than the relationships between individual leaders. But, for King Hussein, the Gulf crisis was as much about his relations with Iraqi President Saddam Hussein and US President George Bush as it was about oil, the preservation of the international order or the defence of Arab nationalism. Much has already been said about the King's friendship with Saddam, and his belief that the Iraqi president could provide the leadership needed to restore pride and dignity to the Arab world. These were views which Hussein repeated time and again in private conversation, even with his Mossad contact Efraim Halevy. In the eyes of the Arab man in the street, he emphasised, Saddam was 'a true hero'. What Westerners might see as Saddam's 'ruthlessness and cruelty' was seen by the Arabs as 'courage and strength and pride'; the King stressed time and again to Halevy that 'the element of pride must never be forgotten'.[1] By the end of the 1980s the King had become so close to Saddam personally that he even acted as a sort of family counsellor for the Iraqi leader. When Saddam's violent elder son, Uday, murdered his father's bodyguard in a fit of rage on 18 October 1988, it was Hussein whom Saddam's wife Sajida telephoned, desperately begging him to come to Baghdad at once and mediate the family dispute. The King spent several days with Saddam's family, talking through the crisis and helping them towards its successful resolution.[2]

The King had also built up a closer personal relationship with George Bush than with any of his predecessors. The connection between the two men went back at least to the mid-1970s, when Bush, as the director of the CIA during 1976–7, had worked closely with the King. They developed a mutual respect, even an admiration, which was based at least in part on the sense that they were kindred spirits. Hussein believed that Bush was committed to a just resolution of the Arab–Israeli conflict, and in one of his many letters to the president he referred back to the stand taken by the United States at the United Nations in September 1971, opposing Israeli appropriation of property and the incorporation of occupied territory in Jerusalem. 'This was one of the few times since 1967 that the United States has publicly and unequivocally reaffirmed basic American policy on these issues,' Hussein recalled, continuing, 'I have always assumed that it was no coincidence that the American Ambassador to the United Nations at that time was yourself, Mr President.'[3]

The sense that Bush shared his ideals shines through elsewhere in their correspondence. Writing to Bush after he was elected vice-president on 7 November 1980, Hussein termed his and Ronald Reagan's victory 'a rejuvenation of faith, confidence, and hope as far as we are concerned. If my assessment is accurate, then, my friend, I am surely right in feeling that it holds great promise of a new future of genuine Arab–American relations.'[4] Although the King's high hopes for the Reagan administration were not fulfilled, he still retained his personal confidence in Bush himself, and greeted the latter's election as president in November 1988 with undisguised joy. For his part Bush reciprocated the King's sentiments: 'I am tremendously cheered', he wrote to Hussein, 'by the knowledge that I will be able to work with outstanding world leaders like yourself in the search for peace and justice around the world. Your friendship means much to me.'[5]

The King was also delighted by the tough stand Bush took as president on issues such as Israeli settlement-building in the occupied territories, writing:

> Like so many millions in this part of the world, I have been tremen-dously heartened by your recent public expressions of opposition to continued Israeli settlement activity in the occupied territories, including Jerusalem. But since I have known how earnestly you have felt about the settlement issue and Jerusalem over the years, the views you expressed did not surprise me.[6]

Here, as always, the King signed himself off personally to Bush with the words 'I am sir, your sincere friend, Hussein'. Of the nine presidents with whom he corresponded during his reign, the only other man with whom he consistently used such terms of familiarity was Bush's successor in the White House, Bill Clinton. But, if the personal relationship between the two men was so strong, how was it that during 1990–91 it came so close to complete rupture? In order to understand this, we have to consider the other forces at work in shaping King Hussein's policy during the Gulf crisis.

One such factor was the state of public opinion in Jordan. Some commentators have claimed that the King's hands were tied in reacting to the Iraqi invasion of Kuwait by the mood of his own people.[7] But, although it is clear that pro-Iraqi sentiment was widespread in Jordan, this is an incomplete explanation for the King's approach.[8] In order to understand why Hussein behaved as he did, we need to consider other factors including the background in Iraqi–Jordanian relations, the domestic political and economic situation in the wake of the April 1989 riots, the influence of the King's close circle of advisers, and, perhaps most importantly of all, his own perception of his proper role in the crisis, and its relationship to his personal sense of Hashemite destiny.

The spring of 1989 represented what was probably the low point of Hussein's reign in terms of domestic politics, with the riots in the south of the country significantly shaking his self-confidence. In terms of foreign policy, though, the picture looked at first sight to be much more positive. The creation of the Arab Cooperation Council (ACC), linking together Egypt, Iraq, Jordan and North Yemen, which was agreed at a summit meeting held in Baghdad in February 1989, seemed to reconcile two of the key strands of Hussein's Arab policy during the second half of the 1980s: rehabilitating Egypt and promoting ties to Iraq. To be sure, Syria remained outside the organisation, but it said much for the credit the King had accrued in Damascus through his wooing of President Asad since the end of 1985 that the Syrians made it clear they would not oppose the new organisation, even though they would not join it.[9] Asad accepted at face value the King's assurances about the positive purpose of the ACC, even congratulating him on the establishment of the new organisation.

In fact, one Jordanian source who was closely involved in the negotiations to secure Syrian accession to the ACC (and thereby an Iraqi–Syrian rapprochement, which had been the third goal of King Hussein's Arab policy in the late 1980s) argues that the attempt came very close to success.[10] The only outstanding question left to resolve between Asad and Saddam by April 1989, he recalls, was a minor procedural one: would Syria restore relations with Iraq before joining the organisation, as Saddam Hussein wanted, or would the mere act of joining the ACC, of which Iraq was a member, be taken as indicative of the restoration of relations, as Asad wanted? The event which blocked Syrian accession, he continues, was the outbreak of rioting in Jordan and the fall of the Rifai government, since Rifai, with his excellent connections in Damascus, was probably the only Jordanian politician who could have secured Asad's final agreement to join the ACC. The source also argues that although the domestic unrest in Jordan had other longer-term causes, the April riots were sparked off by members of the Jordanian intelligence services with links to Israel. The Israelis would have seen the creation of a united Arab eastern front, linking Iraq, Syria and Jordan, as a serious threat. The fact that the riots started when the King and prime minister were both out of the country and unable to exercise direct oversight of the domestic situation may lend support to this argument. Moreover, as the main, long-term conduit of covert relations between the two states the Jordanian intelligence service would have been the most obvious target for any Israeli attempt at subversion. As with all such conspiracy theories, however, there is no archival evidence available to support this claim, although on a strategic level it is persuasive. Perhaps the most that can be said with certainty is that if there was any chance of Syrian accession to the ACC, the fall of the Rifai government ended it.

Israel was not the only state in the region to entertain concerns about the ACC's purpose. From the Saudi perspective, the ACC looked like an attempt to encircle the kingdom. King Fahd's feathers were further ruffled by the fact that Hussein had not consulted him about it in advance, as he had President Asad.[11] This oversight perhaps reflected lingering tensions in Saudi–Jordanian relations caused by differences over the Jordanian role in the occupied territories between 1986 and 1988. It was to prove costly; the price of Saudi discontent was immediately apparent, and was reflected in a reluctance to continue aid payments to Jordan which helped deepen the domestic economic crisis.[12] When the April riots broke out, King Fahd was near the end of the queue of fellow Arab leaders who telephoned King Hussein to offer their support and assistance. So, how far were Saudi suspicions about the ACC justified?

Despite Hussein's assurances, from the outset there remained a crucial unanswered question about the organisation: what was it actually for? Each of the four participating states seems to have had a different view of the ACC's real purpose. For Egypt, the ACC was essentially an economic organisation, which had one strictly limited additional political goal: securing Egypt's re-admission to the Arab League. Once this was achieved at the May 1989 Arab summit in Casablanca, Egypt resisted any attempt to seek broader political or military-strategic roles for the organisation. Iraq, meanwhile, viewed the ACC as a riposte to the Gulf Cooperation Council, established in 1981, which had drawn together the rich Gulf emirates and Saudi Arabia, pointedly excluding Iraq. It also saw the ACC as an instrument of its anti-Syrian and anti-Israeli policies, and hence sought to politicise and militarise the organisation.[13]

Jordan, and to a large extent Yemen, saw the ACC as a primarily economic grouping, which, in the longer run, might accomplish the political goal of drawing the Arab states closer together.[14] Jordan had two additional short-term objectives. Firstly, it sought to galvanise the ACC as an instrument for Jordan's defence against any threat from Israel. Secondly, it saw potential membership of the organisation by any future Palestinian state as a good way to avoid the awkward issue of a possible Palestinian confederation with Jordan. These goals were linked in effect by the considerable impact that the wave of immigration of Soviet Jews to Israel between 1989 and 1991 had on King Hussein's own thinking. The King feared that the new Soviet immigrants would be settled in the occupied West Bank, which, coupled with the ongoing Intifada, might lead to increased pressure for the 'transfer' of its Palestinian population across the River Jordan.[15] This in turn might disturb the delicate political balance in the kingdom, at a time when social stability was already under extra strain as a result of the economic austerity measures prescribed by the IMF.

In turn, Saddam Hussein sought to exploit these fears for his own increasingly aggressive and expansionist purposes. Iraqi–Jordanian military cooperation, which began in the intelligence and surveillance fields, soon extended to encompass a reconnaissance patrol by Iraqi F-1 Mirage fighter jets in the Jordan valley in the summer of 1989, and the establishment of a joint Iraqi-Jordanian air squadron early in 1990.[16] Although the King pleaded economic hardship as the reason for the cooperation between the two air forces, arguing that Jordan could not afford to provide its own pilots with sufficient flying hours without Iraqi assistance, neither the Israelis nor the Americans were convinced by his explanation.

Indeed, part of the reason for the King's failure to distance himself from Saddam during the spring of 1990 was no doubt his worsening relationship with Israel. Towards the end of 1989, the Israeli–Jordanian border, which had been quiet for much of the preceding two decades, witnessed a series of incidents. In January 1990 an armed Jordanian conscript was killed by the Israelis after crossing the border, and later in the month the Jordanian army foiled an attempt by guerrillas to fire surface-to-surface missiles from Jordanian territory against Israeli targets. In March, there were further border incidents. The Jordanian authorities claimed that these were part of a Syrian campaign designed to warn Jordan against establishing closer ties with Iraq. This was a plausible explanation, but from the Israeli perspective the incidents were evidence of a worrying rise in instability on the Jordanian front. The change in government in Israel between March and June 1990, with the grand coalition of the Labour and Likud parties being replaced by a narrower, Likud-led right-wing coalition, also threatened a further deterioration in relations. The border tensions, and the deepening military ties with Iraq, were grist to the mill of those who argued that King Hussein could not be relied upon to maintain security on Israel's eastern front.

Hussein's increasingly close ties with Iraq also had a detrimental impact on his relations with the United States and Britain, Jordan's traditional protectors. Had he been able to extract greater political coordination from Baghdad as the price for military cooperation, his position might have been less uncomfortable. Unfortunately, however, during the spring of 1990 an increasingly belligerent and self-confident Saddam Hussein embarked on a campaign of threats and propaganda directed against both Israel and the Western powers.

It was in these circumstances that the dispute between Iraq and Kuwait flared up during the summer of 1990. There was an Iraqi territorial claim to Kuwait of much longer standing, which had been periodically revived by successive governments in Baghdad since independence from Britain in 1932. Even the supposedly Anglophile Iraqi Prime Minister Nuri Said had gone so far as to threaten the emirate when the British had dragged their feet about the question of allowing it to join the Iraqi-Jordanian Arab Union in 1958.[17] Thereafter, in 1961, British forces had been sent to Kuwait to block a supposed invasion threat from the post-revolutionary Iraqi leader Brigadier Abd al-Karim Qasim. While every Iraqi government thereafter continued to maintain the Iraqi territorial claim, in practice the crisis which blew up in the summer of 1990 was a product of Iraqi indebtedness resulting from the Iran–Iraq war, Kuwaiti intransigence and Saddam Hussein's belief that an international conspiracy was in the making against him.[18]

Since the fall of Saddam's regime in 2003, some further insights have been gleaned into its inner functioning and the mind of its leader, which help elucidate his approach during 1990–91. It is clear that Saddam effectively decided Iraqi strategy in isolation, on the basis of his own intuitive grasp of regional and international politics. His record of ruthless suppression of dissent and opposition meant that he rarely received any contrary advice from within the regime.[19] Moreover, once he had decided on a particular course of action, he tended to carry it out whatever obstacles he encountered. As Saddam put it himself, 'when I get something into my head, I act. That's just the way I am.'[20] Nor was he likely to back down once he had acted, since he considered that this would be indicative of weakness. These personal traits should be borne in mind when considering King Hussein's handling of relations with him during the course of 1990.

Tension began to rise with the first-anniversary summit of the ACC, held in Amman on 24 February 1990. Saddam chose the gathering to make a major set-piece foreign policy speech, the theme of which was the dangers posed by the unmitigated power of the United States in the new international order, and specifically the dangers for the Arabs posed by the continued presence of the US navy in Gulf waters. The attention attracted by the speech might have dissipated quickly had it not been followed on 15 March by the hanging, on trumped-up spying charges, of the Iranian-born journalist Farzad Bazoft, who worked for the British Sunday newspaper the *Observer*. King Hussein's handling of this incident prefigured in some respects his handling of the Gulf crisis itself. After a request for assistance on Bazoft's behalf from British Prime

Minister Margaret Thatcher, the King sent a message to Saddam asking for clemency. When the Iraqi leader ignored his request and proceeded with Bazoft's execution, the King defended Saddam's action in the face of Western criticism, speaking of a 'concentrated attack on Iraq'. He also let it be known that he considered Bazoft to be a spy working in the pay of Mossad, and that his appeal to Saddam for clemency had been no more than 'humanitarian' in motivation.[21]

Bazoft's execution was quickly followed on 22 March by the Mossad assassination in Brussels of Gerald Bull, a Canadian scientist who had been engaged by Saddam to build a so-called 'supergun', a massive stationary artillery piece with the range to strike at Israel. The subsequent seizures in late March by British customs officials of parts destined for this Iraqi 'supergun', and of high-speed electrical capacitors designed to be used as nuclear triggers, all drew attention to Saddam's weapons programmes. Finally, on top of this came Saddam's infamous speech to the General Command of the Iraqi armed forces on 2 April in which he promised retaliation with chemical weapons if Israel attempted a strike at Iraq like the one it had undertaken against the Osirak reactor in 1981. 'By God, we will make fire eat half of Israel if it tries to do anything against Iraq,' he blustered.[22]

A tape recording of a 19 April 1990 meeting he held with his close ally PLO Chairman Yasser Arafat gives a further insight into Saddam's state of mind at this stage. 'We are ready for it,' Saddam announced, 'we will fight America, and, with God's will, we will defeat it and kick it out of the whole region.' When, later in the conversation, Arafat had the temerity to mention the United States' swift defeat of the Panamanian dictator General Noriega, Saddam exploded: 'Panama – Panama is nothing compared to us! I swear we are something to defeat . . .'[23] No records have come to light of similar conversations held with King Hussein, and Saddam was no doubt a shrewd enough judge of character to know that a somewhat different tone would have been more appropriate with the Hashemite monarch. But the depth of Saddam's suspicion and hostility towards the West and Israel at this stage, coupled with the failure of Hussein's intercession over the Bazoft affair, should have given the King pause for thought about the Iraqi leader's possible future intentions, and his own inability to influence them. There is no evidence, though, that the King tried to detach Jordan from the Iraqi bandwagon. On the contrary, his personal closeness to the Iraqi president remained evident at the Baghdad summit in May 1990 where the King issued his own more tempered warning about Israel's 'continuous expansionism' and the need to avoid any crack in the Arab front.[24]

At the ACC meeting in February 1990, Saddam had already warned Hussein that he was impatient with the Kuwaiti refusal to compensate Iraq adequately for what he saw as its heroic defence of the Arab world during the Iran–Iraq war. Specifically, Saddam wanted all of Iraq's wartime debts to the Gulf States, including Kuwait, forgiven, together with an additional immediate grant of $30 billion to aid Iraq's reconstruction efforts. 'Let the Gulf States know that if they do not give this money to me, I will know how to get it,' he warned the King.[25] To this initial demand for money, Saddam subsequently added three other accusations. Firstly, that Kuwait was colluding with the United Arab Emirates in a scheme to exceed their agreed OPEC oil quotas and glut the oil market, thus driving the price down and bankrupting Iraq. Secondly, that Kuwait had stolen Iraq's oil by setting up oil installations and extracting oil in the southern sector of the Rumaila oilfield which spanned the border between the two countries. Finally, that Kuwait had set up police posts, military establishments and farms on what Iraq deemed to be its own territory along the border. All of these accusations were bundled together with Kuwait's alleged failure to compensate Iraq sufficiently for its war effort against Iran, in a document presented by Iraqi Foreign Minister Tariq Aziz to the Secretary-General of the Arab League, Chadly Klibi, on 16 July. At the same time, Saddam ordered a military build-up on the Kuwaiti border, which, by 19 July, totalled 35,000 men from three Iraqi divisions.[26]

Jordanian Foreign Minister Marwan Qasim, who flew back from a holiday in the United States to attend the Arab League foreign ministers' meeting which discussed the crisis, had already been made aware in no uncertain terms of American concerns about developments in the region. During his time in the US, he had been asked to attend a specially arranged meeting with US Secretary of State James Baker, in which Baker had delivered a warning about Jordan's relations with Iraq. Did he know, Baker had asked, that the Iraqis had all of the hotels in Amman under surveillance? Was he aware that Iraqi missile groups had been moved up to the Jordanian border? And, finally, what was the explanation for the joint patrols which the Jordanian and Iraqi air forces had been undertaking? Qasim came away from this impromptu meeting with the distinct impression that 'something was brewing' and that Jordan had better tread carefully.[27]

Arriving at the emergency Arab League meeting, Qasim was immediately made aware of the gravity of the situation by Tariq Aziz's stern warning about the effects of falling oil prices on the Iraqi economy. As a member of the ACC, Jordan received the document presented by Aziz to Klibi two hours ahead of the other Arab states. Qasim immediately sensed its importance and went straight to Klibi to warn him of the seriousness of the situation. He also telephoned Hussein but, according to his account, the King was not very pleased by the warning, preferring instead to trust his own instinct that the crisis could be managed. The Arab League now chose President Mubarak of Egypt to act as a mediator between Iraq and Kuwait with the goal of resolving the dispute.

While Mubarak's efforts were under way, the King engaged in his own round of diplomacy, attempting both to convince the Kuwaitis to compromise with Saddam and, during a visit to Baghdad on 29 July, to persuade Saddam to settle the dispute peacefully. The Jordanian delegation to Baghdad found Saddam in an angry frame of mind, evidently convinced that the United States was behind the Kuwaiti attempts to undermine the Iraqi economy. The Jordanian Prime Minister Mudar Badran observed that this was the only occasion on which he had ever seen Saddam truly angry, threatening to 'throw sand in the eyes' of the Kuwaitis, though Qasim recalls that Saddam never showed his anger, and that this meeting was no exception.[28] All of the Jordanian accounts of the meeting agree that the King warned Saddam privately that in his view the Americans would intervene to reverse any Iraqi attempt to invade Kuwait. The best way to resolve the dispute, he told Saddam, was through a negotiated Arab solution. King Hussein and his advisers came away with the belief that Saddam was still open to such a solution at this stage, albeit only on terms favourable to Iraq.[29] As late as 31 July, the King repeated the same message in a phone conversation with President Bush, arguing that the situation was serious but that if the Kuwaitis showed a greater willingness to compromise, it could still be resolved without resort to war.[30]

It would be unfair to criticise the King for failing to anticipate Saddam's invasion of Kuwait on 2 August 1990. Until very late in the day, Saddam apparently remained undecided himself as to whether he should act on a more limited plan, calling for the occupation of the disputed border area and the islands of Warba and Bubiyan, or whether he should risk a full-scale invasion of Kuwait. According to Sa'd al-Bazzaz, a former regime insider, it was only on 29 July, less than four days before the invasion, that Saddam finally decided to implement the full-scale invasion plan. Deputy Prime Minister and Foreign Minister Tariq Aziz also later spoke of a last-minute decision to carry out a full invasion.[31] At the time the Egyptian President Hosni Mubarak, aided by the Saudis, spread rumours that King Hussein was part of some sort of plot with Saddam, also involving the Yemeni and PLO leadership, to invade Kuwait and share the spoils between them.[32] Mubarak told Bush as early as 7 August that Saddam had offered the King and President Saleh of Yemen 'money and spoils' in exchange for backing the invasion, and later claimed that the King had agreed to support the invasion in exchange for a percentage of the oil and other loot which the Iraqis might pillage from Kuwait.[33] There is no evidence to back this claim. In fact it seems that Saddam took his final decision to invade Kuwait alone, having consulted only with his son-in-law, Hussein Kamel al-Majid.[34] Paradoxically, the notion that Saddam sought some sort of deal with King Hussein to back his invasion of Kuwait may well accord the King too much weight in his thinking.

Saddam's self-assurance was such that he did not believe he needed allies to justify or support his actions.

Early on the morning of 2 August Iraqi armoured forces rolled over the Kuwaiti border and sped towards the capital. They encountered very little resistance from the surprised, out-gunned Kuwaiti forces. With no more than a couple of hours' warning, the Kuwaiti emir and his family fled the country for Saudi Arabia where they established themselves in exile. Meanwhile, Saddam's troops entered Kuwait City in jubilation. The map of the region had been redrawn in a matter of hours.

Saddam's invasion came as a profound shock to King Hussein. But it did not change his basic approach to the crisis. He continued to argue that an Arab solution must be sought, albeit one which now also had to involve the withdrawal of Iraqi troops from Kuwait. In hindsight, this approach was clearly a misjudgement. The room for mediation which the King sought never existed, since Saddam had no intention of withdrawing from Kuwait from the outset, and the Americans had no intention of allowing his occupation to stand. On the basis of his experience during the Iran–Iraq war, the King could perhaps be forgiven for thinking that if anyone could act as an intermediary between Iraq and the United States it was him, since he had played that role, with the blessing of both sides, throughout the 1980s. In practice, though, in the circumstances prevailing during 1990–91, his diplomacy was to prove both unsuccessful and damaging to Jordanian national interests. The astute instinct for the likely course of regional and international developments which he had displayed in other crises, such as that of September 1970 or October 1973, seemed to desert him during the autumn and winter of 1990.

The first news of the crisis reached the sleeping King in the early hours of the morning of 2 August through a phone call from King Fahd of Saudi Arabia.[35] In his memoirs of the crisis, Saudi General Khaled bin Sultan comments that although King Fahd was told King Hussein was sleeping when he phoned, it is more likely that the Jordanian monarch simply did not want to take the call.[36] The implication, of course, is that Hussein had something to hide, and that he already knew of the invasion plans. According to Jordanian sources, though, the difficulty in rousing the King was due to the fact that he had taken sleeping pills and anti-histamines to help his sinus problem; one source recalls that the King had been so groggy when the Saudi monarch rang that, by the time he reached the Royal Diwan shortly afterwards, he thought the call might have been a dream.[37] In the meantime, Foreign Minister Marwan Qasim had also taken calls from the Secretary-General of the Arab League, Chadly Klibi, and the Kuwaiti foreign ministry, asking for help in stopping the Iraqi invasion. The King immediately tried to call Saddam Hussein, but, despite repeated attempts on his part, the Iraqi leader did not deign to speak to him until early afternoon. Qasim, who was listening to the King's end of the conversation, recollects that Saddam told him that the Kuwaitis' 'nose had to be rubbed'. The implication of this comment was that they had to be taught a lesson, and thus that the invasion might not yet be final. According to the official Jordanian account of the conversation, Saddam indicated that if the Arab states took a measured approach to the Iraqi invasion, he would begin to withdraw his troops within days and complete his pull-out from the emirate within weeks.[38]

After speaking to Saddam, the King left Amman for a meeting with President Mubarak in Alexandria. Both men agreed that the crisis could only be resolved through action at the level of heads of state, and that a mini-summit, involving the Iraqi, Saudi, Egyptian, Jordanian and Kuwaiti leaders, should be convened; until this summit had met, the Arab League should refrain from directly condemning the Iraqi invasion. They also spoke by phone to President Bush, asking him to delay American action until they had the chance to try to resolve the crisis. 'I really implore you, sir, to keep calm,' the King begged the president. 'We want to deal with this in an Arab context to find a way that gives us a foundation for a better future.'[39] The King repeated what Saddam Hussein had told him: Iraq was planning to pull out, possibly within a matter of days. At this stage, then, there was no significant difference in approach between the King and President Mubarak, who also asked President Bush for two days' breathing space to resolve the crisis diplomatically.

From this point onwards, Egyptian and Jordanian accounts of the Arab mediation effort begin to diverge. According to the Jordanian account, the King went to Baghdad on 3 August, where he secured a commitment from Saddam to a two-pronged solution to the crisis, within an Arab framework. Firstly, Saddam would attend a mini-summit in Jeddah on 5 August, which would also be attended by the heads of state of Egypt, Jordan, Saudi Arabia and Yemen, together with the emir of Kuwait. Secondly, he would start withdrawing from Kuwait within hours, so long as the Arab League refrained from condemning his invasion.[40] The latter point was essential since any direct condemnation would involve a loss of face for Saddam, turning his withdrawal into a humiliation. The King believed that he was making significant progress, only for his diplomacy to be undercut when on 3 August first the Egyptian government and then the Arab League foreign ministers' meeting in Cairo unexpectedly issued formal condemnations of the Iraqi invasion. Qasim himself abstained in the Arab League vote, warning of the danger of encouraging outside intervention.[41] The Jordanians suspected that both the Egyptians and the Saudis had been persuaded by the United States to abandon prematurely the search for a negotiated Arab solution.[42] They argue that as a result of this Arab League condemnation, Saddam subsequently withdrew his consent to attend the mini-summit in Jeddah and abandoned his plans for withdrawal.

The Egyptian account of these events, by contrast, contends that President Mubarak told King Hussein when they met in Alexandria that the mini-summit would be convened contingent on Saddam's unequivocal acceptance of two preconditions: the immediate withdrawal of Iraqi forces from the sovereign state of Kuwait and the restoration of its legitimate rulers, the al-Sabah family. The problem, according to Mubarak, was that King Hussein had been too timid to raise these preconditions with the Iraqi leader when they met in Baghdad the following day. When he discovered this, Mubarak had told the King that the mini-summit could not be convened on such an uncertain basis.[43] In these circumstances, the Egyptians felt that they could not stand in the way of a formal Arab League condemnation of the invasion, for which both the Syrians and the Saudis were now pressing.

Two important questions arise from these differing accounts: firstly, was there ever really a chance of securing an early Iraqi withdrawal from Kuwait under the cover of an Arab mini-summit; and, secondly, was King Hussein sincere in his efforts to secure an Iraqi withdrawal, or was he, all along, sympathetic to Saddam Hussein's invasion of Kuwait? Probably the best evidence in support of King Hussein's contention that Saddam was on the point of beginning a withdrawal is the statement put out by the Iraqi Revolutionary Command Council (RCC) on 3 August, to the effect that Iraqi forces had completed their mission in Kuwait, and would begin withdrawing from the emirate by 5 August 'unless something emerges which threatens the security of Kuwait and Iraq'. Unfortunately, much like the assurances Saddam Hussein himself gave to the King, these words were never backed up by actions, and our knowledge of Saddam's decision-making does not suggest that he would have been prepared to withdraw from Kuwait voluntarily. Nor were King Hussein's warnings about the threat of American intervention likely to have impressed him. The Iraqi Army Chief of Staff Nizar al-Khazraji, who, like the rest of the army high command, had not been party to Saddam's original decision to invade Kuwait, submitted a report shortly after the invasion explaining that war with America was coming, and that Iraq would lose:

> I explained that war with America was now inevitable . . . there were clear indications. I explained the potential dangers for Iraq. I also explained the status of the balance of powers, saying that Iraq would lose the war. A meeting was held at the general command on 18 September to discuss my two reports in Saddam Hussein's presence . . . The commander in chief expressed his anger and ended the meeting before I finished my report.[44]

Khazraji was subsequently dismissed from his post for delivering these unwelcome warnings, and later defected. Saddam preferred to trust his own instincts about American actions rather than to hear contradictory opinions from either the army high command or his intelligence services. As he commented in private discussion with members of the RCC:

> America is a complicated country. Understanding it requires a politician's alertness that is beyond the intelligence community . . . I said I don't want either intelligence organisation to give me analysis – that is my speciality . . . we agree to continue on that basis . . . which is what I used with the Iranians, some of it out of deduction and some of it through invention and connecting the dots, all without having hard evidence.[45]

The balance of the available evidence therefore suggests that Saddam believed he could face down the Americans, and would not have taken the opportunity provided by an Arab mini-summit to agree to an unconditional withdrawal from Kuwait. The question of whether the King's diplomacy was undercut by the Egyptians and the Arab League is thus an academic one. The King placed too much faith both in Saddam's assurances about his intention to withdraw, and in his own ability to mediate a resolution of the dispute. Despite the experience he had gained as an intermediary between the US and Iraq during the 1980s, this was a crisis in which the middle ground for any mediation was lacking from the outset.

Turning to the question of the sincerity of the King's intentions in seeking Iraqi withdrawal, throughout the crisis, Jordan continued to recognise the Sabah regime as the legitimate government of Kuwait. It did not recognise the short-lived puppet Kuwaiti government installed by Saddam Hussein during the first week after the invasion. On 5 August Prime Minister Badran stressed Jordan's respect for the Arab League Charter, and the inadmissibility of the acquisition of territory by force. The difficulty with this form of words, though, was that it implicitly linked the reversal of Iraq's invasion of Kuwait with the ending of the Israeli occupation of the Palestinian territories, a diversionary tactic which Saddam himself soon employed. Moreover, the King was less than discreet in some of his private comments about the Sabah regime. Soon after the 2 August invasion, Thatcher told President Bush, 'King Hussein was not helpful. He told me the Kuwaitis had it coming – they are not well liked. But he grudgingly agreed to weigh in with Saddam.'[46] The King's claim on Jordan television on 4 August that the invasion 'did not come out of the blue', and that Saddam had legitimate grievances towards Kuwait which needed to be addressed, helped create an impression that he sympathised with the Iraqi position.[47] So, although the King genuinely sought a withdrawal of Iraqi forces from Kuwait, his expressions of sympathy for Iraq, and his belief that Iraq would have to be offered concessions to secure a settlement, made his position unacceptable both to the United States and to the majority of the Arab states.

This became crystal clear at the emergency Arab summit convened in Cairo on 10 August. Here a resolution was adopted which once again condemned the Iraqi invasion, and called additionally for the deployment of an Arab force to defend Saudi Arabia. Jordan abstained from the vote, a form of 'neutrality' which was widely perceived as an expression of sympathy for Iraq. In ensuing talks with Saddam on 13 August, the King found no way to bridge the chasm which had now opened up in the Arab world.

If the vote at the Cairo summit had made apparent Jordan's isolation from the majority of the Arab states, King Hussein's subsequent visit to the United States for talks with President George Bush, at Kennebunkport on 16 August, made it clear how far apart the US and Jordanian positions now were. Paradoxically, the high regard the two men entertained for each other may have exacerbated the breach between them. Both men came to the meeting with the expectation that their strong personal bond would help overcome their differences over the crisis. When this did not happen, disappointed expectations fostered a stronger sense of alienation. US Secretary of State James Baker went even further than this in his memoirs, arguing that the president ultimately saw the King's stance during the crisis as 'an act of personal betrayal' which caused him 'enormous anguish . . . [it] elicited uncharacteristic anger from a man who prefers to give friend and foe alike the benefit of the doubt'.[48] In his own account, the president describes himself as having been 'surprised and disappointed' by the King's 'efforts to speak on behalf of Saddam Hussein'. Evidently King Hussein's more welcome role as intermediary during the Iran–Iraq war was now forgotten. Concerning their Kennebunkport encounter, Bush noted, 'it was not a bitter and mean meeting, but it was a disappointment – more of the same'.[49] Hussein continued to try to persuade the president that there was scope for an Arab solution to the crisis, but Bush pointed out that most of the Arabs had come down against Saddam. In his diary, he recorded that the King 'pressed for some middle ground that could solve the problem, and I kept saying, there isn't any – it's got to be withdrawal and restoration of the Kuwaiti regime'.[50]

The King's attempts to shift the president's position were not only unsuccessful, they were counter-productive. At least one source on the Jordanian side has argued that his failure was partly due to the poor advice he received from several of his closest officials, who were pro-Iraqi in outlook, and who had profited from their connections with Saddam's regime during the 1980s. Much of the private conversation within the Jordanian delegation during the trip to the United States, according to this source, concerned the duplicity of the Kuwaitis, and their supposed theft of Iraqi oil.[51] This refrain from within his own entourage served only to reinforce the King's own low opinion of the Kuwaiti royal family, and contributed to his mishandling of the meeting with President Bush.

In the wake of his failure to change the president's position, Hussein did not abandon his mediation attempts. He now focused much of his effort on seeking some sort of formula linking Iraqi withdrawal from Kuwait with US withdrawal from Saudi Arabia. Part of the plan he developed envisaged modelling Kuwait's future relationship with Iraq on that between Monaco and France, with a constitutional monarchy ceding certain functions to Baghdad. On 5 September he held further talks with Saddam in Baghdad, but the Iraqi leader showed no interest in his ideas. When the King urged him to 'make Kuwait negotiable', Saddam is alleged to have called a staff officer into the room and asked him how the military would react to a possible withdrawal from Kuwait. 'Oh, God forbid, sir, please don't utter these words,' the officer replied.[52]

King Hussein followed up his visit to Baghdad with a personal letter sent to Saddam on 22 September, which the Jordanian government later decided to publish as part of its White Paper justifying the Jordanian role in the crisis. In the letter, the King reiterated Jordan's adherence to the principle of the inadmissibility of the acquisition of territory by force, stressing that this was important because 'failure to apply this principle . . . will constitute a dangerous precedent of which Israel will take advantage'.[53] Hussein also asked Saddam to clarify Iraq's conditions for a withdrawal from Kuwait in order to facilitate a peaceful settlement. Finally, as a way of sweetening the pill, he listed five achievements which Baghdad could still claim even if there was now a diplomatic resolution to the crisis. These included 'embarrassing the world which has neglected the Palestine issue' and highlighting the gap between rich and poor in the Arab world. Once again, though, the letter elicited no softening in Saddam's position.[54]

Hussein persisted in his efforts. In a letter sent to Soviet leader Mikhail Gorbachev on 6 October he sought to clarify Jordan's approach to the crisis, making clear that 'we do not accept Iraq's occupation of Kuwait'.[55] But, he added, Jordan was also opposed to the foreign military presence in the region because it complicated the situation. Any solution, he argued, must address the causes of the Iraqi invasion, not just its consequences, and the resolution of the crisis should be linked to a comprehensive solution to the Arab–Israeli conflict within the framework of international law. It is clear that this position went some way towards meeting Iraqi demands, but evidently not far enough to tempt Saddam into considering the King's terms.

King Hussein also received support for his negotiating efforts at this stage from Yasser Arafat. In a letter to the King, Arafat argued that they faced only two options: war, which 'will destroy us all', and peace through negotiations. He emphasised the need for a comprehensive solution to all of the region's problems, and the dangers presented by foreign interference. Arafat claimed to have secured a softening in Saddam's peace terms through his own meetings with the Iraqi leader, and to have detected, somewhat self-servingly, a growing international acceptance of the need to link the resolution of the Kuwaiti crisis to the Palestinian problem. The PLO leader concluded his letter by bemoaning what he saw as the US bias in dealing with problems in the Middle East.[56]

Arafat and Hussein's efforts to find a diplomatic solution to the crisis proved to be of no avail, but one area in which they did have some limited success was in securing Saddam's eventual agreement to release some of the Western hostages he had seized early in the crisis. Initially, Saddam had seen the detaining of foreign nationals unfortunate enough to have found themselves in Iraq or in Kuwait when Iraqi forces invaded as a way of increasing his diplomatic leverage. These so-called 'guests' of the Iraqi regime were dispersed around the country to strategic sites, where they were deployed as 'human shields' intended to deter any coalition attack. President Bush had already expressed his concern about the fate of foreigners detained by the Iraqi regime to King Hussein on 16 August, warning that 'retaining Americans against their will was bad and unacceptable', and that 'Saddam shouldn't push us further by going against civilians'.[57] On 18 August the UN passed Resolution 664, which expressed deep concern over the safety of foreign nationals in Iraq and Kuwait and called for Iraq to facilitate their immediate departure. Saddam's initial response was intransigent. In an open letter to the families of foreigners in Iraq, broadcast by Baghdad Radio on 19 August, he made it plain that they would only be released if the Western powers withdrew their forces from the region and pledged not to attack Iraq. In the meantime, they would remain at vital targets in Iraq to 'prevent military aggression'.[58]

The image of the hostage was a potent one, particularly in the United States, where memories were still fresh of the embassy hostage saga following the 1979 Iranian revolution, when seventy American diplomats had been held against their will in Tehran for 444 days. Nevertheless, Saddam's attempt to use the selective release of hostages as a way to divide the international community was singularly unsuccessful. By the beginning of December he had largely abandoned the ploy, holding on only to the British and American hostages, whom he perhaps saw as bargaining chips of greater weight. Meeting Saddam in Baghdad for a mini-summit on 4 December, King Hussein, alongside Arafat and Yemeni Vice-President Ali Salim al-Bayd, managed to persuade him that releasing all of the hostages would help facilitate a resolution of the crisis.[59] Saddam may have already decided to let the hostages go, but he followed up on the meeting by announcing the hostages' release on 6 December. On the central issue of withdrawal from Kuwait, however, the King's final personal plea to Saddam during the summit was again unsuccessful. According to the King's later recollection, Saddam's last words while bidding him farewell at the airport were: 'The entire universe is against us and God is with us. Victory will be ours, so don't worry and don't trouble yourself.' The King's response was, 'Thank you. I shall return to my country feeling sad, worried and full of sorrow. What I have heard is beyond my ability to deal with. Should you need my help in something good and worthwhile, I shall be in Amman.'[60] The further call for help from Saddam for which the King hoped never came.

Alongside the question of Iraqi withdrawal, two other issues which resulted from the invasion of Kuwait were of pressing concern to Jordan during the early months of the crisis. The first was the effect of the economic sanctions imposed on Iraq by the United Nations, and, linked to this, the second was the wave of refugees who fled from Iraq and Kuwait to Jordan. UN Security Council resolution 661 of 6 August, which imposed an embargo on trade with Iraq, placed Jordan in an awkward position. The Jordanian economy was heavily dependent on Iraq, particularly for its oil, and the Jordanian government feared that if Jordan implemented the UN embargo in full, Iraq might cut off these supplies. Initially, the Jordanians sought 'clarification' from the UN Secretary-General, Perez de Cuellar, as to the scope of the resolution. This was defensible to the extent that the resolution was general in its wording, appearing to exempt certain types of goods, including those intended 'strictly for medical purposes and, in humanitarian circumstances, foodstuffs'. Thereafter, Jordan based the defence of its position on Article 50 of the UN Charter, which permitted any state confronted with special economic problems in enforcing a UN embargo to consult with the Security Council in seeking a solution to those difficulties.[61] In the event, the Jordanians had little choice about the implementation of the maritime embargo, since international shipping avoided the port of Aqaba anyway for fear of contravening the UN resolution.

The resulting blow to the Jordanian economy was made even worse by the influx of something like 500,000 refugees from Iraq and Kuwait during the crisis. On 11 August, Iraq decided to grant Arab and Third World nationals, many of whom had acted as guest workers in Iraq and Kuwait, the right to leave the country. Soon something like 20,000 refugees a day were crossing the desert border between Iraq and Jordan, creating a large and pressing demand for food, water, shelter and medical supplies. By 23 August, King Hussein announced that 185,000 refugees had arrived in the country, with only 67,000 having been moved on. Although the initial crisis was acute, the Jordanian government gradually got on top of the problem, but not without some bitterness at the tardiness of the international relief effort. Prince Hassan was driven to comment in early September that 'the plight of these persons . . . has evoked only the faintest of responses from the world community'.[62]

Jordan's economic plight during the final months of 1990 was worsened still further by the effective breakdown in relations with Saudi Arabia brought on by the King's approach to the crisis. The Saudis, like the Egyptians, quickly came to believe that the King had been complicit in Saddam's invasion of Kuwait, citing his request to be addressed as 'Sharif' shortly after the crisis broke out as evidence that he had revived designs on his family's ancestral lands in the Hejaz.[63] They retaliated by closing oil pipelines to Jordan in mid-September, and announcing shortly afterwards the expulsion of twenty-four Jordanian diplomats charged with engaging in activities designed to 'undermine the security of the kingdom'.[64] The damage caused by the crisis to relations between the two states was lasting. While King Hussein lived, Jordan's relations with Saudi Arabia never returned to their pre-war level of cordiality.

By late December 1990, it was clear to the King that it was time to prepare for the likely outbreak of war. In view of Saddam Hussein's threats to strike at Israel, and the established Israeli military doctrine which required retaliation in the event of an attack, there was a real danger that Jordan, sandwiched between these two enemies, might be dragged into the conflict. Israeli Defence Minister Moshe Arens declared during the first month of the crisis that any movement of Iraqi forces into Jordanian territory would be viewed as an act of war by Israel, a warning that Hussein took very seriously, as he did a warning delivered to him in September by his Mossad contact, Efraim Halevy, that Iraqi reconnaissance flights along the Jordanian–Israeli border must cease.[65] During this meeting with Halevy, the King had indicated his willingness to meet Israeli Prime Minister Yitzhak Shamir to discuss the crisis. With war evidently approaching, the need for the meeting now became more pressing, and it was eventually fixed to take place between 4 and 5 January 1991 at the King's home near Ascot, England.

Before meeting Shamir, Hussein wanted to make clear to Saddam his position should war break out. On 31 December 1990, therefore, he despatched his trusted aide and speechwriter Adnan Abu Odeh on a mission to Baghdad, carrying a personal letter for Saddam Hussein, in which he told Saddam that in the event of war he would not allow Jordanian territory or airspace to be violated. In his reply, Saddam agreed to abide by the King's request to respect Jordan's sovereignty.[66]

Abu Odeh, along with the King's Chief of Diwan, Sharif Zeid bin Shaker, and his communications chief, Ali Shukri, also attended the subsequent meeting with Shamir. The Israeli prime minister for his part was supported by a team which included Mossad's Efraim Halevy, the IDF Deputy Chief of Staff Ehud Barak, Cabinet Secretary Elyakim Rubinstein, and Director-General of the Prime Minister's Office Yossi Ben Aharon. From the Jordanian side, the King, Adnan Abu Odeh, Ali Shukri and Zeid bin Shaker have all offered accounts of the meeting, while, for the Israeli side, Efraim Halevy and Yitzhak Shamir have given their own versions of what transpired.[67] Although there is much common ground between these various accounts of the meeting, there are also some interesting differences in emphasis as to the outcome. All of the accounts agree on the good atmosphere which the King created. The Israeli party arrived in London on Friday 4 January, reaching Ascot before the beginning of the Sabbath that evening. They stayed overnight as the King's guests, and he made sure that kosher food was provided for them. The mutual respect between the two leaders was evident from the outset of the substantive discussions, which began with the two men exchanging gifts.[68] In his recollections of the meeting, Zeid bin Shaker stressed that its main purpose was to ensure that the Jordanian and Israeli armies did not become embroiled in an accidental clash in the Jordan valley.[69] All of the accounts agree that this particular purpose was accomplished; King Hussein made a personal pledge to Shamir that his armed forces were mobilised for purely defensive reasons, and that he would not allow the use of Jordan's territory for a military strike against Israel.

Efraim Halevy, however, recalls that Shamir then raised a second, more difficult issue. Since Jordan could not prevent the use of 'its outer space' by Iraq for the firing of ballistic missiles against Israel, Shamir asked the King to agree that Israel could make limited and peripheral use of Jordanian airspace should it be forced to retaliate against Iraqi attacks on its territory.[70] The King refused, explaining that he could not be seen to be colluding with Israel should it choose to retaliate against Iraq. Not only would he not acquiesce in Israel's use of Jordanian airspace, he stated categorically that he would order his armed forces to defend Jordan's sovereignty. The implication of this was all too clear. If the Israeli air force struck at Iraq through Jordanian airspace, Jordan would activate its air defences, which Israel would then be obliged to destroy. The result would be war between Israel and Jordan, albeit a short-lived and unequal contest. Halevy's conclusion about the meeting thus contrasts with that of other commentators. For him, 'the issue was one of "life and death" and the upshot was that Israel's request and expectations had been rejected'.[71] Nevertheless, Halevy concedes that while there had been no meeting of minds, there had been a meeting of hearts, which perhaps explains the positive impression created by the encounter on both Hussein and Shamir.[72]

With the beginning of the air assault on Iraq on 17 January, the Israeli prime minister's fears about Iraqi missile strikes were quickly realised. The first Scuds fell on Israel on 18 January and, in all, thirty-nine missiles fell on Israeli territory during the course of the war. Hopelessly inaccurate and carrying a very limited payload, the main effect of the Scuds was to act as a psychological weapon. In this respect at least they proved effective, with the morale of the Israeli civilian population being badly damaged by the regular air-raid sirens and the uncertainty surrounding the possible use of chemical warheads. Shamir came under sustained pressure from his cabinet and the defence establishment to retaliate directly, rather than relying on the US to seek out and destroy the Iraqi Scud launchers. Of course, this would be playing into Saddam's hands, since the purpose of the attacks was precisely this: to provoke an Israeli response which might then split the coalition of forces ranged against Iraq, forcing its Arab members to break ranks. Halevy records that, in the final analysis, Shamir's restraint was the result not only of his commitments to the United States, but also of his trust in King Hussein's good faith. Shamir believed that his conduct towards Hussein might somehow be rewarded in future years.[73]

As soon the Scuds began to fall on Israel, Hussein himself received a warning from the Soviet leader Mikhail Gorbachev about the potential dangers of this new development in the crisis.[74] Emphasising how little sympathy he had for Iraq, Gorbachev asked Hussein to take a 'responsible and balanced position' in response to Saddam's attacks on Israel, arguing that the Iraqi leader's attempt to divert Arab attention from his invasion of Kuwait through the instigation of a direct confrontation with Israel should not be allowed to succeed. While he assured Hussein that the Palestinian problem remained a priority in the Soviet Union's foreign policy, Gorbachev made clear his view that 'you can't solve a problem by starting a new one'. If the Arabs heeded his call to stay calm, the Soviet leader argued, Moscow would work with them to ensure real progress in resolving the Arab–Israeli conflict in the aftermath of the crisis. This pro-active Soviet support for the US and Israeli position in the crisis was unprecedented in the Cold War era.

For his part, the King remained a frustrated spectator as war broke out. On 10 January 1991, in a final desperate peace initiative, he wrote an urgent personal letter to President Bush:

> I . . . am and have always been your friend. In this spirit I address you now as we all stand at the edge of the abyss . . . I am now facing the choice, once again, of either committing all my energies and resources to averting the looming horrendous disaster, by actively engaging all concerned towards that end, as I did at the outset of the Gulf crisis, or remain an observer . . . while adhering to our announced policy of preventing, to the best of our ability, any violation of our territory and air space by any side to the impending carnage which will be one of the

greatest setbacks the human race has yet encountered. If you support my intention to act at this eleventh hour then my chances of contributing towards a peaceful solution to the Gulf crisis will be enhanced by both your earliest response to this message and your assistance in opening the way for me to begin immediately a direct dialogue with our Saudi brethren. If this happens it will then facilitate my subsequent actions within the entire Arab world and internationally to salvage the situation.[75]

The King's eleventh-hour initiative was to no avail. President Bush did not respond to his appeal, and Hussein learned of the beginning of the air campaign not from Washington but from Atlanta, via CNN reports.[76] Despite their profound differences in approach, the King and President Bush evidently saw merit in keeping a private channel between them open as the conflict unfolded. Bush asked Richard Armitage, who had been working as a mediator on water issues in the Middle East, to act as his special emissary to the King. During the third week of January, Armitage visited Amman, carrying with him a message from the president to the effect that he still believed that 'Jordan has a positive role to play in shaping the future of the Middle East'. To this end, the president suggested that, despite the evident crisis in relations, they should endeavour to keep channels of communication open. 'Your Majesty', he wrote:

We cannot escape the fact that we differ profoundly concerning events in your part of the world. I am prepared to accept this fact without questioning the permanence of friendly relations between the Hashemite Kingdom of Jordan and the United States. In these extraordinary times, however, when Americans are giving their lives for a cause we believe to be worthy, the need for clear communication is absolutely vital. We must not allow a misunderstanding to undermine something as profound as the friendship between our two countries.[77]

To enable their dialogue to continue, Bush suggested that the King might wish to select a trusted envoy of his own to come to Washington 'for a very low-key round of discussions'. Alternatively, 'if you wish to have another conversation in Amman, I will be pleased to accommodate. Whatever the venue,' the president wrote, 'we should continue this process.'

Hussein replied on 2 February, thanking Bush for having chosen 'an old friend, a man of great integrity and moral courage, Rich Armitage to talk to me'. Explaining the background to his own peace initiatives, the King wrote:

Believe me, my friend, that it was my concern for you and the United States of America which caused me to seek to meet you at the outbreak of the crisis and later in Paris, which was not to happen. Mine is and has possibly been a lone voice, different to many in this region, but before God I am satisfied that whatever happens it was and will be the voice of friendship, peace and honour.

Welcoming the president's suggestion that their dialogue should continue, the King promised to seek out a trusted Jordanian emissary to visit Washington periodically for discussions. Echoing Bush, Hussein declared, 'discussions must continue between us, Sir. Whatever the venue I fully agree we should continue this process.'[78]

As the campaign against Iraq proceeded, however, the King's frustration with American actions mounted further, reaching a peak with a speech which he delivered on 6 February, within days of his apparently conciliatory message to Bush. In this speech, Hussein denounced the US-led attack on Iraq as a 'ferocious' and 'unjust' war, which was being conducted 'against all the Arabs and Muslims, not against Iraq alone . . . Had the same efforts that were exerted to prepare for this war been exerted for a political settlement,' he argued, 'this tragedy would not have taken place.' He added that Washington had rejected such attempts to reach a peaceful settlement because its real objective was 'to destroy Iraq and to rearrange the regional state of affairs in a manner that would be far more serious for the present and future of our nation than what had been arranged by the Sykes–Picot treaty'. Hussein reserved his strongest criticisms for the Arab members of the US-led coalition:

When Arab and Islamic lands are offered as bases for the allied armies from which to launch attacks to destroy the Arab Muslim Iraq, when Arab money is financing this war with unprecedented generosity unknown to us and our Palestinian brothers, while we shoulder our national responsibilities; when this takes place, I say that any Arab or Muslim can realise the magnitude of this crime against his religion and his nation.[79]

The King concluded by praising 'Iraq, its heroic army, and steadfast, courageous people'.

It is important to note that this speech represented Hussein's authentic, unvarnished personal voice. His two main speechwriters at the time were both surprised when the King let them see an advance draft of what he intended to say. Abu Odeh, who received a call from the King asking him to work on the draft whilst he was in discussions with Zeid bin Shaker, was shocked when he received the provisional text. He telephoned the King immediately to advise him that the wording was far too strong, and that he should not make the speech at all. The King was not at all pleased with Abu Odeh's advice, and sent the speech to his other speechwriter for him to look over instead. The King's other speechwriter also thought the language too extreme, and he and Abu Odeh worked together in trying to dilute the text as best they could, without going against the King's wishes.[80] Sure enough, as soon as the King's speech was broadcast, the American ambassador came to see him to ask for an explanation of its contents and tone. Abu Odeh then hit upon the idea of claiming that the speech was only intended for domestic consumption, and that he had written it and not the King himself. This was the explanation which was subsequently given to Washington, to no avail.

The response to Hussein's speech from President Bush was swift, personal and bitter. In a letter sent to Hussein on 9 February, he wrote:

> I am not going to hide my deep disappointment with your speech of February 6. I had not expected . . . to read such a vitriolic attack on the intentions and actions of the multinational coalition that is liberating Kuwait . . . Perhaps what was not in your speech is more telling: there is no mention of Kuwait. Instead, your words exculpate Saddam Hussein for the most serious and most brazen crime against the Arab nation by another Arab in modern times . . . If we do not agree on these matters, so be it. But we must understand that a public, political posture that takes Jordan so far from the international and Arab consensus has damaged very seriously the prospects for eliciting international help for Jordan. If I am circumspect in my own public views on your accusations, it is only because I continue to place value, however unrequited, in your nation's well-being and stability.[81]

Hussein replied, defending himself, a week later:

> I derive no pleasure in expressing my disillusionment and deep disappointment over the divide which seems to increasingly separate genuine Arab and Muslim aspirations and legitimate rights and United States policies towards us.
>
> While I do not, however, question your right to express yourself in defence of your policies and objectives, I am not able to concede mine as a Hashemite Arab Muslim to express myself and to reflect the true feelings of the Arab and Muslim peoples.
>
> I am convinced that time will prove that my relationship with you has been that of an honest friend concerned for you personally and for Jordanian–American and Arab and Muslim–American relations,

principles and mutual interests. As we pass through this difficult phase
in our relations I suggest that we continue our bilateral dialogue in the
interests of our two countries and our region.[82]

Despite the King's concluding suggestion of further dialogue, the break in
relations with the United States was every bit as serious as his advisers had
warned. In addition to the president's personal counter-blast, the Senate
followed up by passing a bill freezing aid to Jordan. The speech also
significantly deepened the breach in relations between Jordan and the Gulf
States, especially Saudi Arabia. But if the King had been warned in advance
about the likely deleterious consequences of the speech, why did he risk so
much damage to Jordan's economic and political interests by insisting on
making it?

Part of the background to the speech was the King's anger at the coalition's
bombing of trucks on the Baghdad to Amman highway, many of which were
carrying legitimate supplies of oil to Jordan. The casualties among civilians
caused by these attacks may well have been the spark which ignited his
explosive reaction. But combustible material in the form of his deep
frustration at the failure of his own mediation efforts, the division of the Arab
world and the isolation of Jordan was already plentiful. His frustration at the
failure of his mediation efforts may have been deepened by his initial belief,
based on his experience during the Iran–Iraq war, that he was ideally placed
to negotiate a resolution of the crisis. The fact that his efforts were largely
ignored by both sides was certainly a blow to his personal sense of dignity.[83]

But this was only part of the picture. Probably the most significant factor
among all of the explanations which might be offered for the King's speech
was his own sense of Arab nationalism. This was inextricably linked to his
sense of Hashemite destiny, to which he alluded in his reply to George Bush
when he wrote that he could not concede his objectives 'as a Hashemite Arab
Muslim'. Throughout his reign, Hussein had maintained his attachment to
the Hashemite brand of Arab nationalism, which stood for the independence
of the Arab nation from outside control or domination, and asserted the
destiny of the Hashemite family to provide leadership for the Arabs.
Furthermore, as we have seen, Hussein continued to see Iraq as part of the
lost Hashemite patrimony, and so was particularly sensitive to any attack on
it. As one scholar has observed, he pointedly excluded any praise for the Iraqi
leadership from his 6 February 1991 speech.[84] While it was too soon to speak
of a rift between the King and Saddam Hussein, since he went on to praise the
Iraqi leader's 'peace initiative' on 16 February,[85] the speech may well be seen
as marking the beginnings of a process of alienation between the two men,
which culminated in the King's support for the CIA-backed attempt to
overthrow Saddam in 1996. Similarly, the speech, which was addressed to

Arabs and Muslims everywhere, went much further than would have been necessary in condemning the coalition attack on Iraq had its only intended audience been domestic; the King had said more than enough already on this subject to satisfy Jordanian opinion. In sum, this was a juncture where the King fell back on his personal ideological code in framing his response. It is clear that ideology trumped any rational calculation of Jordan's interests when he decided to make the speech.

The King's stance made no difference to the progress and outcome of the war, which witnessed the rout of Iraqi forces and their ejection from Kuwait by the end of February. By the time a ceasefire was formally signed on 3 March, the Iraqi army was in tatters. Crucially, though, despite widespread internal revolt in Iraq in the wake of the war, Saddam remained in power. His survival allowed him to claim, and apparently even to convince himself, that the war had been a personal victory. A summary of his reading of the conflict might be that America had spent an inordinately long time bombing Iraq before it had been willing to commit ground troops. Thereafter, American irresolution had allowed key Republican Guard units to escape, and the US had also failed materially to back the ensuing revolt against his rule. Saddam subsequently argued that America was 'in the last stage of elderliness and the beginning of the first stage of old age'.[86] This explained what he came to see as the timidity of the US approach during and after the Gulf conflict.

As the war came to an end, the King, conscious of the need to rebuild bridges to Washington, wrote to President Bush on 28 February expressing his 'deep joy at the conclusion of hostilities'. Mixing self-justification and congratulation, he continued:

> It is a crisis which I had tried so hard to resolve before it escalated. In any event, well done my friend and you will find me more than ever determined to contribute my utmost to the healing of wounds and to the opening of a new and bright chapter in the history of this region for the benefit of its future generations. We shall commit ourselves to the renewal of the best Jordanian/American and Arab/American relations on sound, clear and solid foundations.[87]

Unlike his previous two letters in February, which, uniquely amongst their correspondence, he had merely signed 'sincerely Hussein', here the King resumed his more familiar parting terms with the president. 'I am your sincere friend, Hussein', he wrote.[88]

The American-led peace process which followed the war, and which was to culminate in the convening of the Madrid peace conference at the end of October 1991, was soon to give Hussein the opportunity to demonstrate his commitment to this new beginning in the region. But in other respects his handling of the Gulf crisis had caused serious damage to Jordan's regional and international position. The impact of his approach on Jordan's national interests was serious, if not close to catastrophic. Jordan was now alienated not only from its traditional Western protectors but also from key allies in the Arab world such as Saudi Arabia, Egypt and the Gulf emirates. The political and economic consequences of the crisis were to overshadow Jordanian diplomacy for much of the rest of the decade. For once, the keen political instinct which had served the King so well in previous crises in the region seemed to desert him during the Gulf crisis. Unlike his role during the Iran–Iraq war, when both Washington and Baghdad had been happy to use him as an intermediary, his attempts after the invasion of Kuwait to reconcile the irreconcilable positions of his two former friends, Saddam Hussein and George Bush, were doomed to failure.

CHAPTER 15

FROM MADRID TO OSLO

KING HUSSEIN AND THE PEACE PROCESS, 1991–3

In the spring of 1991, King Hussein stood alone, more isolated inter-nationally than he had ever been in his forty-year reign. In previous decades, he had always been able to count on at least one powerful foreign friend, but after the Gulf crisis there was no one. The United States was alienated as a result of what it saw as his backing for Saddam's invasion of Kuwait. The Gulf States in general, but particularly the Saudis and Kuwaitis, had turned from friends to foes in the space of six months. The depth of hostility between King Hussein and King Fahd of Saudi Arabia was remarkable, composed as it was of a potent mix of revived dynastic rivalry, fear and suspicion. Relations between the King and the emir of Kuwait were, if anything, even worse. Meanwhile, President Mubarak of Egypt had not forgotten the row over the breakdown of his mediation efforts during the Gulf crisis. Even relations with Syria were difficult, since President Asad had joined the anti-Iraqi coalition and was temporarily tacking closer to Washington in the new post-Cold War era. Finally, although the King's stance may have won him some credit in Baghdad, his attempt to distance himself from Saddam Hussein during the final stage of the crisis also placed a question mark over his relations with Iraq. In any event, an internationally isolated Iraq under a UN sanctions regime hardly constituted a reliable or powerful foreign patron.

Hussein, then, had burnt all his bridges. To be sure, his tough anti-American and anti-Saudi rhetoric had won him much credit at home, but by opening up the domestic political system and providing a vent for the opposition, the King had also made himself more answerable to public opinion. He and his government would have to handle future shifts in policy more carefully than had ever been necessary under the martial law regime. Hussein's involvement in the peace process was, therefore, as much the result of political and economic weakness as it was of personal conviction. This is not to say that he was insincere in his protestations of a desire for peace, but rather that his peacemaking was driven as much by necessity as it was by conviction. The King had only one move left which he could make to avoid checkmate.

Hussein was far too astute a player of international politics not to recognise his predicament. Initially, though, this recognition produced paralysis. One former official and close personal associate of the King describes him as 'helpless and hopeless' at this stage.[1] Hussein sank into a deep depression, which also had consequences for his ever-precarious state of health. On 10 June 1991, he was admitted to hospital for heart treatment. Although he was soon discharged with an apparently clean bill of health, the palace announcement acknowledged that he had been suffering from an irregular heartbeat caused by atrial fibrillation, a condition which had affected him before, and which was quite likely to have been associated with the stress under which he had been working. In her memoir of this period, Queen Noor describes the King as having retreated more and more into his own world, avoiding dealing with any complicated problem.[2] The beginnings of the regional peace process, orchestrated by US Secretary of State James Baker, gave him his only outlet.

Having snubbed Hussein during the early rounds of his diplomacy, Secretary Baker decided that it was time to bring him into the process in April 1991, paying a visit to the King's holiday home in Aqaba. While pleasantries replaced the harsh words which had been spoken during the Gulf crisis, Baker made it plain that the damage to US–Jordanian relations was deep, and that it could not be repaired overnight. 'It's going to be a tough row to hoe to repair Jordan's relationship with the United States,' he told the King. Both men were astute readers of the dynamics of power. As Baker later noted, 'it was clear to me the King understood the simple dynamic: for us to help him now, he needed to play on our terms'.[3] For his part, Hussein characterised the talks as 'extensive, frank and constructive'.[4] In essence, the King accepted Baker's proposals concerning the organisation of the planned international peace conference. He also agreed to provide an umbrella for Palestinian attendance as part of a joint delegation with Jordan.

On 22 April the King sent President Bush his own reply to a question posed by Baker at the end of their meeting: 'what is needed for us to resume a relationship between our two governments and ourselves?' To Hussein's own mind what was required was to 'remove from our relationship all the grey areas that have clouded American/Jordanian relations over a number of years, reaching a peak of intensity during the Gulf crisis and war'. Harking back to the foundations of the relationship under Eisenhower in the 1950s, the King declared that he remained at heart the 'young idealist' committed to 'defending with pride mutual ideals and principles', but that he felt 'a sacred duty to be honest with you at the pinnacle of power in the most powerful nation of our times'. Recognising the underlying strength of the bilateral relationship which, according to him, 'permeated and embraced all the elements within the Government of Jordan, its people, its armed forces, its public security and intelligence forces and their opposite numbers in the United States', Hussein concluded by reiterating his openness to the revival of relations, adding, 'Where we go from here is up to you.'[5]

Despite the awkwardness surrounding this first encounter, as Baker's diplomacy advanced Amman became a favoured stopover point for the secretary of state. Here, unlike in Damascus or Jerusalem, he could be guaranteed a sympathetic and cooperative hearing for his plans. While the King still had disagreements with the Americans over the substance of what should be discussed at the planned peace conference, he was prepared to be much more accommodating than either the Syrians or the Israelis on the question of its form. Baker, who had a tough row to hoe in getting all of the protagonists even to attend the conference in the first place, felt that Hussein at least was pulling with him in the same direction. During Baker's second visit to Amman on 14 May, the King agreed to use his private channels to the Israelis to ensure that there would be no unwelcome surprises for them in the composition of the Palestinian part of the Jordanian delegation,[6] and in an interview with the French magazine *Le Point* a few weeks later, the King stated that the 'taboo' on direct talks between Israel and the Arabs must disappear.[7]

The interview may have been part of Hussein's public response to a personal letter sent by US President George Bush on 31 May. Pressing the King to agree formally to Jordan's participation in the conference whether the Syrians attended or not, the president argued, 'it is essential that Jordan decide for itself and not allow any other party to determine Jordan's role'. He added a personal appeal:

Your Majesty, we have known each other for a long time – times of war and peace, times of friendship and friction. Now, the time has come for you and your country to seize the opportunity at hand and shape events lest they shape us. There can be no escape from this opportunity and from the responsibility it brings. We will be there for you, but we can only help you if you are there for yourselves. You told Jim Baker that you were ready to make a historic decision, and that your going to Damascus was only a matter of 'form'. You told me that you would be there. There will never be a better time. I am counting on you, your leadership, and your sense of history.[8]

In reply, Hussein expressed concern about various dimensions of the American-sponsored peace process. Firstly, he was worried that the two tracks of the process – bilateral and multilateral – might become detached, arguing, 'The dual track approach was never intended as a deviant from a comprehensive settlement but rather augments it.'[9] Secondly, he was concerned that discussions were taking place behind Jordan's back on issues which directly concerned its own national interests, specifically regarding possible interim measures in the occupied territories. He made his objections clear: 'we are justified in resenting our exclusion from the formulation of our role only to be ascribed responsibilities as was the case in Camp David'. In a reference to Jordan's own concerns about the Palestinian problem, he wrote, 'the regional challenge of demography requires participation and responsibility'. Responding to the president's challenge to seize the moment, he retorted, 'do you want us to prove our courage by using our credibility for peace? If so assistance should not come as a reward for committing suicide but as an incentive to proceed with the process. Our people must contribute democratically to realising peace . . . no country in the region, including Israel, has publicly matched my forthrightness in the search for peace.'

As the tone of the King's letter implied, tensions and suspicions continued to dog US–Jordanian relations during the summer of 1991. Matters were made considerably worse in August by the publication of a Jordanian government white paper, explaining the kingdom's stance during the Gulf crisis. This offended not only Egypt, through its implied criticisms of President Mubarak's mediatory role in the early stages of the crisis, but also the Americans, and spurred President Bush to write a terse letter to the King, repudiating many of its claims:

> Although I had not intended revisiting with you many of the issues central to the crisis in the Gulf, the contents of the White Paper compel me to do otherwise. I cannot simply let pass the statement that 'action taken by external forces aggravated and escalated the atmosphere of contention', especially as the text goes on to single out the actions of the United States. I find it extraordinary – and disappointing – that you should emphasize the movement of a few ships at a time when Iraq was positioning tens of thousands of troops on Kuwait's borders. And it is no less frustrating to me that you emphasize one vote in the Congress and ignore all that Iraq did to alienate the United States as well as the years of effort on our part to improve relations with Saddam.[10]

The president went on to describe himself as 'somewhat mystified by your emphasis on the possibility of avoiding confrontation in the early days of August'. The fact was, Bush asserted, that Saddam 'never had any intention of giving up Kuwait', adding, 'Your Majesty, I do not wish to make an issue of the White Paper, but I do want you to know that it troubles me, both that it purports to be a reflection of history and that you would choose to release it now.' Stressing the need to work together both to keep pressure on the Iraqi regime and to promote the cause of peace in the Middle East, Bush, with his confidence in the King evidently dented once again, concluded, 'our success in both of these objectives will be affected in no small part by Jordan's and your personal commitment to these objectives'.

In the event, despite the vicissitudes of US–Jordanian relations, Hussein accepted the formal invitation to the Madrid peace conference. Secretary Baker also succeeded in persuading President Asad to authorise Syrian attendance, thus easing Hussein's position in relation to his only other Arab ally. On 12 October, Hussein announced that Jordan would be attending the peace conference in a long speech before a national congress of 2,500 Jordanian elected representatives, including parliamentarians and officials from municipalities and professional associations. The King told them it was their duty to participate in the peace process in order to safeguard their country.[11] His appeal did not go unnoticed in Washington; in another personal message, President Bush thanked him for Jordan's acceptance of the invitation to Madrid, noting that he realised 'this decision could not have been taken without your personal leadership exemplified most notably in your speech of October 12'.[12]

The Madrid peace conference convened formally on 30 October 1991, with all of the main parties in attendance. Hussein had devoted considerable care to selecting the Jordanian part of the joint Palestinian-Jordanian delegation to the conference and the subsequent bilateral talks, making sure that the key East Bank families as well as the army were represented.[13] Alongside this careful political balancing act, though, the King had to face up to a perennial problem: the relative dearth of talent on which he could draw to carry out such complex negotiations. Jordan had produced a number of exceptional diplomats and lawyers, but, compared to the wealth of talented, Western-educated officials on whom Israel could draw, the Jordanian talent pool was very limited. In effect, over the years, Hussein had had no choice but to recycle many of the same officials whether they had been successful in the job or not. This made the challenge which Hussein and his hard-pressed negotiators faced even harder.

Probably the most far-sighted and conciliatory speech at the Madrid conference came from the leader of the Palestinian delegates, Dr Haidar Abdel Shafi, who called on the Israelis to live side by side with the Palestinians, building a new era of hope. The greatest drama – some might say farce – was provided by the Syrian Foreign Minister, Farouk al-Shara, who brandished a 1947 poster of a youthful Yitzhak Shamir, wanted by the British mandatory authorities for terrorist activities. His intention was no doubt to embarrass the Israeli Prime Minister in front of an international audience, but the poster also demonstrated that former 'terrorists' had the opportunity to become peacemakers. Whether they would seize this opportunity was left unclear by the Madrid proceedings themselves, which amounted for the most part to little more than the formal statement of familiar positions.

Despite this lack of progress, the peace conference had domestic political consequences for Jordan, effectively precipitating the fall of the government. The resignation, on 14 November 1991, of Prime Minister Taher al-Masri, after a mere five months in office, offers a fascinating window on some of the forces at work under the surface in Jordanian politics. Masri, a prominent Jordanian of Palestinian origin who had served as foreign minister during the 1980s, had struggled to hold together a cabinet which would support Jordan's engagement in the peace process. This reflected in part the new-found vitality of the parliament, elected in the open poll of 1989, which contained a substantial opposition bloc. In a reshuffle on 3 October before the Madrid conference convened, Masri had dropped a number of ministers opposed to the peace process. Rather than blunting the opposition, though, this move had helped to unite it, and the result was a petition signed by forty-nine members of the eighty-strong parliament, criticising the government. The opposition to the Masri government encompassed not only Islamists and secular Arab nationalists who opposed the peace process, but also Transjordanian nationalists who were suspicious of Jordanians from Palestinian backgrounds. The joint delegation to Madrid, and the looming possibility of peace negotiations which might eventually result in the creation of some form of Palestinian entity, all added to the political tension. The King, despite his position at the apex of the system, could not hope to manage all of these political eddies and cross-currents. What he could do was to remove what had apparently become the largest domestic obstacle to the smooth flow of the peace process, the Masri government. To his credit, Masri himself recognised the problem by this stage, and offered his own resignation, suggesting when he did so that the King would find it easier to gain the support of the chamber of deputies if he appointed a prominent East Bank Jordanian as the next prime minister.[14]

In nominating Taher Masri's successor, the King made an astute tactical choice. He reappointed as prime minister his cousin, Zeid bin Shaker, who had briefly held office before as head of a caretaker government during 1989. Zeid bin Shaker, who had been commander-in-chief of the armed forces during the 1970s and 1980s, was a powerful man in the kingdom. Moreover, in private he was sceptical about the peace process. By making him prime minister at this critical juncture, the King not only brought to office someone with the background to ensure East Bank support for the process, he also directly associated him with its implementation. Zeid bin Shaker later argued that he was reluctant to take on the post and attempted to persuade Taher Masri to stay on, but to no avail.[15]

If the symbolic importance of the Madrid peace conference as the beginning of a new era in the Middle East was great, the bilateral negotiations which followed in its wake did not initially live up to these expectations. At first, the talks focused on little more than procedural wrangling. The United States remained largely on the sidelines as these disputes unfolded during December and January, husbanding its mediatory resources, as Secretary Baker put it in an explanatory letter to the King, for the 'difficult substantive challenges' that lay ahead.[16] The Israelis were determined to preserve the fiction of a joint Jordanian-Palestinian delegation, since this avoided the awkward issue of recognising any separate Palestinian national identity, but this made for a host of extra complications. In advance of the Madrid conference, the King had appointed the former president of Jordan University, Abdul Salam al-Majali, to lead the Jordanian delegation to the bilateral talks. Majali was under no illusions about the difficulty of the task which lay ahead, which would involve not only trying to make progress on the bilateral issues concerning Israel and Jordan, principally those of water rights and territory, but also managing relations within the joint delegation and ensuring that the Palestinian and Jordanian representatives within it coordinated their approaches.[17] This was particularly delicate given that the PLO was directing the Palestinian delegates behind the scenes. Neither party wanted to negotiate on the other's behalf, but Arab politics, or at least King Hussein's reading of them, meant that the Jordanian delegation would not be allowed to resolve bilateral issues with the Israelis unless similar progress had been made on the Palestinian front. The parties were thus locked in an uncomfortable embrace from which there appeared to be no immediate escape.

The Jordanian delegation also faced other difficulties. Unlike the Israeli team which contained a large number of talented lawyers, including Elyakim Rubinstein and Robby Sabel, Jordan could muster only one lawyer qualified to handle the whole range of issues raised in the negotiations: Awn al-Khasawneh.[18] As the bilateral negotiating process unfolded, he persuaded the King and Crown Prince Hassan to give him additional help, in two ways. Firstly, in a departure from cultural norms, he insisted that a stenographer should be called in to make a verbatim Jordanian record of the negotiations. Secondly, to provide him with a further legal sounding-board, he asked for two outside consultants, Professor James Crawford of Cambridge University and Professor Bernard Graefrath, a German professor of law, to be called in to support the Jordanian team.[19]

In shaping Jordan's legal strategy in the negotiations, Khasawneh believed that two issues would matter in the region in the long run: the possession of weapons of mass destruction (WMD) and demographic change. While Israel was the only state in the region then in possession of nuclear weapons, the situation might change in future, and Jordan might find itself caught in the middle of a thermonuclear or biological and chemical battlefield. Thus, Khasawneh wanted any Israeli–Jordanian agreement to commit each side not to use such weapons against the other, and to work for a WMD-free region. The second issue was that of demographic change – also a major Israeli concern, since the Jewish population of Israel was growing at a slower rate than the Arab population of Israel and the occupied territories. Khasawneh was determined that any agreement between the two states would contain provisions preventing the forced movement of the Arab population out of the occupied territories and into Jordan. These concerns were to be reflected, first in the Common Agenda for negotiations agreed in October 1992, and later in the peace treaty itself.

Beyond these strategic concerns, Khasawneh was also well aware of the relative weakness of the Jordanian negotiating position when compared with the Egyptian position in the negotiations with Israel back in 1978–9. Egypt had at least been able to call on substantial US backing for its negotiating position by playing the 'Cold War card' – that is, stressing its value to the US as an anti-Soviet Arab ally, an option which was not open to Jordan after the collapse of the USSR. Nevertheless, Khasawneh believed that Jordan should not settle for less than Egypt had achieved through the 1978 Camp David agreements and the subsequent 1979 bilateral peace treaty.

Beyond this Camp David baseline, Khasawneh had two further key negotiating goals. Firstly, Jordan should not agree to anything which contradicted its obligations under the Charter of the Arab League and the Arab Defence Pact.[20] Behind this lay his concern that the Israeli strategy was designed to pick off the Arab states one by one in peace negotiations, eventually isolating the Palestinians. Secondly, Jordan should not agree to anything which might prejudice the final-status negotiations between Israel and the Palestinians. This applied particularly to the status of refugees and the terms used to delineate the Israeli–Jordanian border. Jordan should resist any attempt to describe the line between the East and West Banks as an 'international' border before the creation of a Palestinian state. In understanding Jordan's conduct of peace negotiations with Israel it is important to keep all of these considerations in mind. As we will see, they help to explain many of the subsequent points of conflict.

Although Jordan's engagement in the Madrid peace process began the task of rehabilitating King Hussein in the eyes of US officials, it did nothing to improve his relations with the Gulf emirates, Saudi Arabia and Egypt. In a letter to British Prime Minister John Major on 20 May 1992, Hussein expressed great bitterness about the 'persistent questioning of our moral integrity' by those states which, he said:

> now have chosen for some unfathomable reason to turn on us with malice and venom: Egypt, Kuwait, the Kingdom of Saudi Arabia, the United Arab Emirates, Qatar and Bahrain. It would seem that all has been forgotten of Jordan's struggles for their stability, progress, and in some cases, their very survival. In the case of Egypt, its very rehabilitation into the Arab world came about largely due to our efforts.[21]

While the King expressed optimism in an interview in early 1992 that Jordan's relations with the US could soon return to 'the long, deep friendship' enjoyed in the past, he admitted that any improvement in relations with Saudi Arabia would take much longer.[22] If anything, the war of words between Amman and Riyadh intensified during 1992, with the Saudi authorities reacting bitterly to an interview given by the King to CNN in March, in which he refused to comment directly on allegations that the Saudis were funding operations by Islamic fundamentalists in Jordan. Then, in May, a dispute flared up between King Fahd and King Hussein over the restoration of the al-Aqsa Mosque and the Dome of the Rock in Jerusalem. Hussein, who guarded his family responsibilities in relation to Jerusalem's holy sites jealously, was deeply offended when Fahd offered UNESCO $10 million to aid the repairs, which he saw as implying that he was failing in his custodianship of the sites. The King responded by donating $8.25 million of his own money, raised through the sale of his private apartment in central London, to fund the restoration work.

In private, the King harboured particular bitterness about the Saudi stance. He wrote:

> It seems clear to me that they have unilaterally chosen to render null and void the agreement drawn by the founder of the kingdom and my late grandfather to close the chapter of hostility between our two Houses . . . I am satisfied that I never once broke my grandfather's commitment in word or in deed, but beyond this point would be unable to remain passive to unwarranted constant hostility to my people, country, House and self.[23]

During this tense period, two further elements contributed to the deepening Saudi–Hashemite feud. The first was continuing rumours about the King's possible dynastic ambitions in Iraq. A report published in the British *Observer*, on 8 March 1992, suggested that in the event of the overthrow of Saddam Hussein, the King might head a revived Iraqi–Jordanian union, with Crown Prince Hassan taking over responsibility for ruling Jordan itself. Although the report was dismissed as completely false by the Jordanian authorities, speculation about the King's dynastic designs continued. It was not unwarranted. Hussein had never abandoned his interest in the lost Hashemite patrimony in Iraq. In July, the *New York Times* quoted US officials as alleging that Saddam had accused the King of complicity in a recently thwarted coup attempt against him. Although the King denied any involvement, reiterating that Jordan would not interfere in the affairs of neighbouring states, rumours that he was supporting the opposition to Saddam's regime continued to circulate.[24]

To add insult to injury from the Saudi perspective, Hussein now embarked on an ideological campaign that emphasised the relevance of the ideals of the Great Arab Revolt at the end of the twentieth century. There was nothing new, of course, in the King proclaiming the virtues of the Arab Revolt, which had been a constant ideological reference point for him throughout his reign. But he now chose to give this familiar theme a new, more explicitly anti-Saudi and anti-Kuwaiti flavour. In a speech to graduating military officers on 23 November 1992, Hussein proclaimed:

> Let us, we the Arabs, have a new Arab order, a united Arab states, or one state. Let us defend its borders, not the borders drawn up by the colonialists, bypassing those Arabs who are motivated by tribal affiliation and arrogance, after they had flooded the nation with their oil and bragged about their seats which were restored at the hands of the foreigner and with its lances stained with the blood of their brothers.[25]

Hussein followed up on this theme in speech after speech, expressing on 16 February 1993 the 'hope that the turn of the twenty-first century heralds a resumption of the Great Arab Revolt, an interpretation of history in terms of freedom not oil'.[26] Hussein's speeches were part of a continuing attempt to highlight what he believed to be the wrong turn the Arab world had taken during the Gulf crisis, when, as he saw it, the pursuit of self-interest had triumphed over the defence of Arab nationalism.

While relations with the Saudis deteriorated further, the King's visit to Washington in March 1992, his first since his failed encounter with President Bush at Kennebunkport in August 1990, was more successful. Writing to the King after the visit, President Bush expressed his 'hope and trust that we are on the road to restoring the relationship between our two countries to what it was and what it should be. As for our personal relationship, please know that you will always have a friend here.'[27]

If the King's relations with the president were on their way to recovery, those with Congress, by contrast, remained frosty, not to say hostile. Congressmen and Senators, much like the Saudis and Kuwaitis, found it difficult to forgive the King for his stance during the Gulf crisis. In April, ten Republican senators wrote to Secretary Baker opposing a proposed aid package for Jordan, and accusing the country of maintaining an open supply line to Iraq in defiance of the UN embargo.[28] The issue of smuggling across the Iraqi border remained a fraught one, with the King rejecting a US proposal in mid-June 1992 to station UN observers on Jordanian soil to monitor the enforcement of sanctions against Iraq. The economic pressure exerted on Jordan through the interception and inspection of ships bound for Aqaba by the US navy proved a continuing irritant in relations until 1994. As late as December 1993, during a meeting between the new US Secretary of State Warren Christopher and King Hussein, the King told Secretary Christopher, 'Aqaba is one of our major problems.' Prime Minister Majali was even blunter: 'we hope we are going to be relieved – to be trusted or not to be trusted . . . I hope this issue will be resolved before the Palestinian problem!' he exclaimed.[29] The Jordanians saw the inspection regime as a means of exerting economic pressure on Jordan to help achieve US political goals, including the isolation of Iraq and the advancement of separate peace negotiations with Israel.

Alongside these continuing political challenges, the King faced two significant personal problems during 1992. The first concerned his marriage and the second his state of health. During the spring, rumours swirled around Amman that the King was having an affair with his twenty-five-year-old press attaché, and that he intended to divorce Queen Noor so that he could marry her instead. This was hardly the first occasion during his reign that such rumours had circulated, but this time the gossip proved persistent. In her memoirs, Queen Noor is candid about the anguish these stories caused her.[30] Having decided to work through this difficult period together, the couple were subsequently pictured almost daily on Jordanian television in the latter part of April and early May attending social functions together. Admittedly, Jordanian news bulletins normally begin with the King's activities, but the focus on the royal couple working together was clearly intended to help quash the rumours about marital problems.

On top of his personal and political travails, the King was confronted in the summer of 1992 by a major health problem, the discovery of cancer in his urinary tract. On 21 August he underwent surgery to remove the tumour at the Mayo Clinic in Minnesota. His doctors were confident that the cancer had been caught at an early stage, and that the operation had been a complete success. Although regular post-operative check-ups would be needed, chemotherapy was not judged to be necessary. Try as they might, though, neither his doctors nor his close family could persuade him to give up smoking, which was a major cause of this type of cancer. Indeed, the very day after his operation, Queen Noor entered his hospital room only to find him sitting up, out of bed, smoking a cigarette next to an open window.[31] Cigarettes were probably Hussein's one true vice. Over the years he had become so accustomed to lighting up as a way to manage stress and help him relax that he was not about to stop now, even on doctors' advice.

Hussein's stay at the Mayo Clinic during the summer of 1992 contributed to a further significant recovery in his personal relations with President Bush. The King was evidently touched by the president's solicitude for his health and wellbeing, a fact which he acknowledged in a glowing letter of thanks he penned as he left the United States during the first week of September. 'I have been made to feel so much at home,' he wrote, 'and the warmth, concern and care I enjoyed, which reflected your friendship for me, I shall never forget.'[32] As the two men came closer together personally, there was also a meeting of minds on the issue that had divided them – Iraq. 'You asked me the other evening about my interpretation of the thinking of the present Iraqi leadership,' the King wrote, 'and, on reflection, I believe it must be a tactic of gaining time and insuring continued survival, though at what price and to what end, I honestly am unable to comprehend.' In a clear shift of his stance against Saddam, the King added, 'I shall work and pray for a united, free Iraq, free of fear and tyranny, where all Iraqis may come together in a national reconciliation and where pluralism and democracy shall be reborn.' The reference to democracy being 'reborn' was particularly interesting, carrying as it did connotations of a return to the pre-1958 'democratic' system under the Hashemite monarchy. In this context it is worth noting that the King held meetings with members of the Iraqi opposition during a three-week stopover in London on his way back to Jordan. In the closest he came to an apology for his stance in the Gulf crisis, the King concluded his letter to President Bush with the words:

> Sir, I may not have been able to assist you as you might have expected over two years ago when overtaken by the tragic and shocking events which unfolded violently on 2 August 1990, and when it might not have made a difference anyway, but I hope that Jordan and I shall be able to do so at the critical times ahead.[33]

Hussein's time at the Mayo Clinic evidently helped concentrate his mind on other matters. The tumultuous welcome which he received when he returned to Amman on 24 September made him realise that he had to break out of his depression and move forward again for the good of the country. But his brush with mortality also led him to think again about the succession to the throne. Some observers date the beginnings of his disillusionment with Prince Hassan as his successor to this period, pointing out that Hussein was evidently disappointed by Hassan's decision not to change the date of his daughter's wedding, which took place the day before his surgery in America. In any case, after his return to Jordan Hussein began to contemplate setting up a 'Family Council' to consider the question of the succession. The ostensible purpose of this would be to form a consensus within the family as to who was most suitable to succeed to the throne after Prince Hassan; the real aim would be to smoke Hassan out on the question of the succession. The King evidently suspected that Hassan would refuse to commit himself on this issue. His longer-term fear was that Hassan would install his own son, Rashid, as Crown Prince, thus removing all of Hussein's sons from the subsequent line of succession. Some of the King's doubts surfaced in a speech he made on 5 November 1992, in which he drew attention to the historic leadership role of the Hashemite family, but omitted any reference to the fact that the line of succession had already been laid down in Hassan's favour. This omission was widely interpreted at the time as a slight to Hassan.[34]

At the same time as Hussein was grappling with these questions, new opportunities began to open up in the peace process. The decisive victory won by the Labour Party led by Yitzhak Rabin in the Israeli election of 23 June 1992 constituted the most important change in the political landscape. Rabin had stood on a platform which emphasised economic development and security over the Likud's ideological attachment to settlement-building in the occupied territories. While he did not propose any radical change in Israel's approach to the peace process, Rabin did promise that he would aim to conclude an agreement on Palestinian self-government within a year. The crucial difference between the Labour government and its Likud predecessor, Rabin told the Knesset, was that Labour would now attempt to use the Madrid framework to reach agreements, rather than simply playing for time.[35] In pursuit of this objective, Rabin proceeded to assemble a coalition which was probably the most doveish in Israel's history, incorporating the left-wing Meretz and centrist Shas parties.[36]

In the wake of a visit to Washington by Rabin in August, President Bush also struck an optimistic note about the possibilities of progress in the peace process. In a 15 August letter to Hussein, he wrote:

> I was struck in my meetings with Prime Minister Rabin by a fundamental shift in Israeli attitudes. Clearly a new Israel Government has brought with it new priorities on a range of issues. Instead of expansion of settlement activity, there are significant restrictions on such activity; instead of efforts to close off dialogue, there are efforts to expand it; and instead of a preoccupation with the status quo, Rabin

speaks of 'peace, reconciliation and international cooperation.' Indeed there is no doubt in my mind that the Israeli Prime Minister is determined to engage in serious negotiations leading toward a comprehensive peace settlement with all of its neighbors.[37]

In terms of relations with Jordan, President Bush told the King:

Prime Minister Rabin and I also explored how we could accelerate negotiations during this coming round. He made clear his determination to reach an early accord on interim self-government for the Palestinians. He also made clear how important a role Israel believes Jordan can play in this process. We both agreed that Jordan's stability under your leadership is critical to regional stability.[38]

Replying with alacrity the following day, Hussein, while welcoming the apparent shift in Israeli attitudes, struck a note of caution:

We persevered in the previous rounds despite the obstacles posed by the Israeli attitude of that period so clearly outlined in your letter: 'expansion of settlements . . . efforts to close off dialogue . . . preoccupation with the status quo'. We hope that the fundamental shift in Israeli attitudes to which you refer will be paralleled by changed perceptions. We need to address not only the different set of priorities but to work on changing those perceptions. Such a fundamental change requires beyond statements, a clear recognition of Palestinian rights.[39]

What was really needed in order to advance the peace process, Hussein believed, was a fundamental shift in the Israeli position on the Palestinian question, of which there was as yet no evidence. Nevertheless, from Hussein's point of view, the election of a Rabin-led Labour government at least represented a return to the devil he knew. He had, after all, spent the years between 1963 and 1977 covertly negotiating with various Labour representatives, including Rabin himself, although this experience also dictated caution: despite goodwill and strong personal relations on both sides they had been unable to reach final agreement.[40] Perhaps the most promising aspect of the new situation from Hussein's point of view was that this time Rabin was firmly in charge of the government. Despite his fixation with Israel's security, Rabin, with his military background, was a man Hussein could understand.

The impact of the new government in Israel was not immediately apparent in the bilateral Israeli–Jordanian talks, which had continued during 1992. Steady progress was made in the talks after their uncertain beginning in late 1991, but there was no major change in 1992 as a result of the switch in Israeli government.[41] The King continued to take a strong personal interest in the negotiations, taking time to meet members of the Jordanian delegation during his convalescence from surgery in the United States.[42] He remained particularly concerned by Israeli settlement-building in the occupied territories. Writing to President Bush on 9 November 1991, shortly after the Madrid conference, the King warned that the settlements posed 'a threat to the security of Jordan', and described Israeli activity in and around Jerusalem as 'the most sensitive and explosive issue', adding, 'Changes made by Israel in the structure and landscape of the city have defaced its historic character.'[43]

Pursuing the same theme in a letter to Secretary Baker on 17 February 1992, the King argued, 'I can never over-emphasize the importance of persuading the Israeli Government to desist forthwith from its settlement policies of beefing up or constructing any further settlements in the territories occupied since June 1967, including Arab Jerusalem.' Such activities, the King argued, threatened to 'destroy the peace process by further violating the occupied territories, rendering the self-government talks meaningless . . . from the Jordanian perspective we also cannot continue to tolerate these changes that create further and real demographic threats to Jordan itself.'[44]

The culmination of this phase of the bilateral negotiations came at the end of October 1992, with the conclusion of a draft Common Agenda for talks between Jordan and Israel. The document agreed on 29 October reflected the Jordanian negotiating strategy developed by Awn Khasawneh. Weapons of mass destruction loomed large, with two sub-clauses devoted to them.[45] In terms of border delineation, the Common Agenda referred to the 'demarcation of the international boundary between Jordan and Israel with reference to the definition under the Mandate without prejudice to the territories presently under Israeli military administration'.[46] Finally, the Common Agenda also included a clause on 'Refugees and Displaced Persons', which made it plain that a solution to this problem would have to be found 'in accordance with international law'.

The Jordanian negotiators were happy with their work, but at home in Jordan the draft Common Agenda caused a political storm. The Muslim Brotherhood described it as a 'declaration of peace principles with the Zionist enemy' which would lead to the normalisation of relations.[47] The PLO too was critical of the document, accusing the Jordanians of agreeing to negotiate on issues such as water and refugees without considering the Palestinian position. Chairman Arafat expressed his concern that Jordan should not move forward too quickly in its negotiations with Israel in a way which might prejudice Palestinian chances of achieving progress.[48] While King Hussein also believed that Jordan should not move too far ahead of the Palestinians, his major concern was the reaction of President Asad, his only significant regional ally.[49] As a result, he asked the leader of the Jordanian delegation to the bilateral talks, Abdul Salam Majali, to spin the negotiations out. Thereafter, the Jordanian delegation negotiated on technicalities rather than substance until the summer of 1993.[50]

During this period, there was little apparent movement in the peace process. But appearances were to prove deceptive. At the end of May, the King appointed Majali as Jordan's prime minister. The new prime minister and the King were immediately embarrassed, though, by an ill-judged public statement on 7 June by Israeli Foreign Minister Shimon Peres, who claimed that peace between Jordan and Israel was only a pen stroke away, and that the Common Agenda constituted a draft peace agreement. The King and prime minister both rejected Peres's claim, emphasising that Jordan would not pre-empt progress on the Palestinian track. But unknown to the Jordanians, behind the scenes, and outside the Madrid framework, negotiations between unofficial Palestinian and Israeli representatives, brokered by Norwegian intermediaries, were well under way. The appeal to both sides of what became known as the Oslo back channel was obvious. Since the talks were secret and informal, ideas could be aired without committing either side, or compro-mising them in the eyes of their harder-line constituents. While the initial sessions, beginning in January 1993, involved little more than brain-storming, the involvement from May onwards of Uri Savir, the director general of the Israeli Foreign Ministry, reflected the growing importance of the talks. Hussein evidently had suspicions that something was afoot; during the summer months he repeatedly asked his Mossad contact, Efraim Halevy, whether covert Palestinian–Israeli contacts were taking place. Halevy relayed the King's questions on to Prime Minister Rabin, who dismissed them with a wave of his hand, saying that Hussein should not worry.[51] How far there was any deliberate attempt to deceive Hussein on the part of either the Israeli or the Palestinian leadership is a moot point. Initially, neither Rabin nor Arafat believed that the back channel would produce results, and it was only during July and August 1993 that real progress was made.[52] Although Arafat admitted to Hussein that he was in contact with Shimon Peres, he evidently did not keep the King up to date with the progress of the negotiations despite the fact that the Jordanians had made it clear publicly that they were waiting for the Palestinians to move before moving forward themselves. Arafat's deputy, Abu Mazen, was embarrassed by this failure to inform the King, noting that he 'shuddered even to contemplate the consequences of King Hussein's anger if we were to reach an agreement with the Israelis which took him completely by surprise'.[53] In the event, this was precisely what happened.

CHAPTER 16

THE BEST OF ENEMIES, THE BEST OF FRIENDS

HUSSEIN, RABIN AND THE JORDANIAN–ISRAELI PEACE TREATY

News about the secret deal in Oslo between PLO and Israeli representatives broke on 29 August 1993, with the agreement put to the Israeli cabinet for approval the following day. Although the agreement was preliminary, representing more of an agenda for negotiations than a full-blown peace treaty, it did commit the Israeli government to hand over Gaza and the West Bank town of Jericho to Palestinian jurisdiction as part of several interim confidence-building measures. The thornier issues concerning the final status of the occupied territories, however, were left for subsequent negotiations.

King Hussein's first response to the agreement, as Abu Mazen had feared, was anger: 'he had every right to be reproachful', Abu Mazen later wrote.[1] Although Hussein confirmed his recognition of the Palestinians' right to negotiate over their own future, he was privately very disappointed at the lack of consultation. But his anger was quickly tempered by the recognition that the Palestinians had made gains from the agreement.[2] Moreover, by freeing him from the need to wait for progress on the Palestinian–Israeli front, it helped open the way for Jordan to pursue its own interests through a bilateral peace settlement, though the Syrian position would still have to be taken into account. As he wrote to President Clinton, 'we will consider the umbrella which enabled the Palestinians to reach this most important juncture in need of folding up and storing in the annals of history. Representing ourselves alone, we shall now move on our own on the Jordanian–Israeli agenda.'[3] This shift was demonstrated symbolically the very day after the signing of the Israeli–Palestinian Declaration of Principles on the White House lawn, by the signature on 14 September of the Jordanian–Israeli Common Agenda for negotiations, in a more subdued ceremony at the US State Department. The King strove to dampen expectations of an early peace agreement with Israel, emphasising that the Common Agenda was merely an outline for substantive talks.

One of the King's reasons for playing down the Common Agenda was the continuing hostility in Jordan to any agreement with Israel. The King had already made one move aimed at reducing parliamentary opposition. This was an amendment to the electoral law, announced on 4 August 1993, to the effect that voters would have only one vote for one candidate, rather than, as under the existing system, a number of votes for candidates in multi-member constituencies.[4] The electoral constituencies themselves would remain unchanged. While 'one man one vote' was an eminently democratic slogan, in Jordan, where kinship loyalty is strong, the measure was expected to reduce support for ideological political parties, and increase that for candidates from large tribes or influential families. Since the latter were more likely to be regime loyalists, the King hoped that the parliament due to be elected under the new law in November 1993 would be more malleable than its predecessor. Sure enough, in the 8 November 1993 general election, the Islamist opposition suffered a reverse, with the Islamic Action Front seeing its representation reduced from twenty-two to sixteen seats.[5] This amendment to the electoral law showed the limits of the King's tolerance for democratisation in Jordan. From this point onwards, peacemaking took him in a more authoritarian direction.

A further reason for playing down the significance of the Common Agenda was that there remained much work to be done before a peace treaty with Israel could be concluded. Initial progress in the negotiations was halting and limited. Hussein evidently felt that the Oslo agreement was 'close to an act of political betrayal' on the part of his former friends in the Israeli Labour Party. In a meeting between Rabin and the King at Aqaba on 26 September, the Israeli prime minister tried to reassure Hussein that Israel would not neglect Jordan's interests in its dealings with the Palestinians. Differences in approach remained, though, with Efraim Halevy describing their talks as 'very unsatisfactory'; they could not agree even on a first step forward towards a full peace treaty.[6] Worse still, a technical fault on Rabin's aircraft held up his planned departure under cover of darkness from Eilat airport, leading to the inadvertent public discovery of the meeting.

During a meeting in Amman at the beginning of December, Hussein described the problem as he saw it to US Secretary of State Warren Christopher:

Our idea is to build from the bottom upwards. We implemented what we agreed earlier on and we hope that at the end the final achievement will be a peace treaty which will be a contribution to the well being of generations to come. Israel wants a peace treaty but we need substance which makes sense to people rather than ratify something and then [argue] about details, which is what is happening.[7]

In essence, Hussein felt the Israelis were trying to persuade him to put the cart before the horse. They wanted him to sign a peace treaty first, and negotiate the details later, a proposal which he could not accept.

With negotiations between the King and Rabin at a stalemate, Foreign Minister Shimon Peres seized the opportunity to step into the breach. Working through Victor Mishcon, the King's friend and lawyer in London, Peres proposed that the King invite him to Amman to discuss the possibility of creating an ambitious regional economic forum, in the hope that economic cooperation might jump-start the political process. A tripartite American-Israeli-Jordanian economic working group, chaired by Dennis Ross, the US State Department's Middle East negotiator, was consequently established.[8] This was followed by a secret visit by Peres to the Jordanian capital on 2 November for further talks. According to Efraim Halevy, who was present, their meeting produced a document stipulating that further discussions would have to take place to resolve the many outstanding issues.[9] But it did not break the political deadlock; on the contrary, Hussein's trust in Peres, already strained following the breakdown of their peace initiative in April 1987, was damaged further when Peres deliberately leaked news of the meeting in an interview with Israeli state television. The King's chagrin was compounded further by two letters he received after the meeting, one from President Clinton and the other from Arafat. President Clinton expressed delight that Jordan and Israel had now agreed to conclude a peace treaty, and suggested that the King might take the opportunity provided by a planned visit to the US in January to attend a White House signing ceremony.[10] The King was astounded by the letter, since no such agreement had been reached. He responded:

> The drive to achieve final results in the peace process by January 1994 is an ambitious goal indeed. While we in Jordan are sparing no effort to arrive at a state of peace as soon as can be, we are doubtful that such an objective is attainable in two months. The smoothness of negotiations on the Jordanian–Israeli track cannot obviate the fact that many agenda items are still in their early stage of discussion and their satisfactory resolution requires intensive and detailed deliberations . . . An early signature of a treaty before the subjects agreed to in the Agenda have had a chance to be thoroughly discussed would not only be too ambitious, but may be harmful to the cause of peace to which we are committed.[11]

Halevy's recollections suggest that the King's position was well founded, but this episode further damaged his credibility in Washington, where it was seen as another example of his unwillingness to take the final plunge for peace with Israel. But Hussein was surely right to resist being bounced by the Israelis and Americans into signing a half-baked peace treaty.

The letter the King had received from Arafat, meanwhile, touched on an even rawer nerve, since in it the PLO leader claimed he had been given guarantees by Israel concerning a special status for the Palestinians in Jerusalem.[12] The King was incensed, fearing not only that further negotiations were taking place behind his back but that the Hashemite role in protecting Jerusalem's holy sites might be threatened. The incident made clear the extent to which competition between the PLO and Jordan remained a fact of life in the peace process. According to Halevy's account, Hussein feared that there might be a further breakthrough on the Israeli–Palestinian track, and that the Israeli government might come to regard Arafat as its preferred negotiating partner. He was particularly worried by rumours that Israel was considering agreeing to a request from Arafat to visit Jerusalem. It was Hussein's fear that his special role in Jerusalem might be undermined by some secret Israeli–Palestinian deal, Halevy argues, more than any other factor that propelled the King into changing from the cautious, step-by-step approach which had led to deadlock in his earlier talks with Rabin to a willingness to reach a comprehensive peace agreement in the spring of 1994.[13] The King's chief of communications, Ali Shukri, is sceptical about this argument, believing that it was the 'broader regional situation', including apparent progress in the Israeli–Syrian negotiations, which led the King to shift position. Rhetorically, Shukri asks: 'do you really think the King believed the Israelis would do a deal with *Arafat* over *Jerusalem*?'[14]

Whatever the King's true motivation, Halevy reported his apparent change of heart in a meeting with US officials during a visit by Secretary Christopher to Israel in late April 1994. The Americans were sceptical. King Hussein had reached this point before, they argued, only to back away when the time for decision came. Halevy now suggested to Dennis Ross, the State Department's Middle East coordinator, that Secretary Christopher should telephone the King and raise three crucial issues with him about the proposed negotiations: their venue, his willingness to negotiate over borders and his preparedness to go it alone regardless of the attitude of other Arab players.[15] Ross did so, and shortly thereafter Halevy heard that the King had answered positively on all three counts. From this point onwards, the Americans started to take the possibility of an Israeli–Jordanian peace agreement seriously.

Shortly afterwards, on 19 May 1994, the King met Rabin secretly in London. With the deadlock now broken, they agreed that the negotiations would take place on the Israeli–Jordanian border, about fifty kilometres north of Eilat and Aqaba. In return for the King's agreement to meet openly in the region for the first time, Rabin agreed to a substantive agenda for negotiations including border demarcation and water allocation. Although the talks would be bilateral, the Americans would be kept informed of progress. Rabin also promised to do what he could to persuade the US to relieve the economic pressure on Jordan, and assist in the re-equipping of its armed forces.[16]

The Hussein–Rabin partnership from now on formed the heart of the Jordanian–Israeli peace process. In view of this fact it is essential to understand each man's perspective on peacemaking. For Hussein, the forging of a historic reconciliation between Arab and Jew was part of his family's destiny, and the first essential step in achieving it was to empathise with those on the other side. Hussein believed that peace could not be made with Israel without understanding the historic tragedy of the Jewish people, and that in order to heal the scars this had left behind one had to be prepared to offer endless reassurance. There was also only a certain type of Israeli leader with whom Hussein felt he could deal. This was the military strongman, the secular Zionist who placed Israel's security ahead of all other considerations. With such a leader the strategy of offering endless reassurance might pay dividends. Moreover, a military man would be able to convince the Israeli public that their security was assured in any peace deal, and so make an agreement stick. By contrast, Hussein did not believe that Zionist revisionists, such as the Likud leaders Begin or Shamir, would ever relinquish their ideological attachment to an expansionist 'Greater Israel'. Hussein dealt with only two Israeli leaders who fully fitted his preferred bill: Moshe Dayan and Yitzhak Rabin. Circumstances had thwarted his attempts to build peace on the foundation of his strong private relationship with Dayan. Now, in Rabin, he had found the right type of Israeli leader at the right time.

Rabin was a unique figure among Israeli prime ministers: the one man who had arrived at a complete and thorough-going conviction that it was time to make a historic compromise between Zionism and Arab nationalism. This was what made him so dangerous a figure for extremists on both sides. Formerly an advocate of strength and coercion, Rabin, who had infamously promised to break the bones of Palestinian demonstrators during the Intifada, came to recognise the futility of force as a means to resolve the conflict. This private conversion coincided with political opportunity in the shape of the peace-making window which opened briefly after the end of the Cold War and the Gulf crisis.

However, there remained a host of practical problems to be overcome before any peace treaty between the two states could be concluded. On a visit to Washington in the second half of June, Hussein told Ross and other US officials that the Jordanian people needed to see benefits flowing from peace, not just sacrifices, and to this end he sought relief for Jordan's heavy debt burden and assistance in modernising its armed forces.[17] Ross made it clear in return that, in view of the economic climate and continuing opposition in Congress, there would be strict limits to what the administration could realistically offer, especially before any actual peace deal had been concluded. In effect, Hussein needed economic aid to justify peace, while Ross argued that aid could only come once peace had been achieved. At the very least, Ross told Jordanian Prime Minister Majali in a subsequent meeting, there would have to be some demonstrable symbol of a Jordanian move forward which the administration could use to win over a sceptical Congress. 'To do more,' Ross admitted candidly, 'we would require much greater drama in Jordan's peacemaking with Israel.'[18]

In the wake of these unsuccessful meetings, negotiations took an ironic turn. To aid his cause, the King enlisted Mossad's Efraim Halevy, who had already flown to the US capital at his request. Halevy also pressed Ross hard on the need for tangible economic and military benefits for Jordan, emphasising that the King needed not debt restructuring but the actual cancellation of the country's's $700 million debt to the US. Halevy also pushed the case for the provision of a squadron of advanced F16 fighter jets for the Jordanian air force, prompting Ross to exclaim, 'tell me, Efraim, who are you representing here? Israel or Jordan?' Halevy's response says much for the closeness of the relationship he had established with the King across the years: 'both,' he replied.[19] 'If the King makes a move toward you on peace we might be able to do more on debt relief,' Ross told Halevy. 'For debt forgiveness, he has to pull a Sadat.'[20] From Hussein's point of view, the Sadat comparison was an unfortunate one. True, the Egyptian president's surprise flight to Jerusalem to address the Knesset in November 1977 had made for great drama. But the resulting Egyptian–Israeli peace deal in 1979 had isolated Egypt in the Arab word for a decade, and cost Sadat his life.

It took the personal intervention of President Clinton to resolve the problem. On 20 June, the King wrote him an impassioned request for help, pleading, 'our situation is serious and it is imperative that the United States makes its historic ties of friendship with Jordan count now, more than ever before'.[21] In a meeting at the end of Hussein's visit, the president, who had taken the time to master the details of the substantial military and economic shopping list presented by the Jordanians, sought to mollify the King. While he could promise nothing more tangible by way of immediate debt relief, he did show that he understood Jordan's needs. Reiterating Ross's argument, he told the King that the best way to get Congress's agreement to debt forgiveness for Jordan would be to give him an argument to use on Jordan's behalf. A public meeting with Rabin, which the president offered to host at their convenience, would give him that argument.

The King was always sensitive to honours and slights. The fact that the president had taken the time to study the Jordanian case in detail, and to empathise with his position, weighed heavily with him.[22] The subtext of Clinton's message was clear, though. To make the political sacrifices necessary to get a substantial package for Jordan through Congress, he needed a corresponding pay-off. Bilateral negotiations conducted by officials in the middle of the desert without any direct American involvement would not do. A high-profile meeting in Washington between Rabin and Hussein, staged under the benevolent sponsorship of the president, would be a different story, and one which was much more likely to make him willing to push Congress to give Jordan's claims a sympathetic hearing.

The first public indication that the King might accept President Clinton's proposal came in a speech he made to the Jordanian parliament on 9 July. Here, he promised that if it would serve Jordan's interests and further the peace process, he would be prepared to meet Rabin publicly.[23] The King still wanted the first meeting to take place on the Israeli–Jordanian border, with perhaps a subsequent meeting in Washington, as he explained in a letter he sent to President Clinton on 12 July.[24] His reason was that he believed it was important to establish a direct channel between himself and Prime Minister Rabin at the outset of the negotiations. Commending the King for his 'courageous decision' to meet publicly with Rabin, President Clinton nevertheless repeated his own view that it was essential to involve key members of Congress in the dramatic moment from the outset: 'I would therefore like to suggest that it would redound to the benefit of Jordan's image in the United States and therefore help me in fulfilling my commitment to you, if you were to have the first, historic meeting with Prime Minister Rabin at the White House.'[25] Rabin and Congress, he argued, could then be immediately enlisted in the process of seeking debt forgiveness for Jordan.

Both Hussein and Rabin were persuaded by the president's argument that Jordan's needs, and the relations of both their countries with the US, would be better served by a meeting in Washington. Rabin wanted to use the opportunity for the public signing of a declaration which would amount in effect to a proto-peace treaty. Negotiations to prepare the document, which became known as the Washington Declaration, got under way in the greatest of secrecy, with Halevy handling the contacts between Rabin and Hussein. Meanwhile Peres, who was not party to these exchanges, attended a meeting with Jordanian Prime Minister Majali on the eastern shore of the Dead Sea on 20 July. This in itself, as the first public visit by an Israeli foreign minister to Jordan, was a historic event.[26] But it was destined to be overshadowed by the greater drama of the meeting between Rabin and Hussein in Washington on 25 July.

The text of the Washington Declaration reflected issues close to the hearts of both men. For Rabin, this meant commitments to strengthen security and begin the process of 'normalisation' between the two countries. These included the setting-up of two border crossing points, the establishment of telephone communications and cooperation between the Israeli and Jordanian police forces. For Hussein, it meant that the Washington Declaration had to acknowledge the Jordanian role in the custodianship of the Islamic holy places in Jerusalem. This provision was the subject of detailed negotiation, with the Israelis trying to square a clause giving priority to the Jordanian role in Jerusalem with commitments already given to the Palestinians.[27] In the event, the following compromise wording was agreed on:

> Israel respects the present special role of the Hashemite Kingdom of Jordan in [the] Muslim Holy shrines in Jerusalem. When negotiations on the permanent status will take place, Israel will give high priority to the Jordanian historic role in these shrines. In addition the two sides have agreed to act together to promote interfaith relations among the three monotheistic religions.[28]

Although Clinton officials had not been party to the negotiating process, they were gratified to see that the final document included fulsome praise for the president's role in bringing the parties together.[29] 'The personal involvement of the President has made it possible to realise agreement on the content of this historic declaration,' it proclaimed. 'The signing of this declaration bears testimony to the President's vision and devotion to the cause of peace.' This language reflected the Washington Declaration's secondary purpose, of securing American economic support for Jordan.

In terms of the drama required to impress the intended American audience, the 25 July signing ceremony lived up to expectations. It was King Hussein who stole the show, as he would do once again at the signing ceremony for the peace treaty in the Arava Desert in October and, in less happy times, at the funeral of Yitzhak Rabin in Jerusalem the following year. Probably the most striking thing about Hussein's oratory on all of these occasions was the way he spoke slowly, with pregnant pauses before key phrases, but never once stumbling in his choice of words in English. It was as though he was articulating thoughts he had rehearsed in his own mind over and over again, eventually arriving at the perfectly weighted phrase to capture the occasion. 'For many, many years and with every prayer, I have asked God, the Almighty, to help me be a part of forging peace between the children of Abraham,' he proclaimed. 'This was the dream of generations before me, and now I see it realised.' Bringing together the 'children of Abraham' was a key theme of Hussein's rhetoric about the making of peace with Israel. It captured for him not only the quasi-religious nature of the process but also the essential historical transience of the Arab–Israeli conflict. We all have common roots and common beliefs, he seemed to be saying, and we lived side by side for countless generations before circumstances came between us.

The day after they had spoken at the White House ceremony, Hussein and Rabin addressed a joint session of Congress.[30] Clinton officials also approached the congressional leadership, pressing the need for Hussein's bold gesture to be rewarded with a generous aid package for Jordan. For once, the formidable lobbying power of the Israeli embassy in Washington was also deployed on behalf of another state, with Israeli officials using their own contacts in Congress to press Jordan's case. Despite the backing of the administration and the Israeli government, though, the write-off of Jordan's debt to the US was to prove a tough slog in Congress. Indeed, the matter was still not settled by the following April, when the King was forced to devote considerable effort during a further visit to the US to the task of persuading Congress to agree to both debt forgiveness and a new economic and military aid package for Jordan.[31] The difficulties and delay surrounding the US package for Jordan constituted one element in what was later to become the 'bitter aftertaste of peace' for Hussein.

Events had moved with such rapidity during June and July 1994 that there had been very little time for the Jordanian people to adjust to the new situation. A small demonstration led by Islamist students took place in Amman on the day of the Hussein–Rabin meeting, while parliamentary deputies from the Islamic Action Front argued that the Washington Declaration did not represent the will of the people. But overall, the opposition was surprisingly limited. Similarly, although the Syrian press criticised Jordan for its supposed abandonment of Arab coordination, President Asad himself refrained from any direct public criticism of Hussein. Probably the most hostile public response came from the PLO, which bitterly resented the references in the Washington Declaration to the special Jordanian role in Jerusalem. From the PLO's perspective, this constituted a violation of the Israeli–Palestinian Declaration of Principles, which, it was argued, had promised that there would be exclusive Israeli–PLO negotiations over the final status of Jerusalem. The Israeli government was no doubt aware that competition between the PLO and Jordan over this issue could only help its own negotiating position.

Hussein followed up on the Washington Declaration with another act of great symbolic importance. On 3 August, the King, piloting the royal jet, made the first peaceful over-flight of Israel by a Jordanian pilot, striking up as he did so a conversation by radio with Yitzhak Rabin, who was observing the flight from the ground. Five days later, as promised in the Washington Declaration, the first border crossing point between Israel and Jordan was opened, at Aqaba and Eilat. After the ceremony, the King entertained Rabin and his entourage to lunch at the royal palace in Aqaba. In a letter sent to

Hussein at the time, President Clinton paid tribute to these peace moves, which he described as 'further testimony to your courageous leadership and bold vision of a new future for Jordan and the region. As you move toward a final peace treaty, I want to reaffirm that the United States will stand by Jordan.'[32]

In the wake of these symbolic public demonstrations of a new era, the focus shifted back to the detailed negotiations needed for a full peace treaty. In theory, the outstanding issues on the Common Agenda were to be resolved by negotiations between the broader Israeli and Jordanian teams led by Elyakim Rubinstein and Fayez Tarawneh. In practice, on the Jordanian side, the responsibility fell to an inner, core group of negotiators comprising Awn Khasawneh, General Tahseen Shurdum, Munther Haddadin, Professor James Crawford and Professor Bernard Graefrath.[33] While the detailed negotiations unfolded at a variety of locations in the region, including on the shores of the Dead Sea, Lake Tiberias and at Aqaba during August, September and October, a series of high-level summits involving the King and Prime Minister Rabin accelerated the process as it neared its conclusion.

The first such summit involving Rabin and Hussein was convened during the final week of September in Aqaba. At the outset the Israeli delegation tried to seize the higher ground by presenting its own draft peace treaty. Had the Israelis succeeded in making their draft text the basic working document, they would have undoubtedly gained a significant advantage in the shaping of the final treaty. The King and Crown Prince Hassan were concerned that any attempt to rewrite the Israeli text might scupper the negotiations, but Professor James Crawford was frank in his advice. 'Your Majesty,' Crawford explained, 'we cannot, in good conscience, advise you to accept this text advanced by the Israelis because this is tantamount to capitulation, and we should not forget that they need a treaty partner.'[34] Awn Khasawneh, aided by the two outside consultants, turned the text around and produced a draft Jordanian counter-text, effectively overnight.

The Israeli delegation was not pleased when the Jordanians faxed their own counter-text to them the next day, and they symbolically delayed their arrival at the negotiations the following morning. It soon became clear that one issue which caused the Israelis particular discomfort was the Jordanian insistence on including a clause relating to the right of return for Palestinian refugees. The Israelis argued that this issue was not relevant to the negotiations with Jordan, and should be dropped altogether from the treaty. Awn Khasawneh's counter-argument was that the issue had been included in the Common Agenda, that it affected the rights of certain Jordanian citizens, and that the Israelis had already agreed that it should be addressed in final-status talks with the Palestinians. Since these were the final-status talks for Jordan, now was the time to address any bilateral issues raised by the refugee problem.[35]

On this principle at least, Khasawneh's case ultimately prevailed, and provisions relating to the resolution of the problems of 'refugees and displaced persons' in 'appropriate forums, in accordance with international law' were included under Article 8 of the final peace treaty.[36]

Although progress was made on a number of other important issues, including water allocation, many problems, including the crucial border question and the issue of the arbitration of disputes, still remained to be agreed by the end of the summit. Even a meeting over dinner between Rabin and Hussein on 29 September could not resolve these outstanding difficulties, though the personal bond between the two leaders was once again very much in evidence.[37] The summit then adjourned, with Prince Hassan, together with a number of members of the Jordanian delegation, flying out to New York where the prince was due to give Jordan's address to the annual General Assembly of the United Nations.

After the delegation returned to Jordan, further detailed negotiations commenced between officials at Aqaba and Eilat. These were interrupted by a high-level summit, convened at Hussein's al-Hashimiyah Palace on 12 October. During this meeting, Rabin emphasised to the King that he 'did not have any designs to take an inch of your territory, nor to take a drop of your water'. The point he wanted to make was simple. He agreed with the King on the big principles, it was now simply a matter of pinning down the final details. This set the tone for the meeting which was once again positive, with further progress made on the outstanding details of the border and water questions.[38] In a radio interview after the meeting, Rabin spoke optimistically about its outcome, arguing, 'I believe that a major step towards peace has been made and that peace is definitely within the boundaries of 1994.'[39]

Thereafter, detailed negotiations continued for several days at Aqaba during which the final terms of the treaty were hammered out. A further Hussein–Rabin summit then convened in Amman on 16–17 October, at the end of which the treaty was initialled. In terms of its final water allocation, Jordan secured a good deal. Overall, the treaty promised to increase Jordan's water supply by more than 25 per cent of its existing total water budget. The bulk of the extra water was expected to come from Israel's agreement to allow Jordan to tap an extra 165 million cubic metres (MCM) of water per annum from the Yarmuk and Jordan Rivers. Israel also agreed, within a year of the signature of the treaty, to help Jordan find a further 50 MCM per annum from as yet unidentified joint sources. In exchange, Jordan agreed to allow Israel to continue to draw water from wells which it had dug in the al-Ghamr area on the Jordanian side of the border in the Wadi Araba. The agreement also permitted Israel to draw up to an extra 10 MCM per annum from this source within the next five years.[40]

While the water provisions at al-Ghamr were part of an acceptable overall trade-off, the terms agreed for the status of the farmland worked by Israeli citizens here, and in another small area abutting the border at Baqoura in the north of the country, proved more controversial. The Israelis claimed that the land at Baqoura had been in the continuous possession of its current owners since 1921. The Jordanians subsequently discovered, through the despatch of non-Jordanian researchers to the Israeli Land Registry in Jerusalem, that this claim was not entirely true: the land had indeed been in the continuous possession of Jewish owners since 1921, but not the present owners.[41] At the outset of the negotiations the Jordanians suggested a clause allowing the Israeli farmers to work the land for a period of no more than ten years after the signature of the treaty, after which the agreement would expire unless both sides accepted its further extension. In the final annex to Article 3 of the peace treaty, though, the Israelis succeeded in securing an alteration of the clause so that it read: 'Without prejudice to private rights of ownership of land within the area, this Annex will remain in force for 25 years, and shall be renewed automatically for the same periods, unless one year prior notice of termination is given by either Party, in which case, at the request of either Party, consultations shall be entered into.'[42] Thus, not only had the period been extended, but the agreement would roll over automatically unless both sides agreed in advance to terminate it. Although Jordan had successfully asserted its territorial sovereignty, in practice the terms of the annex made it unlikely that these admittedly small pieces of land would revert in future to full Jordanian possession.

Similar compromises took place during the final negotiations in relation to the 'arbitration' and 'involuntary movement of persons' clauses. The Israelis had opposed all along a clause requiring disputes to be settled by arbitration, mainly because in 1988 they had lost the Taba area to Egypt as a result of arbitration. Shimon Peres had tried repeatedly to mollify the King on this question, arguing that such a clause was not necessary in an agreement concluded between friends. The Jordanians pointed out in return that the Israelis had included arbitration clauses in agreements they had concluded with the United States, which somewhat undercut their position. Here again, though, in the final treaty, the language used in Article 29 on the 'Settlement of Disputes' was not as specific as the Jordanians would have liked. It stated that disputes would be resolved through negotiations or submitted to arbitration, but no binding arbitration procedure was established.[43] This was one point in the text of the treaty where the 'Camp David' baseline was reached; the wording of the arbitration clause in the Jordanian–Israeli Treaty was identical to that in the earlier Egyptian–Israeli Peace Treaty.[44] This clause in turn had implications for the future status of Baqoura and al-Ghamr, since, should any disagreement arise about the renewal of the annex, it would be the arbitration procedure under Article 29 which would be invoked to resolve it.

Finally came the question of the 'involuntary movement of persons'. It will be recollected that at the heart of the Jordanian negotiating strategy lay the belief that in the long run demographic change would be a major source of tension in the region. The King had made plain his own fears in this respect in his letter to James Baker in March 1992, in which he spoke of Israeli activities in the occupied territories as posing 'further and real demographic threats to Jordan itself'.[45] To help forestall any possibility that a future Israeli government might force the Palestinian population of the West Bank to cross the River Jordan, the Jordanians wanted a clearly worded, separate article included in the treaty, stating that both parties *must not* engage in the forced movement of persons between their two states. What they got instead was a weaker statement, buried under 'General Principles' in Article 2(6), to the effect that both parties 'further believe that within their control, involuntary movements of persons in such a way as to adversely prejudice the security of either Party should not be permitted'.[46] In the language of international law, 'believe' and 'should' are relatively weak terms. Evidently the Israeli negotiators also had an eye on the issues which would matter in the longer run.

The King had made the concessions on Baqoura and al-Ghamr, arbitration, and the involuntary movement of persons himself, as part of his final, personal negotiations with Rabin on 16–17 October. Trade-offs are an essential part of making any agreement, particularly a peace treaty between former enemies, and it is possible that the King did not fully grasp the implications of what, to a lay person, may have seemed like minor shifts of emphasis in the clauses concerned. But, in the post-Rabin era, he would later rue in private some of the concessions he had given, particularly on the 'transfer' clause.[47]

Still, to dwell on these setbacks would be to neglect the gains the Jordanians achieved in other areas. The overall delineation of the border was very satisfactory from the Jordanian point of view, while the references to WMD in the Common Agenda were also carried over into the final peace treaty. Article 4 committed both sides not to use either conventional or non-conventional weapons against each other, and to work as a matter of priority for the creation of a Middle East free from weapons of mass destruction.[48] In terms of Jordan's obligations under the Arab League Charter and Arab Defence Pact, despite Israeli attempts to introduce wording which would have superseded them, the final wording of Article 25 on 'Rights and Obligations' was satisfactory from the Jordanian point of view.[49]

It seems appropriate at this juncture to ask how well the King, as the man with the ultimate responsibility, had managed the peacemaking process from Jordan's perspective. He was under considerable pressure, particularly from the Americans, to reach an agreement quickly, and he was also concerned that the Israel–Jordan negotiations might be overtaken by an agreement between Israel and either the Palestinians or the Syrians, leaving Jordan in a much weaker position to secure its own national interests. All of this contributed to a sense of haste in the negotiations. It is possible that if more time had been taken, and the King had felt able to dig his heels in more deeply, he might have gained slightly better terms. It is equally possible that too much obstinacy might have led Rabin to turn away once again from the Jordanian track, and renew his focus on the negotiations with Syria. We will never know.

Perhaps a more significant criticism of the King's approach concerns its personalised nature. The King set great store by his relationship with Yitzhak Rabin, which for him was the foundation of the whole peace-making process. Here were two soldiers who had decided to lay down their arms, turn away from the battlefield, and make peace together. The King's approach may have been right to the extent that the bilateral peace process could only be advanced through Rabin's personal engagement. Moreover, Rabin was the one Israeli leader who had decided that it was time to make a historic compromise to secure peace. But, with the unfortunate benefit of hindsight, we know that Rabin was destined not to remain on the scene long enough to conclude the kind of comprehensive peace in the region which Hussein sought. For this reason, Hussein's emphasis on his personal bond with the Israeli prime minister proved ultimately to be a misjudgement.

Such fears were far from the King's mind in the heady days of October 1994. During a news conference on 17 October marking the initialling ceremony for the treaty in Amman, he responded to Rabin's comment that 'no one lost, no one won' in reaching the peace agreement, by interjecting with a laugh 'everyone won'.[50] Once again he returned to his theme of the 'children of Abraham' coming together, and waxed eloquent in proclaiming the beginning of a new era of peace:

At this point we are full of hope and confidence that the future will be a future of peace, that this step will be a very important one in what we are all committed to: a comprehensive peace in this region. But between us, hopefully, it is a fresh beginning and a fresh start. We will guard it, and I hope that generations beyond us will guard it, enjoy it and cherish it.[51]

When asked about the controversial provisions of Article 9 of the peace treaty, which related to Jordan's role as custodian of the holy sites in Jerusalem, Hussein replied: 'I hope that Jerusalem, the holy place, will come to symbolise the true peace finally and at long last between the children of Abraham.'[52] The PLO made plain its view when its permanent representative to the Arab League, Muhammad Subayh, submitted an official memorandum on 20 October, claiming that Article 9 fragmented the Arab stance on the issue of Jerusalem.[53] In a speech to parliament on 22 October, the King repeated, 'Jerusalem's holy places remain a trust with the Hashemites, who are resolute on its patronage, construction and on the supervision of its holy sites.' Referring to the criticisms made of the Jordanian role by some Palestinian Authority officials, the King replied that 'under no circumstances or conditions will we relinquish our religious responsibilities towards holy sites'.[54]

After the initialling of the treaty, preparations were made for a formal signing ceremony in the Arava Desert on 26 October in the presence of President Clinton and a host of other international dignitaries. Here, both Hussein and Rabin radiated joy. For Hussein it was 'a day like no other':

This is peace with dignity. This is peace with commitment. This is our gift to our peoples and the generations to come. It will herald the change in the quality of life of people. It will not be simply a piece of paper ratified by those responsible, blessed by the world. It will be real as we open our hearts and minds to each other, for all of us have suffered for far too long.[55]

For his part, Rabin paid tribute to the strength of their personal bond, and to Hussein's own role in forging peace:

Your Majesty: peace between states is peace between peoples. It is an expression of trust and esteem. I have learned to know and admire the quiet and the smiling power with which you guard your nation and the courage with which you lead your people. It is not only our states that are making peace with each other today. Not only our nations that are shaking hands in peace here in the Arava. You and I, Your Majesty, are making peace here, our own peace, the peace of soldiers and the peace of friends . . .[56]

They were fine words indeed, made all the more poignant in hindsight by the knowledge of what was to come: Rabin's assassination, Hussein's progressive disillusionment and early death, and a peace which, although intact more than a decade later, has not become the peace between peoples of which both men spoke.

Even as the peace treaty was being signed, a spontaneous demonstration of about 5,000 protesters took to the streets of Amman, while black flags were hung from the offices of some professional associations, which were later to be at the forefront of the anti-normalisation campaign in Jordan. For these

Jordanians, the peace treaty was a symbol of defeat, not victory. As they saw it, Israel remained the product of Zionist colonialism, a state which had been established on the wreck of Arab Palestine, and which continued to deny the Palestinians their legitimate human rights. For his part, the King had earlier shown some understanding of the difficulties involved for the Jordanian people in accepting the treaty. In a speech to army officers he acknowledged:

> it is difficult for people to move from one situation to another and from one atmosphere to another within moments. But we hope God will enable us to pass this test too and reach our goals. There are only a few people who have been attacking and have gone too far. This is part of our democratic life, and we respect people's rights in expressing their ideas.[57]

The King warned that what he saw as this minority should respect the views of the majority. His impatience with the opposition to the peace treaty soon increased, and was apparent in a speech he made to members of the Jordanian parliament on 30 October. Commenting on the Jordanian press reaction, he noted bitterly, 'our press, media, our columnists – the overwhelming majority of them – do not support this country and never have done. This situation should not continue as it is.' On opposition to the treaty in general, he argued that 'freedom of speech is not there so that the one enjoying it can insult others or attack them and say things against the good conduct that religion preaches. Intellectual terrorism does not come from the government or from the state.'[58] The tension between the normalisation of relations with Israel and the democratisation of Jordan was all too apparent from these comments.

Just before the formal signature of the peace treaty, the King had also made one other announcement which would have significant implications for the future of his dynasty. In a speech to senior army and intelligence officers, he announced the formal establishment of a Family Council to consider the future line of succession in the House of Hashem.[59] The ostensible purpose of the council was to choose the best and fittest person to succeed after Crown Prince Hassan. But the establishment of the council also had implications for Hussein's relations with his brother: it reflected his inability to resolve the succession question to his own satisfaction through private family discussion.

Whatever the clouds on the horizon in the shape of domestic opposition to the peace treaty, and differences within the family over the succession, this was a time of great hope for Hussein, probably the only chink of light in what was otherwise a dark decade for him. Indeed, he spoke figuratively of darkness and light when characterising the opposition to the treaty as 'a small minority, which is against peace and life; which only wants to cry, weep and see black things in life; and which always keeps a grim face'.[60] Sadly for him, though, the chink of light was soon to disappear, to be replaced by darkness. It was an assassin's bullet which would bring him back to Jerusalem for the first time since 1967, to mourn the passing of his partner in peace-making, Yitzhak Rabin.

CHAPTER 17

THE BITTER AFTERTASTE
OF PEACE

It was a eulogy like no other. 'I never thought that the moment would come like this,' Hussein began, 'when I would grieve the loss of a brother, a colleague and a friend, a man, a soldier who met us on the opposite side of a divide, who we respected as he respected us. A man I came to know because I realized, as he did, that we had to cross over the divide.' Speaking from the heart, almost as though he still felt the physical presence of the murdered Yitzhak Rabin by his side, the King held the mourners at Rabin's funeral in Jerusalem in rapt attention:

> I have never been used to standing, except with you next to me, speaking of peace, speaking about dreams and hopes for generations to come . . . You lived as a soldier, you died as a soldier for peace. And I believe it is time for all of us to come out openly and speak of peace. Not here today, but for all times to come. We belong to the camp of peace . . . Let's not keep silent. Let our voices rise high to speak of our commitment to peace for all times to come, and let us tell those who live in darkness, who are the enemies of light, 'This is where we stand. This is our camp.'

Hussein's words came from the bottom of his heart. On 4 November, the evening of Rabin's assassination, he had been almost unable to digest the news, calling the Israeli ambassador in Amman every few minutes for updates on Rabin's struggle for life.[1] The Israeli prime minister had been gunned down while leaving a peace rally by a right-wing zealot, Yigal Amir, who believed he was a traitor intent on trading away part of the biblical 'land of Israel'. Rabin subsequently died of blood loss on the operating table.

The very next day, trying to sum up his feelings, Hussein penned a letter of condolence to Israeli President Ezer Weizman on behalf of the people of Jordan:

> The sense of outrage, horror and sadness that all peace-loving Jordanians share with me on learning of the brutal assassination of Prime Minister Yitzhak Rabin is beyond words. I personally have lost a true friend in this region and our world has lost a true champion of peace . . . Yitzhak Rabin will forever be remembered and respected as a symbol of decency, integrity and courage. He was a soldier who fell a martyr, a true soldier of peace and since life is but a journey, his legacy will ever be a most worthy and honourable one.[2]

For Hussein it was particularly poignant to return to Jerusalem for Rabin's funeral: Jerusalem where nearly half a century earlier he had stood at his grandfather's side as he too fell to an assassin's bullet; Jerusalem which, for Hussein as a Hashemite, was a symbol of his family's destiny and dignity. It was as though his life and reign had come full circle. In July 1951 his grandfather had been a victim of his search for peace and reconciliation. Now Rabin, the King's partner in peace-making, had suffered the same fate. Hussein could be forgiven for thinking that destiny was at work, that he was engaged in a sort of dance to the music of time where the characters and scenes might shift, but always come back to the same place. 'When my time comes,' he told the mourners, 'I hope it will be like my grandfather's, and like Yitzhak Rabin's.'

Even as he mourned Rabin, the King's thoughts were already turning to the future. In a document entitled 'In Memory of Yitzhak Rabin' in his private papers, Hussein argued, 'There is still a great chance for peace. Our achievements thus far must not be allowed to wither. Existing agreements must be given the opportunity to prove not only that peaceful coexistence can prevail, but normality, humanity and cooperation become the mark of the day.'[3] During the year between the signature of the peace treaty and Rabin's assassination much progress had indeed been made in cementing ties between Jordan and Israel, and building the foundation for a multilateral peace process. In terms of economic aid to Jordan, for instance, Rabin had lent his own substantial weight to the King's efforts in overcoming barriers in the US Congress. Writing to Hussein on 10 May 1995 in the wake of a visit to Washington, Rabin told the King, 'I shared with my hosts on Capitol Hill our unique experience – two adversaries who turned away from the battlefield to make peace . . . I had the opportunity directly to address Jewish Senators and Representatives in a private meeting, where I asserted that Jordan's bold and fearless leap towards peace ought to be met with similar bold American commitment. I urged them to be helpful in the settlement of the debt issue and I am happy to relate to you that my statement was received favourably.'[4] There could be no clearer indication of the new climate than the fact that the Israeli prime minister was lobbying for Jordan's interests in Washington.

It was not only in bilateral relations that the new spirit of cooperation was evident. The multilateral peace process which had been set in train in the wake of the Madrid peace conference started to bear fruit in terms of enhanced and expanding economic relations in the region during 1994 and 1995. At the Middle East and North African Conference (MENA) on regional economic cooperation and development held in Casablanca at the end of October 1994, Jordan's Ministry of Planning put forward a number of propo-sals, including the construction of a canal from the Red Sea to the Dead Sea, which, although they had been mooted for some time, were only conceivable in the new era of open relations with Israel. This economic programme was pressed forward at the next annual summit, this time held in Amman itself between 29 and 31 October 1995, where Jordan gave particular priority to the Jordan Rift Valley Joint Master Plan.[5] Hussein himself saw the gathering as a landmark. As far as he was concerned, it showed Israel and Jordan standing side by side, inviting the world to come and share in the dividends of peace.[6] The summit was also the very last occasion at which he would meet Yitzhak Rabin, a matter of days before the latter's assassination.

During this period there was also some progress on what Hussein professed to see as the most important level of peace-making: that of people to people. But it should be stressed that at the popular level there was more enthusiasm for these contacts on the Israeli than on the Jordanian side. Hussein's files contain much correspondence sent during this period both by ordinary Israelis and by former officials and politicians. A few examples stand out. One is the moving letter from the surviving relatives of two Israeli soldiers who had lost their lives in the battle of Karameh in March 1968. During the almost twenty-eight years which had passed since the battle, their surviving relatives had been unable to find out much information about their death and internment beyond the fact that their Centurion tank had remained in Jordan after the battle. But now, in the new era of peace and cooperation, the men's relatives sought the King's help in 'healing the wounds of conflict'.[7]

Then there is the letter from Abba Eban, the former Israeli foreign minister, whom Hussein had met secretly in search of peace after the 1967 war. In mid-March 1995, Hussein entertained Eban and his wife at home in Jordan. It was, by Eban's own account, a meeting 'charged with emotion'.[8] 'We were able to recall', Eban continued, 'the totally different circumstances in which we met in 1968 and on several occasions thereafter.' One can understand the emotional significance of the occasion for Eban. No doubt in 1968 as much as in 1995, he knew that in Hussein he was dealing with a man who wanted peace. But, back in 1968, Eban's hands had been tied by Israeli domestic politics, and no settlement could be reached. After their meeting, 'I felt entitled', Eban wrote, 'to tell Prime Minister Rabin about the high importance that you attach to the Jordan Israel peace treaty. It is true that we also spoke of the difficulties which this relationship faces. But it is a consolation to know that when there is a common interest you, Your Majesty, and our leaders face them in close harmony.'

Eban's letter highlights the fact that although the dominant refrain during this period was of progress, there were still some discordant notes in relations between Jordan and Israel. One such issue concerned what Hussein termed the Israeli government's confiscation of additional Arab land in Jerusalem. Writing to Rabin on 21 May, the King noted that he had followed developments over 'this explosive issue with a concerned and heavy heart . . . I am, my friend deeply concerned, for pre-1967 East Jerusalem has a very special place in my heart and conscience as it does [for] all Jordanians.'[9] Referring to the tense state of relations between Israel and the Palestinians in the wake of a succession of terrorist attacks, Hussein commented, 'I am . . . completely at a loss to understand why now should the Government of Israel contribute to its further serious deterioration by unilateral action in Jerusalem [sic] and the confiscation of even an inch of Arab land. With all due respect my friend, this should not stand.' Appealing to their shared sense of mission as peacemakers, Hussein concluded, 'I have written frankly and candidly my friend, because you have grown to expect I believe, no less from a fellow builder of peace dedicated to it and deeply concerned and committed to realising it for all our future generations.' Rabin subsequently elected to freeze the land confiscation, but his decision probably owed more to domestic politics, in the shape of a no-confidence motion tabled against his government by an unholy alliance of the Arab parties and the Likud in the Knesset, than it did to Hussein's entreaties.[10]

Whatever their differences over important issues such as Jerusalem, though, one thing was clear from the tone of Hussein's letter: he believed that Rabin had accepted the need for peace in his own heart. Thus, although they might differ about specific problems, he always felt with Rabin that he could appeal to their common goal, their shared mission as peacemakers. As we will see, the tone of Hussein's exchanges with Rabin's successors in office, first Shimon Peres and then Binyamin Netanyahu, was different.

While the King credited Peres with a desire for peace, there had been too many missteps in their personal relationship for him to share the same bond of trust as he had with Rabin. The fact that Peres had been largely excluded from the Jordanian–Israeli peace process did not make for an auspicious beginning. During Peres's brief tenure as prime minister between November 1995 and May 1996, the King's relationship with him cooled still further.

Concerned by the internal security situation which he had inherited from Rabin, in early January 1996 Peres authorised what he perhaps hoped would be the morale-boosting assassination of Yahya Ayyash, the so-called 'Engineer', a man believed to be behind a wave of Hamas suicide bombings in Israel during 1994–5. The Israeli security services reached their target, with Ayyash being killed in Gaza on 5 January 1996 by a bomb concealed in a mobile phone, but Hamas vowed revenge. The result was a further wave of bombings in Israel.

Hussein, who had always been a sincere and trenchant critic of terrorism in all its forms, immediately wrote to Israeli President Weizman, expressing his horror at the news of the Hamas bomb attacks in Jerusalem and Eshkelon. Besides expressing his condolences, and his deeply held conviction that all acts of terror should be unreservedly condemned, Hussein also commented pointedly that the eradication of terrorism called for 'continuing our efforts to build a comprehensive peace and understanding in our region'.[11] In a letter to President Clinton on 4 March, the King promised, 'I shall spare no effort in convincing President Arafat of the need to revoke those parts of the Palestinian Covenant, the maintenance of which would be incompatible with the state of peace and in breach of the rules of good faith in implementing a binding obligation that Mr Arafat had undertaken . . . I shall also do all that is possible to impress upon Mr Arafat the need to dismantle the network of terror responsible for these outrages.'[12] Hussein's relationship with Arafat had always been a difficult one, and the peace process had by and large only served to increase these tensions, with the PLO suspicious of what it saw as continuing Jordanian designs on Jerusalem. During this difficult phase, as the peace process began to unravel, Hussein's exasperation focused not just on Israeli actions but also on Arafat's inaction when it came to thwarting terrorism. The King already feared that, with the Syrian and Palestinian negotiations also apparently stalled, the chance for comprehensive peace in the region was beginning to slip away.

Probably the biggest single factor to damage the relationship between Hussein and Peres was the disastrous military intervention Peres launched in Lebanon under the codename Operation 'Grapes of Wrath', in April 1996.[13] Like the Israeli interventions in Lebanon in 1993 and 2006, this operation was intended to bring security to northern Israel by stopping Hezbollah guerrillas launching Katyusha rockets from southern Lebanon into Israel. Also like these other operations, it was a singular failure, sullying Israel's international image and boosting Hezbollah's regional standing and morale rather than eliminating the group's military capability. Not only did the firing of Katyusha rockets continue, despite the massive deployment of Israeli fire-power, but, on 18 April, a week after the beginning of the operation, Israeli shells killed in error more than one hundred civilian refugees who had been sheltering from the fighting at the United Nations base at Qana in south Lebanon. A little over two weeks after it had begun, Operation Grapes of Wrath drew to an ignominious conclusion, with the United States helping to broker a ceasefire on 26 April.

Writing to Hussein on 30 April, Peres attempted both to justify the operation and to claim that it had successfully achieved its goals. Emphasising that he had authorised the operation reluctantly, and then only after two months of diplomatic effort had failed to stabilise the situation, Peres argued that the Israel Defense Forces had done all they could to avoid civilian casualties. He blamed the Qana massacre on Hezbollah, who had fired on northern Israel from positions 'only hundreds of meters from the compound where refugees were seeking shelter, with the full knowledge that this would endanger all those who were in the area'.[14] Peres promised the King that he would now redouble his efforts to further the peace process and, referring to the Israeli–Jordanian bond as a 'special relationship', he expressed the hope that 'we will now be able to move beyond recent events and return to the implementation of all the projects of our peace agreement'.

For his part, the King was relatively restrained in his reply:

> While we understand that no government can remain idle in the face of violence against its citizens, we feel, at the same time, that [the] response to such violence should not be manifestly disproportionate to the original violence. We also feel that the civilian population should be spared – to the greatest extent possible – the effects of retaliation.
>
> In our joint quest to establish peace in our region, we are likely to be met with situations which test not only our mutual commitment to the moral inheritance we share, but also our wisdom in the face of serious provocations. I must share with you our sense of concern at the news of civilian casualties and wide scale civilian displacement in Lebanon.[15]

The King's allusions to a 'manifestly disproportionate' response, and to the need for 'wisdom' in the face of provocation, made clear his disapproval of Peres's actions.

Although he took no obvious public action, privately Hussein now did what he could to signal that he would welcome a victory for Binyamin Netanyahu, the leader of the opposition party Likud, in the Israeli general election.[16] Born in Tel Aviv in 1949, Netanyahu had spent much of his adolescence in the United States, acquiring in the process a sophisticated grasp of American culture. After military service in Israel between 1967 and 1972, Netanyahu returned to the US to further his studies. A landmark in Netanyahu's life was the death of his brother, Yoni, during his command of the rescue operation to release the hostages held by Palestinian terrorists at

Entebbe in 1976. Thereafter, Netanyahu held a number of diplomatic posts in the US during the 1980s, including that of Israel's ambassador to the UN. Articulate and intelligent, Netanyahu quickly emerged as a political figure on the rise. At the end of the 1980s he entered the Knesset as a Likud representative and in 1993 he became chairman of the party and its candidate for prime minister. While no one could question his political talents, there remained doubts about his moral bearings, including his commitment to the peace process.

During 1994 and 1995, both the King and Prince Hassan had put considerable effort into building relations with Netanyahu as the leader of the main Israeli opposition party. The reasoning behind this approach was straightforward and logical: Hussein wanted to build a peace that was accepted across the whole spectrum of Israeli politics, and which would not be prey to changes in government. Thus, in December 1994, Netanyahu was invited to Jordan where he met both the King and Prince Hassan. For his part, Netanyahu made it clear that, unlike the Oslo process with the Palestinians, the peace treaty with Jordan had widespread support in Israel. Both the King and Prince Hassan evidently formed a positive opinion of Netanyahu as a political leader with whom they could work. Others who met him during the December visit were less convinced. The King's cousin, Zeid bin Shaker, who replaced Abdul Salam Majali as Prime Minister in January 1995, recollected being particularly struck by Netanyahu's body language during his visit to Jordan. According to Zeid bin Shaker, Prince Hassan had telephoned him and asked him to come over and meet Netanyahu at his home. Within fifteen minutes of meeting him, Zeid bin Shaker had developed a dislike of Netanyahu, describing how he had sat with legs spread in his chair, as though he were sitting on a throne.[17] True, his opinion may well have been influenced by his own scepticism about the peace process with Israel, but Zeid bin Shaker's doubts about Netanyahu were soon to be shared by other influential Jordanians.

When Netanyahu scraped to a narrow win in the 29 May poll, the King was considerably more positive than any other Arab leader in his public response, emphasising that he believed the peace process would continue irrespective of the change of government in Israel. Netanyahu should be judged, he argued, on his actions as prime minister rather than on preconceived notions as to his intentions. In a tripartite summit held at Aqaba on 3 June, the King succeeded in persuading Egyptian President Hosni Mubarak and Yasser Arafat, now leader of the Palestinian Authority, to adopt a similarly pragmatic stance towards the new Israeli government. Although the summit statement called on Israel to implement agreements already reached with the Palestinians, Mubarak echoed Hussein's own thinking when he stated that it was too early to make a judgement as to the direction likely to be adopted by a Netanyahu-led government.[18]

Hussein was not alone in expecting a measure of continuity in the new Israeli leader's handling of the peace process. Many Israeli and Western commentators also assumed that with the election won, despite his earlier trenchant criticisms of the Oslo process, involving the progressive handing over of Palestinian population centres in the occupied territories to the control of Arafat's Palestinian Authority, Netanyahu would settle for its further implementation, albeit at a cautious pace. Despite these soothing prophecies, the foreign policy programme presented by the new government to the Knesset on 18 June signalled a significant departure in course from that charted by the previous Labour-led governments. There was firm opposition to any kind of Palestinian state, to the Palestinian right of return and particularly to the dismantling of Jewish settlements.[19] In fact, with its emphasis on the role of settlement-building in fulfilling the Zionist mission, the new government seemed headed for confrontation with both the Palestinians and the neighbouring Arab states.

Despite Netanyahu's political programme, King Hussein continued to counsel a cautious and pragmatic Arab response. His approach proved largely successful at the Arab League summit convened in Cairo between 22 and 23 June, the final communiqué from which was relatively moderate in tone, warning only in general terms that if Israel reneged on existing agreements, or abandoned the land for peace formula, the Arab states would have to reconsider their own position on the peace process. A Syrian proposal to suspend all relations with Israel was rejected by the summit.

President Clinton did his best to reinforce Hussein's resolve. Reporting on his initial discussions with Netanyahu in Washington in July, Clinton acknowledged that there were clearly differences on many major questions of policy between the new government and its predecessor. But, more encouragingly, he reported, 'the Prime Minister told me he had not been elected to preside over a stalemate in the peace process nor over a reversal in the positive steps that have been achieved with respect to Israeli–Arab relations . . . Netanyahu assured me that he respects Arafat and will not seek to marginalize him.' This was a far cry from Netanyahu's public descriptions of the Palestinian leader. But the crucial test for progress in their relationship from Netanyahu's point of view would be reciprocity. In particular, Netanyahu stressed the need for the Palestinian Authority to avoid any actions which might make Jerusalem a flash-point in the relationship.[20]

There was a deep irony here, for Hussein's own efforts at conciliation were soon to be undercut by just such actions undertaken by the Netanyahu government itself. In the middle of the night of 24–25 September, Netanyahu ordered the opening of a walled gate leading to an archaeological tunnel near the Haram al-Sharif or 'Noble Sanctuary' in Jerusalem. This move had been consistently opposed by the Jordanian-run Religious Affairs Ministry ever since it had been first proposed by the Israeli authorities in 1987. Netanyahu perhaps saw the move as one which would win him domestic political credit with hardline elements in his Likud Party, but the fact that he ordered the action to be taken by a group of Israeli soldiers in the dead of night showed that he knew it would arouse opposition amongst the Palestinian population of the city. Any such act near the Muslim holy shrines was viewed as part of the supposed Israeli desire to destroy the Haram al-Sharif and rebuild the Jewish Temple of biblical times on the site. At the very least, it was seen by Palestinians as part of an Israeli plan to alter the character of the Muslim quarter of the Old City.

For Hussein himself, the Israeli action was a particular cause of concern for two reasons. Firstly, because under the terms of the Jordanian–Israeli peace treaty, Israel had recognised the continuing custodianship of Jordan over the Islamic holy sites, at least until final-status negotiations took place with the Palestinians. Hussein therefore felt that he had the right to be consulted about or at least warned in advance of any Israeli action which might affect the sites. Secondly, Netanyahu had sent his adviser Dore Gold to Amman for talks shortly before the tunnel was opened. Although Gold had made no mention of Netanyahu's plans, the meeting created the impression that the King had been consulted in advance. He thus felt both that he had been deceived and that his relations with the Palestinians had been compromised.[21] Thereafter, Hussein rebuffed all attempts by Netanyahu to re-establish personal contact, relenting only when Efraim Halevy, his former Mossad liaison, who had since moved on to become Israel's ambassador to the European Union, interceded, temporarily repairing the breach in relations.[22] Meanwhile the Palestinians took to the streets in protest. Serious rioting followed in Jerusalem and elsewhere in the occupied territories. Crucially, for the first time since the beginning of the Oslo process Palestinian police in some locations sided with the demonstrators, firing on Israeli soldiers.

The Netanyahu government's isolation over the issue was amply illustrated at the United Nations. The Security Council passed Resolution 1073, calling for the protection of the Palestinians, the resumption of the peace process, and the immediate cessation of 'acts which have resulted in the aggravation of the situation', by fourteen votes to nil, with the US abstaining.[23] The fact that the US abstained, rather than issuing its customary veto in defence of Israel, said much for the deterioration in relations between Israel and its closest ally under Netanyahu. In an attempt to calm the situation, President Clinton invited Arafat and Netanyahu, together with Hussein and Mubarak, to a hastily convened summit meeting in Washington between 30 September and 2 October. In the event, Mubarak declined the invitation, so it fell to Hussein to act as the only leader representing the other Arab states. The discussions proved largely fruitless. Netanyahu refused to back down by closing the tunnel, even though the King tried to put forward a face-saving compromise involving the suspension of its opening until archaeologists could show that it posed no danger to the structural integrity of the Islamic shrines.[24] The only concession the Israeli prime minister offered in two days of talks was his agreement to enter into intensive negotiations to resolve the problem of Israeli redeployment from Hebron, the last major West Bank city which had not been transferred to Palestinian control. Over lunch on the final day of the summit, King Hussein gave vent to his frustration with Netanyahu, and his fears for the peace process. In what the American negotiator Dennis Ross termed 'an eloquent, emotional and personal attack', the King warned Netanyahu of the dangers posed by the arrogance of power, and accused him of threatening the foundations of the peace process, dashing the hopes of Israelis and Arabs alike. According to the King's recollection, Netanayahu did not reply immediately, but, as they were leaving, he said, 'I am determined to surprise you.'[25]

The subsequent negotiations, which eventually resulted in the signature of the Hebron Protocol on 15 January 1997, reflected the new realities in the region. Unlike earlier agreements between the Israelis and Palestinians concluded since the original Oslo deal, the Hebron agreement was brokered not by the two parties negotiating directly with each other, but through the intensive mediation of the United States. The extent of the difficulties involved in the process can be gleaned from the title US mediator Dennis Ross gave to the relevant chapter in his memoirs: 'the endless Hebron shuttle'.[26] Ultimately, a deal was struck which committed the Israeli government to hand 80 per cent of the town over to Palestinian control and also to carry out further redeployments of its security forces on the West Bank, handing additional areas over to Palestinian control, by mid-1998.

As the negotiations drew to their climax in early January, King Hussein played a valuable role in helping to bring them to a successful conclusion. With Arafat under pressure from the Egyptians to toughen his stance over the final Hebron terms, the Palestinian leader turned to Hussein to provide him with alternative Arab cover for reaching a final deal on the timing of the further Israeli redeployments which would follow that in Hebron.[27] The King was happy to oblige. After an extended telephone briefing on the state of the negotiations from Dennis Ross, he flew to Gaza on 10 January to meet Arafat. Here, he secured the PLO leader's agreement to the less precise terminal date of 'mid-1998' for the next phase of Israeli redeployments. This gave Ross the room for manoeuvre he needed to secure Netanyahu's agreement. With a compromise reached, the King travelled on to Tel Aviv for a meeting that night with Netanyahu, Ross and the Palestinian negotiator Saeb Erekat. Although it took another day and a half for the final details of the Hebron deal to be hammered out, the King's intervention came at a crucial moment, and his willingness to provide Arab cover for a crucial concession on the Palestinian leader's part was a further indication of his dedication to the peace process. Not only that, but it illustrated the good relationship between Jordan and the Palestinian Authority at this juncture. The differences over Jerusalem, which had plagued relations during 1994 and 1995, had been largely resolved through a deal struck in November 1996 between the two sides, in the wake of the 'tunnel' crisis. This had provided for the future transfer of the staff formally employed by the Jordanian Religious Affairs Ministry to the Palestinian Authority, in return for Palestinian agreement that the shrines in Jerusalem would remain a Jordanian responsibility pending final-status talks between Israel and the Palestinian Authority.[28]

Only one discordant note had been struck during the King's intervention over Hebron, and this concerned once again his relations with the Israeli prime minister. When placing his request with Netanyahu to fly over Israel in order to reach Gaza, the King had asked to be allowed to use a fixed-wing aircraft to fly into Gaza airport. This flight would in effect have marked the symbolic opening of the airport to international air traffic, something for which the Palestinians had repeatedly pressed. The King's request was declined by Netanyahu, who, despite the delicate state of the Hebron negotiations and the potentially helpful nature of the King's intervention, still refused to allow any concession over the Gaza airport issue. This was a slight which the King would recall later. For the present, though, he chose not to challenge Netanyahu's refusal, noting that he had accepted it 'only because there were far more important issues at hand'.[29]

While the Hebron Protocol was passed by a wide margin in the Knesset on 16 January, Netanyahu had earlier faced a much rougher ride in getting the deal accepted by his own cabinet. After a marathon session on 14 January, the deal was only accepted by a split vote of eleven in favour and seven against.[30] The hardline Minister of Science and Technology, Benny Begin, resigned in protest at the agreement, claiming that it would set a dangerous precedent, and that he could not support the further proposed Israeli redeployments. This set the tone for what was to follow. Stung by the criticisms of the Hebron Protocol from within his own party, Netanyahu tried to shore up his position by taking a tough line on two issues. The first concerned the extent of the first Israeli redeployment under the terms of the Hebron Protocol. The second concerned the building of a new settlement at Jebel Abu Ghnaim, or Har Homa, which would complete the encirclement of Arab East Jerusalem, cutting it off from its hinterland in the West Bank. The extent of the first redeployment was a critical test of the intentions of the Netanyahu government from the Palestinians' perspective. A generous redeployment would be taken as a sign of good faith, a miserly redeployment as a sign that the Israeli government was determined to hold on to as much of the West Bank as possible.

During the latter part of February and early March 1997, the two issues became bound up together. On 26 February, the Israeli government publicly announced its intention to build a settlement at Har Homa, making a token effort to sweeten the bitter pill for the Palestinians by including provision for a small number of housing units intended for Arabs in the overall construction plan. Hussein, who continued to pay the closest attention to any issue affecting the status of Jerusalem, was incensed. Writing to Netanyahu the day before the plan was officially made public, the King warned, 'your forthcoming decision will create new realities on the ground whose impact is incalculable on the psychology of peace'.[31] Reminding Netanyahu of the Jerusalem clause in the Washington Declaration and the peace treaty, the King pressed him not to make precipitous moves which would 'undermine the need for joint consultation'. In apocalyptic terms, the King warned, 'the action is bound to inflame passion, lead to violence as well as jeopardise the whole enterprise of peace making. I really feel that we should not allow the peace process to stumble again, as it did so dangerously over the issue of the redeployment of Israeli forces in Hebron.'

This was not the end of the matter. While the Israeli government pressed ahead with the Har Homa project, it also announced the offer of what, to the Palestinian leadership and Hussein, sounded like a derisory first-phase redeployment of forces on the West Bank under the Hebron agreement. Although the Clinton administration had pressed for at least a further 10 per cent of the area of the West Bank to be handed over to full or partial Palestinian control (area A or B status in the jargon of the peace process), in the event the Netanyahu government's offer fell short of even this modest target. Only 2 per cent of new land would come under partial Palestinian control (area B status), while a further 7 per cent would be transferred from partial Palestinian control to full authority (area A status). Although the headline total was therefore of a 9 per cent redeployment, only 2 per cent would constitute new areas for the Palestinians. It was this figure on which the Palestinian Authority leadership seized, arguing that, together with the Har Homa project, it indicated that the Israeli government was not serious about pursuing the peace process.

Hussein shared their sentiment wholeheartedly. This was a decisive moment where he felt that the chance for comprehensive peace, of which the Jordanian–Israeli peace treaty had only ever been one part, was slipping away. And he was not about to let it happen without a fight. In a remarkable letter, which was made public, he launched a sustained personal assault on the Israeli prime minister:

My distress is genuine and deep over the accumulating tragic actions which you have initiated at the head of the government of Israel, making peace – the worthiest objective of my life – appear more and more like a distant mirage. I could remain aloof if the very lives of all Arabs and Israelis and their future were not fast sliding towards an abyss of bloodshed and disaster, brought about by fear and despair . . . The saddest reality that has been dawning on me is that I do not find you by my side in working to fulfil God's will for the final reconciliation of all the descendants of the children of Abraham.[32]

On the Israeli redeployment, Hussein asked, 'what good did it serve to offer such an insignificant first phase withdrawal?' Was it, he wondered, a deliberate attempt to humiliate the Palestinian leadership? On Har Homa, the King commented bitterly, 'if it is your intention to maneuver our Palestinian brethren into inevitable violent resistance, then order your bulldozers into the proposed settlement site'. Finally, reflecting bitterly on Netanyahu's second refusal to allow him to fly into Gaza airport, he asked:

Now, suppose I had taken off nonetheless for Gaza, in the full right of a friend, then would you have ordered my fellow pilots in the Israeli Air Force – those who escorted me on the same aircraft over Israel in what became known as the 'First Flight of Peace' – 'it seems so long ago' – to prevent me forcibly from landing or worse? You will never know how close you came to having to make a decision on the subject . . .

The suggestion that the King had even considered calling Netanyahu's bluff, and daring him to force down his plane, was a remarkable one. Indeed, the tone of the whole letter is almost without precedent in relations between leaders of what were supposed to be two friendly states in the region.

Netanyahu struck back the very next day. First of all, he challenged the whole notion that he was responsible for a crisis in the peace process. 'I was chosen to lead Israel,' he argued, 'because of the bitter dissatisfaction of the Israeli people with the way the peace process was progressing. I inherited a process that was failing.'[33] Defending the extent of the further redeployment, he argued that his government could not be expected to do more when the Palestinians were not fulfilling their own obligations to round up and hold suspected terrorists. In what read more like an election address than a letter to a fellow leader, Netanyahu argued, 'only my government can deliver the more stable "peace of consensus"'. Finally, responding to the King's personal attack on his leadership, Netanyahu asserted:

I hold you in the highest esteem and I value your friendship and under-standing. That is why I must confess that I am baffled by the personal level of the attacks against me. In all my exchanges with leaders in the

Middle East – whether in private or in public – I do not use this sort
of idiom.

Finally, Netanyahu called for Jordanian–Israeli relations to be insulated from
any problems which might occur with the Palestinian peace process. For
anyone with any understanding of Hussein's own outlook or of the realities
of Jordanian and Arab politics, such a request was fanciful in the extreme.

Jordanian–Israeli relations at the summit seemed to have hit rock bottom
with this exchange, but potentially worse was to come. On 13 March a
Jordanian soldier named Ahmed Dakamseh opened fire on a party of Israeli
schoolgirls on a field trip at Baqoura, killing seven and wounding six of them
before he was overpowered. Hussein was shocked and mortified by the
incident. Although it quickly became clear that the soldier had acted on his
own, and that he was mentally unstable, the King felt the need to show his
own personal contrition, and his sympathy for the families of the victims. The
crisis showed Hussein at his best, and also said much about his humanity and
commitment to peace. In a remarkable gesture for a monarch, he flew back
from Europe to visit all of the bereaved families, kneeling before them to offer
his condolences and apologies on behalf of Jordan. The impact in Israel of the
King's extraordinary gesture was profound. There could have been no clearer
demonstration of his dedication to the cause of peace than this act of humility
and empathy. It showed how far above the petty political fray the King could
rise when the occasion demanded it. His gesture was deeply appreciated by
the pupils of the Rimon School in Raanana, which the murdered schoolgirls
had attended, all of whom signed a letter of thanks to him.[34] The mayor of
Raanana also wrote thanking him for having taken the trouble personally to
answer the letters sent to him by students at the school:

> Your wonderful personality, personal courage and humanity, which you
> showed when you visited the bereaved families, have further
> strengthened the support and sympathy you have from the citizens of
> Israel. We all see you as one of the most important, central figures in the
> Middle East, striving continuously, for many years, for the establishment
> of true peace between our two countries.[35]

The King's actions had turned what could have been a serious crisis in
relations between Israel and Jordan into an episode which further cemented
the Israeli public's belief in the peace treaty.

In addition to his wooing of Israeli public opinion, the King also put
considerable effort into winning over a broad range of Israeli politicians. Even
while his relations with Prime Minister Netanyahu reached their nadir, the
Israeli Minister of Defense Yitzhak Mordechai wrote to him in the most

cordial and friendly terms, thanking him for the excellent reception he had been given during a visit to Jordan on 11 March. Offering his own tribute to the King's response to the tragedy at Baqoura, Mordechai wrote:

> Despite the gravity of the situation, your reaction to the tragic event – in both word and deed – once again manifested your unshakable commitment to peace and stability. I was deeply affected by your words and even more touched by your decision to return to the region and visit the mourning families in Bet Shemesh. Your actions will hopefully lead to allaying tensions that have been rampant in our region, fortifying bridges of trust our countries have worked so hard to establish, and reinvigorating peacemaking efforts.[36]

Mordechai's letter is typical of a whole range of correspondence in the King's files with Israeli politicians, including Israeli Deputy Prime Minister David Levy; Infrastructure and later Foreign Minister Ariel Sharon; and Ehud Barak, at this point the leader of the Labour opposition. Barak's correspondence in particular gives a sense of the depth of the King's relations with senior Israelis, hinting at exchanges during and before Barak's time as head of the Israeli armed forces. After a visit to Jordan in March 1997, for example, Barak wrote, 'it is always a rare and wonderful experience to be able to sit with you well into the night, sharing common memories of the past and our visions for the future. I have no doubt that the potential for a warm and true peace between our two countries can be measured by the warm personal relationship we share.'[37] Writing to Hussein again three months later, Barak noted:

> it is not by chance that I chose Jordan as my destination on my first visit abroad as Chairman of the Israeli Labor Party and Leader of the Opposition. This choice reveals my deep-seated belief that the Jordanian–Israeli relationship forms the foundation of the peace process, and my personal commitment to maintaining our close ties. The personal role of the Hashemite family has proved critical to the continuation of peace, and I feel that your contribution is the corner-stone of the historical process of peace-making and reconciliation.[38]

Despite the evident tensions in his relations with Netanyahu, the King had cultivated enough contacts elsewhere in the Israeli political establishment to be sure that there would remain a significant element of continuity in relations between the two states whatever the high-level crises. It is perhaps ironic, then, that the greatest test of the strength of the bilateral relationship during the course of 1997 came from a source which had previously proved to be one of the closest and most enduring channels of cooperation between the two states: the intelligence services.

In late September 1997, Netanyahu authorised a Mossad operation intended to assassinate a prominent Hamas leader, Khaled Meshal, in Amman. The plan went badly wrong. Although the members of the Mossad hit squad, who had entered Jordan posing as Canadian tourists, succeeded in injecting a slow-acting poison into Meshal's ear,[39] his bodyguard fought back, pursuing the Israelis and capturing two of them. These agents were subsequently detained by the Jordanian authorities, while another four took refuge in the Israeli embassy in Amman. King Hussein was incensed. Apart from the reckless disregard for Jordanian sovereignty and the peace treaty between the two states, the operation seemed like a personal slap in the face for him. A few days earlier, he had transmitted a proposal from Hamas via Mossad channels for a thirty-year ceasefire with Israel. The assassination attempt against Meshal seemed to him an extraordinary response to this proposal.[40] Not only was the operation a personal insult to the King, threatening to undermine the arguments he had put in Jordan in favour of peace with Israel, it also threatened cooperation between the Israeli and Jordanian security services. As Efraim Halevy, who was brought in by Netanyahu to sort out the mess, observed, it added insult to injury that the operation showed such a remarkable disregard for Jordanian capabilities.[41]

The King came close to severing diplomatic relations with Israel over the affair. He also threatened that if the Mossad agents sheltering in the Israeli embassy were not handed over to the Jordanian authorities, he would order the storming of the building by elite army units. He demanded and received the immediate application by an Israeli physician of the antidote to the poison which had been given to Meshal. On its own, though, this was not enough to repair the breach in relations with the King. More would be needed to atone for the betrayal of his trust. It was Efraim Halevy who suggested what ultimately proved to be the solution to the problem. Israel would release into Hussein's custody Sheikh Ahmed Yassin, the jailed spiritual founder of Hamas. The King would then be able to accompany him back to Gaza as a free man, thus taking the credit for his release, and repairing his own damaged relations with the Muslim Brotherhood in Jordan.[42]

Arriving in Amman alone in an attempt to resolve the crisis, Halevy was quickly briefed about the botched Mossad operation by Crown Prince Hassan and the head of Jordanian intelligence, Samih Batikhi. Although Halevy knew Prince Hassan well from the peace negotiations, he had never met Batikhi, who had been installed as head of General Intelligence in the latter part of 1995, when the King had decisively changed tack in his handling of policy towards Iraq. He was closely tied to the CIA, which had wanted someone trustworthy in place at the head of Jordanian intelligence, which they feared had been widely penetrated by Iraqi agents.[43] Soon to become an extremely powerful figure in Jordan, Batikhi had a difficult relationship with Prince Hassan. Astutely, or perhaps with the benefit of advance information, Halevy sensed the tension between the two men, and tried to play on it to relieve the crisis. Seizing on Prince Hassan's more positive reception for the idea of a possible trade of the Mossad team for Sheikh Yassin, Halevy secured an audience with the King. During their meeting, despite his bitterness, the King accepted the idea of a trade, although he intimated that there would need to be other Hamas prisoners released alongside Yassin.[44] On the Israeli side, the contacts the King had made elsewhere in the political establishment also played a role in cementing the deal. Despite continuing opposition from within the Israeli defence and intelligence establishment to Yassin's release, Yitzhak Mordechai, the defence minister with whom the King had recently had such cordial exchanges, played a key role in backing the deal, as did Ariel Sharon, another of the King's correspondents. Relations with Israel were thus salvaged, although trust between the two sides at all levels reached its lowest ebb since the signature of the peace treaty.

The deepening crisis in relations between the Israeli and Jordanian regimes paralleled the negative perception of the Jordanian public. Indeed, the Dakamseh case became something of a cause célèbre in Jordan. While the King's decision to kneel before the families of Dakamseh's victims was seen in Israel as a gesture of humility, many in Jordan saw it as more of a gesture of humiliation.[45] This sentiment was exacerbated by the evident difficulties in the Palestinian–Israeli peace process under the Netanyahu government. Nevertheless, the anti-normalisation campaign in Jordan, which opposed the creation of political, cultural and economic ties with Israel, had deeper roots. From the outset, Hussein had faced an uphill struggle in securing broader popular support for his decision to make peace with Israel. While the initial opposition to the signature of the peace treaty in October 1994 was relatively muted, the anti-normalisation campaign began to gain ground during 1995 and 1996, expressing itself not just through the stance of certain members of parliament, but also through the activities of the professional associations. From his position at the apex of the political system, the King did what he could, both through prompting the government to take action and through his public statements, to push the process of normalisation forward, but there were limits to what he could achieve in the face of public opinion.

In parliament, the opposition to normalisation found its initial expression in efforts during 1995 to block the repeal of three explicitly anti-Israeli laws, which prohibited land sales, banned trade and imposed an economic boycott on the Jewish state. Although parliament repealed the laws on 26 July 1995, the anti-normalisation campaign continued to gather support. Following the banning of an anti-normalisation conference in May,[46] in November 1995, on instructions from the King, the government indicated its intention to consider measures designed to prevent professional associations meddling in politics. At the same time, the government also began considering possible revisions to the Press and Publications Law which were intended, among other things, to clamp down on the media expressing dissatisfaction with the peace process. Once again the tensions between political freedom and relations with Israel were on display.

In December 1996, a proposed Israeli trade fair in Amman was postponed when the anti-normalisers, led by the former Prime Minister Ahmed Obeidat, made it a focal point of their protests. Attempts by the anti-normalisation lobby to coordinate their activities with Syria during the winter of 1996–7 provoked a sharp response from the government, which opened investigations into whether four leftist political parties might be banned on the grounds of forbidden foreign connections. Official attempts to frustrate the expression of such sentiments were mirrored in the revisions made to the Press and Publications Law by the new Majali government on 17 May 1997.[47] In an amendment to the Press Law with wide-ranging implications, Jordanian papers were prohibited from publishing anything which might threaten national unity or disparage the royal family, the security services or 'friendly states'. Under the controversial new law, the government banned thirteen weekly newspapers during the final months of 1997. In a further sign of the faltering state of democracy in Jordan, the November 1997 general election was boycotted by nine political parties, including the Islamic Action Front. The focal point for disagreement between the regime and the opposition proved once again to be the electoral law, and the apparent bias of the one-man one-vote system against ideological political parties.

Probably the one bright spot for the regime in terms of dividends from the peace with Israel lay in the eventual conclusion in May 1997 of a deal implementing one of the water clauses in the original peace treaty.[48] Although the deal was long overdue, the agreement concluded between the King and Prime Minister Netanyahu at Aqaba on 8 May was quite satisfactory from the Jordanian perspective. In respect of the outstanding 50 million cubic metres (MCM) of potable water per annum which Israel was supposed to find for Jordan through cooperative efforts, the Israelis agreed to install a desalination plant to provide Jordan with water currently used by Israel for fish farming in the Beit Shean Valley. In the interim period, estimated to be three years, until the completion of the plant, Israel agreed to supply Jordan with an additional 25–30 MCM per annum via pipeline from Lake Tiberias. According to Infrastructure Minister Ariel Sharon, who wrote to Crown Prince Hassan confirming the details of the agreement, its implementation would 'not be easy on Israel since it entails a radical change in the mode of operation of the Israel fish farms in the Beit Shean Valley which have been the backbone of the regional economy for tens of years'.[49] Writing to confirm Jordan's acceptance of the deal, Prince Hassan expressed the hope that it would stimulate the integrated development of the Jordan Rift Valley, which remained an important goal for the Hashemite kingdom.[50] Even with the conclusion of this agreement, though, critics of the peace in Jordan were able to point to the fact according to the requirements of the original peace treaty it was over eighteen months late, and that it was wrung only grudgingly from the Israeli government.

It is difficult to avoid the conclusion that the high hopes for the future which the King had entertained when the Israeli–Jordanian peace treaty was signed in October 1994 had been largely dashed in the following three years. Although progress had been made during 1995 in both bilateral and multilateral relations, Rabin's assassination had dealt a mortal blow to the peace process. At a stroke, the one Israeli leader who believed that it was time to make a broader, historic compromise had been removed from the scene. Thereafter, Jordan's relations with Israel deteriorated. Hussein did his best to stem the process. Although his personal relations with both Peres and Netanyahu proved difficult, he tried to build a network of contacts in the Israeli political establishment, and also took every opportunity he could to appeal to Israeli public opinion. In both respects, he chalked up significant successes. But the litany of political crises ranging from Peres's 'Grapes of Wrath' operation through the Jerusalem tunnel incident, the Hebron redeployment and the Har Homa construction project to the Meshal affair was such that he found himself fighting a losing battle. The problem was not that successive Israeli leaders set out to undermine relations with Jordan. In a sense, it was worse than that. Israeli leaders, particularly Netanyahu, simply took Jordan for granted, seeing it either as a pawn in the larger game of regional politics or as a stage on which to act out other rivalries. This approach reached its apotheosis in the Meshal affair. This operation was undertaken not in order to embarrass or undermine King Hussein, but simply without any regard as to how he might react.

Not only did King Hussein find himself fighting a losing battle in relations with Israel, his efforts to entrench the peace treaty at home met with only limited success. True, the necessary legal steps were taken to usher in the new era, but, in terms of broader public and elite opinion in Jordan, the King struggled to overcome the anti-normalisation campaign. The deteriorating climate in high political relations and the travails of the Palestinian–Israeli peace process did not help him, but the depth of suspicion of Israel in Jordan was such that even in the best of circumstances a significant anti-normalisation backlash would have been likely. Far from tasting the fruits of peace as he had hoped, by the beginning of the final year of his life the King was left instead to mull over what had become the bitter aftertaste of peace.

CHAPTER 18

THE LIBERATION OF IRAQ, 1995–7

In addition to the serious difficulties in the peace process, the King's policy towards another critical regional problem, the fate of Iraq, underwent a number of significant shifts during the final years of his life. Iraq, it will be recollected, had always been close to Hussein's heart. In the immediate aftermath of the 1958 revolution, Hussein had wanted to send Jordanian troops into Baghdad to restore the Hashemite monarchy. Thereafter, in a further attempt to destabilise the post-revolutionary regime of Abd al-Karim Qasim, he had backed his ambassador to Iraq Wasfi Tall's manoeuvres in establishing links with the Iraqi opposition. Although such opportunities had not presented themselves again during the 1970s and 1980s, the King had never given up his interest in the lost Hashemite patrimony in Iraq, and after the Gulf War, he had established contact with Iraqi opposition groups in London. He did not press his own claims but indicated his willingness to back the opposition to Saddam's regime, all the while protesting in public that he would not allow Jordan to be used as a springboard for attempts to destabilise Iraq. He hedged his bets by keeping his channels to Saddam open, thus avoiding alienating the powerful constituency among the Jordanian political elite which still supported the Iraqi leader. But his changed personal view of Saddam had already been made clear in a letter to British Prime Minister John Major, in which he described Saddam as one of two 'demi-gods', Nasser being the other, who had 'caused untold damage to our region'.[1] Meanwhile, on the Iraqi side, Saddam played a game of wait and see in his relations with the King. The channel through Jordan to the outside world was too important to Iraq to threaten it without very good reason. In 1995, however, the situation changed dramatically.[2]

In early summer that year, Israeli Prime Minister Yitzhak Rabin launched a bold and remarkable secret initiative: he sought an invitation from Saddam to visit Baghdad with King Hussein. His aim in doing this was both simple and logical: if he could open up relations with Iraq, he would put more pressure on Saddam's enemy, the Syrian leader Hafez Asad, to come to peace terms with Israel. Rabin also regarded Iraq as the key to the eastern Arab world, and a potential bulwark against any future Iranian threat to Israel. King Hussein played his part in the scheme, handling his contacts with Rabin via the usual channel between his communications chief Ali Shukri and Mossad's Efraim Halevy. As agreed with Rabin, in June 1995 the King sent his Chief of the Royal Court, Marwan Qasim, bearing a secret letter to Saddam proposing the joint visit.[3] Saddam indicated that he would not be prepared to work through lower-level intermediaries, but he did not immediately rule out direct contacts with the Israeli leader. Subsequently, King Hussein implicitly acknowledged his own role in catalysing the initiative in a letter which he sent to Major:

> Earlier, in June of this year, I sent an emissary to the Iraqi President to emphasise the need for full co-operation with the United Nations; in the hope that we could help the Iraqi people overcome their tragedy which has resulted from the major errors committed by the regime. If you recall, when we met in Amman early this year, I brought to your attention, Sir, the importance of bringing Iraq into the peace process which in our view would create a more assuring attitude towards the comprehensiveness of peace in our region.[4]

In view of the real mission of the emissary sent in June, it is no surprise that in this letter Hussein coupled the mention of his despatch with the need to bring Iraq into the peace process. Hussein saw this as a unique opportunity to pursue the comprehensive, multilateral peace in the region which he had always sought.

Now a dramatic event interposed. On 8 August 1995, General Hussein Kamel al-Majid, Saddam's son-in-law, suddenly arrived in Amman and requested asylum. Probably the third most powerful man in Iraq after Saddam himself and his son Uday, Hussein Kamel had become the victim of feuding in the family, and had come to fear that Uday had set his sights on out-manoeuvring and eliminating him.[5] He was accompanied to Amman by his brother, Saddam Kamel, and their wives, both of whom were Saddam's daughters. Although the precise timing of his arrival was a surprise to King Hussein, there had been some advance hints that Hussein Kamel was weighing the possibility of fleeing to Jordan. Chief of the Royal Court Marwan Qasim recollects an impromptu meeting with Hussein Kamel, who was accompanied by the Iraqi ambassador in Amman, early in 1995. Nothing was said during this meeting about defection, but in hindsight it is possible that Hussein Kamel was already beginning to weigh the possibility. During the early summer, Hussein Kamel had again passed through Amman and asked to meet with Qasim, although this time the chief of the Royal Court could not find time to see him. Then, on the day of his defection, Hussein Kamel showed up on Qasim's doorstep with his motorcade saying that he needed to see King Hussein at once. Pressing the urgency of the matter, he claimed that he was carrying an important personal message from Saddam for the King. The excuse seemed plausible to Qasim, who knew that the King was still awaiting a formal reply to the secret letter he had sent to Saddam in June.[6]

The King agreed to receive Kamel and spent about twenty minutes talking to him alone. After the meeting, he asked Qasim to arrange secure accommodation for the Iraqi party at the Hashimiyah Palace. He also asked that the Royal Guard be alerted. With Kamel installed under royal protection in Amman, the King's Iraqi policy now shifted decisively. In a press conference on 12 August, Hussein Kamel pledged that he would work for the downfall of the Iraqi regime. The King himself praised Kamel in a speech on 23 August, and made his most direct public criticisms ever of Saddam, describing the invasion of Kuwait in 1990 as a terrible shock, and accusing the Iraqi leader of planning a second such attack.[7] Although he did not directly call for Saddam's overthrow, the King told the Israeli newspaper *Yediot Aharanot* that he was hoping 'there will be a new era in Iraq'.[8]

The initial response to the King's bold initiative from the American and British governments was apparently positive. John Major wrote offering his 'very warm support' for the King's 'brave decision', describing the defections as 'a serious blow to the Iraqi regime'.[9] Tensions soon began to emerge, however, with the Western intelligence agencies evidently much less enthusiastic than their political masters about the King's decision to welcome and support Hussein Kamel. As a former pillar of Saddam's regime, Hussein Kamel had no credibility with the exiled Iraqi opposition groups such as the Iraqi National Congress (INC) led by Ahmed Chalabi or the Iraqi National Accord (INA) led by Iyad Allawi. Similarly, although the Western intelligence agencies hurried to extract as much information from him as they could about the state of Saddam's weapons programmes and the strength of his regime, they quickly lost interest in him as the information he could provide dried up. Crucially, both the British and the American intelligence services already had their own preferred Iraqi surrogates in the shape of the INA and the INC, and were reluctant to lend any backing to Hussein Kamel as a rallying point for the opposition. Both Rabin's attempt to bring Saddam into the regional peace process and the King's subsequent embrace of Hussein Kamel cut across their plans in different ways. That there was a significant difference in approach between the Western intelligence services and the King at this point is apparent from an urgent message sent by the Head of MI6, David Spedding, to King Hussein on 26 August 1995:

> I was sorry to learn of your disappointment at the British Government's reaction to recent important developments. I was also disturbed to hear of your concern over the actions of one of my officers in Amman recently. I have taken steps to ensure that any such misunderstanding will not arise again. I am sure your Majesty will agree that at this sensitive time our two countries should work closely together in the intelligence field and I would assure your Majesty that my Service will continue to exert all efforts to that end.[10]

The MI6 chief concluded by requesting that Hussein meet his Controller for the Middle East, Geoffrey Tantum, on 29 or 30 August 'to review the various issues involved'. Apparently, the offending agent who Spedding referred to in his letter, and who had drawn King Hussein's ire, had seen himself in the role of a latter-day 'Lawrence of Arabia', making contact from Amman with members of the Iraqi opposition without coordinating his actions with the Jordanian Mukhabarat.[11] Aside from reining in this particular individual, Spedding, who knew Hussein well from his time as the MI6 station chief in Amman between 1983 and 1987, evidently managed to smooth matters over at the political level.

He was helped by an emollient letter written on the same day by his political master, Prime Minister John Major. Beginning by thanking the King for giving his personal emissary, Nicholas Soames, prompt access to the Iraqi defectors, the prime minister sought to find the middle ground between the King's enthusiasm for Hussein Kamel as a rallying point for the Iraqi opposition and the scepticism of his own secret intelligence service. 'Only time will tell whether Hussein Kamil [sic] is in a position to lead efforts to achieve a change of government inside Iraq,' he wrote. 'Meanwhile, we must, I believe, maintain and increase pressure on the present regime.'[12] The prime minister also congratulated the King on improving Jordan's relations with the Gulf States, especially Saudi Arabia, and tried to sweeten the pill still further with an apology for failing to invite Jordan to the recent London Conference on Bosnia, a conflict in which the King had taken a personal interest on account of the plight of the Muslim population. 'This was a mistake,' Major wrote. 'The Conference would undoubtedly have benefited from Jordan's perspective.'

The Prime Minister's blandishments, alongside those of his MI6 controller, evidently went some way towards soothing the King's anger. In explaining his own position, the King wrote:

Regarding the refuge of Hussein Kamel Hassan and his colleagues: we granted them political asylum, being one of the closest people to the President in that regime. To have Hussein Kamel come to Jordan and disclose sensitive information that has never been revealed to UNSCOM [the United Nations Special Commission, charged with investigating Iraq's weapons programme], or anyone else before, would, hopefully, create a situation that would help relieve some of the hard suffering of the Iraqi people.

Therefore, they sought our help, as a result of total desperation and pressing need to alert the world to the urgent requirement for change in their country, something which they could not achieve if they stayed in Iraq.[13]

In the same letter, the King informed the prime minister about the message he had sent to Saddam in June. Evidently, this initiative, or at least Hussein's part in it, had now been overtaken by events.

The King's enthusiasm for Hussein Kamel as a possible figurehead for the Iraqi opposition soon cooled. This was partly the result of Hussein Kamel's evident isolation, and partly the result of continuing pressure from the Americans, British and Saudis, none of whom saw him as a suitable rallying figure. The re-emergence of King Hussein's own dynastic interests in Iraq also became clearer around this time. Although he continued to deny that he had any personal ambition to succeed to the Iraqi throne, the King emphasised in a discussion on 26 September that in terms of the Hashemite family, he 'was the second person after the late King Faysal' of Iraq.[14] In an earlier interview given on 6 September, when asked whether the Hashemites would once again be willing to shoulder responsibility in Iraq, the King had replied: 'that is up to the Iraqis themselves. If they found that a particular regime served them in the past or that a certain leadership resolved their differences and achieved their unity, that is up to them.'[15]

Within the Jordanian government, Foreign Minister Abdul Karim Kabariti, who had longer-term American links, also worked hard to bring about a fundamental shift in Jordan's Iraq policy. A powerful and wealthy individual whose background was in banking, Kabariti was highly ambitious and possessed a supreme confidence in his own abilities. He had earlier resigned his post as minister of tourism during the Gulf crisis, in protest against what he saw as the pro-Iraqi drift in Jordan's policy. Now, in changed circumstances, he saw the opportunity to engineer a decisive shift in the government's approach, and in the process to achieve his own personal ambition of becoming prime minister. Kabariti's goal was to secure the King's cooperation in covert operations led by the INA to bring down the Saddam regime. He was to be backed up in this by the equally ambitious new head of Jordanian intelligence, Samih Batikhi, who owed his promotion to the CIA. Meanwhile, those opposing the reorientation in Jordanian policy towards Iraq included the powerful Prime Minister Zeid bin Shaker and the Chief of the Royal Court Marwan Qasim. Zeid bin Shaker had extensive business and financial interests in Iraq, established during his time as head of the Jordanian armed forces, which made him very reluctant to turn against Saddam.

Kabariti moved quickly. Shortly after Hussein Kamel's arrival, the Saudi intelligence chief Prince Turki bin Feisal came to Amman to discuss the possibility of coordinated action against Saddam. Kabariti made a return visit to Riyadh shortly afterwards, where he was received very cordially, with the Saudi authorities letting it be known that he had come at their invitation, in contrast to a previous visit he had made a mere month earlier which had taken place on sufferance. This time round Kabariti was granted an audience with King Fahd, and presented him a letter from King Hussein which called for a new strategic relationship between Jordan and Saudi Arabia.[16]

At the end of September, Kabariti accompanied the King to a meeting at CIA headquarters in Langley, where they were briefed about a plan for an army coup in Iraq to be carried out in cooperation with the Iraqi National Accord led by Iyad Allawi.[17] Allawi had longstanding contacts with MI6, but, in the wake of the failure earlier in the year of efforts launched by the rival Iraqi National Congress to overthrow Saddam, Allawi's organisation had also gained ground with the CIA. This shift in CIA priorities was furthered by a change in leadership at the Agency during 1995. Its new director, John M. Deutch, was committed to bringing about the downfall of Saddam's regime in short order, and receptive to any plans which seemed likely to achieve this. Allawi's INA was well placed to capitalise on this new atmosphere, since it was in contact with individuals within the elite Iraqi Republican Guard, who claimed to be able to raise a military coup against Saddam. It also helped from King Hussein's point of view that Allawi and the INA did not carry the same baggage in Jordan as Ahmed Chalabi, who had been convicted in absentia by the Jordanian courts for embezzlement in connection with the 1989 collapse of the Petra Bank.

It took President Clinton's personal persuasion to secure Hussein's final agreement to participate in the INA-CIA plan. Initially, the King was sceptical about the briefing given to him at CIA headquarters. One source, who had been alerted to the scheme in advance, had already warned the King to expect a half-baked presentation, in which the organisers' basic lack of knowledge about the internal situation in Iraq was disguised through the use of elaborate

graphs, charts and other presentational aids. 'Ask them who's in command of
the various Iraqi units they mention,' he told the King. 'They won't know.
You know far more about what's happening in Iraq than they do.' This was
exactly what transpired. The operation had by this stage already acquired a
dubious reputation in CIA circles, attracting only those within the Agency
who could not find a better posting elsewhere. According to one source, 'it
stunk'. But despite these doubts, when President Clinton took him to one side
in the Oval Office, put his arm round his shoulders, and asked him to back
the plan, the King agreed.[18] Clinton's interest in the success of the operation
is not difficult to divine; the overthrow of Saddam during the summer of 1996
would help ensure his re-election in the presidential election that November.
King Hussein's acquiescence in the scheme, meanwhile, resulted from a
combination of his desire to please the president, his concern for the suffering
of the Iraqi people under Saddam and his own long-cherished dynastic
ambitions. But his suspicions about the goals of the Western intelligence
services in Iraq, fostered by their negative reaction to his welcome for Hussein
Kamel, remained. Remarkably, when Rabin was assassinated shortly after
Hussein's late-September visit to Washington, the King went so far as to ask
one astonished close friend, 'Did the Americans have Rabin killed?'[19]
Although he grudgingly admitted that he had no evidence for this claim
beyond the CIA's hostility to Rabin's Iraqi initiative, the fact that he could
even contemplate such an unlikely conspiracy showed that he was wary of the
differences between his own goals in Iraq and those of the CIA.

Despite these doubts, Hussein allowed the INA-CIA plan to go forward. A
special liaison unit was now set up within Jordan's intelligence service which
reported straight to Batikhi, and a new CIA station chief was despatched to
Amman, along with a special team assembled to handle the INA's Iraqi
operation. At a meeting convened in Riyadh in mid-January 1996, the British,
Saudi and Kuwaiti intelligence services, alongside the Americans and
Jordanians, all agreed to lend their backing to the INA's plans.[20]

At the Jordanian end, the resistance of Zeid bin Shaker and Marwan Qasim
remained an obstacle to the execution of the plan.[21] Zeid bin Shaker's
opposition was a major barrier to full Jordanian cooperation, since he was not
only very close to Hussein personally, he also had a significant support base
in the army, and was arguably the second most powerful man in the kingdom.
Precisely how Kabariti and Batikhi won the domestic power struggle is
unclear, but their victory was confirmed when Kabariti replaced Zeid bin
Shaker as prime minister on 4 February 1996.[22] Kabariti now held
simultaneously the positions of prime minister, defence minister and foreign
minister, an unusually powerful combination. He cemented his position still
further by filling his government with political newcomers; two-thirds of his
thirty-one-member cabinet were joining the government for the first time.[23]

Thus began one of the strangest premierships in Jordan's political history. The domestic platform unveiled by the new government spoke of economic and political reform, the strengthening of pluralism and democracy, and a drive against corruption. These issues were at best peripheral, or rather subservient, to the real purpose of the Kabariti government, which was to bring about a change of regime in Baghdad. It was Kabariti's promise to the King that he could deliver Iraq which probably won him the highest office.

As part of the process of clearing the decks for the INA operation, Kabariti encouraged Hussein Kamel to leave Jordan. In truth, by the end of 1995, Hussein Kamel had long overstayed his welcome. As one of the stalwarts of Saddam's regime, Kamel was an unsavoury character, whose principal amusements were the brutal and unrestrained exercise of power and the acquisition of wealth. In Jordan, however, he quickly became an isolated, impotent and irrelevant figure. Ali Shukri, the King's chief of communications, who had been given the task of minding Kamel during his time in Amman, found the task so uncongenial that he took to counting the days ('182', he recollected bitterly).[24] Hussein Kamel's decision to return to Iraq and throw himself on Saddam Hussein's 'mercy' may have been prompted by a lawsuit launched against him by a Jordanian journalist, Nayef Tawarah. Tawarah, who was a friend of Kabariti, had written a story in which he recorded critical remarks that the Iraqi exile had allegedly made about King Hussein. Now he accused Hussein Kamel of making threats against him as a result. On behalf of the government, Kabariti made clear that Hussein Kamel would have to stand trial. 'We are all living under the law in Jordan,' he observed, with no small irony.[25] The lawsuit, alongside Saddam's skilful blandishments and the complaints of his own family, who were tired of staying cooped up in Amman, finally led to Hussein Kamel's decision to return to Iraq on 20 February. Just before he left, the King called Kabariti to ask whether he should be allowed to depart. 'Let him go,' replied Kabariti. 'It will be a great relief.'[26] Hussein Kamel's fate was predictable. He died in a shoot-out with members of Saddam's presidential guard within days of his return to Iraq.

While the new Kabariti government unveiled its apparent political programme to parliament in February, its real programme was being unveiled elsewhere. On 18 February, the INA's leader Iyad Allawi held a press conference in which he announced the imminent opening of a new headquarters for his organisation in Amman, and pledged that he would work for the overthrow of Saddam's regime. On 26 March the INA's headquarters was duly opened with a publicly declared two-fold mission: to act as an information outlet and to recruit new members for the organisation from within the Iraqi armed forces. During this period King Hussein was also active in meeting members of the Iraqi opposition, though his call for a conference of opposition groups in late 1995 had met with criticism from

Syria and Egypt, both of which saw it as evidence of his wider ambitions. Thereafter, the King confined himself to slightly lower-profile activities, holding a number of meetings with opposition leaders in London in March 1996. During a visit to Washington in the same month, certain members of the Jordanian delegation, including Kabariti and Batikhi, were given a further briefing on the progress of the plans to overthrow Saddam, though the King made it clear that he himself did not want to hear any of the details of what was being planned.[27] The Washington visit also produced an agreement for the short-term deployment of US aircraft to Jordan in mid-April. These aircraft were assigned to help patrol the southern no-fly zone in Iraq.[28] In view of the imminent coup, which was planned for June, the deployment may also have been intended to protect the kingdom should Saddam lash out, or to back up the INA plotters if their plans ran into difficulty.

While these preparations were unfolding, Saddam was making his own plans. At some point during January or February 1996 the Iraqi intelligence services captured one of the satellite communication devices which the CIA team in Amman had been using to communicate with the plotters in Iraq. This capture may have come about as a result of information gleaned by the Iraqis from sources within the INA, which, it was later admitted, had been extensively penetrated by double-agents. Access to this communication device enabled Saddam's intelligence services to assemble at their leisure the names of those directly involved in the army plot. A warning to this effect delivered by the rival head of the INC, Ahmed Chalabi, was evidently disregarded by the CIA. Plans for the coup, which was scheduled for the latter part of June, went ahead. In another display of remarkable indiscretion, in mid-June Iyad Allawi granted an interview to the *Washington Post*, one of only two US publications which Iraqi intelligence was sure to monitor, in which he spoke of a forthcoming secret operation, which would have at its centre the Iraqi armed forces. 'We preach controlled, coordinated military uprising,' Allawi told the *Post* reporter, claiming portentously, 'we believe the end is near. We have entered the final chapter in salvaging Iraq.'[29]

The end was indeed near, but not in the sense Allawi had expected. Perhaps prompted by the publication of the *Washington Post* article citing Allawi's claims on 23 June, Saddam made his move, picking up a number of the key army plotters during the final week of the month. Thereafter, he set in train a wider investigation, led by his son Qusay, which would ultimately result in several hundred arrests and dozens of executions over the ensuing months.[30] The Iraqis apparently even used the captured communication device to inform the CIA team in Amman of the failure of their plans on 26 June.[31] The collapse of the coup was a serious blow to the Kabariti government, with the prime minister adopting thereafter an uncharacteristically reserved public stance on the topic of Iraq.

However, the Iraq-inspired manoeuvres in Jordanian domestic politics were not yet over. Possibly the most sordid gambit remained to be played out in the form of the government's announcement of large bread and fodder price rises on 12 August.[32] Billed as part of the 'economic reform' process in the country, the nature, timing and handling of the move were in fact all dictated by considerations of Iraq policy. The chief of the Royal Court at the time, Awn Khasawneh, a friend of Kabariti's since his youth, recollects pleading with him to reduce the size of the price rise or implement it in stages, since he feared it would provoke popular protest. But this was precisely the point. Kabariti refused to rescind the decision. When, as Khasawneh had feared, protests broke out, beginning in the southern town of Kerak on 16 August, the chief of the Royal Court reacted to what he thought was a genuine economic policy issue and began to telephone the heads of important families in and around Kerak to see if he could dampen down the trouble. Khasawneh recollects Kabariti pacing around the room at the time, with an expression on his face which showed that he was unhappy with these actions, although he did not try directly to stop them.[33]

Now the King intervened. Against the advice of Khasawneh, and others who did not want him directly associated with such an unpopular move, he insisted on calling a press conference to back up his prime minister. At this stage the King was probably not aware of the real motive behind the price rise. In his press conference, he blamed external elements for fomenting the trouble, specifically pro-Iraqi Jordanians.[34] Indeed, Kerak was then one of the few strongholds in Jordan of the Baath Party.[35] This provides the final clue to what was really behind the bread price rise. The goal of the move was to provoke unrest, which could then be used as an excuse to round up Baathists and other leftists who were seen as sympathisers of Saddam.[36] Hence Kabariti's exasperation at Khasawneh's attempts to resolve the crisis: he had entirely missed the point. The riots had to be allowed to continue until the other man behind the plot, Batikhi, had had the opportunity to round up all the Baathist sympathisers on his list. The fact that some of those arrested were nowhere near the scene of the disturbances at the time was little more than a minor inconvenience in the overall scheme of things.

There was a final irony in the unfolding of the plan. The further opposition action in Iraq, for which the round-up of Baathists and leftists in Jordan was supposed to provide support, never took place. Unbeknown to Kabariti and Batikhi, Saddam had already moved against almost all of those concerned.[37] Worse still from Kabariti's perspective, Saddam now seized the opportunity provided by an outbreak of internecine fighting between the two main Kurdish factions, Massoud Barzani's Kurdish Democratic Party (KDP) and Jalal Talabani's Patriotic Union of Kurdistan (PUK), to move his forces north into the Kurdish enclave in Iraq. The Kurdish conflict had begun when Talabani's

PUK launched an offensive against the KDP on 17 August, the day after the outbreak of trouble in Kerak. As the fighting intensified, the Americans prevaricated. Desperate to avoid defeat, the KDP leader Massoud Barzani turned to Saddam for help. Saddam was only too happy to oblige, pushing his armoured forces forward on 31 August and seizing the Kurdish capital of Irbil. In the process, Saddam's troops captured a large number of supporters of the Iraqi National Congress, many of whom were summarily executed. Those who fled were scattered, some making an eventual escape to the United States. In Jordan, Kabariti was evidently shocked by the US failure to prevent Saddam's push north, despite his own pleas. 'It wasn't an embarrassment what happened,' he told his American contacts. 'It was something like treason.'[38]

In the wake of the disaster in northern Iraq, King Hussein evidently got to the bottom of what had happened during the Kerak disturbances. On 12 November, he instructed the government to close the file on the riots and to release all of those who were still in prison for 'connected offences'. All charges relating to the disturbances were dropped.[39] Although the King did not immediately dismiss Kabariti, the prime minister's handling of the affair undoubtedly played a part in the King's subsequent decision to sack him in March 1997. While Kabariti and Batikhi had had the King's licence to pursue a change of regime in Iraq, there were limits to what Hussein was prepared to tolerate within Jordan itself. Still, we can learn something about the King's own continuing appetite for political risk from his private comment after he had finally sacked Kabariti: 'That was exciting: what are we going to do now?'[40] Evidently the experience of the Kabariti government for him had been the political equivalent of flying a jet at treetop level, or driving a sports car at full throttle.

The CIA-backed INA plot to overthrow Saddam in 1996 was carried out with such a degree of incompetence that one is left wondering whether it was ever really intended to succeed. To be sure, the difficulties in organising any kind of conspiracy within a police state like Iraq were formidable. But, to broadcast one's intentions in the way in which the INA did, and to ignore detailed warnings such as that apparently issued by Ahmed Chalabi of the INC, stretches the bounds of credence.

In the wake of the fiasco, King Hussein's approach to the Iraqi problem shifted once again. Part of the reason for the change was Saddam's acceptance of UN Security Council Resolution 986 on 20 May 1996, and the subsequent beginning of oil exports under the oil-for-food programme on 10 December 1996.[41] The resolution, which had originally been passed by the Security Council on 14 April 1995, permitted the sale of a limited quantity of Iraqi oil in order to purchase food and other humanitarian supplies for the population which had been suffering under the UN sanctions regime.[42] In theory, the oil-for-food programme was supposed to be run under strict UN supervision. In practice, as the subsequent Volcker report uncovered, the whole operation became riddled with corruption. Because the Iraqi regime could choose the companies or individuals to whom it awarded oil contracts, it was able to use the scheme as an instrument of its foreign policy, awarding oil contracts to companies from countries it saw as friendly, or which argued the case for the end of the sanctions regime. In the later stages of the programme, from the end of 2000 onwards, Saddam extracted significant kickbacks by imposing a surcharge on the oil sales, which entrenched his regime still further.[43]

These difficulties in the implementation of Resolution 986 were not unexpected. Writing to King Hussein after he had secured re-election in November 1996, and after the first shipment of oil had been made under the terms of the programme, President Clinton observed:

> I believe that Saddam Hussein hopes implementation of UNSCR 986 will be seen as a first step towards phasing out the Iraq sanctions regime. That is a serious misreading of the situation . . . Now that the basic needs of the Iraqi people can be met, there is no justification whatever for adjusting the overall sanctions regime until Iraq has met all its UN obligations.[44]

Clinton warned, 'I remain firmly convinced that, given the opportunity to do so, Saddam Hussein will seek to avenge his defeat in 1991 . . . close, effective cooperation between our countries in the security sphere remains as important as ever.'[45]

From the Jordanian perspective, though, Saddam's acceptance of Resolution 986 offered significant economic opportunities. Jordan remained Iraq's principal economic conduit to the outside world, so however the oil-for-food programme was run Jordan would benefit from it. The King was aware of this, and also of the fact that an overt anti-Saddam policy such as that which he had pursued from August 1995 onwards was likely to hinder Jordan's role in the expanding Iraqi trade. With the dismissal of Kabariti, and his replacement as prime minister by Abdul Salam Majali on 19 March 1997, therefore, the King settled for a much less pro-active Iraqi policy. He would not hinder opposition activities, but nor would he lend them his direct backing, as he had with the INA plot during 1995-6. In this way he hoped to have the best of both worlds: he would accommodate the United States' anti-Saddam strategy while making the most of the economic opportunities available.

Perhaps he hoped that the passage of time might throw up further opportunities to bring about a 'new era' for Iraq. If so, he reckoned without one key factor. His own remaining time on the political scene was now very short. Much of the final year of his reign was taken up with issues much closer to home: his battle for life and the struggle over the succession to the throne.

CHAPTER 19

A DESTINY FULFILLED?

During the final year of King Hussein's life, the broader political picture in the Middle East did not change significantly. The same issues continued to dominate Jordan's foreign policy, even after Prince Hassan assumed the regency. Domestically, as the severity of the King's illness became apparent, the political manoeuvring over the succession to the throne gathered pace. Those who wanted to undercut Hassan used or created political incidents during his regency in a bid to show that he was unsuited to rule the country. Meanwhile, the Crown Prince and his supporters tried to make use of their partial grip on the reins of power to strike back at his enemies.

In terms of Jordan's foreign affairs, relations with Iraq were plunged into a brief crisis in December 1997 by Saddam's decision to execute four Jordanians on smuggling charges. King Hussein reacted furiously to the executions, calling them a 'heinous crime', and warning that 'the blood of Jordanians is not cheap and we will not forgive any party that considers it cheap or spills it'.[1] Seven Iraqi diplomats were expelled from Amman and the Jordanian chargé was withdrawn from Baghdad in diplomatic retaliation. Saddam, meanwhile, tried to dampen down the crisis by commuting the death sentence on a fifth Jordanian prisoner. Thereafter he released a further 140 Jordanian prisoners from Iraqi jails, although the fact that they were handed over to the prominent anti-normaliser and regime critic Laith Shbeilat showed that the Iraqi president had an eye on influencing the domestic political debate in Jordan. Shbeilat was subsequently one of the most consistently favoured Jordanian beneficiaries of Saddam's largesse under the oil-for-food programme.[2] The Iraqi government also publicly confirmed that it had no intention of cutting off oil supplies to Jordan. No doubt Saddam, as well as Hussein, was well aware of Jordan's continuing importance for Iraq as an economic conduit to the outside world.

If the Jordanian regime had hoped that the passions aroused by the executions of the four Jordanians might have turned domestic public opinion against Iraq, events suggested otherwise. In February 1998 the US threatened to use force again against Iraq if the UN weapons inspectors were not allowed to investigate so-called 'presidential sites'. Jordanians were outraged, with demonstrations on the streets of Amman on 13 February and serious unrest in the town of Maan a week later. Although the security forces were deployed to restore order, the domestic situation in Jordan did not return to normal until the crisis in Iraq was temporarily resolved through the mission of UN Secretary-General Kofi Annan to Baghdad, which concluded on 23 February. Even then, the respite was only temporary. Although the secretary-general had brokered a deal which would allow the weapons inspectors supervised access to the 'presidential sites', Saddam's purpose remained unchanged: to erode their mandate and divide the international community. Hussein, though, believed there was another consistent theme behind Saddam's strategy. In a letter to President Clinton on 7 March, he wrote: 'I have expressed my firm belief that the only constant of the Iraqi regime's policy, since 1990 has been to seek to conduct a direct dialogue with the United States Government and not through any intermediaries.'[3] In other words, Saddam had always been open to cutting a deal with Washington, but was only prepared to negotiate it directly with the president. He distrusted other mediators, and felt that dealing with them was beneath his dignity.

On 5 August Saddam moved the confrontation a stage further with the announcement that the Iraqi government would no longer cooperate with the UN inspectors. Then on 1 November he suspended cooperation with the long-term monitoring programme installed by the UN at known weapons sites. Although the order was temporarily rescinded in the face of imminent American attack, a further military confrontation could not long be avoided. On 16 December President Clinton finally ordered a new round of air and missile strikes, carried out in conjunction with British forces and codenamed 'Operation Desert Fox'. This military action played into Saddam's hands, eliciting protests from the other Permanent Members of the UN Security Council and a further upsurge of popular support for Iraq in the Arab world.

For his part the regent Prince Hassan made plain in a letter to British Prime Minister Tony Blair that Jordan wanted to see a change in Western strategy in dealing with Iraq. 'The problem we face now is that we are left with a conundrum,' he wrote. 'It is rather regrettable that Iraq's intransigence and obstinacy must, from now on, be met with more bombing raids. It is nothing short of a dead end policy.' The Crown Prince suggested instead that a quid

pro quo might be introduced to foster resumed Iraqi cooperation with the
weapons inspection regime:

> This could take the form of what in fact would amount to a hollow
> gesture of magnanimity. Knowing that Iraq is not able to export more oil
> than it is doing at present it would make little difference if the oil
> embargo is lifted completely. In return Iraq would be expected to have
> the inspection regime resumed.

Hassan offered one further important piece of advice:

> A word, Prime Minister, regarding the declared policy of cooperating
> with the opposition groups to topple the Baghdad regime. If this is to be
> followed through it would leave no incentive for Saddam Hussein to
> have weapon inspection resume. Therefore a public statement may have
> to be made stating clearly that any change of regime in Iraq is the
> responsibility of the Iraqi people and no other.[4]

It is possible that Prince Hassan had all along been less keen than his brother
to support coup attempts in Iraq, not least since this policy had been pursued
most vigorously during the premiership of his bitter political enemy
Abdel Karim Kabariti. But Hassan was simply articulating the views held by
most of the Jordanian political establishment. Apart from anything else, the
significant expansion of oil sales permitted under the oil-for-food
programme, which had been authorised by UN Resolution 1153 on 20
February 1998, only increased the economic incentive for Jordan to maintain
ties with Baghdad.[5] The programme also affected Jordan's domestic politics,
to the extent that Saddam used it to reward selected individuals in the anti-
normalisation movement with Iraqi oil contracts.[6] This was one of the more
ironic and unintended consequences of the Iraqi sanctions regime.

In terms of relations with Israel, the scars left by the Meshal affair of
September 1997 took some time to heal. Neither the King nor the Crown
Prince attended the MENA economic conference convened in Doha in
November 1997, joining other Arab leaders who boycotted the event in
protest at Israel's failure to advance the peace process with the Palestinians.
Nevertheless, early in 1998 political relations began to improve. The
resignation in February of the Mossad chief who had authorised the Meshal
operation, Danny Yatom, and his replacement by the King's personal friend
and former Mossad liaison, Efraim Halevy, no doubt helped matters along.
Then, on 10 March, Crown Prince Hassan paid a cordial visit to Israel which
symbolically drew a line under the rupture in relations caused by the Meshal
affair. In a letter to the King sent on 16 March, Prime Minister Netanyahu

wrote, 'I want to tell you first how glad I am about the reinvigoration of the relations between our countries. Prince Hassan's visit was, I believe, extremely successful, and I am looking forward to more mutual visits in the near future.'[7] Seizing the opportunity to show goodwill in the wake of the Crown Prince's trip, the prime minister belatedly picked up a suggestion made by the King the previous year that the two countries should cooperate in creating a children's hospital in Jordan modelled on the Schneider Children's Hospital in Tel Aviv. Netanyahu offered to accept Jordanian doctors on residentships at the Schneider Hospital as the first step towards realising the idea, adding, 'it would be my great pleasure to escort you on a tour of the facility on your next visit, and a privilege to be able to contribute to Jordanian medicine'.

On 16 April, the King took up Netanyahu's suggestion that he visit Israel, albeit briefly, holding two hours of unscheduled talks with the Israeli leader at Eilat, which focused on reviving the stalled peace process.[8] Thereafter, he also received a number of other Israeli visitors during the course of the year, including his established friends and contacts Ariel Sharon, Yitzhak Mordechai and Ehud Barak. He remained critical, though, of the Israeli prime minister's handling of the negotiations with the Palestinians, arguing during a meeting with senior officials on 20 May that the long stalemate in negotiations showed that Israeli Prime Minister Netanyahu had 'no respect for the Palestinians and no commitment to the resolutions and agreements signed, such as U.N. Resolutions 242 and 338, and [the] Oslo and Hebron accords'.[9] Although failing health limited his direct engagement in the peace process during the second half of the year, he did intervene personally during the Wye River summit in October to encourage both parties to reach agreement, urging Arafat and Netanyahu: 'it is time now to finish, bearing in mind the responsibility that both leaders have to their people and especially the children'.[10] According to the US negotiator Dennis Ross, 'the King's appearance and words moved us all'. In the wake of the agreement's conclusion, Netanyahu wrote to the King on the occasion of his birthday in unusually glowing terms:

> I hope you know that the love Israelis feel for you is as universal as it is unreserved. The popularity you enjoy here transcends fashion. It is an expression of deep appreciation for your unstinting, indispensable efforts on behalf of peace and friendship between our peoples. Nothing exemplified these efforts more poignantly than your contribution to the success of the Wye River talks.[11]

Uniquely in their often cold correspondence, Netanyahu hand-wrote the words 'dear friend' over the formal printed address of 'your majesty' at the head of the text. His accompanying wishes in the letter for Hussein's good health over the coming year, however, were sadly not to be realised.

In hindsight, it appears that the King's illness dated back to the latter months of 1997. Hussein started to suffer fevers at night and loss of appetite, and appeared increasingly tired and drawn in public. He also complained of enlarged lymph glands. Although a range of tests were carried out in London, Amman and at the Mayo Clinic in Minnesota his doctors could not precisely determine the cause of the problem. Anxious not to cause the King unnecessary discomfort through intrusive procedures, his doctors did not carry out a bone-marrow tap at this stage. This proved to be a fateful decision: a bone-marrow tap was the one test which might have revealed Hussein's true condition at an early stage, and given him a greater chance of recovery. In the absence of conclusive evidence, Hussein's doctors concluded that his ill health was probably the result of an infection in his lymph glands, and prescribed an extended course of antibiotics. Still, the fact that the King had left the country for treatment in the USA a mere two days after the November 1997 election, a time when he would normally have wanted to remain in Jordan, heightened the sense of concern surrounding him. Thereafter, in the first of a series of what proved to be over-optimistic medical reports, the director of Royal Medical Services of the Jordanian Armed Forces, Dr Yousef Qousous, told Jordanian television at the end of January that the King had 'responded well to the treatment and is in good health'. In a letter to Crown Prince Hassan on 31 January, the King also struck an optimistic, if fatalistic, note, telling him, 'I am resting (in London), while continuing medical treatment towards full recovery, God willing.'[12]

The positive messages continued. On 10 February the King told journalists that he was well on the way to recovery, and was receiving a six-week course of two kinds of antibiotics, while a month later, on 14 March, he telephoned Prince Hassan from the Mayo Clinic to tell him that he had been given a clean bill of health.[13] Unfortunately, his body refused to respond to doctors' advice. Despite what the test results had shown, ill health continued to dog him during the spring and early summer, with his night fevers periodically returning. Then, in mid-July came the fateful diagnosis. After further exploratory surgery, the King's doctors at the Mayo Clinic told him that they had discovered abnormal cells at a number of locations in his body and diagnosed non-Hodgkins lymphoma. On 22 July, the King broke the news in public, by means of an open letter to Prince Hassan.

Hussein now had little more than six months to live. In their initial prognosis, though, his doctors struck a much more optimistic note, telling Queen Noor that the odds for his recovery were good.[14] Indeed the King's cancer was publicly described as being in its early stages and 'one hundred per cent curable'.[15] In a live interview on Jordan television on 28 July, the King himself also spoke optimistically, insisting that his general condition was excellent, and that he had 'no worry except that of being away from home'.[16] In hindsight, of course, these statements seem to have been designed to reassure public opinion in Jordan, but in private the King's doctors were also relatively upbeat in their assessment of his condition.[17] With any cancer patient there is an awkward balance to be struck between giving false hope for recovery on the one hand and undermining the patient's will to live on the other. No doubt the relatively optimistic prognosis given by his doctors was statistically accurate for patients of Hussein's age group suffering from his condition. Nor could the King have been given any better care during the final months of his life. Although Mayo itself was more of a general surgical clinic, the team treating the King was able to call in advice as necessary from the top specialists in the field in the United States.[18] To treat his condition they now prescribed six cycles of chemotherapy, for which he would need to remain in America until the end of the year.

From this point onwards, the story of the King's battle for life becomes increasingly intertwined with the struggle over the succession to the throne.[19] As is the nature of Jordanian politics, conspiracy theories about the events of the final six months of the King's reign, and his ultimate decision to change the line of succession, are abundant. But, as we consider the unfolding saga, it is important to keep one central fact in mind: the final decision about the succession was the King's and his alone. For all the political manoeuvring in the background, Hussein ultimately trusted no one else fully. To suggest that he was duped, coerced or smooth-talked into making his choice is to underestimate his accumulated political wisdom. Hussein had seen conspirators come and go before, and he knew the type. He was not about to rely on the advice of others, however persuasive they might be, in making a decision which was crucial to the future of the Hashemite dynasty. Nor is it convincing to suggest that any of the outside players who had an interest in the succession, whether in the region or beyond, had the means at their disposal to decide his choice. They too could try to influence him, but Hussein made his final decision when he had already come to terms with the fact that he was dying. In these circumstances, nothing mattered more to him than the future of his dynasty. Hence, however we approach the question of the succession, we return time and again to one deciding factor: the King's own personal judgement as to the best way to preserve the Hashemite throne.

Much as plotting the King's chances of survival proved an inexact science, the task of pinning down in hindsight when he finally decided to change the line of succession away from Prince Hassan and in favour of Prince Abdullah is necessarily an imprecise one. The King played his hand so close that no one can state with certainty when his final choice was made. What can be said, though, is that he faced in effect two interlinked decisions. Firstly, would Prince Hassan succeed him? Secondly, if not Hassan, who else would he choose?

The Hussein–Hassan relationship had always been a complex one, with some observers describing it as being in some respects more like father and son than brother and brother. Over the years, Hassan had deferred to his elder brother's wishes, occupying himself with tasks in the economic, administrative and intellectual fields, and not seeking to act as a political rival to Hussein. He had often been close to the centre of power, but was not always consulted by his brother about key decisions. During the 1980s, the King had at times questioned the usefulness of the work done by his brother's office, especially since much of its output in the economic and intellectual fields was far too abstract for his own taste. During the 1990s, by contrast, the peace process had given the Crown Prince's office a new lease of life. The key negotiators on the Jordanian team, including Awn Khasawneh and Munther Haddadin, had served the Crown Prince. Thus, although differences had arisen between the two brothers during the King's first visit to the Mayo Clinic in the summer of 1992, with the King feeling that Hassan had shown insufficient solicitude for his wellbeing,[20] these were subsequently partially buried, if not fully forgotten, as the Crown Prince's office provided essential support for the King's subsequent peace-making efforts.

In the midst of these efforts, one further event took place which was crucial in opening the way for Hussein's subsequent decision to change the succession. On 26 April 1994 Queen Zein died in hospital at Lausanne, Switzerland. During the difficult days of King Talal's illness and abdication in the early 1950s, the Queen, aided by Prime Minister Abu'l Huda, had effectively saved the Hashemite dynasty. Then, in the first decade of King Hussein's reign, his mother had been a powerful political figure behind the scenes, exercising what was often a dominating influence over the young King. Although Hussein had moved out of her political shadow from the late 1950s onwards, she remained the pivotal, uniting figure within the extended family. While she lived, she brought all of her children together, and helped to reconcile disputes between them. She was also a steadfast supporter of Hassan's position as Crown Prince. To be sure, Hussein was quite capable of taking decisions about the family which ran against her wishes, but, had she been alive in 1999, it is less likely that the King would have changed the line of succession away from Hassan; at the very least, her advice might have given him further pause for thought. It is, therefore, no coincidence that it was only in October 1994, after Queen Zein's death, that the King formally announced the establishment of the Hashemite Family Council, the ostensible purpose of which was to decide the line of succession in the House of Hashem after Prince Hassan.

Still, there was no immediate threat to Hassan's position during the mid-1990s. The initial success of the peace process provided further evidence of the value of his support for the King, who paid public tribute to his brother's role on several occasions during this period. In a speech on 15 November 1994, the King praised Hassan for exercising his role as Crown Prince with 'loyalty and distinction',[21] and referred to Hassan as 'my right arm' in an open letter in early April 1995.[22] His public expressions of confidence in the Crown Prince continued, and it is arguable that the King's dismissal of Hassan's enemy Prime Minister Abdel Karim Kabariti in March 1997 was a further measure of the Crown Prince's ability to defend his position.

This is not to say that Hassan did not have other powerful opponents. His relationship with his cousin, Sharif Zeid bin Shaker, was a problematical one. The two men were temperamentally different, and held opposing views on important issues such as the peace process with Israel. During the negotiations leading to the agreement of the peace treaty, Zeid bin Shaker had worked behind the scenes, unsuccessfully as it transpired, to discredit the Crown Prince's role. Although Zeid bin Shaker's influence over Hussein was much less pronounced from late 1995 onwards, when the two men fell out over policy towards Iraq, he remained a powerful figure in the Kingdom. One stratagem which he pursued in the final battle over the succession was to circulate the suggestion that Prince Mohammad's son, Prince Talal, might be considered as an alternative compromise candidate for the throne. Although it is most unlikely that the King would have considered such a change, which would have involved the upheaval of disinheriting Prince Hassan without the compensating benefit of installing one of his own sons as heir, the rumour served the purpose of putting Hassan's position under further pressure.

More generally, it is arguable that Hassan was vulnerable because he had failed to build a sufficient personal following in the key institutions which helped underpin the Hashemite regime – the army and the intelligence services. Indeed, in the final phase of the King's reign, when the succession struggle was truly joined, two of the Crown Prince's chief opponents were the Chairman of the Joint Chiefs of Staff, Field Marshal Abdul Hafez Marai Kaabneh, and the Head of General Intelligence, Samih Batikhi. Hassan did of course have his own supporters, but he was not always the best judge of character in others. One source describes the Crown Prince as having attracted the 'worst type of courtier'. Indeed, in his letter of 25 January 1999 to Prince Hassan, the King referred specifically to the activities of Hassan's circle, writing that 'my small family was offended by slandering and falsehoods, and I refer here to my wife and children. When I heard this most of the time, I attributed it to the tendency towards rivalry among those who pretend to be faithful to you and who attribute to you anything good in whatever you do.'[23] It was clear that the King had little time for many of those who clustered around Hassan. But whatever their qualities one fact is evident: the Crown Prince's camp ultimately proved unequal to the challenge of defending Hassan's position as heir to the throne.

One final factor contributing to family tensions should also be mentioned at this stage. Relations between Prince Hassan's wife Princess Sarvath and the King's wife, Queen Noor, were difficult, if not hostile. One of the more persistent rumours about the King's decision to change the succession concerned his apparent dissatisfaction with a series of actions taken by Hassan and Sarvath during his absence in the United States. Of these actions, the one which most titillated the international media was the King's supposed anger at Sarvath's presumption in changing the curtains and other furnishings in the King's offices at the Royal Diwan, which came to be seen as emblematic of an over-hasty attempt to seize the reins of power. Like many of the rumours which circulated during this period, this story was overblown and distorted. It is of course facile to suggest that a difference over drapes influenced the King's final choice over the succession. The root of the tale seems to have lain in the fact that, charged with the task of carrying out official entertainment during the King and Queen's absence, Princess Sarvath had to make some minor alterations when she found that staff at the Diwan had let standards slip somewhat. In the fervid atmosphere of the times, though, these measures were transmuted by the anti-Hassan rumour mill into an attempt to redesign the Diwan interior in premature anticipation of taking permanent charge. Of course, the story was all the more persuasive since it played on the known divide between Sarvath and Noor.

The saga of the curtains was a minor scene in the broader political drama played out from the summer of 1998 onwards. The metaphor is an appropriate one, since what took place in Jordan was effectively a series of staged events, in which the Crown Prince's enemies tried to seize on minor incidents and inflate them into full-blown political crises, while Prince Hassan, for his part, struck back by exercising his expanded prerogatives as regent ever more assertively.[24] In this respect he was aided by a royal decree, issued on 12 August, which empowered him to accept or demand the resignations of ministers and the prime minister, and gave him authority in all areas of governance except for declaring war, entering treaties and amending the constitution.[25] Prince Hassan used this authority to try to manoeuvre his opponents out of important positions and install his own supporters. So, in August, he nominated as Head of the Royal Court Jawad al-Anani, a capable and experienced operator who was to prove one of the Crown Prince's few useful political assets during the course of the succession battle. He acted as Prince Hassan's intermediary to the King, making several trips on his behalf to the Mayo Clinic or the King's private residence at River House, near Washington DC.[26]

If Anani travelled to the United States to defend Prince Hassan's actions, there were others who made the trip with the opposite purpose in mind. One such was Chairman of the Joint Chiefs of Staff, Field Marshal Kaabneh. While the Crown Prince's attempts to interfere in a number of military appointments showed that he realised the importance of installing and promoting his supporters in the army, his actions antagonised Kaabneh, who made his views plain to King Hussein.[27] In his letter of 25 January 1999 to Prince Hassan, the King singled out the latter's actions in this field as having caused him concern, particularly rumours spread by supporters of the prince about possible corruption surrounding a house which was built for the field marshal:

> I have intervened from my sickbed to prevent meddling in the affairs of the Arab Army. This meddling seemed to be meant to settle scores, and included retiring efficient officers known for their allegiance and whose history and bright records are beyond reproach. At the forefront were the Field Marshal and the Chairman of the Joint Chiefs of Staff, who was envied because of a house. I am the one who paid for the house . . . Its costs in no way approach the estimates made by many. That was because of his loyalty and his integrity and because we wanted to give him something commensurate with his rank and position.[28]

Although Kaabneh's role was significant, probably a bigger part in the final campaign against Prince Hassan was played by a triumvirate who are not directly acknowledged in the King's letter: the intelligence chief Samih Batikhi; the former prime minister, Abdel Karim Kabariti, and the Head of Protocol at the Royal Court, Ayman al-Majali. Of these three, Batikhi was the prime mover, and the best placed to undermine the regent. His visits to see Hussein are not recorded in the official archival log, but as head of General Intelligence he had good reason to report to the King in person on developments at home.[29] Meanwhile, Kabariti, who held no official post at this stage, also travelled to the United States to meet the King on 24 October as part of a delegation which included his immediate successor as prime minister, Abdel Salam Majali.[30] Best placed of all to pass on information to the King was Ayman Majali. As the King underwent his painful and debilitating rounds of treatment, punctuated by bouts of recuperation, he was constantly attended only by a very small group of whom Majali was one. The link to Majali gave Batikhi and Kabariti an invaluable direct channel to the King throughout this period.

In terms of their political tactics, the first, and perhaps the most important, of the incidents which was seized on and manipulated by the Batikhi group to try to discredit Prince Hassan was the so-called 'water scandal' of July–August

1998. For a few days during the intense summer heat of July, the water piped into Amman acquired an unusual and unpleasant smell. In fact, this was the result of the unusual heat rather than of any form of pollution. But it was seized on by opponents of the Crown Prince and used as evidence of corruption and negligence in high places. The Water Minister, Munther Haddadin, a known associate of Prince Hassan, and several other current and former Water Authority officials, were accused of failing to exercise proper oversight of the water filtering system. The affair became something of a cause célèbre, with charges of negligence and forgery being brought against nine senior government officials. Munther Haddadin was forced to resign as water minister and he, along with two other former water ministers, was indicted by the Amman Prosecutor's Office for failing to ensure the proper treatment of water delivered to Jordan from Israel's Lake Tiberias. The affair came to the attention of the King, who referred to it in a letter to Prince Hassan, sent from the Mayo Clinic on 7 August.[31] With the purposes of the Batikhi group thus served, the prosecutions against the officials concerned were allowed to languish in court with no further action taken during the course of the year.

At around the same time, another artificial crisis was manufactured surrounding a contract for the disposal of the remaining pipes from the Iraqi Petroleum Company pipeline which, until 1948, had linked the Kirkuk oil refinery to the Mediterranean port of Haifa. A delegation of parliamentary deputies who inspected the pipeline returned claiming that the pipes were still usable and could have been reclaimed to supply water elsewhere in the Kingdom, rather than being sold for scrap. Even to those with the most rudimentary knowledge of hydraulic engineering, the notion that old oil pipes which had lain unused in the ground for fifty years might have a viable second life carrying water must seem fanciful in the extreme. Once again, though, the 'pipeline scandal' served its purpose, streaking briefly across the political firmament and providing further supposed evidence of corruption and incompetence in high places, before disappearing into the black hole of the courts.

In the face of this mounting offensive, Prince Hassan did not remain idle; instead, he promoted two programmes of his own in the hope of out-manoeuvring his enemies. The first was an 'anti-corruption' campaign, and the second a so-called 'national dialogue' with the opposition. The anti-corruption campaign was of course a familiar political device, often used by those with the strongest grip on the reins of power to strike at their opponents. The national dialogue, by contrast, which Prince Hassan persuaded the new government installed under Prime Minister Fayez Tarawneh in August to adopt, was a fresh departure. Its ostensible purpose was to start a dialogue with critics of the regime, such as the Muslim Brotherhood and the anti-normalisation movement, with a view to reuniting the fractured Jordanian body politic. In reality, it may have been a rather desperate attempt on Prince Hassan's part to seek new supporters in unlikely quarters and to distance himself from his reputation as the architect of the unpopular peace with Israel. In any event, the prince met members of the Muslim Brotherhood's executive committee in August, the first such encounter with a senior member of the royal family since 1995.[32] Then, on 12 September, he reappointed to the Senate Taher Masri and Ahmed Obeidat, two former regime stalwarts who had become leading members of the anti-normalisation movement.[33] Finally, in October, the anti-normaliser Laith Shbeilat, who had been jailed for his role in provoking the Maan riots in February, was released from prison. But what had initially seemed a tactically astute move proved to be strategically flawed. Hassan's dialogue with the Islamists caused some alarm in American quarters, and while this on its own would not have been sufficient reason for the United States to oppose his succession, it certainly gave Washington pause for thought.[34] The limited results of the dialogue also called into question Hassan's political judgement, another issue which played a part in Hussein's final decision about the succession to the throne.

But of all the factors which contributed to Hussein's decision to disinherit Hassan, probably the most significant was the Crown Prince's refusal to commit himself through the Family Council to the King's plans for the subsequent succession. Here we do not need to search for hidden plots or conspiracies, because Hussein made his feelings plain in his final letter to Hassan on 25 January 1999:

We differed over [the council] because your opinion was that it should be achieved only when you were at the helm. I placed between your two hands a few papers that I wrote myself. I did not show them to anyone. They consisted of the main tenets of my proposal, and when I received your comments on them, the response did not reflect the spirit of my proposal, nor did they meet the needs of the times.

We have differed, and we still do, over the succession, and who would succeed you. You were completely opposed to this until the time you would have assumed the Throne and decided who would have been your successor.[35]

The King's letter also makes plain why he chose Abdullah as Crown Prince instead. Referring back to Article 28 of the constitution,[36] which provided for primogeniture but which was amended in 1965 to permit Hassan's succession, the King wrote: 'I find that all conditions that originally dictated the exception have passed, and that, therefore, His Royal Highness Prince Abdullah would, in such a case, immediately assume all duties and responsibilities as the Crown Prince of the Hashemite Kingdom of Jordan.'[37] From the constitutional point of view, the case for Abdullah's succession in the event of Hassan's disinheritance was compelling. Indeed, in order to name anyone other than Abdullah or his other brother Mohammad as Crown Prince in place of Hassan, the King would have had to seek a further amendment to the constitution, which as the King himself no doubt recognised, would have risked serious political instability.

What of the widespread rumours that the King had considered the possibility of installing Prince Hamzeh, his eldest son by Queen Noor, as Crown Prince? These dated back to a letter the King wrote to Hamzeh on the occasion of the latter's eighteenth birthday in September 1997. Here the King praised Hamzeh, describing him as being destined for great achievements, and recalling that he himself had acceded to the throne before his eighteenth birthday. There is no doubt that of all his children, Hussein had a particular soft spot for Hamzeh, whom he saw as being closest to him in temperament, outlook and even physical appearance. This affection was made apparent in the King's final letter to Prince Hassan, which included a paragraph praising Hamzeh:

> Hamzeh . . . has been envied since childhood because he was close to me, and because he wanted to know all matters large and small, and all details of the history of his family . . . I have been touched by his devotion to his country and by his integrity and magnanimity as he stayed beside me, not moving unless I forced him from time to time to carry out some duty on occasions that did not exceed the fingers on one hand.[38]

However, at the age of nineteen, Hamzeh lacked the necessary breadth of experience to be chosen ahead of his brothers to accede to the throne. Abdullah, by contrast, aged thirty-seven and with a successful career in the army behind him, could be expected to take up the reins of power immediately. After completing his schooling in Britain and the United States, Prince Abdullah had acquired a wide range of military experience during the 1980s and 1990s, and had steadily advanced through the ranks of the Jordanian officer corps. In this sense Abdullah was out of the same mould as Hussein, a man of action with a military background. His age and experience, alongside the dictates of the constitution, clearly weighed heavily in the King's final decision over the succession. Abdullah's army background and the support of intelligence chief Batikhi meant that there would be no problems in terms of the two key security institutions of the state. Finally, external players, including the main Arab states and the Western powers, would welcome Abdullah's succession. His education in the United States and his subsequent role in the army meant that his American connections were excellent, and he had also successfully cultivated a network of contacts amongst the younger generation of the royal families of the Gulf States.

It is impossible to state exactly when Hussein made his decision to replace Hassan with Abdullah. However, we can make an informed guess based on the King's public statements and the testimony of those close to him. The first and obvious point to make is that the King is unlikely to have made a final decision on the succession until the need became pressing – in other words, when he realised that he would not recover. It is likely that the King saw Hassan's extended regency, especially with the extra powers he delegated to him from 12 August onwards, as a good test of his brother's exercise of power, giving Hussein the opportunity to see what Jordan might look like under Hassan as king. In a letter to Hassan on 7 August, the King expressed his full confidence in him, writing: 'I am following with much appreciation all that you are doing in the service of our homeland and I support you and stand by you; my confidence in you [is] unwavering and my hopes in you [are] great.'[39]

The King's doubts started to grow during September and October, as a succession of visitors, including Field Marshal Kaabneh, former prime minister Kabariti and intelligence chief Batikhi, painted a negative picture of events in Jordan under Hassan's regency. Indeed, the earliest suggested date that the King may have decided on a change in the succession is in mid-October.[40] On 14 October, the King received a telephone briefing from Hassan on meetings he had held with PLO Chairman Arafat and Israeli Prime Minister Netanyahu.[41] The fact that Hassan, citing his responsibilities as regent, did not fly over to spend time at the King's bedside, but contented himself instead with such occasional telephone contact, no doubt furthered the process of alienation between the two brothers. The King was also offended by an interview the Crown Prince gave to the *New York Times*, reported in a 1 November article titled 'King Hussein Ails: His Brother Waits', which he saw as part of an attempt to prepare the ground for his succession.[42] However, Hussein is unlikely to have taken his final decision at this stage. The positive messages issued in mid-November about the outcome of his chemotherapy, including a statement made by the Mayo Clinic on 13 November describing him as being 'in complete remission from lymphoma', also suggest that up to this point the King's health still gave him no pressing need to make the final choice.[43]

However, between this point and his departure from the United States at the beginning of January, the King does appear to have made up his mind. One common theme in all of the oral accounts is that by the time the King arrived in London on 6 January, for a recuperative stopover on his way back to Jordan, he had made his decision about the succession. It is likely that doubts about the duration of his remission and the success of the bone-marrow transplant performed during his sixth cycle of chemotherapy played a role here. So too did the accumulated evidence about the nature of the regency supplied to him by Hassan's enemies. But, with his own mortality pressing on him, it was a father's natural desire to be succeeded by his son, together with his judgement as to who was most likely to secure the future of the Hashemite dynasty, which proved the deciding factors.

What Hussein said to Hassan on the subject when the latter visited him in London on 8 January is unclear. In public neither man gave much away. Hassan told the press after the meeting, that 'for me to have this opportunity as a brother to see my brother for the first time in six months was delightful. I think our eyes dewed.' As Hassan spoke to reporters, tears welled up in his eyes once again.[44] In a major television address delivered from London just over a week later on 16 January, the King promised to launch a programme of sweeping political reforms on his return to Jordan. Unnamed senior political sources hinted that these would include revisiting the issue of the succession.[45]

The final unfolding of the succession saga began with Hussein's return to Jordan on 19 January 1999. During the welcoming ceremony at the airport Hassan was sidelined, a sure sign that his fate had already been decided. Then, in an interview with the CNN correspondent Christiane Amanpour the following day, the King refused to endorse Hassan as his successor. Despite praising his contribution over the years as Crown Prince, the King commented, 'it was I who did bring about and canvass for the alternative in our Constitution that enables a brother to take over at times. But that didn't mean at all that it was the end of the story'.[46] When pressed once again for a straight 'yes' or 'no' as to whether Hassan would succeed him, the King refused to answer, saying, 'I'm not prepared to say anything, so please don't commit me to anything whatsoever because I really haven't come up with anything — I have only thoughts and ideas'. Whatever his thoughts and ideas were, his refusal to endorse Hassan's succession was telling.

On 22 January the King met once again with his brother. There is no independent and reliable account of what passed between them, but, over the next three days, the King devoted all of his remaining energy first to formulating and then drafting a letter to Hassan announcing his replacement as Crown Prince by Abdullah. On the afternoon and evening of 25 January, the King painstakingly wrote the letter out, passing it one page at a time to his son, Prince Hashem, who typed it up. No one else was allowed to enter the room. While Hussein was drafting the letter, Prince Hassan called three times in a desperate last-ditch attempt to change his brother's mind. It was to no avail. Hussein refused to take his calls. The tone of the letter was very harsh. No doubt the King wanted to make his decision about the succession public in such a way that there could be no subsequent questioning of his intentions. Some commentators have subsequently described the letter as 'rambling'.[47] It is true that the letter contained some quite long, and apparently not directly relevant, digressions, but these also had their purpose for those who knew how to interpret them. Perhaps the longest such digression concerned the dangers of biological weapons and the threat posed to mankind by environmental degradation. More specifically, referring to the link between skin cancer and holes in the ozone layer, the King commented, 'no doubt other forms of cancer result from environmental pollution in the atmosphere, in addition to smoking'.[48] The causes of cancer had doubtless been much on the King's mind as he endured his second battle with the disease, which some might see as a sufficient explanation for this particular passage. Another interpretation is that he was trying to signal his belief that his own condition might have been man-made rather than natural. That this question had been on the minds of the royal couple is also reflected in Queen Noor's account of the King's illness. In the wake of the Mossad assassination attempt against Khaled Meshal in September 1997, she notes that 'half in jest I started to call my husband's malady the Bibi virus [Bibi was Netanyahu's nickname], alluding to a bizarre bioterrorism episode that fall'. And later:

> Though I teased about the Bibi virus, one could not help but wonder at times: it was impossible to ignore the fact that my husband was very popular in Israel; many Israelis told us that they would gladly exchange Hussein for Bibi. Might it be politically expedient for Netanyahu to remove a credible moderate Arab voice from the increasingly polarized region?[49]

Noor was not alone in her suspicions. Other members of Hussein's close family who take this theory seriously point to an incident in the autumn of 1997, just after the Meshal affair and shortly before the first symptoms of Hussein's illness appeared. After carrying out a public engagement, Hussein noticed that he had sustained a scratch on his arm which drew blood. The belief of those who accept this theory is that some sort of viral agent had been introduced into his bloodstream via this scratch, which triggered his subsequent illness.[50] However, there is no further evidence to support this theory. In fact, one former member of the King's medical team has directly dismissed it, subsequently insisting that there is no way that the King's condition could have been artificially induced.[51] The lack of hard medical evidence means that, despite the beliefs of close family members, the theory that Hussein did not die a natural death must remain no more than that.

The long-rumoured news of the change in the succession became public with the issuing of a royal decree making Abdullah Crown Prince late on Monday 25 January.[52] The decree was followed by the publication of the

King's letter to Hassan, and was further confirmed in a letter the King sent to Crown Prince Abdullah on 26 January.[53] Whilst these events were unfolding, the King's health had taken a serious turn for the worse. The cancer had returned, and his doctors told him that his only remaining slim chance for survival was to return to the United States for a further bone-marrow transplant. On 26 January, a mere week after his triumphant return to Amman, the King flew out bound once again for the Mayo Clinic. The deterioration in his health within the space of a few days was startling. Hussein himself knew the end was near, and as he left the royal palace for the last time, he made a point of stopping to speak to everyone to say his final farewell. During the flight over to the United States his condition deteriorated dramatically, and he had to be artificially resuscitated.

This time round Hussein proved too weak to endure the aggressive course of chemotherapy necessary before the bone-marrow transplant. Although a letter sent on his behalf to Israeli President Ezer Weizman as late as 2 February still promised, 'I shall be undergoing a further transplant of bone marrow within the next few days', sadly it was not to be.[54] As Hussein's respiration began to fail, it was decided to fly him back to Jordan so that he could die at home. On 5 February, the King's plane landed back in Amman after a long and tense flight. He was rushed to the intensive-care unit at the King Hussein Medical Centre, where his whole family, except Prince Hassan, gathered to pay their final respects. Hassan's absence during the King's final hours was a sad end to what had been, for more than three decades, a successful political and personal partnership. No doubt Hassan had made mistakes as regent, but no one could question his ultimate loyalty to his brother. Indeed, it was his refusal to tell a lie before Hussein, and commit himself to a scheme for the succession in which he did not believe, which proved his final undoing. The fact that Hussein died with the two brothers unreconciled was a burden which Hassan would have to bear for the rest of his life.

Just before noon on 7 February, Hussein died in his hospital bed. It was not the end he had hoped for, having always spoken of dying a martyr, like his grandfather, or Yitzhak Rabin. But no doubt, with his sense of fatalism, he would have accepted his lot anyway. After the drama of the final weeks of January, the succession when the time came was smooth and orderly. King Abdullah cut a dignified figure, articulating his own and the nation's grief in a television address after his father's death. Despite the divisions caused by the succession crisis, the whole family, including Prince Hassan, assumed a united front in support of the new King. The international stature which King Hussein had achieved, not only through the longevity of his reign, but also through his personal dignity and humanity, was amply reflected in the extraordinary gathering of world leaders who flew to Amman for his funeral on 8 February. But although the public spectacle of mourning was a remarkable one, with large crowds lining the streets of Amman to share the King's final journey, the private expressions of sympathy passed on to his son also said much about Hussein the man.

President Clinton, who had come to know Hussein well during the final years of his life, wrote to King Abdullah describing his father as an extraordinary man for whom his friendship and admiration knew no bounds. Reflecting on their final meeting, when Hussein had celebrated the New Year in Washington on his way back from the Mayo Clinic, the president wrote:

> I had the honor of seeing him just a few weeks before he passed away, as he was about to return home. There was no hint of the extraordinary effort he was undertaking to stay alive. Instead, he spoke with his customary passion and humanity about his nation's well-being; the future of the Arab world; the fulfilment of the Palestinians' legitimate rights; and peace with Israel. At that moment, I saw once again the depth of his love for his country, his dedication to peace and his commitment to the universal values of tolerance and mutual respect.
>
> I will forever cherish that memory along with so many others I have of your father. He was an inspiration and a model for us all . . .[55]

Clinton's friendship with the King may have been relatively short in terms of the overall history of his reign, but he had hit upon some of its key themes with uncanny precision. Perhaps the only element missing in his letter is Hussein's concern for the dignity and destiny of the Hashemite family. The King would have been happy to be remembered as someone who fought for Jordan's wellbeing, the future of the Arab world, the Palestinians' rights and peace with Israel. To be sure, he had had to make difficult choices along the way. He had also been faced with setbacks and deep frustrations. Not the least of these was the relative weakness of his position when it came to influencing the future development of the Arab world. This was a theme to which he returned repeatedly over the years, including during his final television interview, when he commented, 'the worst part was that there were many crises that passed through this area that I could see coming and I warned and did whatever I could to prevent them happening. But no one listened. Those are moments of failure and disappointment.'[56] When he thought of such crises no doubt the King was mulling over the fall of the Hashemite dynasty in Iraq in 1958, the 1967 and 1973 Arab–Israeli wars, and the 1990 Iraqi invasion of Kuwait. But it had been in September 1970 that he had had to make the hardest choice of all, ultimately deciding to put the survival of his throne first when faced with the Palestinian fedayeen challenge. This was a move for which some Palestinians would never forgive him.

If the battle in 1970 for the survival of the Hashemite regime was one expression of the contested nature of Hussein's destiny, his turbulent relations with his regional neighbours over the years was another. Probably the most ambivalent of all of these relationships was that with Israel. The view that Hussein maintained what amounted to a covert strategic partnership with Israel from the early 1960s onwards has taken such root in the interpretations of Israeli scholars and of Arabs, especially those hostile to him, that it has become almost a shibboleth. It is true that Hussein pursued a covert dialogue, and that he sought a compromise peace settlement with Israel, especially in the immediate aftermath of the 1967 war. But there are two essential qualifications which need to be made to this thesis. The first is that Hussein continued throughout this period to see Israel as a potential threat to his kingdom. Hussein's handling of relations with Israel was founded on the old adage: keep your friends close, and your enemies closer still. One of the main purposes of his secret dialogue was to establish and maintain contacts on the other side which might help deflect the threat Israel posed to Jordan. During the September 1970 crisis, the King feared Israeli occupation and annexation of Jordanian territory if the collapse of his regime appeared imminent. In later years, particularly after the Likud Party rose to political power, the King's fears were centred more around the demographic threat; might the Likud choose to solve the problem of the occupied West Bank by expelling the Palestinians to Jordan? These fears persisted into the 1990s, and influenced the King's handling of the Madrid peace process, and the subsequent bilateral negotiations.

The second essential qualification is that Hussein steadfastly refused for three decades the Israeli invitation to reach a bilateral peace deal. For him, the covert negotiations were only ever intended to open the way to a comprehensive peace agreement between Israel and the Arab states. He paid a high price for this refusal, particularly in the wake of the 1978 Camp David deal between Israel and Egypt. But it was not until after the Palestinians had made their historic decision to engage in the Oslo process, and after serious negotiations had begun on the Israeli–Syrian track, that Hussein felt able to reach a Jordanian–Israeli peace treaty.

In terms of his broader relations with his Arab neighbours, meanwhile, the King's ideology of Hashemite destiny was an unavoidable source of tension. Hussein's belief that the Hashemites were destined to provide leadership for the Arab nation made it natural that he would concern himself with pan-Arab politics. Specifically, because of the Union of the Two Banks under his grandfather, and the subsequent loss of the West Bank to Israel in 1967, he always believed that he was both destined and duty-bound to play a role in the resolution of the Palestinian question. But, beyond this, the lost Hashemite patrimony in Iraq always remained close to his heart from 1958 onwards, resurfacing in his support in the mid-1990s for direct attempts to overthrow the Baathist regime. Probably the one direction in which his dynastic ambitions did not run was paradoxically that in which they might have had the strongest claim: that of the lost Hashemite lands in the Hejaz. Despite persistent Saudi suspicions, amply illustrated in the Gulf crisis of 1990–91, that the King nurtured secret ambitions to win back the Hejaz, this was the point at which ideology was trumped by realism. Saudi Arabia was under American protection; there was no prospect of a Hashemite restoration, so Hussein did not pursue it.

Hussein's ideology was often an impediment in inter-Arab politics: it made other more powerful players suspicious of his intentions and often limited his room for manoeuvre. So, during 1995–6, both the Egyptian and Syrian regimes opposed his activities in relation to Iraq. Indeed, there was a tendency across the years for all of the big three secular Arab states – Egypt, Iraq and Syria – to treat Jordan under Hussein as an upstart in regional politics which should be better aware of its place in the Arab pecking order. The Egyptian and Syrian regimes, amongst others, sought the overthrow of his regime on several occasions. Whether it was the Baghdad Pact riots of December 1955, the putative army coup of April 1957, the assassination of Hazza Majali in August 1960, the Nasser-backed army plot of April 1963, the Syrian invasion of September 1970, the northern border tensions of December 1980 or the Abu Nidal terror campaign of the mid-1980s, to name but a few, his powerful neighbours maintained a conveyor belt of threats to his regime. That Hussein survived these many challenges is a testimony not only to his own good judgement but also to the strength of the institutions he had built in Jordan to support the Hashemite regime. Vital among these, and certainly pivotal to his survival in September 1970, was the army. But, in addition, the effective internal intelligence services, initially established by Mohammad Rasool Kilani in the 1960s and built up under successive heads of the Mukhabarat, were also a vital prop for the regime. But there remained an essential personal element in his survival. As the King's close friend Prince Charles put it in the memorial service held for him at St Paul's Cathedral, London, on 5 July 1999, 'it was surely the King's magnanimity and far-sightedness, together with his other personal qualities, that enabled him to survive – and triumph over – the enormous challenges to his country and to himself'.[57]

What became, then, of Hussein's Hashemite destiny? In the end, it found no other outlet than the defence and development of Jordan. Indeed, under his son, King Abdullah, 'Jordan first' has become a slogan of the Hashemite regime. In part this is a simple recognition of domestic and regional realities. Hashemite destiny, despite the historical precedent of the Great Arab Revolt, was always a quixotic ideology in the face of the hard-headed realities of power.

Indeed, by the beginning of the 1990s the King himself, at the same time as reasserting his own Hashemite ideology, had already begun to warn of two impending changes in the region. The first, about which he proved to have more foresight than many, was the challenge presented by a new wave of militant Islamism. As early as 1990, Hussein had warned his Mossad contact Efraim Halevy as to the dangers posed by this 'growing trend of extremism' which could 'wreak havoc throughout the Middle East'.[58] The King was also candid about what he saw as the Saudi role in fostering the movement, in part as a counter-weight to accusations of complicity in the Western-led war against Iraq in 1990–91.

The second development of which the King warned was what he termed the imposition of a new Sykes–Picot agreement on the region. Here he had in mind an imperialist redrawing of Arab borders reminiscent of the secret deal between the French and British which had preceded the post-1918 carve-up of the Ottoman Empire. In his controversial 6 February 1991 speech during the Gulf conflict, the King had warned that Washington and its allies sought 'to destroy Iraq and to rearrange the regional state of affairs in a manner that would be far more serious for the present and future of our nation than what had been arranged by the Sykes–Picot treaty. Our homeland, nation, aspirations and resources will thus be placed under direct foreign hegemony'.[59] In the wake of the Anglo-American invasion and occupation of Iraq in 2003, Hussein's fears seem even more prescient. The potential for the collapse and carve-up of the Iraqi nation-state is real. But this is where we return to the apparently quixotic nature of the ideology of Hashemite destiny. The fate of Iraq shows that there was after all scope for revolutionary change in the region, just not of the Hashemite kind championed by Hussein.

If the fulfilment of his broader Hashemite destiny proved ultimately to be beyond Hussein's grasp within his lifetime, what were his real achievements? Certainly, Jordan itself underwent significant change during his reign. But how far the economic, social and political development of the state was due to his personal agency is a matter for debate. What can be said is that the survival of the Hashemite regime under his leadership across half a century provided what was in regional terms an unusually stable political foundation. On this base, longer-term economic and social planning was feasible, even if the ambitious goals set by the regime were not always met. Also his success in overseeing the modernisation of Jordan has to be judged in relation to the assets with which he worked. Jordan was not blessed (some would say cursed) with economically extractable oil reserves. Its natural resources were few. Indeed, in some areas, particularly that of water resources, it was faced with potentially critical shortages. On top of this, the country had to deal with three major influxes of refugees, in 1948–9, 1967 and 1990–91. Viewed against the backdrop of these challenges, Hussein's personal contribution in facilitating the stability and development of the Kingdom was a significant one.

The King himself would no doubt have seen the achievement of peace with Israel via the 1994 treaty as one of his greatest achievements. In view of the weak and isolated position in which he found himself in the wake of the Gulf crisis, the terms of the final agreement were indeed favourable from the Jordanian point of view. Jordan secured a generous water allocation and a satisfactory demarcation of its border with Israel, and also avoided being separated from the wider Arab community. Furthermore, to some extent the treaty neutralised the demographic threat posed by possible Israeli actions in the occupied territories, although the compromise terms of the 'transfer' clause itself later gave the King pause for reflection. But the subsequent dividends of peace were not those for which the King had hoped. The 'cold peace' of which he had often warned was precisely what he got under Rabin's successors. Jordan was taken for granted by Israel, or, at the very least, not accorded the sort of respect for which the King had hoped. From the Jordanian side, Hussein fought a losing battle against the anti-normalisation campaign, which profited from the lack of any significant economic or political advantage for Jordan as a result of the peace treaty.

Closely linked to the development of the peace process and the anti-normalisation movement is the question of Jordan's democratisation under Hussein. Compared to that of other Arab states, the Jordanian political system which he bequeathed to his successor was relatively open, liberal and democratic. But there were clear limits to the King's tolerance for the process of democratisation. In the wake of the 1989 election, there was an effective, Islamist-led parliamentary opposition, but alterations to the electoral law brought in from the 1993 election onwards served to curtail its size and potency. Similarly, the expression of dissenting opinions in the press and in public was permitted, but there were clear red lines which could not be crossed, including criticism of the royal family and of 'friendly states'. As the peace process faltered, Hussein became increasingly exasperated by the activities of the opposition. At heart, he was more of a paternalist than a democrat. He certainly believed that it was he who knew what was best for Jordan.

Perhaps Hussein's greatest legacy, then, lay more in what he strove for than in what he was able to achieve.[60] For all that the element of dynastic self-interest complicated his statecraft over the years he was still a genuine seeker of peace and reconciliation in the Middle East. This search for reconciliation went beyond the simple resolution of national conflicts. For Hussein, it also had an inter-faith dimension. The formulation to which he returned again and again in describing the making of peace with Israel was that of bringing together the 'children of Abraham'. If the tide of peacemaking in the region had begun to ebb by the time he died, it was not for want of dedication on his part. He had striven as best he could to fulfil his contested destiny.

SELECT BIBLIOGRAPHY

Primary Sources

Archives

Jimmy Carter Library, Atlanta, Georgia, USA (JCL)
Dwight D. Eisenhower Library, Abilene, Kansas, USA (DDEL)
Gerald R. Ford Library, Ann Arbor, Michigan, USA (GRFP)
Lyndon B. Johnson Library, Austin, Texas, USA (LBJL)
John F. Kennedy Library, Boston, Mass., USA (JFKL)
National Library of Jordan, Amman, Jordan
Royal Hashemite Archives, Basman Palace, Amman (RHA)
  The following files were consulted: Britain; Egypt; Iran; Iraq; Israel, Post-1992; Kuwait;
  MENA Summit; Organisation of the Islamic Conference; PLO; Qatar; Saudi Arabia;
  Soviet Union; Syria; United States: Files for Presidents Eisenhower, Kennedy, Johnson,
  Nixon, Ford, Carter, Reagan, Bush, Clinton
United Kingdom National Archives, Kew, Surrey, UK (TNA)
  Prime Minister's Office (PREM)
  Foreign Office, later Foreign and Commonwealth Office (FO, FCO)
  Ministry of Defence (DEFE)
  Cabinet (CAB)
United Kingdom Cabinet Office: UK Freedom of Information Act (2000) (UKFOIA)
  Prime Minister's Office Files, records of meetings with King Hussein, 1976–84 (released
  at author's request)
United States National Archives, College Park, Maryland, USA (USNA)
  RG59: State Department Records
  Richard Nixon Presidential Papers (*RNPP*)

Printed Documentary Sources

Documents on the Foreign Policy of Israel, 1947–60 (companion volumes)
White Paper: Jordan and the Gulf Crisis, August 1990 – March 1991 (Amman: Government
  of Jordan, 1991)

Memoirs

Abbas, M., *Through Secret Channels: The Road to Oslo* (Reading: Garnet Publishing, 1995)
Baker, J., *The Politics of Diplomacy* (New York: G. P. Putnam's Sons, 1995)
Brown, G., *In My Way: The Political Memoirs of Lord George-Brown* (London: Victor Gollancz, 1971)
Brzezinski, Z., *Power and Principle: Memoirs of the National Security Adviser, 1977–81* (London: Weidenfeld & Nicolson, 1983)
Bush, G. and Scowcroft, B., *A World Transformed* (New York: Vintage Books, 1999)
Carter, J., *Keeping Faith: Memoirs of a President* (New York: Bantam Books, 1982)
Dayan, M., *The Story of My Life* (London: Weidenfeld & Nicolson, 1976)
Eban, A., *An Autobiography* (London: Weidenfeld & Nicolson, 1977)
——, *Personal Witness* (London: Jonathan Cape, 1992)
Eisenhower, D.D., *Waging Peace* (London: Heinemann, 1966)
Glubb, J., *A Soldier with the Arabs* (London: Hodder & Stoughton, 1957)
Haig, A., *Inner Circles: How America Changed the World* (New York: Warner Books, 1992)
Halevy, E., *Man in the Shadows* (London: Weidenfeld & Nicolson, 2006)
Heath, E., *The Autobiography of Edward Heath: The Course of My Life* (London: Hodder & Stoughton, 1998)
Hussein bin Talal, *Uneasy Lies the Head* (London: Heinemann, 1962)
——, Vance, V. and Lauer, P., *My War with Israel* (London: Peter Owen, 1969)
Khaled bin Sultan, *Desert Warrior* (London: Harper Collins, 1995)
Kirkbride, A., *From the Wings: Amman Memoirs, 1947–51* (London: Frank Cass, 1976)
Kissinger, H., *White House Years* (New York: Little Brown, 1979)
——, *Years of Upheaval* (Boston: Little Brown, 1979)
——, *Years of Renewal* (New York: Simon & Schuster, 1999)
Macmillan, H., *Tides of Fortune, 1945–1955* (London: Macmillan, 1969)
Majali, A.S.A., Anani, J.A. and Haddadin, M.J., *Peacemaking: The Inside Story of the 1994 Jordanian–Israeli Treaty* (Reading: Ithaca Press, 2006)
Meir, G., *My Life* (London: Weidenfeld & Nicolson, 1975)
Noor, Queen, *Leap of Faith: Memoirs of an Unexpected Life* (London: Weidenfeld & Nicolson, 2003)
Peres, S., *Battling For Peace* (London: Orion Books, 1996)
Rabin, Y., *The Rabin Memoirs* (London: Weidenfeld & Nicolson, 1979)
Rafael, G., *Destination Peace: Three Decades of Israeli Foreign Policy* (New York: Stein and Day, 1981)
Riad, M., *The Struggle for Peace in the Middle East* (London: Quartet Books, 1981)
Ross, D., *The Missing Peace* (New York: Farrar, Strauss and Giroux, 2004)
Shamir, Y., *Summing Up: An Autobiography* (London: Weidenfeld & Nicolson, 1994)
Shultz, G., *Turmoil and Triumph: My Years as Secretary of State* (New York: Charles Scribner's Sons, 1993)
Vance, C., *Hard Choices: Critical Years in America's Foreign Policy* (New York: Simon & Schuster, 1983)

Media Sources

BBC Summary of World Broadcasts (SWB)
Daily Mail
The Economist
Economist Intelligence Unit, Country Reports, Jordan (EIU)
Evening Standard
Foreign Broadcast Information Service (FBIS)
The New York Times
Sunday Express

Sunday Telegraph
The Times
Washington Post

Web Sources

Arab Defence Pact http://www.yale.edu/lawweb/avalon/mideast/arabjoin.htm
Arab League Charter http://www.yale.edu/lawweb/avalon/mideast/arableag.htm
Burr, W., *The October War and US Policy*, National Security Archive http://www.gwu.edu/
    ~nsarchiv/NSAEBB/NSAEBB98/index.htm#doc7
CIA Freedom of Information Act Reading Room http://www.foia.cia.gov/
Constitution of Jordan http://www.kinghussein.gov.jo/constitution_jo.html
Declassified Documents Reference System (DDRS) (via university subscription)
Egyptian–Israeli Peace Treaty http://www.yale.edu/lawweb/avalon/mideast/isregypt.htm
Foreign Relations of the United States (FRUS), 1952–68, http://www.state.gov/r/pa/ho/frus/
Israel's Foreign Relations: Selected Documents (Vols 1–18, 1947–2001) http://www.mfa.gov.il/
    MFA/MFAArchive/2000_2009/2002/7/Israel-s%20Foreign%20Relations-
    %20Selected%20Documents
Jordanian–Israeli Peace Treaty http://www.yale.edu/lawweb/avalon/mideast/jordan
    treaty.htm and http://www.kinghussein.gov.jo/peacetreaty.html
King Hussein's office http://www.kinghussein.gov.jo/library.html
King Hussein's letters and speeches http://www.kinghussein.gov.jo/speeches_letters.html
King Hussein's calendar, 1998 http://www.kinghussein.gov.jo/archive.html
Nixon Presidential Library, Virtual Library, Mandatory Review Documents,
    http://nixon.archives.gov/virtuallibrary/documents/mandatoryreview.php#selection
United Nations Charter http://www.un.org/aboutun/charter/chapter7.htm
United Nations official documents system http://daccessdds.un.org
United Nations Security Council Resolutions http://www.un.org/documents/scres.htm
Volcker Report (Independent Inquiry Committee into the United Nations Oil-For-Food
    Programme – IIC) http://www.iic-offp.org/story27oct05.htm
Washington Declaration http://www.yale.edu/lawweb/avalon/mideast/pal06.htm
Woods, K.M., Pease, M.R., Stout, M.E., Murray, W. and Lacey, J.G., *Iraq Perspectives
    Project: A View of Operation Iraqi Freedom from Iraq's Senior Leadership* (2006),
    http://www.jfcom.mil/newslink/storyarchive/2006/ipp.pdf (*IPP*)

Author's Interviews

King Abdullah bin Hussein, Amman, 5 July 2007
Maan Abu Nowar, Oxford, 5 December 2000
Adnan Abu Odeh, Amman, 14 April 2000
Mudar Badran, Amman, 20 May 2001
Princess Basma, London, 4 October 2007
James Crawford, Cambridge, 21 November 2000
Munther Haddadin, Amman, 25 February 2007
Awn al-Khasawneh, The Hague, 24 June 2000, 17 February 2001, 17 March 2007
Turki al-Khraisha, Amman, 22 May 2001
Mohammad Rasool Kilani, Amman, 22 May 2001
Henry Kissinger, New York, 2 June 2003
Ahmed al-Lawzi, Amman, 3 September 2001
Abdul Salam al-Majali, Amman, 11 April 2000.
Mahmud al-Mu'ayta, Amman, 5 September 2001
Richard Murphy, New York, 29 March 2001
Queen Noor, Ascot, 10 July 1999

Hazem Nusseibeh, Amman, 4 September 2001
Thomas Pickering, Washington DC, 28 September 2007
Marwan al-Qasim, Amman, 17 April 2000, 23 May 2001, 26 September 2002
Zeid Rifai, Amman, 24 September 1999, 5 June 2002, 4 July 2007
Zeid bin Shaker, Amman, 23 March 2000
Ali Shukri, Amman, 26 February 2007
Roscoe Suddarth, Washington DC, 23 March 2001
Prince Talal bin Muhammad, Amman, 22 May 2001
Fayez al-Tarawneh, Amman, 6 June 2002

I have spoken to a number of other individuals who asked to remain anonymous.

Secondary Sources

Books

Abidi, A.H., *Jordan: A Political Study, 1948–1957* (London: Asia Publishing House, 1965)
Abu Jaber, K.S., 'Jordan and the Gulf War', in Ismael, T.Y. and Ismael, J.S., *The Gulf War and the New World Order* (Gainesville: University of Florida Press, 1994)
Abu Nowar, M., *The History of the Hashemite Kingdom of Transjordan, Vol. I: The Creation and Development of Transjordan, 1920–1929* (Oxford: Ithaca Press, 1989); *Vol. II: The Development of Trans-Jordan, 1929–1939* (Amman, The National Library, 1997); *Vol. III: The Struggle for Independence, 1939–1947* (Oxford: Ithaca Press, 2001)
Abu Odeh, A., *Jordanians, Palestinians and the Hashemite Kingdom in the Middle East Peace Process* (Washington DC: United States Institute of Peace, 1999)
Alkadiri, R., 'The Palestinian Factor in Jordanian Foreign Policy, 1967–88', in Schulze, K. E. et al. (eds) *Nationalism, Minorities and Diasporas: Identities and Rights in the Middle East* (London: Tauris Academic Studies, 1996)
Almog, O., *Britain, Israel and the United States, 1955–1958: Beyond Suez* (London: Frank Cass, 2003)
Antonius, G., *The Arab Awakening* (London: Hamish Hamilton, 1938)
Aruri, N., *Jordan: A Study in Political Development, 1921–65* (The Hague: Martinus Nijhoff, 1972)
Ashton, N.J., *Eisenhower, Macmillan and the Problem of Nasser* (London: Macmillan, 1996)
Bailey, C., *Jordan's Palestinian Challenge, 1948–1983: A Political History* (Boulder: Westview Press, 1984)
Bar-Joseph, U., *The Best of Enemies: Israel and Transjordan in the War of 1948* (London: Frank Cass, 1987)
——, *The Watchman Fell Asleep: The Surprise of Yom Kippur and Its Sources* (Albany: State University of New York Press, 2005)
Bar-Zohar, M., *Yaacov Herzog: A Biography* (London: Halban Publishers, 2005)
Ben Zvi, A., *The American–Israeli Alliance: Jordanian Origins* (London: Routledge, 2007)
Blackwell, S., *British Military Intervention and the Struggle for Jordan: King Hussein, Nasser and the Middle East Crisis, 1955–58* (London: Routledge, 2009)
Bligh, A., *The Political Legacy of King Hussein* (Brighton: Sussex Academic Press, 2002)
Boulby, M., *The Muslim Brotherhood and the Kings of Jordan, 1945–1993* (Atlanta: Scholars Press, 1999)
Brand, L.A., *Jordan's Inter-Arab Relations: The Political Economy of Alliance Making* (New York: Columbia University Press, 1994)
Braziat, M., *The Jordanian–Palestinian Relationship: The Bankruptcy of the Confederal Idea* (1998)
Caplan, N., *Futile Diplomacy* (London: Cass, 4 vols, 1983–97)
Cockburn, A. and Cockburn, P., *Out of the Ashes: The Resurrection of Saddam Hussein* (New York: Harper Perennial, 2000)

Dallas, R., *King Hussein: A Life on the Edge* (London: Profile Books, 1998)

Dann, U., *King Hussein and the Challenge of Arab Radicalism* (Oxford: OUP, 1989)

Dawn, C.E., 'The Rise of Arabism in Syria', in *From Ottomanism to Arabism: Essays on the Origins of Arab Nationalism* (Urbana: University of Illinois Press, 1973)

Eisenberg, L.Z. and Caplan, N., *Negotiating Arab–Israeli Peace: Patterns, Problems, Possibilities* (Bloomington: Indiana University Press, 1998)

El-Edross, S.A., *The Hashemite Arab Army, 1908–1979* (Amman, 1980)

Freedman, L. and Karsh, E., *The Gulf Conflict, 1990–1991: Diplomacy and War in the New World Order* (Princeton: Princeton University Press, 1993)

Garfinkle, A., *Israel and Jordan in the Shadow of War: Functional Ties and Futile Diplomacy in a Small Place* (New York: St Martin's Press, 1992)

Gelvin, J.L., *The Israel–Palestine Conflict* (Cambridge: CUP, 2005)

George, A., *Jordan: Living in the Crossfire* (London: Zed Books, 2005).

Ghazi bin Muhammad, *The Tribes of Jordan at the Beginning of the Twenty-First Century* (Amman: 1999)

Graves, P. (ed.), *Memoirs of King Abdullah of Transjordan* (London: Jonathan Cape, 1950)

Gubser, P., *Jordan: Crossroads of Middle East Events* (Boulder: Westview Press, 1983)

Hart, A., *Arafat: A Political Biography* (Bloomington: Indiana University Press, 1989)

Heikal, M., *Illusions of Triumph: An Arab View of the Gulf War* (London: Harper Collins, 1992)

——, *Secret Channels: The Inside Story of Arab–Israeli Peace Negotiations* (London: Harper Collins, 1996)

Hiro, D., *The Longest War: The Iran–Iraq Military Conflict* (London: Paladin, 1990)

Horovitz, D. (ed.), *Shalom Friend: The Life and Legacy of Yitzhak Rabin* (New York: Newmarket Press, 1996)

Hourani, A. (ed.), *The Emergence of the Modern Middle East* (London: Macmillan, 1981)

Israeli, R., *Palestinians between Israel and Jordan* (New York: Praeger, 1991)

Jankowski, J., *Nasser's Egypt, Arab Nationalism and the United Arab Republic* (Boulder: Lynne Rienner, 2002)

Jentleson, B.W., *With Friends Like These: Reagan, Bush and Saddam, 1982–1990* (New York: W.W. Norton & Company, 1994)

Joffé, G., *Jordan in Transition, 1990–2000* (London: Hurst & Co., 2002)

Johnston, C., *The Brink of Jordan* (London: Hamish Hamilton, 1972)

Karsh, E. and Kumaraswamy, P.R., *Israel, the Hashemites and the Palestinians: The Fateful Triangle* (London: Frank Cass, 2003)

Khalidi, R. (ed.), *The Origins of Arab Nationalism* (New York: Columbia University Press, 1991)

al-Khazender, S., *Jordan and the Palestine Question: The Role of Islamic and Left Forces in Foreign Policy Making* (Reading: Ithaca Press, 1997)

Kissinger, H., *Crisis: The Anatomy of Two Major Foreign Policy Crises* (New York: Simon & Schuster, 2003)

Kramer, M., *Arab Awakening and Islamic Revival* (New Brunswick: Transaction Publishers, 1996)

Kyle, K., *Suez* (London: Weidenfeld & Nicolson, 1991)

Louis, W.R. and Owen, R., *A Revolutionary Year: The Middle East in 1958* (London: I.B. Tauris, 2002)

Lukacs, Y., *Israel, Jordan and the Peace Process* (Syracuse: Syracuse University Press, 1997)

Lunt, J., *Hussein: A Political Biography* (London: Macmillan, 1989)

Lynch, M., *State Interests and Public Spheres: The International Politics of Jordan's Identity* (New York: Columbia University Press, 1999)

Madfai, M., *Jordan, the United States and the Middle East Peace Process* (Cambridge: CUP, 1993)

Marr, P., *The Modern History of Iraq* (2nd edn, Boulder: Westview Press, 2004)

Melman, Y. and Raviv, D., *Behind the Uprising: Israelis, Jordanians, and Palestinians* (Westport: Greenwood Press, 1989)

Milton-Edwards, B. and Hinchcliffe, P., *Jordan: A Hashemite Legacy* (London: Routledge, 2001)

Morris, B., *Israel's Border Wars: Arab Infiltration, Israeli Retaliation and the Countdown to the Suez War* (Oxford: OUP, 1993)

Mutawi, S., *Jordan in the 1967 War* (Cambridge: CUP, 1987)

Nevo, J., *King Abdallah and Palestine: A Territorial Ambition* (Basingstoke: Macmillan, 1996)

Nevo, J. and Pappe, I., *Jordan in the Middle East, 1948–88* (London: Frank Cass, 1994)

Oren, M., *Six Days of War: June 1967 and the Making of the Modern Middle East* (Oxford: OUP, 2002)

Parker, R.B., *The October War: A Retrospective* (Gainesville: University Press of Florida, 2001)

Paterson, P., *Tired and Emotional: The Life of Lord George-Brown* (London: Chatto & Windus, 1993)

Quandt, W., *Peace Process: American Diplomacy and the Arab–Israeli Conflict since 1967* (Washington DC: Brookings Institution Press, 1993)

Quandt, W.B., *Camp David: Peacemaking and Politics* (Washington DC: Brookings Institution, 1986)

Rathmell, A., *Secret War in the Middle East* (London: Tauris Academic Studies, 1995)

Reynolds, D., *Summits: Six Meetings that Shaped the Twentieth Century* (London: Allen Lane, 2007)

Robins, P., *A History of Jordan* (Cambridge: CUP, 2004)

Rogan, E.L., *Frontiers of the State in the Late Ottoman Empire: Transjordan, 1850–1921* (Cambridge: CUP, 1999)

Ryan, C., *Jordan in Transition: From Hussein to Abdullah* (Boulder: Lynne Rienner Publishers, 2002)

Salibi, K., *The Modern History of Jordan* (London: I.B. Tauris, 1993)

Satloff, R., *From Abdullah to Hussein* (Oxford: OUP, 1994)

Sayigh, Y., *Armed Struggle and the Search for State: The Palestinian National Movement, 1949–1993* (Oxford: OUP, 1997)

Schenker, D., *Dancing With Saddam: The Dangerous Tango of Jordan–Iraq Relations* (Washington DC: Washington Institute for Near East Policy, 2003)

Seale, P., *Asad of Syria: The Struggle for the Middle East* (London: I.B. Tauris, 1988)

Shalom, Z., *The Superpowers, Israel and the Future of Jordan, 1960–3: The Perils of the Pro-Nasser Policy* (Brighton: Sussex Academic Press, 1998)

Shemesh, M., *The Palestinian Entity, 1959–74: Arab Politics and the PLO* (London: Frank Cass, 1988)

Shlaim, A., *Collusion Across the Jordan* (Oxford: Clarendon Press, 1988)

——, *The Iron Wall: Israel and the Arab World* (London: Allen Lane, 2000)

Shlaim, A. and Rogan, E., *The War for Palestine: Rewriting the History of 1948* (Cambridge: CUP, 2001)

Snow, P., *Hussein: A Biography* (London: Barrie & Jenkins, 1972)

Stein, K.W., *Heroic Diplomacy: Sadat, Kissinger, Carter, Begin, and the Quest for Arab–Israeli Peace* (New York: Routledge, 1999)

Susser, A., *On Both Banks of the Jordan: A Political Biography of Wasfi al-Tall* (London: Frank Cass, 1994)

——, *The Hashemites in the Modern Arab World* (London: Cass, 1995)

——, *Jordan: Case Study of a Pivotal State* (Washington DC, 2000)

Tal, L., *Politics, the Military and National Security in Jordan, 1955–67* (Basingstoke: Palgrave Macmillan, 2002)

Tibi, B., *Arab Nationalism: A Critical Inquiry* (London: Macmillan, 1981)

Tripp, C., *A History of Iraq* (2nd edn, Cambridge: CUP, 2002)

Vatikiotis, P.J., *Politics and the Military in Jordan* (London: Frank Cass, 1967)

Wiktorowicz, Q., *The Management of Islamic Activism: Salafis, the Muslim Brotherhood, and State Power in Jordan* (Albany: State University of New York Press, 2000)

Wilson, M., *King Abdullah, Britain and the Making of Jordan* (Cambridge: CUP, 1987)
Yaqub, S., *Containing Arab Nationalism: The Eisenhower Doctrine and the Middle East* (Chapel Hill: The University of North Carolina Press, 2004)

Articles

Alon, Y., 'Tribal Shaykhs and the Limits of British Imperial Rule in Transjordan, 1920–46', *Journal of Imperial and Commonwealth History*, 32/1, 2004
Andoni, L., 'King Abdallah: In His Father's Footsteps?', *Journal of Palestine Studies*, 29/3, 2000
Ashton, N.J., 'Britain and the Kuwait Crisis, 1961', *Diplomacy & Statecraft*, 9/1, 1998
Baram, A., 'Baathi Iraq and Hashemite Jordan: From Hostility to Alignment', *Middle East Journal*, 45/1, 1991
Brand, L.A., 'Liberalization and Changing Political Conditions: The Bases of Jordan's 1990–91 Gulf Crisis Policy', *Jerusalem Journal of International Relations*, 13/4, 1991
——, 'The Effects of the Peace Process on Political Liberalization in Jordan', *Journal of Palestine Studies*, 28/2, 1999
Edmonds, J., 'The Evolution of British Labour Party Policy on Israel from 1967 to the Intifada', *Twentieth Century British History*, 11/1, 2000
Elmusa, S.S., 'The Jordan–Israel Water Agreement', *Journal of Palestine Studies*, 24/3, 1995
Gat, M., 'Letting Someone Else Do the Job: American Policy on the Eve of the Six Day War', *Diplomacy and Statecraft*, 14/1, 2003
——, 'Britain and the Occupied Territories after the 1967 War', *MERIA*, 10/4, 2006
Gause, F.G., 'Iraq's Decision to Go to War: 1980 and 1990', *Middle East Journal*, 56/1, 2002
Gerges, F.A., 'The Kennedy Administration and the Egyptian–Saudi Conflict in Yemen: Co-opting Arab Nationalism', *Middle East Journal*, 49/2, 1995
Greenwood, S., 'Jordan's "New Bargain": The Political Economy of Regime Security', *Middle East Journal*, 57/2, 2003
Jones, M., 'The "Preferred Plan": The Anglo-American Working Group Report on Covert Action in Syria, 1957', *Intelligence and National Security*, 19/3, 2004
Kahana, E., 'Early Warning versus Concept: The Case of the Yom Kippur War 1973', *Intelligence and National Security* 17/2, 2002
Khadduri, M., 'Nuri al-Sa'id's Disenchantment with Britain in his Last Years', *Middle East Journal*, 54/1, 2000
Lesch, A.M., 'Contrasting Reactions to the Persian Gulf Crisis: Egypt, Syria, Jordan and the Palestinians', *Middle East Journal*, 45/1, 1991
Levey, Z., 'US Arms Policy toward Jordan, 1963–8', *Journal of Contemporary History*, 41/3, 2006
Little, D., 'The New Frontier on the Nile: JFK, Nasser, and Arab Nationalism', *Journal of American History*, 75/2, 1988
——, 'A Puppet in Search of a Puppeteer? The United States, King Hussein and Jordan, 1953–1970', *International History Review*, 17/3, 1995
Lucas, R.E., 'Jordan: The Death of Normalization with Israel', *Middle East Journal*, 58/1, 2004
Maddy-Weitzman, B., 'Jordan and Iraq: Efforts at Intra-Hashemite Unity', *Middle Eastern Studies*, 26/1, 1990
Milton-Edwards, B., 'Jordan and Façade Democracy', *British Journal of Middle East Studies*, 20/3, 1993
Mufti, M., 'Elite Bargains and the Onset of Political Liberalization in Jordan', *Comparative Political Studies*, 32/1, 1999
——, 'A King's Art: Dynastic Ambition and State Interest in Hussein's Jordan', *Diplomacy and Statecraft*, 13/3, 2002
Pedatzur, R., 'Coming Back Full Circle: The Palestinian Option in 1967', *Middle East Journal*, 49/2, 1995

Podeh, E., 'To Unite or Not to Unite – That is *Not* the Question: The 1963 Tripartite Unity Talks Reassessed', *Middle Eastern Studies*, 39/1, 2003

Quandt, W.B., 'Lyndon Johnson and the June 1967 War: What Colour Was the Light?', *Middle East Journal*, 46/2, 1992

Raad, Z., 'A Nightmare Avoided: Jordan and Suez 1956', *Israel Affairs*, 1/2, 1994

Robins, P., 'Shedding Half a Kingdom: Jordan's Dismantling of Ties with the West Bank', *British Journal of Middle Eastern Studies*, 16/2, 1989

Robinson, G.E., 'Defensive Democratization in Jordan', *International Journal of Middle East Studies*, 30/3, 1998

Ryan, C., 'Jordan and the Rise and Fall of the Arab Cooperation Council', *Middle East Journal*, 52/3, 1998

Shemesh, M., 'The IDF Raid on Samu: The Turning Point in Jordan's Relations with Israel and the West Bank Palestinians', *Israel Studies*, 7/1, 2002

Shlaim, A., 'His Royal Shyness: King Hussein and Israel', *The New York Review of Books*, 15 July 1999

Terrill, W.A., 'The Political Mythology of the Battle of Karameh', *Middle East Journal*, 55/1, 2001

Wiktorowicz, Q., 'The Limits of Democracy in the Middle East: The Case of Jordan', *Middle East Journal*, 53/4, 1999

Zak, M., 'Israel and Jordan: Strategically Bound', *Israel Affairs*, 3/1, 1996

Working Papers

Shulman, D., 'Amman's About Face: Jordanian Foreign Policy in the US-led Wars against Iraq, 1990–91 and 2003', http://www.yale.edu/polisci/info/Workshops/IR/10-13-06-Shulman.pdf

NOTES

Introduction: A Contested Destiny

1. Hussein to Major, 20 May 1992, British File, RHA.
2. Hussein to Reagan, 7 August 1981, President Reagan File, RHA.
3. Hussein to Reagan, 17 November 1986, President Reagan File, RHA.
4. Hussein, interview with Christiane Amanpour, 24 January 1999, http://www.king hussein.gov.jo/interviews_press.html (accessed 24 April 2007).
5. Group Captain J.M.A. Parker, Annual and Valedictory Report, 1 January 1973, FCO93/87, TNA.
6. Hussein to Bush, 1 November 1989, President Bush File, RHA.
7. Amman to CIA, 22 March 1963, Folder Jordan General 11/62–3/63, Box 125A, National Security File, JFKL.
8. Dann, U., *King Hussein and the Challenge of Arab Radicalism* (Oxford: OUP, 1989), pp. 128–9.
9. Hussein to J.A. Speares, 8 January 1973, British File, RHA.
10. Brown to Kissinger, 2 June 1976, Amman telegram no. 2954, NSA Country File Middle East/South Asia, Box 23, Folder Jordan State Dept telegrams, To SecState Nodis (26), GRFP.

Chapter 1: The Tragedy of King Talal

1. The best study of this is Eugene Rogan's *The Frontiers of the State in the Late Ottoman Empire: Transjordan, 1850–1921*(Cambridge: CUP, 1999).
2. Antonius, G., *The Arab Awakening* (London: Hamish Hamilton, 1938), p. 149.
3. ibid, p. 153.
4. Hussein to Reagan, 7 August 1981, President Reagan File, RHA.
5. Important scholarly contributions to the debate about the origins and nature of Arab nationalism sparked by Antonius include: Dawn, C.E., 'The Rise of Arabism in Syria', in *From Ottomanism to Arabism: Essays on the Origins of Arab Nationalism* (Urbana: University of Illinois Press, 1973); Tibi, B., *Arab Nationalism: A Critical Inquiry* (London: Macmillan, 1981); Hourani, A. (ed.), *The Emergence of the Modern Middle East* (London: Macmillan, 1981); Khalidi, R. (ed.), *The Origins of Arab Nationalism* (New York: Columbia University Press, 1991); Kramer, M., *Arab Awakening and Islamic Revival* (New Brunswick: Transaction Publishers, 1996).

6.   Although most of the letters are brief, Hussein's correspondence with Glubb is more extensive and longer-lasting than that with any other private individual in his files. For the reference to Jordan as 'our country' see Glubb to Hussein, undated [January 1978], British File, RHA. For the comment that he would always remain a Jordanian see Glubb to Hussein, undated [1972], ibid.

7.   Nevo, J., *King Abdallah and Palestine* (London: Macmillan, 1996), pp. 12–15.

8.   ibid, pp. 60–3.

9.   Wilson, M.C., *King Abdullah, Britain and the Making of Jordan* (Cambridge: Cambridge University Press, 1987), pp. 148–50.

10. Rogan, E.L. and Shlaim A., *The War for Palestine* (Cambridge: Cambridge University Press, 2001), pp. 104–24, provides a useful summary of the evolving debate.

11. Bar-Joseph, U., *The Best of Enemies* (London: Frank Cass, 1987), pp. 197–237.

12. Pirie-Gordon to Burrows, 12 July 1949, FO371/75316, TNA.

13. ibid.

14. Kirkbride, A., *From the Wings: Amman Memoirs, 1847–1951* (London: Frank Cass, 1976), p. 121.

15. See for example Troutbeck to Bowker, 17 January 1952, FO371/98898, TNA.

16. Glubb, J.B., *A Soldier with the Arabs* (London: Hodder & Stoughton, 1957), p. 281.

17. Pirie-Gordon to Burrows, 12 July 1949, FO371/75316, TNA.

18. Kirkbride to Burrows, 21 October 1948, FO371/68864, TNA; Satloff, R., *From Abdullah to Hussein* (Oxford: OUP, 1994), pp. 15–16.

19. Pirie-Gordon to Burrows, 12 July 1949, FO371/75316, TNA.

20. Kirkbride, *From the Wings*, p. 122.

21. Pirie-Gordon to Burrows, 12 July 1949, FO371/75316, TNA; Satloff, *From Abdullah to Hussein*, pp. 16–17.

22. Tal, L., *Politics, the Military and National Security in Jordan, 1955–1967* (Basingstoke: Palgrave Macmillan, 2002), p. 16.

23. Pirie-Gordon to Burrows, 12 July 1949, FO371/75316, TNA.

24. ibid.

25. Amman to Foreign Office, 9 May 1951, FO371/91836, TNA.

26. Pirie-Gordon to Burrows, 12 July 1949, FO371/75316, TNA.

27. Amman to Foreign Office, 27 December 1950, FO371/91836, TNA.

28. Amman to Foreign Office, 9 May 1951, ibid.

29. Kirkbride to Furlonge, 17 May 1951, ibid.

30. ibid.

31. ibid.

32. Bailey to Furlonge, 22 May 1951, ibid; Kirkbride to Furlonge, 17 May 1951, ibid; Satloff, *From Abdullah to Hussein*, p. 18.

33. Kirkbride to Furlonge, 2 June 1951, FO371/91836, TNA.

34. Walker to Furlonge, 18 June 1951, ibid; Walker to Furlonge, 2 July 1951, ibid.

35. ibid.

36. Walker to Furlonge, 11 July 1951, ibid. Since this important file was only opened for research on 20 May 2004, there is no discussion of what proved to be Abdullah's most significant, final promise in respect of the succession in Robert Satloff's otherwise comprehensive account of this period (*From Abdullah to Hussein*, pp. 18–22).

37. Hussein bin Talal, *Uneasy Lies the Head* (London: Heinemann, 1962), p. 4.

38. Amman to Foreign Office, 21 July 1951, telegram no. 241, FO371/91836, TNA.

39. Geneva to Foreign Office (for Amman), 21 July 1951, telegram no. 29, ibid.

40. Geneva to Foreign Office (for Amman), 21 July 1951, telegram no. 26, ibid.

41. Amman to Foreign Office (for Geneva), 23 July 1951, telegram no. 249, ibid.

42. Amman to Foreign Office, 22 July 1951, telegram no. 246, ibid.

43. Furlonge to Bowker, 29 September 1952, FO371/98909, TNA.

44. Amman to Foreign Office, 15 August 1951, FO371/91836, TNA.
45. Furlonge to Kirkbride, 14 August 1951, ibid.
46. Snow, P., *Hussein* (London: Barrie & Jenkins, 1972), pp. 38–9.
47. Robert Satloff, who did not have the benefit of seeing the record of Abdullah's last conversation about the succession with Nayif, expresses puzzlement about Nayif's persistence in pursuing his claim to the throne (*From Abdullah to Hussein*, p. 38).
48. To date, no firm evidence has come to light as to why the British government failed to act on King Abdullah's final wishes regarding the succession and support Nayif's claim. However, the successful covert advocacy of Talal's wife, Sharifa Zein, may well have played a role. When I asked Princess Basma, Zein's daughter, about this episode she commented, 'My mother had her own channels to the British government' (Interview, Princess Basma, London, 4 October 2007).
49. Kirkbride to Younger, 'Proposed Federation between Jordan and Iraq', 1 October 1951, FO371/91798, TNA.
50. Troutbeck to Eden, 14 January 1952, FO371/98898, TNA.
51. Hussein, *Uneasy Lies the Head*, pp. 13, 21.
52. Furlonge to Bowker, 31 March 1952, FO371/98898, TNA.
53. Medical Certificate for Queen Zein of Jordan, issued by Prof. Dr A. Vannotti, undated [June 1952], FO371/98904, TNA.
54. Furlonge to Bowker, 31 March 1952, FO371/98898, TNA.
55. ibid.
56. Furlonge to Bowker, 5 April 1952, ibid.
57. 'The Emir Hussein', memorandum by Wardrop, 17 March 1952, ibid.
58. 'The Emir Hussein of Jordan', memorandum by Ross, 3 April 1952, ibid.
59. Stevenson to Barclay, 27 March 1952, ibid.
60. Furlonge to Bowker, 14 April 1952, ibid.
61. Furlonge to Ross, 28 April 1952, FO371/98899, TNA; Furlonge to Ross, 2 May 1952, ibid.
62. Furlonge to Bowker, 15 May 1952, FO371/98900, TNA; Furlonge to Bowker, 19 May 1952, ibid; Furlonge to Eden, 'Summary of Events Leading up to the Departure of King Talal from Jordan', 30 May 1952, ibid.
63. Paris to Foreign Office, 30 May 1952, ibid.
64. Paris to Foreign Office, 31 May 1952, ibid.
65. Paris to Foreign Office, 1 June 1952, ibid. Hussein told his House Matron, Audrey Miskin, about the attack after his return to Harrow (Snow, *Hussein*, p. 45).
66. Paris to Foreign Office, 1 June 1952, FO371/98900, TNA.
67. Paris to Foreign Office, 3 June 1952, ibid.
68. Satloff, *From Abdullah to Hussein*, p. 53.
69. Amman to Foreign Office, enc. message from Jordan Prime Minister to Queen Zein, 7 August 1952, FO371/98906, TNA.
70. Satloff, *From Abdullah to Hussein*, p. 56.
71. Furlonge to Bowker, 29 September 1952, FO371/98909, TNA.
72. Barclay to Furlonge, 30 June 1952, FO371/98904, TNA.
73. Amman to Foreign Office, 28 August 1952, FO371/98908, TNA.
74. Wardrop to Furlonge, 2 September 1952, ibid.
75. 'King Hussein', memorandum by J.M. Hunter, 8 September 1952, FO371/98909, TNA.
76. Bowker to Furlonge, 1 December 1952, FO371/98911, TNA.
77. Report made by the Commandant, The Royal Military Academy Sandhurst on Officer Cadet King Hussein 10 September – 30 November 1952, ibid.
78. Dawnay to Wardrop, 29 November 1952, ibid.
79. Furlonge to Bowker, 11 December 1952, FO371/98912, TNA.
80. Troutbeck to Bowker, 16 December 1952, ibid.
81. Furlonge to Bowker, 10 February 1953, FO371/104960, TNA.
82. Memorandum by A.D.M. Ross, 15 January 1953, FO371/104959, TNA.

83.   'A King's Romance', 19 January 1953, *Evening Standard*.
84.   'Royal Tunes', 1 March 1953, *Sunday Express*.
85.   For a summary of Hussein's final weeks in Britain see Baker to Furlonge, 6 April 1953, FO371/104962, TNA.
86.   Amman to Foreign Office, 19 March 1953, FO371/104961, TNA.
87.   Furlonge to Bowker, 14 April 1953, FO371/104890, TNA.
88.   Furlonge to Eden, 9 May 1953, FO371/104963, TNA.
89.   Hussein, *Uneasy Lies the Head*, p. 20.
90.   The High Tribunal, headed by the President of the Senate, Zeid Rifai, could have been requested to judge the conformity of the King's actions to the provisions of the constitution. See Article 122: http://www.kinghussein.gov.jo/constitution_jo.html (accessed 16 May 2007).
91.   Satloff, *From Abdullah to Hussein*, p. 74.

Chapter 2: Breaking the British Connection, 1953–6

1.   Robins, P., *A History of Jordan* (Cambridge: CUP, 2004), pp. 73–4; 82–7.
2.   http://www.kinghussein.gov.jo/constitution_jo.html
3.   Shlaim, A., 'His Royal Shyness: King Hussein and Israel', *New York Review of Books*, 15 July 1999, p. 14.
4.   'Queen Zein of Jordan', 4 December 1952, PREM11/188, TNA.
5.   Furlonge to Allen, 8 January 1954, FO371/110882, TNA.
6.   Amman to Foreign Office, 17 February 1954, ibid.
7.   Furlonge to Allen, 8 January 1954, ibid.
8.   Satloff, *From Abdullah to Hussein*, p. 75.
9.   Interview, Mahmud Mu'ayta, Amman, 5 September 2001.
10.   Interviews, Marwan Qasim, Amman, 17 April 2000, 26 September 2002.
11.   Satloff, *From Abdullah to Hussein*, p. 76.
12.   Summary Record of the Conference of US Chiefs of Mission in the NEA Area, Istanbul, 11–14 May 1954, WHO, NSC Staff, OCB Central File Series, Box 77, Folder OCB 091.4 Near East, File #17(1) May 1954 – March 1955, DDEL.
13.   See: Morris, B., *Israel's Border Wars: Arab Infiltration, Israeli Retaliation and the Countdown to the Suez War* (Oxford: OUP, 1993), pp. 246–7; Glubb, J.B., *A Soldier with the Arabs* (London: Hodder & Stoughton, 1957), p. 313; Satloff, *From Abdullah to Hussein*, p. 82 for different estimates of the casualty figures. The editors of Volume 8 (1953) of the series *Documents on the Foreign Policy of Israel* (hereafter *DFPI*) estimate between 42 and 56 persons killed (editorial note, document 426, pp. 357–8).
14.   Eban to Rafael, 15 October 1953, document 432, *DFPI*, Vol. 8, 1953.
15.   Satloff, *From Abdullah to Hussein*, p. 82.
16.   Summary Record of the Conference of US Chiefs of Mission in the NEA Area, Istanbul, 11–14 May 1954, WHO, NSC Staff, OCB Central File Series, Box 77, Folder OCB 091.4 Near East, File #17(1) May 1954 – March 1955, DDEL.
17.   'Queen Dina of Jordan', undated [1955], character sketch, FO371/115717, TNA.
18.   Duke to Macmillan, 25 April 1955, FO371/115715, TNA.
19.   Duke to Hadow, 14 July 1955, FO371/115718, TNA.
20.   'Sharif Nasir bin Jamil', undated character profile, NSF, Country File, Box 148, Folder Jordan: Informal Working Visit of Hussein 11/6–9/67 [2 of 2], LBJL.
21.   Richmond to Shuckburgh, 21 May 1955, FO371/115716, TNA.
22.   Amman to Foreign Office, 26 November 1955, FO371/115720, TNA.
23.   Amman to Foreign Office, 25 May 1955, FO371/115716, TNA.
24.   Duke to Hadow, 4 June 1955, FO371/115717, TNA.
25.   Brant to Hadow, 23 February 1956, FO371/121602, TNA.
26.   Bowker to Rose, 21 August 1956, FO371/121603, TNA.

27.   Duke to Cheke, 3 August 1956, ibid.
28.   Mason to Rose, 13 September 1956, ibid.
29.   ibid.
30.   Hussein, *Uneasy Lies the Head*, p. 57.
31.   'Hussein's Friend Flavia Races Away From It All', *Daily Mail,* 16 October 1956.
32.   Johnston to Rose, 5 March 1957, FO371/127990, TNA.
33.   Weir to Figg, 19 January 1962, FO371/164142, TNA.
34.   Henniker-Major to Figg, 17 February 1962, ibid.
35.   Hussein to Prime Minister John Major, 20 May 1992, British File, RHA.
36.   Snow, *Hussein*, p. 71.
37.   Satloff, *From Abdullah to Hussein*, p. 105.
38.   ibid.
39.   Meeting with Malik, 9 February 1955, Box 1, John Foster Dulles, General Correspondence, DDEL.
40.   Ashton, N.J., *Eisenhower, Macmillan and the Problem of Nasser* (London: Macmillan, 1996), pp. 49–50.
41.   Dann, *King Hussein*, p. 26.
42.   Macmillan, H., *Tides of Fortune, 1945–1955* (London: Macmillan, 1969), p. 656.
43.   Shuckburgh to Kirkpatrick, 24 October 1955, PREM11/1418, TNA.
44.   ibid.
45.   Satloff, *From Abdullah to Hussein*, pp. 112–14.
46.   Kyle, K., *Suez* (London: Weidenfeld & Nicolson, 1991), p. 90.
47.   Amman to Foreign Office, 10 December 1955, PREM11/1418, TNA.
48.   ibid.
49.   Amman to Foreign Office, 7 December 1955, ibid.
50.   Amman to Foreign Office, 10 December 1955, ibid.
51.   Amman to Foreign Office, 13 December 1955, ibid.
52.   ibid.
53.   Report by General Sir Gerald Templer on his Mission to Jordan, 16 December 1955, FO371/115658, TNA.
54.   Amman to Foreign Office, 21 December 1955, PREM11/1418, TNA.
55.   Dann, *King Hussein*, p. 29.
56.   Jankowski, J., *Nasser's Egypt, Arab Nationalism and the United Arab Republic* (Boulder: Lynne Rienner, 2002), pp. 79–81, argues that the Egyptian role in fomenting the riots has been overstated.
57.   Saud to Hussein, 21 January 1956, Saudi Arabia File, RHA.
58.   Hussein to Saud, 26 January 1956, ibid.
59.   Glubb, *Soldier*, p. 300.
60.   Interview, Turki al-Khraisha, Amman, 22 May 2001.
61.   Interview, Mahmud Mu'ayta, Amman, 5 September 2001.
62.   According to Marwan Qasim, the officers normally met at Zerqa which accounts for Mahmud Mu'ayta's recollection. However, on this particular occasion, he argues, they met instead at Zeid bin Shaker's house (interview, Marwan Qasim, Amman, 26 September 2002).
63.   Contact had been in abeyance since Hussein's spring 1953 meeting with Abu Shahut and Ali Abu Nowar at Ambassador Mulqi's reception (interview, Mahmud Mu'ayta, Amman, 5 September 2001).
64.   Interview, Mahmud Mu'ayta, Amman, 5 September 2001. See also Satloff, *From Abdullah to Hussein*, pp. 138–41.
65.   Glubb, *Soldier*, pp. 422–8.
66.   Duke to Foreign Office, 1 March 1956, PREM11/1419, TNA.
67.   Duke to Foreign Office, 6 March 1956, ibid.
68.   Duke listed their names as being Ali Hiyari, Ali Abu Nowar, Radhi Abdulla, Mazen Ajlouni, Lieutenant Qussous (Duke to Foreign Office, 4 March 1956, telegram no. 317, ibid).

69. Duke to Foreign Office, 2 March 1956, ibid.
70. Note by Kirkbride, 8 March 1956, ibid.
71. 'Notes on the Jordan Situation by Sir A. Kirkbride', 8 March 1956, ibid.

Chapter 3: To Hold a Throne, 1956–7

1. Hussein to Saud, Quwatly and Nasser, 17 March 1956, Saudi Arabia File, RHA.
2. This passage is based on conversations with Maan Abu Nowar, Marwan Qasim and Mahmud Mu'ayta. For detailed analysis of the factions which developed within the army see Tal, *Politics, the Military and National Security in Jordan, 1955–1967*, pp. 31–2.
3. See Duke's report of an abortive move against Abu Nowar by Mahmud Rusan, his former superior, whom he had had posted to Arab Legion HQ as his assistant (Amman to Foreign Office, 17 April 1956, PREM11/1420, TNA).
4. Graham to Cairncross, 4 April 1956, PREM11/1415, TNA.
5. Eden to Lloyd, 15 April 1956, PREM11/1420, TNA.
6. Note by Bishop, 16 April 1956, ibid. Duke to Foreign Office, 7 April 1956, ibid.
7. Foreign Office to Amman, 17 April 1956, ibid.
8. Interview, Mahmud al-Mu'ayta, Amman, 5 September 2001.
9. 'The Situation in Jordan Following General Glubb's Dismissal', Duke to Lloyd, 22 March 1956, PREM11/1420, TNA.
10. 'My conclusions and queries', memorandum by Kirkbride, 8 March 1956, PREM11/1419, TNA.
11. Hussein's letter in Amman to Foreign Office, 28 July 1956, PREM11/1422, TNA.
12. Duke to Foreign Office, 29 July 1956, ibid.
13. Foreign Office to Amman, 3 August 1956, ibid.
14. Note by Bishop, 9 August 1956, ibid.
15. Duke to Foreign Office, 29 July 1956, ibid.
16. Text of Hussein's letter in Amman to Foreign Office, 28 July 1956, ibid.
17. Raad, Z., 'A Nightmare Avoided: Jordan and Suez 1956', *Israel Affairs*, 1/2, 1994, p. 290.
18. Duke to Foreign Office, 4 September 1956, PREM11/1422, TNA.
19. Quwatly to Hussein, 3 October 1956, Syria File, RHA.
20. Raad, 'A Nightmare Avoided', pp. 291–7.
21. Foreign Office to Amman, 30 September 1956, PREM11/1422, TNA.
22. Duke to Foreign Office, 4 October 1956, ibid.
23. Morris, *Israel's Border Wars*, pp. 397–400.
24. Hussein to Saud, undated [early November 1956], Saudi Arabia File, RHA.
25. Duke to Foreign Office, 1 November 1956, PREM11/1422, TNA.
26. Dann, *King Hussein*, p. 41; interview with Hazem Nusseibeh, Amman, 4 September 2001; Kyle, *Suez*, p. 399.
27. Hussein to Eisenhower, 2 November 1956, AWF, International Series, Box 35, Folder Jordan, The (4), DDEL. Eisenhower replied in cordial terms on 4 November, ibid.
28. Satloff, *From Abdullah to Hussein*, p. 156.
29. Johnston, C., *The Brink of Jordan* (London: Hamish Hamilton, 1972), pp. 35, 37.
30. Foreign Office to Washington, 16 January 1957, FO371/127900, TNA.
31. Satloff, *From Abdullah to Hussein*, p. 159.
32. See Quwatly to Hussein, 26 March 1957, Syria File, RHA; Quwatly to Hussein, 27 March 1957, ibid.
33. Satloff, *From Abdullah to Hussein*, p. 162.
34. This information comes from private sources and I have been asked to withhold the full name of the individual.
35. Private information. For the 'suitcases of cash' story see Little, 'A Puppet in Search of a Puppeteer', p. 523.

36. Satloff, *From Abdullah to Hussein*, pp. 164–5.
37. Hussein, *Uneasy Lies the Head*, pp. 134–5.
38. This account is based on Hussein, *Uneasy Lies the Head*, pp. 137–51; Satloff, *From Abdullah to Hussein*, pp. 166–8; Dann, *King Hussein*, pp. 57–9; Johnston, *The Brink of Jordan*, pp. 51–64, and author's interviews with Mahmud al-Mu'ayta, Maan Abu Nowar and Zeid bin Shaker.
39. Johnston to Foreign Office, 15 April 1957, PREM11/1913, TNA.
40. Tal, *Politics*, pp. 46–9.
41. Hussein, *Uneasy Lies the Head*, p. 145.
42. Telephone Call from Allen Dulles, 29 April 1957, John Foster Dulles Papers, Telephone Calls Series, Box 6, Folder Memoranda Tel.Con.-General March 1957 – 30 April 1957(1), DDEL.
43. 'The Crisis in Jordan: The Trial of Strength', Johnston to Lloyd, 3 June 1957, PREM11/1913, TNA.
44. Wright (in Baghdad) to Foreign Office, 15 April 1957, FO371/127878, TNA.
45. Little, 'A Puppet in Search of a Puppeteer', p. 524; Caccia to Foreign Office, 24 April 1957, PREM11/1913, TNA.
46. Telephone Call, Augusta, 25 April 1957, AWF, DDE Diary Series, Box 23, Folder April 1957 Phone Calls, DDEL.
47. Satloff, *From Abdullah to Hussein*, pp. 171–2.
48. Telephone Call from Allen Dulles, 25 April 1957, John Foster Dulles Papers, Telephone Calls Series, Box 6, Folder Memoranda Tel.Con.-General March 1957 – 30 April 1957(1), DDEL.
49. Record of a meeting between King Hussein and King Saud, Riyadh, 26 April 1957, Saudi Arabia File, RHA. The document is headed 'secret and not for publication'.
50. Hussein to Saud, 25 June 1957, Saudi Arabia File, RHA.
51. Johnston to Foreign Office, 3 July 1957, FO371/127880, TNA.
52. ibid.
53. Johnston to Foreign Office, 'The Crisis in Jordan: The Trial of Strength', 3 June 1957, PREM11/1913, TNA.

Chapter 4: A Dynasty Under Threat, 1957–61

1. Dann, *King Hussein*, pp. 68–70.
2. State to Amman, 7 May 1957, RG59, Central Decimal File, 785.5-MSP/5-757, USNA.
3. Dann, *King Hussein*, p. 71. For alternative methods of supplying military assistance to Jordan see Rountree to Dulles, 7 June 1957, RG59, Central Decimal File, 785.5-MSP/6-757, USNA; Mallory to State, 16 June 1957, 785.5-MSP/6-1657, ibid.
4. Hussein to Saud, 18 August 1957, Saudi Arabia File, RHA.
5. This description of the 'Preferred Plan' is based on Jones, M., 'The "Preferred Plan": The Anglo-American Working Group Report on Covert Action in Syria, 1957', *Intelligence and National Security*, 19/3, 2004.
6. Yaqub, S., *Containing Arab Nationalism: The Eisenhower Doctrine and the Middle East* (Chapel Hill: The University of North Carolina Press, 2004), pp. 159–60.
7. ibid, p. 163.
8. ibid, p. 168.
9. Ashton, *Eisenhower*, pp. 130–31.
10. Jankowski, *Nasser's Egypt*, pp. 81–2, presents a more positive picture of Egyptian–Jordanian relations during this period.
11. ibid, pp. 106–14.
12. Hussein to Saud, 7 February 1958, Saudi Arabia File, RHA.

13. Hussein, *Uneasy Lies the Head*, pp. 155–9.
14. Amman to FO, 2 June 1958, PREM11/3026, TNA; Acland to Phelps, 'King Hussein's Visit, April 1959', 20 April 1959, ibid.
15. Ashton, *Eisenhower*, p. 146.
16. Hussein to Saud, 6 June 1958, Saudi Arabia File, RHA.
17. Dann, *King Hussein*, p. 80.
18. Memorandum of Conversation, 9 June 1958, AWF, International Series, Box 24, Folder Macmillan–President, 6/1/58–9/30/58 (7), DDEL.
19. Private information.
20. Interview, Mohammad Rasool Kilani, Amman, 22 May 2001.
21. Private information.
22. See also Hussein, *Uneasy Lies the Head*, pp. 160–61.
23. Dann, *King Hussein*, p. 87.
24. Record of a conversation between the Prime Minister and the President, 14 July 1958, PREM11/2387, TNA.
25. Eisenhower, D.D., *Waging Peace* (London: Heinemann, 1966), p. 273.
26. Conference with the President, 16 July 1958, Box 35, DDE Diary Series, Ann Whitman File, DDEL.
27. Amman to State, 16 July 1958, *FRUS*, 1958–60, Vol. XI, pp. 312–13.
28. Lawson to Dulles, 16 July 1958, RG59, Central Decimal File, 785.00/7-1658, USNA; private information.
29. See documents 3, 5, 6 and 7, 15–17 July 1958, *DFPI*, 1958–9, Vol. 13, for the sequence of British consultations with the Israeli government about overflights.
30. Editorial Note, *FRUS*, 1958–60, Vol. XI, p. 317; London to State, telegram no. 371, 17 July 1958 Central Decimal File, 785.00/7-1758, RG59, USNA.
31. Almog, O., *Britain, Israel and the United States, 1955–1958: Beyond Suez* (London: Frank Cass, 2003), pp. 184–6, 189–94, 196–9. See also Pappé, I., 'The Junior Partner: Israel's Role in the 1958 Crisis', in Louis, W.R. and Owen, R., *A Revolutionary Year: the Middle East in 1958* (London: I.B. Tauris, 2002), pp. 245–74.
32. Memorandum of a Conference with the President, White House, Washington, July 20 1958, 3.45pm, *FRUS*, 1958–1960, Vol. XI, p. 349.
33. Memorandum of a Conference with the President, White House, Washington, July 16 1958, 11am, ibid, p. 308.
34. Amman to State, 18 July 1958, ibid, pp. 323–5.
35. Memorandum of a Conversation, British Embassy, Washington, 19 July 1958, 6pm, ibid, p. 342.
36. Telegram from the embassy in Jordan to the Department of State, 22 July 1958, 1am, ibid, p. 364.
37. Dann, *King Hussein*, p. 91.
38. Synopsis, Intelligence and State Department Items Reported to the President, 30 July 1958, WHO, Office of the Staff Secretary, Subject Series, Alphabetical Subseries, Box 14, Folder Intelligence Briefing Notes Vol. I(1), DDEL.
39. Johnston, *The Brink of Jordan*, p. 106.
40. Johnston to Foreign Office, 7 August 1958, FO371/134108, TNA.
41. Telegram from the Embassy in Ethiopia to the Department of State, 8 August 1958, *FRUS*, 1958–1960, Vol. XI, pp. 439–43.
42. Memorandum of Telephone Conversation, 23 August 1958, Christian Herter Papers, Box 5, Folder Chronological File August 1958 (1), DDEL.
43. Johnston to Foreign Office, 18 August 1958, PREM11/2381, TNA.
44. Johnston to Foreign Office, 6 October 1958, FO371/134109, TNA.
45. Telegram from the Embassy in Jordan to the Department of State, 12 August 1958, *FRUS*, 1958–1960, Vol. XI, pp. 453–5.
46. Ashton, *Eisenhower*, p. 187.
47. Hussein, *Uneasy Lies the Head*, pp. 179–85; Dann, *King Hussein*, pp. 102–3.
48. Johnston, *The Brink of Jordan*, p. 128.

49. Amman to Foreign Office, telegram no. 2050, 10 November 1958, PREM11/3028, TNA.
50. One exception is Tal, *Politics*, pp. 73–5.
51. Record of a Conversation between the Secretary of State and Mr Herter in Geneva on 13 May 1959, PREM11/3028, TNA.
52. Sanger to Meyer, 'Reactions of King Hussein to US Visit', 22 April 1959, Folder Background, Work Drafts etc. re King Hussein Visit, 1959, Box 1, Records of the Iraq-Jordan Affairs Desk, 1959–64, Lot Files, RG59, USNA.
53. 'Susan flies in – and it looks like a royal romance', *Daily Herald*, 14 April 1959.
54. Memorandum of Conversation, 24 March 1959, Folder Memos of Conversations, 1959, Box 3, Records of the Iraq-Jordan Affairs Desk, 1959–64, Lot Files, RG59, USNA.
55. Memorandum of Conference with the President, [prepared by John S.D. Eisenhower], 25 March 1959, WHO, Office of the Staff Secretary, International Series, Box 9, Folder Jordan (1) [January 1959 – June 1960], DDEL.
56. Telephone Call, 25 March 1959, AWF, DDE Diary Series, Box 39, Folder Telephone Calls, March 1959, DDEL.
57. Synopsis of State Material Reported to the President, 10 and 11 June 1959, WHO, Office of Staff Secretary, Subject Series, Alphabetical Subseries, Box 14, Folder Intelligence Briefing Notes, Vol. I(8), DDEL.
58. Amman to State, 14 May 1959, *FRUS*, 1958–1960, Vol. XI, pp. 715–16. See also Memcon, Department of State, Washington, 20 October 1959, ibid, pp. 730–1.
59. Record of Meeting between the Prime Minister and King Hussein of Jordan, 12.15pm, Friday, 11 December 1959, at No.10 Downing Street, PREM11/3431, TNA. Nasser also made use of Iraqi émigrés in his propaganda battle with Qasim (Rathmell, *Secret War in the Middle East*, pp. 156–7).
60. Duke to Boothby, 23 April 1960, FO371/151131, TNA.
61. Beith to Duke, 18 May 1960, ibid.
62. Dann, *King Hussein*, p. 107. Jankowski (*Nasser's Egypt*, pp. 155–6, 158) may overstate the case when he speaks of a rapprochement in UAR–Jordanian relations during the second half of 1959 and early 1960.
63. Dann, *King Hussein*, pp. 109–10.
64. Hussein, *Uneasy Lies the Head*, pp. 192–4.
65. ibid, p. 188.
66. Johnston to Foreign Office, telegram no. 749, 9 September 1960, PREM11/4327, TNA.
67. Zak, M., 'Israel and Jordan: Strategically Bound', *Israel Affairs*, 3/1, 1996, p. 43.
68. Synopsis of State and Intelligence Material Reported to the President, 27 January 1960, WHO, Office of Staff Secretary, Subject Series, Alphabetical Subseries, Box 14, Folder Intelligence Briefing Notes, Vol. II(1), DDEL.
69. Foreign Office to Amman, telegram no. 1076, 10 September 1960, ibid. See 'Jordan', C.O.S.(60)255, 14 September 1960, DEFE13/423, TNA, for the British government's assessment of the contingencies surrounding any Jordanian attack on the UAR at this point.
70. Synopsis of State and Intelligence Material Reported to the President, 13 September 1960, WHO, Office of Staff Secretary, Subject Series, Alphabetical Subseries, Box 14, Folder Intelligence Briefing Notes, Vol. II(5), DDEL.
71. Johnston to Foreign Office, 11 September 1960, PREM11/4327, TNA.
72. Johnston, *The Brink of Jordan*, pp. 158–9.
73. Snow, *Hussein*, p. 139.
74. Lunt, *Hussein*, pp. 69–70.
75. Dann, *King Hussein*, pp. 116–17; Hussein, *Uneasy Lies the Head*, pp. 220–33.
76. Dann, *King Hussein*, pp. 114–15, 117.
77. Susser, A., *On Both Banks of the Jordan: A Political Biography of Wasfi al-Tall* (London: Frank Cass, 1994), pp. 32–3; Dann, *King Hussein*, pp. 112–13.

78. Ashton, N.J., 'Britain and the Kuwaiti Crisis, 1961', *Diplomacy & Statecraft*, 9/1, 1998, pp. 174–5.
79. Susser, *On Both Banks*, pp. 33–4.
80. Amman to Foreign Office, 29 September 1961, FO371/158788, TNA; Amman to Foreign Office, 2 October 1961, ibid; Foreign Office to Amman, 4 October 1961, ibid.
81. Dann, *King Hussein*, pp. 118–19.
82. Foreign Office to Amman, 4 October 1961, FO371/158788, TNA.
83. Susser, *On Both Banks*, p. 34.
84. Record of a Meeting between the Prime Minister, Foreign Secretary and King Hussein of Jordan at Admiralty House, 18 December 1961, PREM11/4327, TNA.
85. Amman to Foreign Office, 27 December 1961, ibid.

Chapter 5: Arab Cold War and Détente, 1962–6

1. Amman to State, 30 January 1962, Folder Jordan General, 1/61–3/62, Box 125, National Security File, JFKL.
2. These biographical details are drawn from Susser, *On Both Banks*.
3. Interview, Awn Khasawneh, The Hague, 17 February 2001.
4. Susser, *On Both Banks*, p. 37.
5. Macomber to State, 1 February 1962, Folder Jordan General 1/61–3/62, Box 125, National Security File, JFKL.
6. Little, 'A Puppet in Search of a Puppeteer?', p. 529.
7. Memorandum from the Director of Intelligence and Research (Hilsman) to Secretary of State Rusk, 13 September 1962, *FRUS*, 1961–63, Vol. XVIII, pp. 91–2.
8. Feisal was engaged in a protracted power struggle with his brother King Saud. From October 1962 onwards when he became prime minister and foreign minister he was clearly the dominant political figure in the kingdom. He formally succeeded Saud as King in November 1964.
9. Record of a Conversation between the Prime Minister and H.M. King Hussein of Jordan held at 10 Downing Street at 10am on Friday 22 July 1966, PREM13/988, TNA.
10. For Jordanian–Saudi relations see Nevo, J., 'Jordan and Saudi Arabia: The Last Royalists', in Nevo, J. and Pappé, I., *Jordan in the Middle East: The Making of a Pivotal State, 1948–1988* (London: Frank Cass, 1994), pp. 103–18.
11. For further discussion of US policy towards the conflict see: Gerges, F.A., 'The Kennedy Administration and the Egyptian–Saudi Conflict in Yemen: Co-opting Arab Nationalism', *Middle East Journal*, 49/2, 1995, pp. 292–311; Little, D., 'The New Frontier on the Nile: JFK, Nasser, and Arab Nationalism', *Journal of American History*, 75/2, 1988, pp. 501–27.
12. Amman to State, 15 August 1962, Folder Jordan General 4/62–10/62, Box 125A, National Security File, JFKL.
13. Hussein to Kennedy, 21 September 1962, Folder Jordan Security 1961–63, Box 120, President's Office File, JFKL; Kennedy to Hussein, 13 September 1962, *FRUS*, 1961–63, Vol. XVIII, pp. 92–4.
14. Amman to State, 17 October 1962, Folder Jordan General 4/62–10/62, Box 125A, National Security File, JFKL.
15. State to Amman, 7 November 1962, Folder Jordan General 11/62–3/63, Box 125A, National Security File, JFKL.
16. Amman to State, 14 November 1962, (section three of three), Folder Jordan General 11/62–3/63, Box 125A, National Security File, JFKL.
17. Interview, Hazem Nusseibeh, Amman, 4 September 2001.
18. Amman to State, 14 November 1962, (section three of three), Folder Jordan General 11/62–3/63, Box 125A, National Security File, JFKL.

NOTES TO PAGES 92–98

19. See for example State to Amman, 4 January 1963, Folder Jordan General 11/62–3/63, Box 125A, National Security File, JFKL.

20. Amman to CIA, 21 March 1963, Folder Jordan General 11/62–3/63, Box 125A, National Security File, JFKL.

21. Amman to CIA, 22 March 1963, Folder Jordan General 11/62–3/63, Box 125A, National Security File, JFKL.

22. Dann, *King Hussein*, pp. 128–9. Information about the CIA warning was not available to Dann when he was writing, which explains his statement 'nothing is known of an actual army plot at that time'.

23. Susser, *On Both Banks*, p. 68.

24. Amman to State, 21 April 1963, Folder Jordan General 4/63, Box 125A, National Security File, JFKL.

25. Memorandum of a Telephone Conversation between Under Secretary of State (Ball) and Secretary of Defense McNamara, 8.50am, 27 April 1963, *FRUS*, 1961–63, Vol. XVIII, p. 483. Nasser insisted on retaining the title 'UAR' for the rump state of Egpyt even after the collapse of the union with Syria.

26. Memorandum for the Record: Meeting with the President on Situation in Jordan, 10.15–11.00am, 27 April 1963, *FRUS*, 1961–63, Vol. XVIII, pp. 484–6.

27. Komer to Bundy, 27 April 1963, Folder Jordan General 4/63, Box 125A, National Security File, JFKL. See also Footnote 1, *FRUS*, 1961–63, Vol. XVIII, p. 487.

28. Memorandum of Telephone Conversation between Bundy and Ball, 12.20pm, 29 April 1963, *FRUS*, 1961–63, Vol. XVIII, p. 497.

29. Memorandum of Conversation, 27 April 1963, *FRUS*, 1961–63, Vol. XVIII, pp. 489–92.

30. Bligh, A., *The Political Legacy of King Hussein* (Brighton: Sussex Academic Press, 2002), pp. 8–26. For a different perspective see Shalom, Z., *The Superpowers, Israel and the Future of Jordan, 1960–1963: The Perils of the Pro-Nasser Policy* (Brighton: Sussex Academic Press, 1998), pp. 38–104. The Israeli attitude is also discussed in Podeh, E., 'To Unite or Not to Unite – That is *Not* the Question: The 1963 Tripartite Unity Talks Reassessed', *Middle Eastern Studies*, 39/1, 2003, pp. 155–62; and Dann, *King Hussein*, pp. 133–4.

31. Memorandum, Komer to Bundy, 30 April 1963, *FRUS*, 1961–63, Vol. XVIII, pp. 503–5.

32. Ben Gurion's diary entry, quoted in Shalom, *The Superpowers*, p. 101.

33. Shalom, *The Superpowers*, p. 100.

34. For further discussion of the divisions which undermined the prospective union see Podeh, 'To Unite or Not to Unite', pp. 166–79.

35. Amman to State, 1 August 1963, Folder Jordan General 5/63, Box 125A, National Security File, JFKL.

36. Amman to State, 5 July 1963, Folder Jordan General 5/63, Box 125A, National Security File, JFKL.

37. Private information.

38. Bar-Zohar, M., *Yaacov Herzog: A Biography* (London: Halban Publishers, 2005), pp. 226–31.

39. Amman to State, 23 July 1964, Folder Jordan Cables [2 of 2] Vol. I 11/63–2/65, Box 146, NSF: Country File, LBJL.

40. Dann, *King Hussein*, pp. 137–8.

41. Morris to Harrison, 1 May 1964, PREM11/4882, TNA.

42. Bar-Zohar, *Herzog*, pp. 246–50.

43. Memo, Komer to Johnson, 6 August 1964, Folder Jordan Memos Vol. I 11/63–2/65, Box 146, NSF: Country File, LBJL; telegram, State to Cairo, 15 August 1964, Folder Jordan Cables [1 of 2] Vol. I 11/63–2/65, ibid.

44. Amman to State, 30 May 1964, Folder Jordan Cables [2 of 2] Vol. I 11/63–2/65, Box 146, NSF, Country File, LBJL.

45. Talbot to Rusk, 22 July 1964, Document 78, *FRUS*, 1964–68, Vol. XVIII.

46. Komer to Bundy, 7 February 1965, Document 140, *FRUS*, 1964–68, Vol. XVIII.
47. Memo, Komer to Bundy, 4 August 1964, Folder Jordan Memos Vol. I 11/63–2/65, Box 146, NSF: Country File, LBJL.
48. Israel to State, 11 March 1965, Document 185, *FRUS*, 1964–68, Vol. XVIII.
49. Komer to Johnson, 22 February 1966, Document 273, *FRUS*, 1964–68, Vol. XVIII; State to Jordan, 26 February 1966, Document 276, ibid.
50. Hussein to Johnson, 9 April 1966, Folder Jordan, King Hussein Correspondence, Box 31, NSF: Special Heads of State Correspondence File, LBJL.
51. Abu Odeh, A., *Jordanians, Palestinians and the Hashemite Kingdom* (Washington DC: US Institute of Peace, 1999), pp. 91–2, 115.
52. Interview, Hazem Nusseibeh, Amman, 4 September 2001.
53. Susser, *On Both Banks*, p. 80.
54. Dann, *King Hussein*, pp. 141–2.
55. Amman to State, 13 April 1964, Folder Jordan Cables [2 of 2] Vol. I 11/63–2/65, Box 146, NSF: Country File, LBJL.
56. Susser, *On Both Banks*, p. 81.
57. Dann, *King Hussein*, pp. 147–8.
58. Susser, *On Both Banks*, p. 86.
59. ibid, pp. 88–9.
60. Bar-Zohar, *Herzog*, pp. 253–6.
61. ibid, p. 286.
62. Dann, *King Hussein*, p. 145.

Chapter 6: The Path to Disaster, 1966–7

1. Susser, *On Both Banks*, pp. 100–101; Abu Odeh, *Jordanians*, pp. 125–6.
2. Dann, *King Hussein*, pp. 150–51.
3. Report of a Conversation between the Prime Minister and King Hussein, 22 July 1966, PREM13/988, TNA.
4. Brown to Phillips, 15 August 1966, ibid.
5. Mutawi, S., *Jordan in the 1967 War* (Cambridge: Cambridge University Press, 1987), p. 76.
6. Susser, *On Both Banks*, p. 110.
7. Shemesh, M., 'The IDF Raid on Samu: The Turning Point in Jordan's Relations with Israel and the West Bank Palestinians', *Israel Studies*, 7/1, 2002, pp. 151–2.
8. For this case see Bligh, *The Political Legacy*, pp. 27–46.
9. For accounts of Samu which rely largely on this explanation see: Bligh, *The Political Legacy*, pp. 27–46; Oren, M., *Six Days of War: June 1967 and the Making of the Modern Middle East* (Oxford: OUP, 2002), pp. 31–5; Shlaim, *The Iron Wall* (London: Allen Lane, 2000), pp. 233–4. Dann, *King Hussein*, pp. 154–5 offers a nuanced explanation of the motives behind the attack. See also Tel Aviv to State, 5 December 1966, telegram no. 1942, *DDRS*, CK3100498314.
10. Shlaim, *The Iron Wall*, pp. 233–4; Oren, *Six Days of War*, p. 33.
11. The Director General of the Israeli Foreign Office, Levavi, subsequently claimed that it was only at a meeting on 20 November that the cabinet had been informed of the actual size of the raid. Rabin, in the same meeting, claimed that 'he could hardly believe that "those stupid people" would deliberately take on an armoured column . . .' (Tel Aviv to State, telegram no. 1742, 21 November 1966, Folder POL 32-1, 11/1/66, ISR-JORDAN, Box 2352, CFPF, 1964–6, RG59, USNA).
12. Rostow to Johnson, 15 November 1966, Document 333, *FRUS*, 1964–8, Vol. XVIII. See also Amman to State, telegram no. 1104, 14 November 1966, Folder POL 32-1, 11/1/66, ISR-JORDAN, Box 2352, CFPF, 1964–6, RG59, USNA.
13. Memorandum for the Record, 15 November 1966, Document 334, *FRUS*, 1964–8, Vol. XVIII.

14. Quoted in Oren, *Six Days of War*, p. 34.
15. Amman to State, 23 November 1966, Folder POL 32-1, 11/1/66, ISR-JORDAN, Box 2352, CFPF, 1964–6, RG59, USNA.
16. Amman to State, 14 November 1966, ibid. See also: Bligh, *The Political Legacy*, p. 44; Oren, *Six Days of War*, p. 36; Dann, *King Hussein*, p. 155; Lunt, *Hussein*, p. 81.
17. Memorandum, Wriggins and Saunders to Rostow, 16 November 1966, Document 337, *FRUS*, 1964–8, Vol. XVIII.
18. Amman to State, telegram no. 1105, 14 November 1966, Folder POL 32-1, 11/1/66, ISR-JORDAN, Box 2352, CFPF, 1964–6, RG59, USNA.
19. Memorandum, Rostow to Johnson, 12 December 1966, Document 364, *FRUS*, 1964–8, Vol. XVIII.
20. Memorandum, Katzenbach to Johnson, 27 June 1967, Document 329, *FRUS*, 1964–8, Vol. XIX, p. 578.
21. Amman to State, telegram no. 1457, 11 December 1966, Folder Jordan Memos Vol. III 12/66–5/67, Box 146, NSF: Country File, LBJL.
22. Memo, Rostow to Johnson, 12 December 1966, Document 364, *FRUS*, 1964–8, Vol. XVIII.
23. CIA Information Cable, 23 November 1966, Folder Jordan Cables [2 of 2] Vol. II 3/65–11/66, Box 146, NSF: Country File, LBJL. On disaffection in the JAA see also Amman to State, 6 December 1966, Folder Jordan Cables Vol. III 12/66–5/67, ibid.
24. Amman to State, 26 November 1966, Folder Jordan Cables [1 of 2] Vol. II 3/65–11/66, ibid.
25. CIA Information Cable, 24 December 1966, Folder Jordan Cables Vol. III 12/66–5/67, ibid.
26. Mutawi, *Jordan in the 1967 War*, p. 73.
27. Amman to State, 4 December 1966, Folder Jordan Cables Vol. III 12/66–5/67, Box 146, NSF: Country File, LBJL.
28. Oren, *Six Days of War*, p. 37.
29. Quoted in Mutawi, *Jordan in the 1967 War*, pp. 83–4.
30. Quoted in Oren, *Six Days of War*, p. 42.
31. ibid, p. 48.
32. Susser, *On Both Banks*, p. 117.
33. ibid, p. 122.
34. Mutawi, *Jordan in the 1967 War*, p. 91.
35. Amman to State, telegram no. 3699, 23 May 1967, Folder Middle East Crisis Vol. 13 Appendix S [May 23–24], Box 22, NSF: NSC Histories: Middle East Crisis, LBJL.
36. Eban, A., *Abba Eban: An Autobiography* (New York: Random House, 1977), p. 319.
37. For further discussion see: Parker, R.B., *The Six Day War: A Retrospective* (Gainesville: University of Florida Press, 1996), pp. 13–73; Oren, *Six Days of War*, pp. 54–5.
38. In a meeting with British Prime Minister Harold Wilson on 24 May, Israeli Foreign Minister Abba Eban called Thant's decision 'an error that will reverberate in history' (PREM13/1618, TNA).
39. Amman to Foreign Office, 23 May 1967, PREM13/1617, TNA.
40. Amman to State, telegram no. 3711, 23 May 1967, Folder Middle East Crisis Vol. 13 Appendix S [May 23–24], Box 22, NSF: NSC Histories: Middle East Crisis, LBJL.
41. Amman to Foreign Office, 23 May 1967, PREM13/1617, TNA.
42. Adams to Brown, 29 June 1967, PREM13/2742, TNA.
43. Quoted in Mutawi, *Jordan in the 1967 War*, p. 100.
44. For shrewd assessments of the calculations that led Hussein to war see Dann, *King Hussein*, pp. 161–3; Susser, *On Both Banks*, pp. 125–6. For a very different perspective see Bligh, *The Political Legacy*, pp. 47–72. For a contemporary assessment of Hussein's plight see Amman to State, telegram no. 3774, 25 May 1967, 'GOJ dilemma in Arab–Israel crisis', Folder Middle East Crisis, Vol. 14, Appendix S [May 25–27], Box 22, NSF: NSC Histories: Middle East Crisis, LBJL.

45. Mutawi, *Jordan in the 1967 War*, p. 103.
46. ibid, p. 107.
47. Private information; see also, Little, 'A Puppet in Search of a Puppeteer?', p. 536.
48. CIA, Intelligence Memorandum, 30 May 1967, Folder Middle East Crisis, Vol. 10 Appendix Q [I], Box 21, NSF: NSC Histories, Middle East Crisis, LBJL.
49. Lunt, *Hussein*, pp. 90–91.
50. CIA, Intelligence Memorandum, 30 May 1967, Arab–Israeli Situation Spot Report (as of 0930 EDT), Folder Middle East Crisis, Vol. 10 Appendix Q [I], Box 21, NSF: NSC Histories, Middle East Crisis, LBJL.
51. Mutawi, *Jordan in the 1967 War*, pp. 108–11.
52. Amman to State, 3 June 1967, Folder POL 15-1, Jordan 1/1/67, Box 2253, Central Foreign Policy File, RG59, USNA.
53. Amman to Foreign Office, telegram no. 525, 4 June 1967, PREM13/1619, TNA; Adams to Brown, 29 June 1967, PREM13/2742, TNA.
54. See for example 'Note of a meeting between the Prime Minister and the Minister of State for Foreign Affairs (Mr George Thomson) at No. 10 Downing Street before midnight', 23 May 1967, PREM13/1617, TNA; Washington to Foreign Office, 23 May 1967, PREM13/1617, TNA. See also Gat, M., 'Letting Someone Else Do the Job: American Policy on the Eve of the Six Day War', *Diplomacy and Statecraft*, 14/1, 2003; and Quandt, W.B., 'Lyndon Johnson and the June 1967 War: What Colour Was the Light?', *Middle East Journal*, 46/2, 1992.
55. For this debate see Hathaway, R.M. and Smith, R.J., *Richard Helms as Director of the CIA*, pp. 144–5, http://www.foia.cia.gov/
56. ibid, pp. 141, 143; and private information.
57. Private information.
58. Dann, *King Hussein*, p. 162.
59. Mutawi, *Jordan in the 1967 War*, p. 123.
60. http://www.israel-mfa.gov.il/MFA/Foreign+Relations/Israels+Foreign+Relations+since+1947/1947-1974/16+Message+from+Prime+Minister+Eshkol+to+King+Huss.htm (accessed 29 July 2007). Hussein in fact received two such warnings from the Israelis on 5 June: the first through Bull and the second through the US embassy in Amman (State to Amman, 5 June 1967, Document 160, *FRUS*, 1964–68, Vol. XIX).
61. Shlaim, A., 'His Royal Shyness: King Hussein and Israel', *New York Review of Books*, 15 July 1999, p. 16. See also Bligh, *The Political Legacy*, pp. 66–7.
62. Shlaim, *The Iron Wall*, p. 244. See also Oren, *Six Days of War*, pp. 184–6.
63. This was a matter of controversy, with the Israelis insisting that the Jordanians had targeted civilians. Hussein's response to the allegation was to assert bitterly that 'unfortunately for us, they are always able to tell their story better than we are'. (Amman to State, 6 June 1967, Folder Middle East Crisis: Vol. 15, Appendix S [June 3–6], Box 23, NSF: NSC Histories: Middle East Crisis, LBJL.)
64. Oren, *Six Days of War*, pp. 187–96.
65. State to Amman, 5 June 1967, footnote 2, Document 153, *FRUS*, 1964–8, Vol. XIX.
66. During the night of 5–6 June, Hussein initially used the phrase an 'end to the violent attacks', although by mid-morning on 6 June he was calling unequivocally for a ceasefire. See State to Amman, 6 June 1967, Document 170, *FRUS*, 1964–68, Vol. XIX; Amman to State, telegram no. 4095, 6 June 1967, Folder Middle East Crisis: Vol. 15, Appendix S [June 3–6], Box 23, NSF: NSC Histories: Middle East Crisis, LBJL.
67. Amman to State, telegram no. 4084, 6 June 1967, Folder Middle East Crisis: Vol. 15, Appendix S [June 3–6], Box 23, NSF: NSC Histories: Middle East Crisis, LBJL; Oren, *Six Days of War*, pp. 225–6.
68. Oren, *Six Days of War*, p. 238.
69. ibid, p. 244.
70. State to Tel Aviv, 8 June 1967, Document 201, *FRUS*, 1964–68, Vol. XIX.

71.   Mutawi, *Jordan in the 1967 War*, p. 140.
72.   Hussein, *My "War" With Israel* (London: Peter Owen, 1969), p. 110.
73.   All figures are taken from Mutawi, *Jordan in the 1967 War*, pp. 163–80.

Chapter 7: Lost in a Sandstorm: Hussein and the Peace Process, 1967–8

1.   During August 1968 Hussein travelled to London for major dental surgery.
      A chronic jaw complaint may have been one of the causes of his headaches
      and generally run-down condition during the preceding months. (Amman to
      State, 16 August 1968, Folder POL7 Jordan, 1/1/68, Box 2253, Central Foreign
      Policy Files (hereafter CFPF), 1967–9, RG59, USNA. See also Lunt, *Hussein*,
      pp. 114–15.)
2.   Private information.
3.   Text of Hussein interview with Pauline Fredericks on NBC's 'Today Show' on 27
      June 1967 in FCO to Certain Missions, 28 June 1967, PREM13/1622, TNA.
4.   These were the terms Hussein put to US Ambassador Burns when he put out his first
      peace feeler on 13 July 1967 (Amman to State, telegram no. 4941, 13 July 1967,
      Folder Jordan: Filed by LBJ Library, Box 148, NSF: Country File, LBJL).
5.   Halevy, E., *Man in the Shadows: Inside the Middle East Crisis with a Man Who Led
      the Mossad* (London: Weidenfeld & Nicolson, 2006), pp. 6–8. This passage is rather
      obtuse, but conveys a strong sense that Halevy wants to pay tribute to an unsung
      role played by Angleton.
6.   There is a folder titled 'Arab–Israeli Private Talks', in Box 12, NSF: Files of Walt W.
      Rostow, LBJL, which evidently contains detailed reports on at least some of
      Hussein's meetings with Israeli representatives, including Abba Eban. The only
      declassified portions are a series of cover notes from Rostow to the president during
      August–October 1968 which give very little away. My own attempt to secure
      declassification of these records under FOI was unsuccessful.
7.   This was a CIA codeword.
8.   Amman to State, telegram no. 732, 8 August 1967, Folder Jordan Cables [3 of 3] Vol.
      V 3/68–1/69, Box 147, NSF: Country File, LBJL.
9.   Bar-Zohar, *Herzog*, pp. 300–305.
10.   Record of a Conversation between the Prime Minister and the King of Jordan, 3 July
      1967, FCO17/240, TNA.
11.   ibid.
12.   One very well-informed source who was close to Hussein at this stage has further
      confirmed Brown's role as intermediary (private information).
13.   Brown to Hussein, 5 March 1970, British File, RHA [my italics].
14.   Gat, M., 'Britain and the Occupied Territories after the 1967 War', *MERIA*, 10/4,
      2006.
15.   Edmonds, J., 'The Evolution of British Labour Party Policy on Israel from 1967 to
      the Intifada', *Twentieth Century British History*, 11/1, 2000, p. 25.
16.   Brown, G., *In My Way: The Political Memoirs of Lord George-Brown* (London: Victor
      Gollancz, 1971), pp. 227–32.
17.   Paterson, P., *Tired and Emotional: The Life of Lord George-Brown* (London: Chatto
      & Windus, 1993), pp. 88–91.
18.   Helms to Johnson, 28 October 1968, Document 294, *FRUS*, 1964–8, Vol. XX.
19.   Private information.
20.   Hathaway and Smith, *Richard Helms as Director of Central Intelligence*, p. 146.
21.   Bar-Zohar, *Herzog*, p. 305.
22.   The State–CIA split over the initiative is the one declassified portion of the CIA
      History by Hathaway and Smith, *Richard Helms as Director of Central Intelligence*,
      p. 147.

23. Bar-Zohar, *Herzog*, pp. 331–2.

24. Memorandum of meeting, 15 July 1967, 'Sandstorm: First Special Meeting', Document 368, *FRUS*, 1964–8, Vol. XIX.

25. State to USUN, 13 July 1967, Document 360, ibid.

26. Amman to State, telegram 4941, 13 July 1967, Folder Jordan: Filed by LBJ Library, Box 148, NSF: Country File, LBJL.

27. Eban was in New York participating in discussions at the UN (State to USUN, 13 July 1967, Document 360, *FRUS*, 1964–8), Vol. XIX.

28. Record of a meeting between the Foreign Secretary and the Israeli Foreign Minister, 21 October 1967, PREM13/1623, TNA.

29. For more detail on the positions adopted by different members of the Israeli cabinet over this issue see Shlaim, *The Iron Wall*, pp. 254–6.

30. Tel Aviv to State, 14 July 1967, Document 366, *FRUS*, 1964–8, Vol. XIX.

31. Memcon, 15 July 1967, Document 367, ibid.

32. Memcon, 15 July 1967, 'Sandstorm: First Special Meeting', Document 368, ibid.

33. State to Amman, 21 July 1967, Document 386, ibid.

34. Amman to State, 28 July 1967, Document 393, ibid.

35. Rostow to Johnson, 5 September 1967, Folder Jordan Memos and Misc. Vol. IV 5/67–2/68, Box 147, NSF: Country File, LBJL; Helms to Johnson, 5 September 1967, enc Khartoum report, ibid. In addition to accounts gleaned from Saudi and Jordanian sources, the CIA had successfully bugged the summit and so had a full record of its proceedings (private information).

36. Hussein to Johnson, 7 October 1967, Folder Jordan 8/1/67–7/31/68, Box 31, NSF: Special Head of State Correspondence File, LBJL.

37. Amman to State, telegram no. 732, 16 August 1967, Folder Jordan Cables [3 of 3] Vol. V 3/68–1/69, Box 147, NSF: Country File, LBJL.

38. Battle to Rusk, 5 November 1967, Folder Jordan: Informal Working Visit of Hussein 11/6–9/67 [1 of 2], Box 148, ibid.

39. USUN to State, 13 November 1967, Document 522, *FRUS*, 1964–8, Vol. XIX.

40. Private information.

41. http://www.un.org/documents/sc/res/1967/scres67.htm

42. For Hikmat al-Masri's activities see: Amman to State, 8 April 1968, Folder Jordan Cables [3 of 3] Vol. V 3/68–1/69, Box 147, NSF: Country File, LBJL. For the broader use of West Bank notables see Memcon, 26 April 1968, Document 152, Vol. XIX, *FRUS*, 1964–8.

43. Bar-Zohar, *Herzog*, p. 306.

44. ibid, pp. 316–20.

45. Interview, Zeid Rifai, Amman, 5 June 2002.

46. ibid.

47. The Allon Plan called for the incorporation into Israel of a strip of land 10–15 kilometres wide along the Jordan River, most of the Judean Desert along the Dead Sea, and a substantial area around Jerusalem. Israel would build settlements and army bases to protect these areas. The plan was designed to incorporate as few as possible of the Arab population centres in the West Bank into Israel. Initially Allon envisaged negotiating with local Palestinian leaders for the creation of an autonomous region that would be linked to Israel economically. Only in April 1968, by which point it was clear that no local leadership could be found which would cooperate in the implementation of the plan, did he turn his attention to the possibility of negotiating with King Hussein instead. Shlaim, *The Iron Wall*, pp. 256, 262; Pedatzur, R., 'Coming Back Full Circle: The Palestinian Option in 1967', *Middle East Journal*, 49/2, 1995, pp. 269–91.

48. Interview, Zeid Rifai, Amman, 5 June 2002.

49. State to Amman, 17 August 1968, Folder Jordan Cables [3 of 3] Vol. V 3/68–1/69, Box 147, NSF: Country File, LBJL.

50. According to CIA sources, the May 1968 meetings extended across a two-week

period from 4 to 16 May (Helms to Johnson, 4 June 1968, Document 187, *FRUS*, 1964–8, Vol. XX).

51. Eban, A., *An Autobiography* (London: Weidenfeld & Nicolson, 1977), p. 446.
52. USUN to State, 3 November 1968, telegram no. 7546, DDRS: CK3100481976; Pedatzur, 'Coming Back Full Circle', p. 283.
53. USUN to State, 3 November 1968, telegram no. 7546, DDRS: CK3100481976.
54. Rostow to Johnson, 30 September 1968, Folder Arab–Israeli Private Talks, Box 12, NSF: Files of Walt W. Rostow, LBJL.
55. Pedatzur, 'Coming Back Full Circle', p. 285; Shlaim, *The Iron Wall*, p. 263.
56. Pedatzur, 'Coming Back Full Circle', p. 283.
57. Tel Aviv to State, 21 November 1968, telegram no. 6186, DDRS: CK3100505563.
58. Interview, Zeid Rifai, Amman, 5 June 2002.
59. Pedatzur, 'Coming Back Full Circle', p. 273.
60. Hadow (Tel Aviv) to Allen, 25 April 1968, FCO17/550, TNA.
61. FCO to Tel Aviv, 26 February 1968, FCO17/221, TNA.
62. Hadow (Tel Aviv) to Allen, 25 April 1968, FCO17/550, TNA.
63. For an insider's account of the political divisions over a West Bank settlement in the Israeli cabinet at this stage, see the comments made by the Prime Minister's Political Secretary, Yafeh, reported in Tel Aviv to State, 21 November 1968, telegram no. 6186, DDRS: CK3100505563.
64. Interview, Zeid Rifai, Amman, 5 June 2002.
65. Amman to State, 30 December 1968, Document 373, *FRUS*, 1964–68, Vol. XX.
66. Amman to State, 19 December 1968, Document 353, ibid.
67. Note of a Conversation at the Prime Minister's Dinner for King Hussein, 22 February 1978, UKFOIA.
68. Text of King Hussein interview for BBC *Panorama* programme, recorded 21 January 1978, *FBIS*, MEA-78-16, F3, Vol. V, 24 January 1978.

Chapter 8: 'Seven Questions of Israel': The September 1970 Crisis

1. Hussein, *Uneasy Lies the Head*, pp. 68–70, 75–7, 94, 106.
2. Symmes to Battle or Davies, 9 January 1968, Folder: DEF12.5 Jordan, 1/1/68, Box 1564, CFPF, 1967–9, RG59, USNA.
3. Helms to Johnson, 25 January 1968, Folder Jordan Memos [2 of 2] Vol. V 3/68–1/69, Box 148, NSF: Country File, LBJL.
4. Tripp to Moore, 20 January 1968, FCO17/248, TNA.
5. Hussein to Johnson, 2 March 1968, Folder: DEF12.5 Jordan, 3/1/68, Box 1564, CFPF, 1967–9, RG59, USNA.
6. Middle East Discussions, March 1969, Folder Middle East 1969 (3), Box 148, Robert B. Anderson Papers, DDEL.
7. Extracts from an interview between Dayan and the Haaretz Board of Directors, 19 January 1968, FCO17/550, TNA.
8. Dayan, M., *The Story of My Life* (London: Weidenfeld & Nicolson, 1976), pp. 351–3. I view Dayan's relatively dismissive treatment of Hussein in his memoirs as a cover for a closer personal relationship.
9. The British embassy in Tel Aviv was informed of this move by its American counterpart (Tel Aviv to FCO, 19 March 1968, FCO17/625, TNA).
10. See the after-action report complied by the British military attaché in Amman, Colonel J.F. Weston-Simons, for more details on the engagement ('Report on Operations in Karama YA 4539 and SAFI YV 3535 Areas on 21 March 1968', 24 March 1968 FCO17/633, TNA). Also Lunt, *Hussein*, pp. 116–17.
11. For more on the myth-building surrounding Karameh see Terrill, W.A., 'The Political Mythology of the Battle of Karameh', *Middle East Journal*, 55/1, 2001, pp. 91–111.

12. 'The Karama Raid', Hadow to Stewart, 1 April 1968, FCO17/633, TNA.

13. Rafael, G., *Destination Peace: Three Decades of Israeli Foreign Policy: A Personal Memoir* (New York: Stein and Day, 1981), pp. 202–3.

14. Abu Odeh, *Jordanians*, p. 172.

15. Interview, Hazem Nusseibeh, Amman, 4 September 2001.

16. Abu Odeh, *Jordanians*, p. 173.

17. El-Edross, S.A., *The Hashemite Arab Army, 1908–1979* (Amman: The Publishing Committee, 1980), p. 442.

18. Amman to State, 20 March 1968, Folder Jordan Cables [3 of 3] Vol. V 3/68–1/69, Box 147, NSF: Country File, LBJL.

19. Adams to Moore, 19 February 1968, FCO17/221, TNA.

20. Middle East Discussions, March 1969, Folder Middle East 1969 (3), Box 148, Robert B. Anderson Papers, DDEL.

21. According to Yigal Allon, the Israeli government signalled to the King at this juncture that if he wanted to bring troops into Amman to deal with the 'terrorists', 'they would not take advantage of the situation.' (Record of the Prime Minister's meeting with Yigal Allon, 26 February 1970, PREM13/3331, TNA.)

22. Brown, *In My Way*, pp. 236–7.

23. ibid, p. 237.

24. Brown to Hussein, 5 March 1970, British File, RHA.

25. Hussein to Brown, 11 April 1970, ibid.

26. Brown, *In My Way*, p. 240.

27. Brown to Hussein, 5 March 1970, British File, RHA.

28. Hussein to Nixon, undated [November 1968], President Nixon File, RHA.

29. Hussein to Nixon, dated 'after Xmas 1969', ibid. The syntax and spelling of the handwritten original are unusually confused, perhaps reflecting the King's state of mind. I have corrected the errors in the quotations offered here.

30. Memorandum of conversation, King Hussein of Jordan, 8 April 1970, Folder Middle East 1970 (2), Box 148, Robert B. Anderson Papers, DDEL.

31. See Symmes's own report of the reasons for the decision in Amman to State, 16 April 1970, Folder Jordan IV, Box 614, National Security Council Files, Country Files, Middle East, RNPP, USNA.

32. Private information.

33. Amman to State, 28 February 1970, Folder Jordan III, Box 614, NSC Files, Country File, Middle East, RNPP, USNA.

34. Abu Odeh, *Jordanians*, p. 175–6.

35. Amman to FCO, 2 September 1970, PREM15/123, TNA; Kissinger, H., *White House Years* (Boston: Little Brown, 1979), p. 598–9.

36. Interview, Zeid Rifai, Amman, 4 July 2007.

37. Amman to CIA, 22 March 1963, Folder Jordan General 11/62–3/63, Box 125A, National Security File, JFKL.

38. Quoted in Lunt, *Hussein*, p. 126.

39. Quandt, W.B., *Peace Process: American Diplomacy and the Arab–Israeli Conflict since 1967* (Washington DC: Brookings Institution Press, 1993), p. 76.

40. Prime Minister Edward Heath presents a rather different picture of the British and American positions in his memoirs (*The Autobiography of Edward Heath: The Course of My Life* (London: Hodder & Stoughton, 1998), pp. 322–3).

41. Amman to State, no. 4997, 8.50am, 21 September 1970, Folder Jordan V, Box 615, NSC, Country Files, Middle East, RNPP, USNA; State to Amman, no. 155208, 5.55am, 22 September 1970, ibid.

42. Interviews, Zeid Rifai, Amman, 5 June 2002 and 4 July 2007. Interestingly, in view of Speares' role in facilitating communications between the King and the Israeli government, the British Diplomatic Service List reveals the apparent presence of two Bill 'Speares' or 'Speirs' in the Middle East at this time, one in Amman and one in Tel Aviv. William James McLaren Speirs (born 22 November 1924) is listed as

having served as first secretary at the British embassy in Tel Aviv between June 1970 and July 1972. Meanwhile, John Alan Speares (born 11 July 1919) is listed as the first secretary at the Amman embassy from January 1969 until December 1973. The surnames are phonetically identical, and both individuals evidently used 'Bill' as their first name. Since the Amman Bill Speares established the secure link to the King in the late spring of 1970, it seems a reasonable speculation to assume that MI6 then decided to send their other 'Bill Speirs' out to Tel Aviv shortly afterwards in June 1970. I have considered the possibility that the two men might in fact be one, but each of them has a trail of postings back through the 1960s in volumes of the Diplomatic Service List which were published long before it could have known that they would take on a significant role in the Middle East in 1970. The Jordanians, in any event, were unaware of the existence of the second, Tel Aviv 'Bill Speirs'.

43. Amman to FCO, 15 September 1970, FCO17/1043, TNA.
44. Private information.
45. Kissinger to Nixon, 'Options in Jordan', undated, Folder Jordan V, Box 615, NSC, Country Files, Middle East, RNPP, USNA.
46. Kissinger, *White House Years*, p. 605.
47. Tel Aviv to Ministry of Defence, 19 September 1970, FCO17/1043, TNA; Haig, A. M., *Inner Circles: How America Changed the World* (New York: Warner Books, 1992), pp. 243–4.
48. Amman to State, 11.15pm, 16 September 1970, Folder Jordan V, Box 615, NSC, Country Files, Middle East, RNPP, USNA.
49. Kissinger, *White House Years*, pp. 598–9.
50. Kissinger to Nixon, 'Options in Jordan', undated, Folder Jordan V, Box 615, NSC, Country Files, Middle East, RNPP, USNA. Kissinger told me that this claim was 'pure speculation', not based on any hard evidence from Israeli or Jordanian sources (interview, Henry Kissinger, New York, 2 June 2003).
51. This was one contingency suggested to British Prime Minister Edward Heath at the time ('Jordan', undated, PREM15/124, TNA).
52. Kissinger to Nixon, 'Options in Jordan', undated, Folder Jordan V, Box 615, NSC, Country Files, Middle East, RNPP, USNA.
53. Amman to State, no. 4766, 12.11pm, 15 September 1970, ibid.
54. Abu Odeh, *Jordanians*, pp. 181–2.
55. Interview, Zeid Rifai, Amman, 4 July 2007.
56. Private information.
57. Kissinger to Nixon, 18 September 1970, Folder Jordan V, Box 615, NSC, Country Files, Middle East, RNPP, USNA. See also Amman to State, no. 4918, 8.00pm, 18 September 1970, ibid.
58. Abu Odeh, *Jordanians*, pp. 185–6.
59. FCO to Tel Aviv, 201000Z, 20 September 1970, FCO17/1044, TNA; Middle East Crisis SITREP at 0700 hours [London time], 21 September 1970, PREM15/123, TNA.
60. 'The Situation in Jordan', GEN 14 (70) 1st Meeting, 7.15pm, 20 September 1970, CAB130/479, TNA.
61. FCO to Amman, 202041Z, 20 September 1970, FCO17/1044, TNA.
62. 'The Situation in Jordan', GEN (14) 70 2nd meeting, 10.30pm, 20 September 1970, CAB130/479, TNA.
63. Conversation between Sir Denis Greenhill and a member of Dr Kissinger's staff, 2am [London time], 21 September 1970, PREM11/123, TNA.
64. Amman to State, no. 4984, 11.55pm, 20 September 1970, Folder Jordan Crisis, Box 619, NSC, Country Files, Middle East, RNPP, USNA.
65. Amman to State, 0124Z, 21 September 1970, http://nixon.archives.gov/virtuallibrary/documents/mr/092170_jordan.pdf (accessed 30 November 2007).
66. Seale, P., *Asad of Syria: The Struggle for the Middle East* (London: I. B. Tauris, 1988), p. 158; interview, Zeid Rifai, Amman, 4 July 2007.

67. Kissinger now argues that the Soviets 'tolerated' Syrian intervention in Jordan 'but did not sponsor it' (interview, Henry Kissinger, New York, 2 June 2003).
68. Kissinger, *White House Years*, pp. 618–19.
69. ibid, p. 621.
70. Rabin, *The Rabin Memoirs*, p. 187.
71. Kissinger, *White House Years*, p. 623.
72. Rabin, *The Rabin Memoirs*, p. 187.
73. State to Amman and Tel Aviv, no. 155166, 12.19am, 22 September 1970, Folder Jordan Crisis, Box 619, NSC, Country Files, Middle East, RNPP, USNA; Kissinger, *White House Years*, p. 626; Rabin, *The Rabin Memoirs*, p. 188; Rafael, *Destination Peace*, pp. 246–7.
74. State to Amman and Tel Aviv, no. 155203, 3.38am, 22 September 1970, Folder Jordan V, Box 615, NSC, Country Files, Middle East, RNPP, USNA.
75. Tel Aviv to State, 9.47am, 21 September 1970, Folder Jordan Crisis, Box 619, ibid; State to Amman, 4.16pm, 21 September 1970, ibid.
76. Interview, Henry Kissinger, New York, 2 June 2003.
77. State to Amman, no. 154462, 12.33pm, 21 September 1970, Folder Jordan Crisis, Box 619, NSC, Country Files, Middle East, RNPP, USNA.
78. Amman to State, no. 5008, 1.45pm, 21 September 1970, ibid.
79. Amman to State, no. 5015, 2.35pm, 21 September 1970, ibid.
80. State to Amman, 4.23pm, 21 September 1970, ibid.
81. Tel Aviv to State, no. 5232, 4.35pm, 21 September 1970, ibid.
82. Amman to State, no. 5020, 4.38pm, 21 September 1970, ibid.
83. State to Tel Aviv, no. 154558, 6.24pm, 21 September 1970, ibid.
84. Kissinger told me that it is not inconceivable that there could have been circumstances in which he would have approved action by Israel over King Hussein's objections, for instance if a Syrian takeover of Jordan was judged to be imminent (interview, Henry Kissinger, New York, 2 June 2003).
85. State to Tel Aviv and Amman, no. 155203, 3.38am, 22 September 1970, Folder Jordan V, Box 615, NSC, Country Files, Middle East, RNPP, USNA.
86. Amman to State, no. 5049, 1.25pm, 22 September 1970, ibid.
87. Amman to State, no. 5061, 4.20pm, 22 September 1970, ibid.
88. Amman to State, no. 5065, 6.40pm, 22 September 1970, Folder Jordan Crisis, Box 619, ibid.
89. Tel Aviv to FCO, 11.15am, 23 September 1970, FCO17/1044, TNA.
90. Middle East Sitrep, 7.00am, 23 September 1970, PREM15/124, TNA.
91. Rafael, *Destination Peace*, pp. 244–7; Rabin, *The Rabin Memoirs*, p. 187.
92. Quoted in Zak, 'Israel and Jordan', p. 48.
93. ibid, p. 59.
94. ibid, pp. 48–9. Kissinger told me that he knew nothing of this debate at the time. But he argues that the Israelis would have been aware that any move to undermine Hussein would have provoked a crisis in their relations with Washington (interview, Henry Kissinger, New York, 2 June 2003).
95. There seems to be no foundation for Alexander Haig's claim that the Israeli air force participated in this process (*Inner Circles*, pp. 250–1).
96. Amman to Tel Aviv, 10am, 23 September 1970, FCO17/1044, TNA; Teleprinter Conference with Amman, 1400Z, 23 September 1970, PREM15/124, TNA; Moon to Heath, 23 September 1970, ibid; interview, Zeid Rifai, Amman, 4 July 2007.
97. London to State, 1100Z, 22 September 1970, Folder Jordan Crisis, Box 619, NSC, Country Files, Middle East, RNPP, USNA.
98. Tel Aviv to FCO, 1100Z, 22 September 1970, FCO17/1044, TNA.
99. Record of Prime Minister's meeting with King Hussein, 4 December 1970, PREM15/540, TNA.
100. Tel Aviv to Ministry of Defence, 0950Z 24 September 1970, FCO17/1044, TNA.

101. State to Amman, 0251Z, 23 September 1970, Folder Jordan Crisis, Box 619, NSC, Country Files, Middle East, RNPP, USNA

102. Kissinger, *White House Years*, pp. 630–1; Rabin, *The Rabin Memoirs*, p. 189. See also Alexander Haig's memoirs for a classic expression of the Jordan crisis as seen in Cold War terms (*Inner Circles*, pp. 241–51).

103. Kissinger to Nixon, 'The Situation in Jordan', 28 September 1970, Folder Jordan V, Box 615, ibid.

104. Susser, *On Both Banks*, p. 141.

105. Podgorny to Hussein, 30 September 1970, Soviet File, RHA: Kosygin to Hussein, [undated, early] October 1970, ibid. Both letters are unofficial translations of the Russian originals.

106. Susser, *On Both Banks*, pp. 141–3.

107. ibid, pp. 151–2.

108. ibid, p. 154.

109. Abu Odeh, *Jordanians*, p. 188.

110. See the assessment of the immediate implications of the assassination in Eliot to Kissinger, 29 November 1971, Folder Jordan VII, 1 January – 31 December 1971, Box 616, NSC, Country Files, Middle East, RNPP, USNA.

111. Teleprinter Conference with Amman, 0930Z, 24 September 1970, PREM15/124, TNA.

Chapter 9: The October War

1. 'Jordan: First Impressions', Balfour Paul to Home, 26 September 1972, FCO17/1690, TNA.

2. Kissinger, H., *Years of Renewal* (New York: Simon & Schuster, 1999), p. 369.

3. Interview, Zeid bin Shaker, Amman, 23 March 2000.

4. Amman to FCO, 9 November 1972, FCO17/1683, TNA.

5. Phillips to Home, 2 December 1971, ibid.

6. ibid.

7. The framework of the plan was outlined in personal letters to Arab and Western leaders including Syrian President Hafez Asad, US President Nixon and British Prime Minister Heath in advance of its public announcement. See: Hussein to Asad, 13 March 1972, Syria File, RHA; Hussein to Nixon, 13 March 1972, White House Central File, Subject File, Countries, Box 46, Folder CO76, Jordan 1/1/71, RNPP, USNA; and Hussein to Heath, 13 March 1972, PREM15/1764, TNA. See also: Alkadiri, R., 'The Palestinian Factor in Jordanian Foreign Policy, 1967–1988', in Schulze, K.E., Stokes, M. and Campbell, C. (eds), *Nationalism, Minorities and Diasporas: Identities and Rights in the Middle East* (London: Tauris Academic Studies, 1996), pp. 71–4.

8. Amman to FCO, 'United Kingdom of Jordan and Palestine', 9 March 1972, PREM15/1764, TNA.

9. Phillips to FCO, 11 March 1972, FCO17/1687, TNA. Zeid Rifai denies the plan was discussed with the Israelis in advance. He argues that it was aimed at an Arab audience (interview, Zeid Rifai, Amman, 4 July 2007).

10. Statement to the Knesset by Prime Minister Meir, 16 March 1972, http://www.israel-mfa.gov.il/MFA/Foreign+Relations/Israels+Foreign+Relations+since+1947/1947-1974/37+Statement+to+the+Knesset+by+Prime+Minister+Meir.htm (accessed 24 July 2007). See also Eliot to Kissinger, 'Reactions to King Hussein's Federation Plan', 22 March 1972, NSC, Country Files, Middle East, Box 617, Folder Jordan Vol. VIII, 1972, RNPP, USNA.

11. Tel Aviv to FCO, 22 March 1972, PREM15/1764, TNA.

12. Amman to State, 'Jordan–Israel West Bank Deal', 13 March 1972, NSC, Country File, Middle East, Box 617, Folder Jordan Vol. VIII, 1972, RNPP, USNA.

13. Zak, 'Israel and Jordan', pp. 50–51.
14. Hart, A., *Arafat: A Political Biography* (Bloomington: Indiana University Press, 1989), pp. 356–7.
15. Hussein to Asad, 13 March 1972, Syria File, RHA.
16. Abu Odeh, *Jordanians*, pp. 205–8.
17. Amman to FCO, 'United Kingdom of Jordan and Palestine', 9 March 1972, PREM15/1764, TNA.
18. Rogers to Nixon, 'Hussein Visit', 23 March 1972, NSC, VIP Visits, Box 929, Folder Jordan – King Hussein, 28 March 1972, RNPP, USNA.
19. 'Color Report: Stag Dinner Honoring King Hussein', 29 March 1972, White House Central File, Subject File, Countries, Box 46, Folder CO76 Jordan 1/1/71, ibid.
20. 'Hiya King: Hussein in Florida', *Washington Post*, 23 April 1972.
21. Gore-Booth to Evans, 27 January 1972, FCO17/1705, TNA.
22. Hussein to Douglas-Home, 5 January 1972, British File, RHA. There are two copies of this letter in Hussein's files: the undated handwritten draft and a typed copy which bears the date 5 January 1972.
23. Amman to State, 'Schooling for King Hussein's Children in the US', 13 September 1972, NSC, Country File, Middle East, Box 617, Folder Jordan Vol. VIII, 1972, RNPP, USNA.
24. Balfour Paul to Parsons, 'Relations with Jordan: The Royal Children', 2 October 1972, FCO17/1693, TNA.
25. Hussein to Douglas-Home, 25 September 1972, British File, RHA.
26. Amman to State, 'School for King Hussein's Children in US', 19 September 1972, NSC, Country File, Middle East, Box 617, Folder Jordan Vol. XIII, 1972, RNPP, USNA.
27. Balfour Paul to Douglas-Home, 'Jordan: Annual Review, 1972', 8 January 1973, FCO93/79, TNA.
28. Amman to State, 7 December 1972, NSC, Country File, Middle East, Box 617, Folder Jordan Vol. XIII, 1972, RNPP.
29. J.A. Speares to Hussein, 31 December 1972 (handwritten note on British Embassy notepaper), British File, RHA.
30. Hussein to J.A. Speares, 8 January 1973, ibid.
31. D.E. Speares to Hussein, 15 December 1972, ibid.
32. Hussein to D.E. Speares, 8 January 1973, ibid. There are two copies of this letter in Hussein's files, one his handwritten draft and the other a typed final version.
33. Kissinger to Nixon, 'Visit of King Hussein of Jordan', 22 January 1973, White House Central File, Subject Series, Countries, Box 46, Folder CO76 Jordan 1/1/73, RNPP, USNA.
34. Amman to State, 9 January 1973, NSC, Country File, Middle East, Box 618, Folder Jordan, Vol. IX, Jan.–Oct. 1973, ibid.
35. Champion to Douglas-Home, 14 July 1972, FCO17/1707, TNA.
36. Interview, Henry Kissinger, New York, 2 June 2003; Kissinger to Nixon, 'Your Meeting with King Hussein – Summary of Main Points', undated, NSC, VIP Visits, Box 929, Folder Jordan King Hussein Visit, 6 February 1973 [1 of 2], RNPP, USNA.
37. Kissinger to Nixon, 'Your meeting with King Hussein on February 6', 5 February 1973, ibid. For Kissinger's account of the February talks see *Years of Upheaval*, pp. 216–60.
38. Kissinger, *Years of Upheaval*, p. 219.
39. Record of a Conversation between the Prime Minister and His Majesty King Hussein bin Talal, 12 July 1973, FCO93/97, TNA. According to Uri Bar Joseph (*The Watchman Fell Asleep*, Albany: State University of New York Press, 2005, p. 89), the King passed a similar warning to Israel via intelligence channels on 17 July.
40. Record of a Conversation between the Foreign and Commonwealth Secretary and King Hussein, 11 July 1973, FCO93/97, TNA.

41. Shlaim, 'His Royal Shyness', p. 17.
42. Pickering to Scowcroft, 'Hussein's Meeting in Cairo with Sadat and Assad', 19 September 1973, NSC, Country File, Middle East, Box 618, Folder Jordan Vol. IX, Jan.–Oct. 1973, RNPP, USNA.
43. Shlaim, 'His Royal Shyness', p. 17.
44. ibid.
45. Documentary evidence of this comes from a subsequent telegram from US Ambassador Pickering in Amman, reporting absolutely sensitive intelligence Hussein passed on in the summer of 1974 about a Syrian military build-up on the Golan Heights. 'This comes from the same source', the ambassador noted, 'which so accurately predicted [the] October War' (Amman to State, 28 August 1974, National Security Adviser, Country File, Middle East and South Asia, Box 22, Folder Jordan – State Dept. Telegrams, To SECSTATE NODIS (1), GRFP). Further information to substantiate this has come from American and Jordanian sources who wish to remain anonymous.
46. Interview, Thomas Pickering, Washington DC, 28 September 2007.
47. Bar-Joseph, Watchman, pp. 90–91. See also Kahana, E., 'Early Warning versus Concept: The Case of the Yom Kippur War 1973', Intelligence and National Security, 17/2, 2002, pp. 88–9. Moshe Zak also suggests that Hussein 'warned Israel of Syria's offensive preparations' during this meeting ('Israel and Jordan', p. 50). For further archival confirmation of Hussein's warning see: Deputy Assistant to the President for National Security Brent Scowcroft to Kissinger, 5 October 1973, enclosing message from Israeli Prime Minister Golda Meir (passed through Israeli chargé Shalev), NPMP, HAKO, box 136, Dinitz June 4, 1974 [sic]–Oct. 31, 1973, in Burr, W. (ed.), The October War and US Policy, National Security Archive (http://www.gwu.edu/~nsarchiv/NSAEBB/NSAEBB98/index.htm#doc7) (accessed 14 December 2006).
48. This information comes from American and Jordanian sources who wish to remain anonymous. In factual terms, their accounts complement and enhance what we know from Israeli sources, even if the interpretation they offer of the King's intentions in sharing this information with the Israelis is different.
49. Shlaim, 'His Royal Shyness', p. 17.
50. Shlaim, The Iron Wall, p. 319.
51. Amman to State, 7 October 1973, NSC, Country File, Middle East, Box 618, Folder Jordan Vol. IX, Jan.–Oct. 1973, RNPP, USNA.
52. Quandt, Peace Process, p. 158.
53. State to Amman, 9 October 1973, NSC, Country File, Middle East, Box 618, Folder, Jordan Vol. IX, Jan.–Oct. 1973, RNPP, USNA.
54. Amman to State, 11 October 1973, NSC, ibid.
55. Lunt, Hussein, p. 167.
56. Amman to FCO, 11 October 1973, PREM15/1765, TNA.
57. Telephone Conversation between the Prime Minister and Henry Kissinger at approx. 1.00am, 12 October 1973, PREM15/1765, TNA; Kissinger, H., Crisis: The Anatomy of Two Major Foreign Policy Crises (New York: Simon & Schuster, 2003), pp. 189–90.
58. Kissinger, Crisis, p. 190.
59. This followed an inconclusive telephone conversation between Kissinger and Ambassador Dinitz on the morning of 12 October (ibid, pp. 194–5).
60. State to Amman, 13 October 1973, NSC, Country File, Middle East, Box 618, Folder Jordan Vol. IX, Jan.–Oct. 1973, RNPP, USNA.
61. Tel Aviv to FCO, tel. no. 131620Z, 13 October 1973, PREM15/1765, TNA.
62. State to Amman, 0149Z, 15 October 1973, NSC, Country File, Middle East, Box 618, Folder Jordan Vol. IX, Jan.–Oct. 1973, RNPP, USNA.
63. Amman to State, O405Z, 13 October 1973, ibid.
64. Private information.

65. State to Amman, 1815Z, 15 October 1973, NSC, Country File, Middle East, Box 618, Folder Jordan Vol. IX, Jan.–Oct. 1973, RNPP, USNA.
66. Amman to State, 0105Z 16 October 1973, ibid.
67. State to Amman, 0211Z, 19 October 1973, ibid.
68. Amman to FCO, 22 October 1973, PREM15/1766, TNA.
69. Amman to State, 26 October 1973, NSC, Country File, Middle East, Box 618, Folder Jordan Vol. IX, Jan.–Oct. 1973, RNPP, USNA.
70. State to Amman, 27 October 1973, ibid.
71. Amman to State, 27 October 1973, ibid.

Chapter 10: Disengagement and Disillusionment, 1973–7

1. Interview, Henry Kissinger, New York, 2 June 2003.
2. ibid; also, interview, Zeid Rifai, Amman, 5 June 2002. See also Kissinger, *Years of Upheaval*, pp. 846–8, 976–7.
3. State to Amman, 5 March 1974, NSC, Country File, Middle East, Box 618, Folder Jordan Vol. X, Nov. 1973–, RNPP, USNA. Zeid Rifai subsequently also spoke positively about a meeting in London with 'one Israeli with whom they had worked hard to develop [a] bilateral relationship' (Amman to State, 2 April 1974, telegram no. 1699, ibid).
4. Record of a Conversation between the Foreign and Commonwealth Secretary and Dr Henry Kissinger at London Airport, 20 January 1974, PREM15/2153, TNA.
5. Interview, Zeid Rifai, Amman, 5 June 2002; Shlaim, *The Iron Wall*, pp. 331–4. Madfai, M.R.A., *Jordan, the United States and the Middle East Peace Process, 1974–1991* (Cambridge: CUP, 1993), pp. 19.
6. Record of a Conversation between the Prime Minister and the Prime Minister of Israel, 28 June 1974, PREM16/200, TNA.
7. Record of a Conversation between the Prime Minister and the US Secretary of State Kissinger, 8 July 1974, ibid.
8. Gelvin, J. L., *The Israel–Palestine Conflict* (Cambridge: CUP, 2005), p. 185.
9. Record of a conversation between the Minister of State for Foreign and Commonwealth Affairs and HRH Crown Prince Hassan, 29 May 1974, FCO93/423, TNA.
10. Record of a Conversation between the Prime Minister and King Hussein, 9 September 1974, PREM16/201, TNA.
11. Kissinger, *Years of Upheaval*, p. 757. According to a report from the US embassy in Amman, the Algiers conference brought the Hashemite regime to a state of 'near despondency' (Amman to State, 6 December 1973, NSC, Country File, Middle East, Box 618, Folder Jordan Vol. X, Nov. 1973–, RNPP).
12. Balfour Paul to Craig, 5 November 1974, FCO93/332, TNA.
13. Abu Odeh, *Jordanians*, p. 210.
14. Interview, Zeid Rifai, Amman, 5 June 2002. Kissinger did not recollect receiving a warning in these specific terms, but conceded that it sounded authentic (interview, Henry Kissinger, New York, 2 June 2003).
15. Interview, Zeid Rifai, Amman, 5 June 2002.
16. Interview, Henry Kissinger, New York, 2 June 2003. See also Kissinger, *Years of Upheaval*, pp. 1138–42; and *Years of Renewal*, pp. 355–84.
17. Kissinger, *Years of Renewal*, p. 383. See also Yitzhak Rabin's account of Kissinger's comments during the run-up to Rabat in *The Rabin Memoirs*, pp. 248–9.
18. Alkadiri, 'The Palestinian Factor', pp. 73–4.
19. Interview, Zeid Rifai, Amman, 5 June 2002; Abu Odeh, *Jordanians,* pp. 210–12.
20. 'Queen's Tenant' in 'Albany at Large', *Sunday Telegraph*, 8 December 1974.
21. Craig to Balfour Paul, 3 September 1974, FCO93/424, TNA.
22. Craig to Melhuish, 23 September 1974, ibid.
23. Richardson to Tait, 10 December 1974, ibid.

24. Amman to State, 6 March 1975, NSA Country File Middle East/South Asia, Box 22, Folder Jordan – State Dept telegrams To SecState Nodis 7, GRFP.
25. Brown to Kissinger, 2 June 1976, Amman telegram no.2954, NSA Country File Middle East/South Asia, Box 23, Folder Jordan – State Dept telegrams To SecState Nodis (26), GRFP.
26. Amman to State, 15 June 1975, NSA Country File Middle East/South Asia, Box 22, Folder Jordan – State Dept telegrams To SecState Nodis 10, GRFP.
27. ibid.
28. Amman to State, 24 March 1976, NSA Country File Middle East/South Asia, Box 23, Folder Jordan – State Dept telegrams To SecState Nodis 23, GRFP; Quandt, *Peace Process*, pp. 247–8.
29. 'Issues and Answers', 4 April 1976, Folder King Hussein interview, Box 68, GRFP.
30. Shlaim, *The Iron Wall*, p. 344; Rafael, *Destination Peace*, p. 363.
31. State to Amman, 18 July 1976, NSA Country File Middle East/South Asia, Box 21, Folder Jordan – State Dept telegrams From SecState to Nodis (8), GRFP; Kissinger, *Years of Renewal*, pp. 1048–9.
32. Kissinger to Hussein, 12 July 1976, President Ford File, RHA.
33. State to Amman, 17 October 1976, NSA Country File Middle East/South Asia, Box 21, Folder Jordan – State Dept telegrams From SecState to Nodis (8), GRFP.
34. Atherton and Vest to Kissinger, 4 March 1975, NSA Country File Middle East/South Asia, Box 20, Folder Jordan (2), GRFP; Amman to State, 18 April 1975, NSA Country File Middle East/South Asia, Box 21, Folder Jordan – State Dept telegrams, To SecState Exdis (2).
35. Kissinger to Ford, 15 January 1975, NSA Country File Middle East/South Asia, Box 20, Folder Jordan (1), GRFP.
36. Kissinger to Hussein, 22 July 1975, NSA Country File Middle East/South Asia, Box 21, Folder Jordan – State Dept telegrams From SecState to Nodis (5), GRFP.
37. Hussein to Kissinger, 23 July 1975, NSA Country File Middle East/South Asia, Box 22, Folder Jordan – State Dept telegrams To SecState Nodis (11), GRFP.
38. There is extensive correspondence on this issue in the NSA files at the Ford Library. See for example: Amman to State, telegram nos 6326 and 6328, 18 September 1975, NSA Country File Middle East/South Asia, Box 22, Folder Jordan – State Dept telegrams To SecState Nodis (14); Amman to State, telegram no. 6329, 18 September 1975, NSA Country File Middle East/South Asia, Box 21, Folder Jordan – State Dept telegrams, To SecState Exdis (2), ibid.
39. Kissinger to Pickering enc. Ford to Hussein, 20 September 1975, NSA Country File Middle East/South Asia, Box 21, Folder Jordan – State Dept telegrams From SecState to Nodis (6), GRFP.
40. Robins, *A History of Jordan*, pp. 142–3.
41. ibid, pp. 144–5.
42. Carter to Hussein, 20 February 1977, President Carter File, RHA.
43. 'CIA Paid Millions to Jordan's King Hussein', 18 February 1977, *Washington Post*, p. A1. For one critical comment on the Woodward story see Lofton to Powell, 25 February 1977, enc. 'Payments to Hussein? Check the Editorializing!', 22 February 1977, WHCF, Subject File, Box C)-40, Folder CO79 1/20/77–2/20/78, JCL.
44. See the discussion in chapter 3 above.
45. 'White House Reviewing Intelligence Operations', 19 February 1977, *Washington Post*, p. A1.
46. Private information.
47. This was precisely the fear that Hussein expressed in the immediate aftermath of the revelations (Amman to FCO, 21 February 1977, UKFOIA).
48. 'King Hussein', Associated Press report, 27 February 1977.
49. Note of a Meeting between the Prime Minister and King Hussein, 24 February 1977, UKFOIA.
50. Carter to Hussein, 12 March 1977, President Carter File, RHA.

Chapter 11: The Camp David Disaster, 1977–9

1. Reynolds, D., *Summits: Six Meetings that Shaped the Twentieth Century* (London: Allen Lane, 2007), p. 271.
2. Memcon, Brzezinski–Hassan, 2 June 1977, (7)NSA Brzezinski, Subject File, Box 33, Folder Memcons Brzezinski 1–9/77, JCL.
3. For Hussein's negative appraisal of the prospects for peace see: Brzezinski to Carter, 'Middle East Reports', 21 February 1977, Vertical File, Box 79, Folder Middle East, JCL; memorandum by Quandt, 'Current Negotiating Positions of the Parties', undated [February 1977], ibid. Also, 'Private Visit of King Hussein', Owen to Moberly, 28 February 1977, UKFOIA.
4. Callaghan's annotation on Amman to FCO, 17 August 1977, UKFOIA.
5. Shlaim, 'His Royal Shyness', p. 17.
6. Carter to Hussein, 30 July 1977, President Carter File, RHA.
7. Carter to Hussein, 16 August 1977, ibid.
8. Hussein to Carter, 16 August 1977, ibid.
9. Meeting of Foreign Minister Dayan with President Carter, 19 September 1977, Brzezinski Papers, Geographic File, Box 13, Folder Middle East – Negotiations (9/75–9/77), JCL.
10. Quandt to Brzezinski, 5 October 1977, Brzezinski Papers, Geographic File, Box 13, Folder Middle East – Negotiations (10/77–12/77), JCL.
11. Carter to Hussein, 15 October 1977, President Carter File, RHA.
12. Hussein to Carter, 26 October 1977, ibid.
13. Carter to Hussein, 30 October 1977, ibid.
14. Brzezinski, meeting with King Hussein, 18 March 1979, (7)NSA Brzezinski, Subject File, Box 33, Folder Memcons Brzezinski, 3–6/79, JCL.
15. King Hussein's interview for BBC *Panorama* programme, recorded 21 January 1978, FBIS, MEA-78-16, F2, Vol. V, 24 January 1978.
16. Brzezinski, meeting with King Hussein, 18 March 1979, (7)NSA Brzezinski, Subject File, Box 33, Folder Memcons Brzezinski, 3–6/79, JCL.
17. M.S. Weir, 'US Comments on Arab/Israel Peace Negotiations', 20 February 1978, UKFOIA.
18. Note of a Conversation at the Prime Minister's Dinner for King Hussein, 22 February 1978, UKFOIA.
19. King Hussein interview for BBC *Panorama* programme, recorded 21 January 1978, FBIS, MEA-78-16, F3, Vol. V, 24 January 1978.
20. Hussein to Callaghan, 14 December 1977, British File, RHA.
21. Note of a Conversation at the Prime Minister's Dinner for King Hussein, 22 February 1978, UKFOIA.
22. Brzezinski, meeting with King Hussein, 18 March 1979, (7)NSA Brzezinski, Subject File, Box 33, Folder Memcons Brzezinski, 3–6/79, JCL.
23. For more detail on the Administration's change of course see Quandt, W.B., *Camp David: Peacemaking and Politics* (Washington DC: Brookings Institution, 1986), pp. 135–67.
24. Carter to Hussein, 1 January 1978, President Carter File, RHA.
25. Hussein to Carter, 13 March 1978, ibid.
26. Carter to Hussein, [with Hussein's annotations], 18 March 1978, ibid.
27. Carter to Hussein, 13 May 1978, ibid.
28. Sadat to Hussein, 28 December 1978, Egypt File, RHA. See also Stein, *Heroic Diplomacy*, pp. 238–42, for an account of the Ismailiya summit.
29. Hussein to Sadat, 12 January 1978, Egypt File, RHA.
30. Arafat to Hussein, 28 February 1978, PLO File, RHA.
31. Hussein to Arafat, 22 March 1978, ibid.
32. Sadat to Hussein, 28 April 1978, Egypt File, RHA.
33. Carter to Hussein, 15 August 1978, President Carter File, RHA.

34. Hussein to Carter, 27 August 1978, ibid.

35. Dayan commented indirectly on his meeting with Hussein in his 19 September 1977 discussions with Carter (Brzezinski Papers, Geographic File, Box 13, Folder Middle East – Negotiations (9/75–9/77), JCL). See also Shlaim, 'His Royal Shyness', p. 17.

36. Vance to Carter, 'Study Papers for the Camp David Talks', undated [September 1978], Vertical File, Box 8(1), Folder Camp David Study Papers, JCL; Quandt, *Camp David*, pp. 219–20.

37. Sadat to Hussein, 16 August 1978, Egypt File, RHA.

38. Hussein to Sadat, 23 August 1978, ibid.

39. Quandt, *Camp David*, p. 243. See also Carter, J., *Keeping Faith: Memoirs of a President* (New York: Bantam Books, 1982), pp. 396–7.

40. Interview, Mudar Badran, Amman, 20 May 2001.

41. For the text of the agreement see Quandt, *Camp David*, appendix G, pp. 376–81.

42. Brzezinski, meeting with King Hussein, 18 March 1979, (7)NSA Brzezinski, Subject File, Box 33, Folder Memcons Brzezinski, 3–6/79, JCL.

43. Carter to Hussein, 18 September 1978, President Carter File, RHA.

44. Carter to Hussein, 19 September 1978, ibid. It was the 'threatening' tone of the letter which Jordanian Prime Minister Mudar Badran recollected (interview, Mudar Badran, Amman, 20 May 2001).

45. Sadat to Hussein, 28 September 1978, Egypt File, RHA.

46. Quandt, *Camp David*, pp. 264–6. For the full text of the Jordanian questions and the American answers see Appendix H, pp. 388–96. See also Vance, C., *Hard Choices: Critical Years in America's Foreign Policy* (New York: Simon & Schuster, 1983), pp. 229–31.

47. King Hussein's 23 September 1978 Press Conference, FBIS, MEA-78-188, F4, Vol. V, 27 September 1978.

48. King Hussein's speech, Amman Domestic TV, 10 October 1978, FBIS, MEA-78-197, F4, Vol. V, 11 October 1978.

49. Hussein to Sadat, 14 October 1978, Egypt File, RHA.

50. Quandt, *Camp David*, pp. 274–5.

51. Hussein to Carter, [final] 31 October 1978, and Hussein to Carter [draft], 30 October 1978, President Carter File, RHA.

52. Hussein to Carter, 31 October 1978, ibid.

53. Brzezinski, meeting with King Hussein, 18 March 1979, (7)NSA Brzezinski, Subject File, Box 33, Folder Memcons Brzezinski, 3–6/79, JCL. Brzezinski later described the King as negative and resentful at having been left out of the process (*Power and Principle*, p. 286).

54. Hussein to Carter, 29 December 1978, President Carter File, RHA.

55. Carter, *Keeping Faith*, p. 410.

56. Carter to Hussein, 14 March 1979, President Carter File, RHA.

57. Carter to Hussein, 16 March 1979, ibid.

58. Madfai, *Jordan*, p. 55.

59. Hussein interview as reported in *Ad-Dustur*, 30 March 1979, FBIS, MEA-79-063, F2, Vol. V, 30 March 1979.

60. Hussein interview with *al-Hawadith*, FBIS, MEA-079-073, F1, Vol. V, 13 April 1979.

61. Quandt, *Camp David*, p. 312.

62. Hussein interview with *al-Hawadith*, FBIS, MEA-079-073, F4, Vol. V, 13 April 1979.

63. Hussein to Carter, 29 November 1979, President Carter File, RHA.

64. Hussein to Carter, 30 December 1979, ibid.

65. Brzezinski to Carter, 20 December 1979, (7)NSA Brzezinski Subject File, Box 50, Folder Presidential Determinations, 8/79–5/80, JCL. For Vance's recommendation see Vance to Carter, 5 December 1979, ibid.

66. For press reports of the visit see: First Lady's Press Office, Press Clips, State Dinners, Box 43, Folder King Hussein of Jordan, 17 June 1980, JCL.

67. Queen Noor, *Leap of Faith*, pp. 193–4.
68. *Washington Star*, 18 June 1980, First Lady's Press Office, Press Clips, State Dinners, Box 43, Folder King Hussein of Jordan, 17 June 1980, JCL.
69. Memcon, 3.30pm, 18 June 1980, DDRS.

Chapter 12: The Iran–Iraq War, 1980–88

1. King Hussein's interview with *al-Mustaqbal*, FBIS, MEA-81-061, F5, Vol. V, 31 March 1981.
2. For instance, Dallas (*A Life on the Edge*) makes little mention of the King's backing for Saddam in the Iran–Iraq war, while Lunt devotes only just over two pages to a brief discussion of the war and its consequences for Jordan (*Hussein*, pp. 214–16).
3. See for example King Hussein to Saddam Hussein, 21 March 1985, Iraq File, RHA; and Saddam Hussein to King Hussein, 31 May 1986, ibid.
4. Baram, A., 'Baathi Iraq and Hashemite Jordan: From Hostility to Alignment', *Middle East Journal*, 45/1, 1991, p. 64.
5. Handwritten letter, Saddam Hussein to King Hussein, 31 May 1986, Iraq File, RHA.
6. Robins, *A History of Jordan*, p. 151.
7. For discussion of the economic aspects of the Iraqi–Jordanian relationship during this period see Brand, L., *Jordan's Inter-Arab Relations: The Political Economy of Alliance Making* (New York: Columbia University Press, 1994), pp. 196–241.
8. Amman TV report, 25 February 1981, news digest, FBIS, MEA-81-038, Vol. V, 26 February 1981.
9. King Hussein, al-Karameh day speech, 21 March 1981, FBIS, MEA-81-055, F5, Vol. V, 23 March 1981.
10. Interview, Roscoe Suddarth, New York, 23 March 2001. Hussein's comment was made specifically in response to a US protest about Saddam's use of Aqaba in 1989 to ship missiles to the anti-Syrian Lebanese leader, Michel Aoun.
11. Text of King Hussein's 'Pan-Arab' speech, 6 October 1980, FBIS, MEA-80-196, F1–4, Vol. V, 7 October 1980.
12. Hussein quoted in Mufti, 'A King's Art', p. 19. Mufti argues convincingly that Jordanian foreign policy under Hussein can only be understood fully through an interpretation which blends national interest with dynastic ambition.
13. Interview, Awn Khasawneh, The Hague, 17 February 2001.
14. King Hussein's BBC interview, FBIS, MEA-80-199, F3, Vol. V, 10 October 1980.
15. Hussein to Reagan, 30 January 1982, President Reagan File, RHA.
16. Hussein to Reagan, 15 February 1982, ibid.
17. Hussein to Reagan, 18 May 1982, ibid.
18. Hussein to Reagan, 6 December 1986, ibid.
19. Hussein to Reagan, 15 February 1982, ibid.
20. Hussein to Reagan, 6 December 1986, ibid.
21. Hussein to Reagan, 18 May 1982, ibid.
22. Hussein to Reagan, 4 July 1982, ibid.
23. Hussein letter as broadcast on Amman Domestic Service, FBIS, MEA-81-112, F1, Vol. V, 11 June 1981. The original, dated 10 June 1981, is in the President Reagan File, RHA. The King later apologised for the fact that the text of the letter was publicised before it reached Reagan (Hussein to Reagan, 7 August 1981, RHA).
24. Hussein interview as broadcast on Amman Domestic Service, FBIS, MEA-81-115, F1, Vol. V, 16 June 1981.
25. Hussein speech as broadcast on Amman Domestic Service, FBIS, MEA-81-114, F2, Vol. V, 15 June 1981.
26. Hussein interview as broadcast on Amman Domestic Service, FBIS, MEA-81-130, F2, Vol. V, 8 July 1981.

27. King Hussein interviewed by Kuwaiti editors, FBIS, MEA-82-032, F8, Vol. V, 17 February 1982.
28. ibid, F9.
29. Hussein to Reagan, 30 January 1982, President Reagan File, RHA.
30. Reagan to Hussein, 9 February 1982, ibid.
31. The King may also have had advance warning from Saddam of his intention to invoke the Arab League's 1950 Joint Defence Pact, a call which the Iraqi president duly made on 23 May. In the absence of any American commitment to aid Iraq, the King might have felt obliged to answer this call with the provision of Jordanian forces (Hiro, D., *The Longest War: The Iran–Iraq Military Conflict* (London: Paladin, 1990), p. 60).
32. Hussein to Reagan, 18 May 1982, President Reagan File, RHA.
33. Hussein to Reagan, 22 May 1982, ibid.
34. King Hussein to Saddam Hussein, 21 March 1985, Iraq File, RHA.
35. King Hussein to Saddam Hussein, 11 April 1985, ibid.
36. The March 1985 offensive had also taken place in this area, but the references in Hussein's letter back to Iraqi failures during this operation lead me to believe that the intelligence report cannot simply be misdated.
37. Hussein's account of this episode is in Hussein to Reagan, 17 November 1986, President Reagan File, RHA.
38. King Hussein interview with *Le Monde*, FBIS, MEA-87-010, F1-2, Vol. V, 15 January 1987.
39. Reagan to Hussein, 15 November 1986, President Reagan File, RHA.
40. ibid.
41. Hussein to Reagan, 17 November 1986, ibid.
42. For more on Operation Staunch see Jentleson, B. W., *With Friends Like These: Reagan, Bush and Saddam, 1982–1990* (New York: W. W. Norton & Company, 1994), p. 57.
43. Reagan to Hussein, 26 November 1986, President Reagan File, RHA.
44. Hussein to Reagan, 6 December 1986, ibid.
45. ibid.
46. Reagan to Hussein, 28 December 1986, ibid.
47. King Hussein interview with Radio Monte Carlo, FBIS, MEA-87-009, F1-3, Vol. V, 14 January 1987.
48. Saddam Hussein to King Hussein, 31 May 1986, Iraq File, RHA.
49. King Hussein to Saddam Hussein, 5 August 1986, ibid.
50. Hussein to Asad, 26 March 1987, Syria File, RHA.
51. This detail comes from a member of the Hashemite family who was present during the meeting.
52. See for example British Prime Minister Margaret Thatcher's report to Hussein on her discussion of the issue with President Reagan, in Thatcher to Hussein, 24 July 1987, British File, RHA.
53. Hussein to Thatcher, 4 August 1988, ibid; Hussein to Reagan, 4 August 1988, President Reagan File, RHA.
54. ibid.
55. Hussein to Reagan, 3 October 1988, President Reagan File, RHA; Hussein to Thatcher, 3 October 1988, British File, RHA.
56. Thatcher to Hussein, 21 October 1988, British File, RHA.

Chapter 13: Fishing in the Dead Sea: Hussein and the Peace Process, 1980–89

1. Hussein to Bush, 7 November 1980, President Reagan File, RHA.
2. Interview, Richard Murphy, New York, 29 March 2001.
3. King Hussein's press conference, FBIS, MEA-81-215, F1, Vol. V, 6 November 1981.

4. Peres, S., *Battling for Peace: Memoirs* (London: Orion, 1996), p. 357.
5. Interview, Zeid Rifai, Amman, 24 September 1999.
6. Hussein to Reagan, 15 February 1982, President Reagan File, RHA.
7. Record of a Conversation between the Prime Minister and King Hussein, 17 November 1981, UKFOIA.
8. Interview, King Abdullah, Amman, 5 July 2007.
9. Hussein to Reagan, 7 August 1981, President Reagan File, RHA.
10. ibid.
11. ibid.
12. Associated Press report, 20 November 1981.
13. Djerejian to Hussein, 21 November 1981, President Reagan File, RHA.
14. Hussein to Reagan, 21 November 1981, ibid. Hussein also wrote to Prime Minister Thatcher, asking her to use her influence with the president to 'clarify the position in a satisfactory way' (see Thatcher to Hussein, 4 December 1981, British File, RHA).
15. Reagan to Hussein, 23 November 1981, President Reagan File, RHA.
16. Reagan to Hussein, 12 January 1982, ibid.
17. Hussein to Reagan, 22 June 1982, ibid.
18. See his letters to Reagan, dated 13, 14 and 22 June 1982, ibid; and his letter to Thatcher, 14 June 1982, British File RHA.
19. Quandt, *Peace Process*, p. 345.
20. Hussein to Reagan, 24 August 1982, President Reagan File, RHA.
21. Reagan to Hussein, 28 August 1982, ibid.
22. Hussein to Reagan, 29 August 1982, ibid.
23. Hussein to Reagan, 10 April 1983, ibid.
24. Record of a conversation between the Prime Minister and the King of Jordan, 22 July 1982, UKFOIA.
25. Reagan to Hussein, 16 September 1982, President Reagan File, RHA.
26. Hussein to Reagan, 11 October 1982, ibid.
27. Brezhnev to Hussein, 27 September 1982, Soviet File, RHA.
28. See Hussein to Brezhnev, 20 July 1981, ibid, for the King's expression of satisfaction at this burgeoning relationship.
29. Reagan to Hussein, 23 December 1982, President Reagan File, RHA.
30. In a document summarising the reasons for the collapse of the agreement in his private files, Hussein noted that five days after Arafat's departure from Amman to seek the final approval of the PLO, he received a PLO emissary carrying 'new ideas and methods' which would, as far as he was concerned, have brought them back to where they had started their negotiations in October 1982. This was why he had chosen to break off their discussions (Summary of Jordanian–PLO negotiations, 10 April 1983, PLO File, RHA).
31. Hussein to Reagan, 10 April 1983, President Reagan File, RHA.
32. Hart, *Arafat*, pp. 461–2; Sayigh, *Armed Struggle*, pp. 556–8.
33. See Begin's comments to US envoy Philip Habib in Jerusalem to State, 25 November 1982, Document no. CK3100540820, *DDRS*.
34. Queen Noor, *Leap of Faith*, pp. 235–6.
35. Seale, *Asad*, pp. 464–5.
36. Hussein to Reagan, 27 February 1984, President Reagan File, RHA.
37. Hussein to Reagan, 9 December 1983, ibid.
38. Shultz, *Turmoil and Triumph*, pp. 444–5.
39. Interview, Richard Murphy, New York, 29 March 2001.
40. King Hussein to Saddam Hussein, 31 March 1984, Iraq File, RHA. Hussein expressed similar frustration with the US approach in a letter sent to the new Soviet leader Chernyenko on 25 April 1984 (Soviet File, RHA).
41. Hussein to Reagan, 22 March 1985, President Reagan File, RHA.
42. 'A Proposal for Joint Action', with attachment 'Our Interpretation of Articles Two and Five', 11 February 1985, ibid.

43. Arafat to Hussein, 14 February 1985, PLO File, RHA.
44. Baghdad to State, 28 March 1985, telegram no. 0892, National Security Archive.
45. Lukacs, *Israel*, p. 163; Sayigh, *Armed Struggle*, pp. 578–9.
46. Reagan to Hussein, 2 March 1985, President Reagan File, RHA.
47. Shultz, *Turmoil and Triumph*, p. 444.
48. See for example Thatcher to Hussein, undated [February 1986], British File, RHA.
49. Thatcher to Hussein, 27 February 1985, ibid.
50. See Thatcher to Hussein, 24 July 1987, ibid. British files provide much further evidence of this link throughout the 1980s. See for example Thatcher to Reagan, 22 December 1983, UKFOIA: 'We, the West, should consider urgently what kind of support we can best give to Hussein at this difficult time.'
51. Hussein to Reagan, 22 March 1985, President Reagan File, RHA.
52. Reagan to Hussein, 19 May 1985, ibid.
53. Shultz, *Turmoil and Triumph*, pp. 448, 451.
54. Interview, Zeid Rifai, Amman, 5 June 2002.
55. Interview, Richard Murphy, New York, 29 March 2001.
56. Apart from the inevitable Arab opposition, the new Soviet leader Mikhail Gorbachev made it clear that the Kremlin also opposed any separate agreement with Israel signed under US pressure (Gorbachev to Hussein, 28 September 1985, Soviet File, RHA).
57. Interview, Zeid Rifai, Amman, 5 June 2002.
58. Shlaim, *The Iron Wall*, pp. 432–5.
59. Hussein to Reagan [draft letter], 30 June 1986, President Reagan File, RHA.
60. Seale, *Asad*, p. 466.
61. Hussein's words as reported by Rifai to Shultz, *Turmoil and Triumph*, p. 461.
62. As quoted in Madfai, *Jordan*, p. 176.
63. Abu Odeh, *Jordanians*, p. 223.
64. ibid.
65. Mufti, 'A King's Art', p. 8.
66. ibid, p. 9.
67. Peres, *Battling for Peace*, pp. 356–61.
68. Interview, Zeid Rifai, Amman, 5 June 2002.
69. ibid.
70. Shultz, *Turmoil and Triumph*, p. 938.
71. ibid, p. 939.
72. Peres, *Battling for Peace*, p. 361.
73. Shamir, *Summing Up*, p. 169.
74. Shultz, *Turmoil and Triumph*, pp. 940–41.
75. Shlaim, 'His Royal Shyness', p. 18.
76. Shlaim, 'His Royal Shyness', p. 18.
77. King Hussein's interview with the *Boston Globe*, as quoted in the *Jordan Times*, FBIS, MEA-87-087, F1, Vol. V, 6 May 1987.
78. Queen Noor, *Leap of Faith*, pp. 276–7.
79. Shultz, *Turmoil and Triumph*, pp. 942–3.
80. Thatcher to Hussein, 24 July 1987, British File, RHA.
81. ibid.
82. Lukacs, *Israel*, pp. 167–70.
83. Abu Odeh, *Jordanians*, pp. 224–5. This appeal was issued in defiance of the mainstream leadership of the PLO (Sayigh, *Armed Struggle*, p. 635).
84. Interview, Adnan Abu Odeh, Amman, 14 April 2000.
85. Abu Odeh, *Jordanians*, p. 225.
86. Interview, Adnan Abu Odeh, Amman, 14 April 2000.
87. For the full text of the speech see: http://www.kinghussein.gov.jo/88_july31.html (accessed 4 January 2007). See also Lukacs, *Israel*, pp. 174–6, for discussion of the possible reasons for Hussein's decision.

88. Abu Odeh, *Jordanians*, p. 226.
89. Interview, Zeid Rifai, Amman, 5 June 2002.
90. Hussein to Arafat, 30 July 1988, PLO File, RHA.
91. Ambassador Roscoe Suddarth had picked up some advance indications that a change in Jordanian strategy was being contemplated, as had Wat Cluverius, the president's special adviser on Middle East Affairs (interview, Roscoe Suddarth, Washington DC, 23 March 2001).
92. Shultz, *Turmoil and Triumph*, p. 1033.
93. Hussein to Reagan, 28 July 1988, President Reagan File, RHA; Hussein to Thatcher, 28 July 1988, British File, RHA.
94. Robins, *A History of Jordan*, pp. 163–4; Mufti, 'A King's Art', p. 10.
95. Garfinkle, *Israel and Jordan*, p. 148.
96. For more detail on the rise of Hamas see Sayigh, *Armed Struggle*, pp. 627–32.
97. Shlaim, *The Iron Wall*, p. 459.
98. Lukacs, *Israel*, pp. 177–9.
99. Thatcher to Hussein, 20 November 1988, British File, RHA.
100. Garfinkle, *Israel and Jordan*, p. 150.
101. EIU Country Report, Jordan, No. 1, 1989, p. 9.
102. Robins, *A History of Jordan*, pp. 166–70.
103. Robinson, G.E., 'Defensive Democratization in Jordan', *International Journal of Middle East Studies*, 30/3, 1998, p. 391.
104. EIU Country Report, Jordan, No. 3, 1989, p. 9.
105. Ryan, C., 'Jordan and the Rise and Fall of the Arab Cooperation Council', *Middle East Journal*, 52/3, 1998, p. 393. For a discussion of how the King arrived at the decision to hold elections see Mufti, M., 'Elite Bargains and the Onset of Political Liberalization in Jordan', *Comparative Political Studies*, 32/1, 1999, pp. 105–6.
106. Robinson, 'Defensive Democratization', p. 392. See also Milton-Edwards, B., 'Façade Democracy and Jordan', *British Journal of Middle Eastern Studies*, 20/2, 1993, pp. 194–6.
107. EIU Country Report, Jordan, No. 1, 1990, p. 10.
108. For the full text of the National Charter see: http://www.kinghussein.gov.jo/charter-national.html (accessed 4 January 2007). For further discussion of its implications see Robinson, 'Defensive Democratization', pp. 393–4; Mufti, 'Elite Bargains', pp. 114–16.
109. George, A., *Jordan: Living in the Crossfire* (London: Zed Books, 2005).
110. Interview, Queen Noor, Ascot, 10 July 1999. See also Queen Noor, *Leap of Faith*, p. 279.
111. ibid, pp. 271–3.

Chapter 14: Between Iraq and a Hard Place: King Hussein and the Gulf Crisis, 1990–91

1. Halevy, E., *Man in the Shadows* (London: Weidenfeld & Nicolson, 2006), pp. 27–8.
2. Cockburn, A. and Cockburn, P., *Out of the Ashes: The Resurrection of Saddam Hussein* (New York: Harper Perennial, 2000), p. 155.
3. Hussein to Bush, 9 April 1990, President Bush File, RHA.
4. Hussein to Bush, 7 November 1980, President Reagan File, RHA.
5. Bush to Hussein, 16 December 1988, President Bush File, RHA.
6. Hussein to Bush, 9 April 1990, ibid.
7. Bouillon, M., 'Walking the Tightrope: Jordanian Foreign Policy from the Gulf Crisis to the Peace Process and Beyond', in Joffé, G. (ed.), *Jordan in Transition, 1990–2000* (London: Hurst & Co., 2002), pp. 6–7; Milton-Edwards, 'Façade Democracy', p. 197.
8. Lynch, M., *State Interests and Public Spheres: the International Politics of Jordan's Identity* (New York: Columbia University Press, 1999), pp. 150–1.

9. Ryan, C.R., 'Jordan and the Rise and Fall of the Arab Cooperation Council', *Middle East Journal*, 52/3, 1998, pp. 390–91.

10. This Jordanian official asked to remain anonymous. His account is backed up in general terms by at least one other anonymous Jordanian source.

11. Khaled bin Sultan, *Desert Warrior: A Personal View of the Gulf War by the Joint Forces Commander* (New York: Harper Collins, 1995), p. 157.

12. EIU, Country Report, Jordan, No. 3, 1989, pp. 8–9.

13. Ryan, 'ACC', p. 399.

14. Brand, *Jordan's Inter-Arab Relations*, pp. 230–1.

15. Baram, A., 'Baathi Iraq and Hashimite Jordan', pp. 61–2.

16. EIU, Country Report, Jordan, No. 2, 1990, p. 10.

17. Khadduri, M., 'Nuri al-Sa'id's Disenchantment with Britain in his Last Years', *Middle East Journal*, 54/1, 2000, pp. 91–6.

18. Gause, F.G., 'Iraq's Decision to Go to War, 1980 and 1990', *Middle East Journal*, 56/1, 2002, p. 55–9.

19. For a discussion of Saddam's mindset based on interviews with regime members and captured Iraqi documents see Woods, K.M., Pease, M.R., Stout, M.E., Murray, W. and Lacey, J.G., *Iraq Perspectives Project: A View of Operation Iraqi Freedom from Iraq's Senior Leadership* (2006), pp. 12–14 http://www.jfcom.mil/newslink/storyarchive/2006/ipp.pdf (accessed 12 January 2007), hereafter *IPP*.

20. *The Economist*, 6 January 2007, p. 31.

21. EIU, Country Report, Jordan, No. 2, 1990, pp. 10–11.

22. Saddam quoted in Freedman, L. and Karsh, E., *The Gulf Conflict, 1990–1991: Diplomacy and War in the New World Order* (Princeton: Princeton University Press, 1993), p. 32.

23. *IPP*, p. 6.

24. EIU, Country Report, Jordan, No. 3, 1990, p. 7.

25. Freedman and Karsh, *The Gulf Conflict*, p. 45.

26. ibid, pp. 47–8.

27. Interviews, Marwan Qasim, Amman, 17 April 2000, 23 May 2001.

28. Interview, Mudar Badran, Amman, 20 May 2001.

29. Interviews, Marwan Qasim, Amman, 17 April 2000, 23 May 2001, 26 September 2002; interview, Mudar Badran, Amman, 20 May 2001; interview, Adnan Abu Odeh, Amman, 14 April 2000.

30. Freedman and Karsh, *The Gulf Conflict*, p. 60.

31. Gause, 'Iraq's Decision', pp. 53–4.

32. Khaled, *Desert Warrior*, pp. 180–1; Robins, *A History of Jordan*, pp. 177–8; Baker, J., *The Politics of Diplomacy* (New York: G. P. Putnam's Sons, 1995), pp. 290–1.

33. Bush and Scowcroft, *A World Transformed* (New York: Vintage Books, 1999), pp. 339–40. In a subsequent letter to Bush sent on 10 January 1991, Hussein wrote: 'I am sure you know by now that we never engaged nor were we ever involved in any plan or action against any of our Arab brethren . . .' (President Bush File, RHA).

34. *IPP*, p. 12.

35. *White Paper*, p. 3.

36. Khaled, *Desert Warrior*, p. 17.

37. Interview, Mudar Badran, Amman, 20 May 2001; interview, Marwan Qasim, Amman, 26 September 2002.

38. *White Paper*, p. 3.

39. Bush and Scowcroft, *A World Transformed*, p. 318.

40. *White Paper*, p. 4.

41. *White Paper*, pp. 5, 22.

42. *White Paper*, p. 5.

43. Freedman and Karsh, *The Gulf Conflict*, p. 70.

44. Quoted in *IPP*, pp. 13–14.

45. Captured media tape, September/October 1990, quoted in *IPP*, p. 12.

46. Bush and Scowcroft, *A World Transformed*, p. 320.
47. Lesch, A. M., 'Contrasting Reactions to the Persian Gulf Crisis: Egypt, Syria, Jordan and the Palestinians', *Middle East Journal*, 45/1, 1991, p. 44.
48. Baker, *The Politics of Diplomacy*, p. 450.
49. Bush and Scowcroft, *A World Transformed*, p. 349.
50. ibid, p. 348.
51. Interview with former senior Jordanian official, 24 June 2000.
52. Heikal, M., *Illusions of Triumph: An Arab View of the Gulf War* (London: Harper Collins, 1992), p. 256.
53. *White Paper*, pp. 33–4.
54. ibid, p. 10.
55. Hussein to Gorbachev, 6 October 1990, Soviet File, RHA.
56. Arafat to Hussein, 24 September 1990, PLO File, RHA.
57. Bush and Scowcroft, *A World Transformed*, p. 348.
58. Freedman and Karsh, *The Gulf Conflict*, p. 137.
59. EIU, Country Report, Jordan, No. 1, 1991, p. 10.
60. This exchange is quoted in a later letter, from Hussein to Hassan, 1 February 1998, http://www.kinghussein.gov.jo/speeches_letters.html (accessed 24 April 2007).
61. http://www.un.org/aboutun/charter/chapter7.htm (accessed 10 April 2007).
62. Freedman and Karsh, *The Gulf Conflict*, p. 134.
63. Robins, *A History of Jordan*, p. 178; Khaled, *Desert Warrior*, pp. 181, 210.
64. EIU, Country Report, Jordan, No. 4, 1990, p. 10.
65. Halevy, *Man in the Shadows*, p. 27.
66. Interview, Adnan Abu Odeh, Amman, 14 April 2000.
67. For King Hussein's account see Shlaim, 'His Royal Shyness', p. 18; for Adnan Abu Odeh, interview, Amman, 14 April 2000; for Ali Shukri, interview, Amman, 26 February 2007; for Zeid bin Shaker, interview, Amman, 23 March 2000. For Yitzhak Shamir's version see Zak, 'Israel and Jordan', pp. 53–4. Efraim Halevy's account is in *Man in the Shadows*, pp. 30–32.
68. Interview, Adnan Abu Odeh, Amman, 14 April 2000.
69. Interview, Zeid bin Shaker, Amman, 23 March 2000.
70. Halevy, *Man in the Shadows*, p. 31.
71. ibid, p. 32.
72. ibid, p. 35.
73. ibid, p. 34.
74. Gorbachev to Hussein, 18 January 1991, Soviet File, RHA.
75. Hussein to Bush, 10 January 1991, President Bush File, RHA.
76. Queen Noor, *Leap of Faith*, 328.
77. Bush to Hussein, 29 January 1991, President Bush File, RHA.
78. Hussein to Bush, 2 February 1991, ibid.
79. Hussein's 6 February 1991 speech in *White Paper*, p. 63.
80. Interview, Adnan Abu Odeh, Amman, 14 April 2000. It should be noted that Abu Odeh referred to the other speechwriter as 'Mr X' in this interview.
81. Bush to Hussein, 9 February 1991, document no. CK3100554218, *DDRS*.
82. Hussein to Bush, 16 February 1991, President Bush File, RHA.
83. Interview, Adnan Abu Odeh, Amman, 14 April 2000.
84. Mufti, 'A King's Art', p. 15.
85. Gause, 'Iraq's Decision', p. 61; Freedman and Karsh, *The Gulf Conflict*, p. 379.
86. *IPP*, p. 16.
87. Hussein to Bush, 28 February 1991, document no. CK3100554220, *DDRS*.
88. Hussein's annotation can be found on the copy of this letter in his personal files (Hussein to Bush, 28 February 1991, President Bush File, RHA).

Chapter 15: From Madrid to Oslo: King Hussein and the Peace Process, 1991–3

1. Interview with former Jordanian official.
2. Queen Noor, *Leap of Faith*, pp. 340–41.
3. Baker, *The Politics of Diplomacy*, p. 451.
4. Hussein to Bush, 22 April 1991, President Bush File, RHA.
5. ibid.
6. Baker, *The Politics of Diplomacy*, pp. 464–5.
7. EIU, Country Report, Jordan, No. 3, 1991, p. 11; Lukacs, *Israel*, p. 187.
8. Bush to Hussein, 31 May 1991, document no. CK3100554831, *DDRS*. There is also a copy of this letter in Hussein's own files.
9. Hussein to Bush, 3 June 1991, President Bush File, RHA.
10. Bush to Hussein, 19 September 1991, ibid. See *White Paper*, pp. 2–3, for the specific points Bush challenges in this letter.
11. Majali, A.S.A., Anani, J.A. and Haddadin, M.J., *Peacemaking: The Inside Story of the 1994 Jordanian–Israeli Treaty* (Reading: Ithaca Press, 2006), p. 13.
12. Bush to Hussein, undated (October 1991), document no. CK3100554833, *DDRS*. This letter can also be found in Hussein's own files.
13. Conversation, Awn Khasawneh, The Hague, 17 March 2007.
14. Interview, Adnan Abu Odeh, Amman, 14 April 2000. See also Brand, L., 'The Effects of the Peace Process on Political Liberalization in Jordan', *Journal of Palestine Studies*, 28/2, 1999, pp. 56–7.
15. Interview, Zeid bin Shaker, Amman, 23 March 2000.
16. Baker to Hussein, 10 February 1992, President Bush File, RHA.
17. Interview, Abdul Salam Majali, Amman, 11 April 2000. See also, Majali, Anani and Haddadin, *Peacemaking*, pp. 14, 25.
18. What follows is based on numerous conversations with Awn Khasawneh, but especially one in The Hague on 17 March 2007. Both Munther Haddadin (interview, Amman, 25 February 2007), the author of *Peacemaking*, and Professor James Crawford (interview, Cambridge, 21 November 2000) have confirmed the centrality of Awn Khasawneh's legal role for Jordan in their comments to me on the negotiations. Nevertheless, there were other negotiators on the Jordanian team who also handled their briefs well, especially Munther Haddadin who was responsible for the water negotiations.
19. They were both men whom Khasawneh knew and respected from his own legal career, which included his continuing service on the International Law Commission. Graefrath in particular had impressed him as a former East German academic who had not joined the rush to recant his earlier ideological positions simply because the Berlin Wall had fallen. He also regarded both men as holding sound positions from an Arab perspective on the rights and wrongs of the Arab–Israeli conflict.
20. For the texts of the Arab League Charter and Arab Defence Pact see: http://www.yale.edu/lawweb/avalon/mideast/arabjoin.htm and http://www.yale.edu/lawweb/avalon/mideast/arableag.htm (accessed 2 April 2007).
21. Hussein to Major, 20 May 1992, British File, RHA.
22. EIU, Country Report, Jordan, No. 2, 1992, p. 7.
23. Hussein to Major, 20 May 1992, British File, RHA.
24. EIU, Country Report, Jordan, No. 3, 1992, p. 10.
25. Hussein speech, 23 November 1992, SWB, ME1547/A4-5.
26. 'King Hussein Addresses Human Rights Center Committee', FBIS-NES-93-029, 16 February 1993, p. 47. See also Mufti, 'A King's Art', p. 18.
27. Bush to Hussein, 3 April 1992, President Bush File, RHA.
28. EIU, Country Report, Jordan, No. 2, 1992, p. 14.
29. Minutes of Meeting between His Majesty King Hussein I and U.S. Secretary of State Warren Christopher, at the Royal Hashemite Court, 13.10–13.40, 6 December 1993, President Clinton File, RHA.

30. Queen Noor, *Leap of Faith*, pp. 347–9.
31. ibid, p. 354.
32. Hussein to Bush, 4 September 1992, President Bush File, RHA.
33. ibid.
34. Hussein speech, Jordanian TV, 5 November 1992, SWB, ME/1532/A9-13; EIU, Country Report, Jordan No. 1, 1993, p. 10.
35. Eisenberg, L.Z. and Caplan, N., *Negotiating Arab–Israeli Peace: Patterns, Problems, Possibilities* (Bloomington: Indiana University Press, 1998), pp. 81, 205–9.
36. Shlaim, *The Iron Wall*, p. 503.
37. Bush to Hussein, 15 August 1992, President Bush File, RHA.
38. ibid.
39. Hussein to Bush, 16 August 1992, President Bush File, RHA.
40. Eisenberg and Caplan, *Negotiating*, p. 91.
41. Interview, Abdul Salam Majali, Amman, 11 April 2000.
42. Majali, Anani and Haddadin, *Peacemaking*, p. 169.
43. Hussein to Bush, 9 November 1991, President Bush File, RHA.
44. Hussein to Baker, 17 February 1992, ibid.
45. Jordan–Israel Track Common Agenda, in Majali, Anani and Haddadin, *Peacemaking*, Appendix 3, pp. 329–30. See also pp. 179–88 for discussion of the final negotiations which produced the Common Agenda.
46. This wording was amended in the ninth round of negotiations during April–May 1993 to read 'without prejudice to the status of any territories that came under Israeli Military Government control in 1967'. See Majali, Anani and Haddadin, *Peacemaking*, Appendix 3, pp. 329–30.
47. EIU, Country Report, Jordan, No. 1, 1993, p. 7.
48. Majali, Anani and Haddadin, *Peacemaking*, p. 193.
49. Conversation, Awn Khasawneh, The Hague, 17 March 2007.
50. Interview, Abdul Salam Majali, Amman, 11 April 2000.
51. Halevy, *Man in the Shadows*, pp. 49–50.
52. Shlaim, *The Iron Wall*, p. 515.
53. Abbas, M., *Through Secret Channels: The Road to Oslo* (Reading: Garnet Publishing, 1995), p. 187.

Chapter 16: The Best of Enemies, the Best of Friends: Hussein, Rabin and the Jordanian–Israeli Peace Treaty

1. Abbas, *Through Secret Channels*, p. 187.
2. Majali, Anani and Haddadin, *Peacemaking*, p. 234.
3. Hussein to Clinton, 4 September 1993, President Clinton File, RHA.
4. See Brand, 'Effects of the Peace Process', pp. 58–9; Robinson, 'Defensive Democratization', pp. 397–8; Mufti, 'Elite Bargains', pp. 118–21.
5. The Islamic Action Front was formed as an umbrella body encompassing the Muslim Brotherhood and other independent Islamists, in the wake of the legalisation of political parties in 1992.
6. Halevy, *Man in the Shadows*, p. 106.
7. Minutes of meeting between His Majesty King Hussein and U.S. Secretary of State Warren Christopher, Royal Hashemite Court, 13.10–13.40, 6 December 1993, President Clinton File, RHA.
8. Ross, *The Missing Peace*, p. 167.
9. Halevy, *Man in the Shadows*, pp. 105–9.
10. Clinton to Hussein, 15 November 1993, President Clinton File, RHA.
11. Hussein to Clinton, 18 November 1993, ibid.
12. I have been unable to locate a copy of this letter from Arafat in the Royal Hashemite Archives.

13. Halevy, *Man in the Shadows*, pp. 82–3. Dennis Ross also emphasises the Jerusalem factor in his account of the King's change of heart (*The Missing Peace*, pp. 167–8), although he dates this as being after the Israeli–PLO 4 May 1994 Gaza–Jericho agreement.

14. Interview, Ali Shukri, Amman, 26 February 2007 (italics added to show the original verbal emphasis). Otherwise Shukri sees Halevy's account as being accurate.

15. Halevy, *Man in the Shadows*, pp. 84–5.

16. ibid, pp. 86–8; Ross, *The Missing Peace*, pp. 168–9.

17. Interview, Fayez Tarawneh, Amman, 6 June 2002; Ross, *The Missing Peace*, pp. 170–73.

18. Ross, *The Missing Peace*, p. 172.

19. Halevy, *Man in the Shadows*, p. 88.

20. Ross, *The Missing Peace*, p. 173.

21. Hussein to Clinton, 20 June 1994, President Clinton File, RHA.

22. Ross, *The Missing Peace*, pp. 174–6; Halevy, *Man in the Shadows*, pp. 88–9.

23. Eisenberg and Caplan, *Negotiating*, p. 98.

24. Hussein to Clinton, 12 July 1994, President Clinton File, RHA.

25. Clinton to Hussein, 14 July 1994, ibid.

26. Majali, Anani and Haddadin, *Peacemaking*, p. 263.

27. Halevy, *Man in the Shadows*, pp. 90–93.

28. http://www.yale.edu/lawweb/avalon/mideast/pal06.htm (accessed 6 February 2007). Ali Shukri claims he wrote this particular clause, while much of the rest of the Declaration was drafted by Prince Hassan (interview, Ali Shukri, Amman, 26 February 2007).

29. Ross, *The Missing Peace*, pp. 183–4.

30. The text of Hussein's speech is at http://www.kinghussein.gov.jo/speeches_letters.html (accessed 16 February 2007)

31. EIU, Country Report, Jordan, No. 2, 1995, p. 10.

32. Clinton to Hussein, undated [August 1994], President Clinton File, RHA.

33. Crawford was not present for the final rounds of talks in Amman in October, but was consulted by telephone.

34. Crawford's comments as reported by Awn Khasawneh, in Majali, Anani and Haddadin, *Peacemaking*, pp. 280–81. Also, interview, Awn Khasawneh, The Hague, 24 June 2000.

35. Interview, Awn Khasawneh, The Hague, 24 June 2000.

36. http://www.yale.edu/lawweb/avalon/mideast/jordan_treaty.htm#art8 (accessed 3 April 2007).

37. Voice of Israel and New Channel 2 TV reports, Jerusalem, 30 September 1994, SWB, ME/2115 MED/4-5; Majali, Anani and Haddadin, *Peacemaking*, p. 282–3.

38. Majali, Anani and Haddadin, *Peacemaking*, pp. 289–91.

39. Voice of Israel, Jerusalem, 13 October 1994, SWB, ME/2127 MED/14.

40. Elmusa, S. S., 'The Jordan–Israel Water Agreement: A Model or an Exception', *Journal of Palestine Studies*, 24/3, 1995, pp. 63–73.

41. According to Jordanian sources, the Israeli government had to rely on a note issued by its own Foreign Ministry to support this claim, since officials at the Land Registry apparently refused to issue an inaccurate supporting document.

42. http://www.yale.edu/lawweb/avalon/mideast/jordan_treaty_annex1.htm (accessed 8 February 2007).

43. http://www.yale.edu/lawweb/avalon/mideast/jordan_treaty.htm (accessed 12 February 2007).

44. Compare Article 29, Jordanian–Israeli Peace Treaty, http://www.yale.edu/lawweb/avalon/mideast/jordan_treaty.htm (accessed 12 February 2007) with Article VII, Egyptian–Israeli Peace Treaty, http://www.yale.edu/lawweb/avalon/mideast/isregypt.htm (accessed 2 April 2007). The wording is identical although the layout is slightly different.

45. Hussein to Baker, 17 February 1992, President Bush File, RHA.
46. http://www.yale.edu/lawweb/avalon/mideast/jordan_treaty.htm   (accessed   8
     February 2007).
47. Private information.
48. http://www.yale.edu/lawweb/avalon/mideast/jordan_treaty.htm#art4 (accessed 4
     April 2007).
49. http://www.yale.edu/lawweb/avalon/mideast/jordan_treaty.htm#art25 (accessed 4
     April 2007)
50. Jordanian TV, Amman, 17 October 1994, SWB, ME2130 MED/2.
51. Voice of Israel, Jerusalem, 17 October 1994, SWB, ME2129 MED/1.
52. Jordanian TV, Amman, 17 October 1994, SWB, ME2130 MED/2.
53. MENA news agency, Cairo, 22 October 1994, SWB, ME/2134 MED/5.
54. Jordanian TV, Amman, 22 October 1994, SWB, ME/2134 MED/2.
55. Jordanian TV, Amman, 26 October 1994, SWB, ME/2137 MED/5–6.
56. Voice of Israel, Jerusalem, 26 October 1994, ibid.
57. Jordanian TV, Amman, 24 October 1994, SWB, ME/2136 MED6/8.
58. Hashemite Kingdom of Jordan Radio, Amman, 30 October 1994, SWB, ME2141
     MED/23.
59. Jordanian TV, Amman, 25 October 1994, SWB, ME/2137 MED/17–18.
60. ibid.

Chapter 17: The Bitter Aftertaste of Peace

1.   Horowitz, D., *Shalom Friend: The Life and Legacy of Yitzhak Rabin* (New York:
     Newmarket Press, 1996), pp. 251–2.
2.   Hussein to Weizman, 5 November 1995, Post-1992 Israel File, RHA.
3.   'In Memory of Yitzhak Rabin', undated memorandum, ibid.
4.   Rabin to Hussein, 10 May 1995, ibid.
5.   See the letter of invitation to the MENA summit, 15 July 1995, ibid.
6.   Shlaim, 'His Royal Shyness', p. 19.
7.   Private letter to Hussein, 30 August 1995, Post-1992 Israel File, RHA. In view of the
     nature of the communication, I have protected the names of the senders.
8.   Eban to Hussein, 21 March 1995, ibid.
9.   Hussein to Rabin, 21 May 1995, ibid.
10. Lynch, *State Interests*, p. 208; Lucas, R. E., 'Jordan: the Death of Normalization with
     Israel', *Middle East Journal*, 58/1, 2004, p. 97.
11. Hussein to Weizman, 25 February 1996, Post-1992 Israel File, RHA.
12. Hussein to Clinton, 4 March 1996, President Clinton File, RHA.
13. Lynch, *State Interests*, p. 210; Lucas, 'The Death of Normalization', p. 97.
14. Peres to Hussein, 30 April 1996, Post-1992 Israel File, RHA.
15. Hussein to Peres, 'Urgent Special Message Regarding Events in Lebanon', undated,
     ibid.
16. Author's interview with former Jordanian official. Also Halevy, *Man in the Shadows*,
     p. 147.
17. Interview, Zeid bin Shaker, Amman, 23 March 2000.
18. EIU, Country Report, Jordan, No. 3, 1996, pp. 8–9.
19. Shlaim, *The Iron Wall*, p. 571.
20. Clinton to Hussein, 14 July 1996, President Clinton File, RHA.
21. Lucas, 'The Death of Normalization', pp. 97–8.
22. Halevy, *Man in the Shadows*, pp. 147–8.
23. http://daccessdds.un.org/doc/UNDOC/GEN/N96/257/24/PDF/N9625724.pdf?Open
     Element (accessed 30 July 2007).
24. Ross, *The Missing Peace*, p. 267.
25. ibid; Shlaim, 'His Royal Shyness', p. 19.

26. Ross, *The Missing Peace*, p. 269.

27. ibid, pp. 318–19.

28. EIU, Country Report, Jordan, No. 1, 1997, p. 11.

29. Hussein to Netanyahu, 9 March 1997, Post-1992 Israel File, RHA. Hussein made this letter public.

30. Shlaim, *The Iron Wall*, p. 580; Ross, *The Missing Peace*, p. 322.

31. Hussein to Netanyahu, 25 February 1997, Post-1992 Israel File, RHA. Hussein made this letter public.

32. Hussein to Netanyahu, 9 March 1997, ibid.

33. Netanyahu to Hussein, 10 March 1997, ibid.

34. Students of Junior High School 'Rimon' to Hussein, 18 March 1997, ibid.

35. Zeev Bielski, Mayor of Raanana, to Hussein, 1 June 1997, ibid.

36. Mordechai to Hussein, 16 March 1997, ibid.

37. Barak to Hussein, 13 March 1997, ibid.

38. Barak to Hussein, 10 June 1997, ibid.

39. Halevy claims rather less exotically that the poison was smeared on Meshal's neck (*Man in the Shadows*, p. 171).

40. ibid, pp. 165–6. Halevy's account is the most detailed we have of this episode. See also Kumaraswamy, P.R., 'Israel, Jordan and the Masha'al Affair', in Karsh, E. and Kumaraswamy, P.R. (eds), *Israel, the Hashemites and the Palestinians: The Fateful Triangle* (London: Frank Cass, 2003), pp. 111–28.

41. Halevy, *Man in the Shadows*, p. 172.

42. ibid.

43. Cockburn, and Cockburn, *Out of the Ashes*, p. 219.

44. Halevy, *Man in the Shadows*, pp. 172–5.

45. Interview, Zeid bin Shaker, Amman, 23 March 2000; Lucas, 'The Death of Normalization', p. 98.

46. Lynch, *State Interests*, p. 223; Lucas, 'The Death of Normalization', p. 100.

47. Brand, 'The Effects of the Peace Process', p. 62; Lucas, 'The Death of Normalization', pp. 103–4; Wiktorowicz, Q., 'The Limits of Democracy in the Middle East: The Case of Jordan', *Middle East Journal*, 53/4, 1999, pp. 616–17.

48. See Article 1.3 of Annex II http://www.kinghussein.gov.jo/peacetreaty.html (accessed 26 March 2007). Agreement should have been reached on this point within one year of the signature of the treaty. See also Elmusa, 'The Jordan–Israel Water Agreement', pp. 67–8.

49. Sharon to Hassan, 20 May 1997, Post-1992 Israel File, RHA.

50. Hassan to Sharon, 21 May 1997, ibid.

Chapter 18: The Liberation of Iraq, 1995–7

1. Hussein to Major, 20 May 1992, British File, RHA.

2. Mufti, 'A King's Art', pp. 19–20, follows a similar line of argument. See also Schenker, *Dancing with Saddam: The Dangerous Tango of Jordan–Iraq Relations* (Washington DC: Washington Institute for Near East Policy, 2003), pp. 16–19.

3. Interview, Ali Shukri, Amman, 26 February 2007; conversation, Awn Khasawneh, The Hague, 17 February 2001; and other private information. Marwan Qasim declined to disclose the contents of Hussein's letter (interview, 26 September 2002).

4. Hussein to Major, 28 August 1995, British File, RHA.

5. For further discussion of the implications of Hussein Kamel's defection see IIC report, Management of the Oil-for-Food Programme, Volume II, Chapter II, pp. 58–60, http://www.iic-offp.org/documents/Sept05/Mgmt_V2.pdf (accessed 26 March 2007); and Cockburn and Cockburn, *Out of the Ashes*, pp. 192–3.

6. Interview, Marwan Qasim, Amman, 26 September 2002.

7. Lynch, *State Interests*, p. 239.

8.   EIU, Country Report, Jordan, No. 4, 1995, p. 8.
9.   Major to Hussein, undated [mid-August 1996], British File, RHA.
10. Spedding to Hussein, 26 August 1995, ibid.
11. Private information.
12. Major to Hussein, 26 August 1995, British File, RHA.
13. Hussein to Major, 28 August 1995, British File, RHA.
14. Hussein, 26 September interview with members of the European Parliament, FBIS, 27 September 1995, NES-95-187. See also Schenker, *Dancing with Saddam*, p. 17.
15. Hussein's 6 September 1995 interview, as reported on Amman Radio, FBIS, 8 September 1995, NES-95-174.
16. EIU, Country Report, Jordan, No. 4, 1995, pp. 9–10.
17. Cockburn and Cockburn, *Out of the Ashes*, p. 219.
18. Private information.
19. Private information.
20. Cockburn and Cockburn, *Out of the Ashes*, p. 220.
21. Interview, Marwan Qasim, Amman, 26 September 2002. I also asked Zeid bin Shaker about the arrival of the Iraqi defectors, but a look passed over his face which led me not to pursue the issue further (interview, Zeid bin Shaker, Amman, 23 March 2000).
22. Marwan Qasim was also subsequently replaced as chief of the Royal Court.
23. EIU, Country Report, Jordan, No. 2, 1996, p. 8.
24. Interview, Ali Shukri, Amman, 26 February 2007.
25. Cockburn and Cockburn, *Out of the Ashes*, p. 206.
26. ibid, p. 208.
27. Conversation, Awn Khasawneh, The Hague, 12 May 2007.
28. EIU, Country Report, Jordan, No. 2, 1996, pp. 11–12.
29. 'With CIA's Help, Group in Jordan Targets Saddam; U.S. Funds Support Campaign to Topple Iraqi Leader from Afar', *Washington Post*, 23 June 1996, p. A01; Cockburn and Cockburn, *Out of the Ashes*, pp. 226–7.
30. The news of the arrests and executions became public in September. See 'CIA-Backed Iraqi Dissidents Killed', *Washington Post*, 10 September 1996, p. A01; 'Conflict in Iraq: The CIA', *The New York Times*, 11 September 1996, p. A6.
31. Cockburn and Cockburn, *Out of the Ashes*, pp. 228–30.
32. Mufti, 'Elite Bargains', pp. 121–2.
33. Conversation, Awn Khasawneh, The Hague, 17 March 2007.
34. Ryan, C., *Jordan in Transition: From Hussein to Abdullah* (Boulder: Lynne Rienner Publishers, 2002), p. 59. See also Schenker, *Dancing with Saddam*, pp. 83–4. Lynch, *State Interests*, p. 250, notes that the King's claims were met with scepticism at the time.
35. EIU, Country Report, Jordan, No. 4, 1996, p. 13.
36. Ryan, *Jordan in Transition*, p. 60, also notes that Baathists, leftists and nationalists were the main targets of the government crackdown.
37. The extent of Saddam's success in rounding up INA sympathisers did not become fully apparent until early September (see 'CIA-Backed Iraqi Dissidents Killed', *Washington Post*, 10 September 1996, p. A01; 'Conflict in Iraq: The CIA', *The New York Times*, 11 September 1996, p. A6).
38. Cockburn and Cockburn, *Out of the Ashes*, p. 245.
39. Brand, 'The Effects of the Peace Process', p. 61; EIU, Country Report, Jordan, No. 1, 1997, p. 13.
40. Private information.
41. See Volcker Report, Vol. II, p. 70: http://www.iic-offp.org/documents/Sept05/Mgmt_V2.pdf (accessed 23 March 2007).
42. For the text of the resolution see: http://daccessdds.un.org/doc/UNDOC/GEN/N95/109/88/PDF/N9510988.pdf?OpenElement (accessed 23 March 2007).
43. See IIC, Report on Programme Manipulation, Chapter II, pp. 11–13,

http://www.iic-offp.org/documents/Final%20Report%2027Oct05/IIC%
20Final%20Report%20-%20Chapter%20Two.pdf (accessed 24 March 2007).
44. Clinton to Hussein, 22 December 1996, President Clinton File, RHA.
45. ibid.

Chapter 19: A Destiny Fulfilled?

1.   Lynch, *State Interests*, pp. 251–2; EIU, Country Report, Jordan, No. 1, 1998, p. 14.
2.   Shbeilat received oil allocations totalling 18.5 million barrels during phases 6, 7, 8,
     10, 11, 12 and 13 of the programme. See IIC, 'Summary of Oil Sales by Non-
     Contractual beneficiary', http://www.iic-offp.org/documents/CommitteeTables
     27oct05/Table%203%20-%20Committee%20oil%20beneficiary%20table.pdf
     (accessed 16 April 2007).
3.   Hussein to Clinton, 7 March 1998, President Clinton File, RHA.
4.   Hassan to Blair, 23 December 1998, British File, RHA.
5.   UNSC Resolution 1153: http://daccessdds.un.org/doc/UNDOC/GEN/N98/039/34/
     PDF/N9803934.pdf?OpenElement (accessed 16 April 2007)
6.   Amongst those who subsequently benefited from Saddam's largesse through the
     awarding of oil contracts under the oil-for-food programme were the prominent
     anti-normalisers Toujan Faisal and Laith Shbeilat. See: IIC, 'Summary of Oil Sales
     by Non-Contractual Beneficiary', http://www.iic-offp.org/documents/Committee
     Tables27oct05/Table%203%20-%20Committee%20oil%20beneficiary%
     20table.pdf (accessed 16 April 2007).
7.   Netanyahu to Hussein, 16 March 1998, Post-1992 Israel File, RHA.
8.   See http://www.kinghussein.gov.jo/archive.html (accessed 17 April 2007) [hereafter
     Hussein Web Archive – 'HWA'].
9.   ibid.
10. Ross, *The Missing Peace*, p. 448.
11. Netanyahu to Hussein, 14 November 1998, Post-1992 Israel File, RHA.
12. For this medical bulletin see HWA.
13. HWA.
14. Queen Noor, *Leap of Faith*, p. 403.
15. Archive entry, 27 July 1998, HWA.
16. Archive entry, 28 July 1998, ibid.
17. Interview, Queen Noor, Ascot, 10 July 1999.
18. Informal conversation with one of the King's physicians, Oxford, 11 November
     2002.
19. This discussion of the succession is based on many conversations with various
     members of the Hashemite family and senior political figures. The overall synthesis
     of the saga, though, is of my own making.
20. In his letter disinheriting Prince Hassan, the King spoke of having been 'offended by
     slandering and falsehoods' against his wife and children delivered by supporters of
     the Crown Prince on his return to Jordan from the Mayo Clinic in 1992, Hussein to
     Hassan, 25 January 1999, http://www.kinghussein.gov.jo/archive.html (accessed 19
     April 2007) [hereafter '25 January letter'].
21. http://www.kinghussein.gov.jo/speeches_letters.html (accessed 18 April 2007).
22. EIU, Country Report, Jordan, No. 2, 1995, p. 8.
23. 25 January letter.
24. Andoni, L., 'King Abdallah: In His Father's Footsteps', *Journal of Palestine Studies*,
     29/3, 2000, p. 79.
25. Archive entry, 15 August 1998, HWA.
26. See archive entries: 12 September; 4 and 24 October; 23 November, HWA.
27. For Kaabneh's visits see archive entries, 19 September and 24 October, HWA.
28. 25 January letter.

29. Andoni, 'King Abdallah', p. 79.
30. Archive entry, 24 October, HWA.
31. http://www.kinghussein.gov.jo/98-aug7.html (accessed 19 April 2007).
32. EIU, Country Report, Jordan, No. 4, 1998, p. 13.
33. Archive entry, 1 October, HWA.
34. Andoni, 'King Abdallah', p. 80.
35. 25 January letter.
36. Article 28(a) states: 'The Royal title shall pass from the holder of the Throne to his eldest son, and to the eldest son of that son and in linear succession by a similar process thereafter. Should the eldest son die before the Throne devolves upon him, his eldest son shall inherit the Throne, despite the existence of brothers to the deceased son. The King may, however, select one of his brothers as heir apparent. In this event, title to the Throne shall pass to him from the holder of the Throne.' (As amended in the Official Gazette No. 1831 of 1 April 1965.) http://www.king hussein.gov.jo/constitution_jo.html (accessed 20 April 2007).
37. 25 January letter.
38. ibid.
39. http://www.kinghussein.gov.jo/98-aug7.html (accessed 20 April 2007).
40. This information comes from one of Hussein's visitors at the Mayo Clinic who wishes to remain anonymous.
41. Archive entry, 14 October 1998, HWA.
42. The New York Times, 1 November 1998, p. 8; Queen Noor, Leap of Faith, p. 417.
43. Archive entry, 13 November 1998, HWA.
44. Associated Press report, Saturday 9 January 1999.
45. Agence France Presse report, Monday 18 January 1999.
46. Christiane Amanpour, interview with King Hussein, Amman, 20 January 1999, http://www.kinghussein.gov.jo/interviews_press.html (accessed 23 April 2007).
47. Robins, A History of Jordan, p. 196.
48. 25 January letter.
49. Queen Noor, Leap of Faith, pp. 399–400.
50. This information comes from several family members who must remain anonymous.
51. Informal conversation with one of the King's physicians, Oxford, 11 November 2002.
52. Royal Decree, 25 January 1999, http://www.kinghussein.gov.jo/speeches_letters.html (accessed 23 April 2007).
53. Hussein to Abdullah, 26 January 1999, ibid.
54. Hussein to Weizman, 2 February 1999, Post-1992 Israel File, RHA.
55. Clinton to Abdullah, 17 March 1999, President Clinton File, RHA.
56. Hussein, interview with Christiane Amanpour, 24 January 1999, http://www.king hussein.gov.jo/interviews_press.html (accessed 24 April 2007).
57. A tribute by HRH The Prince of Wales at King Hussein's memorial service, St Paul's Cathedral, 5 July 1999, http://www.princeofwales.gov.uk/speechesandarticles/index.html (accessed 24 April 2007).
58. Halevy, Man in the Shadows, pp. 26–7.
59. Text of Hussein's speech in FBIS, NES-91-026, 7 February 1991, pp. 27–9. Hussein made a similar reference in a speech to graduating officers on 9 December 1990, when he spoke of the Arab nation 'facing a situation reminiscent of the dangerous one in which it found itself in 1918. Then it discovered that its course had been set for it through the Sykes–Picot Agreement, the Balfour Declaration, and at a later stage, by the League of Nations.' http://www.kinghussein.gov.jo/speeches_letters.html (accessed 25 April 2007).
60. Mufti, 'A King's Art', p. 20.

INDEX